Y0-CRP-191

WITHDRAWN

Index to
BOOK REVIEWS
IN
HISTORICAL PERIODICALS
1973

by

John W. Brewster

and

Joseph A. McLeod

The Scarecrow Press, Inc.

Metuchen, N.J.   1976

ISBN 0-8108-0893-5

LC 75-18992

DEDICATION

To Joseph A. McLeod, Sr.
    Annie Barber McLeod (in memoriam)
    Weldon Brewster
    Margaret Howard Brewster

INTRODUCTION

The Index to Book Reviews in Historical Periodicals has developed out of a recognized need among the students at North Texas State University for aid in locating reviews of books assigned for class readings. The present volume includes 93 of the better-known scholarly journals and historical society organs. Although the reviews concentrate on U. S. history, an effort has been made to include materials relating to other countries as well. The index includes only English-language periodicals. Books written in foreign languages are included if the review is in English. The original title is indicated except where a translation is given, in which case the English version is used. In some periodicals, works are included which stress other disciplines than history. These are included for the sake of completeness; such entries comprise a very small minority of the total index.

In most cases, the complete title of the work is indicated although in the case of an exceptionally long title, an abridged form may appear. In all cases, the policy has been to include enough of the title to enable the researcher to identify the work. In regard to imprint, the editors have endeavored to provide enough information to identify the work clearly. Well-known publishers whose works appear frequently are cited by abbreviations (a key to academic press abbreviations appears before the beginning of the index proper). States are included only when needed to identify a city.

Although designed primarily as a tool for locating book reviews, because the index includes some 5000 titles, most of which are current publications, it may also serve as a bibliographic guide in history. As nearly as possible, the editors have used the format of the University of Chicago Style Manual. Standard abbreviations for months and seasons are used. In cases where reviewers' entries conflict, <u>Books in Print</u> has been followed.

The editors present this work with the belief that it will be a useful tool for the scholar, the student, and the general reader with an interest in history.

John W. Brewster
Joseph A. McLeod

Denton, Texas
April 8, 1975

ACKNOWLEDGMENTS

The authors of the index recognize that their efforts have been made much easier by the indulgence and cooperation of others. Not least among these who have made the task easier were the families of the authors who bore with good grace and a minimum of complaint the cluttering of their homes with file cards, trays, and volumes of periodicals. In addition they have rendered valuable assistance in the compilation, typing, and proof-reading and in offering timely suggestions.

Besides members of their immediate families, the authors express appreciation to members of the library staffs in the Fort Worth-Dallas-Denton metroplex. At North Texas State University, special mention should be made of the encouragement given by Director of Libraries Dr. David A. Webb and Assistant Director, Central Services, George D. Mitchell. Indeed it was Mr. Mitchell who first made the observation which led to the compilation of the index. Valuable assistance also came from William B. Floyd and his staff of the Social Science division of the North Texas State University Library. Dr. Gustave L. Seligman, Jr. of the NTSU history faculty offered helpful suggestions.

PERIODICALS INDEXED (1973)

A & W	Arizona and the West
AfAf	African Affairs
Africa	Africa
AgH	Agricultural History
A H	American Heritage
A H I	American History Illustrated
A H R	The American Historical Review
A J H Q	The American Jewish Historical Quarterly
AmAnt	American Antiquity
AmArc	The American Archivist
Antiquity	Antiquity
Archaeology	Archaeology
Archives	Archives
ArkHQ	The Arkansas Historical Quarterly
B H R	Business History Review
C H I Q	The Concordia Historical Institute Quarterly
ChOk	Chronicles of Oklahoma
C H Q	California Historical Quarterly
C H R	The Canadian Historical Review
CoMag	Colorado Magazine
Crisis	The Crisis
C S S H	Comparative Studies in Society and History
CurH	Current History
C W H	Civil War History
C W T I	Civil War Times Illustrated
F C H Q	Filson Club Historical Quarterly
F H Q	Florida Historical Quarterly
G H Q	Georgia Historical Quarterly
G R	The Georgia Review

H A H R	The Hispanic American Historical Review
H & T	History and Theory
Historian	The Historian: A Journal of History
History	History
H J	The Historical Journal
H R N B	History: Reviews of New Books
H T	History Teacher
HTo	History Today
IMH	Indiana Magazine of History
I S	Inland Seas
JAfH	The Journal of African History
JAH	The Journal of American History
JAriH	The Journal of Arizona History
J E H	The Journal of Economic History
J I H	The Journal of Interdisciplinary History
J I S H S	The Journal of the Illinois State Historical Society
J M H	Journal of Modern History
JMiH	Journal of Mississippi History
J N H	Journal of Negro History
J O W	Journal of the West
J S H	The Journal of Southern History
LaH	Louisiana History
L H	Lincoln Herald
Mankind	Mankind
M H M	Maryland Historical Magazine
M H R	Missouri Historical Review
MiA	Mid-America
MilAf	Military Affairs
MinnH	Minnesota History
NCHR	North Carolina Historical Review
N D H	North Dakota History
N E Q	New England Quarterly
N H	Nebraska History
N H B	Negro History Bulletin
N H S Q	Nevada Historical Society Quarterly

N J H	New Jersey History
N M H R	New Mexico Historical Review
N Y H	New York History
N Y H S Q	New York Historical Society Quarterly
O H	Ohio History
OrHQ	Oregon Historical Quarterly
PacH	Pacific Historian
P H	Pennsylvania History
P H R	Pacific Historical Review
P M H B	Pennsylvania Magazine of History and Biography
P N Q	Pacific Northwest Quarterly
R A C H S P	Record of the American Catholic Historical Society Publication
R K H S	Register of the Kentucky Historical Society
S C H M	South Carolina Historical Magazine
S C Q	Southern California Quarterly
S S	The Social Studies
S W H Q	The Southwestern Historical Quarterly
TAm	The Americas
T & C	Technology and Culture
T H Q	The Tennessee Historical Quarterly
Texana	Texana
U H Q	Utah Historical Quarterly
V H	Vermont History
V M H B	Virginia Magazine of History and Biography
W H Q	Western Historical Quarterly
W M H	The Wisconsin Magazine of History
W M Q	William and Mary College Quarterly--3rd series
W P H M	The Western Pennsylvania Historical Magazine
W V H	West Virginia History

ABBREVIATIONS OF PUBLISHERS

Standard abbreviations are used for commercial publishers ("& Sons, " "Co., " "Inc., " and the like are omitted). The following abbreviations are used for university presses and educational presses:

Cam U Press	Cambridge University Press, Cambridge, England
Cath U Amer Press	Catholic University of America Press, Washington, D. C.
Coll and U Press	College and University Press, New Haven, Conn.
Cor U Press	Cornell University Press, Ithaca, N. Y.
CWRU Press	Case Western Reserve University Press, Cleveland, Ohio
Edin U Press	Edinburgh University Press, Edinburgh, Scotland
Har U Press	Harvard University Press, Cambridge, Mass.
Heb Union Coll Press	Hebrew Union College Press, Cincinnati, Ohio
Huntington	Huntington Library, San Marino, California
Ia St U Press	Iowa State University Press, Ames, Ia.
Ind U Press	Indiana University Press, Bloomington, Indiana
JHU Press	Johns Hopkins University Press, Baltimore, Md.
La St U Press / LSU Press	Louisiana State University Press, Baton Rouge, La.
MHS	Maryland Historical Society, Baltimore, Maryland
MIT Press	Massachusetts Institute of Technology Press, Cambridge, Mass.
N Ill U Press	Northern Illinois University Press, DeKalb, Ill.
NW St U La Press	Northwest State University of Louisiana, Natchitoches, La.
NWU Press	Northwestern University Press, Evanston, Illinois

NYU	New York University Press, New York, N. Y.
Ox U Press	Oxford University Press, New York, N. Y.
PHMC	Pennsylvania Historical and Museum Commission
Prin U Press	Princeton University Press, Princeton, N. J.
S Ill U Press / So Ill U Press	Southern Illinois University Press, Carbondale, Ill.
Stan U Press	Stanford University Press, Stanford, California
Syr U Press	Syracuse University Press, Syracuse, N. Y.
TCU Press	Texas Christian University Press, Ft. Worth, Texas
U and Coll Press Miss	University and College Press of Mississippi, Hattiesburg, Mississippi
UBC Press	University of British Columbia Press, Vancouver, B. C.
U Cal Press	University of California Press, Berkeley and Los Angeles
U Chi Press	University of Chicago Press, Chicago, Illinois
U Ga Press	University of Georgia Press, Athens, Georgia
U Ia Press	University of Iowa Press, Iowa City, Iowa
U Ill Press	University of Illinois Press, Urbana, Ill.
U Kan Press / U Ks Press	University of Kansas Press, Lawrence, Kansas
U Mich Press	University of Michigan Press, Ann Arbor, Michigan
U Minn Press	University of Minnesota Press, Minneapolis, Minn.
U Mo Press	University of Missouri Press, Columbia, Mo.
U Mont Press	University of Montana Press, Missoula, Mont.
UNC Press	University of North Carolina Press, Chapel Hill, N. C.
UNM Press	University of New Mexico Press, Albuquerque, N. M.
U Ok Press / U Okla Press	University of Oklahoma Press, Norman, Oklahoma
U Press Ky	University Press of Kentucky, Lexington, Ky.
U Press NE	University Press of New England, Hanover, Vt.
U Press Va	University Press of Virginia, Charlottesville, Va.
USC Press / USCar Press	University of South Carolina Press, Columbia, S. C.

USNI	United States Naval Institute, Annapolis, Md.
U Tenn Press	University of Tennessee Press, Knoxville, Tenn.
U Tex Press / U Tx Press	University of Texas Press, Austin, Texas
U Tor Press	University of Toronto Press, Toronto, Ontario
U Utah Press	University of Utah Press, Salt Lake City, Utah
U Wash Press	University of Washington Press, Seattle, Washington
U Wis Press	University of Wisconsin Press, Madison, Wisconsin
Van U Press	Vanderbilt University Press, Nashville, Tenn.
W St U Press	Wayne State University Press, Detroit, Mich.
West U Press	Wesleyan University Press, Middletown, Conn.

THE INDEX: 1973

Abbas, S. A. see Brecher, Irving

Abbott, Richard H. Cobbler in Congress: The Life of Henry Wilson, 1812-1875. Lexington: U Press Ky., 1972. Rev. by J. G. Barrett, RKHS, 71(Ja 1973):114-17; W. B. Parrish, JSH, 39(May 1973):296-7; H. L. Trefousse, JAH, 60(Je 1973): 136-7; V. B. Howard, FCHQ, 47(Apr 1973):196-8.

Abels, Jules. Man on Fire: John Brown and the Cause of Liberty. New York: Macmillan, 1971. Rev. by J. H. Silbey, NYHSQ, 57(Ja 1973):83-4.

Abrahams, William see Stansky, Peter

Abrahamsson, Bengt. Military Professionalization and Political Power. Beverly Hills: Sage, 1972. Rev. by S. L. Harrison, MilAf, 37(Oct 1973):113.

Abramowitz, Morton see Moorsteen, Richard

Abu-Lughod, Janet L. Cairo: 1001 Years of the City Victorious. Princeton, N. J.: Prin U Press, 1971. Rev. by J. B. Christopher, AHR, 78(Oct 1973):1107-8; R. P. Mock, MEJ, 27(Win 1973):80-1.

Abun-Nasr, Jamil M. A History of the Maghrib. New York: Cam U Press, 1972. Rev. by R. M. Brace, AHR, 78(Dec 1973): 1505-6.

Acheson, Dean. The Korean War. New York: Norton, 1971. Rev. by L. J. Korb, MilAf, 37(Oct 1973):114-15.

Acuño, Rodolfo. Occupied America: The Chicano's Struggle Toward Liberation. San Francisco: Canfield, 1972. Rev. by V. C. Dahl, WHQ, 4(Jl 1973):339-41; J. S. Olson, A & W, 15(Win 1973):377-8; J. Gomez-Q, HAHR, 53(Aug 1973):558-60.

Adam, Jean-Paul. Instauration de la politique des chemins de fer France. Paris: Presses Universitaires de France, 1972. Rev. by C. E. Freedeman, AHR, 78(Dec 1973):1478.

Adams, Alexander. B. Geronimo: A Biography. New York: Put-

1

nam's, 1971. Rev. by A. M. Gibson, AHR, 78(Dec 1973):
1535; J. C. Lane, FHQ, 52(J1 1973):93-5.

Adams, Arthur E. and Jan Steckelberg Adams. Men Versus Systems: Agriculture in the U S S R, Poland, and Czechoslovakia. New York: Free Press, 1971. Rev. by W. W.
Hagen, AgH, 47(Ja 1973):86-7.

Adams, Clarence S. and Tom E. Brown, Sr. Three Ranches West.
New York: Carlton, 1973. Rev. by C. Rickards, A & W,
15(Win 1973):374-5.

Adams, Henry E., ed. Handbook of Latin American Studies, 32:
Humanities. Gainesville, Fla.: U Fla Press, 1970. Rev. by
J Sommers, HAHR, 53(Feb 1973):117-19.

Adams, Ramon F. The Cowman Says It Salty. Tucson: U Ariz
Press, 1971. Rev. by C. P. Westermeier, Montana, 23(Win
1973):68.

Adams, Richard N., et al. Community Culture and National Change.
New Orleans: Middle American Research Institute, 1972. Rev.
by J. B. Biesauz, HAHR, 53(Aug 1973):567.

Adams, T. F. M. and Iwao Hoshii. A Financial History of the New
Japan. Tokyo: Kodansha, 1972. Rev. by K. Yamamura,
BHR, 47(Spr 1973):136-7.

Adamson, Alan H. Sugar Without Slaves: The Political Economy
of British Guiana, 1838-1904. New Haven, Conn.: Yale U
Press, 1972. Rev. by R. B. Sheridan, AHR, 78(Oct 1973):
1153; W. A. Green, BHR, 47 (Win 1973):544-6; J. R. Mandle,
JEH, 33(Je 1973):470-1.

Addington, Larry H. The Blitzkrieg Era and the German General
Staff, 1865-1941. New Brunswick, N. J.: Rutgers U Press,
1971. Rev. by F. Beck, MilAf, 37(Apr 1973):72-3.

Adeleye, R. A. Power and Diplomacy in Northern Nigeria, 1804-
1906: the Sokoto Caliphate and Its Enemies. London: Longmans, 1971. Rev. by D. E. Allyn, AfAf, 72(Ja 1973):84-5.

Adelman, M. A. The World Petroleum Market. Baltimore: JHU
Press, 1972. Rev. by K. M. Langley, JEH, 33(Dec 1973):
875-6.

Adler, Dorothy R. British Investment in American Railways, 1834-
1898. Charlottesville, Va.: U Press Va., 1970. Rev. by
W. D. Farnham, JAH, 59(Mar 1973):1020-1.

Adoff, Arnold, ed. The Poetry of Black America: Anthology of the
20th Century. New York: Harper and Row, 1973. Rev. by
H. Chatfield, OQ, 16(Win 1973):157-8.

Agarwal, S. K. Aircraft Hijacking and International Law. Bombay:
N. M. Tripathi, 1972. Rev. by B. N. Mehrish, IQ, 29(J1-
Sep 1973):259-60.

Agassi, Joseph. Faraday as a Natural Philosopher. Chicago: U Chi
Press, 1971. Rev. by R. Sviedrys, AHR, 78(Je 1973):653.

Agbodeka, Francis. African Politics and British Policy in the Gold
Coast, 1868-1900: A Study in the Forms and Force of Protest.
London: Longmans, 1971. Rev. by E. Reynolds, AfAf, 72
(Ja 1973):82-3.

Agramonte, Roberto D. Marti y su concepción del mundo. Rio
Piedras, Puerto Rico: Editorial Universitaria, 1971. Rev. by
I. A. Schulman, HAHR, 53(Feb 1973):131-3.

Aguilar, Luis E. Cuba, 1933: Prologue to Revolution. Ithaca,
N. Y.: Cornell U Press, 1972. Rev. by R. F. Smith,
HAHR, 53(Feb 1973):135-7; M. M. Anderburg, CurH, 64(Feb
1973):81.

Ahlstrom, Sydney E. A Religious History of the American People.
New Haven: Yale U Press, 1972. Rev. by W. G. McLaugh-
lin, JAH, 60(Je 1973):102-5; R. D. Cross, AHR, 78(Dec 1973):
1521-3; S. V. James, JSH, 39(Aug 1973):428-31; M. E. Lodge,
PMHB, 97(J1 1973):407-8; S. E. Mead, WMQ, 3rd Ser. , 30
(J1 1973):495-7.

Ajayi, J. F. Ade and Michael Crowder, eds. The History of West
Africa, Volume I. New York: Columbia U Press, 1972. Rev.
by O. E. S. , CurH, 64(Mar 1973):125; W. Gutteridge, Africa,
43(Ja 1973):87; J. B. Wolf, Historian, 35(Feb 1973):299-300;
C. Tyfe, History, 58(Je 1973):324.

Akenson, Donald Harmon. The Church of Ireland: Ecclesiastical
Reform and Revolution, 1800-1885. New Haven, Conn.: Yale
U Press, 1971. D. Bowen, JMH, 45(Mar 1973):136-7.

Akten zur Deutschen Auswärtigen Politik 1918-1945. [4 vols.] Göt
tingen: Vandenhoek und Ruprecht, 1971-72. Rev. by J.
Gimbel, JAH, 60(Sep 1973):504-5.

Albert, William. The Turnpike Road System in England, 1663-1840.
Cambridge: Cam U Press, 1972. Rev. by F. Duckham, His-
tory, 58(Je 1973):297-8; D. Spring, BHR, 47(Aut 1973):407-8;
J. B. Rae, T & C, 14(Apr 1973):307-8.

Albertson, Peter and Margery Barnett. Environment and Society in
Transition: Scientific Developments, Social Consequences,
Policy Implications. New York: Annals of the New York
Academy of Sciences, Vol. 184, 1971. Rev. by M. Leiten-
berg, T & C, 14(Apr 1973):345-6.

Albright, Daniel. The Myth Against Myth: A Study of Yeats' Imagination in Old Age. London: Ox U Press, 1972. Rev. by M. H. Begnal, E-I, 8(Win 1973):114-5.

Alcock, A. E. The History of the South Tyrol Question. London: Michael Joseph, 1970. Rev. by C. Seton-Watson, HJ, 16 (Mar 1973):219-20.

Alcock, Leslie. Arthur's Britain. London: Allen Lane; Penguin, 1971. Rev. by K. Jackson, Antiquity, 47(Mar 1973):80-1.

_____. 'By South Cadbury is that Camelot....' London: Thames and Hudson, 1972. Rev. by P. Rahtz, History, 58(Oct 1972): 423.

Aldcroft, Derek H. and Peter Fearon, eds. British Economic Fluctuations, 1790-1939. London: Macmillan, 1972. Rev. by R. Floud, History, 58(Je 1973):317-8.

Alden, Dauril, ed. Colonial Roots of Modern Brazil: Papers of the Newberry Library Conference. Berkeley: U Cal Press, 1973. Rev. by M. Rodriguez, AHR, 78(Dec 1973):1560-1.

Alderson, Frederick. Bicycling, A History. New York: Praeger, 1972. Rev. by L. T. C. Rolt, T & C, 14(Oct. 1973):644-5.

Al-dîn, Rashîd. The Successors of Genghis Khan. New York: Columbia U Press, 1971. Rev. by T. C. Young, AHR, 78(Dec 1973):1510.

Aldred, Cyril. Jewels of the Pharaohs: Egyptian Jewellery of the Dynastic Period. London: Thames and Hudson, 1971. Rev. by J. Ruffle, Antiquity, 47(Mar 1973):72-4.

Aldunate, José María Bulnes. Unidad y testimonio de las grandes letras hispanomericanas. Cuernavaca: Mexico: Centro intercultural de Documentación, 1970. Rev. by I. A. Leonard, HAHR, 53(Aug 1973):557-8.

Alexander, Edward Porter, ed. The Journal of John Fontaine: An Irish Hugenot Son in Spain and Virginia, 1710-1719. Charlottesville: U Va. Press,... 1972. Rev. by E. G. Evans, JAH, 59 (Mar 1973):979-80; R. D. Cohen, JSH, 39(Feb 1973):1001; L. R. Bishko, MHM, 68(Sum 1973):217-8; B. M. Wilkenfeld, NyH, 54(Jl 1973):376-7; H. M. Ward, VMHB, 81(Ja 1973):99-100; P. Marambaud, WMQ, 3rd Ser. 30(Apr 1973):355-6.

Alexander, Sidney S. see Cooper, Charles A.

Alexander, Thomas B. and Richard E. Beringer. The Anatomy of the Confederate Congress: A Study of the Influence of Member Characteristics on Legislative Voting Behavior, 1861-1865.

Rev. by S. Hackney, JAH, 60(Je 1973):139-41; W. L. Barney,
Historian, 36(Nov 1973):127-8; E. M. Thomas, WMH, 56(Sum
1973):330-1; R. A. Wooster, MHM, 68(Sum 1973):226; J. F.
Marszalek, PH, 40(Apr 1973):223-4.

Alexandre, Philippe. The Duel: De Gaulle and Pompidou. Boston:
Houghton Mifflin, 1972. Rev. by J. C. Cairns, AHR, 78(Dec
1973):1406-20.

Alföldi-Rosenbaum, E. Anamur Nekropolü: the Necropolis of Anemurium. Ankara: Türk Tarih Kurumu, 1971. Rev. by
J. M. C. Toynbee, Antiquity, 47(Je 1973):153-4.

Alford, Harold J. The Proud Peoples: The Heritage and Culture
of Spanish-Speaking Peoples in the United States. New York:
David McKay, 1972. Rev. by J. V. Reese, SWHQ, 76(Ja
1973):339-40.

Algar, Hamid. Mirza Malkum Khan: A Biographical Study of Iranian Modernism. Berkeley: U Cal Press, 1973. Rev. by
J. A. Bill, MEJ, 27(Aut 1973):505-6.

Allard, Sven. Russia and the Austin State Treaty: A Case Study of
Soviet Policy in Europe. University Park, Pa.: Pa St U
Press, 1970. Rev. by A. Dallin, AHR, 78(Feb 1973):132.

Allardyce, Gilbert, ed. The Place of Fascism in European History.
Englewood Cliffs, N. J.: Prentice-Hall, 1971. Rev. by F.
Eisner, SS, 64(Feb 1973):90-1.

Allen, Jules Verne. Cowboy Lore. San Antonio: Naylor, 1971.
Rev. by C. P. Westermeier, Montana, 23(Win 1973):68.

Allen, W. E. D., ed. Russian Embassies to the Georgian Kings
(1589-1605). 2 vols. New York: Cam U Press, 1970. Rev.
by N. G. Garsoïan, AHR, 78(Je 1973):716-8.

Allsop, Bruce. The Study of Architectural History. New York:
Praeger, 1970. Rev. by T. K. Rabb, JIH, 4(Sum 1973):107-
17.

Allswang, John M. A House for All Peoples: Ethnic Politics in
Chicago. Lexington: U Press Ky., 1971. Rev. by R. J.
Wechman, AHR, 78(Feb 1973):175; I. Dillard, JISHS, 66(Win
1973):480.

Allworth, Edward, ed. Soviet Nationality Problems. New York:
Columbia U Press, 1971. Rev. by R. Pipes, RR, 32(Ja 1973):
82-3.

Allyn, Charles. Sociology: An Introduction. Englewood Cliffs,
N. J.: Prentice-Hall, 1972. Rev. by W. C. Neely, SS, 64
(Dec 1973):340-1.

Almaraz, Felix D., Jr. Tragic Cavalier: Governor Manuel Salcedo of Texas, 1808-1813. Austin: U Tx Press, 1971. Rev. by R. V. Haynes, AHR, 78(Feb 1973):160-1.

Al' Perovich, M. S. Spanish America in the Struggle for Independence. Moscow: Izdatel'stvo "Nauka, " 1971. Rev. by T. S. Cheston, AHR, 78(Oct 1973):1148-50.

Al' Perovich, M. S. and L. IU. Slezkin. A New History of the Countries of Latin America. Moscow: Izdatel'stvo "Vysshaia Shkola, " 1970. Rev. by T. S. Cheston, AHR, 78(Oct 1973): 1148-50.

Alpers, E. A. The East African Slave Trade. Nairobi: East African Publishing House, 1967. Rev. by A. Redmayne, AfAf, 72(Ja 1973):91-3.

Alric, Henry-Jean-Antoine. Sketches of a Journey on the Two Oceans and to the Interior of America and of a Civil War in Northern Lower California. Los Angeles: Dawson's, 1971. Rev. by N. J. Stowe, WHQ, 4(Jl 1973):334-5.

Al-Sabūr, Salāh 'Abd. Murder in Baghdad. Leiden: E. J. Brill, 1972. Rev. by T. Le Gassick, MEJ, 27(Aut 1973):526.

Alter, Peter. Die irische Nationalbewegung zwischen Parlament und Revolution: Der konstitutionelle nationalismus in Irland, 1880-1918. Munich: R. Oldenbourg, 1971. Rev. by J. Lee, JHM, 45(Mar 1973):137-8.

Amaury, Francine. Histoire du plus grand quotidien de la IIIᵉ République: Le Petit Parisien, 1876-1944. Vol. 1. "La Société du Petit Parisien": Entreprise de presse, d'éditions et de messageries, " Vol. 2. "Le Petit Parisien": Instrument de propagande au service du Régime. [Paris:] Presses Universitaires de France, 1972. Rev. by A. Sedgwick, AHR, 78(Oct 1973):1079-80.

Ambler, Effie. The Career of Aleksei S. Suvorin, Russian Journalism and Politics, 1861-1881. Detroit: Wayne St U Press, 1972. Rev. by H. J. Ellison, RR, 32(Apr 1973):198-200.

Ambrose, Stephen E. Rise to Globalism. London: Penguin, 1971. Rev. by R. D. Accinelli, CHR, 54(Sep 1973):334-6.

Ambroz, Oton. Realignment of World Power: The Russo-Chinese Schism. 2 vols. New York: Robert Speller & Sons, 1972. Rev. by R. L. Walker, RR, 32(Apr 1973):189-92.

The American Heritage Book of Natural Wonders. New York: American Heritage Publishing Co., 1972. Rev. by G. L. H., IS, 29(Fall 1973):236.

Ames, William E.   A History of the "National Intelligencer."
    Chapel Hill: UNC Press, 1972. Rev. by H. Hamilton, FHQ,
    51(Apr 1973):451-2; E. G. McPherson, NCHR, 50(Win 1973):
    101-3; P. Levine, JISHS, 66(Win 1973):469-70.

Ammon, Alf.   Die Christliche Demokratie Chiles: Partei, Ideologie,
    revolutionäre Bewegung.... Bonn, Germany: Verlag neue
    Geselischaft GmbH., 1972. Rev. by A. Von Lazar, HAHR,
    53(Aug 1973):552-5.

Amuzegar, Jahangir and M. Ali Fekrat.   Iran: Economic Develop-
    ment Under Dualistic Conditions.   London: U Chi Press, 1971.
    Rev. by J. W. Gunter, MEJ, 27(Spr 1973):234-5.

Anderson, Dennis.   James Kerr Pollock: His Life and Letters.
    Ann Arbor: U Mich Press, 1972. Rev. by K. J. Pike,
    AmArc, 36(Jl 1973):411-14.

Anderson, Eugene M.   see Wehlage, Gary

Anderson, Hans.   Urbanisierte Ortschaften und lateinische Termi-
    nologie Studien zur Geschichte des nordeuropäischen Städte
    wesens vor 1350.   Göteborg: Kungl, 1971. Rev. by J. M.
    Jochens, AHR, 78(Feb 1973):84.

Anderson, Jervis.   A. Philip Randolph: A Biographical Portrait.
    New York: Harcourt, Brace, Jovanovich, 1973. Rev. by
    T. Kornweibel, Jr., JNH, 58(Oct 1973):471-4; J. W. Ivy,
    Crisis, 80(Oct 1973):279.

Anderson, John Q., ed.   Brokenburn: The Journal of Kate Stone,
    1861-1868.   Baton Rouge: LSU Press, 1972. Rev. by S. W.
    Wiggins, JAH, 60(Je 1973):137-8.

Anderson, M. S.   The Ascendency of Europe: Aspects of European
    History, 1815-1914.   Totowa, N. J.: Rowman and Littlefield,
    1972. Rev. by S. R. Smith, HT, 7(Nov 1973):110-11; M. D.
    Biddiss, History, 58(Oct 1973):456-7.

Anderson, Michael.   Family Structure in Nineteenth-Century Lanca-
    shire.   New York: Cam U Press, 1971. Rev. by T. R.
    Hareven, AHR, 78(Oct 1973):1062-4; R. Shorthouse, BHR, 47
    (Spr 1973):131-2.

Anderson, Richard Lloyd.   Joseph Smith's New England Heritage:
    Influences of Grandfathers Solomon Mack and Asael Smith.
    Salt Lake City: Deseret, 1971. Rev. by C. S. Peterson,
    JAH, 59(Mar 1973):1004-6.

Anderson, Thomas P.   Matanza, El Salvador's Communist Revolt of
    1932.   Lincoln: U Neb Press, 1971. Rev. by R. L. Wood-
    ward, Jr., HT, 6(May 1973):489-90; R. M. Schneider, AHR,

78(Je 1973):749; P. F. Flemion, HAHR, 53(May 1973):334-6.

Andrews, Kenneth R. , ed. The Last Voyage of Drake and Hawkins.
London: Cam U Press, 1972. Rev. by C. F. Richmond,
HAHR, 53(May 1973):313-14.

Andrews, Wayne. Architecture in New England: A Photographic
History. Brattleboro, Vt. : Stephen Greene, 1973. Rev. by
B. K. Little, PMHB, 97(Oct 1973):548-9.

Andriette, Eugene A. Devon and Exter in the Civil War. Newton
Abbot: David and Charles, 1971. Rev. by B. W. Quintrell,
History, 58(Feb 1973):102.

Andrist, Ralph K. , ed. George Washington: A Biography in His
Own Words. New York: Harper and Row, 1972. Rev. by
R. A. Rutland, VMHB, 81(Jl 1973):372-3.

Anes, Gonzalo, ed. Memoriales y discursos de Francisco Martínez
de Mata. Madrid: Editorial Moneda y Credito, 1971. Rev.
by D. R. Ringrose, JEH, 33(Dec 1973):876-7.

Angel, Lawrence J. Lerna, a Preclassical Site in the Argolid: Results of Excavations Conducted by the American School of Classical Studies. Vol. 2. The People. Washington, D. C. :
Smithsonian Institution, 1971. Rev. by M. Walker, T & C, 14
(Ja 1973):78-81.

_____. The People of Lerna: Analysis of a Prehistoric Aegean
Population. Washington, D. C. : Smithsonian Institution, 1971.
Rev. by M. Walker, T & C, 14(Ja 1973):78-81.

Angell, Alan. Politics and the Labour Movement in Chile. London:
Ox U Press, 1972. Rev. by T. C. Wright, HAHR, 53(Aug
1973):550-2.

Angle, Paul M. The Collected Poetry of Abraham Lincoln. Springfield, Ill. : Lincoln and Herndon Building and Press, 1971.
Rev. by L. Anderson, RKHS, 71(Apr 1973):202-3.

Annual Studies of America, 1971. Moscow, U. S. S. R. : Nauka, 1971.
Rev. by R. F. Byrnes, JAH, 60(Dec 1973):763-5.

Ansari, Z. D. see Sankalia, H. D.

Ansel, Walter. Hitler and the Middle Sea. Durham, N. C. : Duke
U Press, 1972. Rev. by C. Burdick, JMH, 45(Sept 1973):544-5.

Anstruther, Ian. The Scandal of the Andover Workhouse. London:
Geoffrey Bles, 1973. Rev. by R. J. Olney, Archives, 11(Aut
1973):105-6.

Antonovsky, Aaron and Alan Arian. Hopes and Fears of Israelis: Consensus in a New Society. Jerusalem: Jerusalem Academic Press, 1972. Rev. by S. D. Johnston, MEJ, 27(Spr 1973): 239-40.

Antoun, Richard T. Arab Village: A Social Structural Study of a Transjordanian Peasant Community. Bloomington: Ind U Press, 1972. Rev. by F. I. Khuri, MEJ, 27(Sum 1973):391-2.

_____ and Iliya Harik, eds. Rural Politics and Social Change in the Middle East. Bloomington: Ind U Press, 1972. Rev. by A. I. Tannous, MEJ, 27(Aut 1973):521-2.

Aponte, Barbara Bockus. Alfonso Reyes and Spain: His Dialogue Unamuno, Valle-Inclán, Ortega y Gasset, Jiménez and Gomez de la Serna. Austin U Tx Press, 1972. Rev. by W. F. Cooper, HAHR, 53(May 1973):362-3.

Arbeloa, V. M. see Batilori, I.

Arceneaux, William. Acadian General: Alfred Mouton and the Civil War. Lafayette: U SW La, 1972. Rev. by M. Hattaway, LaH, 14(Win 1973):110.

Archer, Leonard C. Black Images in the American Theatre. Brooklyn, N. Y.: Pageant-Poseidon, 1973. Rev. by G. B. Current, Crisis, 80(Dec 1973):352.

Archer, Margaret Scotford see Vaughan, Michalina

Ardery, Julia Spencer. Kentucky Court and Other Records. Baltimore: Genealogical Publishing Co., 1972. Rev. by I. S. Winkler, RKHS, 71(Ja 1973):112.

Ardoin, Robert Bruce L. Louisiana Census Records. Vol. II. (Iberville, Natchitoches, Pointe Coupée and Rapides Parishes, 1810-1820). Baltimore: Genealogical Publishing, 1972. Rev. by B. C. D'Antoni, LaH, 14(Fall 1973):411-12.

Argenti, Philip P. The Religious Minorities of Chios: Jews and Roman Catholics. New York: Cam U Press, 1970. Rev. by S. Skendi, AHR, 78(Oct 1973):1011-12.

Arian, Alan, ed. The Elections in Israel, 1969. Jerusalem: Jerusalem Academic Press, 1972. Rev. by B. Reich, MEJ, 27 (Sum 1973):396-7.

_____. Hopes and Fears of Israelis see Antonovsky, Aaron

Armajani, Yahya. Iran. Englewood Cliffs, N. J.: Prentice-Hall, 1972. Rev. in CurH, 64(Ja 1973):34; E. Lengyel, SS, 64(Nov 1973):296-7.

Armbruster, Frank E. and Doris Yokelson. The Forgotten Americans: A Survey of Values, Beliefs, and Concerns of the Majority. New Rochelle, N. Y.: Arlington House, 1972. Rev. by H. Sitkoff, JAH, 60(Sep 1973):501-2.

Armengaud, André. La population française au XIXe siecle. Paris: Presses Universitaires de France, 1971. Rev. by P. V. Adams, JIH, 4(Aut 1973):321-3.

Armentano, D. T. The Myths of Antitrust: Economic Theory and Legal Cases. New Rochelle, N. Y.: Arlington House, 1972. Rev. by D. Dewey, BHR, 47(Spr 1973):123-5.

Armstrong, Hamilton Fish. Peace and Counterpeace: From Wilson to Hitler. Memoirs of Hamilton Fish Armstrong. New York: Harper and Row, 1971. Rev. by F. G. Campbell, JMH, 45 (Mar 1973):173-5.

Armstrong, Virginia I., comp. I Have Spoken: American History Through the Voices of the Indians. Chicago: Swallow, 1971. Rev. by R. L. Nichols, A & W, 15(Spr 1973):88-9.

Arnakis, George G. The Near East in Modern Times. Vol. I. The Ottoman Empire and the Balkan States to 1900. Austin, Tx.: Pemberton, 1969. Rev. by D. N. Skiotis, AHR, 78(Dec 1973): 1502-4.

_____ and Wayne S Vucinich. The Near East in Modern Times. Vol. II. Forty Crucial Years, 1900-1940. Austin, Tx.: Pemberton, 1972. Rev. by D. N. Skiotis, AHR, 78(Dec 1973):1502-4.

Arndt, Karl J. R. George Rapp's Successors and Material Heirs (1847-1916). Rutherford, N. J.: Fairleigh-Dickinson U Press, 1971. Rev. by C. M. Stotz, WPHM, 56(Apr 1973):198-200.

Arnheim, M. T. W. The Senatorial Aristocracy in the Later Roman Empire. New York: Ox U Press, 1972. Rev. by S. J. Simon, AHR, 78(Oct 1973):1029-30.

Arnold, Joseph L. The New Deal in the Suburbs: A History of the Greenbelt Town Program, 1935-1954. Columbus: Ohio St U Press, 1971. Rev. by K. T. Jackson, NJH, 91(Sum 1973):125-9; J. B. Lane, MHM, 68(Spr 1973):114-5.

Aronson, Shlomo. Reinhard Heydrich und die Frühgeschichte von Gestapo und SD. Stuttgart: Deutsche Verlags-Anstalt, 1971. Rev. by G. H. Stein, JMH, 45(Je 1973):352-5.

Aronson, Theodore. Queen Victoria and the Bonapartes. Indianapolis: Bobbs-Merrill, 1972. Rev. by G. Smith, AHR, 78(Feb 1973):106-7.

Arraes, Miguel. Brazil: The People and the Power. Baltimore:
    Penguin, 1972. Rev. by E. J. Rogers, HAHR, 53(Aug 1973):
    568-9.

The Art of the Possible: The Memoirs of Lord Butler, K. G.,
    C. H. Boston: Gambit, 1972. Rev. by T. Lloyd, AHR, 78
    (Oct 1973):1069-70.

Aruri, Naseer H. Jordan: A Study in Political Development (1921-
    1965). The Hague, Netherlands: Martinus Nyhoff, 1972. Rev.
    in CurH, 64(Ja 1973):34.

Ascher, Abraham. Paul Axelrod and the Development of Menshevism.
    Cambridge, Mass.: Har U Press, 1972. Rev. by A. Wild-
    man, RR, 32(Oct 1973):431-3; S. H. Baron, JMH, 45(Dec
    1973):696-7. NOTE: This title listed as Pavel Axelrod...
    in JMH.

Aschmann, Rudolph. Memoirs of a Swiss Officer in the American
    Civil War. Bern and Frankfurt/M: Herbert Lang, 1972. Rev.
    by J. I. Robertson, Jr., VMHB, 81(Apr 1973):208-9; P. S.
    Thompson, JAH, 60(Je 1973):138-9.

Ash, Roberta. Social Movements in America. Chicago: Markham,
    1972. Rev. by I. H. Bartlett, JAH, 59(Mar 1973):1003-4.

Ashbee, Paul. The Earthen Long Barrow in Britain: An Introduc-
    tion to the Study of the Funerary Practice and Culture of the
    Neolithic People of the Third Millennium B. C. Toronto: U
    Tor Press, 1970. Rev. by L. H. Barfield, AHR, 78(Feb
    1973):74-5.

Ashby, Le Roy. The Spearless Leader: Senator Borah and the Pro-
    gressive Movement in the 1920's. Urbana: U Ill Press, 1972.
    Rev. by M. Malone, Montana, 23(Win 1973):65; R. J. Mad-
    dox, JAH, 59(Mar 1973):1035-6; R. T. Johnson, SS, 64(Oct
    1973):234; J. Penick, Jr., AgH, 47(Oct 1973):370-1; A. R.
    Travis, JISHS, 66(Win 1973):474-5.

Ashford, Gerald. Spanish Texas: Yesterday and Today. Austin,
    Tx.: Jenkins, 1971. Rev. by F. D. Almaraz, Jr., HAHR,
    53(May 1973):306-7.

Ashley, Maurice. Charles II: the Man and the Statesman. New
    York: Praeger, 1971. Rev. by T. W. Perry, WMQ, 3rd
    Ser., 30(Ja 1973):178-9; D. R. Lacey, JMH, 45(Mar 1973):
    100-3.

_____. The Golden Century: Europe 1598-1715. New York:
    Praeger, 1968. Rev. by T. K. Rabb, JMH, 45(Sep 1973):456-
    62.

Asihene, E. V. Introduction to Traditional Art of Western Africa.
    London: Constable, 1972. Rev. by M. D. McLeod, AfAf, 72
    (Oct 1973):461-2.

Aspinall, A. , ed. The Correspondence of George, Prince of Wales,
    1770-1812. Vol. VIII. 1811-1812. New York: Ox U Press,
    1972. Rev. by C. R. Middleton, Historian, 35(Feb 1973):284-5.

Asplin, P. W. A. Medieval Ireland c. 1170-1495: A Bibliography
    of Secondary Works. Dublin: Royal Irish Academy, 1971. Rev.
    by J. A. Watt, History, 58(Oct 1973):419-20.

Association of Russian-American Scholars see Russian-American
    Scholars, Association of

Åstrom, Paul and Lena, M. R. Popham, and V. E. G. Kenna. The
    Swedish Cyprus Expedition. Vol. IV. The Late Cypriote
    Bronze Age. Lund: n. p. 1972. Rev. by R. S. Merrillees,
    Antiquity, 47(Dec 1973):323-4.

Atkinson, James. The Trial of Luther. London: Batsford, 1972.
    Rev. by P. Brooks, HJ, 16(Je 1973):433-5.

Audin, Maurice. Histoire de l'imprimerie. Radioscopie d'une ère:
    De Gutenberg à l'Informatique. Paris: Editions A. & J.
    Picard, 1972. Rev. by P. G. Bietenholz, JMH, 45(Dec 1973):
    644-6.

Auger, Boyd. The Architect and the Computer. New York: Praeger,
    1972. Rev. by C. W. Condit, T & C, 14(Oct 1973):670-2.

Ault, Phil. These Are the Great Lakes. New York: Dodd, Mead,
    1972. Rev. by E. O. C. , IS, 29(Fall, 1973):232.

Ault, Warren O. Open Field Farming in Medieval England. London:
    Allen and Unwin, 1972. Rev. by R. H. Hilton, MH, 2(Spr
    1973):48-9.

Aurand, Harold W. From the Molly Maguires to the United Mine
    Workers: The Social Ecology of an Industrial Union, 1869-
    1897. Philadelphia: Temple U Press, 1971. Rev. by W.
    Graebner, BHR, 47(Spr 1973):112-13.

Austin, Anne L. The Woolsey Sisters of New York: A Family's
    Involvement in the Civil War and a New Profession (1860-1900).
    Philadelphia: American Philosophical Society, 1971. Rev. by
    W. I. Trattner, NYHSQ, 57(Apr 1973):186-7.

Austin, Herbert H. With Macdonald in Uganda. London: Dawson's
    of Pall Mall, 1973. Rev. by M. Twaddle, AfAf, 72(Oct 1973):
    466.

Avary, Myrta Lockett. Dixie After the War. New York: De Capo,

13 AVRICH

1970. Rev. by S. W. Wiggins, AlaRe, 26(Apr 1973):145-6.

Avrich, Paul. Russian Rebels, 1600-1800. New York: Schocken, 1972. Rev. by J. L. Wieczynski, RR, 32(J1 1973):316-8; A. Sinel, HT, 7(Nov 1973):142-3; J. W. Kipp, MilAf, 37(Dec 1973):158-9.

Axelson, Sigbert. Culture Confrontation in the Lower Congo: From the Old Congo Kingdom to the Congo Independent State, With Special Reference to the Swedish Missionaries in the 1880's and 1890's. Folköping, Sweden: Gummessons, 1970. Rev. by J. Vansina, Africa, 43(Ja 1973):85-6.

Aydelotte, William O., Allen G. Bogue, and Robert William Fogel, eds. The Dimensions of Quantitative Research in History. Princeton, N. J.: Prin U Press, 1972. Rev. by C. M. Dollar, JAH, 60(Dec 1973):768-70; R. Higgs, BHR, 47(Aut 1973): 375-6; R. P. Swierenga, PHR, 42(Aug 1973):421-3.

Ayers, H. Brandt and Thomas H. Naylor, eds. You Can't Eat Magnolias. New York: McGraw-Hill, 1972. Rev. by W. D. Lewis, AlaRe, 26(Apr 1973):147-50; J. E. Gonzales, JMiH, 35(Aug 1973):415-7; W. H. J. Thomas, SCHM, 74(Apr 1973):106.

Ayerst, David. The Manchester Guardian: Biography of a Newspaper. Ithaca, N. Y.: Cornell U Press, 1971. Rev. by P. Stanksy, JMH, 45(Mar 1973):134-6.

Ayling, Stanley. George the Third. New York: Knopf, 1972. Rev. by C. R. Ritcheson, AHR, 78(Oct 1973):1015-6; W. D. Jones, Historian, 36(Nov 1973):102-3.

Aylmer, C. E., ed. The Interregnum: The Quest for Settlement, 1646-1660. [Hamden, Conn.:] Archon, 1972. Rev. by R. Schlatter, AHR, 78(Oct. 1973):1052-5.

Aziz, K. K. The All India Muslim Conference (1928-35). [Karachi:] Karachi National Publishing House, 1972. Rev. by I. H. Qureshi, HJ, 16(Dec 1973):874-5.

Baali, Fuad see Reed, John P.

Babington, Anthony. The English Bastille: A History of Newgate Gaol and Prison Conditions in England, 1188-1902. New York: St. Martin's, 1972. Rev. by G. Rudé, AHR, 78(Dec 1973):1453.

Bachrach, Bernard S. A History of the Alans in the West: From Their First Appearances in the Sources of Classical Antiquity Through the Early Middle Ages. Minneapolis: U Minn Press, 1973. Rev. by J. E. Rexine, HRNB, 2(Oct 1973):10-11.

_____. Merovingian Military Organization, 481-751. Minneapolis: U Minn Press, 1972. Rev. by P. D. Thomas,

MilAf, 37(Apr 1973):71; C. Gillmor, T & C, 14(J1 1973):497-8.

Bacon, Francis. The History of the Reign of King Henry the Seventh. New York: Bobbs-Merrill, 1972. Rev. by G. M. Straka, SS, 64(Nov 1973):297.

Badian, E. Publicans and Sinners: Private Enterprise in the Service of the Roman Republic. Ithaca, N. Y.: Cornell U Press, 1972. Rev. by F. S. Lear, BHR, 47(Aut 1973):418-19.

Baecker, Thomas. Die Deutsche Mexikopolitik 1913/1914. Berlin: Colloquium Verlag, 1971. Rev. by W. Schiff, TAm, 30(Oct 1973):281-2.

Bagchi, Amiya Kumar. Private Investment in India, 1900-1939. London: Cam U Press, 1972. Rev. by S. Venu, IQ, 29(Apr-Je 1973):17.

Bagwell, William. School Desegregation in the Carolinas: Two Case Studies. Columbia: U SCar Press, 1972. Rev. by D. M. McFarland, JSH, 39(Feb 1973):142-3.

Bahlman, Dudley, W. R., ed. The Diary of Sir Edward Walter Hamilton, 1880-1885. Oxford: Clarendon, 1972. Rev. by A. Jones, HJ, 16(Feb 1973):215-18.

Bahrenburg, Bruce. The Pacific Then and Now. New York: Putnam's, 1971. Rev. by T. Ropp, SS, 63(Dec 1972):339.

Bailey, A. G. Culture and Nationality. Toronto: McClelland and Stewart, 1972. Rev. by D. A. Muise, CHR, 54(Dec 1973):443-4.

Bailey, Helen Miller and Frank H. Cruz. The Latin Americans: Past and Present. Boston: Houghton Mifflin, 1972. Rev. by A. P. Nasatir, SS, 64(Nov 1973):299.

Bailey, M. Thomas. Reconstruction in Indian Territory: A Story of Avarice, Discrimination, and Opportunism. Port Washington, N. Y.: Kennikat, 1972. Rev. by R. L. Hume, JSH, 39(May 1973):301-2; W. T. Hagan, A & W, 15(Win 1973):379-80; R. N. Satz, HT, 7(Nov 1973):148-9; W. D. Baird, WHQ, 4(Oct 1973):461-3.

Bailey, Paul. Polygamy Was Better Than Monotony. Los Angeles: Westernlore, 1972. Rev. by G. L. Caldwell, PacH, 17(Spr 1973):90-1.

Bailey, Sidney D. Prohibitions and Restraints in War. New York: Ox U Press, 1972. Rev. by W. A. Solf, MilAf, 37(Apr 1973):71.

Bailyn, Bernard and Donald Fleming, eds. Perspectives in American History. Vol. V. Law in American History. Cambridge,
Mass.: Charles Warren Center for Studies in American History, 1971. Rev. by J. E. Cooke, JAH, 59(Mar 1973):975-6;
F. B. Wiener, NYHSQ, 57(Apr 1973):189-9.

Baines, John M. Revolution in Peru: Mariá-tegui and the Myth.
University, Ala.: U Ala Press, 1972. Rev. by M. M.
Urquidi, HAHR, 53(May 1973):338-40.

Baird, W. David. The Osage People. Phoenix: Indian Tribal
Series, 1972. Rev. by T. B. Hinton, JAriH, 14(Aut 1973):
264-5.

_____. Peter Pitchlynn: Chief of the Choctaws. Norman: U Okla
Press, 1972. Rev. by W. M. Evans, FHQ, 52(Oct 1973):211-
12; C. L. Kenner, Montana, 23(Win 1973):60; A. H. DeRosier, Jr., PHR, 42(Apr 1973):245-6; A. H. DeRosier, Jr.,
WHQ, 4(Apr 1973):209-10.

Baker, A. R. H., ed. Progress in Historical Geography. Newton
Abbot: David and Charles, 1972. Rev. by H. Carter, History,
58(Oct 1973):413-4; P. G. Goheen, JMH, 45(Sep 1973):471-2.

Baker, Gordon Pratt, ed. Those Incredible Methodists: A History
of the Baltimore Conference of the United Methodist Church.
Baltimore: Commission on Archives and History, Baltimore
Conference, 1972. Rev. by T. L. Agnew, MHM, 68(Sum 1973):
233-4.

Baker, J. H. An Introduction to English Legal History. London:
Butterworth, 1971. Rev. by D. Jenkins, History, 58(Feb 1973):
162-3.

Baker, Jean H. The Politics of Continuity: Maryland Political
Parties From 1858-1870. Baltimore: JHU Press, 1973. Rev.
by G. L. Seligmann, Jr., HRNB, 2(Oct 1973):16; H. Belz,
JSH, 39(Nov 1973):599-600; R. Duncan, NCHR, 50(Aut 1973):
422-3; P. S. Klein, PMHB, 97(Oct 1973):555-6.

Baker, Norman. Government and Contractors: the British Treasury
and War Supplies, 1775-1883. London: Athlone, 1971. Rev.
by R. J. B. Knight, JMH, 45(Mar 1973):111-12; D. S. Graham, CHR, 54(Sep 1973):316-7; J. Shy, AHR, 78(Je 1973):689-
90; J. Cannon, History, 58(Feb 1973):112.

Baker, Richard D. Judicial Review in Mexico: A Study of the
Amparo Suit. Austin: U Tx Press, 1971. Rev. by F. P. Le
Veness, TAm, 30(Jl 1973):143-5.

Baker, Thomas Harrison. The Memphis Commercial Appeal: The
History of a Southern Newspaper. Baton Rouge: LSU Press,
1971. Rev. by W. L. Brown, ArkHQ, 32(Spr 1973):99-101;

W. D. Miller, JSH, 39(Feb 1973):138-9.

Baker, Timothy. Medieval London. New York: Praeger, 1970. Rev. by R. A. Wertime, Archives, 26(Oct 1973):316.

Bakewell, P. J. Silver Mining and Society in Colonial Mexico, Zacatecas, 1546-1700. New York: Cam U Press, 1971. Rev. by A. M. Gallagher, TAm, 29(Ja 1973):400-2; M. D. Bernstein, AHR, 78(Je 1973):747.

Bakker, Elna and Richard Lillard. The Great Southwest. The Story of a Land and Its People. Palo Alto, Cal.: American West, 1972. Rev. by C. C. Potts, PacH, 17(Win 1973):75-6.

Baldwin, John W. and Richard A. Goldthwaite, eds. Universities in Politics: Case Studies from the Late Middle Ages and Early Modern Period. Baltimore: JHU Press, 1972. Rev. by A. C. Reeves, Historian, 35(Feb 1973):278-9; P. Kibre, AHR, 78(Dec 1973):1433.

Baldwin, Leland. Reframing the Constitution: An Imperative for Modern America. Santa Barbara: A B C Clio, 1971. Rev. by J. G. Smith, WPHM, 56(Oct 1973):435-8; W. D. Gilliam, RKHS, 71(Ja 1973):117-19.

Balfour, Michael and Julian Frisby. Helmuth von Moltke: A Leader Against Hitler. New York: St. Martin's, 1972. Rev. by R. E. Neil, AHR, 78(Dec 1973):1491-2.

Ball, M. Margaret. The "Open" Commonwealth. Durham, N. C.: Duke U Press, 1971. Rev. by J. Flint, CHR, 54(Sep 1973): 323.

Ballard, Allen B. The Education of Black Folk. New York: Harper and Row, 1973. Rev. by D. L. Watson, Crisis, 80(Dec 1973): 322-3.

Balsdon, J P. V. D. Life and Leisure in Ancient Rome. New York: McGraw-Hill, 1969. Rev. by H. F. Guite, Archives, 26(Apr 1973):154.

Bamford, Paul W. Fighting Ships and Prisons: The Mediterranean Galleys of France in the Age of Louis XIV. Minneapolis: U Minn Press, 1973. Rev. by A. N. Hamscher, MilAf, 37(Oct 1973):109-10.

Bandelier, Fanny and Gerald Theisen, trans. The Narrative of Alvar Nuñez Cabeza de Vaca, with Oviedo's Version of the Lost Joint Report. Barre, Mass.: Imprint Society, 1972. Rev. by W. H. Hutchinson, AW, 10(Sep 1973):54.

Bandyopadhyaya, Jayantanuja. Mao Tse-Tung and Ghandi. Calcutta: Allied, 1973. Rev. by B. Sarkar, IQ, 29(J1-Sep 1973):265-6.

Bangert, Dieter Ernst. Die russisch-österreichische militärische
    Zusammenarbeit im Siebenjährigen Kriege in den Jahren 1758-
    1759. Boppard am Rhein: Harald Boldt Verlag, 1971. Rev.
    by W. G. McGill, JMH, 45(Je 1973):312-13.

Barber, James. South Africa's Foreign Policy, 1945-1970. New
    York: Ox U Press, 1973. Rev. by R. W. Strayer, HRNB,
    2(Nov/Dec 1973):35.

Barber, Richard. The Figure of Arthur. London: Longmans, 1972.
    Rev. by K. Hughes, Archives, 11(Spr 1973):45.

Barbour, Brian M., ed. American Transcendentalism: an Anthology
    of Criticism. Notre Dame, Ind.: U Notre Dame Press, 1973.
    Rev. by J. D. Daenecke, HRNB, 2(Oct 1973):15.

Barclay, Glen St. J. The Rise and Fall of the New Roman Empire:
    Italy's Bid for World Power, 1890-1943. New York: St. Mar-
    tin's, 1973. Rev. by H. Cliadakis, HRNB, 2(Nov/Dec 1973):
    28.

_____. Struggle for a Continent: The Diplomatic History of South
    America, 1919-1945. New York: NYU Press, 1972. Rev. by
    N. A. Bailey, AHR, 78(Je 1973):746; H. Blakeware, History,
    58(Feb 1973):146-7.

Barfield, Lawrence. Northern Italy Before Rome. New York:
    Praeger, 1972. Rev. by S. Foltiny, Archives, 26(Ja 1973):69.

Barkdull, Tom. Lonesome Walls: An Odyssey Through Ghost Towns
    of the Old West. New York: Exposition, 1971. Rev. by C.
    Lowe, NHSQ, 16(Win 1973):255.

Barker, A. J. The Rape of Ethiopia, 1936. New York: Ballantine,
    1971. Rev. by D. Koenig, MilAf, 37(Dec 1973):160-1.

Barker, Carol M. and Matthew H. Fox. Classified Files: The
    Yellowing Pages; a Report on Scholars' Access to Government
    Documents. New York: 20th Century Fund, 1972. Rev. by
    L. Morton, JAH, 60(Sep 1973):517-9.

Barker, Charles A. American Convictions: Cycles of Public Thought
    1600-1850. Philadelphia: Lippincott, 1970. Rev. by E. Lurie,
    JAH, 60(Dec 1973):772-4.

Barker, Nancy Nichols, trans. and ed. The French Legation in
    Texas. Austin, Tx.: State Historical Assn., 1973. Rev. by
    E. Hebert, LaH 14(Fall 1973):402-4.

Barker, Rodney. Education and Politics 1900-1951: A Study of the
    Labour Party. [Oxford:] Ox U Press, 1972. Rev. by A. Mar-
    wick, History, 58(Oct 1973):478-9.

Barletta, E. Aleandri, ed. La Depositeria del Concilio di Trento I. Il registro di Antonio Manelli, 1545-9. Rome: Ministero dell'Interno Pubblicazioni degli Archivi di Stato, Fonti e Sussidi, I, 1970. Rev. by D. Fenlon, Archives, 11(Aut 1973):102.

Barley, M. W. The House and Home. London: Studio Vista, 1971. Rev. by L. Butler, History, 58(Feb 1973):161.

Barlow, Frank. Edward the Confessor. Berkeley: U Cal Press, 1970. Rev. by T. Sandquist, CHR, 54(Sep 1973):315.

_____ et al. Leofric of Exeter: Essays in Commemoration of the Foundation of Exeter Cathedral Library in A. D. 1072. Exeter, Eng.: U Exeter, 1972. Rev. by M. R. Godden, Archives, 11(Spr 1973):46-7.

Barmann, Lawrence F. Baron Friedrich von Hügel and the Modernist Crisis in England. Cambridge: Cam U Press, 1972. Rev. by S. Rothblatt, JMH, 45(Je 1973):331-2.

Barnes, Leonard. Africa in Eclipse. London: Gollancz, 1971. Rev. by N. Rubin, AfAf, 72(Oct 1973):448-50.

Barnes, Timothy David. Tertullian: A Historical and Literary Study. [Oxford:] Ox U Press, 1971. Rev. by R. A. Markus, History, 58(Feb 1973):73.

Barnet, Richard J. Roots of War. New York: Atheneum, 1972. Rev. by W. La Feber, JAH, 60(Je 1973):183-4.

Barnett, Margery see Albertson, Peter

Barnett, R. D., ed. The Sephardi Heritage: Essays on the History and Cultural Contribution of the Jews of Spain and Portugal. Vol. 1. The Jews in Spain and Portugal Before and After the Expulsion of 1492. New York: Ktav, 1971. Rev. by J. L. Shneidman, AHR, 78(Oct 1973):1035-6; C. J. Bartlett, History, 58(Oct 1973):476-7; T. Lloyd, JMH, 45(Sep 1973):530-1.

Barney, Keith Richard. The History of Springfield, Vermont, 1885-1961: With an Introductory Chapter to 1885. Springfield, Vt.: William L. Bryant Foundation, 1972. Rev. by S. B. Hand, JAH, 60(Sep 1973):470-1; H. Jordan, VH, 41(Sum 1973):173-5.

Barney, William. The Road to Secession: A New Perspective on the Old South. New York: Praeger, 1972. Rev. by T. H. O'Connor, JAH, 60(Sep 1973):449-50.

Barnhart, John D. and Dorothy L. Riker. Indiana to 1816: The Colonial Period. Indianapolis: Indiana Historical Bureau and Indiana Historical Society, 1971. Rev. by D. L. Parman, WHQ, 4(Jl 1973):331-3; L. L. Sylvester, JISHS, 66(Spr 1973):103-4.

19   BARNIKOL

Barnikol, Ernst. Bruno Bauer: Studien und Materialien. Assen:
    Van Gorcum, 1972. Rev. by D. McLellan, AHR, 78(Oct 1973):
    1091.

Baron, Salo Wittmayer. A Social and Religious History of the Jews:
    Late Middle Ages and the Era of European Expansion, 1200-
    1650. Vol. 13. Inquisition, Renaissance, and Reformation.
    Vol. 14. Catholic Restoration and Wars of Religion. New
    York: Columbia U Press; Philadelphia: Jewish Publication
    Society of America, 1969. Rev. by R. H. Popkin, AHR, 78
    (Oct 1973):1043-6.

Baroni, Geno see Wenk, Michael

Barr, Alwyn. Reconstruction to Reform: Texas Politics 1876-1906.
    Austin: U Tx Press, 1971. Rev. by R. Holland, JOW, 12(Jl
    1973):505.

Barr, Robert D. , ed. Values and Youth (Teaching Social Studies in
    An Age of Crisis, No. 2). Washington, D. C. : National Coun-
    cil for the Social Studies, 1972. Rev. by J. L. Browne, SS,
    64(Feb 1973):87-8.

Barrell, John. The Idea of Landscape and the Sense of Place, 1730-
    1840: An Approach to the Poetry of John Clare. New York:
    Cam U Press, 1972. Rev. by T. Bender, AgH, 47(Jl 1973):
    271-2.

Barrett, Ward J. The Sugar Hacienda of the Marquesses del Valle.
    Minneapolis: U Minn Press, 1970. Rev. by T. F. Glick,
    T & C, 14(Apr 1973):292-3.

Barringer, Richard E. War. Patterns of Conflict. Cambridge,
    Mass. : M I T Press, 1972. Rev. by J. B. Bell, MilAf, 37
    (Dec 1973):155-7.

Barron, Caroline see du Boulay, F. R. H.

Barron, Gloria J. Leadership in Crisis: FDR and the Path to In-
    tervention. Port Washington, N. Y. : Kennikat, 1973. Rev.
    by W. B. Fowler, HRNB, 2(Oct 1973):20.

Barros, James, ed. United Nations: Past, Present and Future. New
    York: Free Press, 1972. Rev. by W. C. Clemens, Jr. , AHR,
    78(Dec 1973):1428-30.

Barrow, G. W. S. , ed. Regesta Regum Scottarum. Vol. II: The
    Acts of William I. Edinburgh: Edinburg U Press, 1971. Rev.
    by N. F. Shead, History, 58(Feb 1973):83-4; J. C. Holt, EHR,
    88(Oct 1973):846-8.

Barry, James P. The Fate of the Lakes: A Portrait of the Great
    Lakes. Grand Rapids, Mich. : Baker Book House, 1972. Rev.

by G. L. H. , IS, 29(Spr 1973):76-7.

_____. Ships of the Great Lakes; 300 Years of Navigation.
Berkeley, Cal.: Howell-North, 1973. Rev. by G. L. H. , IS,
29(Win 1973):317.

Barry, Louise. The Beginning of the West: Annals of the Kansas
Gateway to the American West, 1504-1854. Topeka: Kansas
State Historical Society, 1972. Rev. by D. A. Smith, NMHR,
48(Ja 1973):96; C. T. Edwards, PHR, 42(Aug 1973):426-7;
Editor, NDH, 40(Fall 1973):32-3; L. E. Oliva, AW, 10(Mar
1973):50.

Bartoccini, Fiorella. La "Roma dei Romani." Rome: the institute,
1971. Rev. by D. A. Limoli, AHR, 78(Feb 1973):122; M. S.
Miller, JMH, 45(Mar 1973):141-3.

Basler, Roy P. A Touchstone for Greatness: Essays, Addresses,
and Occasional Pieces About Abraham Lincoln. Westport,
Conn: Greenwood, 1973. Rev. by K. J. Brauer, HRNB, 2
(Nov/Dec 1973):52.

Bass, George F. , ed. A History of Seafaring: Based on Underwater
Archaeology. New York: Walker, 1972. Rev. by A. R.
Lewis, AHR, 78(Je 1973):651-2; L. Casson, Archives, 26(Apr
1973):152-3; J. du P. Taylor, Antiquity, 47(Je 1973):165.

Batho, G. R. , ed. A Calendar of the Shrewsbury and Talbot Papers.
London: H M S O, 1971. Rev. by C. Cross, Archives, 11
(Spr 1973):52-3.

Batllori, I. and V. M. Arbeloa, eds. Arxiu Vidal i Barraquer: Església
i estat durant la Segona República Espanyola 1931-1936. 2 vols.
Montserrat: Monestir de Montserrat, 1971. Rev. by P. A.
Linehan, HJ, 16(Sep 1973):652-6.

Batowski, Henryk. German Diplomacy, 1919-1945, An Outline
Sketch. Katowice: Slaski Instytut Naukowy, 1971. Rev. by
R. A. Woytak, EEQ, 7(Sum 1973):223-5.

Baudi di Vesme, Carlo. Studi sul XVIII secolo: Le prime manifestazioni della rivoluzione d'occidente in Francia e nelle repub-
bliche oligarchiche (1748-1775). Turin: Deputazione Subalpina
di Storia Patria, 1972. Rev. by E. P. Noether, AHR, 78(Dec
1973):1451-2.

Baudot, Marcel, ed. Millénaire monastique du mont Saint-Michel.
Vol. 3. Culte de Saint Michel et pèlerinages au Mont. Paris:
P. Lethielleux Editeur, 1971. Rev. by J. W. Baldwin, AHR,
78(Je 1973):669-70.

Bauer, Rolf. Osterreich: Ein Jahrtausend Geschichte im Herzen
Europas. Berlin: Haude & Spenersche Verlagsbuchhandlung,

1970. Rev. by J. A. Mears, AHR, 78(Je 1973):712-3.

Baughman, James P. The Mallorys of Mystic: Six Generations in
    American Maritime Enterprise. Middletown, Conn.: Wesleyan
    U Press, 1972. Rev. by K. L. Bryant, Jr., SWHQ, 76(Apr
    1973):491-2; D. T. Gilchrist, JSH, 39(May 1973):315-7; L.
    Galambos, AHR, 78(Oct 1973):1130-1; E. A. Mueller, FHQ,
    52(Jl 1973):76-7; P. J. Coleman, JAH,   60(Je 1973):121-2;
    E. C. Kirkland, BHR, 47(Spr 1973):103-4.

Bauman, Richard. For the Reputation of Truth: Politics, Religion
    and Conflict Among the Pennsylvania Quakers, 1750-1800. Bal-
    timore: JHU Press, 1971. Rev. by M. Egnal, CHR, 54(Mar
    1973):93-4; R. A. Burchell, History, 58(Feb 1973):151; K. L.
    Carroll, MHM, 68(Spr 1973):104-5.

Baumgart, Winfried. Der Friede von Paris 1856: Studien zum Ver-
    hältnis von Kriegsfuhrüng, Politik, und Friedensbewahrung.
    Munich: R. Oldenbourg, 1972. Rev. by E. L. Presseisen,
    JMH, 45(Dec 1973):692-3; P. W. Schroeder, AHR, 78(Je 1973):
    677-8; E. Anderson, RR, 32(Oct 1973):449-50.

Baumgartner, Jakob. Mission and Liturgie in Mexiko. Beekenreid,
    Switzerland: Administration der Neuen Zeitschrift für Mission-
    swissenschaft, 1971-1972. Rev. by J. B. Warren, TAm, 30
    (Jl 1973):137-8; G. S. Yeager, HAHR, 53(Aug 1973):505-6.

Bausani, Alessandro. The Persians From the Earliest Days to the
    Twentieth Century. New York: St. Martin's, 1971. Rev. by
    Y. Armajani, SS 64(Feb 1973):89-90.

Bautier, Robert-Henri. The Economic Development of Medieval
    Europe. London: Thames & Hudson, 1971. Rev. by R. B.
    Dobson, History, 58(Feb 1973):78-80.

Baxter, T. W. and E. E. Burke. Guide to Historical Manuscripts
    in the National Archives of Rhodesia. Salisbury: National
    Archives of Rhodesia, 1970. Rev. by E. D. Anthony, AmArch,
    36(Ja 1973):78-9.

Bayerle, Gustav. Ottoman Diplomacy in Hungary. Bloomington: Ind
    U Press, 1972. Rev. by H. N. Howard, MEJ, 27(Sum 1973):
    411-12.

Bayum, Max I. A History of Literary Aesthetics in America. New
    York: Frederick Ungar, 1973. Rev. by J. W. Tuttleton, JAH,
    60(Dec 1973):771-2.

Bazylow, Ludwik. Dzieje Rosji, 1801-1917. Warsaw: Panstowowe
    Wydawnictwo Naukowe, 1970. Rev. by W. Sukiennicki, RR,
    32(Jl 1973):329.

_____. Ostatnie Lata Rosji Carskiej: Rzady Stolypina. Warsaw:

Panstwowe Wydawnictwo Naukowe, 1972. Rev. by M. K. Dziewanowski, RR, 32(Oct 1973):450.

Beach, Vincent W. Charles X of France: His Life and Times. Boulder, Colo.: Pruett, 1971. Rev. by S. Schama, History, 58(Je 1973):302-3; D. Higgs, CHR, 54(Dec 1973):470-2.

Beales, Derek. From Castlereagh to Gladstone: 1815-1885. London: Nelson, 1969. Rev. by M. Hurst, HJ, 16(Mar 1973): 212-15.

Bean, George E. Turkey Beyond the Maeander: An Archaeological Guide. Totowa, N. J.: Rowman and Littlefield, 1971. Rev. by E. L. Kohler, Archives, 26(Ja 1973):66.

Bearman, Robert. The Gregorys of Stivichall in the Sixteenth Century. Coventry: Coventry Branch of the Historical Assn., 1972. Rev. by P. Styles, MH, 2(Sep 1973):49-50.

Bearss, Edwin C., ed. Historical Base Map: Proposed Lincoln Home National Historical Park, Springfield, Illinois. n. p.: n. d. Rev. by G. R. Planck, LH, 75(Spr 1973):39-40.

_____ . A Louisiana Confederate: Diary of Felix Pierre Poché. Natchitoches, La.: NW St U Press, 1972. Rev. by R. O. Hatton, LaH, 14(Spr 1973):221-2; A. Barr, JSH, 39(Feb 1973):124-5.

Beasley, W. G. The Meiji Restoration. Stanford, Cal.: Stan U Press, 1972. Rev. by J. C. Lebra, Historian, 36(Nov 1973): 116-7.

Beattie, John. The Nyoro State. London: Clarendon, 1971. Rev. by H. F. Morris, AfAf, 72(Ja 1973):88.

_____ and John Middleton. Spirit Mediumship and Society in Africa. London: Routledge and Kegan Paul, 1969. Rev. by A. Redmayne, AfAf, 72(Oct 1973):450-1.

Beck, Warren A. and David A. Williams. California: A History of the Golden State. New York: Doubleday, 1972. Rev. by A. F. Rolle, CHQ, 52(Sum 1973):180-1.

Becker, Raymond B. John Gorrie, M. D.: Father of Air Conditioning and Mechanical Refrigeration. New York: Carlton, 1972. Rev. by W. M. Straight, FHQ, 51(Apr 1973):445-6.

Beckford, George L. Persistent Poverty: Underdevelopment in the Plantation Economies of the Third World. New York: Ox U Press, 1972. Rev. by F. W. Knight, HAHR, 53(Aug 1973): 547-8.

Beckham, Stephen Dow. Requiem for a People: The Rogue Indians

and the Frontiersmen. Norman: U Ok Press, 1971. Rev. by
H. Temperley. History, 58(Oct 1973):493; G. R. Lothrop,
WHQ, 4(Apr 1973):212-3.

Beckhart, Benjamin Haggott. Federal Reserve System. New York:
American Institute of Banking (Columbia U Press): 1972. Rev.
by B. J Klebaner, JEH, 33(Sep 1973):669-70; E. Wicker,
JAH, 60(Je 1973):168-9.

Beckman, George M., et al. Dilemmas of Growth in Pre-War
Japan. Princeton, N. J.: Prin U Press, 1971. Rev. by
G. R. Falconeri, AHR, 78(Feb 1973):138.

[Beckwourth, James.] The Life and Adventures of James Beckwourth: As Told to Thomas D. Bonner see Oswald, Delmont R.

Bedford, Denton R. and Dan B. Timmons. Tsali. San Francisco:
Indian Historian Press, 1972. Rev. by B. Lee, AW, 10(Sep
1973):53.

Beeler, John. Warfare in Feudal Europe, 730-1200. Ithaca, N. Y.:
Cornell U Press, 1972. Rev. by C. M. Flail, Jr., HT, 7
(Nov 1973):135-6.

Beeman, Richard R. The Old Dominion and the New Nation, 1788-
1801. Lexington: U Press Ky, 1972. Rev. by N. K. Risjord, JSH, 39(May 1973):282-4; C. E. Prince, JAH, 60(Sep
1973):429-30; J. T. Main, WVH, 34(Apr 1973):305-6; N. E.
Cunningham, Jr., VMHB, 81(Apr 1973):206-7; D. P. Jordan,
MHM, 68(Win 1973):459-60; R. M. Bauman, PMHB, 97(Apr
1973):265-7; H. Ammon, WMQ, 3rd Ser., 30(Jl 1973):510-12.

Beers, Paul B. Profiles From the Susquehanna Valley. Harrisburg,
Pa.: Stackpole, 1973. Rev. by H. Collins, WPHM, 56(Oct
1973):434-5.

Beik, Paul H., ed. The French Revolution. Selected Documents.
London: Macmillan, 1971. Rev. by C. H. Church, ESR, 3
(Oct 1973):397-8.

Beilharz, Edwin A. Felipe de Neve: First Governor of California.
San Francisco: California Historical Society, 1971. Rev. by
G. Thiesen, JOW, 12(Ja 1973):183.

Beitzell, Edwin W. Point Lookout Prison Camp for Confederates.
Abell, Md.: E. W. Beitzell, 1971. Rev. by J. L. Nichols,
MHM, 68(Fall 1973):345.

Beitzinger, A. J. A History of Political Thought. New York: Dodd,
1972. Rev. by T. P. Donovan, JAH, 59(Mar 1973):987-8.

Beja, Morris. Epiphany in the Modern Novel. Seattle: U Wash

Press, 1971. Rev. by K. E. Williams, E-I, 8(Win 1973):117-8; D. D. Anderson, OQ, 16(Spr 1973):23-5.

Bek, Alexander. Novoe naznachenie (New Appointment). Frankfurt/Main: Possev Verlag, 1972. Rev. by D. Pospielovsky, RR, 32(Ja 1973):96.

Belford, Richard A. The Man Who Searched for Henry Hudson. Cleveland, Ohio: n. p., 1973. Rev. by E. D. C., IS, 29 (Sum 1973):159.

Belinkov, Nadezhda, et al., eds. Novy kolokol: Literaturno-publisticheski sbornik. London: n.p., 1972. Rev. by M. Friedberg, RR, 32(Oct 1973):452-3.

Bell, Coral. The Conventions of Crisis: A Study in Diplomatic Management. London: Oxford-Royal Institute of International Affairs, 1971. Rev. by D. S. Dutt, IQ, 29(Ja - Mar 1973):60.

Bell, John Patrick. Crisis in Costa Rica: The 1948 Revolution. Austin: U Tx Press, 1971. Rev. by W. M. Clegern, AHR, 78(Oct 1973):1152-3; P. F. Flemison, HAHR, 53(May 1973):334-6.

Bell, Leland V. In Hitler's Shadow: The Anatomy of American Nazism. Port Washington, N. Y.: Kennikat, 1973. Rev. by F. E. Hirsch, HRNB, 2(Oct 1973):20.

Bell, Sidney. Righteous Conquest: Woodrow Wilson and the Evolution of the New Diplomacy. Port Washington, N. Y.: Kennikat, 1972. Rev. by R. W. Curry, WVH, 34(Apr 1973):298-9; D. M. Smith, AHR, 78(Oct 1973):1142; A. Rappaport, JAH, 60(Sep 1973):490-2.

Bellamy, John. Crime and Public Order in England in the Later Middle Ages. Toronto: U Tor Press, 1973. Rev. by B. Lyon, AHR, 78(Dec 1973):1439-40.

Belmonte, José. Historia contemporanea de Iberoamerica. 3 vols. Madrid: Guadarrama, 1971. Rev. by C. C. Griffin, HAHR, 53(Aug 1973):514-15.

Benavides, Santos. Seis años de vacaciones Recuerdos de la Guerra del Pacifico, Chile contra Perú y Bolivia, 1879-1884. Buenos Aires: Editorial Francisco de Aguirre, 1967 (1925). Rev. by W. L. Krieg, HAHR, 53(Aug 1974):569-70.

Bendini, Silvio A. The Life of Benjamin Banneker. New York: Scribner's, 1972. Rev. by H. Fruchtbaum, AHR, 78(Je 1973):729-30; V. C. Hopkins, NYHSQ, 57(Jl 1973):269; E. S. Ferguson, PH, 40(Jl 1973):338-9; D. J. Struik, T & C, 14(Ja 1973):84-6.

Bendix, Reinhard and Roth Guenther. Scholarship and Partisanship:
Essays on Max Weber. Berkeley: U Cal Press, 1971. Rev.
by J. Kornberg, CHR, 54(Mar 1973):75-9.

Benedict, Michael Les. The Impeachment and Trial of Andrew
Johnson. New York: Norton, 1973. Rev. by H. L. Trefousse,
CWH, 19(Dec 1973):365-7; J. C. Mohr; JNH, 58(Jl 1973):363-
4.

Benjamin, Jacques. Les Camerounais Occidentaux: la minorité dans
un état bicommunautaire. Montreal: U Montreal Press, 1972.
Rev. by J. F. Bayart, AfAf, 72(Oct 1973):453-4.

Bennett, Daphne. Vicky: Princess Royal of England and German
Empress. London: Collins and Harvill, 1971. Rev. by J.
Steinberg, HJ, 16(Dec 1973):877-8.

Bennett, Geoffrey. Nelson the Commander. New York: Scribner's,
1972. Rev. by D. Syrett, JMH, 45(Sep 1973):494.

Ben-Sasson, H. H. and S. Ettinger, eds. Jewish Society Through
the Ages. New York: Schocken, 1971. Rev. by J. T. Meda,
HT, 7(Nov 1973):109-10.

Benson, Elizabeth P. , ed. Dumbarton Oaks Conference on Chavin.
Washington, D. C.: Dumbarton Oaks Research Library and
Collections..., Har U, 1971. Rev. by C. Morris, AmAn, 38
(Jl 1973):380-1.

Benson, Lee. Toward the Scientific Study of History: Selected Essays. Philadelphia: Lippincott, 1972. Rev. by R. F. Berkhofer, Jr. , JAH, 59(Mar 1973):973-5; W. O. Aydelotte, JIH,
4(Aut 1973):263-72.

Benson, Maxine see Ubbelohde, Carl

Benson, Paul R. The Supreme Court and the Commerce Clause,
1937-1970. New York: Dunellen, 1970. Rev. by R. C. Cort-
ner, JAH, 60(Sep 1973):509-10.

Benthall, Johnathan. Science and Technology in Art Today. New
York: Praeger, 1972. Rev. by R. Weinberg, T & C, 14(Oct
1973):667.

Bentham, Jeremy. An Introduction to the Principles of Morals and
Legislation. London: Athlone, 1970. Rev. by W. Thomas,
EHR, 88(Oct 1973):861-3; S. R. Letwin, HJ, 16(Je 1973):411-
19.

_____. Of Laws in General. London: Athlone, 1970. Rev. by
W. Thomas, EHR, 88(Oct 1973):861-3; S. R. Letwin, HJ, 16
(Je 1973):411-19.

Bentley, Gerald Eades. The Profession of Dramatist in Shakespeare's Time 1590-1642. Princeton, N. J.: Prin U Press,
1971. Rev. by F. D. Hoeniger, AHR, 78(Je 1973):678-9.

Benton, Elbert J. The Movement for Peace Without a Victory During the Civil War. New York: Da Capo, 1972. Rev. by
I. H. Bartlett, WPHM, 56(Apr 1973):192-3.

Béranger, Jean. Nathaniel Ward (c. 1578-1652). Bordeaux: Sobodi,
1969. Rev. by N. R. N. Tyacke, History, 58(Je 1973):287-8.

Beresford, Maurice and John G. Hurst, eds. Deserted Medieval
Villages: Studies. New York: St. Martin's, 1971. Rev. by
D. Herlihy, JIH, 4(Aut 1973):299-302; P. D. A. Harvey, His-
tory, 58(Oct 1973):437-9.

Bergamini, David. Japan's Imperial Conspiracy. New York: Morrow, 1971. Rev. by H. Webb, PHR, 42(Feb 1973):124-5.

Berger, Ernst. Das Basler Arztrelief: Studien zum griechischen
Grab- und Votivrelief um 500 v. Chr. und zur vorhippokrati-
schen Medizin. Basel: Philipp von Zabern, 1970. Rev. by
B. S. Ridgway, Archives, 26(Ja 1973):67.

Berger, Morroe. Islam in Egypt Today. Social and Political Aspects of Popular Religion. Cambridge: Cam U Press, 1970.
Rev. by B. M. Borthwick, MEJ, 27(Win 1973):83-4.

Berger, Suzanne. Peasants Against Politics: Rural Organization in
Brittany, 1911-1967. Cambridge, Mass.: Har U Press, 1972,
Rev. by E. Weber, JMH, 45(Dec 1973):704-5; B. C. Weber,
AgH, 47(Oct 1973):355-6.

Bergeron, David M. English Civic Pageantry. London: Edward
Arnold, 1971. Rev. by D. M. Palliser, History, 58(Feb
1973):100-1.

Bergeron, Paul H. see Weaver, Herbert

Berghahn, Volker R. Der Tirpitz Plan. Genesis and Verfall einer
innen politischen Krisen strategie. Dusseldorf: Droste Verlag,
1971. Rev. by J. Steinberg, HJ, 16(Mar 1973):196-204.

Bergwitz, Hubertus. Die Partisanenrepublik Ossola: Vom 10 September biz zum 23. Oktober 1944. Hanover: Verlag für Lit-
eratur und zeitgeschehen, 1972. Rev. by M. Salvadori, AHR,
78(Dec 1973):1495.

Beringer, Richard see Alexander, Thomas B.

Berkhofer, Robert F. A Behavioral Approach to Historical Analysis.
New York: Free Press, 1969. Rev. by M. Brichford, Am
Arch, 36(Jl 1973):397-402.

Berman, Bruce D. Encyclopedia of American Shipwrecks. Boston:
Mariners' Press, 1972. Rev. by J. C. S., IS, 29(Spr 1973):
80.

Bernal, J. D. The Extension of Man: A History of Physics Before
the Quantum. Cambridge, Mass.: M I T Press, 1972. Rev.
by L. P. Williams, AHR, 78(Je 1973):651.

Bernard, Paul P. Jesuits and Jacobins: Enlightenment and En-
lightened Despotism in Austria. Urbana: U Ill Press, 1971.
Rev. by J. G. Gagliardo, JMH, 45(Mar 1973):123-4; A. G.
Haas, AHR, 78(Dec 1973):1492-3.

Bernstein, Samuel. Auguste Blanqui and the Art of Insurrection.
London: Lawrence and Wishart, 1971. Rev. by R. J. Bezucha,
JMH, 45(Je 1973):319-21; I. Collins, History, 58(Je 1973):
310-11.

Beros, Mateo Martiné. Magallanes, sintesis de tierra y gentes.
Buenos Aires, Argentina: Editorial Francisco de Aguirre,
1972. Rev. by G. Marcella, HAHR, 53(Nov 1973):670.

Berque, Jacques. Egypt: Imperialism and Revolution. New York:
Praeger, 1972. Rev. by H. A. B. Rivlin, AHR, 78(Oct
1973):1108-9; M. E. Yapp, History, 58(Je 1973):329; P. K.
Bechtold, MEJ, 27(Spr 1973):232-3.

Berreman, Gerald D. Hindus of the Himalayas: Ethnography and
Change. Berkeley: U Cal Press, 1972. Rev. by N. M.
Khilnani, IQ, 29(Jl-Sep 1973):276-7.

Berry, Mary Frances. Black Resistance/White Law: A History of
Constitutional Racism in America. New York: Appleton-Cen-
tury-Crofts, 1971. Rev. by A. H. Spear, SS, 64(Ja 1973):37-8.

Berthoff, Rowland. An Unsettled People: Social Order and Disorder
in American History. New York: Harper and Row, 1971. Rev.
by B. W. Sheehan, WMQ, 3rd Ser., 30(Ja 1973):154-7; D. M.
Scott, JISHS, 66(Spr 1973):107-8.

Bertier de Sauvigny, Guillaume de. Metternich et al France après
le Congrès de Vienne. Vol. 3. Au temps de Charles X,
1824/1830. Paris: Presses Continentales, 1972. Rev. by
A. J. Reinerman, JMH, 45(Je 1973):319.

Berton, Pierre. The Impossible Railway: The Building of the
Canadian Pacific. New York: Knopf, 1972. Rev. by R. C.
Overton, JAH, 60(Je 1973):188-9; H. C. Miner, Historian,
36(Nov 1973):137-8; R. W. Hidy, BHR, 47(Sum 1973):284-5.

Best, Geoffrey. Mid-Victorian Britain, 1851-75. New York:
Schocken, 1972. Rev. by P. N. Stearns, T & C, 14(Jl 1973):
503-5; G. Smith, HT, 7(Nov 1973):137-8; F. B. Smith, AHR,

78(Feb 1973):107-8; C. F. Mullett, SS, 64(Mar 1973):136.

Beth, Loren P. The Development of the American Constitution, 1877-1917. New York: Harper and Row, 1971. Rev. by M. Keller, AHR, 78(Dec 1973):1534-5.

Beti, Mongo. Main Basse sur le Cameroun: Autopsie d'une de' colonisation. n. p.: Francois Maspero, 1972. Rev. by J. F. Bayart, AfAf, 72(Oct 1973):453-4.

Betjeman, John. London's Historic Railway Stations. London: John Murray, 1972. Rev. by C. W. Condit, T & C, 14(Apr 1973): 303-4

Bezucha, Robert J. Modern European Social History. Lexington, Mass.: D. C. Heath, 1972. Rev. by W. H. Sewell, Jr., JMH, 45(Sep 1973):467-8.

Bhargava, G. S. Crush India or Pakistan's Death Wish. Delhi: Indian School Supply Depot, 1972. Rev. by D. N. B., IQ, 29 (Jl-Sep 1973):270-1.

_____. Success or Surrender?: The Simla Summit. New Delhi: Sterling, 1972. Rev. by A. K. Bahl, IQ, 29(Apr-Je 1973): 179-80.

Bharier, Julian. Economic Development in Iran: 1900-1970. New York: Ox U Press, 1971. Rev. by M. A. Fekrat, MEJ, 27 (Spr 1973):233-4.

Bhatt, V. V. Structure of Financial Institutions. Bombay: Vora, 1972. Rev. by S. Venu, IQ, 29(Jan-Mar 1973):74-5.

Bianco, Lucien. Origins of the Chinese Revolution, 1915-1949. London: Ox U Press, 1971. Rev. by D. Latifi, IQ, 29(Jan-Mar 1973):63.

Bigler, Robert M. The Politics of German Protestantism: The Rise of the Protestant Church Elite in Prussia, 1815-1848. Berkeley: U Cal Press, 1972. Rev. by J. S. Conway, AHR, 78 (Je 1973):710; J. E. Groh, JMH, 45(Dec 1973):688-9.

Bilgrami, Asghar H. Afghanistan and British India, 1793-1907: A Study in Foreign Relations. New Delhi: Sterling, 1972. Rev. by L. B. Poullada, MEJ, 27(Aut 1973):511.

Bill, E. G. W. A Catalog of Manuscripts in Lambeth Palace Library: MSS. 1222-1860. Oxford: Clarendon, 1972. Rev. by R. E. Walton, AmArc, 36(Jl 1973):409-10; A. G. Watson, History, 58(Oct 1973):417.

Bill, James Alban. The Politics of Iran: Groups, Classes and Modernization. Columbus, Ohio: Chas. E. Merrill, 1972.

Rev. by W. G. Miller, MEJ, 27(Aut 1973):504-5.

Billerbeck, Rudolf. Die Abgeordneten der ersten Landtage (1946-1951) und der Nationalsozialismus. Dusseldorf: Droste Verlag, 1971. Rev. by P. H. Merkl, JHM, 45(Sep 1973):547-8.

Billias, George Athan see Vaughan, Alden T.

Billington, Ray Allen, ed. "Dear Lady": The Letters of Frederick Jackson Turner and Alice Forbes Perkins Hooper. San Marino, Cal.: Huntington Library, 1970. Rev. by G. M. Gressley, AHR, 78(Feb 1973):173-5.

_____. Frederick Jackson Turner: Historian--Scholar--Teacher. New York: Ox U Press, 1973. Rev. by B. C. Shafer, A & W, 15(Aut 1973):275-7; E. Pomeroy, AHR, 78(Dec 1973):1541-2; H. A. Fleming, JOW, 12(Oct 1973):645-6; W. Rundell, Jr., JAH, 60(Dec 1973):832-3; J. B. Frantz, Montana, 23 (Aut 1973):63; G. M. Guessley, AHR, 78(Feb 1973):173-5; R. E. Morrow, JSH, 39(Aug 1973):426-8; J. Caughey, Montana, 23(Win 1973):63; J. Caughey, PHR, 42(Aug 1973):419-21; D. Lavender, AW, 10(Jl 1973):49; L. Atherton, WHQ, 4(Jl 1973):327-8; J. M. Cooper, Jr., WMH, 56(Spr 1973):236-8.

_____ and Vern Carnes, eds. People of the Plains and Mountains: Essays in the History of the West Dedicated to Everett Dick. Westport, Conn.: Greenwood, 1973. Rev. by E. B. Robinson, NDH, 40(Fall 1973):30.

Bingham, Edwin R. see Hine, Robert V. The American Frontier....

Bingham, Madeleine. Scotland Under Mary Stuart. London: Allen and Unwin, 1971. Rev. by I. B. Coman, History, 58(Feb 1973):98.

Bird, Traveller. Tell Them They Lie, The Sequoyah Myth. Los Angeles: Westernlore, 1972. Rev. by R. E. Smith, PacH, 17(Spr 1973):92.

Birley, A. Septimus Severus, the African Emperor. London: Eyre and Spottiswood, 1971. Rev. by R. Seager, History, 58(Feb 1973):73-4.

Birnbaum, Eleazar. Books on Asia From the Near East to the Far East: A Guide for the General Reader. Toronto: U Tor Press, n. d. Rev. by S. Ganguly, IQ, 29(Jl-Sep 1973):265.

Bischof, Henning. Die Spanisch-Indianisch auseinandersetzund in der nördlichen Sierra Nevada de Santa Marta, 1501-1600. Bonn: Rheinische Frederich-Wilhelms-Universitat, 1971. Rev. by L. Necker, HAHR, 53(Aug 1973):506-8.

Bishop, A. S. The Rise of a Central Authority for English Education. Cambridge: Cam U Press, 1971. Rev. by R. Johnson, History, 58(Feb 1973):121-2.

Biskup, Peter. Not Slaves, Not Citizens. New York: Crane Russak, 1973. Rev. by R. M. Perry, PacH, 17(Win 1973):76-7.

Bivins, John, Jr. The Moravian Potters in North Carolina. Chapel Hill: UNC Press, 1972. Rev. by E. P. Alexander, JSH, 39 (Feb 1973):105-6; S. Ragan, NCHR, 50(Win 1973):93-4.

Bizzarro, Salvatore. Historical Dictionary of Chile. Metuchen, N. J.: Scarecrow, 1972. Rev. by S. F. Edwards, HAHR, 53(Aug 1973):497-8; E. Echevarría, TAm, 30(Oct 1973):291-2.

Bjork, Kenneth O., ed. Norwegian-American Studies. Northfield, Minn.: Norwegian-American Historical Assn., 1972. Rev. by K. W. Olson, SS, 64(Nov 1973):299-300.

Blacker, Carmen, et al. Tradition and Modernization in Japanese Culture. Princeton, N. J.: Prin U Press..., 1971. Rev. by B. K. Marshall, AHR, 78(Oct 1973):1113-4.

Blackley, F. D. and G. Hermansen, eds. The Household Book of Queen Isabella of England. Edmonton, Alta.: U Alta Press, 1971. Rev. by J. R. L. Maddicott, History, 58(Je 1973):260.

Blaffer, Sarah C. The Black-man of Zinacantan: A Central American Legend. Austin: U Tx Press, 1972. Rev. by P. Thomas, HAHR, 53(Aug 1973):558-60.

Blake, Edward L. Farm Bureau in Mississippi. Jackson, Miss: Mississippi Farm Bureau Federation, 1971. Rev. by D. G. Sansing, JMiH, 35(Feb 1973):101-2.

Blakeley, Brian L. The Colonial Office, 1868-1892. Durham, N. C.: Duke U Press, 1972. Rev. by D. M. L. Farr, CHR, 54 (Sep 1973):319-20; R. A. Austen, JMH, 45(Je 1973):317-8; V. Cromwell, History, 58(Je 1973):314.

Blanchard, I. S. W., ed. The Duchy of Lancaster's Estates in Derbyshire 1485-1540. n. p.: Derbyshire Record Society ... 1971. Rev. by A. Rogers, Archives, 11(Spr 1973):49-50.

Blanché, Wendell. Juarez of Mexico. New York: Praeger, 1971. Rev. by E. B. Couturier, SS, 64(Ja 1973):37.

Blassingame, John W. Black New Orleans, 1860-1880. Chicago: U Chi Press, 1973. Rev. by J. E. Fickle, HRNB, 2(Nov/Dec 1973):54.

_____. The Booker T. Washington Papers.... see Harlan, Louis R.

_____. The Slave Community: Plantation Life in the Old South. New York: Ox U Press, 1972. Rev. by W. L. Rose, JAH, 66(Je 1973):131-3; M. D. DeB. Kilson, AHR, 78(Oct 1973): 1132-3; O. W. Taylor, JNH, 58(Oct 1973):470-1; K. W. Porter, JSH, 39(May 1973):293-4; G. Wright, BHR, 47(Aut 1973):386-8; D. R. Goldfield, AgH, 47(Jl 1973):277-9*; G. W. Mullin, WMQ, 3rd Ser., 30(Jl 1973):513-6*; R. Cassimere, WMH, 56(Spr 1973):287-8*. NOTE: Asterisk indicates these periodicals render the title of this work: The Slave Community: Plantation Life in the Ante-Bellum South.

Blewett, Neal. The Peers, the Parties, and the People: The British General Elections of 1910. Toronto: U Tor Press, 1971. Rev. by S. E. Koss, AHR, 78(Je 1973):696-7; E. David, HJ, 16 (Sep 1973):646; P. Stansky, JMH, 45(Dec 1973):699-701; P. F. Clarke, History, 58(Oct 1973):466.

Blit, Lucjan. The Origins of Polish Socialism: The History and Ideas of the First Polish Socialist Party, 1878-1886. New York: Cam U Press, 1971. Rev. by M. K. Dziewanowski, AHR, 78(Feb 1973):127.

Bliven, Bruce, Jr. Under the Guns--New York: 1775-1776. New York: Harper and Row, 1972. Rev. by D. R. Palmer, MilAf, 37(Oct 1973):110.

Bloch, Marc. The Ile-de-France: The Country Around Paris. London: Routledge and Kegan Paul, 1971. Rev. by P. S. Lewis, History, 58(Feb 1973):81-2. NOTE: This work was originally published in 1912.

Bloom, Edward A. and Lillian D. Joseph Addison's Sociable Animal: In the Market Place, on the Hustings, in the Pulpit. Providence, R. I.: Brown U Press, 1971. Rev. by J. G. A. Pocock, JMH, 45(Je 1973):306-9; T. K. Meier, BHR, 47(Spr 1973):128-9.

Blower, James. Gold Rush. New York: American Heritage, 1971. Rev. by P. Gellatly, LJ, 97(Ja 1973):68.

Blue, Frederick J. The Free Soilers: Third Party Politics 1848- 54. Urbana: U Ill Press, 1973. Rev. by L. Ratner, HT, 7(Nov 1973):146; H. Hamilton, GHQ, 57(Win 1973):593; J. G. Rayback, PMHB, 97(Oct 1973):552-3.

Blumberg, Arnold. The Diplomacy of the Mexican Empire, 1863- 1867. Philadelphia: American Philosophical Society, 1971. Rev. by L. L. Blaisdell, AHR, 78(Feb 1973):186-7; T. Schoon- over, TAm 30(Oct 1973):280-1; R. F. Smith, CWH, 19(Dec 1973):364-5.

Blumenkranz, Bernhard. Histoire des Juifs en France. Toulouse:

Edouard Privar, 1972. Rev. by L. Kochan, History, 58(Oct 1973):422.

Blumenson, Martin. The Patton Papers: I, 1885-1940. Boston: Houghton Mifflin, 1972. Rev. by A. R. Millett, MilAf, 37 (Oct 1973):108.

Blyth, Henry. Caro: The Fatal Passion. New York: Coward, McCann and Geohegan, 1973. Rev. by R. Merrill, Mankind, 4(Aug 1973):8.

Boand, Nell Holladay. Nannie Scott of "Bel-air" School. Richmond: Dietz, 1971. Rev. by J. M. Jennings, VMHB, 81(Ja 1973): 114-5.

Boardman, John, et al., eds. The European Community in Later Prehistory. Totowa, N. J.: Rowman and Littlefield, 1971. Rev. by M. Gimbutas, AHR, 78(Feb 1973):73-4.

Boase, T. S. R. Kingdoms and Strongholds of the Crusades. London: Thames and Hudson, 1971. Rev. by R. C. Smail, History, 58(Oct 1973):433-4.

Bode, Carl, comp. and ed. Midcentury America: Life in the 1850's. Carbondale: S Ill U Press, 1972. Rev. by D. B. Marti, IMH, 69(Mar 1973):77-9.

Bödy, Paul. Joseph Eötvös and the Modernization of Hungary, 1840-1870: A Study of Ideas of Individuality and Social Pluralism in Modern Politics. Philadelphia: American Philosophical Society, 1972. Rev. by K. Hitchins, JMH, 45(Je 1973):330-1.

Boesel, David and Peter H. Rossi, eds. Cities Under Siege: An Anatomy of the Ghetto Riots, 1964-1968. New York: Basic Books, 1971. Rev. by T. R. Frazier, SS, 64(Mar 1973):140.

Bogue, Allen G. see Aydelotte, William O.

Bohemia: Jahrbuch des. Collegium Carolinum. Vol. X. Muenchen: Verlag Robert Lerche, 1970. Rev. by B. M. Garver, EEQ, 7(Sep 1973):91-4.

Bohr, Paul Richard. Famine in China and the Missionary: Timothy Richard as Relief Administrator and Advocate of National Reform, 1876-1884. Cambridge, Mass.: Har U Press, 1972. Rev. by P. A. Cohen, PHR, 42(May 1973):260-1.

Boles, John B. The Great Revival, 1787-1805. Lexington: U Press Ky., 1972. Rev. by J. C. Dann, FCHQ, 47(Ja 1973):58-9; C. Eaton, AHR, 78(Je 1973):728-9; D. G. Matthews, JSH, 39 (Feb 1973):108-10; W. G. Loughlin, JAH, 60(Je 1973):118-20; A. R. Tanks, IMH, 69(Mar 1973):75-7; T. L. Agnew, GHQ, 57(Spr 1973):148; S. S. Hill, Jr., FHQ, 51(Ja 1973):324-5;

33   BOLES

D. T. Stokes, SCHM, 74(Ja 1973):43-4; C. R. Allen, Jr.,
VMHB, 81(Ja 1973):105-6; G. W. Pilcher, WMQ, 3rd Ser.,
30(Apr 1973):349-51. NOTE: Full title of this work: The
Great Revival, 1787-1805: The Origins of the Southern
Evangelical Mind. It appears only in the review cited in
VMHB.

_____. A Guide to the Microfilm Edition of the William Wirt
Papers. Baltimore: Md Historical Society, 1971. Rev. by
B. E. Marks, MHM, 68(Spr 1973):106.

Boller, Henry A. Among the Indians: Four Years on the Upper
Missouri, 1858-1862. Lincoln: U Neb Press, 1972. Rev. by
W. E. McFarland, JOW, 12(Oct 1973):656; N. G. Franke,
NDH, 40(Fall 1973):33.

Bolt, Christine. Victorian Attitudes to Race. London: Routledge
and Kegan Paul, 1971. Rev. by R. T. Shannon, History, 58
(Feb 1973):125-6; L. H. Lees, JIH, 4(Sum 1973):140-5.

Bolus, Malvina, ed. People and Pelts: Selected Papers; Second
North American Fur Trade Conference. Winnipeg: Peguis,
1972. Rev. by J. E. Sunder, Montana, 23(Spr 1973):73; H.
A. Dempsey, AW, 10(Ja 1973):55.

Bonachea, Rolando E. and Nelson P. Valdés, eds. Revolutionary
Struggle, 1947-1958: Vol. 1 of The Selected Works of Fidel
Castro. Cambridge, Mass.: M I T Press, 1972. Rev. by
L. E. Aguilar, HAHR, 53(Nov 1973):699-702; R. H. Fitzgib-
bon, AHR, 78(Feb 1973):184-5; S. B. Liss, Historian, 35(Feb
1973):321-2.

Bond, Brian. The Victorian Army and the Staff College, 1854-1914.
London: Eyre, Methuen, 1972. Rev. by R. L. Blanco, AHR,
78(Dec 1973):1468-9; W. S. Hamer, JMH, 45(Sep 1973):509-
10; T. Ropp, MilAf, 37(Oct 1973):111; A. J. A. Morris,
History, 58(Oct 1973):464-5.

Bond, Maurice F. Guide to the Records of Parliament. London:
H M S O, 1971. Rev. by D. A. L. Morgan, History, 58(Feb
1973):163.

Bone, Quentin. Henrietta Maria: Queen of the Cavaliers. Urbana:
U Ill Press, 1972. Rev. by D. Underdown, AHR, 78(Je 1973):
683; M. Lee, Jr., Historian, 36(Nov 1973):100-1; J. Richardson, HTo, 23(Je 1973):443-4.

Bonelli, Franco. La crisi del 1907: Una tappa della sviluppo industriale in Italia. Turin: Fondazione Luigi Einaudi, 1971.
Rev. by S. Saladino, JMH, 45(Sep 1973):551-2.

Boney, F. N., ed. Slave Life in Georgia. A Narrative of the Life,
Sufferings, and Escape of John Brown, a Fugitive Slave. Sa-

vannah: Beehive, 1972. Rev. by J. L. Franklin, CWH, 19
(Sep 1973):285-7; J. E. Talmadge, GR, 27(Spr 1973):143-5.
NOTE: This work was originally published in England in 1855.

Bonner, James C. Georgia's Last Frontier. Athens: U Ga Press,
1971. Rev. by E. D. Odom, AgH, 47(Jl 1973):276-7.

Bonomi, Patricia U. A Factious People: Politics and Society in
Colonial New York. New York: Columbia U Press, 1971. Rev.
by J. A. Henretta, AHR, 78(Feb 1973):150; J. Gwyn, CHR,
54(Dec 1973):465-6; Sung Bok Kim, NYHSQ, 57(Ja 1973):72-3;
M. W. Hamilton, PH, 40(Ja 1973):96-7.

Bontemps, Arna, ed. The Harlem Renaissance Remembered. New
York: Dodd, Mead, 1972. Rev. by H. E. Thornton, JNH,
58(Apr 1973):214-17.

Bontinck, François, tr. and ed. Diarie congolais de Fra Luca da
Caltanisella. Louvain: Naumelaerts, 1970. Rev. by D. Bir-
mingham, Africa, 43(Ja 1973):80-1.

Boorstin, Daniel J. The Americans: The Democratic Experience.
New York: Random, 1973. Rev. by M. Y. Kujovich, BHR,
47(Win 1973):520-2; R. H. Ferrell, HRNB, 2(Nov/Dec 1973):
39; J. J Heslin, NYHSQ, 57(Oct 1973):363.

Borah, Woodrow see Cooke, Sherburne F.

Borchardt, Frank L. German Antiquity in Renaissance Myth. London: JHU Press, 1972. Rev. by D. Hay, History, 58(Je
1973):267.

Bordes, F., ed. The Origin of Homo sapiens ... Proceedings of
the Paris Symposium on Ecology and Conservation. Paris:
UNESCO, 1972. Rev. by R. M. Rowlett, T & C, 14(Oct
1973):614-5.

Borg, Dorothy, Shumpei Okamoto, and Dale K. A. Finlayson, eds.
Pearl Harbor as History: Japanese-American Relations, 1931-
1941. New York: Columbia U Press, 1973. Rev. by J.
Davids, HRNB, 2(Oct 1973):19.

Bork, June Baldwin, comp. Wayne County, Kentucky, Marriages
and Vital Records, 1801-1860. (3 vols.). Order from: Mrs.
June B. Bork, 17352 Drey Lane, Huntington Beach, California
92647. Rev. in FCHQ, 47(Oct 1973):363.

Born, Irene, trans. The Born-Einstein Letters. Correspondence
Between Albert Einstein and Max and Hedwig Born from 1916
to 1955, With Commentaries by Max Born. London: Macmillan, 1970. Rev. by P. M. Heimann, ESR, 3(Apr 1973):198-9.

Bose, Sisir K., ed. A Becon[sic] Across Asia: A Biography of

Subhas Chandra Bose. New Delhi: Orient Longmans, 1973.
Rev. by K. K. Ghosh, IQ, 29(Oct-Dec 1973):361-2.

Bourke, John C. On the Border With Crook. Lincoln: U Neb
Press, 1971. Rev. by R. L. Limbaugh, PacH, 17(Fall 1973):
62-3.

Bousquet-Mélou, Jean. Louis Barthou et la circonscription d'Oloron
(1889-1914). Paris: Pedone, 1972. Rev. by S. Jessner,
AHR, 78(Dec 1973):1480.

Boutruche, Robert. Seigneurie et Féodalite: L'Apogée (XIe-XIIIe
siècles.) Paris: Aubier, 1970. Rev. by J. C. Holt, History,
58(Oct 1973):434-6.

Bowden, Henry Warner. Church History in the Age of Science: His-
toriographical Patterns in the United States, 1876-1918. Chapel
Hill: UNC Press, 1971. Rev. by D. D. Van Tassel, JAH, 59
(Mar 1973):1013-14.

Bowden, J. J. Spanish and Mexican Land Grants in the Chihuahuan
Acquisition. El Paso, Tx.: Western Press, 1971. Rev. by
W. H. Beezley, A & W, 15(Spr 1973):98-9.

Bowen, E. G. Britain and the Western Seaways. London: Thames
and Bowen, 1972. Rev. by L. Alcock, History, 58(Je 1973):
251; E. E. Evans, Antiquity, 47(Je 1973):157-8.

Bowman, Amos see Marsh, Andrew J.

Bowsky, William M. The Finance of the Commune of Siena, 1285-
1355. Oxford: Ox U Press, 1970. Rev. by J. K. Hyde, History, 58(Feb 1973):84-5.

Boyd, Julian P., ed. The Papers of Thomas Jefferson. Vol. 17.
6 July to 3 November 1790. Princeton, N. J.: Prin U Press,
1965. Rev. by M. Jensen, JAH, 60(Je 1973):98-100.

_____ et al., eds. The Papers of Thomas Jefferson. Vol. 18.
4 November 1790--24 January, 1791. Princeton, N. J.: Prin
U Press 1971. Rev. by M. Jensen, JAH, 60(Je 1973):98-100.

Boyer, Dwight. True Tales of the Great Lakes. New York: Dodd,
Mead, 1971. Rev. by W. Havighurst, JISHS, 66(Spr 1973):
110-11; C. Dunathan, MichH, 57(Spr 1973):69-70.

Boyer, Paul and Stephen Nissenbaum, eds. Salem--Village Witchcraft: A Documentary Record of Local Conflict in Colonial New
England. Belmont, Cal.: Wadsworth, 1972. Rev. by C. Hansen, WMQ, 3rd Ser., 30(Jl 1973):528-9.

Boyer, Paul S. see James, Edward T.

Boyer, Richard O.   The Legend of John Brown: A Biography and a
    History. New York: Knopf, 1973. Rev. by H. Aptheker,
    JAH, 60(Dec 1973):812-3.

Boyers, Robert, ed.   The Legacy of the German Refugee Intellec-
    tuals. New York: Schocken, 1972. Rev. by J. J. Weingart-
    ner, Historian, 35(Feb 1973):291-2; M. Jay, JMH, 45(Je
    1973):360.

Boylan, Brian Richard.   Benedict Arnold: The Dark Eagle. New
    York: Norton, 1973. Rev. by R. Higham, HRNB, 2(Nov/Dec
    1973):45.

Boyle, John Hunter.   China and Japan at War, 1937-1945: The
    Politics of Collaboration. Stanford: Stan U Press, 1972. Rev.
    by A. D. Coox, MilAf, 37(Apr 1973):71-2.

Bracegirdle, Brian.   The Archaeology of the Industrial Revolution.
    London: Heinemann, 1973. Rev. by E. Course, Antiquity, 47
    (Dec 1973):333-4.

Braddy, Haldeen.   Mexico and the Old Southwest: People, Palaver,
    and Places. Port Washington, N. Y.: Kennikat, 1971. Rev.
    by G. Barth, TAm, 30(Oct 1973):282-3.

Braden, Spruille.   Diplomats and Demagogues. New Rochelle, N. Y.:
    Arlington House, 1971. Rev. by M. Falcoff, TAm, 30(Jl 1973):
    148-9.

Bradwin, Edmund.   The Bunkhouse Man: Life and Labour in the
    Northern Work Camps. Toronto: U Tor Press, 1972. Rev.
    by G. Porter, BHR, 47(Sum 1973):285-6.

Braeman, John, Robert H. Bremner, and David Brody, eds.
    Twentieth-Century American Foreign Policy. Columbus, O.:
    Ohio St U Press, 1971. Rev. by K. D. Eagles, CHR, 54(Mar
    1973):97-101.

Braider, Donald.   The Niagara. New York: Holt, Rinehart and
    Winston, 1972. Rev. by C. D. S., IS, 29(Spr 1973):78-9; A.
    Runte, NYHSQ, 57(Apr 1973):191-2.

Braisted, William Reynolds.   The United States Navy in the Pacific,
    1909-1922. London: U Tx Press, 1971. Rev. by E. Ranson,
    History, 58(Feb 1973):155; E. Andrade, Jr., AHR, 78(Je
    1973):739-40.

Bramstead, Ernest K.   Germany. Englewood Cliffs, N. J.: Pren-
    tice-Hall, 1972. Rev. by W. Carr, History, 58(Oct 1973):421.

Branco, Renato Castelo.   Pré-história brasileiro. Fatos and lendas.
    São Paulo, Brazil: Quatro Artes Editora, 1971. Rev. by J.
    Magalis, HAHR, 53(Aug 1973):564.

37 BRANCOURT

Brancourt. Jean-Pierre. Le duc de Saint-Simon et la monarchie. Paris: Editions Cujas, 1971. Rev. by R. Mettam, JMH, 45 (Dec 1973):663-4.

Brandes, Detlef. Die Tachechen unter deutschen Protektorat. Vol. 1. Besatzungspolitik Kollaboration und Widerstand in Protektorat Bohmen und Mahren bis Heydricks Tod (1939-1942). Munich: R. Oldenbourg, 1969. Rev. by D. H. Perman, AHR, 78(Feb 1973):124-5.

Brandes, Joseph. Immigrants to Freedom, Jewish Communities in Rural New Jersey. Philadelphia: U Pa Press, 1971. Rev. by M. H. Ebner, NJH, 91(Spr 1973):53-7; A. A. Goren, NYH, 54 (Ja 1973):109-10.

Brandon, William, ed. The Magic World: American Indian Songs and Poems. New York: Morrow, 1971. Rev. by T. E. Brown, ChOk, 51(Fall 1973):371.

Branigan, K., et al. Latimer: Belgic, Roman, Dark Age and Early Modern Farm. Bristol: Chess Valley Archaeological and Historical Society, 1971. Rev. by A. L. F. Rivet, Antiquity, 47 (Mar 1973):75-7.

Branson, Noreen and Margot Heineman. Britain in the Nineteen Thirties. London: Weidenfeld and Nicolson, 1971. Rev. by G. Phillips, History, 58(Feb 1973):139-40.

Brathwaite, Edward. The Development of the Creole Society in Jamaica. New York: Ox U Press, 1971. Rev. by G. J. Heuman, AHR, 78(Feb 1973):185-6; J. Walmin, History, 58(Feb 1973):147; R. D. Ralston, JNH, 58(Oct 1973):475-9.

Brecher, Irving and S. A. Abbas. Foreign Aid and Industrial Development in Pakistan. New York: Cam U Press, 1972. Rev. by S. J Burki, MEJ, 27(Sum 1973):399-400.

Breen, T. H The Character of the Good Ruler, Puritan Political Ideas in New England, 1630-1730. London: Yale U Press, 1971. Rev. by R. C. Simmons, History, 58(Oct 1973):486-7.

Bremner, Robert H. see Braeman, John

Brenner, Anita. The Wind That Swept Mexico: The History of the Mexican Revolution, 1910-1942. Austin: U Tx Press, 1971. Rev. by R. E. Quirk, HAHR, 53(Feb 1973):128-9.

Brennig, Charles. The Age of Revolution and Reaction, 1789-1850. London: Weidenfeld and Nicolson, 1971. Rev. by R. Bullen, History, 58(Feb 1973):113-14.

Brentjes, Burchard. African Rock Art. New York: Clarkson N. Potter, 1970. Rev. by B. M. Fagan, Archaeology, 26(Ja 1973): 77

Brett-Smith, Richard. The Eleventh Hussars (Prince Albert's Own).
New York: Hilary House, 1969. Rev. by E. Andrade, Jr.,
Historian, 35(Feb 1973):287-8.

Bridenbaugh, Carl and Roberta. The Beginnings of the American
People. Vol. II. No Peace Beyond The Line: The English in
the Caribbean, 1624-1690. New York: Ox U Press, 1972.
Rev. by E. V. Goveia, WMQ, 3rd ser., 30(Ja 1973):149-52;
F. W. Knight, JMH, 45(Sep 1973):478-80; C. R. Ritcheson,
NYHSQ, 57(Apr 1973):172-4; R. R. Rea, FHQ, 51(Apr 1973):
449-50.

Bridge, F. R. From Sadowa to Sarajevo: The Foreign Policy of
Austria-Hungary, 1866-1914. Boston: Routledge and Kegan
Paul, 1972. Rev. by R. A. Kann, AHR, 78(Je 1973):713-14.

Bridges, Katherine. A Calendar of the Egan Family Collection.
Natchitoches, La.: NW St. Coll., 1971. Rev. by A. L. Nolen,
AmArch, 36(Ja 1973):76-8.

Bridges, Roger D. see Simon, John Y.

Briggs, Asa and John Saville, eds. Essays in Labour History, 1886-
1923. Hamden, Conn.: Archon, 1971. Rev. by B. B. Gilbert,
AHR, 78(Feb 1973):108-9; W. H. Sewell, Jr., JMH, 45(Sep
1973):513; G. A. Phillips, History, 58(Oct 1973):467-8.

Brill, Robert H., ed. Science and Archaeology. Cambridge, Mass.:
M I T Press, 1971. Rev. by M. Walker, T & C, 14(Ja 1973):
77-8.

Brinckerhoff, Sidney B. Metal Uniform Insignia of the Frontier U. S.
Army 1846-1902. Tucson, Ariz.: Ariz Historical Society,
1972. Rev. by R. A. Murray, NHSQ 16(Fall 1973):200-2.

_____ and Pierce A. Chamberlain. Spanish Military Weapons in
Colonial America, 1700-1821. Harrisburg, Pa.: Stackpole,
1972. Rev. by O. L. Jones, Jr., A & W, 15(Aut 1973):283-4;
R. E. Belous, AW, 10(Mar 1973):56.

Brinkworth, E. R. C. Shakespeare and the Bawdy Court of Stratford. [Chichester:] Phillimore, 1972. Rev. by P. Styles,
MH, 2(Aut 1973):123-4.

Brocher, Karl Dietrich. The German Dictatorship. The Origins,
Structure, and Effects of National Socialism. London: Weidenfeld and Nicolson, 1971. Rev. by A. J. Ryder, ESR, 3(Apr
1973):196-8.

Brock, Peter. Pacifism in Europe to 1914. Princeton, N. J.: Prin
U Press, 1972. Rev. by C. Chatfield, AHR, 78(Je 1973):654-
5.

_____. Twentieth-Century Pacifism. New York: Van Nostrand
Reinhold, 1970. Rev. by C. Chatfield, AHR, 78(Je 1973):654-
5.

_____ and H. G. Skilling, eds. The Czech Renascence in the
Nineteenth Century: Essays Presented to Otokar Odlozilek.
Toronto: U Tor Press, 1971. Rev. by N. C. Masterson,
History, 58(Je 1973):309-10.

Brockett, Oscar G. and Robert R. Findlay. Century of Innovation;
A History of European Theatre and Drama Since 1870. Engle-
wood Cliffs, N. J.: Prentice-Hall, 1973. Rev. by G. B.
Wilson, JAH, 60(Dec 1973):818-9.

Brody, David see Braeman, John

Brody, Ervin C. The Demetrius Legend and Its Literary Treatment
in the Age of the Baroque. Rutherford, N. J.: Fairleigh-
Dickinson U Press, 1972. Rev. by L. Turkevich, RR, 32(Jl
1973):329-30.

Bromley, J. S. and E. H. Kossmann, eds. Britain and the Netherlands. Vol. IV. Metropolis, Dominion, and Province. The
Hague: Martinus Nijhoff, 1971. Rev. by A. C. Carter, History, 58(Feb 1973):168.

_____. Statesmen, Scholars, and Merchants: Essays in Eight-
eenth Century History.... see Whiteman, Anne

Brooke, John. King George III. New York: McGraw-Hill, 1972.
Rev. by C. R. Ritcheson, AHR, 78(Oct 1973):1015-16; W. D.
Jones, GHQ, 57(Spr 1973):151-2; R. Middleton, JAH, 60(Sep
1973):428-9; L. F. S. Upton, PMHB, 97(Apr 1973):258-9;
R. R. Rea, VMHB, 81(Apr 1973):204-5; I. D. Gruber, MHM,
68(Win 1973):452-3; J. J. Heslin, NYHSQ, 57(Oct 1973):350-2;
T. W. Perry, WMQ, 3rd Ser., 30(Jl 1973):531-3.

Brookins, Jean A. see Holmquist, June Drenning

Brooks, H. Allen. The Prairie School: Frank Lloyd Wright and His
Midwest Contemporaries. Toronto: U Toronto Press, 1972. Rev.
by R. C. Twombly, WMH, 56(Spr 1973):241-2; C. W. Condit,
JISHS, 66(Win 1973):470-1.

Broome, Harvey. Faces of the Wilderness. Missoula, Mont.:
Mountain Press ... Wilderness Society, 1972. Rev. by D. H.
Strong, AW, 10(Nov 1973):53.

Brophy, A. Blake. Foundlings on the Frontier: Racial and Religious
Conflict in Arizona Territory, 1904-1905. Tucson: U Ariz,
1972. Rev. by J. S. Olson, A & W, 15(Win 1973):377-8.

Brophy, James D. see Porter, Raymond J.

Brose, Olive J. Frederick Denison Maurice: Rebellious Conformist.
    Athens, Ohio: Ohio U Press, 1971. Rev. by L. F. Barmann,
    JMH, 45(Je 1973):317.

Brotel, Dieter. Französischer Imperialismus in Vietnam: Die ko-
    loniale Expansion und die Errichtung des Protektorates Anmam-
    Tongking 1880-1885. Zürich: Atlantis, 1971. Rev. by H. J.
    Warmenhoven, JMH, 45(Sep 1973):517-18; J. Mirsky, AHR,
    78(Je 1973):658.

Broué, Pierre. La révolution espagnole (1931-1939). Paris: Flam-
    marion, 1973. Rev. by G. Jackson, AHR, 78(Dec 1973):1484-
    5.

_____ and Émile Temine. The Revolution and the Civil War in
    Spain. London: Faber and Faber, 1972. Rev. by R. A. H.
    Robinson, History, 58(Feb 1973):139; H. Hamilton, HRNB, 2
    (Oct 1973):67.

Brown, Anne S. K. see Rice, Howard C. , Jr.

Brown, Charles H. William Cullen Bryant. New York: Scribner's,
    1971. Rev. by E. S. Vesell, NYHSQ, 57(Ja 1973):84-6.

Brown, John A. see Ruby, Robert H.

Brown, Jonathan. The History and Present Condition of St. Domingo.
    2 vols. London: Frank Cass, 1971, 1972. Rev. by M. M.
    Ortega, HAHR, 53(Aug 1973):565-6. NOTE: This work previ-
    ously published in 1837.

Brown, Letitia Woods. Free Negroes in the District of Columbia:
    1790-1846. New York: Ox U Press, 1972. Rev. by R. R.
    Duncan, CWH, 19(Mar 1973):82-3; C. S. Contee, Historian,
    35(Feb 1973):308-9; C. M. Green, AHR, 78(Oct 1973):1124;
    A. Zilversmit, JAH, 59(Mar 1973):991-2; G. W. Mullin, WMQ,
    3rd Ser. , 30(Jl 1973):513-6.

Brown, Malcolm. The Politics of Irish Literature: London: Allen
    and Unwin, 1972. Rev. by R. W. Uphaus, E-I, 8(Aut 1973):
    151-3.

Brown, Maurice F. Estranging Dawn: The Life and Works of Wil-
    liam Vaughn Moody. Carbondale: S Ill U Press, 1973. Rev.
    by J. T. Flanagan, IMH, 69(Dec 1973):377-9.

Brown, Peter. The World of Late Antiquity. London: Thames and
    Hudson, 1971. Rev. by R. A. Markus, History, 58(Feb 1973):
    74-5.

Brown, Sanborn C. , ed. Collected Works of Count Rumford, 5,
    Public Institutions. Cambridge, Mass. : Belknap Press of Har
    U Press, 1971. Rev. by M. J Heale, ESR, 3(Jl 1973):291-7.

Brown, Theodore M. Margaret Bourke-White, Photojournalist.
Ithaca, N. Y.: Cornell U Press, 1972. Rev. by R. V. Jenkins, T & C, 14(Oct 1973):669-70.

Brown, Tom E. , Sr. see Adams, Clarence S.

Browne, J. Ross. Adventures in the Apache Country. New York:
Arno, 1973. Rev. by W. A. Duffen, JAriH, 14(Win 1973):
390-2.

Browne, Robert S. , Howard E. Freeman, and Charles V. Hamilton,
eds. The Social Scene. Cambridge, Mass.: Winthrop, 1972.
Rev. by J S. Roucek, SS, 64(Nov 1973):288.

Browning, Sr. Mary Carmel, O. S. U. Think Big. Owensboro, Ky.:
Winkler, n. d. Rev. by H. C. Mayer, FCHQ, 47(Ja 1973):64.

Brownlie, Ian, ed. Basic Documents on African Affairs. London:
Clarendon, 1971. Rev. by A. M. Chambati, AfAf, 72(Ja 1973):
79.

Brundtland, A. O. see Schou, A.

Brunhouse, Robert L. Sylvanus G. Morley and the World of the
Ancient Mayas. Norman: U Ok Press, 1971. Rev. by M. D.
Coe, HAHR, 53(Feb 1973):116-7.

Brunk, Harry Anthony. History of the Mennonites in Virginia, 1900-
1960. Verona, Va.: McClure, 1972. Rev. by K. Wust,
VMHB, 81(Ja 1973):120-1.

Brunn, Gerhard. Deutschland und Brasilien (1889-1914). Cologne:
Böhlau Verlag, 1971. Rev. by T. E. Skidmore, AHR, 78(Je
1973):658-9.

Brunschwig, Henri, et al. Brazza explorateur: Les traités Makoko,
1880-1882. Paris: Mouton, 1972. Rev. by D. E. Gardiner,
AHR, 78(Oct 1973):1111-2.

Bryan, Bruce. Archaeological Explorations on San Nicolas Island.
Los Angeles: Southwest Museum, 1970. Rev. by C. Jennings,
AmAnt, 38(Apr 1973):253.

Bryant, Clifton D. , ed. The Social Dimensions of Work. Englewood Cliffs, N. J.: Prentice-Hall, 1972. Rev. by A. Bos-
koff, SS, 64(Dec 1973):341.

Bryant, Keith L. , Jr. Arthur E. Stillwell: Promoter With a Hunch.
Nashville: Van U Press, 1971. Rev. by R. C. Overton, JAH,
59(Mar 1973):1021-2; B. A. Storey, AHR, 78(Oct 1973):1140-1;
J. Kilfoil, JOW, 12(Jl 1973):510; J. L. Forsythe, SWHQ, 76
(Ja 1973):343-4; J. B. Frantz, T & C, 14(Ja 1973):88-9.

Buchanan, R. A. Industrial Archaeology in Britain. Harmondsworth, Middlesex: Penguin, 1972. Rev. by T. Sande, T & C,
14(Oct 1973):618-20.

Buchanan, R. H., et al. Man and His Habitat--Essays Presented
to Emyr Estyn Evans. London: Routledge and Kegan Paul,
1971. Rev. by G. R. J. Jones, History, 58(Feb 1973):162.

Buck, Lawrence P. and Jonathan W. Zophy, eds. The Social History of the Reformation. Columbus, Ohio: Ohio St U Press,
1972. Rev. by C.-P. Clasen, AHR, 78(Dec 1973):1445-8;
N. L. Roelker, JMH, 45(Dec 1973):647-9.

Buckland, Patrick. Irish Unionism. Dublin: Gill and Macmillan,
1973. Rev. by P. Pyne, E-I, 8(Win 1973):155-6.

Budhraj, Vijay Sen. Soviet Russia and the Hindustan Subcontinent.
Bombay: Somaiya Publications, 1973. Rev. by J. A. Naik,
IQ, 29(Oct-Dec 1973):358-9.

Buel, Richard, Jr. Securing the Revolution: Ideology in American
Politics, 1789-1815. Ithaca, N. Y.: Cornell U Press, 1972.
Rev. by J. S. Chase, Historian, 36(Nov 1973):122-3; J. M.
Banner, JAH, 60(Sep 1973):431-2; N. K. Risjord, MHM, 68
(Fall 1973):342-3; D. Higginbotham, NCHR, 50(Sep 1973):219-
20; H. Ammon, PMHB, 97(Apr 1973):267-8; R. M. Bauman,
PH, 40(Oct 1973):485-6; G. C. Rogers, Jr., SCHM, 74(Jl
1973):173; G. G. Shackelford, VMHB, 81(Oct 1973):495-6;
L. K. Kerber, WMQ, 3rd Ser., 30(Jl 1973):503-5; R. Leffler,
WMH, 56(Spr 1973):253-4.

Bugnicourt, Jacques. Disparités Régionales et Aménagement du Territoire en Afrique. n. p.: Librairie Armand Colin, 1971.
Rev. by J. v. d. M., AfAf, 72(Jl 1973):346.

Buhite, Russell D. Patrick J. Hurley and American Foreign Policy.
Ithaca, N. Y.: Cornell U Press, 1973. Rev. by W. I. Cohen,
JAH, 60(Dec 1973):854-5.

Buhler, Kathryn C. American Silver, 1655-1825, in the Museum of
Fine Arts, Boston. 2 vols. Boston: Museum of Fine Arts,
1972. Rev. by I. M. G. Quimby, PMHB, 97(Oct 1973):545-7.

Bullard, William R., Jr. Monographs and Papers in Maya Archaeology. Cambridge, Mass.: Peabody Museum, 1970. Rev. by
D. M. Pendergast, Archives, 26(Ja 1973):78.

Bulletin Philalogique et Historique (jusqu' a 16/10) du Comite des
travaux historiques des sociètés savantes. Année 1968. Actes
due 93e congrès national des sociétés savantes. Paris: Bibliothèque nationale, 1971. Rev. by R. H. Hilton, EHR, 88(Jl
1973):590-2.

Bulliet, Richard W. The Patricians of Nishapur: A Study in Medi-
    eval Islamic Social History. Cambridge, Mass.: Har U Press,
    1972. Rev. by G. R. G. Hambly, AHR, 78(Dec 1973):1505.

Bullitt, Orville H. , ed. For the President--Personal and Secret:
    Correspondence Between Franklin D. Roosevelt and William C.
    Bullitt. Boston: Houghton Mifflin, 1972. Rev. by B. Farns-
    worth, AHR, 78(Oct 1973):1142-3; G. A. Craig, PMHB, 97(Jl
    1973):423-4.

Bullough, Bonnie and Vern L. Poverty, Ethnic Identity and Health
    Care. New York: Appleton-Century-Crofts, 1972. Rev. by
    J. Leiby, JAH, 60(Sep 1973):499.

Bullough, D. A. and R. L. Storey, eds. The Study of Medieval
    Records: Essays in Honour of Kathleen Major. Oxford: Ox
    U Press, 1971. Rev. by C. H. Lawrence, History, 58(Feb
    1973):80-1.

Bulman, T. Alex. Kamloops Cattlemen: One Hundred Years of
    Trail Dust! Sidney, British Columbia: Gray's, 1972. Rev.
    by D. H. Breen, Montana, 23(Sum 1973):57.

Bumsted, J. M. Henry Alline, 1748-1784. Toronto: U Tor Press,
    1971. Rev. by J. W. Davidson, WMQ, 3rd Ser., 30(Jl 1973):
    526-8.

Bunche, Ralph J. The Political Status of the Negro in the Age of
    F D R. Chicago: U Chi Press, 1973. Rev. by M. Kranz,
    HRNB, 2(Oct 1973):18.

Burago, Alla and Burton Raffel, trans. Selected Works of Nikolai
    S. Gumilev. Albany: SUNY, 1972. Rev. by H. W. Tjalsma,
    RR, 32(Apr 1973):208-10.

Burch, Philip H. , Jr. The Managerial Revolution Reassessed:
    Family Control in America's Large Corporations. Lexington,
    Mass.: D. C. Heath, 1972. Rev. by A. M. Johnson, BHR,
    47(Spr 1973):125-6.

Burckhardt, Carl J. Richelieu and His Age. Vol. III. Power
    Politics and the Cardinal's Death. London: Allen and Unwin,
    1971. Rev. by R. Mettam, History, 58(Oct 1973):447.

Burford, Alison. Craftsmen in Greek and Roman Society. London:
    Thames and Hudson, 1972. Rev. by J. A. Crook, Antiquity,
    47(Mar 1973):68.

_____. The Greek Temple Builders at Epidauros: A Social and
    Economic Study of Building in the Asklepian Sanctuary During
    the Fourth and Early Third Centuries B. C. Toronto: U Tor
    Press, 1969. Rev. by J. Wisemen, Archaeology, 26(Oct 1973):
    314-16.

Burggraaff, Winfield J. The Venezuelan Armed Forces in Politics, 1935-1959. Columbia, Mo.: U Mo Press, 1972. Rev. by J. Malloy, TAm, 30(Oct 1973):295-6.

Burke, E. E. see Baxter, T. W.

Burke, Peter. Culture and Society in Renaissance Italy, 1420-1540. New York: Scribner's, 1972. Rev. by R. Trexler, AHR, 78 (Je 1973):714-15; D. S. Chambers, History, 58(Je 1973):271-2.

_____, ed. Economy and Society in Early Modern Europe: Essays from Annales. New York: Harper and Row, 1972. Rev. B. Lyon, JEH, 33(Dec 1973):877-9; P. H. Ramsey, History, 58 (Je 1973):273-4.

Burke, Russell see Gerdts, William H.

Burlinson, Irene. Yesterday and Today in the Life of the Apaches. Philadelphia: Dorrance, 1973. Rev. by L. Davisson, JAriH, 14(Sum 1973):169.

Burman, Ben Lucien. Look Down That Winding River: An Informal Profile of the Mississippi. New York: Taplinger, 1973. Rev. by J. W. Webb, JMiH, 35(Aug 1973):414-5.

Burney, Charles and David Marshall Lang. The Peoples of the Hills: Ancient Ararat and Caucasus. New York: Praeger, 1972. Rev. by A. O. Saukisson, AHR, 78(Feb 1973):71; J. E. Curtis, Antiquity, 47(Mar 1973):71-2.

Burns, E. Bradford. Latin America: A Concise Interpretative History. Englewood Cliffs, N. J.: Prentice-Hall, 1972. Rev. by H. M. Hamill, Jr., HAHR, 53(Feb 1973):113-14; J. L. Helguera, SS, 64(Nov 1973):285; D. L. Roby, CHR, 54(Sep 1973):313-4.

Burros, Ernest J., ed. Kino and Manje: Explorers of Sonora and Arizona, Their Vision of the Future. St. Louis: Jesuit Historical Institute, 1971. Rev. by A. P. Nasatir, HAHR, 53(Nov 1973):679-81.

Burston, W. H. and C. W. Green, eds. Handbook for History Teachers. London: Methuen, 1972. Rev. by H. F. Mahon, HT, 6(Feb 1973):323.

Burt, Jesse and Robert B. Ferguson. Indians of the Southeast: Then and Now. Nashville: Abingdon, 1972. Rev. by J. F. Corn, THQ, 32(Spr 1973):95-7.

Bush, George P., ed. Technology and Copyright: Annotated Bibliography and Source Materials. Mt. Airy, Md.: Lomond Systems, 1972. Rev. by J. G. Jackson, T & C, 14(Oct 1973):684.

Busse, Heribert, trans. History of Persia Under Qajar Rule. New
    York: Columbia U Press, 1972. Rev. by H. F. Farmayan,
    MEJ, 27(Aut 1973):502-4.

Buszello, Horst. Der Deutsche Bavernkrieg von 1525 als Politische
    Bewegung. Berlin: Colloquium Verlag, 1969. Rev. by H. J.
    Cohn, History, 58(Feb 1973):96-7.

Butcher, Margaret Just. The Negro in American Culture. New
    York: Knopf, 1972. Rev. by J. F. Marszalek, Jr., Histor-
    ian, 36(Nov 1973):129-30.

Butler, R. A. see The Art of the Impossible: The Memoirs of ...

Butler, R. M., ed. Soldier and Civilian in Roman Yorkshire.
    Leicester: Leicester U Press, 1971. Rev. by R. G. Livens,
    History, 58(Feb 1973):72.

Butterfield, L. H. see Friedlander, Marc

Cadbury, Henry J. John Woolman in England, 1772: A Documentary
    Supplement. London: Friends Historical Society, 1971. Rev.
    by K. L. Carroll, PMHB, 97(Ja 1973):112.

Cadenhead, Ivie E. Jesús González Ortega and Mexican National
    Politics. Fort Worth: T C U Press, 1972. Rev. by D. B.
    Adams, SWHQ, 76(Apr 1973):497.

Caldwell, Malcolm and Lek Tan. Cambodia in the Southeast Asian
    War. New York: Monthly Review Press, 1973. Rev. by
    B. M. Kaushik, IQ, 29(Oct-Dec 1973):359.

Caldwell, Oliver J. A Secret War: Americans in China, 1944-1945.
    Carbondale: S Ill U Press, 1972. Rev. by K. Tolley, Histor-
    ian, 35(Feb 1973):316-7.

Callahan, North. George Washington: Soldier and Man. New York:
    Morrow, 1972. Rev. by A. Keller, AHI, 8(Jl 1973):49; D. R.
    Palmer, MilAf, 37(Oct 1973):110; D. C. Skaggs, Historian,
    35(Feb 1973):305-6; H. F. Rankin, PMHB, 97(Jl 1973):412-3.

Callahan, William J. Honor, Commerce, and Industry in Eighteenth-
    Century Spain. Boston: Baker Library, Harvard Grad. School Bus-
    iness Admin., 1972. Rev. by R. Herr, JEH, 33(Je 1973):472-3.

Calvocoressi, Peter and Guy Wint. Total War: The Story of World
    War II. New York: Pantheon, 1972. Rev. by G. O. Kent,
    AHR, 78(Dec 1973):1427-8.

Cameron, Ian. The Impossible Dream: The Building of the Panama
    Canal. New York: Morrow, 1972. Rev. by C. D. Ameringer,
    HAHR, 53(May 1973):333-4.

Cameron, Rondo, ed. Banking and Economic Development: Some

Lessons of History. New York: Ox U Press, 1972. Rev. by
R. W. Weiss, JMH, 45(Sep 1973):468-70; D. F. Good, JEH,
33(Je 1973):473-5.

Campbell, John C. and Helen Caruso. The West and the Middle
East. New York: Council on Foreign Relations, 1972. Rev.
by J. D. Anthony, MEJ, 27(Win 1973):101-2.

Campbell, O. B. Mission to the Cherokees. Oklahoma City: Metro
Press, 1973. Rev. by W. B. Morris, Jr., ChOk, 51(Fall
1973):367-8.

Campbell, Penelope. Maryland in Africa. The Maryland State Colonization Society, 1831-1857. Urbana: U Ill Press, 1971. Rev.
by B. Wyatt-Brown, AHR, 78(Oct 1973):1133-4.

Campbell, Rosemae Wells. From Trappers to Tourists: Fremont
County, Colorado, 1830-1950. Palmer Lake, Colo.: Filter,
1972. Rev. by J. E. Ophus, CoMag, 50(Spr 1973):167-8.

Campbell, Stanley W. The Slave Catchers: Enforcement of the
Fugitive Slave Law, 1850-1860. Chapel Hill: UNC Press,
1970. Rev. by A. Grundman, MichH, 57(Sum 1973):175-7;
S. G. F. Spockman, History, 58(Feb 1973):152; B. W. Collins, HJ, 16(Sep 1973):644-6.

Campbell, Thomas M. Masquerade Peace: America's UN Policy,
1944-1945. Tallahassee: Fla St U Press, 1973. Rev. by
G. B. Ostrower, HRNB, 2(Nov 16 1973):55.

Cancian, Frank. Change and Uncertainty in a Peasant Economy:
The Maya Corn Farmers of Zinacantan. Stanford, Cal.: Stan
U Press, 1972. Rev. by P. Thomas, HAHR, 53(Aug 1973):
558-60; W. Dusenberry, AgH 47(Oct 1973):357-8.

Canney, Margaret and David Knott, comps. Printed Books to 1800.
Vol. I. Cambridge: Cam U Press, 1970. Rev. by N. Rosenburg, JEH, 33(Je 1973):475-6.

Cannon, Elizabeth Roberts, ed. My Beloved Zebulon: The Corres-
pondence of Zebulon Baird Vance and Harriet Newell Espy.
Chapel Hill: UNC Press, 1971. Rev. by J. H. Schroeder,
CWH, 19(Dec 1973):360-1.

Cannon, John. Parliamentary Reform, 1640-1832. New York: Cam
U Press, 1973. Rev. by I. R. Christie, AHR, 78(Dec 1973):
1456.

Cantamine, Philippe. Guerre, état et société à la fin du Moyen Age:
Études sur les armées des rois de France, 1337-1494. Paris:
Mouton, 1972. Rev. by P. Solon, AHR, 78(Je 1973):672-3.

Cantor, Milton, ed. Black Labor in America. Westport, Conn.:

Negro U's Press, 1970. Rev. by D. J. MacLeod, History,
58(Feb 1973):156-7.

Cantril, Albert H. see Roll, Charles W., Jr.

Caplan, Gerald L. The Elites of Barotseland 1878-1969: A Political
History of Zambia's Western Province. Berkeley: U Cal
Press, 1970. Rev. by P. Silverman, CHR, 54(Dec 1973):455-7.

Capp, B. S. The Fifth Monarchy Men: A Study in Seventeenth-
Century English Millennarianism. Totowa, N. J.: Rowman
and Littlefield, 1972. Rev. by L. F. Solt, AHR, 78(Oct 1973):
1057-8; A. Woolrych, History, 58(Je 1973):289-91.

Capps, Benjamin and Time-Life Editors. The Indians. New York:
Time-Life Books, 1973. Rev. by R. N. Ellis, Montana, 23
(Aut 1973):74.

Capron, William M., ed. Technological Change in Regulated Industries. Washington, D. C.: Brookings Institution, 1971. Rev.
by G. Rosegger, T & C, 14(Apr 1973):329-30.

Carden, Moren Lockwood. Oneida: Utopian Community to Modern
Corporation. Baltimore: JHU Press, 1969. Rev. by J. Fack-
ler, VH, 41(Spr 1973):107-10.

Carden, Patricia. The Art of Isaac Babel. Ithaca: N. Y.: Cornell U Press, 1972. Rev. by T. L. Aman, RR, 32(Apr 1973):
212-3.

Cardwell, D. S. L. Technology, Science and History. London:
Heinemann, 1972. Rev. by A. E. Musson, History, 58(Oct
1973):415.

_____. Turning Points in Western Technology: A Study of Tech-
nology, Science and History. New York: Science History Publications, 1972. Rev. by E. S. Ferguson, T & C, 14(Jl 1973):
477-9.

Carleton, Willian [sic]. The Black Prophet: A Tale of Irish Famine.
Shannon: Irish U Press, 1972. Rev. by L. V. Harrod, E-I,
8(Win 1973):119-21.

Carlisle, Lilian Baker, ed. Look Around Jericho, Underhill, and
Westford, Vermont. Burlington: Chittenden, County Historical
Society, 1972. Rev. by C. H. Liebs, VH, 41(Spr 1973):101-2.

_____, ed. Look Around Winooski, Vermont. Burlington: Chit-
tenden County Historical Society, 1972. Rev. by C. H. Liebs,
VH, 41(Spr 1973):101-2.

Carlson, Andrew R. Anarchism in Germany. Vol. 1. The Early
Movement. Metuchen, N. J.: Scarecrow, 1972. Rev. by

J. J. Sheehan, JMH, 45(Sep 1973):525.

Carlson, Lewis H. and George A. Colburn, eds. In Their Place: White Defines Her Minorities, 1850-1950. New York: Wiley, 1972. Rev. by R. M Johnson, HT, 6(Feb 1973):327.

Carner, Vern see Billington, Ray Allen

Carone, Edgar D. A Republica velha. 2 vols. São Paulo: Difusão Européia do Livro, 1970. Rev. by J. L. Love, HAHR, 53(Feb 1973):146-8.

Carpenter, Jesse Thomas. Competition and Collective Bargaining in the Needle Trades, 1910-1917. Ithaca, N. Y.: Cornell U Press, 1972. Rev. by D. Montgomery, JAH, 59(Mar 1973): 1031-2; R. Ozanne, BHR, 47(Win 1973):537-9.

Carpenter, Kenneth E., ed. British Labour Struggles: Contemporary Pamphlets, 1727-1850. New York: Arno, 1972. Rev. by J. F. C. Harrison, BHR, 47(Aut 1973):409-11.

Carr, Edward Hallett and R. W. Davies. Foundations of a Planned Economy, 1926-1929. Vol. I, Parts 1 and 2. New York: Macmillan, 1971. Rev. by G. Grossman, RR, 32(Apr 1973):195-6; R. W. Campbell, AHR, 78(Feb 1973):128-30.

Carr, John Laurence. Robespierre, The Force of Circumstances. [London:] Constable, n. d. Rev. by J. Richardson, HTo, 23 (Ja 1973):68.

Carr, Raymond, ed. The Republic and the Civil War in Spain. London: Macmillan and St. Martin's, 1971. Rev. by R. M. Blinkhorn, ESR, 3(Ja 1973):81-7; V. S. Kiernan, History, 58(Feb 1973):138-9.

Carr, William. Arms, Autarky and Aggression: A Study in German Foreign Policy, 1933-1939. New York: Norton, 1973. Rev. by T. S. Hamerow, HRNB, 2(Nov/Dec 1973):26.

Carranza de Mirando, Bartolome. Commentarios sobre el Catechismo Christiano. Vols. 1 and 2. Madrid: Biblioteca de Autores Christianos, 1972. Rev. by W. B. Jones, HAHR, 53 (Nov 1973):676-7.

Carroll, Daniel B. Henri Mercier and the American Civil War. Princeton, N. J.: Prin U Press, 1971. Rev. by L. Wilson, JISHS, 66(Spr 1973):113-4; R. Bullen, History, 58(Oct 1973): 491.

Carroll, John M., ed. The Black Military Experience in the Middle West. New York: Liveright, 1971. Rev. by R. McConnell, JNH, 58(Jl 1973):365-7; B. A. Glasrud, JOW, 12(Jl 1973): 515-16.

49   CARROLL

_____. The Grand Duke Alexis in the United States of America.
New York: Interland, 1972. Rev. by J. W. Bailey, MilAf,
37(Oct 1973):115.

Carson, Gerald. Men, Beasts, and Gods: A History of Cruelty and
Kindness to Animals. New York: Scribner's, 1972. Rev. by
M. Z. Langsam, JAH, 60(Dec 1973):770-1.

Carsten, F. L. Revolution in Central Europe: 1918-1919. Berkeley: U Cal Press, 1972. Rev. by A. Mitchell, JMH, 45(Je
1973):336-8.

Carter, Charles H. The Western European Powers, 1500-1700.
Ithaca, N. Y.: Cornell U Press, 1971. Rev. by D. Jensen,
JMH, 45(Dec 1973):647-9; H. Kamen, History, 58(Oct 1973):
440.

Carter, Paul A. The Spiritual Crisis of the Gilded Age. De Kalb:
N Ill U Press, 1971. Rev. by T. D. Clark, FHQ, 51(Apr
1973):454-6.

Carter, Samuel, III. Blaze of Glory: The Fight for New Orleans,
1814-1815. New York: St. Martin's, 1971. Rev. by F. L.
Owsley, Jr., FHQ, 52(Jl 1973):75-6; T. Brown, MilAf, 37
(Feb 1973):33; R. Horsman, SS, 64(Apr 1973):186.

_____. The Cowboy Capital of the World: The Saga of Dodge
City. [Garden City, N. Y.:] Doubleday, 1973. Rev. by J. W.
Snell, Montana, 23(Aut 1973):74.

Carter, William. Bolivia: A Profile. New York: Praeger, 1971.
Rev. by J. M. Malloy, HAHR, 53(Aug 1973):570-1.

Caruso, Helen see Campbell, John C.

Case, Gladys Calhoon. The Bayou Chene Story: A History of the
Atchafalaya Basin and Its People. Detroit: Harlo, 1973. Rev.
by F. Kniffen, LaH, 14(Fall 1973):406.

Casebier, Dennis. Carleton's Pah-Ute Campaign. Norco, Cal.:
Published by the Author, 1972. Rev. by C. Lowe, NHSQ, 16
(Spr 1973):37-9.

Casey, Kevin, ed. Winter's Tales From Ireland. Dublin: Gill and
Macmillan, 1972. Rev. by T. J. Murray, E-I, 8(Sum 1973):
154-7.

Cash, Joseph H. The Sioux People (Rosebud). Phoenix: Indian
Tribal Series, 1971. Rev. by J. D. McDermott, A & W, 15
(Win 1973):372-4; T. B. Hinton, JAriH, 14(Aut 1973):264-5.

_____ and Herbert T. Hoover, eds. To Be an Indian: An Oral
History. New York: Holt, Rinehart and Winston, 1971. Rev.

by R. Anderson, Montana, 23(Win 1973):70.

Cassar, George H. The French and the Dardanelles: A Study of
    Failure in the Conduct of War. London: Allen and Unwin,
    1971. Rev. by J. Gooch, History, 58(Feb 1973):132.

Cassara, Ernest, ed. Universalism in America: A Documentary
    History. Boston: Beacon, 1971. Rev. by H. Segal, PH, 40
    (Ja 1973):100-1.

Cassell, Frank A. Merchant Congressmen in the Young Republic:
    Samuel Smith of Maryland, 1752-1839. Madison: U Wis Press,
    1971. Rev. by R. Hoffman, AHR, 78(Feb 1973):153-4; A. C.
    Land, JAH, 59(Mar 1973):988-9; D. S. Spencer, NYHSQ, 57
    (Ja 1973):78-80; J. C. Morton, PH, 40(Jl 1973):339-41; R. S.
    Klein, WMH, 56(Spr 1973):246-7.

Casso, Evans J. Lorenzo: The History of the Casso Family in
    Louisiana. New Orleans: Jackson Square Press, 1972. Rev.
    by P. H. LeBlanc, LaH, 14(Fall 1973):401-2.

Casson, Lionel. Ships and Seamanship in the Ancient World. Prince-
    ton, N. J.: Prin U Press, 1971. Rev. by F. H. VanDoor-
    ninck, Jr., Archives, 26(Ja 1973):70, 72.

Castellion, Sébastien. De l'impunité des hérétiques, "De Haereticis
    non Puniendis." Geneva: Librairie Droz, 1971. Rev. by
    R. H. Bainton, JMH, 45(Je 1973):299.

Castelot, Andre. Napoleon. New York: Harper and Row, 1971.
    Rev. by E. L. Newman, Historian, 35(Feb 1973):288-9.

Castro, Américo. The Spaniards: An Introduction to Their History.
    Berkeley: U Cal Press, 1972. Rev. by G. Jackson, AHR, 78
    (Feb 1973):114-6; P. A. Linehan, History, 58(Oct 1973):427-8.

Castro, Fidel. Fidel in Chile: A Symbolic Meeting Between Two
    Historical Processes. Selected Speeches of Major Fidel Castro
    During His Visit to Chile, November 1971. New York: Inter-
    national, 1972. Rev. by R. H. Fitzgibbon, AHR, 78(Oct 1973):
    1150-1; R. M., HAHR, 53(Aug 1973):571.

_____. Revolutionary Struggle--1947-1958. Vol. 1, of Selected
    Works of Fidel Castro. Cambridge, Mass.: M I T Press,
    1972. Rev. R. H. Fitzgibbon, AHR, 78(Feb 1973):184-5; S. B.
    Liss, Historian, 35(Feb 1973):321-2; L. E. Aguilar, HAHR,
    53(Nov 1973):699-702.

Catalog of the Sophia Smith Collection. Northampton, Mass.: Smith
    College, n. d. Rev. by A. L. Nolen, AmArch, 36(Ja 1973):
    76-8.

Catherine May: An Indexed Register of Her Congressional Papers,

1959-1970, in the Washington State University Library. Pull-
man: Washington: Wash St U Press, 1972. Rev. by K. J.
Pike, AmArch, 36(Jl 1973):411-14.

Catton, Bruce. Waiting for the Morning Train. An American Boyhood. New York: Doubleday, 1972. Rev. by F. C. McLaughlin, WPHM, 56(Oct 1973):441-2.

Catudal, Honoré M., Jr. Steinstücken: A Study in Cold War Politics. New York: Vantage, 1971. Rev. by E. Plischke, SS
(Apr 1973):181.

Caughey, John Walton. Bernardo de Galvez in Louisiana, 1776-1783.
New Orleans: Pelican, 1972. Rev. by R. R. Rea, AlaRe, 26
(Jl 1973):232-3; M. Peoples, LaH, 14(Sum 1973):325-6.

Caughey, John and LaRue. To Kill a Child's Spirit: The Tragedy
of School Segregation in Los Angeles. Itasca, Ill.: F. E.
Peacock, 1973. Rev. by I. G. Hendrick, PHR, 42(Nov 1973):
592-4.

Cecil, Robert. The Myth of the Master Race: Alfred Rosenberg and
Nazi Ideology. London: Batsford, 1972. Rev. by M. D. Biddiss, History, 58(Oct 1973):471-2.

Cerchione, Angelo J., Victor E. Rothe and James Vercellina, eds.
Master Planning the Aviation Environment. Tucson: U Ariz
Press, 1970. Rev. by J. B. Rae, T & C, 14(Oct 1973):656-7.

Chafe, William Henry. The American Woman: Her Changing Social,
Economic, and Political Roles, 1920-1970. New York: Ox U
Press, 1972. Rev. by M. C. Davis, JSH, 39(May 1973):312-
13; D. M. Kennedy, JAH, 60(Sep 1973):493-5; N. Schrom,
WMH, 56(Sum 1973):332-3.

The Chain Reaction. Frankfurt/Main: Possev, 1971. Rev. by D.
V. Pospielovsky, RR, 32(Oct 1973):441-2.

Chaitanya, Krishna. A History of Malayalam Literature. New Delhi: Orient Longmans, 1971. Rev. by O. M. Ánajun, IQ, 29
(Jl-Sep 1973):279-80.

Chaliand, Gérard and Juliette Minces. L'Algérie Indépendante.
Paris: François Maspero, 1972. Rev. by D. B. Ottaway,
MEJ, 27(Sum 1973):397-8.

Challener, Richard D. Admirals, Generals, and American Foreign
Policy, 1898-1914. Princeton, N. J.: Prin U Press, 1973.
Rev. by R. W. Leopold, AHR, 78(Dec 1973):1537-8; T. A.
Bryson, GHQ, 57(Win 1973):595-6; P. Karsten, JAH, 60(Dec
1973):826-8; R. W. Turk, MilAf, 37(Dec 1973):159-60.

Chalmers, Douglas A. Changing Latin America: New Interpreta-

tions of Its Politics and Society. New York: Columbia U
Press, 1972. Rev. by H. Dietz, HAHR, 53(May 1973):347-9;
M. M. Anderberg, CurH, 64(Feb 1973):82.

Chamberlain, Joseph, et al. The Radical Programme. Brighton:
Harvester Press, 1971. Rev. by R. T. Shannon, History, 58
(Je 1973):315-6.

Chamberlain, Pierce A. see Brinckerhoff, Sidney B.

Chambers, Clarke A. Paul U. Kellogg and the Survey: Voices for
Social Welfare and Social Justice. Minneapolis: U Minn
Press, 1971. Rev. by J. S. Olson, WPHM, 56(Apr 1973):190-
1.

Chancellor, Sir Christopher, ed. An Englishman in the American
Civil War: The Diaries of Henry Yates Thompson: 1863.
New York: NYU Press, 1971. Rev. by F. N. Boney, CWH,
19(Mar 1973):85-6.

Chand, Tara. History of the Freedom Movement in India. (Vols. 3
and 4). New Delhi: Publication Division, Government of India,
1972. Rev. by S. L. Poplai, IQ, 29(Apr-Je 1973):167-8.

Chandler, Alfred Jr. and Stephen Salsbury. Pierre S. Du Pont and
the Making of the Modern Corporation. New York: Harper
and Row, 1971. Rev. by M. Keller, AHR, 78(Feb 1973):177-8.

Chandler, Billy Jaynes. The Feitosas and the Sertão dos Inhamuns:
The History of a Family and a Community in Northeast Brazil,
1700-1930. Gainesville, Fla.: U Fla Press, 1972. Rev. by
S. Gross, HAHR, 53(Aug 1973):526-7.

Chandler, David. Marlborough as Military Commander. New York:
Scribner's, 1973. Rev. by R. L. Blanco, HRNB, 2(Nov-Dec
1973):30; M. Ashley, HTo, 23(Aug 1973):593.

Chaney, William A. The Cult of Kingship in Anglo-Saxon England:
The Transition from Paganism to Christianity. Berkeley: U
Cal Press, 1970. Rev. by C. W. Hollister, AHR, 78(Feb
1973):80-1.

Chantraine, Georges. "Mystère" et "Philosophie du Christ" selon
Érasme. Etude de la lettre à P. Volz et la "Ratio Verae The-
ologiae" (1518). Namur: Secrétariat des publications; Gem-
bloux: Editions J. Duculot, 1971. Rev. by L. W. Spitz,
JMH, 45(Sep 1973):472-3.

Chapelle, Howard I. The American Fishing Schooners, 1825-1835.
New York: Norton, 1973. Rev. by V. Lignori, HRNB, 2
(Nov-Dec 1973):44-5.

Chapelow, Allan, ed. Shaw "The Chucker-Out." A Biographical

Exposition and Critique. n. p. : AMS press, n. d. Rev. by
S. Weintraub, E-I, 8(Spr 1973):135-42.

Chaplais, Pierre. English Royal Documents: King John--Henry IV,
    1199-1461. Oxford: Ox U Press, 1971. Rev. by A. L.
    Brown, History, 58(Feb 1973):84.

Chapman, Carleton B. Dartmouth Medical School: The First 175
    Years. Hanover, N. H. : U Press New England, 1973. Rev.
    by J. Duffy, VH, 41(Sum 1973):177-8.

Chapman, J. K. , ed. A Political Correspondence of the Gladstone
    Era: The Letters of Lady Sophia Palmer and Sir Arthur
    Gordon, 1884-1889. Philadelphia: American Philosophical
    Society, 1971. Rev. by M. Hurst, HJ, 16(Je 1973):442-4.

Chapman, S. D. , ed. The History of Working-Class Housing--A
    Symposium. Newton Abbot: David and Charles, 1971. Rev.
    by R. W. Brunskill, MH, 2(Aut 1973):126-7.

Chappell, Fred. The World Between the Eyes. Baton Rouge: LSU
    Press, 1971. Rev. by K. S. Byer, GR, 27(Spr 1973):110-21.

Chappell, Gordon S. Logging Along the Denver and Rio Grande:
    Narrow Gauge Logging Railroads of Southwestern Colorado and
    Northern New Mexico. Golden, Colo. : Colo Railroad Museum,
    1971. Rev. by H. C. Miner, Montana, 23(Win 1973):61.

_____ . The Search for the Well-Dressed Soldier, 1865-1890.
    Tucson: Ariz Historical Society, 1972. Rev. by R. A. Mur-
    ray, NHSQ, 16(Fall 1973):200-2; D. F. Giese, NMHR, 48
    (Oct 1973):337.

Chaput, Donald. The Cliff: America's First Great Copper Mine.
    Kalamazoo, Mich. : Sequoia, 1971. Rev. by M. Whiteman,
    BHR, 47(Win 1973):528-9.

Charanis, Peter. Studies on the Demography of the Byzantine Em-
    pire: Collected Studies. London: Variorum Reprints, 1972.
    Rev. by A. E. Laiou, AHR, 78(Oct 1973):1039.

Charnay, Jean-Paul, ed. L'Ambivalence dans la Culture Arabe.
    Paris: Editions Antropos, 1967. Rev. by N. Bitar, MEJ, 27
    (Spr 1973):223-4.

Chaudhuri, Dipak B. R. Aspects of Parliament and Government in
    India. New Delhi: Rachna Prakashan, 1972. Rev. by S.
    Ganguly, IQ, 29(Jl-Sep 1973):271.

Chavez, Angelico, ed. and trans. The Oroz Codex: The Oroz Re-
    lacion, or Relation of the Description of the Holy Gospel Pro-
    vince in New Spain and the Lives of the Founders and Other
    Noteworthy Men of Said Province, Composed by Fray Pedro

Oroz, 1584-1586. Washington, D. C. Academy of American Franciscan History, 1972. Rev. by E. B. Adams, TAm, 30 (Jl 1973):136-7.

Checkland, S. G. The Gladstones: A Family Biography, 1764-1851. Cambridge: Cam U Press, 1971. Rev. by C. R. Middleton, Historian, 35(Feb 1973):286-7; W. L. Arnstein, JMH, 45(Je 1973):314-5; H. Perkin, History, 58(Oct 1973):455-6.

Chelkowski, Peter J., ed. Iran: Continuity and Variety. New York: NYU Press, 1971. Rev. by H. Algar, MEJ, 27(Spr 1973):246-7.

Cheney, C. -R. Notaries Public in England. Oxford: Ox U Press, 1972. Rev. by E. L. G. Stones, History, 58(Je 1973):260-1; M. M. Sheehan, Archives, 11(Aut 1973):99-100.

Cheney, Roberta C. Names on the Face of Montana: The Story of Montana's Place Names. Missoula: U Montana, n. d. Rev. by S. Davison, Montana, 23(Aut 1973):68.

Chernov, O. O., et al., eds. History of the Cities and Villages of the Ukrainian SSR. Kiev: Institut Istorii Akademii Nauk URSR, 1971. Rev. by J. A. Armstrong, AHR, 78(Je 1973):716.

Cherns, A. B., R. Sinclair and W. L. Jenkins, eds. Social Science and Government: Policies and Problems. New York: Barnes and Noble, 1972. Rev. by B. F. Hoselitz, SS, 64 (Nov 1973):274-5.

Cheshire, Noel see Quinn, David B.

Chesneaux, Jean. Peasant Revolts in China, 1840-1949. New York: Norton, 1973. Rev. by M. Gasster, HRNB, 2(Nov/Dec 1973): 36-7.

Chesney, Kellow. The Victorian Underworld. New York: Schocken, 1972. Rev. by G. Smith, HT, 7(Nov 1973):137-8; C. F. Mullett, SS, 64(Dec 1973):343.

Chidester, Otis B., ed. Brand Book 2 of the Tucson Corral of Westerners: A Collection of Smoke Signals, Numbers 11-20, 1965-1969. Tucson: Tucson Corral of the Westerners, 1971. Rev. by D. Russell, A & W, 15(Spr 1973):100.

Chidsey, Donald Barr. Louisiana Purchase: The Story of the Biggest Real Deal in History. New York: Crown, 1972. Rev. by H. Lane, Montana, 23(Aut 1973):62.

Chilcote, Ronald H. Emerging Nationalism in Portugese Africa: Documents. Stanford, Cal.: Hoover Institution Press, 1972. Rev. by O. E. S., CurH, 64(Mar 1973):135.

55   CHILCOTE

_____, ed. Protest and Resistance in Angola and Brazil: Com-
parative Studies. Berkeley: U Cal Press, 1972. Rev. by W.
Dean, HAHR, 53(Nov 1973):667-9; W. G. Clarence-Smith,
JAfH, 14(3rd Qr 1973):517-18.

Chirovsky, Nicholas L. A History of the Russian Empire. Vol. 1.
New York: Philosophical Library, 1973. Rev. by D. R.
Papazian, HRNB, 2(Nov/Dec 1973):31-2.

Chopra, Surendra. U. N. Mediation in Kashmir: A Study in Power
Politics. n. p.: Vishal Kurukshetra, 1971. Rev. by D. C.
Jha, IQ, 29(Apr-Je 1973):180-1.

Choudhary, Sukhbir. Peasants and Workers Movement in India, 1905-
1929. New Delhi: People's Publishing House, 1971. Rev. by
S. Chakravarty, IQ, 29(Apr-Je 1973):173-4.

Chrimes, S. B. Henry VII. Berkeley: U Cal Press, 1972. Rev.
by B. C. Weber, Historian, 36(Nov 1973):97; G. R. Elton,
HJ, 16(Sep 1973):627-9; M. J. Tucker, AHR, 78(Dec 1973):
1453-4; A. L. Rowse, HTo, 23(Ja 1973):67.

Christensen, C. A. and Herluf Nielsen, eds. Diplomatrium Danicum. 3rd Ser., 1340-1412. Vol. 7. 1364-1366. Copenhagen:
Munksgaard, 1972. Rev. by W. G. Jones, AHR, 78(Oct 1973):
1036-7.

Christian, Marcus. Negro Ironworkers of Louisiana, 1718-1900.
Gretna, La.: Pelican, 1972. Rev. by D. E. Davis, LaH,
14(Sum 1973):328.

Christie, Ian B., ed. The Correspondence of Jeremy Bentham.
Vol. 3, January 1781-October 1788. London: Athlone, 1971.
Rev. by W. Thomas, EHR, 88(Oct 1973):861-3.

Christoff, Peter K. An Introduction to Nineteenth-Century Russian
Slavophilism: A Study in Ideas. Vol. II. I. V. Kireevskij.
The Hague; Mouton, 1972. Rev. by N. V. Riasanovsky, RR,
32(Oct 1973):434-5.

Christovich, Mary Louise, et al., comps and eds. New Orleans
Architecture. Vol. II. The American Sector. Gretna, La.:
Pelican, 1972. Rev. by W. V. Trufant, LaH, 14(Fall 1973):
406-7.

Chudacoff, Howard P. Mobile Americans: Residential and Social
Mobility in Omaha, 1880-1920. New York: Ox U Press, 1972.
S. B. Warner, Jr., JAH, 60(Sep 1973):474-5.

Chyet, Stanley F. Lopez of Newport; Colonial American Merchant
Prince. Detroit: Wayne St U Press, 1970. Rev. by E. S.
Bruchey, MHM, 68(Fall 1973):340.

Civilization and Science: In Conflict or Collaboration. London: Churchill, 1972. Rev. by I. S. Spiegel-Rösing, T & C, 14 (Oct 1973):678-81.

Clanchy, M. T., ed. Civil Pleas of the Wiltshire Eyre, 1249. n. p. Wiltshire Record Society ... 1971. Rev. by S. F. C. Milsom, Archives, 11(Apr 1973):47-8.

Clark, Francis and James Lynch. The New York Volunteers in California. Glorieta, N. Mex.: Rio Grande, 1970. Rev. by J. Yates, CHQ, 52(Sum 1973):183-4.

Clark, G. Kitson. Churchmen and the Condition of England 1832-1885. London: Methuen, 1973. Rev. by O. Chadwick, HJ, 16(Dec 1973):870-4.

Clark, Sir George. English History: A Survey. Oxford: Ox U Press, 1971. Rev. by R. R. Rea, LJ, 97(Ja 1973):68.

Clark, James A. and Michel T. Halbouty. The Last Boom. New York: Random House, 1972. Rev. by P. H. Giddens, JAH, 60(Dec 1973):845-6.

Clark, John D. Ignition! An Informal History of Liquid Rocket Propellants. New Brunswick, N. J.: Rutgers U Press, 1972. Rev. by M. R. Sharpe, T & C, 14(Jl 1973):514-5.

Clark, John G. Towns and Minerals in Southeastern Kansas, 1890-1930. Lawrence: State Geological Survey of Kansas, 1970. Rev. by G. Lamson, JEH, 33(Dec 1973):879-80.

Clark, Patricia P. see Graf, LeRoy

Clark, Peter and Paul Slack, eds. Crisis and Order in English Towns, 1500-1700: Essays in Urban History. Toronto: U Tor Press, 1972. Rev. by R. Howell, Jr., AHR, 78(Feb 1973): 94-5; D. Hirst, HJ, 16(Je 1973):432-3.

Clark, Thomas D. Pleasant Hill in the Civil War. Shakertown, Ky.: Pleasant Hill Press, 1972. Rev. by J. Neal, FCHQ, 47(Apr 1973):198-9.

Clarke, Dwight L. William Tecumseh Sherman: Gold Rush Banker. San Francisco: Cal Historical Society, 1969. Rev. by J. H. Madison, JAH, 60(Je 1973):129-30.

Clarke, J I. and W. B. Fisher, eds. Populations of the Middle East and North Africa: A Geographical Approach. London: U Lon Press, 1969; New York: Africana, 1972. Rev. by D. R. Harris, AfAf, 72(Jl 1973):338; C. Issawic, MEJ, 27(Spr 1973): 244.

Clarke, Mary Whatley. Chief Bowles and the Texas Cherokees.

Norman: U Ok Press, 1971. Rev. by K. F. Neighbors, WHQ, 4(Jl 1973):337-8.

Clarkson, L. A. The Pre-Industrial Economy in England, 1500-1750. New York: Schocken, 1972. Rev. by G. E. Mingay, AgH, 47(Ja 1973):88-90; P. H. Ramsey, History, 58(Je 1973): 272-3; W. E. Minchinton, BHR, 47(Aut 1973):412-14.

Clasen, Claus-Peter. Anabaptism: A Social History, 1525-1618. Ithaca, N. Y.: Cornell U Press, 1972. Rev. by G. R. Elton, EHR, 88(Oct 1973):853-6; R. R. Liebowitz, JMH, 45(Sep 1973):474-5; P. C. Matheson, History, 58(Oct 1973):442-3.

Clawson, Marion. The Bureau of Land Management. New York: Praeger, 1971. Rev. by J. L. Artz, NHSQ, 16(Sum 1973): 139-40.

Clay, James W. and Douglas, M. Orr, Jr., eds. Metrolina Atlas. Chapel Hill: UNC Press, 1972. Rev. by R. F. Knapp, NCHR, 50(Win 1973):94-5.

Clayton, Bruce. The Savage Ideal. Intolerance and Intellectual Leadership in the South, 1890-1914. Baltimore: JHU Press, 1972. Rev. by L. M. Simms, Jr., JNH, 58(Apr 1973):225-7; GHQ, 57(Spr 1973):154-5; W. B. Gatewood, Jr., FHQ, 52(Jl 1973):81-3; D. W. Noble, CHR, 54(Dec 1973):466-7; J. T. Moore, NCHR, 50(Spr 1973):216; D. W. Grantham, Jr., JSH, 39(May 1973):304-6.

Cleary, Edward L., ed. Shaping a New World: An Orientation to Latin America. New York: Orlis, 1971. Rev. by S. M. N., HAHR, 53(Aug 1973):572-3.

Cleaveland, Norman. The Morleys: Young Upstarts on the Southwest Frontier. Albuquerque: Calvin Horn, 1971. Rev. by W. J. Donlon, A & W, 15(Spr 1973):91-3; R. N. Ellis, AHR, 78(Oct 1973):1139-40; V. G. Spence, Montana, 23(Win 1973): 62.

Clemens, Diane Shaver. Yalta. New York: Ox U Press, 1970. Rev. by R. D. Schulzinger, H & T, 12(1973):146-62.

Clemens, Samuel see Marsh, Andrew J.

Clemoes, Peter, et al., eds. Anglo-Saxon England. Vol. I. New York: Cam U Press, 1972. Rev. by J. D. A. Ogilvy, AHR, 78(Dec 1973):1434-5; C. E. Wright, Antiquity, 47(Sep 1973): 245-6.

_____ and Kathleen Hughes, eds. England Before the Conquests: Studies in Primary Sources Presented to Dorothy Whitelock. Cambridge: Cam U Press, 1971. Rev. by E. John, History, 58(Je 1973):254-5.

Clepper, Henry. Professional Forestry in the United States. Baltimore: JHU Press, 1971. Rev. by W. D. Rasmussen, JAH, 59(Mar 1973):1029-30; L. Rakestraw, PHR, 42(Feb 1973):117-8.

Cleveland, William L. The Making of an Arab Nationalist: Ottomanism and Arabism in the Life and Thought of Sati^c al-Husri. Princeton, N. J.: Prin U Press, 1971. Rev. by J. P. Jankowski, AHR, 78(Oct 1973):1105-6; M. Khadduri, MEJ, 27(Win 1973):77-8.

Clifford, John Gary. The Citizen Soldiers: The Plattsburg Training Camp Movement, 1913-1920. Lexington, Ky.: U Press Ky, 1972. Rev. by D. R. Beaver, JAH, 60(Je 1973):161-3; M. E. Fletcher, RKHS, 71(Ja 1973):119-20; D. J. Mrozek, MilAf, 37(Oct 1973):109.

Clissold, Stephen. Latin America: New World, Third World. New York: Praeger, 1972. Rev. by J. P. Harrison, TAm, 30 (Oct 1973):277-8; J. E. Fagg, HAHR, 53(Aug 1973):490-1.

Clive, John. Macaulay: The Shaping of the Historian. New York: Knopf, 1973. Rev. by L. D. Lafore, AHR, 78(Dec 1973):1464-5.

Clough, Raymund Gore. Oil Rivers Trader. London: C. Hurst, 1972. Rev. by A. J. H. Latham, JAfH, 14(No. 2 1973):354.

Clowse, Converse D. Economic Beginnings in Colonial South Carolina, 1670-1730. Columbia, S. C.: U SCar Press, 1971. Rev. by J. J. McCusker, History, 58(Feb 1973):148; L. Lee, AgH, 47(Jl 1973):275-6.

Cloyd, E. L. James Burnett, Lord Monboddo. Oxford: Ox U Press, 1972. Rev. by S. Piggot, Antiquity, 47(Mar 1973):79-80.

Clubb, O. Edmund. China and Russia: The "Great Game." New York: Columbia U Press, 1971. Rev. by K. L. London, AHR, 78(Oct 1973):1012-3.

Coakley, Leo J. Jersey Troopers: A Fifty-Year History of the New Jersey State Police. New Brunswick, N. J.: Rutgers U Press, 1971. Rev. by K. Jordan, NJH, 91(Aut 1973):271-3.

Coben, Stanley, ed. Reform, War and Reaction: 1912-1932. Columbia, S. C.: U SCar Press, 1973. Rev. by F. L. Grubbs, Jr., NCHR, 50(Sum 1973):344.

Cochise, Ciyé. "Nino" and A. Kenny Griffith. The First Hundred Years of Nino Cochise: The Untold Story of an Apache Indian Chief. New York: Abelard-Schuman, 1971. Rev. by R. N. Ellis, JOW, 12(Jl 1973):517.

Cochran, Bert. Harry Truman and the Crisis Presidency. New
    York: Funk and Wagnalls, 1973. Rev. by A. Yarnell, HT,
    6(May 1973):488-9.

Cochran, Thomas C. American Business in the Twentieth Century.
    Cambridge, Mass.: Har U Press, 1972. Rev. by G. T.
    White, BHR, 47(Aut 1973):400-1.

_____. Business in American Life: A History. New York:
    McGraw-Hill, 1972. Rev. by S. Salisbury, IMH, 69(Sep 1973):
    293-4; H. D. Woodman, BHR, 47(Aut 1973):372-3; W. D.
    Lewis, PMHB, 97(Apr 1973):268-71; S. Bruchey, JAH, 59
    (Mar 1973):993-4.

_____. Social Change in Industrial Society. London: Allen and
    Unwin, 1972. Rev. by A. Lindsey, SS(Nov 1973):296.

Cochran, William C. The Western Reserve and the Fugitive Slave
    Law: A Prelude to the Civil War. New York: Da Capo,
    1972. Rev. by J. F. Marszalek, Jr., WPHM, 56(Ja 1973):
    92-3.

Cochrane, Eric. Florence in the Forgotten Centuries, 1527-1800: A
    History of Florence and the Florentines in the Age of the Grand
    Dukes. Chicago: U Chi Press, 1973. Rev. by F. J. Coppa,
    HRNB, 2(Nov/Dec 1973):27.

Cockburn, J. S., ed. Somerset Assize Orders, 1640-1659. Somer-
    set: Somerset Record Society, 1971. Rev. by D. H. Penning-
    ton, History, 58(Feb 1973):101-2; W. Prest, Archives, 11(Aut
    1973):105.

Coffey, Brian. Selected Poems. Dublin: Zozimus Books, 1971.
    Rev. by F. S. Kiley, E-I, 8(Aut 1973):148-50.

Cohen, Bernard. Sociocultural Changes in American Jewish Life as
    Reflected in Selected Jewish Literature. Rutherford, N. J.:
    Fairleigh-Dickinson Press, 1972. Rev. by A. H. Rosenfeld,
    AJHQ, 63(Sep 1973):97-8.

Cohen, Claude. L'Islam des Origines au début de L'Empire Ottoman.
    Paris: Bordas, 1970. Rev. by M. A. Cook, History, 58(Feb
    1973):76-7.

Cohen, David W. and Jack P. Greene, eds. Neither Slave nor Free:
    The Freedmen of African Descent in the Slave Societies of the
    New World. Baltimore: JHU Press, 1972. Rev. by C. N.
    Degler, HAHR, 53(Aug 1973):491-3; A. J. Lane, JSH, 39(Aug
    1973):450-2; R. M. Morse, AHR, 78(Dec 1973):1426-7.

Cohen, Henry. Business and Politics in America from the Age of
    Jackson to the Civil War: The Career Biography of W. W.
    Corcoran. Westport, Conn.: Greenwood, 1971. Rev. by

R. P. Sharkey, AHR, 78(Feb 1973):163-4; T. L. Hardin, JISHS, 66(Spr 1973):105-6.

Cohen, William B. Rulers of Empire: The French Colonial Service in Africa. Stanford, Cal.: Hoover Institution Press, 1971. Rev. by M. A. Klein, CHR, 54(Mar 1973):109-10; M. A. Klein, JMH, 45(Je 1973):333-4; R. C. O'Brien, JAfH, 14(3rd Qr 1973):527; P. Hatton, History, 58(Je 1973):326.

Cohn, Gabriel. Petróleo e nacionalismo. São Paulo, Brazil: Difusão Européia do Livro, 1968. Rev. by A. Q. Tiller, HAHR, 53(Aug 1973):568.

Cohn, H J., ed. Government in Reformation Europe, 1520-1560. London: Macmillan, 1971. Rev. by G. Parker, History, 58 (Je 1973):276-7.

Coke, James G. see Gargan, John J.

Coke, Van Deren. The Painter and the Photograph From Delcaroix to Warhol. Albuquerque: U NM Press, 1972. Rev. by R. V. Jenkins, T & C, 14(Jl 1973):485-6.

Colburn, George A. see Carlson, Lewis

Coldstream, J. N. and G. L. Huxley, eds. Kythera: Excavations and Studies Conducted by the University of Pennsylvania Museum and the British School at Athens. London: Faber, 1972. Rev. by P. Warren, Antiquity, 47(Dec 1973):321-3.

Cole, Herbert M. see Fraser, Douglas

Cole, William. Poems from Ireland. New York: Crowell, 1972. Rev. by A. Bradley, E-I, 8(Aut 1973):150-1.

Coleman, J. Winston, Jr. The Squire's Sketches of Lexington. Lexington, Ky.: Henry Clay Press, 1972. Rev. by W. T. C., LH, 75(Spr 1973):39; J. R. Bentley, FCHQ, 47(Oct 1973):361.

Coleman, Terry. Going to America. New York: Pantheon, 1972. Rev. by V. Greene, WMH, 56(Spr 1973):247-8.

Coles, John. Field Archaeology in Britain. London: Methuen, 1972. Rev. by R. J. C. Atkinson, Antiquity, 47(Je 1973):163-4.

Coles, Robert. Farewell to the South. Boston: Little, Brown, 1972. Rev. by L. C. Lamon, JSH, 39(Aug 1973):422-3.

Coletta, Paolo E. The Presidency of William Howard Taft. Lawrence: U Press Ks., 1973. Rev. by J. L. Penick, Jr., JSH, 39(Nov 1973):617-18; J. L. Nethers, OQ, 16(Win 1973):151-4.

Coley, W. B. see Arthur S. Weinsinger

Collaer, Paul, ed. Music of the Americas: An Illustrated Music
  Ethnology of the Eskimo and American Indian Peoples. New
  York: Praeger, 1973. Rev. by D. S. Gaus, TAm, 30(Oct
  1973):278-9.

Colley, Charles C., comp. Documents of Southwestern History: A
  Guide to the Manuscript Collections of the Arizona Historical
  Society. Tucson: Ariz Historical Society, 1972. Rev. by
  R. S. Dunn, A & W, 15(Aut 1973):295-7; D. M. Powell, NMHR,
  48(Jl 1973):270-1.

Collias, Joe G. The Search for Steam. Berkeley: Howell-North,
  1972. Rev. by L. Carranco, JOW, 12(Jl 1973):511; J. C.
  Thode, Montana, 23(Spr 1973):67.

Collier, Christopher. Roger Sherman's Connecticut. Middletown,
  Conn.: Wes U Press, 1971. Rev. by R. T. Warfle, HT, 6
  (Feb 1973):326-7; D. S. Lovejoy, AHR, 78(Feb 1973):157.

Collier, John. American Indian Ceremonial Dances. New York:
  Crown, 1972. Rev. by H. A. Howard, JOW, 12(Apr 1973):
  341-2; L. C. Kelly, SWHQ, 76(Ja 1973):350-1.

Collier, Richard. Duce! A Biography of Benito Mussolini. New
  York: Viking, 1971. Rev. by D. Koenig, MilAf, 37(Feb
  1973):160.

Collins, Larry and Dominique Lapierre. O Jerusalem! New York:
  Simon and Schuster, 1972. Rev. by E. M. Wilson, MEJ, 27
  (Win 1973):91-2.

Collins, Robert. Land Beyond the Rivers: The Southern Sudan,
  1898-1918. New Haven, Conn.: Yale U Press, 1971. Rev.
  by I. R. Smith, AfAf, 72(Ja 1973):87-8.

Collison, Robert L. Abstracts and Abstracting Services. Santa
  Barbara: Clio, 1971. Rev. by D. Harrison, AmArch, 36(Ja
  1973):73-4.

Colloque universitaire pour la commémoration du centenaire de la
  commune de 1871. Paris: Les Editions Ouvrieres, 1972. Rev.
  by P. N. Stearns, JMH, 45(Dec 1973):684-5.

Coman, Ian B., ed. The Enigma of Mary Stuart. London: Victor
  Gollancz, 1971. Rev. by D. M. Loades, History, 58(Feb 1973):
  97-8.

Conacher, J. B. The Peelites and the Party System, 1846-52.
  Newton Abbot: David and Charles, 1972. Rev. by N. Gash,
  History, 58(Je 1973):307-9; W. L. Arnstein, JMH, 45(Sep
  1973):506-9.

Conlin, Joseph Robert. Bread and Roses Too: Studies of the Wobblies. Westport, Conn.: Greenwood, 1969. Rev. by J. Sullivan, JOW, 12(Ja 1973):180-1.

Connell, John, ed. Semnan: Persian City and Region. London:
University College, 1970. Rev. by E. J. Hoogland, MEJ, 27
(Aut 1973):526-7.

Connelley, William E. see Root, Frank A.

Connell-Smith, Gordon and Howell A. Lloyd. The Relevance of History. London: Heinemann, 1972. Rev. by G. R. Elton, History, 58(Oct 1973):410.

Connelly, Owen. The Epoch of Napoleon. New York: Holt, Rinehart and Winston, 1972. Rev. by F. X. J. Homer, HT, 7
(Nov 1973):113.

Connelly, Thomas Lawrence. Autumn of Glory: The Army of Tennessee, 1862-1865. Baton Rouge: LSU Press, 1971. Rev. by
G. H. Lobdell, JISHS, 66(Spr 1973):102-3; G. McWhiney, JAH,
60(Dec 1973):814-6.

_____ and Archer Jones. The Politics of Command: Factions
and Ideas in Confederate Strategy. Baton Rouge: LSU Press,
1973. Rev. by J. I. Robertson, Jr., GHQ, 57(Win 1973):589-
90; R. E. Dalton, THQ, 32(Win 1973):391-2.

Connor, Seymour V. Texas: A History. New York: Crowell,
1971. Rev. by B. Procter, JAH, 59(Mar 1973):1006.

_____ and Odie B. Faulk. North America Divided: the Mexican
War, 1846-1848. New York: Ox U Press, 1972. Rev. by
M. M. Anderberg, CurH, 64(Feb 1973):82; G. W. Price,
PacH, 17(Spr 1973):97-9; D. J. Weber, PHR, 42(Feb 1973):
113-14; A. Castel, AHI, 8(Apr 1973):49.

Connors, Richard J. A Cycle of Power: The Career of Jersey City
Mayor Frank Hague. Metuchen, N. J.: Scarecrow, 1971.
Rev. by H. K. Platt, NJH, 91(Aut 1973):273-7.

Conover, Helen F. and Donald H. Mugridge. An Album of American
Battle Art, 1755-1918. New York: Da Capo, 1972. Rev. by
D. L. DeBerry, JOW, 12(Oct 1973):648.

Conrad, Robert. The Destruction of Brazilian Slavery, 1850-1888.
Berkeley: U Cal Press, 1972. Rev. by R. H. Mattoon, Jr.,
BHR, 47(Win 1973):548-9.

Conrad, W. P. Conococheague: A History of the Greencastle--An-
trim Community, 1736-1971. Greencastle, Pa.: Greencastle-
Antrim School District, 1971. Rev. by H. T. Rosenberger,
PH, 40(Oct 1973):495.

Conroy, Hilary and T. Scott Miyakawa, eds. East Across the Pa-
    cific: Historical and Sociological Studies of Japanese Immigra-
    tion and Assimilation. Santa Barbara: Clio, 1972. Rev. by
    J. Modell, JAH, 60(Dec 1973):839-40; H. B. Melendy, PHR,
    42(Aug 1973):435-6.

Constable, G. and B. Smith, eds. and trans. Libellus de diversis
    ordinibus et professionibus qui sunt in aecclesia. New York:
    Ox U Press, 1972. Rev. by C. R. Cheney, AHR, 78(Oct
    1973):1031-2.

Constantinescu, Miron, et al. Unification of the Romanian National
    State: The Union of Transylvania With Old Romania. Bucha-
    rest: Publishing House of the Academy of the Socialist Repub-
    lic of Romania, 1971. Rev. by W. O. Oldson, EEQ, 7(Fall
    1973):343-4.

Cook, Ann, Marilyn Gittell and Herb Mack, eds. City Life, 1865-
    1900: Views of Urban America. New York: Praeger, 1973.
    Rev. by P. L. Simon, HRNB, 2(Nov/Dec 1973):47.

Cook, M. A. Population Pressure in Rural Anatolia, 1450-1600.
    New York: Ox U Press, 1972. Rev. by D. R. Sadat, AHR,
    78(Oct 1973):1104-5.

Cook, R. M. Greek Art: Its Development, Character and Influence.
    London: Weidenfeld and Nicolson, 1972. Rev. by H. Plom-
    mer, Antiquity, 47(Je 1973):151-2.

Cook, Warren L. Flood Tide of Empire: Spain and the Pacific
    Northwest, 1543-1819. New Haven, Conn.: Yale U Press,
    1973. Rev. by A. P. Nasatir, HT, 7(Nov 1973):144-5; T. E.
    Treutlein, CHQ, 52(Win 1973):371-2; A. P. Nasatir, JAH, 60
    (Dec 1973):779-81.

Cooke, A. B. and J. R. Vincent, eds. Lord Carlingford's Journal:
    Reflections of a Cabinet Minister 1885. [Oxford:] Clarendon,
    1971. Rev. by M. Hurst, HJ, 16(Je 1973):442-4.

Cooke, A. M. A History of the Royal College of Physicians of Lon-
    don. Vol. III Oxford: Clarendon, 1972. Rev. by E. Clarke,
    EHR, 88(Jl 1973):607-8.

Cooke, Sherburne F. and Woodrow Borah. Essays in Population His-
    tory: Mexico and the Caribbean. London: U Cal Press, 1972.
    Rev. by D. A. Brading, History, 58(Oct 1973):481; M. Mör-
    ner, HAHR, 53(Feb 1973):109-12.

Cooling, B. Franklin, III see Millett, Allan R.

Coombs, Norman. The Black Experience in America. New York:
    Twayne, 1972. Rev. by B. Fladeland, JAH, 60(Je 1973):106-7.

Cooper, Bryan. Alaska: The Last Frontier. New York: Morrow, 1973. Rev. by J. A. Hussey, AW, 10(Jl 1973):58.

Cooper, Charles A. and Sidney S. Alexander. Economic Development and Population Growth in the Middle East. New York: Elsevier, 1972. Rev. by I. Oweiss, MEJ, 27(Spr 1973):243-4.

Cooper, J. P., ed. The New Cambridge Modern History. Vol. IV. The Decline of Spain and the Thirty Years War, 1609-48/59. n. p.: Cam U Press, 1970. Rev. by G. V. Scammell, HJ, 16(Sep 1973):637-8.

_____ see Thirsk, Joan

Coppa, Frank J. Planning, Protectionism and Politics in Liberal Italy: Economics and Politics in the Giolittian Age. Washington, D. C.: Cath U Amer Press, 1971. Rev. by R. S. Cunsolo, JMH, 45(Sep 1973):552-3.

Corbett, Charles D. The Latin American Military as a Socio-Political Force: Case Studies of Bolivia and Argentina. Coral Gables, Fla.: U Miami Press, 1972. Rev. by M. Needler, HAHR, 53(May 1973):343-4; T. M Bader, CHR, 54(Dec 1973):437-8; C. D. Ameringer, MilAf. 37(Dec 1973):157.

Corbin, Henry. Creative Imagination in the Sufism of Ibn 'Arabī. Princeton, N. J.: Prin U Press, 1969. Rev. by C. E. Butterworth, MEJ, 27(Win 1973):92-6.

Cordier, Andrew W. and Wilder Foote, eds. Public Papers of the Secretaries-General of the United Nations. Vol. 2. Dag Hammarskjold, 1953-1956. New York: Columbia U Press, 1972. Rev. by W. C. Clemens, Jr., AHR, 78(Dec 1973):1428-30; W. F. Kuehl, JAH, 60(Dec 1973):760-2.

Corkran, Herbert, Jr. Patterns of International Cooperation in the Caribbean, 1942-1969. Dallas: SMU Press, 1970. Rev. by D. D. Burks, AHR, 78(Feb 1973):184.

Cornelius, Janet. Constitution Making in Illinois, 1818-1970. Urbana: U Ill Press, 1972. Rev. by M. G. Baxter, IMH, 69 (Mar 1973):67-9; J. H. Krenkel, JAH, 59(Mar 1973):1046-7.

Corner, George W. Doctor Kane of the Arctic Seas. Philadelphia: Temple U Press, 1972. Rev. by W. L. Fox, JAH, 60(Dec 1973):810-11; J. Cadwallader, PMHB, 97(Apr 1973):276-8.

Corráin, D. Ó. Ireland Before the Normans. Dublin: Gill and Macmillan, 1972. Rev. by A. P. Smyth, History, 58(Je 1973):253.

Corro, Alejandro del. Movimentos revolucionarios de Latin America. Louvain, Belgium: Información Documental de América Latina.

Rev. by W. E. Ratliff, HAHR, 53(Nov 1973):717-8.

Cortada, James W. United States-Spanish Relations, Wolfram and
World War II. Barcelona: Manuel Pareja, 1971. Rev. by
R. L. Proctor, JAH, 60(Dec 1973):852-3.

Cosmos, Graham A. An Army for Empire: The United States Army
in the Spanish-American War. Columbia, Mo.: U Mo Press,
1972. Rev. by J K. Mahon, FHQ, 52(Oct 1973):203-4; J. M.
Gates, MilAf, 37(Feb 1973):34; H. W. Morgan, SWHQ, 76(Apr
1973):490-1.

Cosseboom, Kathy. Grosse Pointe Michigan: Race Against Race.
East Lansing: Mich St U Press, 1972. Rev. by C. R. Os-
thaus, MichH, 57(Fall 1973):274-5; N. Lederer, Crisis, 80
(Oct 1973):279-80. NOTE: Author's name appears as Cose-
boom in the Crisis citation.

Costamagna, Giorgio. Il notoio a Genova tra prestigio e potere.
Rome: Consiglio Nazionale del Notariato, 1970. Rev. by A.
Andrews, AHR, 78(Feb 1973):121-2.

Costello, David F. The Desert World. New York: Crowell, 1972.
Rev. by G. Monson, JAriH, 14(Sum 1973):169-70.

Couland, Jacques. Le mouvement syndical au Liban (1919-1946):
Son évolution pendant le mandat francais de l'occupation a
l'évacuation et au Code du travail. Paris: Éditions Sociales,
1970. Rev. by A. G. Gerteiny, AHR, 78(Oct 1973):1109-10.

Coulter, E. Merton. Daniel Lee, Agriculturist: His Life North and
South. Athens, Ga.: U Ga Press, 1972. Rev. by K. Coleman, GHQ, 57(Spr 1973):149-50; F. J. Huffman, JSH, 39(May
1973):289-90; J. C. Bonner, FHQ, 52(Jl 1973):77-8; V.
Wiser, AgH, 47(Oct 1973):352-3.

Courlander, Harold. The Fourth World of the Hopis. New York:
Crown, 1971. Rev. by M. Syasz, WHQ, 4(Ja 1973):71-3;
H. A. Howard, JOW, 12(Jl 1973):502.

Cowden, Joanna Dunlap see Curry, Richard O.

Cowdrey, H. E. J., ed. and trans. The 'Epistolae Vagantes' of
Pope Gregory VII. [Oxford:] Ox U Press, 1972. Rev. by
J. H. Denton, History, 58(Oct 1973):430-1.

Cox, J. Halley and Edward Stasack. Hawaiian Petroglyphs. Honolulu: Bishop Museum, 1970. Rev. by R. Shutler, Jr.,
Archives, 29(Jl 1973):235-6.

Cox, Joseph W. Champion of Southern Federalism: Robert Goodloe
Harper of South Carolina. Port Washington, N. Y.: Kennikat,
1972. Rev. by M. Borden, MHM, 68(Win 1973):458-9; L. A.

Rose, JAH, 60(Je 1973):124-5; R. R. Beeman, JSH, 39(May
1973):284-6; W. Blanton, FHQ, 52(Oct 1973):196; G. C.
Rogers, Jr., SCHM, 74(Apr 1973):105.

Cracraft, James. The Church Reform of Peter the Great. Stanford, Cal.: Stan U Press, 1971. Rev. by R. Hellie, JMH,
45(Mar 1973):120-1.

Craddock, Patricia B., ed. The English Essays of Edward Gibbon.
New York: Ox U Press, 1972. Rev. by V. G. Wexler, AHR,
78(Dec 1973):1457-8; P. Quennell, HTo, 23(Jl 1973):513, 515.

Craig, F. W. S., comp. and ed. British Parliamentary Election
Results 1950-1970. Chichester: Political Reference Publishers, 1971. Rev. by P. F. Clarke, History, 58(Feb 1973):143.

Craig, Richard B. The Bracero Program: Interest Groups and
Foreign Policy. Austin: U Tx Press, 1971. Rev. by L. A.
Cardozo, HAHR, 53(Feb 1973):168-9; D. T. Leary, A & W,
15(Spr 1973):89-91.

Cramer, C. H. Open Shelves and Open Minds: A History of the
Cleveland Public Library. Cleveland: Press CWR U, 1972. Rev.
by J. Y. Cole, AHR, 78(Oct 1973):1135-6.

Cramer, Clarence H. American Enterprise: Free and Not So Free.
Boston: Little, Brown, 1972. Rev. by T. C. Cochran, AHR,
78(Je 1973):723; A. Spencer, JEH, 33(Dec 1973):880-1; W.
Greenleaf, JAH, 60(Je 1973):109-10.

Crandall, Ruth, comp. Tax and Valuation Lists of Massachusetts
Towns Before 1776. Cambridge, Mass.: Chas. Warren Center
for Studies in American History. Rev. by E. M. Cook, Jr.,
AHR, 78(Feb 1973):146-8.

Crane, Sylvia E. White Silence: Greenough, Powers, and Crawford, American Sculptors in Nineteenth-Century Italy. Coral
Gables, Fla.: U Miami Press, 1972. Rev. by L. B. Miller,
AHR, 78(Oct 1973):1132; P. R. Baker, JAH, 60(Sep 1973):
483-5.

Crapanzano, Vincent. The Fifth World of Forster Bennett: Portrait
of a Navaho. New York: Viking, 1972. Rev. by F. J. Johnston, JOW, 12(Jl 1973):508.

Crassweller, Robert D. The Caribbean Community: Changing Societies and United States Policy. New York: Praeger, 1972.
Rev. by F. G. Gil, HAHR, 53(May 1973):318-20.

Craven, Wesley Frank. White, Red, and Black, The Seventeenth-
Century Virginian. Charlottesville: U Press Va., 1972. Rev.
by G. C. Rogers, Jr., FHQ, 51(Ja 1973):321-2.

Creason, Joe. Joe Creason's Kentucky. Louisville, Ky.: The
    Louisville Times and the Courier Journal, 1972. Rev. by T.
    Pfeiffer, FCHQ, 47(Apr 1973):194-5.

Creighton, Donald. Towards the Discovery of Canada. Toronto:
    Macmillan, 1972. Rev. by I. R. Robertson, CHR, 54(Dec
    1973):441-3.

Crespo, R. Alberto. El Corregimiento de la Paz, 1548-1600. La
    Paz, Bolivia: Editora Urquizo, 1972. Rev. by R. G. Keith,
    HAHR, 53(Aug 1973):508-9.

Creswell, John. British Admirals of the Eighteenth Century: Tactics
    in Battle. Hamden, Conn.: Archon, 1972. Rev. by D. A.
    Baugh, AHR, 78(Oct 1973):1059.

Crews, Clyde F. Presence and Possibility: Louisville Catholicism
    and Its Cathedral. Louisville, Ky.: Clyde F. Crews, 1973.
    Rev. by C. C. Boldrick, FCHQ, 47(Jl 1973):289-90.

Crocker, Lester G. Jean-Jacques Rousseau: The Prophetic Voice,
    1753-1778. Vol. 2. New York: Macmillan, 1973. Rev. by
    D. Felix, HRNB, 2(Oct 1973):6.

Croft, Pauline. The Spanish Company. London: London Record
    Society, 1973. Rev. by R. Pike, HAHR, 53(Nov 1973):727-8;
    C. H. Carter, AHR, 78(Dec 1973):1483-4.

Crompton, Rosemary see Wedderburn, Dorothy

Crosby, Alfred W., Jr. The Columbian Exchange: Biological and
    Cultural Consequences of 1492. Westport, Conn.: Greenwood,
    1972. Rev. by D. B. Cooper, HAHR, 53(Aug 1973):498-500;
    R. S. Dunn, JAH, 60(Sep 1973):420-2; W. D. Rasmussen,
    AgH, 47(Jl 1973):267-9; G. S. Dunbar, WMQ, 3rd Ser., 30
    (Jl 1973):542-3.

Cross, A. G. N. M. Karamzin: A Study of His Literary Career
    1783-1803. Carbondale: S Ill U Press, 1971. Rev. by W. G.
    Jones, ESR, 3(Apr 1973):184-7.

Cross, Eleanor P., ed. The Voyages of Frederick Williams. Ches-
    apeake, Va.: Norfolk County Historical Society, 1972. Rev.
    by T. C. Parramore, NCHR, 50(Spr 1973):207.

Cross, K. G. W. and R. T. Dunlop. A Bibliography of Yeats Crit-
    icism. New York: Macmillan, 1971. Rev. by R. Kent, E-I,
    8(Win 1973):139-40.

Crossman, Carl L. and Ernest S. Dodge. The China Trade: Ex-
    port Paintings, Furniture, Silver and Other Objects. Prince-
    ton, N. J.: Pyne, 1972. Rev. by B. Penrose, PMHB, 97
    (Oct 1973):545.

CROUZET   68

Crouzet, Francois, ed. Capital Formation in the Industrial Revolu-
    tion. London: Methuen, 1972. Rev. by J. J. Pincus, JEH,
    33(Dec 1973):381-2.

Crowder, Michael, ed. West African Resistance. London: Hutch-
    inson, 1971. Rev. by D. Birmingham, History, 58(Je 1973):
    327.

_____   see Ajayi, J. F. Ade

Crowley, F. K. Forrest, 1847-1918. I. 1847-1891, Apprenticeship
    to Premiership. Brisbane: U Queensland Press; Portland,
    Ore.: International Scholarly Book Services, 1972. Rev. by
    R. A. Shields, CHR, 54(Dec 1973):453-4.

Crowley, Frances G. Domingo Faustino Sarmiento. New York:
    Twayne, 1972. Rev. by B. D. Ansel, HAHR, 53(Nov 1973):
    710-11.

_____. Garcilaso de la Vega, el Inca and His Sources in Com-
    mentarios Reales de los Incas. The Hague: Mouton, 1971.
    Rev. by H. V. Livermore, HAHR, 53(May 1973):307-9.

Cruden, Robert. The War That Never Ended: The American Civil
    War. Englewood Cliffs, N. J.: Prentice-Hall, 1973. Rev. by
    L. Cox, JAH, 60(Sep 1973):453.

Cruz, Frank H. see Bailey, Helen Miller

Cudahy, Brian J. Change at Park Street Under: The Story of Bos-
    ton's Subways. Brattleboro, Vt.: Stephen Green, 1972. Rev.
    by R. V. Bruce, T & C, 14(Oct 1973):642-3; C. W. Cheape,
    BHR, 47(Aut 1973):397-8.

Cuff, Robert D. The War Industries Board: Business-Government
    Relations During World War I. Baltimore: JHU Press, 1973.
    Rev. by G. D. Nash, AHR, 78(Dec 1973):1543; J. W. Cham-
    bers, BHR, 47(Win 1973):518-20.

Cullen, L. M. An Economic History of Ireland Since 1660. London:
    Batsford, 1972. Rev. by J. Lee, History, 58(Oct 1973):418-9.

Cumberland, Charles C. Mexican Revolution: The Constitutionalist
    Years. Austin: U Tx Press, 1972. Rev. by D. C. Villegas,
    HAHR, 53(May 1973):327-8; A. Bryan, SWHQ, 76(Apr 1973):
    489-90. NOTE: The Villegas review is in Spanish.

Cumming, W. P., R. A. Skelton, and D. B. Quinn. The Discovery
    of North America. London: Elek, 1971; New York: American
    Heritage, 1972. Rev. by G. V. Scammell, History, 58(Oct
    1973):440-1; L. De Vorsey, Jr., NCHR, 50(Spr 1973):218-9.

Cummings, Charles M. Yankee Quaker Confederate General: The

Curious Career of Bushrod Rust Johnson. Rutherford, N. J.:
Fairleigh-Dickinson U Press, 1971. Rev. by R. M. McBride,
THQ, 32(Sum 1973):195-6.

Cummins, Duane and William Gee White. The Origins of the Civil
War. New York: Benziger, 1972. Rev. by A. C. Ashcraft,
JOW, 12(Jl 1973):516.

Cumpston, I. M., ed. The Growth of the British Commonwealth,
1880-1932. New York: St. Martin's, 1973. Rev. by W. G.
Simon, HRNB, 2(Oct 1973):3.

Cunha, George Martin and Dorothy Grant Cunha. Conservation of
Library Materials: A Manual and Bibliography on the Care,
Repair and Restoration of Library Materials. Vol. 2. Me-
tuchen, N. J.: Scarecrow, 1972. Rev. by J. C. Wright, Am-
Arch, 36(Oct 1973):555-8.

Cunha, George Martin and Norman Paul Tucker, eds. Library and
Archives Conservation. Boston: Library, Boston Atheneum,
1972. Rev. by J. C. Wright, AmArch, 36(Oct 1973):555-8.

Cunliffe, Barry. Roman Bath Discovered. Boston: Routledge and
Kegan Paul, 1971. Rev. by R. Brilliant, AHR, 78(Feb 1973):
75.

Cunliffe, Marcus. American Presidents and the Presidency. New
York: American Heritage, 1972. Rev. by M. Borden, WVH,
34(Apr 1973):297-8.

Cunningham, John T. University in the Forest: The Story of Drew
University. Madison, N. J.: Afton, n.d. Rev. by G. P.
Schmidt, NJH, 91(Aut 1973):196-8.

Cüppers, Heinz. Die Trierer Rommerbrücken. Mainz: Philipp von
Zabern, 1969. Rev. by A. Frantz, Archaeology, 26(Apr 1973):
153-4.

Curia Regis Rolls of the Reign of Henry III Preserved in the Public
Record Office. Vol. 15. London: H M S O, 1972. Rev. by
S. Reynolds, Archives, 11(Aut 1973):100-1.

Current Africanist Research International Bulletin. London: Research
International African Institute. 1971. Rev. by M. D. McKee,
JAfH, 14(3rd Qr 1973):529-30.

Current-Garcia Eugene and Dorothy B. Hatfield, eds. Shem, Ham
and Japheth. The Papers of W. O. Tuggle, Comprising His
Indian Diary, Sketches and Observations, Myths and Washington
Journal in the Territory and at the Capital, 1879-1882. Athens,
Ga.: U Ga Press, 1973. Rev. by D. Brown, AHI, 8(Oct
1973):49-50; GHQ, 57(Win 1973):602-3; H. S. Marks, AlaRe,
26(Jl 1973):233-4; R. N. Ellis, JSH, 39(Nov 1973):610-11.

Currey, Cecil B. Code # 72, Ben Franklin. Franklin: Patriot and Spy?
    Englewood Cliffs, N. J.: Prentice-Hall, 1972. Rev. by A.
    Bakshian, Jr., Mankind, 4(Aug 1973):8, 52; C. L. Egan, His-
    torian, 36(Nov 1973):121-2.

Curry, Richard O. and Joanna Dunlap Cowden, eds. Slavery in
    America: Theodore Weld's American Slavery As It Is. Itasca,
    Ill.: F. E. Peacock, 1972. Rev. by W. F. Mugleston, HT,
    7(Nov 1973):127; J. G. Taylor, LaH, 14(Fall 1973):401.

Curtis, L. P. Apes and Angels: The Irishman in Victorian Carica-
    ture. Newton Abbot: David and Charles, 1971. Rev. by N.
    Mansergh, HJ, 16(Je 1973):436-41; L. H. Lees, JIH, 4(Sum
    1973):140-5; E. D. Steele, History, 58(Oct 1973):461-2.

Curtis, L. Perry, Jr. Anglo-Saxons and Celts: A Study of Anti-
    Irish Prejudices in Victorian England. Bridgeport, Conn.:
    Conference on British Studies ... 1968. Rev. by L. H. Lees,
    JIH, 4(Sum 1973):140-5.

Curtis, L. P., Jr., ed. The Historian's Workshop: Original Es-
    says by Sixteen Historians. New York: Knopf, 1970. Rev.
    by E. Ions, History, 58(Feb 1973):158-9.

Curwen, Samuel. The Journal of Samuel Curwen, Loyalist. Cam-
    bridge, Mass.: Harvard, 1972. Rev. by R. D. Brown, WMQ,
    3rd Ser., 30(Oct 1973):675-6.

Cushner, Nicholas P., S. J. Spain in the Philippines: From Con-
    quest to Revolution. Quezon City, Philippines: Ateneo de
    Manilla U., 1971. Rev. by V. R. Pilapil, HAHR, 53(May
    1973):315-6.

Cuttino, G. P. English Diplomatic Administration. Oxford: Ox U
    Press, 1971. Rev. by E. L. G. Stones, History, 58(Je 1973):
    260-1.

Dabbs, James McBride. Haunted by God. Richmond: John Knox,
    1972. Rev. by F. G. Davenport, JAH, 60(Sep 1973):455-6;
    W. H. Daniel, JSH, 39(May 1973):321-3.

Dabney, Virginius. Virginia: The New Republic. New York:
    Doubleday, 1971. Rev. by J. P. Cullen, AHI, 8(Apr 1973):49.

D'Addario, Arnaldo. Aspetti della Controriforma a Firenze. Rome:
    Ministero dell'Interno Publicazioni degli Archivi di Stato,
    LXXVII, n. d. Rev. by D. Fenlon, Archives, 11(Aut 1973):102-
    3.

Da Fonseca, Gondin. A Revolução Francesca e a vida de José Boni-
    fácio. Rio de Janeiro, 1971. Rev. by W. A. Harrell, HAHR,
    53(Nov 1973):730.

Dagli, Vadilal, ed. Twenty-Five Years of Independence: A Survey
   of Indian Economy. Bombay: Vora, 1973. Rev. by K. Kas-
   turi, IQ, 29(Oct-Dec 1973):362-3.

Dain, Phyllis. The New York Public Library: A History of Its
   Founding and Early Years. New York: N Y Public Library,
   1972. Rev. by R. D. Marcus, JAH, 60(Je 1973):156-7; J. Y.
   Cole, AHR, 78(Oct 1973):1135-6; J. F. Guido, NYH, 54(Ja
   1973):107-9; J. J Heslin, NYHSQ, 57(Apr 1973):190-1.

Dakin, Douglas. The Unification of Greece, 1770-1923. London:
   Ernest Benn, 1972. Rev. by L. P. Morris, History, 58(Je
   1973):302; W. H. McNeill, JMH, 45(Sep 1973):554-5.

D'Albissin, Nelly Girard. Genèse de la frontière franco-belge: Les
   variations des limites septentrionales de la France de 1659 à
   1789. Paris: Editions A and J Picard, 1970. Rev. by J. B.
   Wolf, JMH, 45(Je 1973):309-10.

Dalby, David, ed. Language and History in Africa. London: Cass,
   1970. Rev. by P. Alexandre, Africa, 43(Ja 1973):81-2.

Daly, George Anne and John J. Robrecht. An Illustrated Handbook
   of Fire Apparatus. Philadelphia: Insurance Co. North America, 1972. Rev. by J. H. White, Jr., T & C, 14(Oct 1973):
   630-2.

Dalzell, Robert F., Jr. Daniel Webster and the Trial of American
   Nationalism, 1843-1852. Boston: Houghton Mifflin, 1973. Rev.
   by L. Harrison, AHI, 8(Dec 1973):49; R. N. Current, AHR,
   78(Dec 1973):1530-1; R. Carpol, Mankind, 4(Aug 1973):6, 8;
   N. D. Brown, JAH, 60(Sep 1973):442-3.

Dancey, William S. Archaeological Survey of Mossyrock Reservoir.
   Seattle: U Wash, 1969. Rev. by B. R. Butler, AmAnt, 38
   (Oct 1973):508-9.

Danelski, David and Joseph S. Tulchin, eds. The Autobiographical
   Notes of Charles Evans Hughes. Cambridge, Mass.: Har U
   Press, 1973. Rev. by D. C. Brown, HRNB, 2(Oct 1973):18.

Dangberg, Grace. Carson Valley: "Historical Sketches of Nevada's
   First Settlement." Reno, Nev.: A Carlisle, 1972. Rev. by
   L. J. Higgins, Jr., NHSQ, 16(Sum 1973):142-3.

Daniel, Glyn. Megaliths in History. London: Thames and Hudson,
   1973. Rev. by E. G. Bowen, Antiquity, 47(Sep 1973):240.

_____. The Origins and Growth of Archaeology. New York:
   Crowell, 1971. Rev. by F. J. Johnston, JOW, 12(Jl 1973):
   513-4.

Daniel, Pete. The Shadow of Slavery: Peonage in the South, 1901-

1969. Urbana: U Ill Press, 1972. Rev. by L. J. Friedman, AHR, 78(Feb 1973):179-80; W. I. Hair, JSH, 39(Feb 1973): 132-3; H. C. Bailey, FHQ, 52(Oct 1973):205-6; C. V. Woodward, JAH, 59(Mar 1973):1030-1; N. Lederer, AgH, 47(Oct 1973):367-9; W. F. Holmes, WMH, 56(Spr 1973):256-7.

Daniel, Robert L. American Philanthropy in the Near East, 1820-1960. Athens, O.: Ohio U Press, 1970. Rev. by J. B. Gidney, AHR, 78(Feb 1973):134-5.

Daniels, Jonathan. The Randolphs of Virginia. New York: Doubleday, 1972. Rev. by M. W. Schlegel, JSH, 39(May 1973):314-15.

Daniels, Robert V., ed. The Russian Revolution. Englewood Cliffs, N. J.: Prentice-Hall, 1972. Rev. by R. C. Elwood, RR, 32 (Jl 1973):330-1.

Daniels, Roger. The Bonus March: An Episode of the Great Depression. Westport, Conn.: Greenwood, 1971. Rev. by T. K. Nenninger, MilAf, 37(Oct 1973):112.

_____. Concentration Camps, U. S. A.: Japanese Americans and World War II. New York: Holt, Rinehart and Winston, 1971. Rev. by A. Hoffman, JOW, 12(Ja 1973):179-80; A. R. Millett, MilAf, 37(Feb 1973):34-5; L. B. Chan, NHSQ, 16(Spr 1973): 36-7; M. Hane, SS, 64(Nov 1973):276-7.

_____, ed. Essays in Western History in Honor of T. A. Larson. Laramie: U Wyo, 1971. Rev. by E. R. Bingham, PHR, 42 (May 1973):241-2.

Darby, William J. see Patwardhan, Vinayak N.

Darrah, William Culp. Pithole, the Vanished City: A Story of the Early Days of the Petroleum Industry. Gettysburg, Pa.: William C. Darrah, 1972. Rev. by H. B. Powell, JAH, 59(Mar 1973):1018-19; J. H. Madison, BHR, 47(Spr 1973):120-1; C. A. Newton, PH, 40(Apr 1973):228-9; A. M. Johnson, T & C, 14(Apr 1973):311-12.

Das, Durga, ed. Sardar Patel's Correspondence 1945-1950. 5 vols. Ahmedabad: Navajivan Press, 1971-72. Rev. by S. L. Poplai, IQ, 29(Apr-Je 1973):185-6.

Da Silva, Antonio. Trent's Impact on the Portugese Patronage Missions. Lisbon: Centro de Estudos Historicos Ultramarinos, 1969. Rev. by C. N. McDonnell, TAm, 30(Jl 1973):139.

Da Silva, José Gomes. A Reforma agrarïa no Brasil. Rio de Janeiro: Zahar Editores, 1971. Rev. by M. Cebelsky, HAHR, 53 (May 1973):353-4.

Datar, Asha L. India's Economic Relations with the U. S. S. R. and
   Eastern Europe, 1953-54 and 1969-70. New York: Cam U
   Press, 1972. Rev. by A. Z. Rubenstein, CurH, 64(May 1973):
   224.

Daumas, General E. The Ways of the Desert. [Austin:] U Tx
   Press, 1971. Rev. by S. K. Lazarov, NO, 16(Je 1973):44-5.

Daumas, Maurice. Scientific Instruments of the Seventeenth and
   Eighteenth Centuries and Their Makers. London: Batsford,
   1972. Rev. by M B. Hall, History, 58(Je 1973):297.

David, Paul T. Party Strength in the United States, 1872-1970.
   Charlottesville: U Press Va., 1972. Rev. by J. L. Mc-
   Carthy, AHR, 78(Je 1973):736-7.

Davidson, Basil. Africa: History of a Continent. New York: Macmillan, 1972. Rev. by O. E. S., CurH, 64(Mar 1973):125.

_____. In the Eye of the Storm--Angola's People. London: Long-
   mans, 1972. Rev. by W. G. Clarence-Smith, JAfH, 14(#4,
   1973):703-4.

Davidson, Chalmers Gaston. The Last Foray: The South Carolina
   Planter of 1860: A Sociological Study. Columbia, S. C.: U
   SCar Press, 1971. Rev. by L. Lee, AgH, 47(Jl 1973):275-6.

Davidson, Chandler. Biracial Politics: Conflict and Coalition in the
   Metropolitan South. Baton Rouge: LSU Press, 1972. Rev. by
   T. A. Krueger, JAH, 60(Je 1973):186-8; H. D. Graham, JNH,
   58(Apr 1973):209-10; D. W. Grantham, FHQ, 52(Jl 1973):89-
   90; H. Sitkoff, JSH, 39(May 1973):311-12; A. G. Belles,
   JISHS, 66(Win 1973):478-9; D. McComb, SWHQ, 76(Ja 1973):
   342-3.

Davies, Horton. Worship and Theology in England: From Cranmer
   to Hooker, 1534-1603. Princeton, N. J.: Prin U Press,
   1970. Rev. by W. D. J. Cargill-Thompson, History, 58(Je
   1973):277-9; P. Brooks, HJ, 16(Je 1973):433-5.

Davies, J. Conway, ed. Catalogue of Manuscripts in the Library of
   the Honourable Society of the Inner Temple. 3 vols. New
   York: Ox U Press, 1972. Rev. by J. F. Preston, AmArch,
   36(Jl 1973):407-9.

Davies, Norman. White Eagle, Red Star: The Polish-Soviet War,
   1919-1920. New York: St. Martin's, 1972. Rev. by A.
   Parry, RR, 32(Apr 1973):196-8; J. Korbel, JMH, 45(Dec
   1973):710; J. W. Kipp, MilAf, 37(Oct 1973):114.

Davies, R. W. and Edward Hallett Carr. Foundations of a Planned
   Economy, 1926-1929. Vol. I, parts 1 and 2. New York:
   Macmillan, 1971. Rev. by R. W. Campbell, AHR, 78(Feb 1973):
   128-30.

Davis, Allen F.   American Heroine: The Life and Legend of Jane
  Addams.   New York: Ox U Press, 1973.   Rev. by A. L.
  Hamby, HRNB, 2(Nov/Dec 1973):49.

Davis, Bertram H.   A Proof of Eminence: The Life of Sir John
  Hawkins.   Bloomington: Ind U Press, 1973.   Rev. by M.
  Golden, AHR, 78(Dec 1973):1458-9.

Davis, Daniel S.   Marcus Garvey.   New York: Franklin Watts, 1972.
  Rev. by D. L. Watson, Crisis, 80(Ja 1973):31-2.

Davis, Harold Eugene.   Latin American Thought: A Historical In-
  terpretation.   Baton Rouge: LSU Press, 1972.   Rev. by W. R.
  Crawford, TAm, 30(Jl 1973):131-2;   C. A. Hale, HAHR, 53
  (Aug 1973):516.

Davis, Kenneth S.   FDR: The Beckoning of Destiny, 1882-1928: A
  History.   New York: Putnam's, 1972.   Rev. by A. F. Mc-
  Clure, JSH, 39(Nov 1973):621-3;   R. S. Kirkendall, WMH, 56
  (Sum 1973):339-40.

Davis, Lance and Douglas C. North.   Institutional Change and American Economic Growth.   Cambridge: Cam U Press, 1971.
  Rev. by R. Floud, History, 58(Feb 1973):156.

Davis, Lawrence B.   Immigrants, Baptists and the Protestant Mind
  in America.   Urbana: U Ill Press, 1973.   Rev. by I. G.
  Blake Blake, IMH, 69(Dec 1973):370-2.

Davis, Michael.   The Image of Lincoln in the South.   Knoxville: U
  Tenn Press, 1971.   Rev. by H. C. Bailey, JISHS, 66(Spr
  1973):116-17;   R. Lowe, MHM, 68(Spr 1973):109-10;   S. G. F.
  Spackman, History, 58(Oct 1973):491-2.

Davis, Moshe, ed.   Study Circle Diaspora Jewry at the Home of the
  President of Israel.   Jerusalem: The Institute of Contemporary
  Jewry at the Hebrew U., 1971-72.   Rev. by I. T. Naamani,
  AJHQ, 68(Sep 1973):100-2.

Davis, O. L., Jr., et al.   Exploring the Social Sciences....   New
  York: American Book Co., 1971.   Rev. by J. M. Larkin, SS,
  64(Ja 1973):43-4.

Davis, Ralph.   The Rise of the Atlantic Economies.   Ithaca, N. Y.:
  Cornell U Press, 1973.   Rev. by P. P. Abrahams, HRNB, 2
  (Nov/Dec 1973):32.

Davis, Richard Beale.   Literature and Society in Early Virginia,
  1608-1840.   Baton Rouge: LSU Press, 1973.   Rev. by E.
  Cometti, NCHR, 50(Aut 1973):421-2.

Davis, Richard W.   Political Change and Continuity, 1760-1885: A
  Buckinghamshire Study.   Hamden, Conn.:   Archon, 1972.   Rev.

by J. Cannon, AHR, 78(Dec 1973):1460.

Davison, Kenneth E.   The Presidency of Rutherford B. Hayes.   Westport, Conn.: Greenwood, 1972. Rev. by W. P. Vaughn, JSH,
39(Aug 1973):456-7; W. F. Zornow, CWH, 19(Dec 1973):367-
8; T. C. Reeves, AHR, 78(Oct 1973):1140; H. W. Morgan,
JAH, 60(Sep 1973):459; H. D. Hunt, PMHB, 97(Jl 1973):421-2.

Dawn, C. Ernest. From Ottomanism to Arabism: Essays on the
Origins of Arab Nationalism. Urbana: U Ill Press, 1973.
Rev. by R. H. Davison, HRNB, 2(Oct 1973):11-12.

Dawson, Christopher. The Dividing of Christendom. London: Sidgwick and Jackson, 1972. Rev. by P. C. Matheson, History,
58(Je 1973):275-6.

_____. The Gods of Revolution. New York: NYU Press, 1972.
Rev. by J. G. Smith, WPHM, 56(Oct 1973):438-40; M. J.
Sydenham, CHR, 54(Dec 1973):434-5.

Day, Richard B. Leon Trotsky and the Politics of Economic Isolation. New York: Cam U Press, 1973. Rev. by W. Lerner,
HRNB, 2(Oct 1973):8.

Deakin, F. W. D. The Embattled Mountain. London: Ox U Press,
1971. S. K. Pavlowitch, ESR, 3(Ja 1973):88-95.

Dean, Jill and Susan Smith, eds. Wisconsin: A State for All Seasons. Madison: Wis Tales and Trails, 1972. Rev. by D.
Anderson, WMH, 56(Win 1972-73):164-5.

de Benavente O Mololinía, Fray Taribio. Memoriales o Libro de las
Cosas de la Nueva España y de las Naturales de Ella. Mexico:
Universidad Nacional Autónoma de Mexico, 1971. Rev. by
J. L. Phelan, HAHR, 53(Feb 1973):120-2.

De Bèze, Théodore. Du Droit des Magistrats. Geneva: Librairie
Droz, 1970. Rev. by T. N. Tentler, AHR, 78(Feb 1973):92;
N. M. Sutherland, History, 58(Je 1973):283-5.

Debouzy, Marianne. Le Capitalisme "Sauvage" aux Etats-Unis (1860-
1900). Paris: Editions du Seuil, 1972. Rev. by H. Sales,
BHR, 47(Aut 1973):389-90.

DéCarli, Gileno. Politica de desenvolvimento do Nordeste. Recife,
Brazil: Universidade Federale de Pernambuco, 1971. Rev. by
R. H. Chilcote, HAHR, 53(Feb 1973):155-7.

de Clementi, Andreina. Amadeo Bordiga. Turin: Giulio Einaudi
Editore, 1971. Rev. by E. Craver, JMH, 45(Dec 1973):706-8.

Decleva, Enrico. Da Adua a Sarajevo: La politica estera italiana
e la Francia, 1896-1914. Bari: Laterza, 1971. Rev. by C.

Seton-Watson, HJ, 16(Mar 1973):218-9; W. C. Askew, JMH, 45(Mar 1973):158-9.

De Conde, Alexander. Half Bitter, Half Sweet: An Excursion into Italian-American History. New York: Scribner's, 1971. Rev. by M Klein, AHI, 8(Jl 1973):49-50; H. S. Nelli, AHR, 78 (Je 1972):730-1; R. J. Vecoli, JAH, 59(Mar 1973):1032-4.

Defoe, Daniel. A General History of the Pyrates. Columbia, S. C.: U SCar Press, 1972. Rev. by K. Coleman, GHQ, 57(Fall 1973):442-3.

De Gaulle, Charles. Memoirs of Hope: Renewal and Endeavor. New York: Simon and Schuster, 1971. Rev. by J. C. Cairns, AHR, 78(Dec 1973):1406-20.

Degler, Carl N. Neither Black Nor White: Slavery and Race Relations in Brazil and the United States. New York: Macmillan, 1971. Rev. by R. W. Logan, JAH, 60(Je 1973):130-1; S. M. Elkins, JNH, 58(Ja 1973):86-90.

De Graw, Ronald. The Red Arrow: A History of One of the Most Successful Suburban Transit Companies in the World. Haverford, Pa.: Haverford Press, 1972. Rev. by H. E. Cox, PMHB, 97(Jl 1973):424-6.

de Haas, Elsa and G. D. G. Hall, eds. Early Registers of Writs. London: Bernard Quaritch, 1970. Rev. by D. W. Sutherland, AHR, 78(Dec 1973):1436-7.

Deininger, Jürgen. Der politische Widerstand gegen Rom in Griechenland, 217-86 v. Chr. Berlin: Walter de Gruyter, 1971. Rev. by E. S. Gruen, JIH, 4(Aut 1973):273-86.

Deist, Wilhelm see Schottelius, Herbert

De Jong, L. The Kingdom of the Netherlands in the Second World War. Vol. 4. May 1940-March 1941. The Hague: Martinus Nijhoff, 1972. Rev. by W. Warmbrunn, AHR, 78(Oct 1973): 1085-6.

de Kadt, Emanuel, ed. Patterns of Foreign Influence in the Caribbean. London: Ox U Press, 1972. Rev. by R. V. Salisbury, HAHR, 53(Aug 1973):542-3.

Dekmejian, R. Hrair. Egypt Under Nasir: A Study in Political Dynamics. Albany, N. Y.: SUNY Press, 1971. Rev. by I. Harik, MEJ, 27(Win 1973):82-3.

de Kostianovsky, Olinda Massare. La Mujer Paraguaya: Su Participación en la Guerra Grande. Asunción: Tallereo Gráficos de la Escuela Técnica Salesiana, 1970. Rev. by D. J. Vodarsik, TAm, 30(Oct 1973):294-5.

De Laet, S. J. , A. VanDoorselaer, P. Spitaels and H. Thoen. Le
Nécropole Gallo-Romaine de Blicquy. Vol. XIV. Bruges: De
Tempel, 1972. Rev. by R. Jessup, Antiquity, 47(Je 1973):
152-3.

Delaney, Norman C. John McIntosh Kell of the Raider Alabama. University: U Ala Press, 1973. Rev. by W. S. Still, Jr. , NCHR,
50(Sum 1973):333; GHQ, 57(Win 1973):604; R. Mann, HT, 7
(Nov 1973):147; H. M. Hattaway, JSH, 39(Nov 1973):604-5.

Delaney, Robert W. see Jefferson, James

de las Casas, Bartolome. History of the Indies. New York: Harper
and Row, 1971. Rev. by B. Hamilton, ESR, 3(Jl 1973):303-7.

Delassus, Jean-Francois. The Japanese: A Critical Evaluation of
the Character and Culture of a People. New York: Hart, 1972.
Rev. by M. Hane, SS, 64(Nov 1973):285-6.

Deléry, Simone de la Souchère. Napoleon's Soldiers in America.
Gretna, La. : Pelican, 1972. Rev. by J. D. L. Holmes, FHQ,
52(Oct 1973):197-8; J. Pancake, JAH, 60(Dec 1973):806-7.

Delobelle, André. Die Katholische Universität in Lateinamerika.
Cuernavaca, Mexico: Centro Intercultural de Documentación,
1968. Rev. by Augustus F. Faust, HAHR, 53(May 1973):359-
61.

Delpar, Helen, ed. The Barzoi Reader in Latin American History.
2 vols. New York: Knopf, 1972. Rev. by S. L. Wagner,
HAHR, 53(May 1973):304-5.

Del Solar, Alberto. Diario de campaña. Recuerdos intimos de la
Guerra del Pacifico, 1879-1884. Buenos Aires, Argentina:
Editorial Francisco de Aguirre, 1967 (1886). Rev. by W. L.
Krieg, HAHR, 53(Aug 1973):569-70.

de Lumley, H. , et al. La Grotte Moustérienne de l'Hortus. n. p. :
Université de Provence, 1972. Rev. by D. Collins, Antiquity,
47(Sep 1973):251-2.

de Lumley-Woodyear, Henry. Le paléolithique inférieur et moyen
du midi méditerranean dan son cadre géologique. Paris: Centre National de la Recherche Scientifique, 1969, (Vol. I), 1971,
(Vol. II). Rev. by D. Collins, Antiquity, 47(Mar 1973):86-7.

de Medina, Pedro. A Navigator's Universe: The Libro Cosmog-
raphia 1538. Chicago: ... U Chi Press, 1972. Rev. by R. H.
Fuson, HAHR, 53(Nov 1973):674-5.

De Molen, Richard L. , ed. Erasmus of Rotterdam: A Quincenten-
nial Symposium. New York: Twayne, 1971. Rev. by J. F.
Davis, History, 58(Je 1973):276.

Demolon, Pierre. Le Village mèrovingien de Brebieres (VIe-VIIe
siècles). Arras: Archives du Pas-de-Calais, 1972. Rev. by
B. S. Bachrach, AHR, 78(Oct 1973):1034-5.

Dempsey, Hugh A. Crowfoot, Chief of the Blackfeet. Norman: U
Ok Press, 1972. Rev. by W. E. Unrau, Montana, 23(Sum
1973):54-5; K. A. Murray, AW, 10(Jl 1973):58; J. C. Olson,
PHR, 42(Nov 1973):583-4.

De Murville, Maurice Couve. Une politique étrangère, 1958-1969.
Paris: Plon, 1971. Rev. by J. C. Cairns, AHR, 78(Dec
1973):1406-20.

de Navarro, J. M. The Finds from the Site of La Tene. Vol. I.
Scabbards and the Swords Found in Them. Oxford: Ox U
Press, 1972. Rev. by O.-H. Frey, Antiquity, 47(Sep 1973):
248-50.

Dennis, Peter. Decision by Default: Peacetime Conscription and
British Defense, 1919-39. Durham, N. C.: Duke U Press,
1972. Rev. by W. R. Rock, JMH, 45(Sep 1973):530.

Denzer, Horst. Moralphilosophie und Naturrecht bei Samuel Pufendorf: Ein geistes-und wissenschaftsgeschichtliche Untersuchung
zur Geburt des Naturrecht aus der Praktischen Philosophie.
Munich: Verlag C. H. Beck, 1972. Rev. by L. Krieger,
AHR, 78(Je 1973):674-6.

Deo, Z. B., see Sankalia, H. D.

De Oliveira Marques, A. H. History of Portugal, Vol. 1. From
Lusitania to Empire. New York: Columbia U Press, 1972.
Rev. by S. C. Schneider, HAHR, 53(Aug 1973):535-7; J. Vogt,
AHR, 78(Dec 1973):1485-6; T. B. Duncan, JMH, 45(Dec 1973):
646-7.

_____. History of Portugal. Vol. II. From Empire to Corpo-
rate State. New York: Columbia U Press, 1973. Rev. by
A. Z. Rubenstein, CurH, 64(Apr 1973):179; J. Vogt, AHR, 78
(Dec 1973):1485-6; T. B. Duncan, JMH, 45(Dec 1973):646-7.

De Pauw, Linda Grant, ed. Documentary History of the First Fed-
eral Congress of the United States of America. Vol. I. The
Senate Legislative Journal. Baltimore: JHU Press, 1972.
Rev. by M. Borden, JAH, 60(Sep 1973):412-14; J. A. Treon,
MHM, 68(Fall 1973):341; P. Goodman, WMQ, 3rd ser., 30
(Jl 1973):508-10; B. Henry, AmArch, 36(Jl 1973):415-16;
D. P. Jordan, NCHR, 50(Aut 1973):430-1.

Derry, John W. Charles James Fox. London: Batsford, 1972.
Rev. by I. R. Christie, History, 58(Je 1973):301-2; R. W.
Greaves, AHR, 78(Je 1973):687-8; P. Langford, JMH, 45(Sep
1973):493-4.

Derry, T. K. A History of Modern Norway, 1814-1972. New York:
    Ox U Press, 1973. Rev. by E. Anderson, HRNB, 2(Nov/Dec
    1973):32-3.

Desaive, Jean-Paul, et al. Médecins, climat et epidémies à la fin
    du XVIIIᵉ siècle. Paris: Mouton, 1972. Rev. by D. B.
    Weiner, AHR, 78(Oct 1973):1076-7.

De Salis, Jean-Rodolphe. Switzerland and Europe: Essays and Re-
    flections. University: U Ala Press, 1971. Rev. by J. Tom-
    linson, HT, 7(Nov 1973):142.

Deschamps, Hubert, ed. Histoire génerale de l'Afrique noire, de
    Madagascar, et des archipelo. Tome 1: Des origines à 1800.
    Tome 2: De 1800 à nos jours. Paris: Presses universitaires
    de France, 1971. Rev. by R. Austen, JMH, 45(Sep 1973):
    463-5.

Desdunes, Rodolphe Lucien. Our People and Our History. Baton
    Rouge: LSU Press, 1973. Rev. by R. M. McMurray, GHQ,
    57(Fall 1973):445; R. V. Haynes, JSH, 39(Nov 1973):629-30.

des Montaignes, Francois. The Plains: Being No Less Than a Col-
    lection of Veracious Memoranda Taken During the Expeditions
    of Exploration in the Year 1845, From the Western Settlements
    of Missouri to the Mexican Border, and from Bent's Fort on
    the Arkansas to Fort Gibson, Via South Fork of the Canadian-
    North Mexico and North-Western Texas. Norman: U Ok
    Press, 1972. Rev. by D. Dean, Montana, 23(Spr 1973):74;
    R. J. Chaffin, JOW, 12(Ja 1973):182.

Desroche, Henri. The American Shakers: From Neo-Christianity
    to Presocialism. Amherst: U Mass Press, 1971. Rev. by
    R. F. W. Meader, NYH, 54(Ja 1973):110-3.

De Ste. Croix, G. E. M. The Origins of the Peloponnesian War.
    Ithaca, N. Y.: Cornell U Press, 1972. Rev. by C. G. Starr,
    AHR, 78(Je 1973):662-3.

Destler, I. M. Presidents, Bureaucrats, and Foreign Policy: The
    Politics of Organizational Reform. Princeton, N. J.: Prin U
    Press, 1972. Rev. by W. H. Heinrichs, JAH, 59(Mar 1973):
    1043-4.

Detailed Reports on the Salzburger Emigrants Who Settled in America.
    Edited by Samuel Urlsperger. Volume II: 1734-1735. Edited
    by George Fenwick Jones.... Volume III: 1736. Edited and
    translated by George Fenwick Jones and Marie Hahn. Athens,
    Ga.: U Ga. Press, 1969, 1972. Rev. by W. C. Smith, FHQ,
    51(Ja 1973):323-4; M. Rubincam, JSH, 39(Feb 1973):101-2;
    M. L. Brown, Jr., WMQ, 3rd ser., 30(Jl 1973):533-5.

The Development of a Revolutionary Mentality. Washington, D. C.:

DE VORSEY 80

Library of Congress, 1972. Rev. by J. G. Smith, WPHM, 56
(Oct 1973):435-8; R. M. Weir, NCHR, 50(Sum 1973):336-8;
H. M. Ward, PMHB, 97(Oct 1973):540-1; L. M. Simms, Jr.,
GHQ, 57(Fall 1973):442; C. Ubbelohde, JAH, 60(Dec 1973):
789-90; R. M. Calhoon, MHM, 68(Win 1973):453-5; B. W.
Sheehan, IMH, 69(Sep 1973):281-3.

De Vorsey, Louis, Jr. De Brahm's Report of the General Survey
in the Southern District of North America. Columbia, S. C.:
U SCar Press, 1971. Rev. by H. S. Marks, JOW, 12(Jl
1973):500; P. Spalding, GHQ, 57(Win 1973):588-9.

de Vries, Leonard and Ilonka van Amstel. Victorian Inventions.
New York: American Heritage, 1971. Rev. by B. A. Storey,
CoMag, 50(Spr 1973):166-7.

de Vries, Margaret G., et al. The International Monetary Fund,
1945-1965: Twenty Years of International Monetary Cooperation. Vol. II. Analysis. Washington, D. C.: International
Monetary Fund, 1969. Rev. by J. H. Furth, JEH, 33(Sep
1973):676-8.

Dewey, Donald O. Marshall Versus Jefferson: The Political Background of Marbury v. Madison. New York: Knopf, 1970. Rev.
by P. R. Benson, Jr., JAH, 59(Mar 1973):996-7.

Dewindt, Edwin Brezette. Land and People in Holywellcum-Needing-
worth; Structures of Tenure and Patterns of Social Organization in an East Midlands Village: 1252-1457. Toronto: Pontifical Institute of Medieval Studies, 1972. Rev. by F. A.
Cazel, Jr., AHR, 78(Je 1973):667-8.

Dharampal. Indian Science and Technology in the Eighteenth Century.
Delhi: Impex India, 1971. Rev. by S. K. Ghaswala, T & C,
14(Apr 1973):293-4.

Dibble, Ernest F. and Earle W. Newton, eds. Spain and Her Rivals
on the Gulf Coast. Pensacola, Fla.: Historic Pensacola Preservation Board, 1971. Rev. by J. L. Wright, PHR, 42(May
1973):247-8.

Dibbs, Paul. Siberia and the Pacific: A Study of Economic Development and Trade Prospects. New York: Praeger, 1972.
Rev. by R. H Fisher, RR, 32(Jl 1973):314-5.

Di Bona, Joseph. Change and Conflict in the Indian University.
Bombay: Lalvani Publishing House, 1973. Rev. by A. Ray,
IQ, 29(Jl-Sep 1973):274-5.

Dick, William M. Labor and Socialism in America: The Gompers
Era. Port Washington, N. Y.: Kennikat, 1972. Rev. by
J. G. Rayback, IMH, 69(Sep 1973):292-3; J. L. Blackman,
Jr., JAH, 60(Je 1973):159-60; M. Dubofsky, CHR, 54(Dec

1973):467-8; K. E. Hendrickson, NYH, 54(Jl 1973):381-2.

Dickens, A. G. The Age of Humanism: Europe in the Fourteenth,
    Fifteenth, and Sixteenth Centuries. Englewood Cliffs, N. J.
    Prentice-Hall, 1972. Rev. by E. Lucki, Historian, 36(Nov
    1973):96; B. C. Weber, SS, 64(Nov 1973):297-8.

Dickerman, Edmund H. Bellièvre and Villeroy: Power in France
    Under Henry III and Henry IV. Providence, R. I.: Brown U
    Press, 1971. Rev. by D. Jensen, JMH, 45(Je 1973):299-300.

Dickert, D. Augustus. History of Kershaw's Brigade. Dayton, O.:
    Morningside, 1973. Rev. by W. Ripley, SCHM, 74(Oct 1973):
    320-1.

Dickson, P. G. M. see Whiteman, Anne

Dickson, Paul. Think Tanks. New York. Atheneum, 1972. Rev.
    by L. F. Gore, T & C, 14(Jl 1973):522-5.

Di Clari, Roberto. La Conquista de Constantinopoli (1198-1216).
    Genoa: Universita de Genova ... 1972. Rev. by J. Geanakop-
    los, AHR, 78(Oct 1973):1040-1.

Dienes, C. Thomas. Law, Politics and Birth Control. Urbana: U
    Ill Press, 1972. Rev. by D. M. Kennedy, AHR, 78(Dec 1973):
    1532-3; C. E. Larson, JAH, 60(Dec 1973):822-3.

Diggins, John P. Mussolini and Fascism: The View From America.
    Princeton, N. J.: Prin U Press, 1972. Rev. by A. Mann,
    JAH, 59(Mar 1973):1037-8; A. Cassels, AHR, 78(Je 1973):
    743-4; F. H. Matthews, CHR, 54(Sep 1973):328-9.

Dilke, O. A. W. The Roman Land-Surveyors: An Introduction to
    the Agrimensores. Newton Abbot: David and Charles, 1971.
    Rev. by J. E. Skydsgaard, T & C, 14(Ja 1973):81-2.

Dillard, J. L. Black English: Its History and Usage. New York:
    Random House, 1972. Rev. by B. Jackson, JNH, 58(Ja 1973):
    90-6.

Dillon, Richard. Burnt-Out Fires: California's Modoc Indian War.
    Englewood Cliffs, N. J.: Prentice-Hall, 1973. Rev. by F.
    Egan, AW, 10(May 1973):54; F. Egan, NHSQ, 16(Win 1973):
    252-3.

Dinnerstein, Leonard and Mary Dale Palsson, eds. Jews in the
    South. Baton Rouge: LSU Press, 1973. Rev. by GHQ, 57
    (Fall 1973):449-50; N. Hirschberg, NCHR, 50(Sum 1973):344-
    5; Myron Berman, VMHB, 81(Oct 1973):502-3; J. Burt, THQ,
    32(Fall 1973):300-1.

Dobbin, Christine. Urban Leadership in Western India. New York:

Ox U Press, 1972. Rev. by I. H. Qureshi, HJ, 16(Dec 1973): 874-5.

Dobbs, Farrell. Teamster Rebellion. New York: Monad, 1972. Rev. by M. Comack, Historian, 35(Feb 1973):314-5.

Dobie, Bertha McKee, et al. Growing Up in Texas: Recollections of Childhood. Austin, Tx.: Encino, 1972. Rev. by R. Rouillard, JOW, 12(Oct 1973):647.

Dobney, Frederick J., ed. Selected Papers of Will Clayton. Baltimore: JHU Press, 1971. Rev. by D. O. Whitten, AgH, 47 (Apr 1973):172-3; R. H. Ferrell, JSH, 39(May 1973):308-10; R. D. McKinzie, SWHQ, 76(Ja 1973):341-2.

Dobson, John M. Politics in the Gilded Age: A New Perspective on Reform. New York: Praeger, 1972. Rev. by R. H. Pulley, JAH, 59(Mar 1973):1023-4; R. H. Williams, AHR, 78(Feb 1973):171-3.

Dobyns, Henry F. The Apache People (Coyotero). Phoenix: Indian Tribal Series, 1971. Rev. by D. O. Fowler, AW, 15(Aut 1973):287-8.

_____ and Robert C. Euler. The Havasupai People. Phoenix: Indian Tribal Series, 1971. Rev. by D. O. Fowler, AW, 15 (Aut 1973):287-8.

_____, Paul L. Doughty and Harold D. Lasswell, eds. Peasants, Power and Applied Social Change: Vicos as a Model. Beverley Hills, Cal.: Sage, 1971. Rev. by P. F. Klarén, HAHR, 53 (Aug 1973):549-50.

Doctoral Students in Social Sciences. New Delhi: Indian Council of Social Science Research, 1971. Rev. by B. K. R. Burman, IQ, 29(Apr-Je 1973):184-5.

Documents Concerning the Foreign Policy of the USSR. Vol. 17. (1934). Moscow: Diplomatic Publications Commission of the Ministry of Foreign Affairs of the USSR, 1971. Rev. by J. Harris, JMH, 45(Dec 1973):711.

Documents Relative to the Manufactures in the United States. United States House of Representatives, Executive Document No. 308. collected and transmitted by the Secretary of the Treasury. New York: B. Franklin, 1969. (3 vols.). Rev. by N. Rosenberg, BHR, 47(Sep 1973):106-7.

Dodds, Gordon B. Hiram Martin Crittenden: His Public Career. Lexington, Ky.: U Press Ky., 1973. Rev. by T. F. Andrews, HRNB, 2(Nov/Dec 1973):51.

Dodge, Ernest S. see Crossman, Carl L.

Doe, Brian. Southern Arabia. New York: McGraw-Hill, 1971. Rev.
    by W. S. Thomas, Archaeology, 26(Jl 1973):230, 232.

Doherty, Francis. Samuel Beckett. London: Hutchinson, 1971. Rev.
    by C. F. Thomas, E-I, 8(Win 1973):137-9.

Doherty, James L. Race and Education in Richmond. Richmond:
    Privately Printed, 1972. Rev. by V. Dabney, VMHB, 81(Oct
    1973):503-4.

Dokumente zur Kirchenpolitik des Dritten Reiches. Band I: Das
    Jahr 1933. Munich: Chr. Kaiser Verlag, 1971. Rev. by E.
    C. Helmreich, JMH, 45(Mar 1973):183-4.

Dolgoff, Sam, ed. and trans. Bakumin on Anarchy: Selected Works
    by the Activist-Founder of World Anarchism. New York: Knopf,
    1972. Rev. by F. C. Griffin, Historian, 35(Feb 1973):293-4.

Donaldson, Scott. Poet in America: Winfield Townley Scott. Austin:
    U Tx Press, 1972. Rev. by H. G. McCurdy, GR, 27(Spr 1973):
    132-5.

Donelan, M. D. see Northedge, F. S.

Donnachie, Ian. Industrial Archaeology of Galloway. Newton Abbot:
    David and Charles, 1971. Rev. by J. R. Hume, History, 58
    (Feb 1973):114-5.

Donoso, José. Hell Has No Limits. New York: Dutton, 1966. Rev.
    by R. D. Souza, HAHR, 53(Nov 1973):732.

Dorey, T. A., ed. Livy. Toronto: U Tor Press, 1971. Rev. by
    W. V. Harris, AHR, 78(Feb 1973):65.

Doria, Giorgio. Uomini e terre di um borgo collinare dal XVI al
    XVIII secolo. Milan: Giuffre, 1968. Rev. by D. Sella, JEH,
    33(Dec 1973):882-3.

Dornberg, John. The New Tsars: Russia Under Stalin's Heirs.
    Garden City, N. Y.: Doubleday, 1972. Rev. by A. Parry,
    RR, 32(Apr 1973):211.

Dornbusch, C. E., comp. Military Bibliography of the Civil War,
    Volume 3. New York: New York Public Library, 1972. Rev.
    by B. I. Wiley, CWTI, 12(Dec 1973):49.

Dorner, Peter, ed. Land Reform in Latin America: Issues and
    Cases. Madison, Wis.: Wis U Press, 1971. Rev. by C.
    Zuvekas, Jr., JEH, 33(Dec 1973):884-5.

Dörries, Hermann. Constantine the Great. London: Harper and
    Row, 1972. Rev. by R. A. Markus, History, 58(Je 1973):250-
    1.

Dorson, Richard M., ed. Folklore and Folklife, An Introduction.
    Chicago: U Chi Press, 1972. Rev. by J. A. Anderson, PMHB,
    97(Ja 1973):119-20.

Dorwart, Reinhold August. The Prussian Welfare State Before 1740.
    Cambridge, Mass.: Har U Press, 1971. Rev. by D. Gerhard,
    AHR, 78(Oct 1973):1090-1; H. P. Liebel, JMH, 45(Mar 1973):
    103-4.

Doty, Gresdna Ann. The Career of Mrs. Anne Brunton Merry in
    the American Theatre. Baton Rouge: LSU Press, 1972. Rev.
    by D. Grimsted, MHM, 68(Sum 1973):224; G. B. Wilson,
    AHR, 78(Feb 1973):157-8.

Doughty, Paul see Dobyns, Henry F.

Douglas, Mary, ed. Witchcraft Confessions and Accusations. Lon-
    don: Tavistack, 1970. Rev. by J. L. Teall, AHR, 78(Feb
    1973):67-9.

Douglas, Roy. The History of the Liberal Party, 1895-1970. Lon-
    don: Sidgwick and Jackson, 1971. Rev. by V. Bogdanor,
    History, 58(Feb 1973):143-4; P. Rowland, JMH, 45(Mar 1973):
    157-8.

Douglass, Elisha P. The Coming of Age of American Business:
    Three Centuries of Enterprise, 1600-1900. Chapel Hill, N. C.:
    UNC Press, 1971. Rev. by A. P. Chandler, Jr., AHR, 78
    (Feb 1973):142-3.

Dovring, Folke and Karin. The Optional Society: An Essay on Eco-
    nomic Choice and Bargains of Communication in an Affluent
    World. The Hague: Martinus Nijhoff, 1971. Rev. by J. Ra-
    poport, JEH, 33(Dec 1973):886-7.

Dowdell, Dorothy and Joseph. The Chinese Helped Build America.
    New York: Messner, 1972. Rev. by A. Hoffman, JOW, 12
    (Ja 1973):178.

Downer, L. J., ed. Leges Henrici Primi. Oxford: Clarendon
    Press, 1972. Rev. by G. D. G. Hall, EHR, 88(Oct 1973):
    844-6; J. N. Sutherland, AHR, 78(Feb 1973):82.

Downton, James V. Rebel Leadership, Commitment and Charisma
    in the Revolutionary Process. New York: Free Press, 1973.
    Rev. by J. B. Bell, MilAf, 37(Dec 1973):155-7.

Dozy, Reinhart. Spanish Islam: A History of Moslems in Spain.
    London: Frank Cass, 1972. (1913). Rev. by L. P. Harvy,
    HAHR, 53(Aug 1973):563-4.

Drachkovitch, Melorad M. and Branko Lazitch. Lenin and the Com-
    munist International. Vol. I. Stanford, Cal.: Hoover Institu-

tion Press, 1972. Rev. by S. Hook, RR, 32(Ja 1973):1-14.

Drake, W. Magruder and Robert R. Jones, eds. Edward King's The
    Great South. Baton Rouge: LSU Press, 1972. Rev. by J. E.
    Gonzales, JMiH, 35(Aug 1973):328-9; R. L. Zuber, NCHR, 50
    (Spr 1973):213-14. See also King, Edward.

Draznin, Yaffa. It Began With Zade Usher. Los Angeles: Jamy,
    1972. Rev. by P. A. Kalisch, AJHQ, 63(Sep 1973):95-7.

Dreifort, John E. Yvon at the Quai D'Orsay, French Foreign Policy
    During the Popular Front, 1936-1938. Lawrence: U Press
    Ks., 1973. Rev. by R. M Brace, Historian, 36(Nov 1973):
    108-9.

Drew, Benjamin. The Refugee: A North-Side View of Slavery.
    Reading, Mass.: Addison-Wesley, 1969. Rev. by J. L.
    Franklin, CWH, 19(Sep 1973):285-7.

Drinnon, Richard. White Savage: The Case of John Dunn Hunter.
    New York: Schocken, 1972. Rev. by A. D. Aberbach, JAH,
    60(Sep 1973):434-5; R. W. Etulain, PHR, 42(Nov 1973):582-3;
    D. F. Behen, WHQ, 4(Oct 1973):460-1.

Drosdoff, Daniel. El Gabierno de Las Vacas, 1933-1956. Buenos
    Aires: Ediciones La Bastilla, 1972. Rev. by T. M. Bader,
    HAHR, 53(Nov 1973):712-13.

Droz, Eugénie. Chemins de l'hérésie. (Vol. 2). Geneva: Slatkine,
    1971. Rev. by R. H. Bainton, JMH, 45(Je 1973):299.

Druhe, David N. Russo-Indian Relations, 1466-1917. New York:
    Vantage, 1970. Rev. by S. K. Gupta, RR, 32(Ja 1973):96-7.

Duberman, Martin. Black Mountain: An Exploration in Community.
    New York: Dutton, 1972. Rev. by P. K. Conkin, JAH, 60
    (Sep 1973):510-12; H. C. Ferrell, Jr., JSH, 39(Aug 1973):
    469-70; G. B. Tindall, NCHR, 50(Spr 1973):197-9.

DuBois, Shirley Graham. His Day is Marching On: A Memoir of
    W. E. B. DuBois. New York: Lippincott, 1971. Rev. by R.
    Walters, JNH, 58(Ja 1973):106-9.

du Boulay, F. R. H. and Caroline Barron, eds. The Reign of
    Richard II: Essays in Honour of May McKisack. London:
    Athlone, 1971. Rev. by J. R. Maddicott, History, 58(Feb
    1973):89-90.

Duckett, Eleanor. Medieval Portraits from East and West. Ann
    Arbor: U Mich Press, 1972. Rev. by K. G. Holum, AHR,
    78(Dec 1973):1433.

Dudden, Arthur Power. Joseph Fels and the Single-Tax Movement.

Philadelphia: Temple U Press, 1971. Rev. by D. A. Shannon, AHR, 78(Feb 1973):175-6; R. H. Zieger, SS, 64(Nov 1973):278.

Duhnke, Horst. Die K P D von 1933 bis 1945. Köln: Kiepenheuer and Witsch, 1972. Rev. by C. Landauer, JMH, 45(Je 1973): 355-6.

Duignan, Peter, ed. Guide to Research and Reference Works on Sub-Saharan Africa. Stanford, Cal.: Hoover Institution Press, 1972. Rev. by O. E. S., CurH, 64(Mar 1973):126.

_____, Victor Turner, and L. H. Gann, eds. Colonialism in Africa, 1870-1960. Vol. 3. Profiles of Change: African Society and Colonial Rule. Cambridge: Cam U Press, 1971. Rev. by R. O. Collins, JMH, 45(Je 1973):332-3.

Duke, Benjamin C. Japan's Militant Teachers: A History of Left-Wing Teachers' Movement. Honolulu: U Press Hawaii, 1973. Rev. by M. Patoski, HRNB, 2(Oct 1973):22.

Dukore, Bernard F. Bernard Shaw, Director. Seattle: U Wash Press, 1971. Rev. by M. Levin, E-I, 8(Win 1973):115-7.

Dulles, Foster Rhea. American Policy Toward Communist China: The Historical Record, 1949-1969. New York: Crowell, 1972. Rev. by A. Iriye, PHR, 42(Feb 1973):132-4.

Dumbarton Oaks Papers. No. 25. Washington: Dumbarton Oaks Center for Byzantine Studies, 1971. Rev. by D. A. Miller, AHR, 78(Feb 1973):85-7.

Dumont, Fernand, Jean-Paul Montminy, et Jean Hamelin. Idéologies au Canada Français, 1850-1900. Rev. by A. I. Silver, CHR, 54(Dec 1973):450-1.

Duncan, G. I. O. The High Court of Delegates. Cambridge: Cam U Press, 1971. Rev. by P. A. Howell, HJ, 16(Mar 1973): 189-95.

Duncan, Lyle Kinnear. The First 100 Years: A History of Virginia Polytechnic Institute and State University. Blacksburg, Va.: Va Polytechnic Institute Educational Foundation, 1972. Rev. by L. G. Geiger, AHR, 78(Oct 1973):1137-9.

Duncan, Quince see Meléndez, Carlos

Duncan, T. Bentley. Atlantic Islands: Madeira, the Azores, and the Cape Verdes in Seventeenth-Century Commerce and Naviga-tion. Chicago: U Chi Press, 1972. Rev. by M. Cordozo, TAm, 30(Jl 1973):133-4; C. R. Boxer, JMH, 45(Je 1973):305-6; A. J. R. Russell-Wood, AHR, 78(Dec 1973):1425; H. B. Johnson, HAHR, 53(Nov 1973):677-8; B. Penrose, PMHB, 97 (Apr 1973):251-2; D. Alden, WMQ, 3rd ser., 30(Oct 1973):671-3.

Dunlop, D. M.   Arab Civilization to A. D. 1500.   New York:
    Praeger, 1971.   Rev. by W. B. Bishai, AHR, 78(Oct 1973):
    1103-4;   J. Lampe, MEJ, 27(Win 1973):98-9.

Dunlop, John B.   Staretz Amvrosy: Model for Dostoevsky's Staretz
    Zossima.   Belmont, Mass.: Nordland, 1972.   Rev. by H. A.
    Stammler, RR, 32(Jl 1973):331.

Dunlop, R. T.   see   Cross, K. G. W.

Dunn, John.   Modern Revolutions: An Introduction to the Analysis
    of a Political Phenomenon.   London: Cam U Press, 1972.
    Rev. by P. Pant, IQ, 29(Oct-Dec 1973):352.

Dunn, Richard S.   The Age of Religious Wars, 1559-1689.   London:
    Weidenfeld and Nicolson, 1971.   Rev. by M. Hughes, History,
    58(Je 1973):274-5.

_____.   Sugar and Slaves: The Rise of the Planter Class in the
    English West Indies, 1624-1713.   Chapel Hill: UNC Press,
    1972.   Rev. by M. Craton, JAH, 59(Mar 1973):978-9; R. R.
    Rea, FHQ, 52(Oct 1973):190-1; R. B. Sheridan, JSH, 39(Feb
    1973):98-9;   C. R. Ritcheson, NYHSQ, 57(Apr 1973):172-4;
    F. W. Knight, JMH, 45(Sep 1973):478-80; A. C. Land, NCHR,
    50(Win 1973):110-11; I. K. Steele, PMHB, 97(Ja 1973):107-8;
    S. A. Lily, SCHM, 74(Jl 1973):174; R. C. Batie, JEH, 33(Je
    1973):477-8; E. V. Goveia, WMQ, 3rd ser., 30(Ja 1973):149-
    52.

Dunn, Walter S., Jr., ed.   History of Erie County, 1870-1970.
    Buffalo, N. Y.: Buffalo and Erie County Historical Society,
    1972.   Rev. by B. McKelvey, JAH, 60(Je 1973):158-9.

Dunne, Gerald T.   Justice Joseph Story and the Rise of the Supreme
    Court.   New York: Simon and Schuster, 1970.   Rev. by A. H.
    Kelly, AHR, 78(Feb 1973):159-60.

DuPre, Flint O.   Hap Arnold: Architect of American Air Power.
    New York: Macmillan, 1972.   Rev. by R. P. Hallion, T & C,
    14(Oct 1973):653-5.

Dupuy, R. Ernest.   The Compact History of the United States Army.
    New York: Hawthorn, 1973.   Rev. by R. L. Blanco, HT, 7
    (Nov 1973):132.

_____.   The National Guard: A Compact History.   New York:
    Hawthorn, 1971.   Rev. by M. K. Gordon, MilAf, 37(Feb 1973):
    32.

Dupuy, Roger.   La Garde nationale et les débuts de la révolution en
    Ille-et-Vilaine (1789-mars 1793).   Paris: Librairie C. Klinck-
    sieck, 1972.   Rev. by D. Sutherland, JMH, 45(Dec 1973):665-
    6.

Dupuy, Trevor Nevitt. The Military Life of Abraham Lincoln: Commander-in-Chief. New York: Franklin Watts, 1969. Rev. by G. R. Planck, LH, 75(Win 1973):191.

Duran, Fray Diego. Book of the Gods and Rites and the Ancient Calendar. Norman: U Ok Press, 1972. Rev. by J. H. Elliott, History, 58(Feb 1973):97.

Durand, Yves. Les Fermiers Généraux au XVIIIe siècle. Paris: Presses Universitaries de France, 1971. Rev. by O. Hufton, History, 58(Oct 1973):451-2.

Durden, Robert F. The Gray and the Black: The Confederate Debate on Emancipation. Baton Rouge: LSU Press, 1972. Rev. by E. M. Thomas, JSH, 39(May 1973):300-1; P. D. Klingman, FHQ, 52(Oct 1973):201-3; C. W. Harper, JNH, 58(Jl 1973): 369-70; T. P. Govan, JAH, 60(Dec 1973):813-4; B. Quarles, MHM, 68(Fall 1973):345-6; M. Abbott, NCHR, 50(Spr 1973): 212-3; F. N. Boney, VMHB, 81(Apr 1973):209-10; J. J. Halstead, WMH, 56(Sum 1973):348-9.

Durnbaugh, Donald F., ed. The Church of the Brethren: Past and Present. Elgin, Ill.: Brethren Press, 1971. Rev. by J. B. Frantz, PH, 40(Jl 1973):342-3.

Duster, Alfreda M., ed. Crusade for Justice: The Autobiography of Ida B. Wells. Chicago: U Chi Press, 1970. Rev. by E. Gertz, JISHS, 66(Win 1973):479-80.

Dyer, George Carroll. The Amphibians Come to Conquer: The Story of Admiral Richmond Kelly Turner. 2 vols. Washington: Government Printing Office, 1972. Rev. by G. E. Wheeler, JAH, 59(Mar 1973):1039-40; K. J. Bauer, AHR, 78(Je 1973): 744.

Dykes, Jeff C., comp. The Grand Duke Alexis in the United States of America. New York: Interland, 1972. Rev. by J. D. W. Guice, Montana, 23(Spr 1973):67.

Eagly, Robert V., ed and trans. The Swedish Bullionist Controversy: P. N. Christiernin's Lectures on the High Price of Foreign Exchange in Sweden (1761). Philadelphia: American Philosophical Assn., 1971. Rev. by J. H. Furth, JEH, 33 (Sep 1973):670-2.

Earle, Alice Morse. Two Centuries of Costume in America: 1620-1820. New York: Dover, 1970. Rev. by V. M. Griner, JOW, 12(Oct 1973):644.

Early American Bookbindings from the Collection of Michael Papantonio. New York: Pierpont Morgan Library ... 1972. Rev. by E. Wolf, II, PMHB, 97(Ja 1973):124-5.

89   EATON

Eaton, Leonard K. American Architecture Comes of Age: European
Reaction to H. H. Richardson and Louis Sullivan. Cambridge,
Mass.: M I T Press, 1972. Rev. by I. Abrams, JAH, 60
(Sep 1973):485-7.

Eaves, Richard Glen. Henry VIII's Scottish Diplomacy, 1513-1524.
New York: Exposition, 1971. Rev. by J. M. Brown, History,
58(Oct 1973):443.

Ebel, Arnold. Das Dritte Reich und Argentinien Die diplomatischen
Beziehungen unter besonderer Berucksichtigung der Handelspoli-
tik, 1933-1939. Cologne, Germany: Böhlau Verlag Koln Wien
... 1971. Rev. by S. E. Hilton, HAHR, 53(Nov 1973):709-10.

Eccles, W. J. France in America. New York: Harper and Row,
1972. Rev. by R. D. Smith, JSH, 39(Aug 1973):432-3; Y. F.
Zoltvany, PHR, 42(May 1973):246-7; L. Kennett, PMHB, 97
(Jl 1973):409-10; R. C. Alltmont, WMH, 56(Sum 1973):338-9.

Echaiz, René León. Evolución histórica de los partidos políticos
chilenos. Buenos Aires and Santiago de Chile: Editorial Francisco de Aguirre, 1971. Rev. by A. von Lazar, HAHR, 53
(Aug 1973):552-5.

Ecke, Melvin W. From Ivy Street to Kennedy Center: Centennial
History of the Atlanta Public School System. Atlanta: Atlanta
Board of Education, 1972. Rev. by J. C. Kiger, JSH, 39(Nov
1973):632-3.

Eckley, Grace. Benedict Kiely. New York: Twayne, 1972. Rev.
by A. Bradley, E-I, 8(Win 1973):147-8.

Economic Growth of Colombia: Problems and Prospects. Baltimore: JHU Press, 1972. Rev. by C. O. Andrew, AgH, 47
(Jl 1973):269-70; M. Urrutia, HAHR, 53(Nov 1973):731-2.

Edgar, Walter B., ed. The Letterbook of Robert Pringle. 2 vols.
Columbia, S. C.: U SCar Press, 1972. Rev. by P. G. E.
Clemens, BHR, 47(Aut 1973):380-1; K. J. Bauer, AmArch,
36(Jl 1973):417-8; J. M. Clifton, NCHR, 50(Win 1973):95-6;
J. R. Morrill, JSH, 39(Feb 1973):102-3; R. N. Lokken, JAH,
60(Je 1973):114-5; GHQ, 57(Spr 1973):159-60; G. C. Rogers,
Jr., SCHM, 74(Ja 1973):41-2; P. M. Van Ee, WMQ-3, 30(Apr
1973):362-3.

Editors, Army Times. Pearl Harbor and Hawaii: A Military History. New York: Walker, 1971. Rev. by A. N. Garland,
MilAf, 37(Feb 1973):35.

Edmonds, A. O. Joe Louis. Grand Rapids, Mich.: Eerdmans,
1973. Rev. by N. Lederer, MichH, 57(Fall 1973):269-71.

Edmunds, Pocahontas Wight. Virginians Out Front. Richmond, Va.:

Whittet and Shepperson, 1972. Rev. by M. W. Schlegel,
NCHR, 50(Spr 1973):207-8; V. Dabney, VMHB, 81(Apr 1973):
212-3.

Edwardes, Michael. Nehru: A Political Biography. London: Allen
Lane; Penguin, 1971. Rev. by J. M. Brown, History, 58(Je
1973):332-3.

Edwards, David L. Leaders of the Church of England, 1828-1944.
Oxford: Ox U Press, 1971. Rev. by D. M. Thompson, History, 58(Feb 1973):131.

Edwards, I., C. Gadd, and N. Hammond, eds. The Cambridge An-
cient History. Vol. I, Part 2. Early History of the Middle
East. Cambridge: Cam U Press, 1971. Rev. by H. N.
Howard, MEJ, 27(Win 1973):99-100.

Edwards, I. E. S. Treasures of Tutankhamun. New York: Viking,
1973. Rev. by R. Brilliant, HRNB, 2(Nov/Dec 1973):33-6.

Edwards, R. Dudley. A New History of Ireland. Dublin: Gill and
Macmillan, 1972. Rev. by A. Cohen, E-I, 8(Spr 1973):153-5.

Edwards, Stewart, ed. The Communards of Paris, 1871. Ithaca,
N. Y.: Cornell U Press, 1973. Rev. by S. C. Tucker, HRNB,
2(Nov/Dec 1973):29.

_____. The Paris Commune, 1871. New York: Quadrangle,
1971. Rev. by P. N. Stearns, JMH, 45(Dec 1973):684-5; P.
Pilbeam, History, 58(Oct 1973):461.

Egan, Ferol. Sand in a Whirlwind: The Paiute Indian War of 1860.
Garden City, N. Y.: Doubleday, 1972. Rev. by R. N. Ellis,
NMHR, 48(Apr 1973):179-80; J. W. Hulse, A & W, 15(Aut
1973):277-8; R. G. Lillard, AW, 10(Mar 1973):52; G. C.
Thompson, CoMag, 50(Sum 1973):252-4; W. D. Rowley, Mon-
tana, 23(Aut 1973):62; R. C. Wood, PacH, 17(Fall 1973):61-2.

Ehrenfeld, David W. Conserving Life on Earth. New York: Ox U
Press, 1972. Rev. by T. R. Cox, AgH, 47(Oct 1973):366-7.

Ehrenkreutz, Andrew S. Saladin. Albany: SUNY Press, 1972. Rev.
by R. W. Bulliet, MEJ, 27(Sum 1973):407-8.

Eichwede, Wolfgang. Revolution und internationale Politik: Zur
Kommunistischen Interpretation der kapitalistischen Welt, 1921-
1925. Cologne and Vienna: Böhlau Verlag, 1971. Rev. by
F. G. Campbell, JMH 45(Sep 1973):558-9.

Eighmy, John Lee. Churches in Cultural Captivity: A History of
the Social Attitudes of Southern Baptists. Knoxville: U Tenn
Press, 1972. Rev. by D. E. Harrell, Jr., JAH, 59(Mar
1973):999-1000; H. W. Mann, JSH, 39(Feb 1973):137-8; M.

Abbott, RKHS, 71(Ja 1973):108-9; W. Flynt, FHQ, 52(Oct 1973):210-11.

Einhard. Vita Karoli Magni: The Life of Charlemagne. Coral Gables, Fla.: U Miami Press, 1972. Rev. by A. Cabaniss, AHR, 78(Oct 1973):1035.

Ellenbogen, George. The Night Unstones. Cambridge, Mass.: Identity, 1971. Rev. by K. S. Byer, GR, 27(Spr 1973):110-21.

Elliot, R. S. P. and John Hickie. Ulster: A Case Study in Conflict Theory. New York: St. Martin's, 1971. Rev. by L. A. Curtis, E-I, 8(Sum 1973):145-7.

Elliott, Russell R. History of Nevada. Lincoln: U Neb Press, 1973. Rev. by R. C. Lillard, NHSQ, 16(Sum 1973):129-31; J. A. Brennan, CoMag, 50(Sum 1973):264-6.

Ellis, Conleth. Under the Stone. Dublin: Gill and Macmillan, 1971. Rev. by F. S. Kiley, E-I, 8(Win 1973):131-2.

Ellis, E. L. The University College of Wales, Aberystwyth: 1872-1972. Cardiff: U Wales Press, 1972. Rev. by K. O. Morgan, History, 58(Oct 1973):420.

Ellis, John Tracy, ed. The Catholic Priest in the United States: Historical Investigations. Collegeville, Minn.: St. John's, 1971. Rev. by W. S. Hudson, AHR, 78(Feb 1973):139-40.

Ellis, Myriam, et al. Historia geral da civilizacão brasileira, Tomo II: O Brasil monarquico. Vol. IV: Declinio e quedo do império. Sao Paulo: Difusão Europeia do Livro, 1971. Rev. by R. H. Matoon, Jr., HAHR, 53(Feb 1973):144-5.

Ellis, P. Berresford. A History of the Irish Working Class. New York: Braziller, 1973. Rev. by W. H. Cohn, HT, 7(Nov 1973):137.

Ellis, Richard E. The Jeffersonian Crisis: Courts and Politics in the Young Republic. [Oxford:] Ox U Press, 1971. Rev. by J. A. Woods, History, 58(Oct 1973):489-90.

Ellis, Richard N. General Pope and U. S. Indian Policy. Albuquerque: U NM Press, 1970. Rev. by H. E. Fritz, AHR, 78 (Je 1973):735-6.

_____, ed. New Mexico Past and Present: A Historical Reader. Albuquerque: U NM Press, 1971. Rev. by G. M. Jenks, JOW, 12(Ja 1973):187.

_____, ed. The Western American Indian, Case Studies in Tribal History. Lincoln: U Neb Press, 1972. Rev. by D. A. Walker, NDH, 40(Spr 1973):38-9; V. DeLoria, Jr., A & W,

15(Aut 1973):282-3; J. A. Greene, JOW, 12(Oct 1973):635.

Ellis, Richard S. A Bibliography of Mesopotamian Archaeological
Sites. Wiesbaden: Otto Harrassowitz, 1972. Rev. by J.
Oates, Antiquity, 47(Sep 1973):252.

Ellison, Mary. Support for Secession: Lancashire and the American
Civil War. Chicago: U Chi Press, 1972. Rev. by N. Lederer, Historian, 36(Nov 1973):104-5; J. F. Gentry, JSH, 39(Aug
1973):455-6; B. Cresap, JMiH, 35(Aug 1973):327-8.

Ellsworth, Lucius F., ed. The Americanization of the Gulf Coast,
1803-1850. Pensacola, Fla.: Historic Pensacola Preservation
Board, 1972. Rev. by P. H. Bergeron, THQ, 32(Spr 1973):
99; R. R. Rea, JAH, 60(Je 1973):122-3; H. P. Owens, FHQ,
51(Apr 1973):442-4; J. D. L. Holmes, JMiH, 35(May 1973):
209-10; W. M. Drake, NCHR, 50(Spr 1973):208-9; R. D.
Hebert, LaH, 14(Sum 1973):327-8; J. L. Wright, Jr., PHR,
42(May 1973):247-8.

_____ see Taylor, George Rogers

Ellsworth, S. George. Utah's Heritage. Santa Barbara and Salt
Lake City: Peregrine Smith, 1972. Rev. by R. R. Elliott,
Montana, 23(Aut 1973):70.

Elton, G. R. Policy and Police: The Enforcement of the Reforma-
tion in the Age of Thomas Cromwell. Cambridge: Cam U
Press, 1972. Rev. by C. Zinberg, HT, 6(May 1973):481-2;
C. M. Gray, JMH, 45(Mar 1973):96-8; P. Williams, EHR, 88
(Jl 1973):594-7; A. J. Slavin, AHR, 78(Feb 1973):95-6; J. R.
Rilling, Historian, 35(Feb 1973):283-4.

Elton, Geoffrey R. The Practice of History. London: Sydney U
Press, 1967. Rev. by M. Brickford, AmArch, 36(Jl 1973):
397-402.

Emerson, Dorothy. Among the Mescalero Apaches: The Story of
Father Albert Braun, O. F. M. Tucson: U Ariz Press, 1973.
Rev. by E. Ball, JAriH, 14(Win 1973):386-7.

Emerson, Everett, ed. Major Writers of Early American Literature.
Madison: U Wis Press, 1972. Rev. by T. Martin, JAH, 60
(Dec 1973):777-8; E. Wolf, 2nd, PMHB, 97(Jl 1973):427-8;
C. R. Dolmetsch, VMHB, 81(Apr 1973):201-2; S. Lanier,
WMQ, 3rd ser., 30(Oct 1973):667-9.

Emmerson, John K. The Japanese Dilemma: Arms, Yen, and
Power. New York: Dunellen, 1971. Rev. by M. Hane, SS
64(Mar 1973):138-9.

Enemark, Poul. Studies in the Documents of the Customs Accounts
at the Beginning of the Sixteenth Century: With Special Attention

to the Danish Cattle Exports. 2 vols. Arhus: Arhus Univer-
sitet, 1971. Rev. by H. E. Ellersieck, AHR, 78(Je 1973):707.

Engel, Madeline H. Inequality in America: A Sociological Perspective. New York: Crowell, 1971. Rev. by W. C. Neely, SS,
64(Ja 1973):42-3.

Engelhardt, Fr. Zephyrin, O. F. M. Mission San Antonio de Padua:
The Mission in the Sierras. Ramona, Cal.: Ballena, 1972.
Rev. by W. R. Enger, JOW, 12(Oct 1973):655-6.

Engel-Janosi, Frederick. Vom Chaos zur Katastrophe: Vatikamsche
Gespräche 1918 bis 1938, vornehmlich auf Grund der Berichte
der osterreichen Gesandten beim heiligen Stuhl. Vienna and
Munich: Verlag Herold, 1971. Rev. by S. A. Stehlin, JMH,
45(Mar 1973):181-3.

Engelman, Rose C., ed. A Decade of Progress; The United States
Army Medical Department 1959-1969. Washington: Government
Printing Office, 1971. Rev. by D. F. Harrison, MilAf, 37
(Feb 1973):36.

Engels, Max see Marx, Karl

Enno, Van Gelder. Temperate Freedom: An Essay on the Relationship of the Church and State in the Republic of the United
Netherlands and on Freedom of Expression in Religion, Press,
and Education During the Seventeenth Century. Groningen:
Wolters-Noordhoff, 1972. Rev. by H. H. Rowen, AHR, 78(Je
1973):706-7.

Epstein, Fritz T. Germany and the East: Selected Essays. Bloomington: Ind U Press, 1973. Rev. by C. M. Kimmich, AHR,
78(Dec 1973):1489; R. G. Wesson, RR, 32(Oct 1973):451.

Epstein, Melech. Pages from a Colorful Life: An Autobiographical
Sketch. Miami Beach, Fla.: I Block, 1971. Rev. by E. Lif-
schultz, AJHQ, 62(Mar 1973):321-2.

Erdoes, Richard and John (Fire) Lame Deer. Lame Deer, Seeker
of Visions: The Life of a Sioux Medicine Man. New York:
Simon and Schuster, 1972. Rev. by R. Ellis, Montana, 23(Spr
1973):71.

Erickson, Arvel B see Jones, Wilbur Devereux

Erickson, Charlotte. Invisible Immigrants: The Adaptation of Eng-
lish and Scottish Immigrants in Nineteenth-Century America.
Coral Gables, Fla.: U Miami Press, 1972. Rev. by M. Klein,
AHI, 8(Jl 1973):49-50; W. S. Shepperson, Historian, 36(Nov
1973):124-5; W. W. Wasson, AmArch, 36(Jl 1973):418-19; D.
E. Pitzer, IMH, 69(Dec 1973):369-70; R. Boston, JISHS, 66
(Aut 1973):359-60; P. A. Kalisch, RKHS, 71(Ja 1973):113-14;

C. Wilson, NCHR, 50(Win 1973):106-7; M. B. Bogue, JEH, 33(Sep 1973):672-5; B. A. Guthrie, Jr., FCHQ, 47(Apr 1973): 200; D. B. Cole, JAH, 60(Je 1973):148-9; R. Berthoff, AHR, 78(Je 1973):731-2; M. Walsh, BHR, 47(Aut 1973):388-9.

Erickson, Erling A.   Banking in Frontier Iowa, 1836-1865.   Ames: Ia St U Press, 1971. Rev. by G. Lamson, JEH, 33(Je 1973): 478-9; J. Olson, AOI, 41(Spr 1973):1279-80; T. P. Govan, BHR, 47(Spr 1973):108-9; P. W. Gates, PHR, 42(May 1973): 249-50; M. B. Bogue, AgH, 47(Apr 1973):183-4.

Errington, Robert M.   The Dawn of Empire: Rome's Rise to World Power. London: Hamish Hamilton, 1971. Rev. by E. S. Gruen, JIH, 4(Aut 1973):273-86.

Ershkowitz, Miriam and Joseph Zikmund, II, eds.   Black Politics in Philadelphia. New York: Basic Books, 1973. Rev. by H. Sitkoff, HRNB, 2(Nov/Dec 1973):54-5.

Erwin, Wallace M.   A Basic Course in Iraqi Arabic. Washington, D. C.: Georgetown U Press, 1969. Rev. by E. N. McCarus, MEJ, 27(Sum 1973):404-5.

Esson, D. M. R.   The Curse of Cromwell: A History of the Iron-side Conquest of Ireland, 1649-53. Totowa, N. J.: Rowman and Littlefield, 1971. Rev. by F. G. James, AHR, 78(Feb 1973):102-3; H. Hattaway, MilAf, 37(Oct 1973):110.

Estrada, Ezequiel Martinez.   X-Ray of the Pampa. Austin: U Tx Press, 1971. Rev. by J. T. Criscenti, TAm, 29(Ja 1973): 411-13.

Eterovich, Adam S.   Yugoslavs in Nevada, 1859-1900. San Fran-cisco: R and E Research Assn., 1973. Rev. by L. M. Kosso, NHSQ, 16(Win 1973):255-7.

Etheridge, Elizabeth W.   The Butterfly Caste: A Social History of Pellegra in the South. Westport, Conn.: Greenwood, 1972. Rev. by L. M. Simms, Jr., JAH, 60(Je 1973):172-3; J. H. Young, FHQ, 52(Jl 1973):90-92; J. Duffy, JSH, 39(May 1973): 318-19.

Etter, Don D.   Auraria: Where Denver Began. Boulder, Col.: Col. Associated Univ Press, 1972. Rev. by M. S. Wolle, CoMag, 50(Spr 1973):257-9.

Ettinger, S. see Ben-Sasson, H. H.

Euler, Robert C. see Dobyns, Henry F.

Evans, E. Estyn.   The Personality of Ireland: Habitat, Heritage, and History. New York: Cam U Press, 1973. Rev. by L. J. McCaffrey, HRNB, 2(Oct 1973):3.

Evans, G. N. D. Uncommon Obdurate: The Several Public Careers
of J. F. W. DesBarres. Toronto: U Tor Press, 1970. Rev.
by R. Middleton, History, 58(Feb 1973):149.

Evans, J. D. The Prehistoric Antiquities of the Maltese Islands:
A Survey. London: Athlone, 1971. Rev. by D. Evett, AHR,
78(Feb 1973):71-3.

_____ and Colin Renfrew. Excavations at Saliagos Near Anti-
paros. London: Thames and Hudson, 1968. Rev. by S. S.
Weinberg, Archaeology, 26(Jl 1973):232-3.

Evans, John X. The Works of Sir Roger Williams. Oxford:
Clarendon, 1972. Rev. by P. J. Berger, JMH, 45(Sep 1973):
477.

Everett, Frank Edgar, Jr. Brierfield, Plantation Home of Jefferson
Davis. Hattiesburg: U and C Press Miss., 1971. Rev. by
H. Monroe, CWH, 19(Dec 1973):356-8.

Everett, Mark R. Medical Education in Oklahoma: The University
of Oklahoma School of Medicine and Medical Center, 1900-1931.
Norman: U Ok Press, 1972. Rev. by J. O. Breeden, JSH,
39(May 1973):320-1.

Everitt, Alan. The Pattern of Rural Dissent: The Nineteenth Cen-
tury. [Leicester:] Leicester U Press, 1972. Rev. by S. D.
Chapman, MH, 2(Spr 1973):54-5; R. W. Ambler, Archives 11
(Spr 1973):55-7.

Evers, Alf. The Catskills: From Wilderness to Woodstock. Garden
City, N. Y.: Doubleday, 1972. Rev. by W. Chazanof, JAH,
60(Sep 1973):433-4; M. Kudish, NYH, 54(Jl 1973):370-1.

Eversley, D. E. C. and Jane S. Williams, eds. Third International
Conference of Economic History, Munich, 1965. Vol. 4. Dem-
ography and Economy. Paris: Mouton, 1972. Rev. by L. K.
Berkner, AHR, 78(Oct 1973):1008-9.

Faber, J. A. Friesland Over Three Centuries: Economic and So-
cial Developments From 1500 to 1800. 2 vols. Wageningen:
Afdeling Agrarisch Geschiedenis Landbouwhogeschool, 1972.
Rev. by J. De Vries, AHR, 78(Oct 1973):1083-4.

Fagen, Richard R. and William S. Tuohy. Politics and Privilege in
a Mexican City. Stanford, Cal.: Stan U Press, 1972. Rev.
by R. E. Scott, HAHR, 53(May 1973):331-3.

Fagg, William. Divine Kingship in Africa. London: British Museum, 1970. Rev. by M. D. McLeod, AfAf, 72(Oct 1973):
461-2.

_____, ed. The Living Arts of Nigeria. London: Studio Vista,

1971. Rev. by G. Lienhardt, AfAf, 72(Oct 1973):460-1.

_____. Miniature Wood Carvings of Africa. Greenwich, Conn.:
N. Y. Graphic Society, 1970. Rev. by M. W. Mount, Archaeology, 26(Ja 1973):77-8.

_____. The Tribal Image. London: British Museum, 1970.
Rev. by M. D. McLeod, AfAf, 72(Oct 1973):461-2.

_____ and Michael Foreman. The Living Art of Nigeria. New
York: Macmillan, 1972. Rev. by O. E. S., CurH, 64(Mar
1973):125.

_____ and John Picton. The Potter's Art in Africa. London:
British Museum, 1970. Rev. by J. Kesby, AfAf, 72(Oct 1973):
462-3.

Fahey, Edmund. Rum Road to Spokane. Missoula: U Mont Publications in History, 1972. Rev. by H. Lane, Montana, 23(Aut
1973):68.

Fahey, John. The Ballyhoo Bonanza: Charles Sweeny and the Idaho
Mines. Seattle: U Wash Press, 1971. Rev. by W. Barnes,
JEH, 33(Je 1973):480; W. T. Jackson, AHR, 78(Feb 1973):
168-9; G. M. Gressley, BHR, 47(Aut 1973):391-3.

Fairman, Charles. History of the Supreme Court of the United
States. Vol. VI. Reconstruction and Reunion, 1864-88, Part 1.
New York: Macmillan, 1971. Rev. by H. Belz, JAH, 59(Mar
1973):1012-13.

Fairservis, Walter A., Jr. The Roots of Ancient India. New York:
Macmillan, 1971. Rev. by J. M. Casal, Antiquity, 47(Sep
1973):239-40.

Fakhouri, Hani. Fafr El-Elow: An Egyptian Village in Transition.
New York: Holt, Rinehart and Winston, 1972. Rev. by E. W.
Fernea, MEJ, 27(Sum 1973):393-4.

Faludy, George. Erasmus of Rotterdam. London: Eyre and Spottiswoode, 1970. Rev. by J. F. Davis, History, 58(Je 1973):
276.

Fanton, Jonathan F. see Warch, Richard

Farber, Bernard. Guardians of Virtue: Salem Families in 1800.
New York: Basic Books, 1972. Rev. by J. K. Somerville,
WMQ, 3rd ser., 30(Apr 1973):359-62.

Faris, James C. Nuba Personal Art. London: Duckworth, n. d.
Rev. by M. Shinnie, JAfH, 14(2nd Qr 1973):353.

Farming in the New Nation: Interpreting American Agriculture,

1790-1840. Darwin P. Kelsey, ed. Washington, D. C.: Agricultural History Society, 1972. Rev. by G. M Herndon, WMQ,
3rd ser., 30(Apr 1973):358-9; W. Graebner, PH, 40(Oct 1973):
489-90; D. O. Whitten, JEH, 33(Sep 1973):679-81.

Farnham, Eliza W. California In-Doors and Out: Or, How We
Farm, Mine, and Live Generally in the Golden State. Nieuw-
koop, Netherlands: De Graaf, 1972. Rev. by D. R. Anderson,
JOW, 12(Apr 1973):336-7.

_____. Life in Prairie Land. Nieuwkoop, Netherlands: De
Graaf, 1972. Rev. by M. Rodriguez, JOW, 12(Apr 1973):337.

Farnie, D. A. East and West of Suez: The Suez Canal in History,
1854-1956. Oxford: Clarendon Press, 1969. Rev. by R. P.
Mitchell, MEJ, 27(Win 1973):81-2.

Farrell, Brian. Chairman or Chief? The Role of Taoiseach in
Irish Government. Dublin: Gill and Macmillan, 1971. Rev.
by R. T. Reilly, E-I, 8(Win 1973):135-7.

Fatout, Paul. Indiana Canals. West Lafayette, Ind.: Purdue U
Press, 1972. Rev. by S. F. Strausberg, JAH, 60(Je 1973):
134-5.

Faulk, Odie B. Destiny Road: The Gila Trail and the Opening of
the Southwest. New York: Ox U Press, 1973. Rev. by L.
L. Morrison, JOW, 12(Oct 1973):638.

_____. Tombstone: Myth and Reality. New York: Ox U Press,
1972. Rev. by W. H. Lyon, WHQ, 4(Jl 1973):342-3; G. L.
Roberts, A & W, 15(Aut 1973):302-4; R. Holland, JOW, 12(Jl
1974):505; W. B. Hughes, JAH, 60(Sep 1973):464-5; R. L.
Nichols, PHR, 42(May 1973):254-5; W. K. Zellmer, AW, 10
(Jl 1973):53.

_____. see Connor, Seymour V.

Fauré, Henri. Changement et continuité chez les mayas du mexique:
contribution à l'étude de la situation coloniale en amerique
latine. Paris: Editions Anthropos, 1971. Rev. by J. V.
Murra, HAHR, 53(Feb 1973):159-60.

_____. Les Incas. Paris: Presses Universitaires de France,
1972. Rev. by T. F. Lynch, HAHR, 53(Aug 1973):531-2.

Fearon, Peter see Aldcroft, Derek H.

Featherstone, Donald F. MacDonald of the Forty-Second. London:
Seeley Service, 1971. Rev. by A. M. J. Hyatt, MilAf, 37
(Dec 1973):159.

_____. War Games Through the Ages, 3,000 B. C. to 1500 A. D.

London: Stanley Paul, 1972. Rev. by R. J. Sommers, MilAf, 37(Dec 1973):158.

Feder, Ernest. The Rape of the Peasantry: Latin America's Land-holding System. Garden City, N. Y.: Doubleday Anchor, 1971. Rev. by D. Butterworth, AgH, 47(Apr 1973):164-7; R. W. Wilkie, HAHR, 53(Aug 1973):539-40.

Feder, Ernst. Heute sprach ich mit...: Tagebücher eines berliner Publizisten, 1926-1932. Stuttgart: Deutsche Verlags-Anstalt, 1971. Rev. by O. J. Hale, JMH, 45(Je 1973):347-8.

Fedyshyn, Oleh H. Germany's Drive to the East and the Ukrainian Revolution, 1917-1918. n. p.: n. d. Rev. by R. J. Cramp-ton, History, 58(Feb 1973):131-2.

Fehrenbacher, Don, ed. History and American Society: Essays of David M. Potter. New York: Ox U Press, 1973. Rev. by C. Strout, JSH, 39(Aug 1973):425-6; R. A. Billington, JAH, 60(Dec 1973):762-3; G. B. Tindall, AHR, 78(Dec 1973):1519-21.

Fein, Albert. Frederick Law Olmsted and the American Environ-mental Tradition. New York: Braziller, 1972. Rev. by N. Harris, JAH, 60(Je 1973):157-8; D. Simon, NYHSQ, 57(Apr 1973):184-6; C. C. McLaughlin, AHR, 78(Je 1973):734-5.

Feingold, Henry L. The Politics of Rescue; The Roosevelt Admin-istration and the Holocaust, 1938-1945. New Brunswick, N. J.: Rutgers U Press, 1970. Rev. by F. Friedel, MilAf, 37(Feb 1973):36-7.

Feinstein, C. H. National Income, Expenditure and Output of the United Kingdom, 1855-1965. Cambridge: Cam U Press, 1972. Rev. by D. H. Aldcroft, BHR, 47(Aut 1973):404-5.

Feinstein, Elaine, trans. Marina Tsvetayeva's Selected Poems. New York and Toronto: Ox U Press, 1971. Rev. by S. Karlinsky, RR, 32(Ja 1973):101-2.

Feiwel, George R. The Soviet Quest for Economic Efficiency: Is-sues, Controversies and Reforms. New York: Praeger, 1972. Rev. by G. E. Schroeder, RR, 32(Ja 1973):88-9.

Fekrat, M. Ali see Amuzegar, Jahangir

Fell, Clare. Early Settlement in the Lake Counties. Clapham: Dalesman, 1972. Rev. by A. King, Antiquity, 47(Sep 1973):253.

Felloni, Guiseppe. Gli Investimenti Finanziari Genovesi In Europa Tra Il Seicento e la Restaurazione. Milano: Dott A. Giuffre, 1971. Rev. by J. S. Cohen, JEH, 33(Je 1973):481-2.

Fellow-Gordon, Ian. The Magic War, the Battle for North Burma.

New York: Scribner's, 1971. Rev. by J. B. Bell, MilAf, 37
(Dec 1973):155-7.

Fenlon, Dermot. Heresy and Obedience in Tridentine Italy: Cardinal
    Pole and the Counter Reformation. New York: Cam U Press,
    1972. Rev. by P. F. Grendler, AHR, 78(Dec 1973):1494-5.

Fenyo, Mario D. Hitler, Horthy, and Hungary: German-Hungarian
    Relations 1941-44. New Haven, Conn.: Yale U Press, 1972.
    Rev. by B. K. Király, JMH, 45(Dec 1973):709-10; T. L. Sak-
    myster, AHR, 78(Oct 1973):1051-2.

Ferguson, Alan D. see Pushkarev, Sergei, et al, comps. and eds.

Ferguson, Blanche E. Countee Cullen and the Negro Renaissance.
    New York: Dodd, Mead, 1966. Rev. by A. Hoffman, JOW,
    12(Ja 1973):176-7.

Ferguson, John. English Diplomacy, 1422-1461. New York: Ox U
    Press, 1972. Rev. by S. B. Chrimes, AHR, 78(Oct 1973):
    1034.

_____. The Yorubas of Nigeria. Bletchley, Bucks, England:
    Open U, 1970. Rev. by J. Goody, Africa 43(Ja 1973):82.

Ferguson, Robert B. see Burt, Jesse

Ferguson, Yale H., ed. Contemporary Inter-American Relations:
    A Reader in Theory and Issues. Englewood Cliffs, N. J.:
    Prentice-Hall, 1972. Rev. by W. A. Chaffee, HAHR, 53(May
    1973):346-7.

Ferris, Robert G., ed. Soldier and Brave: Historic Places Asso-
    ciated With Indian Affairs and the Indian Wars in the Trans-
    Mississippi. Washington, D. C.: National Park Service, 1971.
    Rev. by R. E. Smith, WPHM, 56(Ja 1973):93-4; C. T. McIn-
    tosh, PacH, 17(Sum 1973):83-4; W. L. Bailey, NDH, 40(Fall
    1973):31-2; M. W. M. Hargreaves, RKHS, 71(Ja 1973):110-11,
    L. Barry, JISHS, 66(Spr 1973):97-8; W. G. Bell, MilAf, 37
    (Dec 1973):159.

Ferris, William R., Jr. Mississippi Folklore: A Research Bibli-
    ography and Discography. Hattiesburg: U and C Press Miss.,
    1971. Rev. by L. D. S. Harrell, JMiH, 35(Feb 1973):99.

Fetscher, Iring. Marx and Marxism. New York: Herder and
    Herder, 1971. Rev. by R. H. W. Theen, JMH, 45(Dec 1973):
    675-8.

Feuchtwanger, E. J. Israeli, Democracy and the Tory Party: Con-
    servative Leadership and Organization After the Second Reform
    Bill. Oxford: Ox U Press, 1968. Rev. by J. Cornford, His-
    tory, 58(Feb 1973):127-9.

Ffrench-Blake, R. L. V. The Crimean War. Hamden, Conn.:
    Archon, 1972. Rev. by A. Brett-James, MilAf, 37(Apr 1973):
    72.

Field, Saul and Morton P. Levitt. Bloomsday: An Interpretation of
    James Joyce's Ulysses. Greenwich, Conn.: N. Y. Graphic
    Society, 1972. Rev. by M. H. Begnal, E-I, 8(Win 1973):142-4.

Fielding, Raymond. The American Newsreel, 1911-1967. Norman:
    U Ok Press, 1972. Rev. by L. C. Waffen, AmArch, 36(Oct
    1973):561-2.

Fiester, Mark. Blasted, Beloved Breckenridge. Boulder, Col.:
    Pruett, 1973. Rev. by B. A. Storey, CoMag, 50(Sum 1973):
    267-8; D. A. Smith, Montana, 23(Sum 1973):51.

Fifer, J. Valerie. Bolivia: Land, Location, and Politics Since 1825.
    New York: Cam U Press, 1972. Rev. by R. J. Alexander,
    AHR, 78(Oct 1973):1153-4; D. B. Heath, HAHR, 53(Aug 1973):
    523-4.

Fifoot, C. H. S. Frederic William Maitland: A Life. Cambridge,
    Mass.: Har U Press, 1971. Rev. by T. A. Sandquist, CHR,
    54(Sep 1973):320-1.

Filby, P. W. and Edward G. Howard, comps. Star-Spangled Books:
    Books, Sheet Music, Newspapers, Manuscripts, and Persons
    Associated With "The Star-Spangled Banner." Baltimore: Md
    Historical Society, 1972. Rev. by E. Wolf, 2nd, PMHB, 97
    (Ja 1973):123-4; R. Harwell, VMHB, 81(Ja 1973):107-8.

Finberg, H. P. R., ed. The Agrarian History of England and
    Wales. Vol. I, Part 2. A. D. 43-1042. New York: Cam
    U Press, 1972. Rev. by G. E. Fussell, T & C, 14(Jl 1973):
    491-3.

Findlay, Robert R. see Brockett, Oscar G.

Findley, Rowe. Great American Deserts. Washington, D. C.:
    National Geographic Society, 1972. Rev. by K. Black, JOW,
    12(Oct 1973):637; A. W. Wilson, JAriH, 14(Aut 1973):262-3;
    D. Bowers, NHSQ, 16(Sum 1973):133-5; R. H. Lister, AW,
    10(Sep 1973):52.

Fine, Lenore and Jesse A. Remington. United States Army in World
    War II: The Technical Services--The Corps of Engineers: Con-
    struction in the United States. Washington: Office of the Chief
    of Military History, U. S. Army, 1972. Rev. by R. F.
    Weigley, JAH, 60(Dec 1973):849-50.

Fingerhut, Eugene R. The Fingerhut Guide: Sources in American
    History. Santa Barbara: Clio, 1973. Rev. by C. R. Mc-
    Clure, ChOk, 51(Win 1973-74):503-4.

Finlayson, Dale K. A. see Borg, Dorothy

Finley, Joseph E. The Corrupt Kingdom: The Rise and Fall of the
    United Mine Workers. [New York:] Simon and Schuster, 1972.
    Rev. by R. D. Bonham, OQ, 16(Win 1973):168-70.

Finn, R. Welldon. The Making and Limitations of the Yorkshire
    Domesday. York, Eng.: St. Anthony's, 1972. Rev. by J.
    Cooper, Archives, 11(Spr 1973):45-6.

Fiori, Guiseppe. Antonio Gramsci: Life of a Revolutionary. New
    York: Dutton, 1971. Rev. by C. F. Delzell, AHR, 78(Dec
    1973):1544-5; M. Clark, JMH, 45(Je 1973):341-2.

Firpo, Massimo. Pietro Bizzari Esule del Cinquecento. Turin:
    Università di Torino Facultà di Lettere e Filosofia, 1971. Rev.
    by R. H. Bainton, JMH, 45(Sep 1973):486.

The First One Hundred: A Catalog of Manuscripts and Special Col-
    lections [in the John C. Pace Library--U W Fla Library.]
    Pensacola: U W Fla., 1972. Rev. by K. J. Pike, AmArch,
    36(Jl 1973):411-14.

Fischer, David H. Historians' Fallacies: Toward a Logic of His-
    torical Thought. New York: Harper and Row, 1970. Rev. by
    M. Brickford, AmArch, 36(Jl 1973):397-402.

Fischer, John L. , see Taylor, Walter W.

Fischer, Louis. The Road to Yalta: Soviet Foreign Relations, 1941-
    1945. New York: Harper and Row, 1972. Rev. by G. A.
    Morgan, RR, 32(Ja 1973):77-9; A. Iriye, JMH, 45(Dec 1973):
    711-14.

Fisher, Allan G. B. and Humphrey J. Slavery and Muslim Society
    in Africa. London: n. p. , 1970. Rev. by A. Atmore, JAfH,
    14(3rd Qr 1973):509-10.

Fisher, Ralph T. see Pushkarev, Sergei, et al.

Fisher, Roger. Dear Israelis, Dear Arabs: A Working Approach
    to Peace. New York: Harper and Row, 1972. Rev. by D. E.
    Long, MEJ, 27(Aut 1973):523-4.

Fisher, W. B. see Clarke, J. I.

Fitch, James Marston. American Building: The Environmental
    Forces That Shape It. Boston: Houghton Mifflin, 1972. Rev.
    by C. W. Condit, T & C, 14(Jl 1973):509-11.

_____ . American Building: The Historical Forces That Shaped
    It. New York: Schocken, 1973. Rev. by S. Sternlicht, HRNB,
    2(Nov/Dec 1973):46-7.

Fitting, James Edward. The Schultz Site at Green Point. Ann
    Arbor: U Mich Press, 1972. Rev. by R. J Salzer, MichH,
    57(Spr 1973):76-7.

_____. The Archaeology of Michigan: A Guide to the Prehistory
    of the Great Lakes Region. Garden City, N. Y.: Natural His-
    tory Press, 1970. Rev. by N. E. T., IS, 29(Win 1973):319.

Fitzgerald, Frances. Fire in the Lake: The Vietnamese and the
    Americans in Vietnam. Boston: Little, Brown, 1972. Rev.
    by D. A Wilson, PHR, 42(May 1973):264-5.

Fitzgerald, Gerald E., ed. The Political Thought of Bolivar: Se-
    lected Writings. The Hague: Martinus Nijhoff, 1971. Rev.
    by P. K. Liss, AHR, 78(Feb 1973):187-8.

FitzGibbon, Louis. Katyn: A Crime Without Parallel. New York:
    Scribner's, 1971. Rev. by A. D. Coox, MilAf, 37(Feb 1973):
    35-6.

Fitzhugh, Lester Newton, ed. Cannon Smoke: The Letters of Cap-
    tain John J. Good, Good-Douglas Texas Battery, C. S. A.
    Hillsboro, Tx.: Hill Jr. Coll Press, 1971. Rev. by R. D.
    Hoffsommer, CWTI, 12(Aug 1973):50.

Fitzpatrick, Doyle C. The King Strang Story, A Vindication of
    James J. Strang, The Beaver Island Mormon King. Lansing,
    Mich: National Heritage, 1970. Rev. by D. Rowley, WMH,
    56(Sum 1973):328-9; B. Stinson, AHI, 8(Dec 1973):50.

FitzSimons, Neal, ed. The Reminiscences of John B. Jervis, Engi-
    neer of the Old Croton. Syracuse, N. Y.: Syr U Press, 1971.
    Rev. by W. D. Lewis, PH, 40(Oct 1973):490-1.

Fladeland, Betty. Men and Brothers: Anglo-American Antislavery
    Cooperation. Urbana: U Ill Press, 1972. Rev. by R. Det-
    weiler, HT, 6(May 1973):485; J. C. Mohr, JNH, 58(Mar
    1973):210-12; B. Wyatt-Brown, AHR, 78(Oct 1973):1133-4; His-
    torian, 36(Nov 1973):126-7; E. M. Steel, Jr. WVH, 34(Jl
    1973):390-1; A. S. Kraditor, JAH, 60(Sep 1973):447-8; R. B.
    Drake, JSH, 39(Aug 1973):448-9; R. B. Nye, MHM, 68(Fall
    1973):343-5; D. D. Wax, VMHB, 81(Jl 1973):373-4.

Flaherty, David H. Privacy in Colonial New England. Charlottes-
    ville: U Press Va., 1972. Rev. by J. J. Waters, WMQ, 3rd
    Ser., 30(Ja 1973):168-70; R. D. Cohen, NYHSQ, 57(Apr 1973):
    176-7.

Fleischer, David M. O Recrutamento politico em Minos, 1890-1918.
    Análise dos Antecédentes socias e das carreiras politícas de
    151 deputados federais. Belo Horizonte, Brazil: Edições da
    Revista Brasileira de Estudos Politícos, n. d. Rev. by C.
    O'Neil, HAHR, 53(Nov 1973):730-1.

Fleisher, Martin, ed. Machiavelli and the Nature of Political
Thought. New York: Atheneum, 1972. Rev. by J. Kirshner,
JMH, 45(Sep 1973):484-5; W. T. Jones, SS, 64(Apr 1973):183.

Fleming, Donald see Bailyn, Bernard

Fleming, Thomas, ed. Benjamin Franklin: A Biography in His Own
Words. New York: Harper and Row, 1972. Rev. by J. J.
Zimmerman, PMHB, 97(Apr 1973):261-2.

Flemion, Philip F. Historical Dictionary of El Salvador. Metuchen,
N. J.: Scarecrow, 1973. Rev. by B. B. Solnick, HAHR, 53
(Aug 1973):494-5.

Flexner, James Thomas. George Washington and the New Nation
(1783-1793). Boston: Little, Brown, 1969. Rev. by E.
Wright, JAH, 60(Dec 1973):791-3.

_____. George Washington. Vol. IV. Anguish and Farewell
(1793-1799). Boston: Little, Brown, 1972. Rev. by A. Keller, AHI, 8(Jl 1973):49; M. Jensen, AHR, 78(Oct 1973):1124-
5; G. W. Gawalt, FHQ, 52(Oct 1973):194-5; E. Wright, JAH,
60(Dec 1973):791-3; E. G. Evans, JSH, 39(Aug 1973):440-1;
J J. Heslin, NYHSQ, 57(Jl 1973):268-9; J. Cary, PMHB, 97
(Jl 1973):413-4; R. R. Beeman, WMQ, 3rd ser., 30(Oct 1973):
663-5.

Fligge, Jörg Rainer. Herzog Albrecht von Preussen und der Osiandrismus, 1522-1568. Bonn: The Author, 1972. Rev. by
H. J Grimm, AHR, 78(Oct 1973):1090.

Florin, John W. Death in New England: Regional Variations in
Mortality. Chapel Hill: UNC Press, 1971. Rev. by S. B.
Hand, VH, 41(Win 1973):57-8.

Floud, Roderick. An Introduction to Quantitative Methods for Historians. Princeton, N. J.: Prin U Press, 1973. Rev. by
A. D. Anderson, BHR, 47(Win 1973):554-5.

Fogarty, Robert S., ed. American Utopianism. Itasca, Ill.: F. E.
Peacock, 1972. Rev. by S. C. Scholl, HT, 7(Nov 1973):124-5.

Fogel, Robert William see Aydelotte, William O.

Fogle, French, ed. Complete Prose Works of John Milton. Vol. V,
Part I. 1648?-1671. The History of Britain. London: Yale U
Press, 1971. Rev. by V. Pearl, History, 58(Oct 1973):448-9.

Folkman, David I., Jr. The Nicaragua Route. Salt Lake City: U
Utah Press, 1972. Rev. by R. Mann, WHQ, 4(Je 1973):341-2;
H. R Grant, HT, 6(May 1973):486-7; M. M Smith, ChOk,
51(Win 1973-74):495-6; H H. Hague, NHSQ, 16(Win 1973):
253-4; J. Caughey, PHR, 42(May 1973):251-2.

Folsom, Franklin. Red Power on the Rio Grande: The Native
    American Revolution of 1680. Chicago: Follett, 1973. Rev.
    by G. Theisen, NMHR, 48(Oct 1973):338.

Foner, Philip S. The Spanish-Cuban-American War and the Birth of
    American Imperialism, 1895-1902. 2 vols. New York: Monthly
    Review Press, 1972. Rev. by R. F. Smith, HAHR, 53(Nov
    1973):697-9; H. W. Morgan, PHR, 42(Jl 1973):432-3.

Foote, Wilder see Cordier, Andrew W.

Foreign Relations of the United States. The Conferences at Washing-
    ton and Quebec, 1943: The Conference at Quebec, 1944. Wash-
    ington: Government Printing Office, 1970, 1972. Rev. by W.
    F. Kimball, AHR, 78(Dec 1973):1551-3.

Foreign Relations of the United States, 1947. Vol. II. Council of
    Foreign Ministers: Germany and Austria. Washington: Govern-
    ment Printing Office, 1972. Rev. by R. A. Divine, JAH, 60
    (Dec 1973):755-6.

Foreign Relations of the United States, 1947. Vol. IV. Eastern
    Europe: The Soviet Union. Washington: Government Printing
    Office, 1972. Rev. by M. Jonas, JAH, 60(Dec 1972):757-9.

Foreign Relations of the United States, 1947. Vol. V. The Near
    East and Africa. Washington: Government Printing Office,
    1971. Rev. by H. N Howard, AHR, 78(Oct 1973):1146-7; H.
    N. Howard, MEJ, 27(Spr 1973):245.

Foreign Relations of the United States ... 1947. Vol. VI. The Far
    East. Washington: Government Printing Office, 1972. Rev.
    by R. G. O'Connor, PHR, 42(Feb 1973):131-2.

Foreign Relations of the United States, 1947. Vol. VIII. The Amer-
    ican Republics. Washington: Government Printing Office, 1972.
    Rev. by R. R. Trask, JAH, 60(Dec 1973):759-60.

Foreign Relations of the United States ... 1947. Vol. X. The Far
    East: China. Washington: Government Printing Office, 1972.
    Rev. by R. G. O'Connor, PHR, (Feb 1973):131-2.

Foreman, Michael see Fagg, William

Forester, Margaret. Michael Collins--The Lost Leader. London:
    Sidgwick and Jackson, 1971. Rev. by R. T. Reilly, E-I, (Spr
    1973):155-6.

Forman, James A. Law and Disorder. New York: Thomas Nelson,
    1972. Rev. by R. F. Allen, SS, 64(Feb 1973):87.

_____. The Making of Black Revolutionaries: A Personal
    Account. New York: Macmillan, 1972. Rev. by L. M. Simms,

Jr., WMH, 56(Sum 1973):329-30.

Forman, Robert E. Black Ghettos, White Ghettos, and Slums.
  Englewood Cliffs, N. J.: Prentice-Hall, 1972. Rev. by P. C.
  Sharma, SS, 64(Dec 1973):341-3.

Forman, Shephard. The Raft Fishermen: Tradition and Change in
  the Brazilian Peasant Economy. Bloomington: Ind U Press,
  1970. Rev. by T. Summons, TAm, 29(Ja 1973):410-11.

Formisano, Ronald P. The Birth of Mass Political Parties: Michigan, 1827-1861. Princeton: Prin U Press, 1971. Rev. by
  P. Levine, IMH, 69(Mar 1973):69-70; S. Nathan, NYH, 54(Ja
  1973):118-19; R. J Jensen, WMH, 56(Win 1972-3):165-6.

Forney, John W. Anecdotes of Public Men. New York: Da Capo,
  1970. Rev. by K. R. Nodyne, WPHM, 56(Jl 1973):319-21.

Forrest, A. C. The Unholy Land. Old Greenwich, Conn.: Devin
  Adair, 1972. Rev. by J. P. Richardson, MEJ, 27(Win 1973):
  101.

Forster, Colin and G. S. L. Tucker. Economic Opportunity and
  White American Fertility Ratios, 1800-1860. New Haven,
  Conn.: Yale U Press, 1972. Rev. by M. A. Minovskis, JAH,
  60(Sep 1973):432-3.

Forster, Robert. The House of Saulx-Tavanes: Versailles and Bur-
  gundy, 1700-1830. Baltimore: JHU Press, 1971. B. C.
  Weber, AgH, 47(Apr 1973):177-8; J. S. Wozniak, JEH, 33
  (Sep 1973):675-6; R. R. Palmer, AHR, 78(Feb 1973):111; J.
  Mackrell, JMH, 45(Dec 1973):664-5; D. Higgs, CHR, 54(Dec
  1973):470-2; N. Hampson, History, 58(Feb 1973):111; L. A.
  Tilly, JIH, 4(Aut 1973):315-21.

Forsyth, Alice D. and Earlene L. Zerinque, comps. and trans.
  German "Pest Ships." New Orleans: The Genealogical Re-
  search Society of New Orleans, 1969. Rev. by E. Vicknair,
  LaH, 14(Fall 1973):407-8.

Forsythe, David P. United Nations Peacemaking: The Conciliation
  Commission for Palestine. Baltimore: JHU Press, 1972. Rev.
  by E. H. Buehrig, MEJ, 27(Sum 1973):389-90.

Fortier, Alcee. A History of Louisiana, Vol. II. Baton Rouge:
  Claitor's, 1972. Rev. by A. P. Nasatir, LaH, 14(Spr 1973):
  223-4.

Foss, Michael. The Age of Patronage: The Arts in England, 1660-
  1750. Ithaca, N. Y.: Cornell U Press, 1972. Rev. by J. L.
  Clifford, AHR, 78(Je 1973):683-4.

Foster, Douglas W. Successful Management in Developing Countries:

Product and Market Management, 3. New Delhi: Orient Longmans, 1972. Rev. by S. Venu, IQ, 29(Apr-Je 1973):162-3.

_____. Successful Management in Developing Countries: Vol. 4.
Finance, Distribution and Promotion. [New Delhi:] Orient
Longmans, n. d. Rev. by S. Venu, IQ, 29(Jl-Sep 1973):262-3.

[Foster, Pops] ... Pops, Foster: The Autobiography of a New Orleans Jazzman ... Berkeley: U Cal Press, 1971. Rev. by E.
F. Dyson, JNH, 58(Apr 1973):221-2.

Foster, Stephen. Their Solitary Way: The Puritan Social Ethics in
the First Century of Settlement in New England. New Haven,
Conn.: Yale U Press, 1971. Rev. by P. J. Greven, Jr.,
AHR, 78(Feb 1973):145-6; R. C. Simmons, History, 58(Je
1973):286-7.

Foushee, Ola Maie. Art in North Carolina: Episodes and Developments, 1585-1970. Charlotte, N. C.: Author and Heritage
Pringers, 1972. Rev. by B. Wolter, NCHR 50(Sum 1973):323-
4.

Fowler, Don D. In A Sacred Manner We Live. Barre, Mass.:
Barre Publishers, 1972. Rev. by R. A. Weinstein, AW, 10
(Ja 1973):49.

_____. "Photographed All the Best Scenery:" Jack Hiller's
Diary of the Powell Expeditions, 1871-1875. Salt Lake City:
U Utah Press, 1972. Rev. by H. R. Grant, HT, 7(Nov 1973):
149; D. F. Schafer, ChOk, 51(Win 1973-74):496-7; R. J.
Roske, NHSQ, 16(Sum 1973):132-3; M. J. Mattes, AW, 10(Ja
1973):53; L. B. Lee, PHR, 42(May 1973):253-4.

Fowler, George L., ed. Locomotive Dictionary: Railroad Gazette,
1906. Novato, Cal.: Newton K. Gregg, 1972 (reprint). Rev.
by J. H. White, T & C, 14(Jl 1973):304-5.

Fowler, P. J., ed. Archaeology and the Landscape: Essays for
L. V. Grinsell. London: John Baker, 1972. Rev. by L. Alcock, History, 58(Oct 1973):412-3.

Fox, Carl. The Doll. New York: Harry N. Abrams, 1972. Rev.
by M. Black, NYHSQ, 57(Jl 1973):270-1.

Fox, Edward Walling. History in Geographic Perspective: The
Other France. New York: Norton, 1971. Rev. by J. Bow-
ditch, JMH, 45(Dec 1973):644-6.

Fox, Levi. In Honor of Shakespeare. Norwich: Jarrold, 1972.
Rev. by C. Carpenter, Archives, 11(Aut 1973):108.

Fox, Matthew H. see Barker, Carol M.

Frakes, George Edward. Laboratory for Liberty: The South Carolina Legislative Committee System, 1719-1776. Lexington, Ky.: U Press Ky, 1970. Rev. by W. R. Higgins, AHR, 78(Feb 1973):151-2.

France, Peter, trans. Diderot's Letters to Sophie Volland. New York: Ox U Press, 1972. Rev. by A. M. Wilson, AHR, 78 (Oct 1973):1074.

François, Michel and Nicolas Tolu, eds. International Bibliography of Historical Sciences. Vol. 35, 1966; Vol. 36, 1967. Paris: Librarie Armond Colin, 1969. Rev. by O. H. Orr, Jr., AHR, 78(Feb 1973):63-4.

Françoise, Henry. Irish Art in the Romanesque Period, 1020-1170 A. D. Ithaca, N. Y.: Cornell U Press, 1970. Rev. by A. Hamlin, AHR, 78(Je 1973):669.

Frank, Louis F. German-American Pioneers in Wisconsin and Michigan. Milwaukee: Milwaukee County Historical Society, 1971. Rev. by R. A. Suelflow, MichH, 57(Spr 1973):86-7.

Frankel, Francine R. India's Green Revolution: Economic Gains and Political Costs. Princeton, N. J.: Prin U Press, 1971. Rev. by T. N. Madan, IQ, 29(Jan-Mar 1973):74.

Franklin, Benjamin. The Papers of Benjamin Franklin. Vol. 11, 1764. Vol. 12, 1765. Vol. 13, 1766. Vol. 14, 1767. Ed. by Leonard W. Labaree. Vol. 15, 1768. Ed. by William B. Willcox. New Haven, Conn.: Yale U Press, 1967, 1968, 1969, 1970, 1972. Rev. by C. WMQ, 3rd ser., 30(Apr 1973): 343-7; B. Hindle, JAH, 60(Je 1973):96-8.

Franklin, Jimmie Lewis. Born Sober: Prohibition in Oklahoma, 1907-1959. Norman: U Ok Press, 1971. Rev. by B. H. Johnson, A & W, 15(Aut 1973):288-9.

Franzwa, Gregory M. The Oregon Trail Revisited. St. Louis: Patrice, 1972. Rev. by E. W. Harris, NHSQ, 16(Fall 1973): 199-200.

Fraser, Colin. Harry Ferguson, Inventor and Pioneer. London: John Murray, 1972. Reav by J. B. Rae, T & C, 14(Jl 1973): 511-13.

Fraser, Douglas and Herbert M. Cole, eds. African Art and Leadership. Madison: U Wis Press, 1972. Rev. by G. Lienhardt, AfAf, 72(Oct 1973):460-1.

Fraser, George MacDonald. The Steel Bonnets: The Story of the Anglo-Scottish Border Reiners. New York: Knopf, 1972. Rev. by S. A. Burrell, AHR, 78(Je 1973):681-2.

Fraser, Ronald. In Hiding: The Life of Manuel Cortes. New York: Pantheon, 1972. Rev. by J. C. Harvey, Historian, 36(Nov 1973):114.

Fraser, Stewart E., ed. Ludvig Holberg's Memoirs: An Eighteenth-Century Danish Contribution to International Understanding. Leiden: E. J. Brill, 1970. Rev. by O. J. Falnes, AHR, 78(Je 1973):708-9.

Frederick, Pierce G. The Sepoy and the Cossack. New York: New American Library, 1971. Rev. by R. W. Winks, JAH, 60(Ja 1973):41.

Frederickson, George M. The Black Image in the White Mind: The Debate on Afro-American Character and Destiny, 1817-1914. New York: Harper and Row, 1971. Rev. by R. L. Harris, Jr., JNH, 58(Apr 1973):219-21.

Freeman, Howard E. see Browne, Robert S., et al., eds.

Freeth, Zahra and Victor Winstone. Kuwait: Prospect and Reality. New York: Crane, Russak, 1972. Rev. by J. Twinam, MEJ, 27(Spr 1973):247.

Freiberg, Malcolm, Intro. The Journal of Madam Knight. Boston: Godine, 1972. Rev. by M. J. Dowd, AmArch, 36(Oct 1973):563-4.

Freimark, Vincent and Bernard Rosenthal, eds. Race and the American Romantics. New York: Schocken, 1972. Rev. by Erik S. Lunde, SS, 64(Nov 1973):294.

French, Herbert E. Love of Barth. New York: Putnam's, 1973. Rev. by M. J. Mattes, AW, 10(Jl 1973):54.

French, Peter J. John Dee. The World of an Elizabethan Magus. London: Routledge and Kegan Paul, 1972. Rev. by S. Clark, History, 58(Je 1973):281-2; S. E. Lehmberg, AHR, 78(Feb 1973):97-8; N. H. Clulee, JMH, 45(Je 1973):298-9.

Frend, W. H. C. The Rise of the Monophysite Movement. [Cambridge:] Cam U Press, 1972. Rev. by R. A. Oliver, JAfH, 14(No. 4 1973):699-70.

Frere, Sheppard, I. W. Cornwall, R. Goodburn, B. R. Hartley, K. F. Hartley, W. H. Manning, H. Waugh and M. G. Wilson. Verulamium Excavations I. London: Ox U Press, 1972. Rev. by G. Webster, Archaeology, 26(Jul 1973):229; C. B. Ruger, Antiquity, 47(Je 1973):156-7.

Frey, Otto-Herman. Die Entstehung der Situlenkunst: Studien zur figürlich verzierten Toreutik von Este. Römisch-Germanische Forschungen 31. Berlin: Walter de Gruyter, 1969. Rev. by

J. Collis, Antiquity, 47(Mar 1973):77-78.

Friar, Ralph and Natasha Friar. The Only Good Indian: The Holly-
    wood Gospel. New York: Drama Book Specialists, 1972. Rev.
    by M. T. Isenberg, Montana, 23(Aut 1973):61.

Fridenson, Patrick. Histoire des Usines Renault: Naissance de la
    Grande Enterprise, 1898-1939. Paris: Editions du Seuil,
    1972. Rev. by R. F. Kuisel, BHR, 47(Win 1973):549-52.

Friede, Juan. La Otra verdad. La Independencia Americana vista
    por los españoles. Bogata, Colombia: Ediciones Tercer
    Mundo, n. d. Rev. by M. E. Goldstein, HAHR, 53(Nov 1973):
    689-91.

_____ and Benjamin Keen, eds. Bartolomé de las Casas in His-
    tory: Toward an Understanding of the Man and His Work.
    DeKalb: N Ill U Press, 1972. Rev. by M. V. Gannon, FHQ,
    51(Ja 1973):318-21; J. A. Fernandez-Santamaría, HAHR, 53
    (Feb 1973):122-5; S. Poole, AHR, 78(Dec 1973):1482-3.

Friedlander, Marc and L. H. Butterfield, eds. The Adams Papers:
    Series II, Adams Family Correspondence. Vol. 3. April 1778-
    September 1780; Vol. 4. October 1780-September 1782. Cam-
    bridge, Mass.: Belknap Press, Har U Press, 1973. Rev. by
    H. A. Barnes, HRNB, 2(Nov/Dec 1973):42-3; AH, 24(Apr
    1973):98-9.

Friedrich, Otto. Before the Deluge: A Portrait of Berlin in the
    1920's. New York: Harper and Row, 1972. Rev. by P. R.
    Waibel, HT, 7(Nov 1973):141.

Friedrich, Paul. Agrarian Revolt in a Mexican Village. Englewood
    Cliffs, N. J.: Prentice-Hall, 1970. Rev. by H. A. Lands-
    berger, CSSH, 15(Je 1973):378-88.

Friesel, Uwe and Walter Grab. Noch ist Deutschland nicht verloren:
    Eine historisch-politische Analyse unterdrückter Lyrik von der
    Französischen Revolution bis zur Reichsgründung. Munich:
    Carl Hanser Verlag, 1970. Rev. by E. Wangermann, JMH,
    45(Sep 1973):520-2.

Frisby, Julian see Balfour, Michael

Frisch, Michael H. Town Into City: Springfield, Massachusetts,
    and the Meaning of Community, 1840-1880. Cambridge, Mass.:
    Har U Press, 1972. Rev. by W. S. Glazer, AHR, 78(Je 1973):
    733-4; P. R. Knights, JAH, 59(Mar 1973):1007-9.

Fritz, Jean. Cast for a Revolution: Some American Friends and
    Enemies, 1728-1814. Boston: Houghton Mifflin, 1972. Rev.
    by N. Callahan, JAH, 60(Je 1973):120-1.

Fritz, Paul and David Williams, eds. The Triumph of Culture: Eighteenth-Century Perspectives. Toronto: A. M. Hakkert, 1972. Rev. by A. M. Wilson, AHR, 78(Dec 1973):1449-1450.

Froidefond, Christian. Le mirage égyptien dans la littérature grecque d'Homère à Aristotle. Aix-en Provence: Ophrys, 1971. Rev. by S. M. Burstein, AHR, 78(Dec 1973):1431-2.

Frost, J. William. The Quaker Family in Colonial America: A Portrait of the Society of Friends. New York: St. Martin's, 1973. Rev. by S. E. Mead, HRNB, 2(Nov/Dec 1973):42.

Frost, Richard H. The Mooney Case. Stanford, Cal.: Stan U Press, 1968. Rev. by J. Penick, JOW, 12(Ja 1973):176.

Fry, Geoffrey Kingdon. Statesmen in Disguise: The Changing Role of the Administrative Class of the British Home Civil Service, 1853-1966. New York: Humanities Press, 1969. Rev. by R. M. MacLeod, AHR, 78(Dec 1973):1386-1405.

Fry, Michael G. Illusions of Security: North Atlantic Diplomacy, 1918-22. Toronto: U Tor Press, 1972. Rev. by F. G. Campbell, JMH, 45(Sep 1973):536-9.

Fuchs, Estelle and Robert J. Havighurst. To Live on This Earth: American Indian Education. [Garden City, N. Y.:] Doubleday, 1972. Rev. by J. S. Phillipson, OQ, 16(Sum 1973):89-91.

Fuentes, Carlos. Triple Cross: Holy Place. New York: Dutton, 1972. Rev. by R. D. Souza, HAHR, 53(Nov 1973):732.

Fuhrmann, Joseph T. The Origins of Capitalism in Russia: Industry and Progress in the Sixteenth and Seventeenth Centuries. Chicago: Quadrangle, 1972. Rev. by J. D. Clarkson, AHR, 78 (Je 1973):718; W. L. Blackwell, T & C, 14(Apr 1973):315-7; W. B. Walsh, RR, 32(Ja 1973):83-5.

Fukutake, Tadashi. Japanese Rural Society. Ithaca, N. Y.: Cornell U Press, 1972. Rev. by K. H. Kim, AgH, 47(Oct 1973): 361-2.

Fulford, Roger, ed. Your Dear Letter: Private Correspondence of Queen Victoria and the Crown Princess of Prussia, 1865-1871. New York: Scribner's, 1971. Rev. by G. Smith, AHR, 78 (Feb 1973):106-7.

Fuller, Margaret. Summer on the Lakes. Nieuwkoop, Netherlands: De Graaf, 1972. Rev. by P. S. Mulvihill, JOW, 12(Apr 1973): 335-6.

Fuller, Wayne E. The American Mail: Enlarger of the Common Life. U Chi Press, 1972. Rev. by M. F. Taylor, CoMag, 50(Spr 1973):171-2; A. Hoogenboom, JAH, 60(Sep 1973):457-8;

S. Lottinville, JSH, 39(May 1973):319-20;   D. N. Kelly, MHM,
68(Sum 1973):230-1;   E. P. L. Apfelbaum, PMHB, 97(Apr
1973):272-3;   O. W. Homes, WHQ, 4 (Jl 1973):329-31;   A.
Hecht, T & C, 14(Oct 1973):628-30.

Fundaburk, Emma Lila. Reference Materials in Economics: An International List in Five Volumes. Vol. 1: Agriculture. Metuchen, N. J.: Scarecrow, 1971. Rev. by J. R. Blanchard,
AgH, 47(Apr 1973):173-4.

Furneaux, Rupert. The Pictorial History of the American Revolution
as Told by Eyewitnesses and Participants. Chicago: J. G.
Ferguson, 1973. Rev. in GHQ, 57(Win 1973):605; by W. S.
Price, Jr., NCHR, 50(Aut 1973):429-30.

Fussell, G. E. The Classical Tradition in West European Farming.
Rutherford, N. J.: Fairleigh Dickinson U Press, 1972. Rev.
by D. Herlihy, AgH, 47(Jl 1973):272-3; W. K. Hackmann,
JEH, 33(Dec 1973):887-8; B. B. Blaine, T & C, 14(Jl 1973):
493-5.

Fynn, J. K. Asante and Its Neighbours, 1700-1807. London: Longmans, 1971. Rev. by K. Arhin, AfAf, 72(Jl 1973):339-40.

Gabert, Glen. In Hoc Signo? A Brief History of Catholic Parochial
Education in America. Port Washington, N. Y.: Kennikat,
1973. Rev. by R. D. Cohen, HRNB, 2(Oct 1973):17.

Gabriel, Ralph H. see Wood, Leonard C.

Gadd, C. see Edwards, I.

Gaddis, John Lewis. The United States and the Origins of the Cold
War, 1941-1947. New York: Columbia U Press, 1972. Rev.
by G. A. Morgan, RR, 32(Ja 1973):77-9; A. Iriye, JMH, 45
(Dec 1973):711-14; M. A. Stoler, WMH, 56(Spr 1973):254-6.

Gailey, Harry A. The Road to Aba. London: U London Press,
1971. Rev. by C. Fyfe, History, 58(Je 1973):327-8.

Gainer, Bernard. The Alien Invasion: The Origins of the Aliens
Act of 1905. New York: Crane, Russak, 1972. Rev. by F.
M. Leventhal, AHR, 78(Dec 1973):1470-1.

Gajendragadkar, P. B. The Indian Parliament and the Fundamental
Rights. Calcutta: Eastern Law House, 1972. Rev. by R.
Rattan, IQ, 29(Apr-Je 1973):168-70.

Galai, Shmuel. The Liberation Movement in Russia 1900-1905. New
York: Cam U Press, 1973. Rev. by T. Emmons, RR, 32
(Oct 1973):430-1.

Galbraith, John S. Mackinnon and East Africa, 1878-1895: A Study

in the 'New Imperialism.' New York: Cam U Press, 1972.
Rev. by M. Hay, AHR, 78(Oct 1973):1112; R. A. Austen,
JMH, 45(Dec 1973):680.

Galeano, Eduardo. Open Veins of Latin America: Five Centuries
of the Pillage of a Continent. New York: Monthly Review
Press, 1973. Rev. by G. Breathett, HRNB, 2(Oct 1973):21.

Gallacher, Tom. Mr. Joyce Is Leaving Paris. London: Calder
Boyars, n. d. Rev. by A. S. Jennings, E-I, 8(Win 1973):140-
2.

Galler, Meyer and Harland E. Marques, comps. Soviet Prison
Camp Speech: A Survivor's Glossary. Madison: U Wis Press,
1972. Rev. by N. S. Pashin, RR, 32(Apr 1973):211-12.

Gallet, Michel. Stately Mansions: Eighteenth-Century Paris Architecture. New York: Praeger, 1972. Rev. by T. F. Sheppard, AHR, 78(Feb 1973):110-11.

Gallo, Max. Mussolini's Italy: Twenty Years of the Fascist Era.
New York: Macmillan, 1973. Rev. by C. P. Delzell, HRNB,
2(Nov/Dec 1973):33.

Gallup, George H. The Gallup Poll: Public Opinion, 1935-1971.
3 vols. New York: Random House, 1972. Rev. by M. C.
Cummings, Jr., AHR 78(Oct 1973):1145-6; R. Jensen, JAH,
60(Sep 1973):499-500.

Galvin, John and Warren R. Howell, comp. The Etchings of Edward
Borein: A Catalogue of His Work. San Francisco: John
Howell, 1971. Rev. by P. H. Hassrick, SWHQ, 76(Ja 1973):
349-50.

Ganelin, R. Sh. Russia and the U. S. A., 1914-1917: Essays on
the History of Russian-American Relations. Leningrad:
Idzatel'stvo 'Nauka,'' 1969. Rev. by A. Dallin, AHR, 78(Oct
1973):1018.

Gann, Lewis H. Central Africa: The Former British States. Englewood Cliffs, N. J.: Prentice-Hall, 1971. Rev. by D. Birm-
ingham, History, 58(Je 1973):326-7; R. H. Davis, Jr., SS, 64
(Nov. 1973):290-1.

Gara, Larry, Intro. The Narrative of William W. Brown: A Fugitive Slave. Reading, Mass.: Addison-Wesley, 1969. Rev. by
W. F. Mugleston, HT, 7(Nov 1973):127; J. L. Franklin, CWH,
19(Sep 1973):285-7.

García-Baquero González, Antonio. Comercio colonial y guerras
revolucionarias. La Decadencia economica de Cádiz a raíz de
la emancipación americana. Seville, Spain: ... Escuela de
Estudios Hispano-Americanos de Sevilla, 1972. Rev. by A.

McFarlane, HAHR, 53(Nov 1973):685-6.

Gardner, Lloyd C., ed. The Korean War. Chicago: Quadrangle, 1972. Rev. by T. Ropp, SS, 64(Nov 1973):286.

Gardner, R. K. A., M. J. Antsee, and C. L. Patterson, eds. Africa and the World. London: Ox U Press, 1970. Rev. by J. Murray, AfAf, 72(Oct 1973):451-2.

Gargan, John J. and James G. Coke. Political Behavior and Public Issues in Ohio. Kent, Ohio: Kent St U Press, 1972. Rev. by F. C. Luebke, JAH, 60(Dec 1973):865-6.

Garlake, Peter S. Great Zimbabwe. London: Thames and Hudson, 1973. Rev. by B. M. Fagan, Antiquity, 47(Dec 1973):330-1.

Garlick, Peter. African Traders and Economic Development in Ghana. London: Clarendon, 1971. Rev. by G. Hart, AfAf, 72(Ja 1973):83.

Garlinski, Jozef. Poland, SOE and the Allies. London: Allen and Unwin, 1969. Rev. by T. Hunizak, EEQ, 7(Spr 1973):98.

Garnel, Donald. The Rise of Teamster Power in the West. Berkeley: U Cal Press, 1972. Rev. by H. Weintraub, PHR, 42 (May 1973):258-9.

Garner, Frank H., ed. Modern British Farming Systems: An Introduction. New York: Barnes and Noble, 1972. Rev. by J. A. Casada, AgH, 47(Oct 1973):362-3.

Garzouzi, Eva. Economic Growth and Development: The Less Developed Countries. New York: Vantage, 1972. Rev. by I. Oweiss, MEJ, 27(Aut 1973):524.

Gascon, Richard. Grand Commerce et vie Urbaine au XVIe Siècle: Lyon et ses Marchands. Paris: École Pratique des Hautes Études, 1971. Rev. by C. Fairchilds, BHR, 47(Aut 1973):414-6.

Gash, Norman. Sir Robert Peel: The Life of Sir Robert Peel After 1830. Totowa, N. J.: Rowman and Littlefield, 1972. Rev. by W. O. Aydelotte, AHR, 78(Oct 1973):1065-7; Rev. by J. A. Casada, HT, 6(May 1973):482-3.

Gasman, Daniel. The Scientific Origins of National Socialism. London: McDonald, 1971. Rev. by H. W. Koch, History, 58(Feb 1973):136; R. Herzstein, JMH, 45(May 1973):145-7; R. H. Bowen, AHR, 78(Je 1973):711-2.

Gastaldi, Ugo. Storia dell'Anabattismo, dalle origini a Münster (1525-1535). Turin: Editrice Claudiana, 1972. Rev. by R. P. Liebowitz, JMH, 45(Sep 1973):474-5; P. C. Matheson, History,

58(Oct 1973):441-2.

Gatell, Frank Otto <u>see</u> Weinstein, Allen

Gates, John M. <u>Schoolbooks and Krags: The United States Army in the Philippines, 1898-1902.</u> Westport, Conn.: Greenwood, 1973. Rev. by R. Spector, MilAf, 37(Dec 1973):159.

Gatewood, Willard B., Jr. <u>Smoked Yankees and the Struggle for Empire: Letters from Negro Soldiers, 1898-1902.</u> Urbana: U Ill Press, 1971. Rev. by D. F. Tingley, JISHS, 66(Aut 1973): 355-6.

Gaudio, Attilio. <u>Allal el Fassi ou l'Histoire de l'Istiqlal.</u> Paris: Alain Moreau Editions, 1972. Rev. by C. H Moore, MEJ, 27(Win 1973):88-90; L. B. Blair, AHR, 78(Oct 1973):1110-11.

Gayle, Addison. <u>Oak and Ivy: A Biography of Paul Laurence Dun</u>-bar. Garden City, N. Y.: Doubleday, 1971. Rev. G. H. Hudson, JNH, 58(Ja 1973):114-16.

Gebbie, John H. <u>An Introduction to the Abercorn Letters (As Relat</u>-ing to Ireland 1736-1816). Omagh, Northern Ireland: Strule Press, 1971. Rev. by S. N. Bogorad, E-I, 8(Win 1973):153-5.

Geffen, William, ed. <u>Command and Commanders in Modern Warfare: The Proceedings of the Second Military History Symposium, United States Air Force Academy, 2-3 May 1968.</u> Washington: Office of Air Force History, 1971. Rev. by H. L. Coles, JAH, 60(Je 1973):174-5.

Geiger, Hans-Ulrich. <u>Der Beginn der Gold-und Dickmunzen pragung Munzund Geldgeschichte des 15 Jahrhunderts.</u> Bern: the Verein, 1968. Rev. by H. L. Adelson, AHR, 78(Feb 1973): 84-5.

Geiger, Theodore. <u>The Fortunes of the West: The Future of the Atlantic Nations.</u> Bloomington: Ind U Press, 1973. Rev. by T. L. Thompson, CurH, 64(Apr 1973):180.

Gendzier, Irene L. <u>Frantz Fanon: A Critical Study.</u> New York: Pantheon, 1973. Rev. by V. M. Smith, AHR, 78(Oct 1973): 1023; J. W. Ivy, Crisis, 80(Nov 1973):321-2.

<u>The Genesis of the Frontier Thesis: A Study in Historical Crea</u>-tivity. San Marino, Cal.: Huntington Library, 1971. Rev. by M. S. O'Bryan, PacH, 17(Sum 1973):84-6.

George, Victor and Paul Wilding. <u>Motherless Families.</u> Boston: Routledge and Kegan Paul, 1972. Rev. by S. Jacobs, SS, 64 (Nov 1973):287-8.

Georgescu, Vlad. <u>Political Ideas and the Enlightenment in the</u>

Rumaniån Principalities (1750-1831). Boulder, Colo.: East
European Quarterly, 1971. Rev. by K. Hitchins, AHR, 78(Dec
1973):1495-6; J. Tucker, JMH, 45(Dec 1973):673-4.

Georgetta, Clel. Golden Fleece in Nevada. Reno, Nev.: Venture,
1972. Rev. by G. Dangberg, NHSQ, 16(Spr 1973):41-2.

Gérard-Libois, J. and José Gotovitch. L'an 40. La Belgique Occupée. Brussels: Editions du Crisp, 1971. Rev. by A.
Adamthwaite, History, 58(Oct 1973):474; W. Warmbrunn, JMH,
45(Sep 1973):549-50.

Gerbaud, G., A. Lamadon, and D. Martin, and J. Pételet. La
revolution dans le Puy-de-Dôme. Paris: Bibliothèque Nationale, 1972. Rev. by J. R. Vignery, JMH, 45(Sep 1973):498-9.

Gerdts, William H. and Russell Burke. American Still-Life Painting.
New York: Praeger, 1971. Rev. by C. C. Sellers, NYHSQ,
57(Ja 1973):93-4.

Gerhard, Peter. A Guide to the Historical Geography of New Spain.
Cambridge: Cam U Press, 1972. Rev. by W. B. Taylor,
Historian, 35(Feb 1973):318-9; W. Osborn, HAHR, 53(Aug
1973):504-5.

Gerstell, Vivian S. Silversmiths of Lancaster, Pennsylvania, 1730-
1850. Lancaster: Lancaster Co. Historical Society, 1972.
Rev. by L. C. Madeira, PMHB, 97(Apr 1973):255-6.

Gerteis, Louis S. From Contraband to Freedman: Federal Policy
Toward Southern Blacks, 1861-1865. Westport, Conn.: Greenwood, 1973. Rev. by J. A. Hodges, HRNB, 2(Nov/Dec 1973):
53-4.

Gestrin, Ferdo. Mitninski knifge 16. in 17. stoletja na Slovenskem.
Ljubljana: Slovenska akademija znanosti im umetnosti, 1972.
Rev. by T. Hocevar, JEH, 33(Dec 1973):888-9.

Geyl, P. Pennestrud over Staat en Histoire. Opstellen over de
Vaderlandse Geshidenis Aangeunld met Geyl's Levensverhaal
(Tot 1945). Groningen Wolters-Noordhoff, 1971. Rev. by J.
L. Price, History, 58(Feb 1973):103-4.

Gibb, Sir Hamilton A. R. The Life of Saladin: From the Works of
Imad ad-Din and Baha' ad-Din. New York: Ox U Press, 1973.
Rev. by W. Spencer, HRNB, 2(Oct 1973):12.

_____. The Travels of Ibn Battuta (A.D. 1325-1354). Vol. III.
New York: Cam U Press, 1972. Rev. by G. F. Hourani,
MEJ, 27(Spr 1973):221-2.

Gibson, Arrell M. The Chickasaws. Norman: U Ok Press, 1971.
Rev. by D. H. Corkran, WHQ, 4(Ap 1973):211-12.

. Wilderness Bonanza: The Tri-State District of Missouri,
Kansas, and Oklahoma. Norman: U Ok Press, 1972. Rev.
by W. S. Greener, JAH, 60(Je 1973):144-5; G. G. Suggs, Jr.,
A & W, 15(Aut 1973):278-9; S. Carroll, Montana, 23(Aut 1973):
73; J. D. Norris, BHR, 47(Aut 1973):390-1; C. C. Spence,
JSH, 39(Nov 1973):628-9.

Gibson, James R. Feeding the Russian Fur Trade: Provisionment
of the Okhotsk Seaboard, 1639-1856. Milwaukee: U Wis Press,
1969. Rev. by L. K D. Kristof, CHR, 54(Mar 1973):104-5.

Gibson, Richard. African Liberation Movements: Contemporary
Struggles Against White Minority Rule. New York: Ox U
Press, 1972. Rev. by O. E. S., CurH, 64(Mar 1973):126;
J. B. Bell, MilAf, 37(Dec 1973):155-7.

Gibson, William. American Primitive: The Words of John and
Abigail Adams. New York: Atheneum, 1972. Rev. by R. A.
Brown, SS, 64(Mar 1973):139.

Gies, Joseph and Frances. Merchants and Moneymen: The Commercial Revolution, 1000-1500. New York: Crowell, 1972.
Rev. by J. C. Russell, BHR, 47(Spr 1973):127-8.

Gifford, James F., Jr. The Evolution of a Medical Center: A History of Medicine at Duke University to 1941. Durham, N. C.:
Duke U Press, 1972. Rev. by J H. Young, JSH, 39(Feb
1973):139-41; D. Long, NCHR, 50(Aut 1973):419-20.

Gifford, Prosser and William Roger Louis, eds. France and Britain
in Africa: Imperial Rivalry and Colonial Rule. New Haven,
Conn.: Yale U Press, 1967. Rev. by J. R. Dukes, HT, 6
(Feb 1973):324; R. Bullen, EHR, 88(Oct 1973):864-6; P. Hatton, History, 58(Je 1973):325; O. E. S., CurH, 64(Mar 1973):
125; I. R. Smith, AfAf, 72(Oct 1973):447-8.

Gilbert, Bentley B. British Social Policy 1914-1939. Ithaca, N. Y.:
Cornell U Press, 1970. Rev. by G. Sutherland, HJ, 16(Je
1973):420-31.

Gilbert, Charles, ed. The Making of a Conglomerate. Hempstead,
N. Y.: Hofstra U Yearbook, 1972. Rev. by N. Berg, BHR,
47(Win 1973):539-40.

Gilbert, Edmund W. British Pioneers in Geography. New York:
Barnes and Noble, 1972. Rev. by D. G. G. Kerr, AHR, 78
(Je 1973):652-3.

Gilbert, Felix. The End of the European Era, 1890 to the Present.
London: Weidenfeld and Nicolson, 1971. Rev. by R. Bullen,
History, 58(Feb 1973):113-14.

and Stephen R. Graubard, eds. Historical Studies Today.

New York: Norton, 1972. Rev. by R. H. Bradford, WVH, 34(Ja 1973):212-13; R. H., MilAf, 37(Feb 1973):31; M. Curti, PHR, 42(Feb 1973):101-2; W. Rundell, Jr., SS, 64(Oct 1973): 235.

Gilbert, James. Designing the Industrial State: The Intellectual Pursuit of Collectivism in America, 1880-1940. Chicago: Quadrangle, 1972. Rev. by M. Levine, WMH, 56(Spr 1973): 244-5; J. P. Diggins, JAH, 59(Mar 1973):1016-18; A. Hoogenboom, JSH, 39(Feb 1973):128-9; E. C. Kirkland, BHR, 47 (Win 1973):516-18; C. L. Sanford, T & C, 14(Apr 1973):333-7.

Gilbert, Martin. Winston S. Churchill. Vol. 3. 1914-1916. London: Heineman, 1971. Rev. by H. Pelling, History, 58(Feb 1973):133-5.

Gilbreath, Kent. Red Capitalism: An Analysis of the Navajo Economy. Norman: U Ok Press, 1973. Rev. by D. L. Smith, JAriH, 14(Aut 1973):259-61.

Gilchrist, J. and W. J. Murray, eds. The Press in the French Revolution. London: Ginn, 1971. Rev. by C. Lucas, History, 58(Oct 1973):453.

Gildas, Bernard. Le Secrétariat d'État et le Conseil Espagnol des Indes (1700-1808). Geneve-Paris: Librairie Droz, 1972. Rev. by J. Lynch, ESR, 3(Jl 1973):309-10; R. Pike, JMH, 45(Sep 1973):500.

Giles, F. J. Ikhnaton: Legend and History. Cranbury, N. J.: Fairleigh Dickinson U Press, 1970. Rev. by J. Weinstein, Archaeology, 26(Jl 1973):232.

Gilhooley, Leonard. Contradiction and Dilemma: Orestes Brownson and the American Idea. New York: Fordham U Press, 1972. Rev. by J. L. Wakelyn, CWH, 19(Dec 1973):358-9; R. Lora, JAH, 60(Sep 1973):438-9.

Gilison, Jerome M. British and Soviet Politics: Legitimacy and Convergence. Baltimore: JHU Press, 1972. Rev. by J. S. Reshetar, Jr., RR, 32(Jl 1973):321-2.

Gill, Harold B., Jr. The Apothecary in Colonial Virginia. Charlottesville: U Press Va, 1972. Rev. by G. W. Jones, VMHB, 81(Apr 1973):202-3.

Gilliam, Harold. For Better or For Worse: The Ecology of an Urban Area. San Francisco: Chronicle Books, 1972. Rev. by T. J. Kent, Jr., CHQ, 52(Win 1973):373.

Gillis, John R. The Prussian Bureaucracy in Crisis, 1840-1860: Origins of an Administrative Ethos. Stanford, Cal.: Stan U Press, 1971. Rev. by W. Carr, History, 58(Je 1973):309;

P. R. Duggan, JMH, 45(Mar 1973):143-5.

Gillispie, Charles Coulson, ed. Dictionary of Scientific Biography. Vol. 1, Pierre Abelard--L. S. Berg; Vol. 2, Hans-Berger-- Christoph Ballot. New York: Scribner's, 1970. Rev. by R. G. Colodny, AHR, 78(Feb 1973):64-5.

_____. Lazare Carnot, Savant. Princeton, N. J.: Prin U Press, 1971. Rev. by W. Coleman, JMH, 45(Sep 1973):495-6; D. S. L. Cardwell, T & C, 14(Oct 1973):624-6.

Gillman, Joseph M. The B'nai Khaim in America. Philadelphia: Dorrance, 1969. Rev. by P. A. Kalisch, AJHQ, 63(Sep 1973): 95-7.

Gillmor, C. Stewart. Coulomb and the Evolution of Physics and Engineering in Eighteenth-Century France. Princeton, N. J.: Prin U Press, 1971. Rev. by R. M. McKeon, T & C, 14 (Apr 1973):294-6; W. Coleman, JMH, 45(Sep 1973):495-6.

Gilman, Stephen. The Spain of Fernando de Rojas: The Intellectual and Social Landscape of La Celestina. Princeton, N. J.: Prin U Press, 1972. Rev. by W. D. Phillips, Jr., HAHR, 53(Aug 1973):532-4.

Gilmore, Myron P., ed. Studies on Machiavelli. Florence: G. C. Sansoni Editore, 1972. Rev. by J. Kirshner, JMH, 45(Sep 1973):484-5.

Gimbutas, Marija. The Slavs. New York: Praeger, 1971. Rev. by W. S. Vucinich, RR, 32(Ja 1973):95.

Gippius, Zinaida. Selected Works. Urbana: U Ill Press, 1972. Rev. by J. Brooks, RR, 32(Jl 1973):332.

Gitelman, Zvi Y. Jewish Nationality and Soviet Politics: The Jewish Sections of the CPSU, 1917-30. Princeton, N. J.: Prin U Press, 1972. Rev. by W. Korey, RR, 32(Oct 1973):438-40.

Gittell, Marilyn, Ann Cook, and Herb Mack, eds. City Life, 1865- 1900: Views of Urban America. New York: Praeger, 1973. Rev. by P. L. Simon, HRNB, 2(Nov/Dec 1973):47.

Gjevre, John A. Saga of the Soo: West from Shoreham. n. p.: Privately Printed by Author, 1973. Rev. by D. L. Hofsommer, NDH, 40(Fall 1973):30-1.

Gladstone, William Ewart. The Prime Ministers' Papers: W. E. Gladstone. I. Autobiographical. London: H. M. S. O., 1971. Rev. by A. Ramm, Archives 11(Spr 1973):57-8.

Glanz, Rudolf. The Jew in Early American Wit and Graphic Humor. New York: KTAV, 1973. Rev. by M. R. Rubinoff, WPHM,

56(Oct 1973):431-3; L. J. Iorizzo, HRNB, 2(Oct 1973):14; GHQ,
57(Win 1973):605-6.

_____. Studies in Judaica Americana. New York: KTAV, 1971.
Rev. by J. A. Feld, MHM, 68(Spr 1973):115.

Glaskow, General Wasili G. History of the Cossacks. New York:
Speller, 1972. Rev. by B. W. Menning, RR, 32(Apr 1973):
205-7.

Gleason, Abbott. European and Muscovite: Ivan Kireevsky and the
Origins of Slavophilism. Cambridge, Mass.: Har U Press,
1972. Rev. by J. A. Rogers, JMH, 45(Dec 1973):694-5; P. P.
Dunn, RR, 32(Ja 1973):91-2.

Glenny, Michael and G. R. Urban, eds. Can We Survive Our Future.
New York: St. Martin's, 1972. Rev. by H. J. Muller,
T & C, 14(Ja 1973):100-8.

Glick, Thomas F. Irrigation and Society in Medieval Valencia. Cambridge, Mass.: Belknap Press, 1970. Rev. by R. I. Burns,
JIH, 4(Aut 1973):302-4.

_____. The Old World Background of the Irrigation System of
San Antonio, Texas. El Paso: Texas Western Press, 1972.
Rev. by J. A. Garcia-Diego, T & C, 14(Oct 1973):622-4; M.
Simmons, HAHR, 53(Nov 1973):727.

Glines, Carroll V. Jimmy Doolittle: Daredevil Aviator and Scientist.
New York: Macmillan, 1972. Rev. by R. P. Hallion, T & C,
14(Oct 1973):653-5.

Glob, P. V. The Bog People: Iron-Age Man Preserved. Ithaca,
N. Y.: Cornell U Press, 1969. Rev. by S. Foltiny, Archaeology, 26(Ja 1973):74.

Glover, Michael. Legacy of Glory: The Bonaparte Kingdom of Spain,
1808-1813. New York: Scribner's, 1971. Rev. by W. J. Callahan, JMH, 45(Je 1973):313-4; J. G. Gallaher, MilAf, 37
(Oct 1973):112.

Glyn, Andrew and Bob Sutcliffe. Capitalism in Crisis. New York:
Pantheon, 1972. Rev. by D. F. Channon, BHR, 47(Win 1973):
552-4.

Godin, Andre. Spiritualite Franciscaine en Flandre au XVIe Siècle:
L'Homéliaire de Jean Vitrier. Geneva: Droz, 1971. Rev. by
M. M Phillips, ESR, 3(Oct 1973):395-6.

Goebel, Julius, Jr. History of the Supreme Court of the United
States. Vol. I. Antecedents and Beginnings to 1801. New
York: Macmillan, 1971. Rev. by F. McDonald, JAH, 59(Mar
1973):994-6.

Goetze, Sigmund. Die Politik des schwedischen Reichskanzlers Axel
    Oxenstierna gegenüber Kaiser und Reich. Kiel: Kommissions-
    verlag Walter G. Mühlau, 1971. Rev. by W. Kirchner, AHR,
    78(Oct 1973):1086-8; M. Roberts, JMH, 45(Je 1973):302-5.

Goetzmann, William H. , ed. The Colonial System: America in the
    Sixteenth and Seventeenth Centuries. Reading, Mass.: Addi-
    son-Wesley, 1969. Rev. by J. L. Susskind, HT, 7(Nov 1973):
    122-3.

Goitein, S. D. A Mediterranean Society, the Jewish Community of
    the Arab World as Portrayed in the Documents of the Cairo
    Geniza. Vol. II. The Community. Berkeley: U Cal Press,
    1971. Rev. by W. B. Bishai, MEJ, 27(Sum 1973):392-3.

Golan, Galia. The Czechoslovak Reform Movement: Communism in
    Crisis, 1962-1968. London: Cam U Press, 1972. Rev. by
    A. Z. Rubenstein, CurH, 64(May 1973):224.

_____. Reform Rule in Czechoslovakia: The Dubček Era 1968-
    1969. New York: Cam U Press, 1973. Rev. by A. Z.
    Rubenstein, CurH, 64(May 1973):224.

Goldberg, Gerry and George Wright, eds. I Am a Sensation. To-
    ronto: McClelland and Stewart, 1971. Rev. by T. Benjamin,
    PacH, 17(Spr 1973):96.

Goldberg, Harvey. Cave Dwellers and Citrus Growers: A Jewish
    Community in Libya and Israel. New York: Cam U Press,
    1972. Rev. by A. Weingrod, MEJ, 27(Spr 1973):237-9.

Goldbold, E. Stanley, Jr. Ellen Glasgow and the Woman Within.
    Baton Rouge: LSU Press, 1972. Rev. by F. G. Davenport,
    Jr. , JSH, 39(Feb 1973):131-2.

Goldhamer, Herbert. The Foreign Powers in Latin America.
    Princeton, N. J.: Prin U Press, 1972. Rev. by R. Fontaine,
    HAHR, 53(Nov 1973):713-5.

Goldman, Marshall I. The Spoils of Progress: Environmental Pol-
    lution in the Soviet Union. Cambridge, Mass.: M I T Press,
    1972. Rev. by J. G. Tolpin, RR, 32(Apr 1973):213-4.

Goldsby, Richard A. Race and Races. New York: Macmillan, 1971.
    Rev. by B. P. Bradley, JNH, 58(Ja 1973):104-6.

Goldstein, Milton. The Magnificent West: Yosemite. New York:
    Doubleday, 1972. Rev. by S. Warrick, ChOk, 51(Win 1973-
    74):498-9.

Goldthwaite, Richard A. see Baldwin, John W.

Goldwert, Marvin. Democracy, Militarism and Nationalism in

Argentina, 1930-1966--An Interpretation. Austin: U Tx Press, 1972. Rev. by L. Hogan, TAm, 30(Oct 1973):284-5; P. Snow, HAHR, 53(Jl 1973):341-3.

Golson, J. and D. J. Mulvaney, eds. Aboriginal Man and Environment in Australia. Canberra: Australian National U Press, 1971. Rev. by R. A. Gould, AmAn, 38(Oct 1973):507-8.

Góngora, Mario. Encomenderos y estancieros: Estudios acerea de constitución social aristocratica de Chile después de la conquista, 1580-1660. Santiago de Chile: Editorial Universitaria, 1970. Rev. by T. S. Floyd, AHR, 78(Feb 1973):189.

González Orellana, Carlos. Historia de la educación en Guatemala. Guatemala: Editorial José de Pineda Ibarra, 1968, 1970. Rev. by J. M. Lay, HAHR, 53(Aug 1973):494-5.

Goodman, Anthony. The Loyal Conspiracy: The Lords Appellant Under Richard II. Coral Gables, Fla.: U Miami Press, 1971. Rev. by B. C. Weber, Historian, 35(Feb 1973):281-2; J. R. Maddicott, History, 58(Feb 1973):89-90.

Goodspeed's General History of Tennessee. Nashville, Tenn.: Charles and Randy Elder, 1973. Rev. by S. F. Horn, THQ, 32(Fall 1973):299-300.

Gopalan, A. K. In the Cause of the People: Reminiscences. New Delhi: Orient Longman's, 1973. Rev. by K. C. Kohli, IQ, 29 (Oct-Dec 1973):363-4.

Gordon, David C. Self-Determination and History in the Third World. Princeton, N. J.: Prin U Press, 1971. Rev. by R. L. Tignor, AHR, 78(Oct 1973):1022-3.

Gordon, Dudley. Charles F. Lummis: Crusader in Corduroy. Los Angeles: Cultural Assets Press, 1972. Rev. by J. W. Caughey, CHQ, 52(Sum 1973):177; W. H. Lyon, JOW, 12(Oct 1973):637; D. M. McComb, PacH, 17(Fall 1973):63-5.

Gordon, Harold J., Jr. Hitler and the Beer Hall Putsch. Princeton, N. J.: Prin U Press, 1972. Rev. by P. Pulzer, AHR, 78(Oct 1973):1093; F. Dumin, Historian, 36(Nov 1973):111-12.

Gordon, Roxy. Some Things I Did. Austin, Tx.: Encino, 1971. Rev. by J. B. Pearson, Jr., SWHQ, 76(Ja 1973):351-2.

Gorewicz, Jerzy. Technical Thought and Protection Against Moisture in Industrial Building in the Polish Kingdom of the First Half of the XIXth Century. Warsaw: Polish Academy of Sciences, 1972. Rev. by C. W. Condit and J. Zbilut, T & C, 14(Jl 1973):505-6.

Gossman, Lionel. French Society and Culture: Background for

Eighteenth Century Literature. Englewood Cliffs, N. J.: Prentice-Hall, 1972. Rev. by K. M. Baker, AHR, 78(Dec 1973):
1475-6.

Gotovitch, José see Gerard-Libois, J.

Gott, Richard. Guerilla Movements in Latin America. Garden City,
N. Y.: Doubleday, 1971. Rev. by H. A. Candsberger, CSSH,
15(Je 1973):378-88.

Gottschalk, Louis and Margaret Maddox. Lafayette in the French
Revolution: From the October Days Through the Federation.
Chicago: U Chi Press, 1973. Rev. by G. Downum, HRNB,
2(Nov/Dec 1973):26-7.

Goubert, Pierre. Louis XIV and Twenty Million Frenchmen. London: Penguin, 1970. Rev. by J. H. Shennan, History, 58(Oct
1973):450.

Gough, Barry M. The Royal Navy on the Northwest Coast of North
America, 1810-1914: A Study of the British Maritime Ascendency. Vancouver: U BC Press, 1971. Rev. by C. J. Bartlett, History, 58(Feb 1973):154-5.

Gould, Lewis L. Progressives and Prohibitionists: Texas Democrats in the Wilson Era. Austin: U Tx Press, 1973. Rev.
by M Cantor, HRNB, 2(Oct 1973):13-14.

Goulder, Grace. John D. Rockefeller. The Cleveland Years. Cleveland, O.: Western Reserve Historical Society, 1972. Rev. by
C. D. S., IS, 29(Sum 1973):158.

Goulet, Denis. The Cruel Choice: A New Concept in the Theory of
Development. New York: Atheneum, 1971. Rev. by D. H.
Pollock, TAm, 29(Ja 1973):395-7.

Goure, Leon see Harvey, Mose L.

Le Gouvernement de Vichy, 1940-1942: Institutions and politiques.
Paris: Armand Colin, 1972. Rev. by P. C. F. Bankwitz,
AHR, 78(Oct 1973):1081-2.

Grab, Walter see Friesel, Uwe

Graber, Kay and Thomas Henry Tribbles, eds. The Ponca Chiefs:
An Account of the Trial of Standing Bear. Lincoln: U Neb
Press, 1972. Rev. by L. J. White, JOW, 12(Oct 1973):640.

Grabert, G. F. The Astor Fort Okanogan. Seattle: U Wash Press,
1968. Rev. by B. R. Butler, AmAnt, 38(Oct 1973):508-9.

_____. North-Central Washington Prehistory. Seattle: U Wash,
1968. Rev. by B. R. Butler, AmAnt, 38(Oct 1973):508-9.

Grade, Arnold, ed. Family Letters of Robert and Elinor Frost.
   Albany: SUNY Press, 1972. Rev. by R. L. Cook, VH, 41
   (Win 1973):55-7.

Gradwohl, David Mayer. Prehistoric Villages in Eastern Nebraska.
   Lincoln: Neb State Historical Society, 1969. Rev. by W. R.
   AmAnt, 38(Apr 1973):246-7.

Graells, Eudald. La indústria dels claus a Ripoll. Contribució a
   l'estudi de la farga catalana. Barcelona: Fundació Vives
   Casajuana, 1972. Rev. by T. F. Glick, T & C, 14(Jl 1973):
   499-500.

Graf, Leroy P., Ralph W. Haskins, and Patricia P. Clark, eds.
   The Papers of Andrew Johnson. Volume III, 1858-1860. Knox-
   ville: U Tenn Press, 1972. Rev. by F. B. Williams, Jr.,
   THQ, 32(Apr 1973):93-5; R. A. Heckman, IMH, 69(Dec 1973):
   372-4; J. H Parks, JAH, 60(Dec 1973):752-3; D. H. Donald,
   NCHR, 50(Sum 1973):330-1.

Graham, Loren R. Science and Philosophy in the Soviet Union. New
   York: Knopf, 1972. Rev. by A. Vucinich, AHR, 78(Feb 1973):
   131-2; W. McClellan, T & C, 14(Oct 1973):676-7.

Graham, Richard. Independence in Latin America: A Comparative
   Approach. New York: Knopf, 1972. Rev. by D. Bushnell,
   HAHR, 53(Feb 1973):126-7.

Grainger, Gervis D. Four Years with the Boys in Gray. Franklin,
   Ky.: Favorite Press, 1902. Reprinted by Press, Morningside
   Bookshop, Dayton, O., 1972. Rev. by G. Tucker, FCHQ, 47
   (Ja 1973):59-60.

Granados, Anastasio. El Cardenal Gomá: Primado de España.
   Madrid: Espasa-Calpe, S. A., 1969. Rev. by P. A. Linehan,
   HJ, 16(Sep 1973):652-6.

Granfelt, Helge. Alliances and Ententes as Political Weapons: From
   Bismarck's Alliance System to Present Time. Lund: C W K
   Gleerup, 1970. Rev. by H. D. Andrews, AHR, 78(Je 1973):659.

Granoien, Neil and Michael Green, eds. and trans. Mikhail Kuzmin's 'Wings: Prose and Poetry.' Ann Arbor, Mich.: Ardis,
   1972. Rev. by J. Brooks, RR, 32(Jl 1973):332-3.

Grant, Charles. The War Game. New York: St. Martin's, 1971.
   Rev. by R. J. Sommers, MilAf, 37(Dec 1973):158.

Grant, George. Time as History. Toronto: Canadian Broadcasting
   Co., 1971. Rev. by W. H. Dray, CHR, 54(Mar 1973):79-80.

Grant, Michael. The Jews in the Roman World. New York: Scribner's, 1973. Rev. by O. W. Reinmuth, HRNB, 2(Oct 1973):10.

_____. The Roman Forum. New York: Macmillan, 1970. Rev. by A. Laidlaw, Archaeology, 26(Ja 1973):69-70.

Grattan-Guinness, I. Joseph Fourier, 1768-1830. Cambridge, Reb. Mass.: M I T Press, 1972. Rev. by C. S. Gillmor, T & C, 14(Jl 1973):501-3.

Graubard, Stephen R. see Gilbert, Felix

Graves, Richard. Bushcraft: A Serious Guide to Survival and Camping. New York: Schocken, 1972. Rev. by G. E. Bessey, JOW, 12(Apr 1973):343.

Graymont, Barbara. The Iroquois in the American Revolution. Syracuse, N. Y.: Syr U Press, 1972. Rev. by C. G. Klopfenstein, WHQ, 4(Apr 1973):207-8; C. M. Johnston, CHR, 54 (Sep 1973):329-30; K. B. West, MichH, 57(Sum 1973):177-8; J. Shy, MilAf, 37(Oct 1973):110; D. M. Roper, NYHSQ, 57 (Ja 1973):89-91; A. S. Brown, HT, 6(Feb 1973):326; A. F. C. Wallace, PHR, 42(Feb 1973):106-7; F. Jennings, PH, 40 (Jl 1973):228-31; R. G. Carlson, VH, 41(Spr 1973):103-4.

Grayson, A. Kirk and Donald B. Redford, eds. Papyrus and Tablet. Englewood Cliffs, N. J.: Prentice-Hall, 1973. Rev. by B. M. Fagan, HRNB, 2(Nov/Dec 1973):34.

Grayson, George. El Partido Demócrata cristiano chileno. Buenos Aires and Santiago de Chile: Editorial Francisco de Aguirre, 1968. Rev. by A. von Lazar, HAHR, 53(Aug 1973):552-5.

Greeley, Andrew M. That Most Distressful Nation: The Taming of the American Irish. Chicago: Quadrangle, 1972. Rev. by J. B. Duff, JAH, 59(Mar 1973):1001-2.

Green, Archie. Only a Miner. Studies in Recorded Coal-Mining Songs. Urbana: U Ill Press, 1972. Rev. by K. R. Bailey, WVH, 34(Ja 1973):215-16; S. Lynd, AHR, 78(Feb 1973):169-70.

Green, Ben K. Some More Horse Tradin'. New York: Knopf, 1972. Rev. by M. Simmons, SWHQ, 76(Apr 1973):492-3.

Green, C. W. see Burston, W. H.

Green, Fletcher M. The Role of the Yankee in the Old South. Athens, Ga.: U Ga Press, 1972. Rev. by P. Kolchin, JSH, 39(May 1973):288-9; H. S. Stroupe, NCHR, 50(Spr 1973):210-1; W. K. Scarborough, WVH, 34(Jl 1973):391-3; C. B. Dew, JAH, 60(Je 1973):125-7; W. H. J. Thomas, SCHM, 74(Apr 1973):105-6.

Green, George D. Finance and Economic Development in the Old South: Louisiana Banking, 1804-1861. Stanford, Cal.: Stan U Press, 1972. Rev. by F. R. Marshall, JSH, 39(Feb 1973):

111-3; H. N. Scheiber, AHR, 78(Oct 1973):1126-7; D. O.
Whitten, LaH, 14(Fall 1973):405-6; H. Rockoff, JEH, 33(Je
1973):482-3; J. R. Sharp, AgH, 47(Apr 1973):182-3.

Green, Louis. Chronicle Into History. Cambridge: Cam U Press,
1972. Rev. by M. B. Becker, Historian, 36(Nov 1973):97-8.

Green, Peter. The Shadow of the Parthenon: Studies in Ancient
History and Literature. Berkeley: U Cal Press, 1972. Rev.
by P. Mackendrick, AHR, 78(Oct 1973):1027.

Greene, A. C. The Last Captive. Austin, Tx.: Encino, 1972.
Rev. by J. Suberi, JOW, 12(Ja 1973):183.

Greenhalgh, P. A. L. Early Greek Warfare. Cambridge: Cam U
Press, 1973. J. K. Anderson, Antiquity, 47(Dec 1973):335-6.

Greenway, D. E., ed. Charters of the House of Mowbray, 1107-
1191. New York: Ox U Press, 1972. Rev. by R. B. Patterson, AHR, 78(Dec 1973):1436; R. H. C. Davis, History, 58
(Oct 1973):432.

Greenwood, John O. Namesakes II. Cleveland, O.: Freshwater
Press, 1973. Rev. by D. T. B., IS, 29(Sum 1973):159-60.

Greenwood, W. Bart and Edwin B. Hooper, comps. The American
Revolution, 1775-1783. An Atlas of Eighteenth-Century Maps
and Charts. Washington: Naval History Div., Dept. of Navy,
1972. Rev. by G. G. Shackelford, VMHB, 81(Oct 1973):493-4;
GHQ, 57(Win 1973):606.

Gregory, Malcolm S. History and Development of Engineering.
London: Longmans, 1971. Rev. by C. O. Smith, Jr., T & C,
14(Apr 1973):288-9.

Gregory, Robert G. India and East Africa: A History of Race Relations Within the British Empire, 1890-1939. Oxford: Clarendon, 1971. Rev. by K. K. Janmohamed, AfAf, 72(Ja 1973):
90; J. Lansdale, History, 58(Je 1973):328-9; N. A. Motani,
JAfH, 14(No. 2 1973):347-9.

Gregory, Ross. The Origins of American Intervention in the First
World War. New York: Norton, 1971. Rev. by R. Simmons,
WVA, 34(Ja 1973):214-15; J. B. Startt, SS, 64(Apr 1973):180.

Grieff, Constance M., ed. Lost America: From the Mississippi to
the Pacific. Princeton, N. J.: Pyne, 1972. Rev. by W.
Carter, AW, 10(Jl 1973):50; J. H. Bernstein, Montana, 23
(Aut 1973):72.

Grewal, J. S. Muslim Rule in India: The Assessments of British
Historians. New York: Ox U Press, 1970. Rev. by F. Lehmann, AHR, 78(Je 1973):721-3.

Grey, Ian.   The Romanovs: The Rise and Fall of a Russian Dynasty.   Newton Abbot: David and Charles, 1971.   Rev. by Paul
Dukes, History, 58(Feb 1973):167-8.

Grez, Vincente.   El combate homérico, 21 de mayo de 1879.
Buenos Aires, Argentina: Editorial Francisco de Aguirre,
1968 (1880).   Rev. by W. L. Krieg, HAHR, 53(Aug 1973):569-
70.

Gribben, William.   The Churches Militant: The War of 1812 and
American Religion.   New Haven, Conn.:   Yale U Press, 1973.
Rev. by J. B. Boles, JAH, 60(Dec 1973):805-6; M. Borden,
JSH, 39(Nov 1973):592-3;   C. J Phillips, NYHSQ, 57(Oct
1973):360-1.

Griest, Guinevere L.   Mudie's Circulating Library and the Victorian
Novel.   Newton Abbot: David and Charles, 1971.   Rev. by
G. Sutherland, History, 58(Oct 1973):463-4.

Griffin, A. R.   Coalmining.   London: Longmans, 1971.   Rev. by
J. E. Williams, History, 58(Oct 1973):479.

Griffin, Charles C., ed.   Latin America: A Guide to the Historical
Literature.   Austin: U Tx Press, 1971.   Rev. by S. B.
Schwartz and P. Johnson, HAHR, 53(May 1973):302-4.

Griffin, Robert A., Intro.   Reminiscences of Alexander Toponce,
Written by Himself.   Norman: U Ok Press, 1971.   Rev. by
P. I. Earl, NHSQ, 16(Sum 1973):135-7.

Griffith, A. Kenny   see   Cochise, Ciyé "Nino"

Griffith, Lucille.   Alabama: A Documentary History to 1900.   University: U Ala Press, 1972.   Rev. by E. C. Williamson,
FHQ, 51(Apr 1973):457-9;   GHQ, 57(Fall 1973):452;   R. E.
Corlew, JMiH, 35(May 1973):212-13;   J. F. Doster, NCHR,
50(Win 1973):100-1.

Griffiths, Ralph A.   The Principality of Wales in the Later Middle
Ages: The Structure and Personnel of Government.   I.   South
Wales, 1277-1536.   Rev. by A. D. Carr, History, 58(Je 1973):
258.

Grindle, Roger L.   Quarry and Kiln: The Story of Maine's Lime
Industry.   Rockland: Courier-Gazette, 1971.   Rev. by G. B.
Engberg, JAH, 59(Mar 1973):1019-20;   J. W. Eastman, BHR,
47(Aut 1973):529-30.

Grohskopf, Bernice.   The Treasure of Sutton Hoo: Ship-Burial for
an Anglo-Saxon King.   New York: Atheneum, 1970.   Rev. by
S. A. Glass, Archaeology, 26(Ja 1973):74-5.

Gromyko, A. A., et al., eds.   Documents on the Foreign Policy of

the USSR. Vols. 16, 17. Moscow: Izdatel'stvo Politicheskoi
Literatury, 1970, 1971. Rev. by R. Himmer, AHR, 78(Oct
1973):1101-2.

Groner, Alex. The History of American Business and Industry.
New York: American Heritage, 1972. Rev. by R. I. Fries,
BHR, 47(Aut 1973):378-80.

Grubbs, Donald. Cry from the Cotton: The Southern Tenant Farmers' Union and the New Deal. Chapel Hill: UNC Press, 1971.
Rev. by A. J. Badger, HJ, 16(Mar 1973):220-2.

Gruber, Ira D. The Howe Brothers and the American Revolution.
New York: Atheneum ... 1972. Rev. by P. Mackesy, WMQ,
3rd ser., 30(Ja 1973):158-60; H. W. Peckham, JAH, 60(Je
1973):117-18; T. C. Barrow, JSH, 39(Feb 1973):107-8; R. F.
Weigley, MHM, 68(Sum 1973):219-20; R. K. Murdock, GHQ,
57(Spr 1973):152-3; P. F. Lambert, NYHSQ, 57(Apr 1973):
179-80; H. F. Rankin, NCHR, 50(Win 1973):108-10.

Gruder, Vivian R. The Royal Provincial Intendants: A Governing
Elite in Eighteenth-Century France. Ithaca, N. Y.: Cornell
U Press, 1968. Rev. by E. Karafiol, JMH, 45(Mar 1973):
116-19.

Grundy, Kenneth W. Guerilla Struggle in Africa: An Analysis and
Preview. New York: Grossman, 1971. Rev. by R. Dale,
AfAf, 72(Oct 1973):452-3.

Gruner, Erich. Die Schweiz seit 1945: Beitrage zur Zeitgeschichte.
Bern: Francke Verlag, 1971. Rev. by J. Steiner and H. E.
Glass, JMH, 45(Mar 1973):188-9.

Gudozhnik, G. S. Scientific-Technical Progress: Essence of Basic
Tendencies. Moscow: Nauka, 1970. Rev. by S. Lieberstein,
T & C, 14(Apr 1973):323-5.

Guerra, Francisco. The Pre-Columbian Mind. New York: Seminar,
1971. Rev. by J. T. Milanich, FHQ, 51(Apr 1973):446-7; G.
Custred, TAm, 30(Jl 1973):132-3; A. Arias-Larreta, HAHR,
53(Feb 1973):158-9.

Guest, Francis F. Fermin Francisco de Lasuen (1736-1803): A Biography. Washington: Academy of American Franciscan History, 1973. Rev. by F. J. Weber, TAm, 30(Oct 1973):287-8;
E. J. Burros, HAHR, 53(Nov 1973):681-2.

Guhin, Michael A. John Foster Dulles: A Statesman and His Times.
New York: Columbia U Press, 1972. Rev. by L. L. Gerson,
JAH, 60(Je 1973):181; J. D. Doenecke, Historian, 36(Nov
1973):135-6; R. E. Bunselmeyer, PHR, 42(May 1973):262-3;
L. C. Gardner, WMH, 56(Sum 1973):347-8.

Guice, John D. W. The Rocky Mountain Bench: The Territorial
Supreme Courts of Colorado, Montana, and Wyoming, 1861-
1890. New Haven: Yale U Press, 1972. Rev. by M. J.
Brodhead, WHQ, 4(Apr 1973):205-6; E. H. White III, A & W,
15(Aut 1973):297-8; L. W. Dorsett, CoMag, 50(Spr 1973):168-
9; A. E. K. Nash, JAH, 60(Je 1973):149-50; J. P. Bloom,
Montana, 23(Spr 1973):73; T. A. Larson, PHR, 42(May 1973):
252-3.

Guido, Margaret. Southern Italy: An Archaeological Guide. London: Faber, 1972. Rev. by D. Ridgway, Antiquity, 47(Sep
1973):250-1.

Guillot, Olivier. Le Comte d'Anjou et son entourage au XIe siècle.
Paris: Editions A. AND J. Picard, 1972. Rev. by M. Chib-
nall, AHR, 78(Je 1973):670-1.

Guinness, Desmond and Julius Trousdale Sadler, Jr. Mr. Jefferson,
Architect. New York: Viking, 1973. Rev. by R. A. Murdock, VMHB, 81(Oct 1973):497-8.

Gujer, Bruno. Free Trade and Slavery: Calhoun's Defense of
Southern Interests Against British Interference, 1811-1848.
Zurich: atu-Fotodruck, 1971. Rev. by A. V. Huff, Jr., JSH,
39(May 1973):286-7.

Gukiina, Peter M. Uganda: A Case Study in African Political De-
velopment. South Bend, Ind.: U Notre Dame Press, 1972.
Rev. by O. E. S., CurH, 64(Mar 1973):126; M. T., AfAf, 72
(Jl 1973):346.

Guldbeck, Per E. The Care of Historical Collections: A Conservation Handbook for the Nonspecialist. Nashville: American
Assn. for State and Local History, 1972. Rev. by A. Neal,
CoMag, 50(Spr 1973):170-1; J. C. Wright, AmArch, 36(Oct
1973):555-8.

Guldescu, Stanko. The Croatian-Slavonian Kingdom, 1526-1792.
The Hague: Mouton, 1970. Rev. by S. Z. Pech, AHR, 78
(Feb 1973):123-4.

Gulhati, Niranjan D. Indus Waters Treaty: An Exercise In International Mediation. Bombay: Allied, 1973. Rev. by T. G.
Ramamurthi, IQ, 29(Oct-Dec 1973):363.

Gumerman, George J. Black Mesa: Survey and Excavation in
Northeastern Arizona, 1968. Prescott, Ariz.: Prescott College, 1970. Rev. by W. J. Judge, AmAnt, 38(Apr 1973):251-3.

Gunn, J. A. W. Factious No More. Attitudes to Party in Government and Opposition in the Eighteenth Century. London: Frank
Cass, 1972. Rev. by I. R. Christie, History, 58(Feb 1973):
111.

Gunter, A. Y. The Big Thicket: A Challenge for Conservation. Austin, Tx.: Jenkins, 1971. Rev. by F. O. Wilson, LaH, 14 (Win 1973):111-12.

Gunther, Erna. Indian Life on the Northwest Coast of North America as Seen by the Early Explorers and Fur Traders During the Last Decades of the Eighteenth Century. Chicago: U Chi Press, 1972. Rev. by B. W. Dippie, AW, 10(Mar 1973):57; A. G Bailey, JAH, 60(Sep 1973):427-8.

Gupta, Bhabani Sen. Communism in Indian Politics. Berkeley: Columbia U Press, 1972. Rev. by R. Rattan, IQ, 29(Apr-Je 1973):172-3.

Gurgani, Fakhr ud-Din. Vis and Ramin. New York: Columbia U Press, 1972. Rev. by P. Avery, MEJ, 27(Win 1973):86-8.

Guterman, Stanley S. Black Psyche: The Modal Personality Patterns of Black Americans. Berkeley, Cal.: Glendessary, 1972. Rev. by R. E. Forman, SS, 64(Nov 1973):289-90.

Guthorn, Peter J. British Maps of the American Revolution. Monmouth Beach, N. J.: Philip Freneau Press, 1973. Rev. by J. D. Black, PMHB, 97(Oct 1973):538-40.

_____. The Seabright Skiff and Other Jersey Shore Boats. New Brunswick, N. J.: Rutgers U Press, 1971. Rev. by F. R. Colie, NJH, 91(Aut 1973):193-4.

Gutman, Herbert G. and Gregory S. Kealey, eds. Many Pasts: Readings in American Social History, 1600-1876. Vol. 1. Englewood Cliffs, N. J.: Prentice-Hall, 1973. Rev. by G. Land, HT, 7(Nov 1973):124; R. J. Palenberg, HRNB, 2(Nov/ Dec 1973):49.

_____ and _____, eds. Many Pasts: Readings in American Social History. Vol. 2. 1865-The Present. Englewood Cliffs, N. J.: Prentice-Hall, 1973. Rev. by R. J. Palenberg, HRNB, 2(Nov/Dec 1973):49.

Gutman, Robert, ed. People and Buildings. New York: Basic Books, 1972. Rev. by C. W. Condit, T & C, 14(Apr 1973): 303-4.

Guttridge, Leonard F. see McGovern, George S.

Gwassa, G. C. K., ed and trans. Kumbukumbu za Vita vya Maji Maji, 1905-1907. Nairobi, Kenya: EAPH, 1969. Rev. by A. Redmayne, AfAf, 72(Oct 1973):464-5.

Gwassa, G. C. K. and John Iliffe, eds. Records of the Maji Maji Rising. (Part 1). Nairobi, Kenya: EAPH, n. d. Rev. by A. Redmayne, AfAf, 72(Ja 1973):91-3.

Haas, Robert Bartlett, ed. William Grant Still and the Fusion of
    Cultures in American Music. Los Angeles: Black Sparrow,
    1972. Rev. by M. D. Hudgins, ArkHQ, 32(Spr 1973):102-4.

Habakkuk, H. J.   Population Growth and Economic Development
    Since 1750. New York: Humanities, 1971. Rev. by P. G.
    Spagnoli, JIH, 4(Aut 1973):312-15.

Hachey, Thomas E. and Ralph E. Weber.   Voices of Revolution.
    Hinsdale, Ill.: Dryden, 1972. Rev. by N. Levine, JNH, 58
    (Oct 1973):482-3.

Hachmann, Rolf. The Ancient Civilization of Germanic Peoples.
    London: Barrie and Jenkins, 1971. Rev. by S. J. DeLaet,
    Antiquity, 47(Mar 1973):82-3.

Hackett, Neil J., et al. The World of Europe. St. Louis: Forum,
    1973. Rev. by J. D. Startt, HT, 7(Nov 1973):111-12; J. L.
    Wieczynski, HT, 7(Nov 1973):112-13.

Hackett, Roger F.   Yamagata Aritomo in the Rise of Modern Japan,
    1838-1922. Cambridge, Mass.: Har U Press, 1971. Rev.
    by K. B. Pyle, AHR, 78(Dec 1973):1513-14.

Haddad, Robert M. Syrian Christians in Muslim Society: An Inter-
    pretation. Princeton, N. J.: Prin U Press, 1970. Rev. by
    F. J. Ziadeh, MEJ, 27(Win 1973):96-7.

Hafen, LeRoy R. and Ann W. The Joyous Journey of LeRoy R. and
    Ann W. Hafen: An Autobiography. Glendale, Cal.: Arthur
    Clark; Denver: Fred A. Rosenstock, 1973. Rev. by G.
    Pfeiffer III, AW, 10(Sep 1973):54.

Hagerman, Robert L. Covered Bridges of Lamoille County. Essex
    Junction: Essex Publishing Co., 1972. Rev. by W. Herning,
    VH, 41(Win 1973):54-5.

Hahn, Marie see Detailed Reports....

Hahn, Richard. The Anatomy of a Scientific Institution: The Paris
    Academy of Sciences, 1666-1803. London: U Cal Press, 1971.
    Rev. by R. Fox, History, 58(Feb 1973):110.

Hahn, Werner G. The Politics of Soviet Agriculture, 1960-1970.
    Baltimore: JHU Press, 1972. Rev. by P. M. Raup, RR, 32
    (Oct 1973):436-7; R. D. Laird, AgH, 47(Oct 1973):356-7.

Haikal, Yusuf. Palestine Before and After. Beirut: Dār al-'Ilm
    lil-Malayīn, 1971. Rev. by E. Ghareeb, MEJ, 27(Sum 1973):
    382-3.

Hainsworth, D. R. The Sydney Traders. Melbourne: Cassell Aus-
    tralia, 1972. Rev. by J. Bach, History, 58(Je 1973):335-6;

A. J. Robinson, JEH, 33(Je 1973):483-4.

Hair, Paul, ed. Before the Bawdy Court. London: Elek, 1972.
Rev. by P. Styles, MH, 2(Aut 1973):123-4.

Halbouty, Michel T. see Clark, James A.

Hale, J. R. Renaissance Europe: Individual and Society, 1480-1520.
New York: Harper and Row, 1971. Rev. by C. Trinkaus,
AHR, 78(Oct 1973):1046.

Haley, J. Evetts and William Curry Holden. The Flamboyant Judge,
James D. Hamlin: A Biography. Canyon, Tx.: Palo Duro
Press, 1972. Rev. by B. Proctor, WHQ, 4(Jl 1973):345-6;
G. Baydo, JAH, 60(Dec 1973):841-2.

Haley, K. D. The Dutch in the Seventeenth Century. London:
Thames and Hudson, 1972. Rev. by J. L. Price, History, 58
(Feb 1973):103-4.

Haley, P. Edward. Revolution and Intervention: The Diplomacy of
Taft and Wilson With Mexico, 1910-1917. Cambridge, Mass.:
M I T Press, 1970. Rev. by R. E. Quirk, HAHR, 53(May
1973):325-7.

Haliburton, Gordon M. The Prophet Harris--A Study of an African
Prophet and His Mass Movement in the Ivory Coast and the
Gold Coast, 1913-1915. New York. Ox U Press, 1973. Rev.
by E. Reynolds, HT, 7(Nov 1973):134-5.

Hall, David D. The Faithful Shepherd: A History of the New England Ministry in the Seventeenth Century. Chapel Hill: UNC
Press, 1972. Rev. by R. F. Scholz, WMQ, 3rd ser., 30(Je
1973):498-500; B. R. Burg, AHR, 78(Oct 1973):1117-18; J.
F. H. New, JAH, 60(Dec 1973):775-6; S. S. Cohen, NYHSQ,
57(Oct 1973):348-9.

Hall, G. D. G. and Elsa de Haas, eds. Early Registers of Writs.
London: Bernard Quaritch, 1970. Rev. by D. W. Sutherland,
AHR, 78(Dec 1973):1436-7.

Hall, Gwendolyn Midlo. Social Control in Slave Planation Societies:
A Comparison of St. Dominique and Cuba. Baltimore: JHU
Press, 1971. Rev. by R. B. Sheridan, WMQ, 3rd ser., 30
(Apr 1973):339-41; R. Cassimere, Jr., WMH, 56(Spr 1973):
257-8; E. Brathwaite, AHR, 78(Feb 1973):183-4; M. K. Cobb,
JNH, 58(Apr 1973):222-4.

Hall, H. Duncan. Commonwealth: A History of the British Commonwealth of Nations. London: Van Nostrand Reinhold, 1971.
Rev. by D. W. Harkness, HJ, 16(Je 1973):446-8.

Hall, Mabel. Upper Beaver Creek: Pioneer Life in Early Colorado.

New York: Exposition, 1972. Rev. by N. J. Bender, Montana, 23(Aut 1973):71.

Hall, Thadd E. France and the Eighteenth-Century Corsican Question. New York: NYU Press, 1971. Rev. by B. R. Kreiser, JMH, 45(Je 1973):310-12.

Hall, Thomas B. Medicine on the Santa Fe Trail. Dayton, O.: Mornside Bookshop, 1971. Rev. by A. Baber, JISHS, 66(Win 1973):473-4.

Hall, Van Beck. Politics Without Parties: Massachusetts, 1780-1791. Pittsburgh: U Pitt Press, 1972. Rev. by R. J. Taylor, WMQ, 3rd ser., 30(Ja 1973):161-3; P. F. Lambert, WMH, 56(Spr 1973):249-50; J. Cary, Historian, 35(Feb 1973): 306-7.

Halperin, Maurice. The Rise and Decline of Fidel Castro: An Essay in Contemporary History. Berkeley: U Cal Press, 1972. Rev. by R. H. Fitzgibbon, AHR, 78(Oct 1973):1150-1.

Haltern, Utz. Die Londoner Weltausstellung von 1851: Ein Beitrag zur Geschichte der bürgerlich-industriellen Gesellschaft im 19. Jahrhundert. Münster: Aschendorff, 1971. Rev. by R. D. Mandell, JMH, 45(Sep 1973):510-11; W. O. Henderson, History, 58(Oct 1973):459.

Hämäläinen, Pekka Kalevi. Nationality Struggle and Language Strife in Finland, 1917-1939. Helsingfors: Holger Schildts Forlag, 1969. Rev. by H. P. Krosby, AHR, 78(Je 1973):709.

Hamann, Richard and Jose Hermand. Gründerzeit. Munich: Nymphenburger Verlagshandlung, 1971. Rev. by C. E. Pletsch, JMH, 45(Je 1973):324-5.

Hamer, D. A. Liberal Politics in the Age of Gladstone and Rosebery: A Study in Leadership and Policy. New York: Ox U Press, 1972. Rev. by W. L. Arnstein, JMH, 45(Sep 1973): 506-9; B. Malament, AHR, 78(Oct 1973):1068-9; P. Smith, History, 58(Je 1973):316.

Hamer, Philip M., et al., eds. The Papers of Henry Laurens. Vol. II: November 1, 1755-December 31, 1758; Vol. III: January 1, 1759-August 31, 1763. Columbia, S. C.: U SCar Press, 1970. Rev. by J. P. Greene, JSH, 39(May 1973):279-81; R. Walsh, FHQ, 52(Oct 1973):191-3 (Vol. II): L. S. Butler, NCHR, 50(Win 1973):96-8. (Vol. III): R. M. Weir, WMQ, 3rd ser, 30(Ap 1973):351-3.

Hamerow, Theodore S. The Social Foundations of German Unification, 1858-1871: Struggles and Accomplishments. Princeton, N. J.: Prin U Press, 1972. Rev. by R. M. Berdahl, JMH, 45(Sep 1973):522-3; G. R. Mork, Historian, 36(Nov 1973):110.

Hamilton, Alistair. The Appeal of Fascism: A Study of Intellectuals and Fascism 1919-1945. London: Anthony Bland, 1971.
Rev. by S. Wilson, History, 58(Feb 1973):135-6.

Hamilton, Charles, ed. Cry of the Thunderbird. Norman: U Ok,
1972. Rev. by R. Anderson, Montana 23(Sum 1973):56.

Hamilton, Charles V. see Browne, Robert S., et al.

Hamilton, Elizabeth. William's Mary. London: Hamish Hamilton,
1972. Rev. by W. A. Speck, History, 58(Je 1973):295.

Hamilton, Raphael W. Marquette's Explorations: The Narratives
Reexamined. Madison: U Wis Press, 1970. Rev. by R. M.
Sutton, Historian, 35(Feb 1973):302-3; H. A. Fleming, JOW,
12(Jl 1973):506-7.

Hamilton, Virginia Van Der Veer. Hugo Black: The Alabama Years.
Baton Rouge: LSU Press, 1972. Rev. by E. C. Johnson, FHQ,
51(Apr 1973):459-61; J. S. Saeger, NCHR, 50(Win 1973):112-
13.

Hammett, A. B. J. The Empresario: Don Martin de León (The
Richest Man in Texas). Victoria, Tx.: Victoria Daily News,
1971. Rev. by I. Vizcaya-Canales, SWHQ, 76(Ja 1973):345-6.

Hammond, George P., ed. A Guide to the Manuscript Collections
of the Bancroft Library, Vol. 2, Manuscripts Relating Chiefly
to Mexico and Central America. Berkeley: U Cal Press, 1972.
Rev. by H. P. Beers, AmArch, 36(Jl 1973):410-11; M. Wells,
JOW, 12(Oct 1973):634; A. K. Johnson, HAHR, 53(Nov 1973):
672-3.

Hammond, Mason. The City in the Ancient World. Cambridge,
Mass.: Har U Press, 1972. Rev. by T. Kelly, Historian, 36
(Nov 1973):92; W. G. Simigen, AHR, 78(Dec 1973):1430-1.

Hammond, N. see Edwards, I.

Hammond, N. G. L. Studies in Greek History, A Companion Volume to A History of Greece to 322 B. C. Oxford: Clarendon
Press, 1973. Rev. by C. G. Starr, Antiquity, 47(Dec 1973):
324-5.

Hampden, John, ed. Francis Drake, Privateer: Contemporary Narratives and Documents. University: U Ala Press, 1972. Rev.
by J. S. McGee, WHQ, 4(Oct 1973):457-8; B. Henry, PacH,
17(Sum 1973):86-7; R. H. Power, CHQ, 52(Sum 1973):175-6;
P. E. Hoffman, FHQ, 52(Jl 1973):74-5; F. A. Cassell, GHQ,
57(Fall 1973):443-4.

Hampton, H. Duane. How the U. S. Cavalry Saved Our National
Parks. Bloomington: Ind U Press, 1971. Rev. by R. A.

Bartlett, AHR, 78(Je 1973):737-8; M. J. Mattes, Montana, 23 (Win 1973):66.

Hamshere, Cyril. The British in the Caribbean. Cambridge, Mass.: Har U Press, 1972. Rev. by A. H. Adamson, AHR, 78(Dec 1973):1559-60; R. B. Sheridan, JAH, 60(Dec 1973):781-2; S. Harcourt-Smith, HTo, 23(May 1973):363, 365.

Handlin, Oscar. The Uprooted. Boston: Atlantic--Little, Brown, 1973. Rev. by T. Saloutos, JAH, 60(Dec 1973):840-1.

Handy, Robert T. , ed. Religion in the American Experience: The Pluralistic Style. Columbia, S. C.: U SCar Press, 1972. Rev. by D. T. Stokes, NCHR, 50(Aut 1973):435-6.

Hanham, H. J. , ed. Dod's Electoral Facts, 1832-1853 (1853). Brighton: Harvester, 1972. Rev. by T. J. Nossiter, History, 58(Je 1973):307.

Hanna, Alfred Jackson and Kathryn Abbey Hanna. Napoleon III and Mexico. Chapel Hill: UNC Press, 1972. Rev. by R. Bullen, History, 58(Je 1973):311; L. L. Blaisdell, AHR, 78(Feb 1973): 186-7.

Hansell, Haywood S. , Jr. The Air Plan That Defeated Hitler. Atlanta: H. S. Hansell, Jr. , 1972. Rev. by E. M. Emme, JAH, 60(Dec 1973):851-2.

Hansen, Edward C. see Wolf, Eric R.

Hansen, Roger D. The Politics of Mexican Development. Baltimore: JHU Press, 1971. Rev. by R. N. Sinkin, HAHR, 53(Feb 1973): 129-31.

Hanson, Donald W. From Kingdom to Commonwealth: The Development of Civic Consciousness in English Political Thought. [Cambridge, Mass.:] Har U Press, 1971. Rev. by M. Wilks, History, 58(Oct 1973):446-7.

Harding, Thomas S. College Literary Societies: Their Contribution to Higher Education in the United States, 1815-1876. New York: Pageant Press International, 1971. Rev. in GHQ, 57(Fall 1973):447-8.

Hardinge, Leslie. The Celtic Church in Britain. London: S. P. C. K. , 1972. Rev. by P. McGurk, History, 58(Je 1973):251-2.

Hardy, James D. , Jr. Judicial Politics in the Old Regime: The Parlement of Paris During the Regency. Baton Rouge: LSU Press, 1967. Rev. by E. Karafiol, JMH, 45(Mar 1973):115-16.

Hardy, P. The Muslims of British India. [Cambridge:] Cam U Press, 1972. Rev. by I. H. Qureshi, HJ, 16(Dec 1973):874-5.

Hare, James M. With Malice Towards None: The Musings of a
   Retired Politician. East Lansing: Mich St U Press, 1972.
   Rev. by H. Ladner, MichH, 57(Fall 1973):273-4.

Hareven, Tamara K. Anonymous Americans: Explorations in Nineteenth-Century Social History. Englewood Cliffs, N. J.: Prentice-Hall, 1971. Rev. by S. Scheinberg, CHR, 54(Mar 1973):
   95-6; J. E. Bodnar and C. Oblinger, PH, 40(Jl 1973):346-8.

Hargrett, Lester, comp. The Gilcrease-Hargrett Catalog of Imprints. Norman: U Ok, 1972. Rev. by R. S. Dunn, A & W,
   15(Aut 1973):295-7; G. M. Jenks, JOW, 12(Oct 1973):651.

Harik, Iliyā. Who Rules Lebanon. Beirut: Dar al-Nahār lil-Nashr,
   1972. Rev. by P. Gubser, MEJ, 27(Sum 1973):395-6.

_____. Rural politics ... see Antoun, Richard

Harkabi, Yehoshafat. Arab Attitudes Toward Israel. New York:
   Hart, 1972. Rev. by F. J. Khouri, MEJ, 27(Win 1973):90-1.

Harlan, Louis R. Booker T. Washington. The Making of a Black
   Leader, 1856-1901. New York: Ox U Press, 1972. Rev. by
   R. L Zangrando, CWH, 19(Dec 1973):353-6; in GHQ, 57(Spr
   1973):153-4; by E. L. Thornbrough, JAH, 60(Sep 1973):487-8;
   H. P. Ownes, JMiH, 35(May 1973):213-15; W. B. Gatewood,
   Jr., JNH, 58(Apr 1973):204-7; I. A. Newby, JSH, 39(May
   1973):302-4; V. Howard, NCHR, 50(Spr 1973):223-5; L. L.
   Gould, SWHQ, 76(Apr 1973):493; O. K. Rice, WVH, 34(Jl
   1973):394-6.

_____, ed. The Booker T. Washington Press, Vol. I.... Ur-
   bana: U Ill Press, 1972. Rev. by W. B. Gatewood, Jr., JNH,
   58(Apr 1973):204-7; V. Howard, NCHR, 50(Spr 1973):223-5.

_____ and John W. Blassingame, eds. The Booker T. Washington Papers. Vol. I. The Autobiographical Writings. Urbana:
   U Ill Press, 1972. Rev. by W. S. Hoole, AlaRe, 26(Apr
   1973):146-7; R. L. Zangrando, CWH, 19(Dec 1973):353-6;
   E. J. Burns, FHQ, 52(Jl 1973):78-80; A. H. Spear, JAH, 60
   (Dec 1973):753-5; E. L. Thornbrough, JSH, 39(Aug 1973):458-
   60; D. W. Grantham, WVH, 34(Apr 1973):299-301.

_____, et al., eds. The Booker T. Washington Papers, Vol. II.
   1860-1889. Urbana: U Ill Press, 1972. Rev. by R. L. Zangrando, CWH, 19(Dec 1973):353-6; A. H. Spear, JAH, 60(Dec
   1973):753-5; W. B. Gatewood, JNH, 58(Apr 1973):204-7; E.
   L. Thronbrough, JSH, 39(Aug 1973):458-60; V. Howard, NCHR,
   50(Spr 1973):223-5; D. W. Grantham, WVH, 34(Apr 1973):299-
   301.

Harmsen, Dorothy B. Harmsen's Western Americana: A Collection
   of 100 Western Paintings With Biographical Profiles of the

Artists. Flagstaff, Ariz.: Northland Press, 1971. Rev. by
R. N. Coen, JISHS, 66(Apr 1973):108-9.

Harner, Charles E. Florida's Promoters: The Men Who Made It
Big. Tampa: Trend House, 1973. Rev. by T. S. Graham,
FHQ, 52(Oct 1973):189-90.

Harner, Michael J. The Jivaro: People of the Sacred Waterfalls.
Garden City, N. Y.: Doubleday Natural History Press, 1972.
Rev. by D. Lathrap, HAHR, 53(Nov 1973):721-3.

Harper, Norman, ed. Pacific Circle 2: Proceedings of the Third
Biennial Conference of the Australian and New Zealand American Studies Association. St. Lucia, Australia: U Queensland
Press, 1972. Rev. by J. A. Dowling, JAH, 60(Dec 1973):765-
7.

Harrāz, Rajab. The Ottoman Empire and the Arabian Peninsula,
1840-1909. Cairo: al Matba'a al-'Alamiyya, 1970. Rev. by
W. L. Ochsenwald, MEJ, 27(Win 1973):99.

Harris, George S. Troubled Alliance: Turkish-American Problems
in Historical Perspective, 1945-1971. Washington, D. C.:
American Enterprise Institute for Public Policy Research, 1972.
Rev. by J. A. De Novo, WMH, 56(Sum 1973):340-1; J. C.
Campbell, MEJ, 27(Sum 1973):402.

Harris, H. A. Sport in Greece and Rome. Ithaca, N. Y.: Cornell U Press, 1972. Rev. by E. G. Huzar, AHR, 78(Oct
1972):1024-5; R. L. Howland, Antiquity, 47(Mar 1973):84-5.

Harris, J. R., ed. The Legacy of Egypt. New York: Ox U Press,
1971. Rev. by S. M. Burstein, AHR, 78(Dec 1973):1431-2.

Harris, José. Unemployment and Politics: A Study in English Social Policy, 1886-1914. New York: Ox U Press, 1972. Rev.
by B. B. Gilbert, AHR, 78(Dec 1973):1469-70; P. P. Poirier,
JMH, 45(Dec 1973):681-3.

Harris, Neil, Arthur Mann, and Sam Bass Warner, Jr. Indiana
Historical Society Lectures: History and the Role of the City
in American Life. Indianapolis: Ind Historical Society, 1972.
Rev. by R. Janis, IMH, 69(Sep 1973):278-9; R. A. Mohl,
AHR, 78(Oct 1973):1115-6.

Harris, W. V. Rome in Erituria and Umbria. New York: Ox U
Press, 1971. Rev. by R. E. Mitchell, AHR, 78(Feb 1973):
77-8.

Harris, Walter D., Jr. The Growth of Latin American Cities.
Athens, O.: Ohio U Press, 1971. Rev. by H. Browning,
HAHR, 53(Nov 1973):691-3.

Harrison, Brian. <u>Drink and the Victorians: The Temperance Ques-</u>
<u>tion in England, 1815-1872.</u> Pittsburgh: U Pitt Press, 1971.
Rev. by W. L. Arnstein, AHR, 78(Oct 1973):1064-5; L. A.
Shiman, JMH, 45(Mar 1973):129-30.

Harrison, James Pinckney. <u>The Long March to Power: A History</u>
<u>of the Chinese Communist Party, 1921-1972.</u> New York:
Praeger, 1972. Rev. by A. Rubenstein, CurH, 64(May 1973):
225.

Harrison, Royden, ed. <u>The English Defense of the Commune 1871.</u>
London: Merlin, 1971. Rev. by I. Prothero, History, 58
(Feb 1973):125.

Harrod, Howard L. <u>Mission Among the Blackfeet.</u> Norman: U Ok
Press, 1971. Rev. by H. E. Fritz, WHQ, 4(Jl 1973):338-9;
R. F. Berkhofer, Jr., PHR, 42(Feb 1973):108-10.

Hart, Ansell. <u>The Life of George William Gordon.</u> Kingston,
Jamaica: Institute of Jamaica, 1972. Rev. by J. Walvin,
History, 58(Oct 1973):483.

Hart, Cyril. <u>The Venderers and Forest Laws of Dean.</u> Newton
Abbot: David and Charles, 1971. Rev. by C. R. Elrington,
History, 58(Feb 1973):163.

Hart, Gillian P. <u>African Entrepreneurship.</u> Grahamstown, South
Africa: Rhodes U, 1972. Rev. by C. Bundy, AfAf, 72(Oct
1973):459-60.

Hart, John L. Jerome. <u>Fourteen Thousand Feet: A History of the</u>
<u>Naming and Early Ascents of the High Colorado Peaks.</u> Den-
ver: Colo Mountain Club, 1972 (reprint). Rev. by L. W.
Arps, CoMag, 50(Sum 1973):256-7.

Hartley, Anthony. <u>Gaullism: The Rise and Fall of a Political</u>
<u>Movement.</u> New York: Outerbridge and Dientsfrey, 1971.
Rev. by A. R. Zolberg, JMH, 45(Mar 1973):190-1.

Hartley, B. R. <u>see</u> Frere, Sheppard, et al.

Hartley, K. F. <u>see</u> Frere, Sheppard, et al.

Hartmann, Axel. <u>Prähistorische Goldfunde aus Europa.</u> Berlin:
Gebr. Mann Verlag, 1970. Rev. by J. Coles, Antiquity, 47
(Dec 1973):327-8.

Hartman, Susan M. <u>Truman and the Eightieth Congress.</u> Columbia, Mo.: U Mo Press, 1971. Rev. by K. McNaught, AHR,
78(Dec 1973):1555-6; T. A. Krueger, JISHS, 66(Spr 1973):
101-2.

Hartung, Horst. <u>Die Zeremonialzentren der Maya: Ein Beitrag</u>

zur Untersuchung der Planungsprinzipien.   Graz, Austria: Aka-
demische Druck-u.   Verlagsanstalt.   Rev. by D. M. Pendergast, HAHR, 53(Nov 1973):725-6.

Hartwell, R. M., ed.   The Industrial Revolution and Economic
Growth.   London: Methuen, 1971.   Rev. by I. M. Drummond,
CHR, 54(Sep 1973):309-11;   A. J. Taylor, History, 58(Oct
1973):453-4.

Harwood, Alan.   Witchcraft, Sorcery and Social Categories Among
the Safwa.   London: Ox U Press, 1970.   Rev. by A. Redmayne, AfAf, 72(Oct 1973):450-1.

Harvey, John, ed.   The Diplomatic Diaries of Oliver Harvey, 1937-
1940.   New York: St. Martin's, 1972.   Rev. by P. Stansky,
SS, 64(Nov 1973):295-6.

Harvey, John.   The Medieval Architect.   New York: St. Martin's,
1972.   Rev. by R. Mark, JIH, 4(Sum 1973):129-32;   E. G.
Carlson, AHR, 78(Je 1973):663-4.

Harvey, John H.   Early Gardening Catalogues.   Chichester, Eng.:
Phillimore, 1972.   Rev. by M. Hadfield, Archives, 11(Spr
1973):54-5.

Harvey, Mose L., Leon Goure, and Vladimir Prokofieff.   Science
and Technology as an Instrument of Soviet Policy.   Miami,
Fla.:   U Miami Press, 1972.   Rev. by K. E. Bailes, MilAf,
37(Dec 1973):158.

Haskins, James.   Pinckney Benton Stewart.   New York: Macmillan,
1973.   Rev. by J. W. Cooke, HRNB, 2(Nov/Dec 1973):51.

Haskins, Ralph W.   see   Graf, LeRoy, P.

Haslip, Joan.   The Crown of Mexico: Maximilian and His Empress
Carlota.   New York: Holt, Rinehart, Winston, 1972.   Lowell
L. Blaisdell, AHR, 78(Feb 1973):186-7.

Hasslof, Olof, Henning Henningsen, and Arne Emil Christensen, Jr.
Ships and Shipyards, Sailors and Fishermen: Introduction to
Maritime Ethnology.   Copenhagen: ... Copenhagen U Press,
1972.   Rev. by H. I. Chapelle, T & C, 14(Apr 1973):296-300.

Hatch, John.   Tanzania: A Profile.   London: Pall Mall, 1971.
Rev. by G. Kitching, AfAf, 72(Ja 1973):83-4.

Hatfield, Dorothy B.   see   Current-Garcia, Eugene

Hauck, Cornelius W.   Narrow Gauge to Central and Silver Plume.
Golden, Colo.:   Colorado Railroad Museum, 1972.   Rev. by
T. J. Noel, Montana, 23(Spr 1973):72;   S. B. Smalley, OQ,
16(Sum 1973):70-2.

Haupt, Georges. Socialism and the Great War: The Collapse of the Second International. Oxford: Clarendon, 1972. Rev. by M. D. Biddiss, History, 58(Je 1973):319-20; R. Wohl, JMH, 45(Je 1973):335-6.

Havard, William C., ed. The Changing Politics of the South. Baton Rouge: LSU Press, 1972. Rev. by J. F. Steelman, JSH, 39(May 1973):309-10; S. Hackney, FHQ, 52(Jl 1973):84-6; G. Osborn, GHQ, 57(Fall 1973):439; J. H. Wilkinson III, VMHB, 81(Ja 1973):98-9; W. L. Brown, ArkHQ, 32(Aut 1973): 287-90.

Havaunisian, Richard G. The Republic of Armenia. Vol. I. The First Year, 1918-1919. Berkeley: U Cal Press, 1971. Rev. by W. J Griswold, Historian, 35(Feb 1973):296-7.

Hawes, Joseph M. Children in Urban Society: Juvenile Delinquency in Nineteenth-Century America. n. p.: Ox U Press, 1971. Rev. by C. Taylor, History, 58(Oct 1973):494.

Hawi, Khalil S. Kahlil Gibran: His Background, Character and Works. Beirut: The Arab Institute for Research and Publishing, 1972. Rev. R. M. A. Allen, MEJ, 27(Sum 1973):405-6.

Hawke, David Freeman. Benjamin Rush: Revolutionary Gadfly. Indianapolis: Bobbs-Merrill, 1971. Rev. by M. M. Dunn, AHR, 78(Feb 1973):156-7; C. C. Robbins, NYHSQ, 57(Apr 1973): 180-2; L. S. King, PH, 40(Ja 1973):101-3; R. A. Brown, SS, 64(Ja 1973):40-1.

Hawkins, Hugh. Between Harvard and America: The Educational Leadership of Charles W. Eliot. New York: Ox U Press, 1972. Rev. by L. Veysey, JAH, 60(Sep 1973):478-80.

Haws, Charles H., ed. Scottish Parish Clergy at the Reformation, 1540-1574. n. p.: Scottish Record Society, 1972. Rev. by F. Heal, Archives, 11(Aut 1973):103-4.

Hayami, Yujiro and Vernon W. Ruttan. Agricultural Development: An International Perspective. Baltimore: JHU Press, 1971. Rev. by J. R. Behrman, AgH, 47(Apr 1973):168-9; J. G. Williamson, JEH, 33(Je 1973):484-7. NOTE: First author's name appears as Hyami in JEH.

Hayes, J. W. Late Roman Pottery: A Catalogue of Roman Fine Wares. London: British School at Rome, 1972. Rev. by H. Comfort, Archaeology, 26(Jl 1973):229-30.

Hayes, Paul M. Quisling: The Career and Political Ideas of Vidkun Quisling, 1887-1945. Bloomington: Ind U Press, 1972. Rev. by L. Bushkoff, MilAf, 37(Dec 1973):161-2.

Haynes, Robert V. Blacks in White America Before 1865: Issues and Interpretations. New York: David McKay, n. d. Rev. by R. Halliburton, Jr., SS, 64(Nov 1973):290.

Hazzard, Shirley. Defeat of an Ideal: A Study of the Self-Destruction of the United Nations. Boston: Atlantic--Little, Brown, 1973. Rev. by W. C. Clemens, Jr., AHR, 78(Dec 1973):1428-30.

Heald, Edward T. Witness to Revolution: Letters from Russia, 1916-1919. Kent, O.: Kent St U Press, 1972. Rev. by R. P. Browder, Historian, 35(Feb 1973):294-5.

Heath, Shirley Brice. Telling Tongues: Language Policy in Mexico, Colony to Nation. New York: Columbia U Press, 1972. Rev. by T. G. Powell, HAHR, 53(Nov 1973):659-6; W. B. Taylor, Historian, 35(Feb 1973):320-1; H. G. Rosenblush, TAm, 30(Jl 1973):134-5.

Heaton, Peter. Yachting, A Pictorial History. New York: Viking, 1973. Rev. by C. D. S., IS, 29(Win 1973):318.

Hecht, Marie B. John Quincy Adams: A Personal History of an Independent Man. New York: Macmillan, 1972. Rev. by H. Ammon, JAH, 60(Sep 1973):441-2; P. P. Hull, WMQ, 3rd ser., 30(Oct 1973):683-4; P. Levine, MHM, 68(Fall 1973):343.

Heer, Nancy Whittier. Politics and History in the Soviet Union. Cambridge, Mass.: M I T Press, 1971. Rev. by G. E. Snow, HT, 7(Nov 1973):143-4.

Heggoy, Alf Andrew. Insurgency and Counterinsurgency in Algeria. Bloomington: Ind U Press, 1972. Rev. by J. B. Bell, MilAf, 37(Dec 1973):155-7.

Heiber, Helmuth. Goebbels. New York: Hawthorne, 1972. Rev. by L. H. Addington, HT 6(May 1973):479-80.

Heimpel, Hermann, Festschrift für, erster Band. Gottingen: Vandenhoeck and Ruprecht, 1972. Rev. by L. Kochan, History, 58(Oct 1973):416-7.

Heimsath, Charles and Surjit Mansingh. A Diplomatic History of Modern India. Bombay: Allied, 1971. Rev. by D. R. SarDesai, IQ, 29(Oct-Dec 1973):360-1.

Heineman, Margot see Branson, Noreen

Heizer, Robert F. and Adam E. Tragenza. Mines and Quarries of the Indians of California. Ramona, Cal.: Ballena Press, 1972. Rev. by M. Rusco, NHSQ, 16(Sum 1973):140-2.

Hellie, Richard. Enserfment and Military Change in Muscovy. London: U Chi Press, 1971. Rev. by R. E. F. Smith, History, 58(Feb 1973):102-3.

Hémardinquer, Jean-Jacques, ed. Pour une histoire de l'alimenta-
    tion. Paris: Librairie Armand Colin, 1970. Rev. by R. F.
    Kierstead, AHR, 78(Feb 1973):89-91.

Hemenway, Abby Maria. Abby Hemenway's Vermont: Unique Por-
    trait of a State. Brattleboro, Vt.: Stephen Greene, 1972.
    Rev. by B. Bandel, VH, 41(Aut 1973):237-9.

Hemmings, F. W. J. Culture and Society in France, 1848-1898:
    Dissidents and Philistines. New York: Scribner's, 1971. Rev.
    by G. J. Becker, AHR, 78(Oct 1973):1078-9; I. Collins, His-
    tory, 58(Je 1973):311-12.

Hemphill, W. Edwin, ed. The Papers of John C. Calhoun. Vol. V:
    1820-1821. Columbia, S. C.: U SCar Press, 1971. Rev. by
    H. Monroe, JISHS, 66(Aut 1973):352-4; T. P. Govan, FHQ,
    51(Ja 1973):325-7; W. S. Hoffmann, NCHR, 50(Spr 1973):205-
    6.

_____, ed. The Papers of John C. Calhoun. Vol. VI: 1821-1822.
    Columbia, S. C.: U SCar Press, 1972. Rev. by H. Ammon,
    JSH, 39(May 1973):287-8; GHQ, 57(Win 1973):600-1; W. S.
    Hoffmann, NCHR, 50(Spr 1973):205-6; J. S. Coussons, SCHM,
    74(Oct 1973):316-7.

Henderson, Moffitt Sinclair. A Long, Long Day for November.
    Philadelphia: Dorrance, 1972. Rev. by J. O. Breeden, RKHS,
    71(Ja 1973):106-8.

Hendre, Sudhir Laxman. Hindus and Family Planning: A Socio-po-
    litical Demography. Bombay: Supraja Prakashan, 1971. Rev.
    by C. B. Mamoria, IQ, 29(Apr-Je 1973):181-2.

Hendrickx, Benjamin. The Political and Military Legal Foundation
    of the Latin Empire of Constantinople During the Early Years
    of Its Existence. Thessalonica: The Author, 1970. Rev. by
    P. Charanis, AHR, 78(Oct 1973):1041.

Henneman, John Bell. Royal Taxation in Fourteenth-Century France.
    The Development of War Financing, 1322-1356. Princeton,
    N. J.: Prin U Press, 1972. Rev. by J. J. N. Palmer, His-
    tory, 58(Je 1973):265; F. J. Pegues, AHR, 78(Dec 1973):
    1443-4; J. H Munro, CHR, 54(Dec 1973):496-70.

Hennessey, R. A. S. The Electric Revolution. London: Oriel, 1971.
    Rev. by P. Fearon, History, 58(Feb 1973):144.

Hennock, E. P. Fit and Proper Persons: Ideal and Reality in Nine-
    teenth-Century Urban Government. London: Edward Arnold,
    1973. Rev. by A. Sutcliffe, MH, 2(Aut 1973):128-30.

Henretta, James A. "Salutary Neglect": Colonial Administration
    Under the Duke of Newcastle. Princeton, N. J.: Prin U

Press, 1972. Rev. by J. Sosin, WMQ, 3rd ser., 30(Apr 1973):329-32; E. C. Papenfuse, Jr., Historian, 35(Feb 1973): 303-5; F. B. Wickwire, NYHSQ, 57(Jl 1973):260-1; S. S. Webb, JAH, 59(Mar 1973):980-2; F. R. Black, NJH, 91(Sum 1973):129; I. R. Christie, History, 58(Je 1973):299; T. C. Barrow, PMHB, 97(Ja 1973):126-7.

Henry, Addison. The First West. Nashville; Aurora, 1972. Rev. by E. S. McKechnie, FCHQ, 47(Jl 1973):293-4.

Hercules, Frank. American Society and Black Revolution. New York: Harcourt Brace Jovanovich, 1972. Rev. by J. W. Ivy, Crisis, 80(Oct 1973):280-1.

Hermanns, William. The Holocaust: From a Survivor of Verdun. New York: Harper and Row, 1972. Rev. by C. Boyd, MilAf, 37(Oct 1973):112.

Hermansen, G. see Blackley, F. D.

Hermassi, Elbaki. Leadership and National Development in North Africa: A Comparative Study. Berkeley: U Cal Press, 1972. Rev. by L. Hahn, MEJ, 27(Sum 1973):398-9.

Herndon, G. Melvin. William Tatham, 1752-1819: American Versatile. Johnson City, Tenn.: ... E. Tenn St U, 1973. Rev. by L. H. Harrison, FCHQ, 47(Jl 1973):284-5; O. K. Rice, JSH, 39(Nov 1973):588-9.

Herr, Richard. Spain. Englewood Cliffs, N. J.: Prentice-Hall, 1971. Rev. by C. E. Lida, JMH, 45(Je 1973):293-4.

Herring, George C., Jr. Aid to Russia 1941-1946: Strategy, Diplomacy, the Origins of the Cold War. New York: Columbia U Press, 1973. Rev. by J. N. Hazard, RR, 32(Oct 1973): 429-30.

Hersey, George L. High Victorian Gothic: A Study in Associationism. Baltimore: JHU Press, 1972. Rev. by G. Howes, AHR, 78(Oct 1973):1060-2.

Hertzberg, Hazel W. The Search for an American Identity: Modern Pan-Indian Movements. Syracuse, N. Y.: Syr U Press, 1971. Rev. by R. Houghton, NHSQ, 16(Spr 1973):33-5.

Hexter, John H. Doing History. Bloomington: Ind U Press, 1971. Rev. by M. Brichford, AmArch, 36(Jl 1973):397-402; C. G. Gustavson, SS, 64(Feb 1973):88-9.

Heyman, Jacques. Coulomb's Memoir on Statics: An Essay in the History of Civil Engineering. Cambridge: Cam U Press, 1972. Rev. by C. S. Gillmor, T & C, 14(Jl 1973):500-1.

Hickel, Walter J. Who Owns America? New York: Paperback Library, 1971. Rev. in NDH, 40(Fall 1973):32.

Hickerson, Harold. The Chippewa and Their Neighbours: A Study in Ethnohistory. New York: Holt, Rinehart and Winston, 1970. Rev. by E. S. Rogers, MichH, 57(Spr 1973):83-6.

Hickin, Patricia see Reese, George H.

Hienton, Louise Joyner. Prince George's Heritage: Sidelights on the Early History of Prince George's County From 1696 to 1800. Baltimore: Md Historical Society, n. d. Rev. by R. Barnes, MHM, 68(Sum 1973):221-2.

Higginbotham, Don. The War of American Independence: Military Attitudes, Policies, and Practice, 1763-1789. New York: Macmillan, 1971. Rev. by M. A. Jones, WMQ, 3rd ser., 30 (Ja 1973):166-7; I. R. Christie, History, 58(Oct 1973):488-9.

Higgins, J. P. P. and S. Pollard, eds. Aspects of Capital Investment in Great Britain, 1750-1850. A Preliminary Survey. London: Methuen, 1971. Rev. by D. Baines, History, 58(Oct 1973):454-5.

Higgs, E. S., ed. Papers in Economic Prehistory. Cambridge: Cam U Press, 1972. Rev. by P. C. Nair, JEH, 33(Dec 1973): 889-90.

Higham, John. Writing American History: Essays on Modern Scholarship. Bloomington: Ind U Press, 1970. Rev. by M. Brichford, AmArch, 36(Jl 1973):397-402.

Higham, Robin. Air Power--A Concise History. New York: St. Martin's, 1972. Rev. by E. B. Haslam, MilAf, 37(Oct 1973): 115.

_____, ed. Civil Wars in the Twentieth Century. Lexington: U Press Ky, 1972. Rev. by R. W. Randall, RKHS, 71(Apr 1973):199-202.

_____, ed. A Guide to the Source of British Military History. Berkeley: U Cal Press, 1971. Rev. by B. Bond, JMH, 45 (Mar 1973):92-3.

Highfield, Roger, ed. Spain in the Fifteenth Century. London: Macmillan, 1972. Rev. by P. Rycroft, History, 58(Je 1973): 270-1.

Higonnet, Patrice L. -R. Pont-de-Montvert: Social Structure and Politics in a French Village, 1700-1914. Cambridge, Mass. : Har U Press, 1971. Rev. by T. W. Margadant, AgH, 47(Apr 1973):178-80.

Hill, Boyd H. , Jr. Medieval Monarchy in Action: The German
Empire From Henry I to Henry IV. New York: Barnes and
Noble, 1972. Rev. by P. Munz, AHR, 78(Je 1973):673-4.

Hill, Christopher. Antichrist in Seventeenth-Century England. Oxford: Ox U Press, 1971. Rev. by C. Russell, History, 58
(Feb 1973):105-6.

_____. The World Turned Upside Down: Radical Ideas During
the English Revolution. New York: Viking, 1972. Rev. by
R. Schlatter, AHR, 78(Oct 1973):1052-5; A. Woolrych, History, 58(Je 1973):289-91.

Hill, Evan. , William F. Stehl, and Roger Tory Peterson. The
Connecticut River. Middletown, Conn.: Wes U Press, 1972.
Rev. by A. J. Holden, Jr., VH, 41(Spr 1973):105-6.

Hill, James M. Broken K Pueblo: Prehistoric Social Organization
in the American Southwest. Tucson: U Ariz, 1970. Rev. by
J. Muller, AmAnt, 38(Apr 1973):249-51.

Hill, Polly. Rural Hausa: A Village and a Setting. New York:
Cam U Press, 1972. Rev. by M. Last, AfAf, 72(Ja 1973):
85-6.

Hill, Samuel S. , Jr. Religion and the Solid South. Nashville:
Abingdon, 1972. Rev. by A. E. Murray, JSH, 39(Feb 1973):
136-7.

Hill, West T. , Jr. The Theatre in Early Kentucky, 1790-1820.
Lexington: U Press Ky., 1971. Rev. by G. B. Wilson, AHR,
78(Feb 1973):158.

Hillerbrand, Hans J. Christendom Divided: The Protestant Reformation. London: Hutchinson, 1971. Rev. by P. Brooks, HJ, 16
(Je 1973):433-5.

Hilliard, Sam Bowers. Hog Meat and Hoecake: Food Supply in the
Old South, 1840-1860. Carbondale: S Ill U Press, 1972. Rev.
by J D. Foust, AgH, 47(Apr 1973):171-2; D. P. Jordan,
JMiH, 35(Feb 1973):100-1; R. W. Twyman, JSH, 39(Feb
1973):119-20; D. Lindstrom, BHR, 47(Aut 1973):385-6; P.
Perry, NCHR, 50(Win 1973):103-4.

_____. Indian Land Cessions: Map Supplement to the "Annuals."
Washington, D. C.: Association of American Geographers,
1972. Rev. by I. Sutton, PHR, 42(Feb 1973):108.

Hillgarth, J. N. Ramon Lull and Lullism in Fourteenth-Century
France. Oxford: Ox U Press, 1971. Rev. by B. Smalley,
History, 58(Je 1973):263-4.

Hilton, George W. The Cable Car in America. Berkeley: Howell-

North, 1971. Rev. by D. F. Myrick, Montana, 23(Win 1973):
71; D. F. Myrick, CHQ, 52(Sum 1973):179; M. Massouth,
T & C, 14(Oct 1973):640-1.

Hinckley, Ted C. The Americanization of Alaska, 1867-1879.
Palo Alto, Cal.: Pacific Books, 1972. Rev. by B. W. Mar-
ley, WHQ, 4(Oct 1973):459-60; W. T. Jackson, AW, 10(Sep
1973):52; T. H. McDonald, JAH, 60(Sep 1973):467-8; S. R.
Tompkins, PHR, 42(Nov 1973):588-9; B. M. Gough, PacH, 17
(Sum 1973):90-1.

Hind, R. J Henry Labouchere and the Empire, 1880-1905. London: Athlone, 1972. Rev. by P. Stansky, JMH, 45(Je 1973):
318.

Hine, Robert V. The American West: An Interpretative History.
Boston: Little, Brown, 1973. Rev. by R. M. Utley, AHI, 8
(Dec 1973):50.

_____ and Edwin R. Bingham, eds. The American Frontier:
Readings and Documents. Boston: Little, Brown, 1972. Rev.
by Editor, NDH, 40(Fall, 1973):34.

_____ and Savoie Lottinville, eds. Soldier in the West: Letters
of Theodore Talbot During His Services in California, Mexico,
and Oregon, 1845-53. Norman: U Ok Press, 1972. Rev. by
M. L. Spence, A & W, 15(Spr 1973):85-7; F. Rochlin, JOW,
12(Jl 1973):505; R. L. Nichols, Montana, 23(Sum 1973):58; G.
Theisen, NMHR, 48(Jl 1973):271-2; F. Egan, AW, 10(Ja 1973):
54; L. E. Oliva, PHR, 42(Feb 1973):112-13; O. B. Faulk,
WHQ, 4(Oct 1973):454-5.

Hingorani, R. C., ed. International Law Through [the] United Nations. Bombay: N. M. Tripathi, 1972. Rev. by B. N. Mehrish, IQ, 29(Jl-Sep, 1973):259-60.

Hinshaw, Seth B. and Mary Edith, eds. Carolina Quakers: Our
Heritage, Our Hope. Tercentenary, 1672-1972. Greensboro:
North Carolina Yearly Meeting, 1972. Rev. by B. Crabtree,
NCHR, 50(Aut 1973):416-17.

Hinton, Harold C. The Bear at the Gate: Chinese Policy Making
Under Soviet Pressure. Washington, D. C.: ... American
Enterprise Institute and Hoover Institution Policy Studies, 1971.
Rev. by R. L., RR, 32(Apr 1973):189-92.

Hirsch, Ernest A. see Petroni, Frank A.

Hirschman, Albert O. A Bias for Hope: Essays on Development of
Latin America. New Haven, Conn.: Yale U Press, 1971.
Rev. by A. G. Frank, HAHR, 53(Nov 1973):663-7.

The Historic Santa Fe Foundation. Old Santa Fe Today. Albuquer-

que: U NM Press, 1966. Rev. by S. J Williams, JOW, 12
(Oct 1973):641.

Historical Office, U. S. Department of State, ed. The Foreign Relations of the United States: The Near East and North Africa.
Washington, D. C.: U. S. Government Printing Office. 1969,
1971. Rev. by H. N. Howard, MEJ, 27(Spr 1973):245.

Hitchman, James H. Leonard Wood and Cuban Independence, 1898-
1902. The Hague: Martinus Nijhoff, 1971. Rev. by H. Por-
tell-Vila, HAHR, 53(Feb 1973):133-5.

Hitt, Rodney. Electric Railway Dictionary. New York: McGraw-Hill,
1911. (Novato, Cal.: Newton K. Gregg, 1972--reprint). Rev.
by J. H. White, T & C, 14(Apr 1973):306-7.

Hitti, Philip K. Capital Cities of Arab Islam. Minneapolis: U
Minn Press, 1973. Rev. by J Abu-Lughod, MEJ, 27(Aut
1973):499-500.

Hnilicka, Karl. Das Ende auf dem Balkan 1944/45: Die militarische
Raumung Jugoslaviens durch die deutsche Wehrmacht. Got-
tingen: Musterschmidt Verlag, 1970. Rev. by J. H. Wolfe,
EEQ, 7(Sum 1973):225-6.

Hobhouse, L. T. Democracy and Reaction [1904]. Brighton: Harvester, 1972. Rev. by R. T. Shannon, History, 58(Je 1973):
315-6.

Hodgett, Gerald A. J. A Social and Economic History of Medieval
Europe. London: Methuen, 1972. Rev. by R. H. Hilton,
History, 58(Oct 1973):426.

Hodson, F. R., et al., eds. Mathematics in the Archaeological and
Historical Sciences: Proceedings of the Anglo-Romanian Con-
ference, Mamaia, 1970.... Edinburgh: Univ. Press, 1971.
Rev. by R. J Jensen, AHR, 78(Je 1973):654.

Hodson, J. H. The Administration of Archives. Vol. 15. International Series in Library and Information Science. Oxford:
Pergamon, 1972. Rev. by F. B. Evans, AmArch, 36(Oct
1973):543-50.

Hoerder, Dirk. Society and Government 1760-1780: The Power
Structure in Massachusetts Townships. Berlin: John F. Ken-
nedy Institut, Freie Universität, 1972. Rev. by C. S. Olton,
JAH, 60(Dec 1973):787-8.

Hoffman, Herbert. Collecting Greek Antiquities. New York: Clarkson N. Potter, 1971. Rev. by J. V. Noble, Archaeology, 26
(Ja 1973):68.

Hoffman, Robert L. Revolutionary Justice: The Social and Political

Theory of P. J. Proudhon. Urbana: U Ill Press, 1972. Rev. by D. Stafford, JMH, 45(Sep 1973):515-6; C. H. Johnson, AHR, 78(Oct 1973):1078-9.

Hofstadter, Richard. America at 1750: A Social Portrait. London: Cape, 1972. Rev. by J. R. Pole, HJ, 16(Sep 1973):639-41.

Hogendorn, Jan S. Managing the Modern Economy. Cambridge: Winthrop, 1972. Rev. by W. Krause, SS, 64(Nov 1973):277-8.

Hohenthal, Helen Alma, et al. Streams in a Thirsty Land: A History of the Turlock Region. Turlock, Cal.: City of Turlock, 1972. Rev. by K. Black, JOW, 12(Apr 1973):338-9.

Höjer, Signe. Mary Kingsley ... (Explorer in West Africa). n. p.: L T's förlag, n. d. Rev. by A. B. Snodin, AfAf, 72(Oct 1973):463-4.

Holden, William Curry see Haley, J. Evetts

Holder, Leonard and W. E. May. A History of Marine Navigation. New York: Norton, 1973. Rev. by R. A. Courtemanche, HRNB, 2(Oct 1973):17.

Holl, Jack M. Juvenile Reform in the Progressive Era: William R. George and the Junior Republic Movement. London: Cornell U Press, 1971. Rev. by M. Simpson, History, 58(Feb 1973):154.

Holland, De Witte and Robert Oliver, eds. A History of Public Speaking in Pennsylvania. n. p.: Pa Speech Association ... 1971. Rev. by C. C. Cole, Jr., PH, 40(Ja 1973):114-15.

Holland, Francis Ross, Jr. America's Lighthouses. Their Illustrated History Since 1716. Brattleboro, Vt.: Stephen Greene, 1972. Rev. by J. W. Carruthers, JOW, 12(Jl 1973):506.

Hollander, A. N. J. Den, ed. Diverging Parallels: A Comparison of American and European Thought and Action. Leiden: E. J Brill, 1971. Rev. by D. Brudnoy, JAH, 60(Je 1973):184-5.

Hollander, Gayle Durham. Soviet Political Indoctrination: Developments in Mass Media and Propaganda Since Stalin. New York: Praeger, 1972. Rev. by I. Vogyes, RR, 32(Jl 1973):323-4.

Hollingsworth, T. H. Historical Demography. Ithaca, N. Y.: Cornell U Press, 1969. Rev. by M. R. Haines, JEH, 33 (Je 1973):488-9.

Holm, Don. The Old-Fashioned Dutch Oven Cook Book: Complete with Authentic Sourdough Baking, Smoking Fish and Game, Making Jerky, Pemmican and other Lost Campfire Arts.

Caldwell, Ida.: Caxton, 1972. Rev. by S. Black, JOW, 12
(Oct 1973):660.

_____ and Myrtle. The Complete Sourdough Cookbook: For
Camp Trail and Kitchen--Authentic and Original Sourdough
Recipes from the Old West. Caldwell: Ida.: Caxton, 1972.
Rev. by S. Black, JOW, 12(Oct 1973):660.

Holman, C. Hugh. The Roots of Southern Writing: Essays on the
Literature of the American South. Athens, Ga.: U Ga
Press, 1972. Rev. I. Malin, GR, 27(Spr 1973):128-31.

Holmes, Beatrice Hort. A History of Federal Water Resources
Programs, 1800-1960. Washington: U S D A, E R S, 1972.
Rev. by L. B. Lee, AgH, 47(Oct 1973):373.

Holmes, Charles S. The Clocks of Columbus: The Literary Career
of James Thurber. n. p.: Atheneum, 1972. Rev. by M. T.
Zimmerman, OQ, 16(Sum 1973):93-4.

Holmquist, June Drenning and Jean A. Brookins. Minnesota's Major Historic Sites: A Guide. St. Paul, Minn.: Minn Historical Society, 1972. Rev. by A. N. E., IS, 29(Fall 1973):
232-3.

Holt, P. M. Studies in the History of the Near East. London:
Frank Cass, 1973. Rev. by J. O. Voll, MEJ, 27(Aut 1973):
517-8.

Holt, P. M. et al., eds. The Cambridge History of Islam. 2 vols.
Cambridge: Cam U Press, 1970. Rev. by J. Janowski,
Historian, 35(Feb 1973):297-9; R. Owen, JIH, 4(Aut 1973):
287-98.

Homan, Gerlof D. Jean-François Reubell: French Revolutionary,
Patriot, and Director. The Hague: Martinus Nijhoff, 1971.
Rev. by C. Lucas, History, 58(Oct 1973):452-3.

Honigsbaum, Frank. The Struggle for the Ministry of Health. London: Bell, 1970. Rev. by G. Sutherland, HJ, 16(Je 1973):
420-31.

Honour, V. G., et al., eds. Jacaranda Junior World Atlas....
Brisbane, Qld.: Jacaranda Press, 1971. Rev. by J. M.
Hunter, SS, 64(Ja 1973):41-2.

Hood, Graham. Bonnin and Morris of Philadelphia: First American
Porcelain Factory, 1770-1772. Chapel Hill: UNC Press,
1972. Rev. by M. M Delhom, PMHB, 97(Jl 1973):412; B.
Liggett, WMQ, 3rd ser., 30(Oct 1973):673-5.

Hood, Sinclair. The Minoans: The Story of Bronze Age Crete.
New York: Praeger, 1970. Rev. by E. Vermeule, Archae-

ology, 26(Apr 1973):151-2.

Hoogenboom, Ari see Klein, Philip S.

Hook, Judith. The Sack of Rome, 1527. n. p. : Macmillan, n. d.
    Rev. by P. Partner, HTo, 23(Jan 1973):65-6.

Hoover, Herbert T. see Cash, Joseph H.

Hopkins, James F. , et al. , eds. The Papers of Henry Clay. Vol.
    IV. Secretary of State, 1825. Lexington: U Press Ky,
    1972. Rev. by G. G. Van Deusen, JAH, 60(Sep 1973):415;
    L. P. Curry, FCHQ, 47(Jl 1973):285-7; L. W. Turner,
    IMH, 69(Sep 1973):284-6.

Hopwood, Derek, ed. The Arabian Peninsula: Society and Politics.
    Totowa, N. J. : Rowman and Littlefield, 1972. Rev. by
    L. G. Landen, AHR, 78(Oct 1973):1104.

Horan, James D. The McKenny-Hall Portrait Gallery of American
    Indians. New York: Crown, 1972. Rev. by F. P. Prucha,
    AHR, 78(Oct 1973):1131; J. E. Sunder, JAH, 60(Sep 1973):
    437-8; J. Monaghen, AW, 10(Mar 1973):49; N. B. Wain-
    wright, PMHB, 97(Jl 1973):418-9.

Horn, Wolfgang. Führerideologie und Parteiorganisation in der
    NSDAP (1919-1933). Düsseldorf: Droste Verlag, 1972. Rev.
    by D. Orlow, JMH, 45(Je 1973):346.

Horsefield, J. Keith, ed. The International Monetary Fund, 1945-
    1965: Twenty Years of International Monetary Cooperation.
    Volumes I and III. Washington, D. C. : International Mone-
    tary Fund, 1969. Rev. by J. H. Furth, JEH, 33(Sep 1973):
    676-8.

Horst, Irwin B. The Radical Brethren: Anabaptism and the English
    Reformation to 1558. Nieuwkoop: B. de Graaf, 1972. Rev.
    by G. R. Elton, EHR, 88(Oct 1973):853-6.

Hoshii, Iwao see Adams, T. F. M.

Hotchkis, Katharine Bixby. Christmas Eve at Rancho Los Alamitos.
    San Francisco: Cal Historical Society, 1971. Rev. by R. E.
    Levinson, JOW, 12(Apr 1973):339-40.

_____. Trip with Father. San Francisco: Cal Historical So-
    ciety, 1971. Rev. by R. E. Levinson, JOW, 12(Apr 1973):
    339-40.

Hotham, David. The Turks. London: John Murray, 1972. Rev.
    by P. Nulty, MEJ, 27(Aut 1973):527-8.

Houghton, D. Hobart and Jennifer Dagut, eds. Source Material on the South African Economy: 1860-1970. Vol. I. 1860-1899. Cape Town: Ox U Press, 1973. Rev. by C. Bundy, JAfH, 14(No. 2 1973):346-7.

Hoult, Thomas Ford. The March to the Right--A Case Study in Political Repression. Cambridge: Schenkman, 1972. Rev. by D. Sharma, IQ, 29(Jl-Sep 1973):263-4.

Houn, Franklin W. A Short History of Chinese Communism. Englewood Cliffs, N. J.: Prentice-Hall, 1973. Rev. by J. W. Killigrew, HRNB, 2(Nov/Dec 1973):37.

Houtart, François and André Rousseau. The Church and Revolution: From the French Revolution of 1789 to the Paris Riots of 1968. Maryknoll, N. Y.: Orbis Books, 1971. Rev. by S. Shapiro, HAHR, 53(May 1973):345-6.

Hovannisian, Richard G. The Republic of Armenia. Vol. I. 1918-1919. Berkeley: U Cal Press, 1972. Rev. by P. Kenez, RR, 32(Oct 1973):435-6.

Howard, Edward G. see Filby, P. W.

Howard, Harold P. Sacajawea. Norman: U Ok Press, 1971. Rev. by R. E. Smith, PacH, 17(Spr 1973):93.

Howard, Oliver O. My Life and Experiences Among Our Hostile Indians: A Record of Personal Observations, Adventures, and Campaigns Among the Indians of the Great West. New York: Da Capo, 1972. Rev. by G. E. Moulton, JOW, 12 (Oct 1973):653.

Howard, Perry H. Political Tendencies in Louisiana. Baton Rouge: LSU Press, 1971. Rev. by H. P. Owens, CWH, 19(Mar 1973):91-2; J. A. Carrigan, LaH, 14(Sum 1973):323-5.

Howard, Robert P. Illinois: A History of the Prairie State. Grand Rapids, Mich.: Eerdmans, 1972. Rev. by D. F. Tingley, WMH, 56(Spr 1973):238; L. H. Fischer, JISHS, 66(Win 1973):468-9; R. M. Sutton, JAH, 60(Sep 1973):445-6.

Howe, Christopher. Wage Patterns and Wage Policy in Modern China, 1919-1972. New York: Cam U Press, 1973. Rev. by E. Rhoads, HRNB, 2(Nov/Dec 1973):36.

Howe, John R. From the Revolution Through the Age of Jackson: Innocence and Empire in the Young Republic. Englewood Cliffs, N. J.: Prentice-Hall, 1973. Rev. by C. B. Smith, HRNB, 2(Nov/Dec 1973):47.

Howell, Warren R. see Galvin, John

Howell, Wilbur Samuel. Eighteenth-Century British Logic and

Rhetoric. Princeton, N. J.: Prin U Press, 1971. Rev. by
R. N. Stromberg, AHR, 78(Feb 1973):98-9.

Howland, Marguerite S. see Poulton, Helen J.

Howse, Derek and Michael Sanderson. The Sea Chart, An Historical
Survey Based on the Collections in the National Maritime Mu-
seum. New York: McGraw-Hill, 1973. Rev. by L. A. P.,
IS, 29(Fall 1973):234.

Hoyle, Fred. From Stonehenge to Modern Cosmology. San Francisco and Reading: W. H. Freeman, 1973. Rev. by D. C.
Heggie, Antiquity, 47(Dec 1973):331.

Hoyt, Edwin P. The Battle of Leyte Gulf: The Death Knell of the
Japanese Fleet. New York: Weybright and Talley, 1972.
Rev. by J. A. Field, Jr., JAH, 60(Je 1973):175-6.

Huang, Philip C. Liang Chi-ch'ao and Modern Chinese Liberalism.
Seattle: U Wash Press, 1972. Rev. by E. Friedman, PHR,
42(Feb 1973):128-30.

Hudson, J H. and Frank B. Evans. The Administration of Archives.
Vol. 15. ... Oxford: Pergamon, 1972. Rev. by AmArch,
36(Oct 1973):543-50.

Hudson, Kenneth. A Guide to the Industrial Archaeology of Europe.
Cranbury, N. J.: Fairleigh Dickinson U Press, 1971. Rev.
by T. Althin, T & C, 14(Apr 1973):352-4.

_____. Air Travel: A Social History. Totowa, N. J.: Rowman
and Littlefield, 1972. Rev. by R. E. Bilstein, T & C, 14
(Oct 1973):651-3.

Huggett, Frank E. How It Happened. New York: Barnes and
Noble, 1972. Rev. by R. G. Cowherd, SS, 64(Nov 1973):281.

Huggins, Nathan Irvin. Protestants Against Poverty: Boston's
Charities, 1870-1900. Westport, Conn.: Greenwood, 1971.
Rev. by S. E. Ahlstrom, AHR, 78(Oct 1973):1127-30.

Hughes, Judith. To the Maginot Line: The Politics of French Military Preparations in the 1920's. Cambridge, Mass.: Har
U Press, 1971. Rev. by P. - H. Laurent, JMH, 45(Mar
1973):179-81.

Hughes, Kathleen. Early Christian Ireland: Introduction to the
Sources. Ithaca, N. Y.: Cornell U Press, 1972. Rev. by
J. P. Reidy, HT, 7(Nov 1973):136; C. Thomas, Antiquity,
47(Sep 1973):247.

_____. England Before the Conquest:... see Clemoes, Peter.

Hull, P. L. , ed. The Caption of Seisin of the Duchy of Cornwall
(1337). n. p.: Devon and Cornwall Record Society ... 1971.
Rev. by E. King, Archives, 11(Spr 1973):48-9.

Humboldt, Alexander von. Political Essay on the Kingdom of New
Spain. New York: Knopf, 1972. Rev. by J. E. Roderiguez
O HAHR, 53(May 1973):314-15.

Hunt, Noreen, ed. Cluniac Monasticism in the Central Middle Ages.
London: Macmillan, 1971. Rev. by R. H. C. Davis, History, 58(Feb 1973):82-3.

Hunter, Louise. Buddhism in Hawaii--Its Impact on a Yankee Community. Honolulu: U Hawaii Press, 1971. Rev. by W.
Kramer, JOW, 12(Apr 1973):340.

Huntington, R. T. Hall's Breechloaders: John H. Hall's Invention
and Development of a Breechloading Rifle With Precision-Made
Interchangeable Parts, and Its Introduction into the United
States Service. New York: Shumway, 1972. Rev. by W. H.
J. Chamberlain, T & C, 14(Ja 1973):86-7; M. R. Smith,
VMHB, 81(Ja 1973):111-13.

Hurewitz, J. C. and Jacques Vernant, eds. Intérets et Politiques
de la France et des Etats-Unis au Moyen Orient et en Afrique
du Nord. n. p.: n. d. Rev. by W. Zartman, MEJ, 27(Aut
1973):516-17.

Hurley, F. Jack. Portrait of a Decade: Roy Stryker and the Development of Documentary Photography in the Thirties. Baton
Rouge: LSU Press, 1972. Rev. by R. L. Heinemann, MHM,
68(Sum 1973):229-30; R. D. McKinzie, JAH, 60(Dec 1973):
846-7.

Hurst, John G. see Beresford, Maurice

Husband, Will W. Old Brownsville Days: An Historical Sketch of
Early Times in Jackson County, Illinois. Carbondale, Ill.:
Jackson County Historical Society, 1973. Rev. by B. B.
Hubbs, JISHS, 66(Aut 1973):357-8.

Huston, James A. Out of the Blue: United States Army Airborne
Operations in World War II. West Lafayette, Ind.: Purdue
U Studies, 1972. Rev. by A. R. Millett, JAH, 60(Je 1973):
176-7.

Hutchinson, Ira A. Some Who Passed This Way. Panama City,
Fla.: Privately Published, 1972. Rev. by J. D. Ware, FHQ,
51(Ja 1973):312-14.

Hutchinson, Sir Joseph. Farming and Food Supply: The Interdepend-
ence of Countryside and Town. Cambridge: Cam U Press,
1972. Rev. by K. P. Fox, JEH, 33(Sep 1973):678-9.

Hutchinson, W. H. California: Two Centuries of Man, Land, and
Growth in the Golden State. San Francisco: Canfield, 1972.
Rev. by T. F. Andrews, HT, 7(Nov 1973):128.

Hutchison, Harold F. Edward II: The Pliant King. London: Eyre
and Spottiswoode, 1971. Rev. by J. R. S. Phillips, History,
58(Feb 1973):87.

Huth, Hans. Lacquer of the West: The History of a Craft and an
Industry, 1550-1950. Chicago: U Chi Press, 1971. Rev.
by R. B. Haas, AHR, 78(Dec 1973):1422-3.

Hutson, James H. Pennsylvania Politics, 1746-1770: The Movement
for Royal Government and Its Consequences. Princeton,
N. J.: Prin U Press, 1972. Rev. by P. Maier, JAH, 59
(Mar 1973):984-6; B. Friedman, Historian, 35(Nov 1973):
119-20; R. S. Klein, PH, 40(Jl 1973):334-6; R. Ketcham,
WMQ, 3rd ser., 30(Apr 1973):327-8; R. M. Bliss, History,
58(Oct 1973):487-8; P. S. Klein, NJH, 91(Spr 1973):58-9;
D. F. Hawke, NYHSQ, 57(Apr 1973):177-9; J. D. Marietta,
PMHB, 97(Ja 1973):114-15.

_____ see Kurtz, Stephen G.

Huttenback, Robert A. Ghandi in South Africa: British Imperialism
and the Indian Question, 1860-1914. Ithaca, N. Y.: Cornell
U Press, 1971. Rev. by H. Tinker, JAfH, 14(3rd Qr 1973):
523-7.

Huxley, G. L. see Coldstream, J. N.

Hvidt, Kristian. The Flight to America: Motives for Mass Emigration From Denmark, 1868-1914. Aarhus: Universitetsforlaget, 1971. Rev. by K. O. Bjork, AHR, 78(Feb 1973):
167.

Hyam, Ronald. The Failure of South African Expansion, 1909-1939.
London: Macmillan, 1972. Rev. by M. Legassick, AfAf, 72
(Oct 1973):458-9; J. E. Spence, JAfH, 14(3rd Qr 1973):522-
3.

Hyde, Montgomery. Stalin: The History of a Dictator. New York:
Farrar, Straus, and Giroux, 1971. Rev. by R. D. Worth,
JMH, 45(Je 1973):338-41; R. M Slusser, AHR, 78(Oct 1973):
1100-1.

Hyman, Louis. The Jews of Ireland. Shannon: Irish U Press,
1972. Rev. by H. F. Beechhold, E-I, 8(Spr 1973):133-5.

Iatrides, John O. Revolt in Athens: The Greek Communist "Second
Round," 1944-1945. Princeton, N. J.: Prin U Press, 1972.
Rev. by G. Frangos, AHR, 78(Oct 1973):1098-9.

IBARRURI   154

Ibarruri, Dolores, et al., eds. Guerra y revolución en España,
1936-1939. Vol. 3. Moscow: Editorial Progreso, 1971.
Rev. by G. Jackson, AHR, 78(Je 1973):702-3.

Ignatus, Paul. Hungary. New York: Praeger, 1972. Rev. by I.
Deak, JMH, 45(Mar 1973):94-5.

Ikime, Obaro. Niger Delta Rivalry: Itsekiri-Urhobo Relations and
the European Presence 1884-1936. London: Longmans, 1969.
Rev. by G. I. Jones, Africa, 43(Ja 1973):78-80.

Iliffe, John. Agricultural Change in Modern Tanganyika: An Outline
History. Nairobi, Kenya: East African Publishing House,
1971. A. Redmayne, AfAf, 72(Oct 1973):464-5.

Immerwahr, S. A. The Neolithic and Bronze Ages. Princeton,
N. J.: American School of Classical Studies at Athens, 1971.
Rev. by S. Diamant, Antiquity, 47(Mar 1973):70-1.

Indebrø, Gustav and Oluf Kolsrud, eds. Learned Letters from and
to P. A. Munch. Vol. 1. 1832-1850. Olso: H. Aschehoug,
1955. Rev. by F. J Bowman, AHR, 78(Oct 1973):1088-9.

_____ and _____, eds. Learned Letters from and to P. A.
Munch. Vol. 2. January 1, 1851--September 30, 1859.
Oslo: H. Aschehoug, 1955. Rev. by F. J Bowman, AHR,
(Oct 1973):1088-9.

Ingle, Clyde R. From Village to State in Tanzania. Ithaca, N. Y.:
Cornell U Press, 1972. Rev. by O. E. S., CurH, 64(Mar
1973):126.

Inglis, Alex I. ... Documents on Canadian External Relations. Vol.
4. 1926-1930. Ottawa: ... Department of External Affairs, 1971. Rev. by N. Hillmer, CHR, 54(Sep 1973):308-9.

Ingraham, Mark H. Charles Sumner Slichter: The Golden Vector.
Madison: U Wis Press, 1972. Rev. by J. D. Hoeveler,
Jr., WMH, 56(Aut 1973):65-6.

Ingrams, Doreen, comp. Palestine Papers, 1917-1922: Seeds of
Conflict. New York: Braziller, 1973. Rev. by A. M.
Lesch, MEJ, 27(Sum 1973):384-5; K. P. Jones, HT, 7(Nov
1973):139-40.

Inlow, Gail M. Values in Transition: A Handbook. New York:
Wiley, 1972. Rev. by R. E. Gross, SS, 64(Nov 1973):280-1.

Innis, Harold A. Empire and Communications. Toronto: U Tor
Press, 1972. Rev. by H. J Muller, T & C, 14(Jl 1973):
483-4.

Innis, P. B. and Walter Dean Innis. Gold in the Blue Ridge. The

True Story of the Beale Treasure. Washington: Robert B.
Luce, 1973. Rev. in GHQ, 57(Win 1973):606.

International Bibliography of Historical Sciences. Vol. 35, 1966;
    Vol. 36, 1967. Michel François and Nicolas Tolu, eds.
    Paris: Librarie Armand Colin, 1969. Rev. by O. H. Orr,
    Jr., AHR, 78(Feb 1973):63-4.

Inter-University Board of India and Ceylon and Indian Council of
    Social Science Research see Doctoral Students....

Investigaciones Contemporáneas sobre Historia de México. Austin:
    U Tx Press, 1971. Rev. by W. Sherman, SWHQ, 76(Ja
    1973):340.

Iorizzo, Luciano J. and Salvatore Mondello. The Italian-Americans.
    New York: Twayne, 1971. Rev. by H. S. Nelli, AHR, 78
    (Je 1973):730-1.

Iredale, David. Enjoying Archives. Newton Abbott: David and
    Charles, 1973. Rev. by L. Rapport, AmArch, 36(Oct 1973):
    553-4.

Ireland, Robert M. The County Courts in Antebellum Kentucky.
    Lexington: U Press Ky., 1972. Rev. by C. T. Cullen,
    WMQ, 3rd ser., 30(Apr 1973):334-6; H. A. Johnson, FCHQ,
    47(Ja 1973):56-8; M. F. Mitchell, JSH, 39(Feb 1973):110-
    11; D. F. Henderson, IMH, 69(Mar 1973):66-7.

Iremonger, Valentin. Horan's Field and Other Reservations. Dublin:
    Dolmen, 1972. Rev. by T. D. Redshaw, E-I, 8(Spr 1973):
    142-51.

Iriye, Akira. Pacific Estrangement: Japanese and American Ex-
    pansion, 1897-1911. Cambridge, Mass.: Har U Press, 1972.
    Rev. by C. E. Neu, AHR, 78(Oct 1973):1017-18; R. A.
    Esthus, JAH, 60(Dec 1973):828-30; B. B. Ray, MilAf, 37
    (Dec 1973):160; W. R. Braisted, PHR, 42(Jl 1973):433-4.

Ischboldin, Boris. History of Russian Non-Marxian Economic
    Thought. New Delhi: New Book Society of India, 1971. Rev.
    by D. R Brower, JEH, 33(Je 1973):489-90.

Isern, J. Pioneros Cubanos en United States of America, 1575-1898.
    Miami, Fla.: Cenit, 1971. Rev. by L. O. Ealy, TAm 29
    (Ja 1973):405.

Isherwood, Robert M. Music in the Service of the King: France in
    the Seventeenth Century. Ithaca, N. Y.: Cornell U Press,
    1973. Rev. D. Stevens, AHR, 78(Dec 1973):1474-5.

Islam, Riazul. Indo-Persian Relations: A Study of the Political and
    Diplomatic Relations Between the Mughal Empire and Iran.

id=9780810808935 page 172

Tehran: Iranian Culture Foundation, 1970. Rev. by M. M.
Mazzaoui, MEJ. 27(Sum 1973):410-11.

Israel, Jerry, ed. Building the Organizational Society: Essays on
Associational Activities in Modern America. New York: Free
Press, 1972. Rev. by J. L. Shover, JAH, 60(Dec 1973):
834-6; J. Higham, JSH, 39(Nov 1973):612-13; R. H. Wiebe,
BHR, 47(Aut 1973):395-7.

Israilevich, E. E., comp. English-Russian General Economic and
Foreign Trade Dictionary. Moscow: Soviet Encyclopaedia
Publishing House, 1972. Rev. by J. Kayaloff, RR, 32(Oct
1973):450-1.

Issawi, Charles ed. The Economic History of Iran, 1800-1914.
Chicago: U Chi Press, 1971. Rev. by F. Kazemzadeh, AHR,
78(Je 1973):719-20.

Jabber, Fuad see Quandt, William B.

Jack, R. Ian. Medieval Wales. Ithaca, N. Y.: Cornell U Press,
1972. Rev. by B. Wilkinson, AHR, 78(Oct 1973):1032.

Jackson, Bruce. Wake Up Dead Man: Afro-American Worksongs
From Texas Prisons. Cambridge, Mass.: Har U Press,
1972. Rev. by G. R. Woolfolk, JNH, 58(Apr 1973):212-14.

Jackson, Gabriel. The Making of Medieval Spain. New York: Harcourt, Brace, Jovanovich, 1972. Rev. by R. I. Burns,
HAHR, 53(Nov 1973):673-4; P. A. Linehan, History, 58(Oct
1973):427-7.

Jackson, Gordon. Hull in the Eighteenth Century: A Study in Economic and Social History. New York: Ox U Press, 1972.
Rev. by G. Rudé, JMH, 45(Sep 1973):491-2.

Jackson, John Brinckerhoff. American Space: The Centennial Years,
1865-1876. New York: Norton, 1972. Rev. by C. W.
Condit, T & C, 14(Oct 1973):643-4; D. D. Gondos, PMHB,
97(Apr 1973):278-9; D. Jensen, AW, 10(Nov 1973):59.

Jackson, W. G. F. Alexander of Tunis. London: Batsford, 1971.
Rev. by B. Bond, History, 58(Feb 1973):142-3.

Jacobs, Clyde E. The Eleventh Amendment and Sovereign Immunity.
Westport, Conn.: Greenwood, 1972. Rev. by D. Mathis,
JAH, 60(Dec 1973):796-7; H. M. Hyman, JSH, 39(Aug 1973):
443-4.

Jacobs, Hubert, ed. and trans. Sources and Studies for the History
of the Jesuits. Vol. III. A Treatice on the Moluccas, c.
1544. Rev. by N. P. Cushner, HAHR, 53(May 1973):317-8.

Jacobs, Wilbur R. Dispossessing the American Indian: Indians and
    Whites on the Colonial Frontier. New York: Scribner's,
    1972. Rev. by N. O. Lurie, WMQ, 3rd ser., 30(Ja 1973):
    179-81; R. Horsman, WHQ, 4(Ja 1973):69-70; A. Debo,
    FHQ, 51(Ja 1973):327-8; E. H. Moseley, JSH, 39(Feb 1973):
    99-100; H. J. Viola, IMH, 69(Mar 1973):72-3; M. Young,
    NYH, 54(Ja 1973):113-14; J. H. Cash, A & W, 15(Win 1973):
    378-9; G. W. Pilcher, Montana, 23(Spr 1973):68; L. M.
    Hauptman, NYHSQ, 57(Apr 1973):175-6; T. J. Eblen and
    J. E. Eblen, PacH, 17(Spr 1973):100-2; F. Jennings, PH,
    40(Jl 1973):328-31; F. W. Turner, III, AHR, 78(Je 1973):
    724-6; A. M. Gibson, PHR, 42(Aug 1973):424-5.

Jacobson, Hans-Adolf. Nationalsozialistische Aussenpolitik 1933-
    1938. Frankfurt am Main: Alfred Metzner Verlag, 1968.
    Rev. by F. T. Epstein, JMH, 45(Je 1973):356-8.

Jacobson, Jon. Locarno Diplomacy: Germany and the West 1925-
    1929. Princeton, N. J.: Prin U Press, 1972. Rev. by
    R. P. Grathwol, JMH, 45(Je 1973):350-2.

Jaffa, Harry V. Crisis of the House Divided: An Interpretation of
    the Issues in the Lincoln-Douglas Debates. Seattle: U Wash
    Press, 1973. Rev. by F. J. Bowman, HRNB, 2(Nov/Dec
    1973):50-1.

Jaffe, Julian F. Crusade Against Radicalism: New York During the
    Red Scare, 1914-1924. Port Washington, N. Y.: Kennikat,
    1972. Rev. by J. B. Lane, NYH, 54(Apr 1973):249-51; L.
    K. Adler, AHR, 78(Je 1973):741-2; R. K. Murray, JAH, 60
    (Sep 1973):489-90.

Jäger, Wolfgang. Politische Partei und Parlamentarische Opposi-
    tion. Eine Studie zum Politischen Denken von Lord Boling-
    broke und David Hume. Berlin: Duncker and Humblot, 1971.
    Rev. by B. W. Hill, History, 58(Feb 1973):110-11.

Jahoda, Gloria. River of the Golden Ibis. New York: Hotl, Rine-
    hart and Winston, 1973. Rev. by F. G. Slaughter, FHQ, 52
    (Oct 1973):185-6.

Jain, A. P., ed. India and the World. Delhi: D. K. Publishing
    House, 1972. Rev. by N. M. Khilnani, IQ, 29(Ja-Mar 1973):
    63-4.

Jain, B. S. Administration of Justice in Seventeenth Century India
    (A Study of Salient Concepts of Mughal Justice). Delhi: Metro-
    politan, 1970. Rev. by F. Lehmann, AHR, 78(Je 1973):721-3.

Jain, C. M. State Legislatures in India: The Rajasthan Legislative
    Assembly, a Comparative Study. New Delhi: S. Chand, 1972.
    Rev. by R. Rattan, IQ, 29(Apr-Je 1973):170.

Jain, J. K. Transport Economics. Allahabad: Chaitanya, 1973.
Rev. by N. M. Khilnani, IQ, 29(Oct/Dec 1973):364-5.

James, Bessie Rowland. Anne Royall's U. S. A. New Brunswick,
N. J.: Rutgers U Press, 1972. Rev. by J. Pulley, JAH,
60(Je 1973):127-8; GHQ, 57(Spr 1973):155-6; L. R. Gerlach,
RKHS, 71(Apr 1973):204-7; H. M. Ward, JOW, 12(Oct 1973):
643-4; L. Griffith, NYHSQ, 57(Apr 1973):183-4; J. E.
Friedman, NJH, 91(Aut 1973):191-3; J. E. Gonzales, NCHR,
50(Spr 1973):217; E. M. Geffen, PMHB, 97(Apr 1973):273-5.

James, Edward T., Janet Wilson James, and Paul S. Boyer, eds.
Notable American Women, 1607-1950: A Biographical Dic-
tionary, 3 vols. Cambridge, Mass.: Har U Press, 1971.
Rev. by M. S. Benson, JAH, 59(Mar 1973):972-3; B. Wel-
ter, WMQ, 3rd ser., 30(Jl 1973):518-22; M. E. Massey,
AHR, 78(Feb 1973):144-5.

James, Francis Godwin. Ireland in the Empire, 1688-1770: A History of Ireland From the Williamite Wars to the Eve of the
American Revolution. Cambridge, Mass.: Har U Press,
1973. Rev. by G. Costigan, HRNB, 2(Oct 1973):2-3.

James, George Wharton. Indian Blankets and Their Makers.
Glorieta, N. M.: Rio Grande, 1970. Rev. by S. Black,
JOW, 12(Apr 1973):342-3.

James, Harold and Denis Sheil-Small. The Undeclared War: The
Story of the Indonesian Confrontation 1962-1966. Totowa,
N. J.: Rowman and Littlefield, 1971. Rev. by D. C. Gordon,
MilAf, 37(Feb 1973):36.

James, Janet Wilson see James, Edward T.

James, Margery Kirkbride. Studies in the Medieval Wine Trade.
Oxford: Clarendon, 1971. Rev. by J. LePatourel, EHR, 88
(Jl 1973):592-4; W. M Daly, JEH, 33(Dec 1973):890-2.

James, Robert E. The Emancipation of the Russian Nobility, 1762-
1785. Princeton, N. J.: Prin U Press, 1973. Rev. by D.
Reinhartz, HRNB, 2(Oct 1973):7-8.

Janis, Irving L. Victims of Groupthink: A Psychological Study of
Foreign-Policy Decisions and Fiascoes. Boston: Houghton
Mifflin, 1972. Rev. by B. Kublick, JAH, 60(Dec 1973):857-8.

Jankovich, Miklós. They Rode Into Europe: The Fruitful Exchange
in the Arts of Horsemanship Between East and West. New
York: Scribner's, 1973. Rev. by J. Beeler, AHR, 78(Dec
1973):1422.

János, Andrew C. and William B. Slottman, eds. Revolution in
Perspective: Essays on the Hungarian Soviet Republic. Lon-

don: U Cal Press, 1972. Rev. by N. Stone, History, 58
(Oct 1973):468-9; I. Volgyes, EEQ, 7(Fall 1973):345-7.

Jaques, Florence Page. Francis Lee Jaques: Artist of the Wilderness World. New York: Doubleday, 1973. Rev. by J.
Campbell, ChOk, 51(Win 1973-74):502-3.

Jarman, Thomas L. Socialism in Britain From the Industrial Revolution to the Present Day. New York: Toplinger, 1972.
Rev. by M. Ratliff, Historian, 35(Feb 1973):285-6.

Jarvis, Rupert C. Collected Papers on the Jacobite Risings. Vol. 2.
Manchester: Manchester U Press, 1972. Rev. by D. Read,
Archives, 11(Spr 1973):53-4; P. D. G. Thomas, History, 58
(Feb 1973):111-12.

Jedin, Hubert. Geschichte des Konzils von Trient. Band III.
Bologneser Tagung (1547-8), Zweite Trienten Tagunsperiode
(1551-2). Freiberg, Basel-Wien: Herder, 1970. Rev. by
J. Bossy, ESR, 3(Apr 1973):183-4; S. Kuttner, AHR, 78
(Feb 1973):91-2.

Jefferson, James, Robert W. Delaney and Gregory C. Thompson.
The Southern Utes: A Tribal History. Ignacio, Colo.:
Southern Ute Tribe, 1972. Rev. by O. C. Stewart, CoMag,
50(Sum1973):263-4.

Jefferson, Thomas see Boyd, Julian T.

Jelavich, Barbara. The Ottoman Empire, The Great Powers, and
the Straits Question, 1870-1887. Bloomington: Ind U Press,
1973. Rev. by K. R. Nelson, HRNB, 2(Nov/Dec 1973):33.

Jenkins, David. The Agricultural Community in Southwest Wales at
the Turn of the Century. Cardiff: U Wales Press, 1971.
Rev. by G. E. Evans, MH, 2(Aut 1973):130-2.

Jenkins, George D. see Post, Kenneth W. J.

Jenkins, W. L. see Cherns, A. B.

Jenkins, William M., Jr. And ... I'll Throw in the Socks. Bowling Green, Ky.: William M. Jenkins, Jr., 1972. Rev. by
B. A. Guthrie, Jr., FCHQ, 47(Oct 1973):362.

Jennings, Laurence C. France and Europe in 1848: A Study of
French Foreign Affairs in Time of Crisis. New York: Ox
U Press, 1973. Rev. by G. Fasel, HRNB, 2(Oct 1973):5-6.

Jennison, Keith W., comp. The Essential Lincoln. n. p.: Franklin
Watts, 1971. Rev. by R. D. Hoffsommer, CWTI, 12(Oct
1973):49.

Jensen, Richard. The Winning of the Midwest: Social and Political Conflict, 1888-1896. Chicago: U Chi Press, 1971. Rev. by W. O. Beck, NDH, 4(Spr 1973):38; M. Hammarberg, JAH, 59(Mar 1973):1024-6; W. V. Hill, MichH, 57(Spr 1973):88-90.

Jequier, François. Une entreprise horlogère du Val-de-Travers: Fleurier Watch Co. SA. De l'atelier familial du XIXe aux Concentrations du XXe siècle. Neuchâtel: Editions de la Baconnière, 1972. Rev. by R. J. Bezucha, JMH, 45(Dec 1973):687-8.

Jeschke, Hubert. U-Bootta Ktik: Zur deutschen U-Boottaktik 1900-1945. Freiberg-im-Breisgau: Verlag Rombach, 1972. Rev. by C. Burdick, JHM, 45(Sep 1973):544-5.

Jessey, Gary D. Letcher County's Pine Mountain Caves. Cromona, Ky.: Superior, 1973. Rev. by A. I. George, FCHQ, 47(Oct 1973):362.

Jewell, Helen M. English Local Administration in the Middle Ages. Newton Abbott: David and Charles, 1972. Rev. by R. F. Hunnisett, Archives, 11(Spr 1973):50-1.

Jha, L. K. Economic Development: Ends and Means. Bombay: Vora, 1973. Rev. by S. Venu, IQ, 29(Jl-Sep 1973):278-9.

Joel, Miriam. African Traditions in Latin America. Cuernavaca, Mexico: Centro Intercultural de Documentacion, 1972. Rev. by P. J. Carroll, HAHR, 53(Nov 1973):728.

Joesting, Edward. Hawaii: An Uncommon History. New York: Norton, 1972. Rev. by B. Melendy, AW, 10(Nov 1973):58.

Joffe, Julian A. Studies in the History of Civilization. New York: Philosophical Library, 1970. Rev. by G. Roberson, JOW, 12(Jl 1973):503; J. S. Roucek, SS, 64(Feb 1973):87.

Johanningmeier, Erwin V. see Johnson, Henry C. Jr.

Johannsen, Robert W. Stephen A. Douglas. New York: Ox U Press, 1973. Rev. by I. Katz, CWH, 19(Sep 1973):277-9; J. Z. Rabun, JSH, 39(Nov 1973):600-2.

Johari, J. C. Naxalite Politics in India. Delhi: Research Publications, 1972. Rev. by B. S. Gupta, IQ, 29(Apr-Je 1973):174.

Johnson, Barry C. Case of Marcus A. Reno. London: English Westerners' Society, 1969. Rev. by T. Wilson, ChOk, 51 (Fall 1973):369-70.

Johnson, Cecil. Communist China and Latin America, 1959-1967. New York: Columbia U Press, 1970. Rev. by W. R. Garner, AHR, 78(Feb 1973):70-1.

Johnson, David. Music and Society in Lowland Scotland in the
     Eighteenth Century. New York: Ox U Press, 1972. Rev.
     by D. Forbes, HJ, 16(Dec 1973):868-9.

Johnson, Dorothy W. The Bloody Bozeman: The Perilous Trail to
     Montana's Gold. New York: McGraw-Hill, 1971. Rev. by
     A. M Gibson, AHR, 78(Oct 1973):1134-5.

Johnson, Douglas, ed. The Making of the Modern World. London:
     Ernest Benn, 1971. Rev. by G. V. Scammell, History, 58
     (Feb 1973):93-4.

Johnson, E. A. J. The Foundations of American Economic Free-
     dom: Government and Enterprise in the Age of Washington.
     Minneapolis: U Minn Press, 1973. Rev. by C. Gilbert,
     HRNB, 2(Nov/Dec 1973):44.

Johnson, F. Roy. The Algonquins: Indians of That Part of the New
     World First Visited by the English. Vol. I. Pre-History.
     Vol. II. History and Traditions. Murfreesboro, Tenn: John-
     son, 1972. Rev. by A. H. DeRosier, Jr., NCHR, 50(Spr
     1973):204-5.

Johnson, Glenn L. and C. Leroy Quance, eds. The Overproduction
     Trap in U. S. Agriculture: A Study of Resource Allocation
     From World War I to Late 1960's. Baltimore: JHU Press,
     1972. Rev. by E. W. Grove, AgH, 47(Jl 1973):266-7.

Johnson, Henry C. and Erwin V. Johanningmeier. Teachers for the
     Prairie: The University of Illinois and the Schools, 1868-
     1945. Urbana: U Ill Press, 1972. Rev. by J. Herbst,
     WMH, 56(Aut 1973):66; D. Sloan, JAH, 60(Je 1973):150-2.

Johnson, J. K. and Carole B. Stelmack, eds. The Papers of the
     Prime Ministers. The Letters of Sir John A. Macdonald.
     2 vols. Ottawa: Public Archives of Canada, 1968, 1969.
     Rev. by B. W. Hodgins, CHR, 54(Mar 1973):85-8.

Johnson, Mary Lynch. A History of Meredith College. Raleigh,
     N. C.: Meredith College, 1972. Rev. by W. H. Wallace,
     NCHR, 50(Spr 1973):200-1.

Johnson, Niel M. George Sylvester Viereck: German-American
     Propagandist. Urbana: U Ill Press, 1972. Rev. by J.
     Grimbel, JAH, 59(Mar 1973):1034-5; S. Weinberg, AHR, 78
     (Je 1973):660-1.

Johnson, Walter and Carol Evans, eds. The Papers of Adlai
     Stevenson. Vol. I. Beginnings of Education. Boston: Little,
     Brown, 1972. Rev. by O. L. Graham, Jr., JAH, 60(Je
     1973):94-6; H. C. Nicholas, AHR, 78(Dec 1973):1539-41;
     R. H. Bremmer, JISHS, 66(Win 1973):475-6.

_____ and _____, eds. The Papers of Adlai Stevenson. Vol.
II. Washington to Springfield, 1941-1948. Boston: Little,
Brown, 1973. Rev. by O. L. Graham, Jr., JAH, 60(Sep
1973):417-18.

Johnson, Willard R. The Cameroon Federation: Political Integration in a Fragmentary Society. Princeton, N. J.: Prin U
Press, 1970. Rev. by J. F. Bayart, AfAf, 72(Oct 1973):
453-4.

Johnston, H. J. M. British Emigration Policy, 1815-1830: 'Shovel-
ling Out the Paupers.' n. p.: Ox U Press, 1972. Rev. by
R. A. Lewis, History, 58(Oct 1973):457.

Johnston, William M. The Austrian Mind: An Intellectual and Social History, 1848-1938. Berkeley: U Cal Press, 1972. Rev.
by C. E. Schorske, AHR, 78(Feb 1973):119-21; M. Jay,
JMH, 45(Dec 1973):689-91; F. Field, History, 58(Je 1973):
312.

Joiner, Edward E. A History of Florida Baptists. Jacksonville,
Fla.: Fla Baptist Convention, 1972. Rev. by W. B. Posey,
FHQ, 51(Ja 1973):311-12; W. Flint, JSH, 39(May 1973):323-4.

Jonas, Gerald. On Doing Good: the Quaker Experiment. New York:
Scribner's, 1971. Rev. by L. Gara, PH, 40(Ja 1973):95-6.

Jones, Andrew. The Politics of Reform, 1884. Cambridge and
New York: Cam U Press, 1972. Rev. by N. Gash, JMH,
45(Sep 1973):511-12.

Jones, Ann. Uncle Tom's Campus. New York: Praeger, 1973.
Rev. by N. Lederer, Crisis, 80(Je-Jl 1973):213-14.

Jones, Archer see Connelly, Thomas Lawrence

Jones, Charles S. From the Rio Grande to the Arctic: The Story
of the Richfield Oil Corporation. Norman: U Ok Press,
1972. Rev. by J. E. Fickle, JOW, 12(Oct 1973):643; H. M.
Larson, BHR, 47(Spr 1973):121-2; E. A. Erickson, PacH,
17(Spr 1973):88-9.

Jones, Eldred D. The Elizabethan Image of Africa. Charlottesville: Va Univ, 1971. Rev. by W. E. M., AfAf, 72(Ja 1973):
97.

Jones, George Fenwick and Marie Hahn, eds. and trans. Detailed
Reports on the Salzburger Emigrants Who Settled in America.
... Vol. III: 1736. Athens, Ga.: U Ga Press, 1972. Rev.
by M. Rubincam, JSH, 39(Feb 1973):101-2; W. C. Smith,
FHQ, 51(Ja 1973):323-4; M. L. Brown, Jr., WMQ, 3d ser.
30(Jl 1973):533-5.

Jones, Michael. <u>Ducal Brittany.</u> Oxford: Ox U Press, 1970. Rev.
    by K. Fowler, History, 58(Je 1973):264-5.

Jones, O. W. <u>Isaac Williams and His Circle.</u> London: S. P. C. K.,
    1971. Rev. by B. Coleman, History, 58(Je 1973):304.

Jones, Ray. <u>The Nineteenth-Century Foreign Office: An Adminis-</u>
    <u>trative History.</u> London: Weidenfeld and Nicolson, 1971.
    Rev. by R. A. Lewis, History, 58(Feb 1973):118-19; R. M.
    MacLeod, AHR, 78(Dec 1973):1386-1405.

Jones, Robert H. <u>Disrupted Decades: The Civil War and Recon-</u>
    <u>struction Years.</u> New York: Scribner's, 1973. Rev. by R.
    Lowe, HRNB, 2(Oct 1973):15-16; J. T. Moore, VMHB, 81
    (Oct 1973):501-2; M. E. Massey, JSH, 39(Nov 1973):606-8.

Jones, Robert R. <u>see</u> Drake, W. Magruder

Jones, Roger. <u>The Rescue of Emin Pasha.</u> n. p.: Allison and
    Busby, 1972. Rev. by J. A. Casada, AfAf, 72(Jl 1973):
    338-9.

Jones, Thomas Firth. <u>A Pair of Lawn Sleeves: A Biography of</u>
    <u>William Smith (1727-1803).</u> Philadelphia: Chilton, 1972.
    Rev. by R. S. Klein, AHR, 78(Feb 1973):152; O. S. Ireland,
    PH, 40(Jl 1973):336-7.

Jones, W. J. <u>Politics and the Bench.</u> London: Allen and Unwin,
    1971. Rev. by D. H. Pennington, History, 58(Feb 1973):
    101-2.

Jones, Wilbur Devereux and Arvel B. Erickson. <u>The Peelites 1846-</u>
    <u>1857.</u> Columbus, O.: Ohio St U Press, 1972. Rev. by W.
    L. Arnstein, JMH, 45(Sep 1973):506-9; N. Gash, History,
    58(Je 1973):307-9.

Jordan, David M. <u>Roscoe Conkling of New York: Voice in the</u>
    <u>Senate.</u> London: Cornell U Press, 1971. Rev. by S. G. F.
    Spackman, History, 58(Feb 1973):152; G. G. Eggert, PH,
    40(Ja 1973):108-10.

Jordan, David P. <u>Gibbon and His Roman Empire.</u> London: U Ill
    Press, 1971. Rev. by N. Hampson, History, 58(Feb 1973):
    113.

Jordan, Ruth. <u>Sophie Dorothea.</u> New York: Barziller, 1972. Rev.
    by S. Biddle, AHR, 78(Je 1973):685-6.

Jordan, W. K. <u>Edward VI: The Threshhold of Power. The Dom-</u>
    <u>inance of the Duke of Northumberland.</u> London: Allen and
    Unwin, 1970. Rev. by P. Williams, EHR, 88(Jl 1973):597-9.

Jorgenson, Joseph G. <u>The Sun Dance Religion: Power for the</u>

Powerless. Chicago: U Chi Press, 1972. Rev. by D.
McNickle, NMHR, 48(Apr 1973):177-9; V. J. Vogel, JAH,
60(Dec 1973):819-20.

Josephson, Matthew and Hannah. Al Smith: Hero of the Cities.
London: Thames and Hudson, 1971. Rev. by M. Simpson,
History, 58(Feb 1973):157.

Josephy, Alvin M., Jr., ed. The Horizon History of Africa. New
York: American Heritage, n. d. Rev. by R. Austen, JMH,
45(Sep 1973):463-5.

Joslin, D. M. see Winter, J. M.

Journal of Glass Studies, Vol. 13. Corning, N. Y.: Corning Museum of Glass, 1971. Rev. by H. J. Haden, T & C, 14(Ja
1973):110-12.

Joyce, R. B. Sir William MacGregor. New York: Ox U Press,
1971. Rev. by H. J. Hanham, AHR, 78(Je 1973):695.

Joyce, Trevor. Pentahedron. Dublin: Zozimus Books, 1972. Rev.
by F. S. Kiley, E-I, 8(Aut 1973):148-50.

Juhasz, Gyula. Magyarorszag kulpolitikaja, 1919-1945. Budapest:
Kossuth Konyukiado, 1969. Rev. by T. Spira, EEQ, 7(Spr
1973):96-7.

Kaelble, Hartmut. Berliner Unternehmer Waehrend der Fruhen Industrialisierung. Berlin: De Gruyter, 1972. Rev. by K.
K. Wolff, BHR, 47(Win 1973):546-8.

Kaestle, Carl F. The Evolution of an Urban School System: New
York City, 1750-1850. Cambridge, Mass.: Har U Press,
1973. Rev. by W. Smith, HRNB, 2(Nov/Dec 1973):48-9.

Kaeuper, Richard W. Bankers to the Crown: The Riccardi of Luc-
ca and Edward I. Princeton, N. J.: Prin U Press, 1973.
Rev. by D. Herlihy, AHR, 78(Dec 1973):1438.

Kahn, Herman and B. Bruce-Briggs. Things to Come: Thinking
About the 70's and 80's. New York: Macmillan, 1972. Rev.
by T. L. Thompson, CurH, 64(Apr 1973):180.

Kahn, Kathy. Hillbilly Women. Garden City, N. Y.: Doubleday,
1973. Rev. by J. E. Talmadge, GHQ, 57(Win 1973):596-7.

Kain, Richard M. Susan L. Mitchell. Lewisburg, Pa.: Bucknell
U Press, 1972. Rev. by T. C. Ware, E-I, 8(Win 1973):
144-7.

Kaiser, Friedhelm Berthold. Die russische Justizreform von 1864.
Zur Geschichte der russischen Justiz von Katharina II bis

1917. Leiden: E. J. Brill, 1972. Rev. by M. Raeff, RR, 32(Jl 1973):318-9.

Kaiser, Karl and Roger Morgan, eds. Britain and West Germany: Changing Societies and the Future of Foreign Policy. New York: Ox U Press, 1971. Rev. by R. W. Carden, JMH, 45(Mar 1973):187-8.

Kalela, Jorma. Neighbors on Separate Roads: Finnish-Swedish Cooperation in the Finnish and Swedish Foreign Policies, 1921-1923. Helsingfors: Suomen Historiallinen Seura, 1971. Rev. by K. Hamalainen, AHR, 78(Dec 1973):1486-7.

Kalicz, Nándor. Clay Gods: The Neolithic Period and Copper Age in Hungary. Budapest: Corvina Press, 1970. Rev. by T. W. Jacobsen, Archaeology, 26(Ja 1973):73-4.

Kamen, Henry. The Iron Century: Social Change in Europe 1550-1660. New York: Praeger, 1971. Rev. by T. K. Rabb, JMH, 45(Sep 1973):456-62; B. Pullan, HJ, 16(Sep 1973):629-35; A. Lossky, AHR, 78(Oct 1973):1047-8.

Kammen, Michael. People of Paradox: An Inquiry Concerning the Origins of American Civilization. New York: Knopf, 1972. Rev. by J. M. Murrin, WMQ, 3rd ser., 30(Jl 1973):491-5; T. L. Haskell, JSH, 39(May 1973):276-7; I. D. Gruber, NCHR, 50(Aut 1973):425; C. Robbins, PMHB, 97(Ja 1973): 110-11; M. D. Peterson, MHM, 68(Fall 1973):347-9; A. P. Kenny, NYH, 54(Apr 1973):253-4.

_____, ed. "What Is the Good of History?" Selected Letters of Carl L. Becker, 1900-1945. Ithaca, N. Y.: Cornell U Press, 1973. Rev. by W. Issel, HRNB, 2(Nov/Dec 1973):39.

Kane, Paul. Paul Kane's Frontier: Including Wandering of an Artist Among the Indians of North America. Austin: U Tx Press, 1971. Rev. by W. D. Hoyt, JOW, 12(Ja 1973):188-9.

Kane, William Everett. Civil Strife in Latin America: A Legal History of U. S. Involvement. Baltimore: JHU Press, 1972. Rev. by J. N. Plank, HAHR, 53(Aug 1973):543-5.

Kantor, Harry. Bibliography of José Figueres. Tempe, Ariz: Ariz St U Press, 1972. Rev. by P. F. Flemion, HAHR, 53(May 1973):334-6.

Kanza, Thomas. Conflict in the Congo. Harmondsworth, England: Penguin, 1972. Rev. by P. Whitaker, AfAf, 72(Oct 1973): 457.

Kapferer, B. Strategy and Transaction in an African Factory. Manchester: Manchester U Press, 1972. Rev. by H. Heisler, AfAf, 72(Ja 1973):96-7.

Kaplan, H. R. and James F. Hunt. This is the Coast Guard. Cambridge, Md.: Cornell Maritime Press, 1972. Rev. by T. R.
Strobridge, MilAf, 37(Feb 1973):31-2.

Kaplan, Harold. Democratic Humanism and American Literature.
Chicago: U Chi Press, 1972. Rev. by J. W. Tuttleton, JAH,
59(Mar 1973):1002-3.

Kaplan, Lawrence S. Colonies Into Nation: American Diplomacy,
1763-1801. New York: Macmillan, 1972. Rev. by J. A.
Combs, WMQ, 3rd ser., 30(Apr 1973):347-9.

Kapoor, Ashok. International Business Negotiations: A Study in
India. New York: NYU Press, 1970. Rev. by S. Venu, IQ,
29(Jl-Sep 1973):258-9.

Kappler, Charles J. Indian Treaties, 1778-1883. New York: Interland, 1973. Rev. by M. R. Blaine, ChOk, 51(Win 1973-74):
500-1. NOTE: This work is a reprint of the original 1904
edition.

Karbar, Yaqub N. Railway Development in the Ottoman Empire,
1856-1914. New York: Vantage, 1972. Rev. by W. L.
Ochsenwald, MEJ, 27(Spr 1973):249.

Karmi, Hasan S. Al-Manar English-Arabic Dictionary. New York:
St. Martin's, 1972. Rev. by Q. I. Al-Sharbati, MEJ, 27
(Spr 1973):247-8.

Karnes, Thomas L., ed. Readings in the Latin American Policy of
the United States. Tucson: U Ari Press, 1972. Rev. by
C. L. Stansifer, HT, 7(Nov 1973):131-2; L. R., HAHR, 53
(Aug 1973):573.

Karngire, S. R. A History of the Kingdom of Nkore in Western
Uganda to 1896. London: Clarendon, 1971. Rev. by C.
Wrigley, AfAf, 72(Ja 1973):89.

Karsten, Peter. The Naval Aristocracy: The Golden Age of Annapolis and the Emergence of Modern American Navalism. New
York: Free Press, 1972. Rev. by W. R. Herrick, Jr.,
JAH, 60(Je 1973):147-8; H. B. Hammett, MHM, 68(Sum
1973):226-7; W. R. Braisted, PHR, 42(May 1973):259-60.

Kaspi, André. La mission de Jean Monnet à Alger: mars-octobre
1943. Paris: Publications de la Sorbonne, 1971. Rev. by
L. S. Kaplan, JAH, 60(Je 1973):177-8; L. R. Blair, AHR,
78(Je 1973):701-2.

Katoke, Israel K. The Making of the Karagwe Kingdom: Tanzanian
History From Oral Traditions. Nairobi, Kenya: EAPH,
1970. Rev. by A. Redmayne, AfAf, 72(Oct 1973):464-5.

Katz, Abraham. The Politics of Economic Reform in the Soviet Union. New York: Praeger, 1972. Rev. by R. W. Campbell, RR, 32(Jl 1973):319-20.

Katz, Friedrich. The Ancient American Civilizations. London: Weidenfeld and Nicolson. 1972. Rev. by W. Bray, History, 58(Oct 1973):479-80; L. C. Faron, HAHR, 53(Aug 1973): 529-31.

Katz, William Loren. The Black West. Garden City, N. Y.: Doubleday, 1971. Rev. by W. D. Rowley, NHSQ, 16(Spr 1973):43-4; W. L. Richter, JISH, 66(Win 1973):471-2; R. C. McConnell, JNH, 58(Jl 1973):365-7.

Kauffman, Henry J. American Axes: A Survey of Their Development and Their Makers. Brattleboro, Vt.: Stephen Greene, 1972. Rev. by P. C. Welsh, T & C, 14(Ja 1973):83-4.

Kaufman, Martin. Homeopathy in America: The Rise and Fall of a Medical Heresy. Baltimore: JHU Press, 1971. Rev. by J. F. Kett, AHR, 78(Feb 1973):164.

Kaufman, Robert R. The Politics of Land Reform in Chile, 1950-1970: Public Policy, Political Institutions and Social Change. Cambridge, Mass.: Har U Press, 1972. Rev. by J. Petras, HAHR, 53(Nov 1973):719-21; A. J. Bauer, AgH, 47(Oct 1973): 358-61.

Kaushik, Susheela. The Agony of Vietnam: The Origin and Background of American Intervention in Vietnam. New Delhi: Sterling, 1972. Rev. by K. C. Kohli, IQ, 29(Jl-Sep 1973): 268-9.

Kavenagh, W. Keith, ed. Foundations of Colonial America: A Documentary History. Vol. I. Northeastern Colonies. Vol. II. Middle Atlantic Colonies. Vol. III. Southern Colonies. New York: Chelsea, 1973. Rev. by S. N. Katz, JAH, 60(Dec 1973):774-5.

Kay, G. B., ed. The Political Economy of Colonialism in Ghana: A Collection of Documents and Statistics, 1900-1960. Cambridge: Cam U Press, 1972. Rev. by T. R. De Gregori, T & C, 14(Jl 1973):517-18; P. Kilby, BHR, 47(Spr 1973): 137-9.

Kealey, Edward J. Roger of Salisbury: Viceroy of England. Berkeley: U Cal Press, 1972. Rev. by R. H. C. Davis, AHR, 78(Feb 1973):82-3; H. C. Krueger, Historian, 35(Feb 1973): 280-1; J. W. Alexander, CHR, 54(Dec 1973):457-8; J. O. Prestwich, History, 58(Oct 1973):431.

Kealey, Gregory S. see Gutman, Herbert G.

_____ and _____, eds. see Gutman, Herbert G.

Keddie, Nikki R. Sayyid Jamāl ad-dīn "Al-Afghānī": A Political
    Biography. Berkeley: U Cal Press, 1972. Rev. by M. H.
    Kerr, MEJ, 27(Sum 1973):402-4.

_____, ed. Sufis, Scholars and Saints: Muslim Religious Insti-
    tutions Since 1500. Berkeley: U Cal Press, 1972. Rev. by
    R. P. Mitchell, MEJ, 27(Aut 1973):518-19.

Keen, Benjamin. The Aztec Image in Western Thought. New Bruns-
    wick, N. J.: Rutgers U Press, 1971. Rev. by M. León-
    Portilla, HAHR, 53(Feb 1973):106-9.

_____ and Juan Friede, eds. see Friede, Juan.

Keen, M. H. England in the Later Middle Ages. [London]:
    Methuen, n. d. Rev. by R. O'Day, HTo, 23(Ja 1973):68-9.

Keenan, Edward L. The Kurbskii-Groznyi Apocrypha: The Seven-
    teenth-Century Genesis of the "Correspondence" Attributed
    to Prince A. M. Kurbskii and Tsar Ivan IV. Cambridge,
    Mass.: Har U Press, 1972. Rev. by S. A. Zenkovsky, RR,
    32(Jl 1973):299-311; R. Hellie, JMH, 45(Sep 1973):489-90.

Keith, Herbert F. Man of the Woods. Syracuse, N. Y.: Syr U
    Press, 1972. Rev. by J. R. Moravek, NYH, 54(Jl 1973):
    372-4.

Keithley, George. The Donner Party. New York: Barziller, 1972.
    Rev. by K. Lamott, CHQ, 52(Sum 1973):182-3; D. M. Bor-
    den, PacH, 17(Sum 1973):88-9.

Kele, Max H. Nazis and Workers: National Socialist Appeals to
    German Labor, 1919-1933. Chapel Hill: UNC Press, 1972.
    Rev. by R. N. Hunt, JMH, 45(Sep 1973):542-3.

Keller, Allan. Colonial America. New York: Hawthorn, 1971.
    Rev. by J. P. Cullen, AHI, 7(Feb 1973):49.

Kelley, Darwin. Milligan's Fight Against Lincoln. New York: Ex-
    position, 1973. Rev. by M. Perman, JSH, 39(Nov 1973):
    605-6; GHQ, 57(Win 1973):606-7; F. L. Klement, IMH, 69
    (Sep 1973):279-81.

Kelley, Sarah Foster. Children of Nashville ... Lineages from
    James Robertson. Nashville: Blue and Gray Press, 1973.
    Rev. by J. R. Bigger, THQ, 32(Sum 1973):190.

Kelly, Daniel T. and Beatrice Chauvenet. The Buffalo Head: A
    Century of Mercantile Pioneering in the Southwest. Santa
    Fe: Vergara, 1972. Rev. by W. I. Robertson, AW, 10(Mar
    1973):54; W. J. Donlon, A & W, 15(Spr 1973):91-3.

Kelsey, Darwin P., ed. Farming in the New Nation: Interpreting American Agriculture, 1790-1840. Washington: Agriculture History Society, 1972. Rev. by W. Graebner, PH, 40(Oct 1973):489-90; D. O. Whitten, JEH, 33(Sep 1973):679-81; G. M. Herndon, WMQ, 3rd ser., 30(Apr 1973):358-9.

Kemeny, John G. Man and the Computer. New York: Scribner's, 1972. Rev. by W. L. Casey, Jr., T & C, 14(Oct 1973): 665-7.

Kemiläinen, Aira. "L'affaire d'Avignon" (1789-1791) From the Viewpoint of Nationalism. Helsinki: Suomalainen Tiedeakatemia, 1971. Rev. by B. C. Shafer, JMH, 45(Dec 1973):668-9.

Kemp, Donald C. Quicksilver to Bar Silver: Tales of Mexico's Bonanzas. Pasadena: Socio-Technical Publications, 1972. Rev. by A. Probert, JOW, 12(Ja 1973):180.

Kemp, Tom. The French Economy 1913-1939. London: Longman, 1972. Rev. by J. Angus, History, 58(Oct 1973):469.

Kendall, Paul Murray. Louis XI. London: Allen and Unwin, 1971. Rev. by M. Jones, History, 58(Feb 1973):85-6.

Kenez, Peter. Civil War in Russia, 1918: The First Year of the Volunteer Army. Berkeley: U Cal Press, 1971. Rev. by P. Avrich, JMH, 45(Mar 1973):167-8.

Kennan, George F. The Marquis de Custine and His Russia in 1839. Princeton, N. J.: Prin U Press, 1971. Rev. by A. Sinel, AHR, 78(Feb 1973):127-8.

_____. Memoirs, 1950-1963. Vol. II. Boston: Little, Brown, 1972. Rev. by T. T. Hammond, RR, 32(Apr 1973):193-5; A. Z. Rubenstein, CurH, 64(May 1973):225.

Kennedy, Kiernan A. Productivity and Industrial Growth. The Irish Experience. Oxford: Clarendon, 1971. Rev. by J. Pincus, JEH, 33(Je 1973):490-1.

Kent, Barry C., Ira F. Smith, III, and Catherine McCann. Foundations of Pennsylvania Prehistory. Harrisburg: Pa Historical and Museum Commission, 1971. Rev. by R. A. Thomas, PH, 40(Ja 1973):213-14.

Kent, Donald H. see Stevens, S. K.

Kenworthy, Leonard S., ed. Ginn Social Science Series. 8 vols. Lexington, Mass.: Ginn, 1972. Rev. by E. G. Campbell, 64(Nov 1973):273-4.

Kenyon, John. The Popish Plot. New York: St. Martin's, 1972. Rev. by W. C. Wilbur, JMH, 45(Sep 1973):477-8; C. Robbins, AHR, 78(Oct 1973):1058-9.

Kerby, Robert L. Kirby Smith's Confederacy: The Trans-Missis-
sippi South, 1861-1865. New York: Columbia U Press, 1972.
Rev. by B. F. Cooling, CWH, 19(Mar 1973):84-5; P. J.
Avillo, Jr., A & W, 15(Aut 1973):281-3; C. P. Roland, JSH,
39(May 1973):289-300; A. Barr, JAH, 59(Mar 1973):1010-11;
G. Tucker, FHQ, 51(Ja 1973):330-1; G. M. Jenks, JOW, 12
(Jl 1973):509; J. D. Winters, LaH, 14(Sum 1973):323; L.
Anders, MoHR, 67(Ja 1973):324-6; L. H. Fischer, AW, 10
(Ja 1973):50; F. H. Smyrl, SWHQ, 76(Apr 1973):495-6.

Kerr, Stanley E. The Lions of Marash: Personal Experiences With
American Near East Relief, 1919-1922. Albany: SUNY Press,
1973. Rev. by J. B. Gidney, HRNB, 2(Oct 1973):12.

Kesavan, K. V. Japan's Relations with South-East Asia, 1952-60.
Bombay: Somaiya, 1972. Rev. by P. Pant, IQ, 29(Ja-Mar
1973):61-2.

Keskar, B. V. and V. K. N. Menon, eds. Acharya Narendra Dev:
A Commemoration Volume. Delhi: National Book Trust,
1971. Rev. by K. P. Misra, IQ, 29(Apr-Je 1973):166-7.

Ketcham, Ralph. James Madison: A Biography. New York: Macmillan, 1971. Rev. by F. C. McLaughlin, WPHM, 56(Ja
1973):87-90; A. Spalt, NYHSQ, 57(Ja 1973):77-9.

Ketchum, Richard. The Winter Soldiers. Garden City, N. Y.:
Doubleday, 1973. Rev. by G. O. Haffner, IMH, 69(Dec 1973):
367-8; R. F. Snow, AH, 25(Dec 1973):94-5; D. Sloan,
ArkHQ, 32(Aut 1973):292-4; R. N. Sheldon, GHQ, 57(Win
1973):592; G. Swetnam, WPHM, 56(Oct 1973):443-4.

Khadduri, Majid, ed. Major Middle Eastern Problems in International Law. Washington, D. C.: American Enterprise Institute of Policy Research, 1972. Rev. by H. J. Liebesny,
MEJ, 27(Win 1973):100-1.

_____. Political Trends in the Arab World: The Role of Ideas
and Ideals in Politics. Baltimore: JHU Press, 1970. Rev.
by F. M. Najjar, MEJ, 27(Spr 1973):227-9.

Kidder, J. Edward. Early Buddhist Japan. New York: Praeger,
1972. Rev. by H. Befu, Archaeology, 26(Apr 1973):155.

Kieft, David Owen. Belgium's Return to Neutrality: An Essay in
the Frustrations of Small Power Diplomacy. n. p.: Ox U
Press, 1972. Rev. by A. Adamthwaite, History, 58(Oct
1973):473-4; P.-H. Laurent, AHR, 78(Je 1973):703-5; W.
Warmbrunn, JMH, 45(Sep 1973):549.

Kiely, Benedict. Poor Scholar: A Study of the Works and Days of

William Carleton (1794-1869).   Dublin: Talbot Press, 1972.
Rev. by L. V. Harrod, E-I, 8(Win 1973):133.

Kienast, W.   Der Herzogstitel in Frankreich und Deutschland (9. bis
12. Jahrhundert) mit Listen der Ältesten deutschen Herzogsurkunden. Munich: Oldenbourg, 1968. Rev. by K. Leyser,
EHR, 88(Jl 1973):584-9.

Kiernan, Bernard P.   The United States, Communism and the Emergent World. Bloomington: Ind U Press, 1972. Rev. by
A. Z. Rubinstein, CurH, 64(Apr 1973):179.

Killion, Ronald and Charles Waller.   Slavery Times When I Was
Chillun Down on Marster's Plantation. Savannah: Beehive,
1973. Rev. in GHQ, 57(Win 1973):597-8.

Kimambo, I. N.   Mbiru: Popular Protest in Colonial Tanzania.
Nairobi, Kenya: EAPH, 1971. Rev. by A. Redmayne, AfAf,
72(Oct 1973):464-5.

Kimball, E. G., ed.   Sessions of the Peace in the City of Lincoln,
1351-1354 and the Borough of Stamford, 1351.   Lincoln?:
Lincoln Record Society ... 1971. Rev. by S. F. C. Milsom,
Archives 11(Spr 1973):47-8.

Kimball, Lorenzo Kent.   The Changing Pattern of Political Power in
Iraq, 1958-1971. New York: Speller, 1972. Rev. by T. Y.
Ismael, MEJ, 27(Aut 1973):523.

Kinchen, Oscar A.   Women Who Spied for the Blue and Gray. Philadelphia: Dorrance, 1972. Rev. by B. M. D. Price, JMiH,
35(Aug 1973):413-14; GHQ, 57(Win 1973):607; M. E. Massey,
NCHR, 50(Aut 1973):434-5; M. Stuart, VMHB, 81(Oct 1973):
499-500.

Kindahl, J. K. see Stigler, G. J.

King, David see Wyndham, Francis

King, Edmund.   Peterborough Abbey, 1086-1310: A Study in the
Land Market. New York: Cam U Press, 1973. Rev. by
R. E. Sullivan, HRNB, 2(Oct 1973):9-10.

King, Edward.   The Great South. Baton Rouge: LSU Press, 1972.
Rev. in GHQ, 57(Spr 1973):156-7. See also Drake, W.
Magruder.... NOTE: Reprint of edition published in 1875.

King, Grace.   Creole Families of New Orleans. Baton Rouge:
Claitor's, 1971. Rev. by W. De Ville, LaH, 14(Spr 1973):
217-18.

King, Hazel.   Richard Bourke. New York: Ox U Press, 1971.
Rev. by S. C. McCulloch, AHR, 78(Dec 1973):1518.

King, Kenneth James. Pan Africanism and Education: A Study of Race Philanthropy and Education in the Southern States of America and East Africa. Oxford: Clarendon, 1971. Rev. by W. M. Marable, WMH, 56(Sum 1973):343-4.

King, P. D. Law and Society in the Visigothic Kingdom. n. p.: Cam U Press, 1972. Rev. by R. J. H. Collins, History, 58(Oct 1973):423-4.

King, T. F., J. P. Carpenter, and N. N. Leonard, III, eds. Archaeological Survey Annual Report, Vol. 10. Los Angeles: U Cal Press, 1968. Rev. by C. M. Warren, AmAnt, 38(Ja 1973):122-3.

_____, _____, and _____, eds. Archaeological Survey Annual Report, Vol. 11. Los Angeles, U Cal Press, 1968. Rev. by R. G. Matson, AmAnt, 38(Ja 1973):123-5.

Kinghorn, A. M. The Chorus of History: Literary-Historical Relations in Renaissance Britain 1485-1558. New York: Barnes and Noble, 1971. Rev. by G. M. Straka, SS, 64(Mar 1973): 135.

Kinnear, Duncan Lyle. The First One Hundred Years: A History of Virginia Polytechnic Institute and State University. Blacksburg: Va Polytechnic Institute Educational Foundation, 1972. Rev. by H. C. Johnson, Jr., JAH, 59(Mar 1973):1014-15; S. Noblin, JSH, 39(Feb 1973):141-2; D. S. Lancaster, VMHB, 81(Ja 1973):118-20. L. G. Geiger, AHR, 78(Oct 1973):1137-9.

Kino, Eusebio Francisco. Sources and Studies for the History of the Americas. Vol. 9: Kino's Biography of Francisco Javier Saeta, S. J. St. Louis: Jesuit Historical Institute, 1971. Rev. by A. P. Nasatir, HAHR, 53(Nov 1973):679-81.

Kinsella, Thomas. Notes from the Land of the Dead. Dublin: Cuala, 1972. Rev. by T. D. Redshaw, E-I, 8(Spr 1973): 142-51.

Kinsey, W. Fred, ed. Archaeology in the Upper Delaware Valley: A Study of the Cultural Chronology of the Tocks Island Reservoir. Harrisburg: Pa Historical and Museum Commission, 1972. Rev. by R. M. Benson, PH, 40(Oct 1973):478-9; D. W. Drago, WPHM, 56(Jl 1973):324-6.

Kipphan, Klaus. Deutsche Propaganda in den Vereinigten Staaten, 1933-1941. Heidelberg: Carl Winter, 1971. Rev. by S. Weinberg, AHR, 78(Je 1973):660-1.

Kipping, Ernst. The Hessian View of America, 1776-1783. Monmouth Beach, N. J.: Philip Freneau Press, 1971. Rev. by R. J. Koke, NYHSQ, 57(Jl 1973):264-6.

Kirby, Jack Temple. Darkness at the Dawning: Race and Reform in the Progressive South. Philadelphia: Lippincott, 1972. Rev. by R. H. Pulley, JAH, 60(Je 1973):154-5; C. U. Smith, FHQ, 52(Jl 1973):83-4; D. W. Grantham, Jr., JSH, 39(May 1973):304-6.

Kirk, Ruth. Desert: The American Southwest. Boston: Houghton Mifflin, 1973. Rev. by M. Y. Martinez, AW, 10(Nov 1973): 56.

_____. Exploring Yellowstone. Seattle: U Wash Press, 1972. Rev. by M. B. Husband, JOW, 12(Oct 1973):636.

Kirk-Greene, A. H. M. Crisis and Conflict in Nigeria: A Documentary Sourcebook, 1966-1969. Vol. 1. January 1966-July 1967. Vol. 2. July 1967-January 1970. New York: Ox U Press, 1971. Rev. by J. Herskovits, AHR, 78(Dec 1973): 1508-10.

Kirova, K. Z. The Russian Revolution and Italy, March-October 1917. Moscow: Izdatel 'stvo "Nauka, " 1968. Rev. by R. Wohl, AHR, 78(Je 1973):676-7.

Kissell, Mary Lois. Basketry of the Papago and Pima Indians. Glorieta, N. M.: Rio Grande, 1972. Rev. by C. L. Tanner, JAriH, 14(Win 1973):388-9. NOTE: Reprint of edition published in 1916.

Kitching, C. J., comp. Tudor Royal Letters. London: HMSO, 1972. Rev. by J. Guy, Archives 11, (Spr 1973):51-2.

Kitsikis, Dimitri. Le rôle des experts à la conférence de la paix de 1919: Gestation d'une technocratie en politique internationale. Ottawa: Editions de l'Université d'Ottawa, 1972. Rev. by L. E. Gelfaud, JMH, 45(Dec 1973):697-9.

Kitson, Frank. Low Intensity Operations, Subversion, Insurgency and Peacekeeping. Harrisburg: Stackpole, n. d. Rev. by J. B. Bell, MilAf, 37(Dec 1973):155-7.

Kiwanuka, M. S. M. Semakula. A History of Buganda, From the Foundation of the Kingdom to 1900. London: Longmans, 1972. Rev. by C. Wrigley, AfAf, 72(Ja 1973):89.

Kizer, Carolyn. Midnight Was My Cry: New and Selected Poems. Garden City, N. Y.: Doubleday, 1971. Rev. by K. S. Byer, GR, 27(Spr 1973):110-21.

Kjeruff, Georgiana. Tales of Old Brevard. Melbourne: South Brevard Historical Society, 1972. Rev. by E. Lyons, FHQ, 52(Oct 1973):186-8.

Klatzman, Joseph, et al., eds. The Role of Group Action in the

Industrialization of Rural Areas. New York: Praeger, 1971.
Rev. by M. E. Kurtzig, MEJ, 27(Spr 1973):249.

Klein, Maury. Edward Porter Alexander. Athens, Ga.: U Ga
Press, 1971. Rev. by R. P. Weinert, Jr., MilAf, 37(Feb
1973):33-4; H. D. Woodman, BHR, 47(Spr 1973):111-12.

_____. History of the Louisville and Nashville Railroad. New
York: Macmillan, 1972. Rev. by P. W. Gates, T & C, 14
(Oct 1973):637-8; J. Burt, THQ, 32(Spr 1973):97-8; C. J.
Kennedy, BHR, 47(Aut 1973):530-2.

Klein, Philip S. and Ari Hoogenboom. A History of Pennsylvania.
New York: McGraw-Hill, 1973. Rev. by E. B. Bronner,
JAH, 60(Sep 1973):423-4; J. A. Munroe, PH, 40(Jl 1973):
332-4; H. M. Tinkcom, PMHB, 97(Oct 1973):547-8.

Klein, Richard G. Man and Culture in the Late Pleistocene: A
Case Study. San Francisco: Chandler, 1969. Rev. by V.
Markotic, Archaeology, 26(Apr 1973):148-9; J. Coles, Anti-
quity, 47(Dec 1973):334.

Klein, Theodore B. The Canals of Pennsylvania and the System of
Internal Improvement. Bethlehem, Pa.: Canal Press, 1973.
Rev. by J. W. Murphy, WPHM, 56(Jl 1973):322-4.

Kleppner, Paul. The Cross of Culture: A Social Analysis of Midwestern Politics, 1850-1900. New York: Free Press, 1970.
Rev. by R. C. Nesmit, WMH, 56(Aut 1973):67-8.

Klessmann, Christoph. Die Selbstbehauptung einer Nation: Nationalsozialistische Kulturpolitik und polnische Widerstandbewegung
im Generalgouvernement 1939-1945. Düsseldorf: Bertelsmann universitätsverlag, 1971. Rev. by V. Mastny, JMH,
45(Je 1973):361-3.

Klima, George J. The Barabaig: East African Cattle-Herders.
New York: Holt, Rinehart, 1970. Rev. by P. Spencer,
Africa, 43(Ja 1973):90.

Klindt-Jensen, Ole. The World of the Vikings. London: Allen and
Unwin, 1971. Rev. by G. Jones, History, 58(Feb 1973):77.

Klinefelter, Walter. Lewis Evans and His Maps. Philadelphia:
American Philosophical Society, 1971. Rev. by L. J. Cappon, AHR, 78(Feb 1973):152-3; W. P. Cumming, WMQ, 3rd
ser., 30(Apr 1973):366-7.

Klingenstein, Grete. Staatsvervialtung und kirchliche autorität im 18.
Jahrhundert. Das Problem der Zensur in der theresianischen
Reform. Vienna: Verlag für Geschichte und Politik, 1970.
Rev. by E. Wangermann, HJ, 16(Mar 1973):208-11.

Klippel, Walter E. The Booth Site: A Late Archaic Campsite. Columbia, Mo.: Mo Archaeological Society, 1969. Rev. by
J. E. Price, AmAnt, 38(Oct 1973):507.

Klonis, N. I. Guerrilla Warfare, Analysis and Projections. New
York: Speller, 1972. Rev. by J. B. Bell, MilAf, 37(Dec
1973):155-7.

Kloss, C. Boden. Andamans and Nicobars. Delhi: Vivek, 1971.
Rev. by L. P. Mathur, IQ, 29(Apr-Je 1973):182-3.

Klotschie, J. Martin. The University of Wisconsin--Milwaukee: An
Urban University. [Milwaukee:] U Wis, Milwaukee, 1972.
Rev. by L. G. Geiger, AHR, 78(Oct 1973):1137-9; J. Herbst,
WMH, 56(Sep 1973):242-4.

Kluger, James R. The Clifton-Morenci Strike: Labor Difficulties
in Arizona, 1915-1916. Tucson: U Ariz Press, 1970. Rev.
by H. Weintraub, PHR, 42(Feb 1973):118-9.

Knauth, Lothar. Confrontación Transpacifica El Japón y el Nuevo
Mundo Hispánico 1542-1639. Cuidad Universitaria: Univer-
sidad Nacional Autónoma de México, 1972. Rev. by C. R.
Boxer, TAm, 30(Oct 1973):276.

Knights, Peter R. The Plain People of Boston, 1830-1860: A Study
in City Growth. New York: Ox U Press, 1971. Rev. by
M. Frisch, AHR, 78(Je 1973):732-3.

Knobloch, Edgar. Beyond the Oxus: Archaeology, Art, and Architecture of Central Asia. Totowa, N. J.: Rowman and Littlefield, 1972. Rev. by W. Trousdale, Archaeology, 26(Ja
1973):75.

Knoles, George H. , ed. Essays and Assays: California History Re-
appraised. San Francisco: Cal Historical Society, 1973.
Rev. by K. Starr, CHQ, 52(Win 1973):375-6.

Knott, David and Margaret Canney, comps. Vol. I. Printed Books
to 1800. Cambridge: Cam U Press, 1970. Rev. by N.
Rosenburg, JEH, 33(Je 1973):475-6.

Knox, J. Wendell. Conspiracy in American Politics, 1787-1815.
New York: Arno, 1972. Rev. by L. K Kerber, JAH, 60
(Dec 1973):795-6.

Knudsen, Trygve and Per Sveaas Andersen, eds. Learned Letters
From and to P. A. Munch. Vol. 3. October 1, 1859--May
7, 1863. Oslo: Universitetsforlaget, 1971. Rev. by F. J.
Bowman, AHR, 78(Oct 1973):1088-9.

Knütter, Hans-Helmuth. Die Juden und die deutsch Linke in der
Weimarer Republik. Düsseldorf: Droste Verlag, 1971. Rev.

by K. von Klemperer, JMH, 45(Je 1973):344-6.

Kobler, John. Capone: The Life and World of Al Capone. New York: Putnam's, 1971. Rev. by D. Holt, JISHS, 66(Spr 1973):119-20.

Koch, Albert C. Journey Through a Part of the United States of North America in the Years 1844 to 1846. Carbondale: S Ill U Press, 1972. Rev. by C. L. Jackson, JSH, 39(Nov 1973):598-9; W. B. Hendrickson, IMH, 69(Sep 1973):289-91; T. D. Clark, NCHR, 50(Aut 1973):433-4.

Koch, Raymond and Charlotte. Educational Commune: The Story of Commonwealth College. New York: Schocken, 1972. Rev. by W. L. Brown, ArkHQ, 32(Aut 1973):285-7.

Koelsch, William A. and Barbara Gutmann Rosenkrantz. American Habitat: An Historical Perspective. New York: Free Press, 1973. Rev. by R. A. Bartlett, HRNB, 2(Nov/Dec 1973):46.

Koenig, Louis W. Bryan: A Political Biography of William Jennings Bryan. New York: Putnam's, 1971. Rev. by R. H. Williams, AHR, 78(Feb 1973):172-3.

Kohlmeier, Louis M., Jr. "God Save This Honorable Court!" New York: Scribner's, 1972. Rev. by A. H. Kelly, JAH, 60 (Dec 1973):861-2.

Kohlmeyer, Fred W. Timber Roots: The Laird Norton Story, 1855-1905. Winona, Minn.: Winona County Historical Society, 1972. Rev. by G. H. Larsen, JAH, 60(Je 1973):145; D. C. Smith, BHR, 47(Spr 1973):114-5; C. S. Peterson, AgH, 47 (Oct 1973):347-8.

Kolchin, Peter. First Freedom: The Responses of Alabama's Blacks to Emancipation and Reconstruction. Westport, Conn.: Greenwood, 1972. Rev. by W. L. Rose, JSH, 39(Nov 1973): 608-9; J. H. Schroeder, WMH, 56(Sum 1973):341-2; A. Meier, AHR, 78(Dec 1973):1535-6.

Kolinsky, Eva. Engagieter Expressionismus: Politik und Literature zwischen Weltkreig und Weimarer Republik: Eine Analyse expressionisticher Zeitschriften. Stuttgart: J. B. Metzlersche Verlag, 1970. Rev. by H. Hirsch, ESR, 3(Apr 1973):193-6.

Kopczyk, Henryk. German Intelligence Activities in Pomerania, 1920-1933. Gdansk: Wydawnictwo Morskie, 1970. Rev. by R. A. Woytak, EEQ, 7(Sum 1973):223-5.

Kopeczi, Béla. La France et la Hongrie au début du XVIIIe siècle: Étude d'histoire des relations diplomatiques et d'histoire des idees. Budapest: Akademiai Kiado, 1971. Rev. by P. Bödy, AHR, 78(Oct 1973):1050-1.

Kornwolf, James D. M. H. Baillie Scott and the Arts and Crafts
    Movement. Baltimore: JHU Press, 1972. Rev. by L. K.
    Eaton, T & C, 14(Apr 1973):301-3.

Korolenko, Vladimir G. The History of My Contemporary. New
    York: Ox U Press, 1972. Rev. by R. F. Byrnes, RR, 32
    (Apr 1973):215.

Kors, Alan C. and Edward Peters, eds. Witchcraft in Europe,
    1100-1700: A Documentary History. Philadelphia: U Pa
    Press, 1972. Rev. by R. H. West, GR, 27(Spr 1973):137-41.

Kortepeter, Carl Max. Ottoman Imperialism During the Reforma-
    tion: Europe and the Caucasus. New York: NYU Press,
    1972. Rev. by R. H. Davison, MEJ, 27(Sum 1973):406-7;
    A. C. Hess, AHR, 78(Dec 1973):1504-5.

Kossmann, E. H. see Bromley, J. S.

Kostof, Spiro. Caves of God: The Monastic Environment of Byzan-
    tine Cappadocia. Cambridge, Mass.: M I T Press, 1972.
    Rev. by N. P. Sevcenko, AHR, 78(Oct 1973):1039-40.

Kovalenko, D. A. Oboronnaia promyshlenmost' sovetskoi Rossii v
    1918-1920 gg. Moscow: "Nauka", 1970. Rev. by J. W.
    Kipp, MilAf, 37(Oct 1973):114.

Kransberg, Melvin and William H. Davenport, eds. Technology and
    Culture: An Anthology. New York: Schocken, 1972. Rev.
    by R. A. Buchanan, T & C, 14(Jl 1973):474-7.

Krashennikov, Stephan Petrovich. Explorations of Kamchatka, North
    Pacific Scimitar: Opsanie Kemli Kamchatki, a Journey Made
    to Explore Eastern Siberia in 1735-1741, by Order of the
    Russian Imperial Government. Portland, Ore.: Ore His-
    torical Society, 1972. Rev. by B. M. Gough, JOW, 12(Ja
    1973):187.

Krenkel, John H., ed. The Life and Times of Joseph Fish, Mor-
    mon Pioneer. Danville, Ill.: Interstate, 1970. Rev. by
    J. M. Haymond, NHSQ, 16(Spr 1973):32-3.

Kreutel, Richard F., ed. and trans. Leben und Taten der türk-
    ischen Kaiser: Die anonyme vulgärgriechische Chronik Codes
    Barberinianus Graecus III (Anonymus Zoras). Graz: Verlag
    Styria, 1971. Rev. by R. P. Lindner, AHR, 78(Oct 1973):
    1042-3.

Kriegel, Annie. The French Communists: A Profile of a People.
    Chicago: U Chi Press, 1972. Rev. by R. Wohl, JMH, 45
    (Sep 1973):533-5.

Krieger, Leonard. Kings and Philosophers, 1689-1789. London:

Weidenfeld and Nicolson, 1971. Rev. by M. Hughes, History, 58(Je 1973):274-5.

Kropp, Simon F. That All May Learn: New Mexico State University, 1888-1964. Las Cruces: NM St U, 1972. Rev. by H. F. Eschenbacher, JAH, 60(Sep 1973):481-2.

Kruchko, John G. The Birth of a Union Local: The History of UAW Local 674, Norwood, Ohio, 1933 to 1940. Ithaca, N. Y.: ... Cornell U Press, 1972. Rev. by D. Montgomery, JAH, 60 (Sep 1973):497-8.

Krug, Edward A. The Shaping of the American High School. Vol. 2. 1920-1941. Madison: U Wis Press, 1972. Rev. by L. Veysey, AHR, 78(Oct 1973):1136-7.

Krüger, Kersten. Die Einnahmen und Ausgaben der dänischen Rentmeister 1588-1628: Ein Beitrag zur frühneuzeitlichen Finanzgeschichte. Marburg: N. G. Elwert, 1970. Rev. by H. E. Ellersieck, AHR, 78(Je 1973):707.

Kruszewski, Anthony Z. The Oder-Neisse Boundary and Poland's Modernization: The Socioeconomic and Political Impact. New York: Praeger, 1972. Rev. by J. Korbel, JMH, 45(Dec 1973):716.

Kubler, George. Portuguese Plain Architecture Between Spices and Diamonds. Middletown, Conn.: Wes U Press, 1972. Rev. by P. Kelemen, HAHR, 53(May 1973):365-6.

Kublin, Hyman. China. Boston: Houghton Mifflin, 1972. Rev. by M. E. Cameron, SS, 64(Apr 1973):182-3.

_____, ed. China: Selected Readings. Boston: Houghton Mifflin, 1972. Rev. by M. E. Cameron, SS, 64(Apr 1973):182-3.

Kuklick, Bruce. American Policy and the Division of Germany: The Clash With Russia Over Reparations. Ithaca, N. Y.: Cornell U Press, 1972. Rev. by A. Iriye, JMH, 45(Dec 1973):711-14; J. L. Gaddis, JAH, 59(Mar 1973):1040-1.

_____. Josiah Royce: An Intellectual Biography. Indianapolis: Bobbs-Merrill, 1972. Rev. by E. Pomeroy, JAH, 59(Mar 1973):1028-9; R. E. Welch, Jr., Historian, 35(Feb 1973):314.

Kula, Witold. Théorie économique du système féodal: Pour un modèle de l'economie polonaise 16e-18e siècles. Paris: Mouton, 1970. Rev. by S. Kieniewicz, AHR, 78(Feb 1973): 125-6.

Kulkarni, A. R. Maharashtra in the Age of Shiraji. Poona: Deshmukh, 1969. Rev. by R. Basu, JEH, 33(Je 1973):491-2.

179   KURBATOV

Kurbatov, G. L. Basic Problems of the Internal Development of
    Byzantine Cities in the Fourth-Seventh Centuries. Leningrad:
    Izdatel'stvo Leningradskogo U., 1971. Rev. by J. Meyen-
    dorff, AHR, 78(Dec 1973):1444-5.

Kurland, Gerald. Seth Low: The Reformer in an Urban and Indus-
    trial Age. New York: Twayne, 1971. Rev. by A. Cerillo,
    Jr., NYHSQ, 57(Ja 1973):91-3.

Kurtz, Stephen and Joseph H. Hutson, eds. Essays on the American
    Revolution. Chapel Hill: UNC Press ... 1973. Rev. by
    R. M. Calhoon, MHM, 68(Win 1973):453-5; P. F. Detweiler,
    JSH, 39(Nov 1973):589-91; P. Carroll, HT, 7(Nov 1973):
    123-4; R. M. Wier, NCHR, 50(Sum 1973):336-8; J. Rabun,
    GHQ, 57(Win 1973):591-2.

Kutakov, Leonid N. Japanese Foreign Policy on the Eve of the
    Pacific War: A Soviet View. Tallahassee, Fla.: Diplomatic
    Press. 1972. Rev. by J. K. Emmerson, RR, 32(Apr 1973):
    204-5; R. Dingman, CHR, 54(Dec 1973):438-9.

Kutler, Stanley I. Privilege and Creative Destruction: The Charles
    River Bridge Case. Philadelphia: Lippincott, 1971. Rev.
    by L. M. Friedman, JIH, 4(Aut 1973):331-6; P. E. Stebbins,
    PH, 40(Apr 1973):219-21.

Kuzmin, Mikhail. Wings: Prose and Poetry. Ann Arbor, Mich.:
    Ardis, 1972. Rev. by J. Brooks, RR, 32(Jl 1973):332-3.

Labaree, Leonard W., ed. [Franklin, Benjamin.] The Papers of
    Benjamin Franklin. Volume 11, 1764; Volume 12, 1765;
    Volume 13, 1766. New Haven, Conn.: Yale U Press, 1967,
    1968, 1969. Rev. by C. Crowe, WMQ, 3rd ser., 30(Apr
    1973):343-7.

_____, et al., eds. The Papers of Benjamin Franklin. Volume
    14, January 1-December 31, 1767. New Haven, Conn.: Yale
    U Press, 1970. Rev. by B. Hindle, JAH, 60(Je 1973):96-8.

Labatut, Jean-Pierre. Les ducs et pairs, de France au XVIIe
    siècle: Étude sociale. Paris: Presses Universitaires de
    France, 1972. Rev. by O. Ranum, AHR, 78(Oct 1973):1070-
    2; W. C. Roth, Historian, 36(Nov 1973):106-7; A. L.
    Moote, JMH, 45(Dec 1973):662.

La Capra, Dominick. Émile Durkheim: Sociologist and Philosopher.
    Ithaca, N. Y.: Cornell U Press, 1972. Rev. by J. M.
    Johnson, JMH, 45(Dec 1973):678-80.

Lademacher, Horst. Die belgische Neutralist als Problem der euro-
    paischen Politik, 1830-1914. Rev. by P. -H. Laurent, AHR,
    78(Je 1973):703-5.

Ladner, Leon J.   The Ladners of Ladner: By Covered Wagon to the
     Welfare State.   Vancouver: Mitchell Press, 1972.   Rev. by
     R. M. Logan, JOW, 12(Oct 1973):655.

Lafferty, R. A.   Okla Hannali.   Garden City, N. Y.:   Doubleday,
     1972.   Rev. by J. E. L. Robertson, RKHS, 71(Apr 1973):
     203-4.

La fine del potere temporale e il ricongiungimento di Roma all'Italia:
     Atti del XLV Congresso di storia del Risorgimento italiano
     (Roma, 21-23 Settembre 1970.   Rome: the Instituto, 1972.
     Rev. by R. Grew, AHR, 78(Oct 1973):1096-7.

La Fontaine, J. S.   City Politics: A Study of Léopoldville, 1962-63.
     Cambridge: [Cam] U, 1970.   Rev. by P. Whitaker, AfAf, 72
     (Ja 1973):94-5.

Laing, Lloyd.   Coins and Archaeology.   New York: Schocken, 1970.
     Rev. by I. L. Merker, Archaeology, 26(Ja 1973):68.

Laiou, Angeliki E.   Constantinople and the Latins: The Foreign
     Policy of Andronicus II, 1282-1328.   Cambridge, Mass.:   Har
     U Press, 1972.   Rev. by A-M, M. Talbot, AHR, 78(Oct
     1973):1042.

Laird, M. A., ed.   Bishop Heber in Northern India: Selections
     From Heber's Journal.   Cambridge: Cam U Press, 1971.
     Rev. E. Stokes, History, 58(Je 1973):330-1.

La Juge, Joseph, et al., eds.   Bordeaux au XXe siècle.   Bordeaux:
     Federation historique du Sud-Quest, 1972.   Rev. by L. Lou-
     bere, AHR, 78(Je 1973):699-701.

Lamadon, A., G. Gerbaud, D. Martin, and J. Pételet.   La revolu-
     tion dans le Puy-de-Dôme.   Paris: Bibliothèque Nationale,
     1972.   Rev. by J. R. Vignery, JMH, 45(Sep 1973):498-9.

Lamb, Ruth S.   Mexican Americans: Sons of the Southwest.   Clare-
     mont, Cal.:   Ocelot, 1970.   Rev. by J. Gómez-Q, HAHR, 53
     (Aug 1973):558-60.

Lamb, W. Kaye, ed.   The Journals and Letters of Sir Alexander
     Mackenzie.   Cambridge: Cam U Press, 1971.   Rev. by G.
     Williams, History, 58(Feb 1973):149-50.

Lambton, A. K. S.   see   Holt, Peter M.

Lame Deer, John (Fire) and Richard Erdoes.   Lame Deer, Seeker
     of Visions: The Life of a Sioux Medicine Man.   New York:
     Simon and Schuster, 1972.   Rev. by R. Ellis, Montana, 23
     (Spr 1973):71.

La Mineria Hispana e Iberoamerica.   Contribución a su investigación

historica: estudios, fuentes, bibliografiå. 7 numbered volumes. Leon, Spain: Catedro de San Isidoro, 1970. Rev.
by R. C. West, HAHR, 53(May 1973):309-11.

Lamson, Peggy. The Glorious Failure: Black Congressman Robert
Brown Elliott and the Reconstruction in South Carolina. New
York: Norton, 1973. Rev. by J. F. Marszalek, Jr., JSH,
39(Nov 1973):609-10; E. A. Cash, JNH, 58(Oct 1973):483-5.

La Nauze, J. A. The Making of the Australian Constitution. Carlton: Melbourne U Press, 1972. Rev. by H. T. Manning,
AHR, 78(Dec 1973):1518-19.

Landau, Jacob M. The Hejaz Railway and the Muslim Pilgrimage:
A Case of Ottoman Political Propaganda. Detroit: Wayne St
U Press, 1971. Rev. by R. L. Chambers, AHR, 78(Oct
1973):1106.

_____, ed. Man, State, and Society in the Contemporary
Middle East. New York: Praeger, 1972. Rev. by R. G.
Landen, MEJ, 27(Aut 1973):526.

Landberg, Hans. The Economy of the War on the Continent: Studies
in the Financing of War in the Period When Sweden Was a
Great Power. Stockholm: Läromedelsförlagen, 1971. Rev.
by W. Kirchner, AHR, 78(Oct 1973):1086-8.

Landes, David S., et al., eds. History as Social Science. Englewood Cliffs, N. J.: Prentice-Hall, 1971. Rev. by R. P.
Swierenga, CHR, 54(Mar 1973):80-2.

Landsberger, Henry A., ed. The Church and Social Change in
Latin America. Notre Dame, Ind.: U Notre Dame Press,
1970. Rev. by M. T. Williams, HAHR, 53(Aug 1973):540-1.

Lane, Ann J. The Brownsville Affair: National Crisis and Black
Reaction. Port Washington, N. Y.: Kennikat, 1971. Rev.
by J. P. Felt, SS, 64(Apr 1973):186-7.

Lang, Berel and Forrest Williams, eds. Marxism and Art: Writings in Aesthetics and Criticism. New York: David McKay,
1972. Rev. by L. H. Legters, RR, 32(Jl 1973):322-3.

Lang, David Marshall see Burney, Charles

Langworthy, Franklin. Scenery of the Plains, Mountains and Mines.
New York: Da Capo Press, 1972. Rev. by O. E. Young,
NMHR, 48(Apr 1973):182-3; B. A. Storey, JOW, 12(Oct
1973):650. First published in 1855.

Lankford, John and David Reimers. Essays on American Social History. New York: Holt, Rinehart, and Winston, 1970. Rev.
by C. E. Hoffecker, PH, 40(Ja 1973):113.

Lannoy, Richard. The Speaking Tree: A Study of Indian Culture and Society. New York: Ox U Press, 1971. Rev. by S. L. Weiner, JIH, 4(Sum 1973):150-4.

Lansing, Elizabeth. The Sumerians: Inventors and Builders. New York: McGraw-Hill, 1971. Rev. by L. R. Johnson, SS, 64 (Feb 1973):92.

Lantz, Herman R. A Community in Search of Itself: A Case History of Cairo, Illinois. Carbondale: S Ill U Press, 1972. Rev. by E. B. Weisel, JISHS, 66(Spr 1973):118-19.

Laqueur, Walter. A History of Zionism. New York: Holt, Rinehart and Winston, 1972. Rev. by A. S. Kliemen, MEJ, 27 (Aut 1973):514-16.

Larner, John. Culture and Society in Italy, 1290-1420. London: Batsford, 1971. Rev. by C. H. Clough, History, 58(Je 1973):262-3.

Larrowe, Charles P. Harry Bridges: The Rise and Fall of Radical Labor in the United States. Westport, N. Y.: Lawrence Hill, 1972. Rev. by S. Lynd, AHR, 78(Dec 1973):1545; B. Mergen, JAH, 60(Dec 1973):847-8; H. Weintraub, PHR, 42 (Nov 1973):591-2.

Larson, Gustive O. The "Americanization" of Utah for Statehood. San Marino, Cal.: Huntington Library, 1971. Rev. by M. S. De Pillis, AHR, 78(Feb 1973):171; W. B. Turner, A & W, 15(Spr 1973):87-8; J. M. Hammond, Montana, 23(Spr 1973): 70.

Larson, Henrietta M., Evelyn H. Knowlton and Charles S. Popple. History of Standard Oil Company (New Jersey), 1927-1950: New Horizons. New York: Harper and Row, 1971. Rev. by S. Salsbury, T & C, 14(Oct 1973):660-3.

Lartéguy, Jean. The Guerillas. New York: New American Library, 1970 (1967). Rev. by S. T., HAHR, 53(Aug 1973):572.

Lasby, Clarence G. Project Paperclip: German Scientists and the Cold War. New York: Atheneum, 1971. Rev. by C. Pursell, JAH, 60(Sep 1973):505-6; B. C. Hacker, T & C, 14 (Oct 1973):659-60.

Laslett, Peter, ed. Household and Family in Past Time: Comparative Studies in the Size and Structure of the Domestic Group Over the Last Three Centuries in England, France, Serbia, Japan, and Colonial North America, With Further Materials From Western Europe. New York: Cam U Press, 1972. Rev. by S. Thernstrom, AHR, 78(Oct 1973):1006-8.

Lass, William E. From the Missouri to the Great Salt Lake: An

Account of Overland Freighting. Lincoln: Neb State Historical Society, 1972. Rev. by H. P. Walker, Montana 23
(Aut 1973):70-1.

La Terreur, Marc, ed. Dictionary of Canadian Biography. Vol. 10.
1871-1880. Toronto: U Tor Press, 1972. Rev. by R. W.
Winks, AHR, 78(Feb 1973):182.

Latham, Charles, Jr. A Short History of Thetford: 1761-1870.
Thetford, Vt.: Thetford Historical Society, 1972. Rev. by
A. R. Foley, VH, 41(Aut 1973):236-7.

Latham, Robert and William Matthews, eds. The Diary of Samuel
Pepys, A New and Complete Transcription. (5 vols.). London: Bell, 1970-1971. Rev. by V. Pearl, History, 58(Feb
1973):106-8.

_____ and _____, eds. The Diary of Samuel Pepys. Vols.
VI and VII. London: Bell, 1970. Rev. by P. Q., HTo, 23
(Feb 1973):139-40.

Launay, Michel. Jean-Jacques Rousseau: Ecrivain politique (1712-
1762). Cannes: C. E. L., 1971. Rev. by R. D. Masters,
AHR, 78(Oct 1973):1073-4.

Laurence Dan H., ed. Bernard Shaw. Collected Letters, 1898-
1910. n. p.: Dodd, Mead, n. d. Rev. by S. Weintraub,
E-I, 8(Spr 1973):135-42.

Laurens, Henry. The Papers of Henry Laurens. Edited by Philip
M. Hamer and George C. Rogers, Jr. Volume 2: November 1, 1755-December 31, 1758. Volume 3: January 1,
1759-August 31, 1763. Columbia, S. C.: U SCar Press ...
1970, 1972. Rev. by R. M. Weir, WMQ, 3rd Ser., 30(Apr
1973):351-3.

Lavender, David. California: Land of New Beginnings. New York:
Harper and Row, 1972. Rev. by A. F. Rolle, CHQ, 52(Sum
1973):180-1.

Lavoie, Yolande. L'emigration de Canadiens aux Etats-Unis avant
1930: Mesure du Phénomène. Montreal: Les Presses de
l'Université de Montréal, 1972. Rev. by S. M. Hoy, JAH,
60(Je 1973):189.

Lawford, J. P. and Peter Young. Wellington's Masterpiece--the
Battle and Campaign of Salamanca. London: Allen and Unwin, 1973. Rev. by D. Chandler, HTo, 23(Je 1973):444-5.

Lawrence, D. H. Movements in European History. New York: Ox
U Press, 1972. Rev. by R. N. Stromberg, SS, 64(Apr 1973):
180-1.

Lawson, R. Alan. The Failure of Independent Liberalism, 1930-
    1941. New York: Putnam's, 1971. Rev. by P. Conklin, SS,
    64(Ja 1973):39-40.

Lawson, Rowena. The Changing Economy of the Lower Volta, 1954-
    67. New York: Ox U, 1972. Rev. by G. Hart, AfAf, 72
    (Ja 1973):83; R. W. Wyllie, Africa, 43(Ja 1973):88-90.

Lazar, Moshe, ed. The Sephardic Tradition: Ladino and Spanish
    Literature. New York: Norton, 1972. Rev. by A. D.
    Carre, AJHQ, 62(Mar 1973):322-7.

Lazerson, Marvin. Origins of the Urban School: Public Education
    in Massachusetts, 1870-1915. Cambridge, Mass.: Har U
    Press, 1971. Rev. by L. Veysey, AHR, 78(Oct 1973):1136-7.

Lazitch, Branko and Melorad M. Drachkovitch. Lenin and the Com-
    munist International. Vol. I. Stanford, Cal.: Hoover Insti-
    tution Press, 1972. Rev. by S. Hook, RR, 32(Ja 1973):1-14.

Lazlo, Ervin, ed. The Relevance of General Systems Theory. New
    York: Braziller, 1972. Rev. by F. A. Rossini, T & C, 14
    (Oct 1973):674-6.

Leach, Barry A. German Strategy Against Russia, 1939-1941. New
    York: Ox U Press, 1973. Rev. by N. Luxemburg, HRNB,
    2(Oct 1973):7.

Leach, Douglas Edward. Arms for Empire: A Military History of
    the British Colonies in North America, 1607-1763. New York:
    Macmillan, 1973. Rev. by J. D. F. Williams, NCHR, 50
    (Aut 1973):426-7; J. C. Rainbolt, VMHB, 81(Oct 1973):489-90.

Leacock, Seth and Ruth. Spirits of the Deep: A Study of an Afro-
    Brazilian Cult. Garden City, N. Y.: Doubleday ... 1972.
    Rev. by D. Warren, Jr. , HAHR, 53(May 1973):349-50.

Leaky, L. S. B., R. D. Simpson, T. Clements, R. Berger and J.
    Witthoff. Pleistocene Man at Calico, a Report on the Inter-
    national Conference on the Calico Mountains Excavations, San
    Bernardino County, California. San Bernardino, Cal.: San
    Bernardino County Museum Assn, 1972. Rev. by R. J. Roske,
    NHSQ, 16(Spr 1973):29-30.

Leary, W. Methodism in the City of Lincoln. n. p.: Published
    Privately, 1969. Rev. by B. J. Biggs, MH, 2(Spr 1973):
    55-6.

_____. Methodism in the Town of Boston. n. p.: Richard Kay,
    1972. Rev. by B. J. Biggs, MH, 2(Spr 1973):55-6.

_____. Two Hundred Years of Methodism in Messingham. Lin-
    coln: The Author, 1971. Rev. by B. J. Biggs, MH, 2(Spr

1973):55-6.

Lebedev, N. M.   Pestel':   The Ideologue and Leader of the Decem-
brists. Moscow: Izdatel'stvo "misl'", 1972. Rev. by A. G.
Mazour, AHR, 78(Oct 1973):1100.

LeBlanc, Steven A. , Patty Jo Watson and Charles A. Redman. Explanation in Archaeology: An Explicitly Scientific Approach.
New York: Columbia U Press, 1971. Rev. by R. L. Schuy-
ler, AmAnt, 38(Jl 1973):372-4.

Lebra, Joyce C.   Jungle Alliance: Japan and Indian National Army.
Singapore: Donald Moore ... 1971. Rev. by Y. Akashi,
AHR, 78(Dec 1973):1512-13.

LeBrun, François. Les Hommes et la mort en Anjou aux 17e et
18e siècles. Paris-La Haye: Mouton, 1971. Rev. by E.
LeGoff, CHR, 54(Sep 1973):325-6.

Lecky, W. E. H. A History of Ireland in the Eighteenth Century.
Chicago: U Chi Press, 1972. Rev. by A. Cohen, E-I, 8
(Sum 1973):147-9.

Leder, Lawrence H. , ed. The Colonial Legacy. Vol. II. Some
Eighteenth-Century Commentaries. New York: Harper and
Row, 1971. Rev. by D. Bernstein, NJH, 91(Spr 1973):60-1;
D. Ammerman, NYH, 54(Apr 1973):252-3; P. H. Smith, JAH,
60(Je 1973):105-6.

Lee, Antoinette and Harold Skramsted. A Biographical Dictionary
of American Civil Engineers. New York: American Society
of Civil Engineers, 1972. Rev. by C. W. Conditt, T & C,
14(Ja 1973):108-9.

Lee, C. H. A Cotton Enterprise, 1795-1840: A History of McConnel and Kennedy, Fine Cotton Spinners. Manchester: Manchester U Press, 1972. Rev. by T. W. Perry, JEH, 33(Je
1973):492-3.

Lee, Chong-sik and Robert A. Scalapino. Communism in Korea.
Part 1: The Movement; Part 2: The Society. Berkeley:
U Cal Press, 1972. Rev. by A. W. Burks, AHR, 78(Dec
1973):1516-17.

Lee, Joseph. The Modernization of Irish Society 1848-1918. Dublin:
Gill and Macmillan, 1973. Rev. by C. J. Woods, E-I, 8
(Win 1973):123-6.

Lee, Maurice, Jr. James I and Henri IV: An Essay in English
Foreign Policy, 1603-10. Urbana: U Ill Press, 1970. Rev.
by A. G. R. Smith, History, 58(Je 1973):291.

Lefeber, Louis and Mrinal Datta-Chaudhuri. Regional Development:

Experiences and Prospects in South and Southeast Asia. The
Hague: Morton 1971. Rev. by S. Venu, IQ, 29(Jl-Sep 1973):
267-8.

Lefferts, Charles M. Uniforms of the American, British, French,
and German Armies in the War of the American Revolution
1775-1783. Old Greenwich, Conn.: W. E., Inc. 1971. Rev.
by C. R. Ferguson, MilAf, 37(Dec 1973):159. NOTE: Originally published in 1926.

Legget, Robert. Rideau Waterway. Toronto: U Tor Press, 1972.
Rev. by N. E. T., IS, 29(Fall 1973):235.

Lehmann, Phyllis William, et al. Samothrace: Excavations Conducted by the Institute of Fine Arts, New York University.
Vol. 3: The Hieron. Princeton, N. J.: Prin U Press,
1969. Rev. by H. A. Thompson, Archaeology, 26(Jl 1973):
228-9.

Lehmann, William C. Henry Home, Lord Kames and the Scottish
Enlightenment: A Study in National Character and in the His-
tory of Ideas. The Hague: Martinus Nijhoff, 1971. Rev. by
J. J. Ellis, WMQ, 3rd ser., 30(Oct 1973):669-71.

Leighton, Albert C. Transport and Communication in Early Medieval Europe, AD 500-1100. New York: Barnes and Noble,
1972. Rev. by J. Beeler, AHR, 78(Oct 1973):1030; R.
Schumann, BHR, 47(Aut 1973):416-17; M. M. Knight, JEH,
33(Dec 1973):892-3.

Leiss, William. The Domination of Nature. New York: Braziller,
1972. Rev. by W. W. Wagar, T & C, 14(Jl 1973):480-2.

Lelo Bellotto, Manoel. Correio Marítimo Hispano-americano. A
Carreira de Buenos Aires, 1767-1779. São Paulo, Brazil:
Faculdade de Filosofia, Ciêncios e Letras de Assis, 1971.
Rev. by P. E. Hoffman, HAHR, 53(Nov 1973):684-5.

Lemay, J. A. Leo. Men of Letters in Colonial Maryland. Knoxville: U Tenn Press, 1972. Rev. by K. Silverman, AHR,
78(Oct 1973):1119-20; D. W. Jordan, JAH, 60(Dec 1973):778-
9; G. A. Wood, MHM, 68(Jl 1973):451-2; G. J. Goodwin,
JSH, 39(Aug 1973):433-5; E. Wolf, 2nd, PMHB, 97(Jl 1973):
427-8; C. C. Davis, VMHB, 81(Apr 1973):200-1; L. P.
Simpson, WMQ, 3rd ser., 30(Oct 1973):665-7.

Lemmon, Sarah McCulloh, ed. The Pettigrew Papers, Vol. I, 1685-
1818. Raleigh: N. C. Dept Archives and History, 1971. Rev.
by C. N. Wilson, SCHM, 74(Oct 1973):321-2; J. H. Smylie,
WMQ, 3rd ser., 30(Apr 1973):363-4.

Lemon, James T. The Best Poor Man's Country: A Geographical
Study of Early Southeastern Pennsylvania. Baltimore: JHU

187   LEMONS

Press, 1972. Rev. by S. J. Crowther, JEH, 33(Je 1973):
494; R. Beach, AgH, 47(Jl 1973):279-80; D. Ward, JIH,
4(Aut 1973):329-31; P. J. Grenen, Jr., NJH, 91(Aut 1973):
194-6; G. S. Dunbar, PHR, 42(Feb 1973):105-6; C. V.
Earle, MHM, 68(Sum 1973):218-9.

Lemons, J. Stanley. The Woman Citizen: Social Feminism in
the 1920's. Urbana: U Ill Press, 1973. Rev. by R.
B. Sherman, JAH, 60(Dec 1973):843-5; A. E. Taylor,
JSH, 39(Nov 1973):620-1; W. A. Wiegand, IMH, 69(Dec
1973):381-2.

Lensen, George A. The Strange Neutrality: Soviet-Japanese Relations During the Second World War, 1941-1945. Tallahassee, Fla.: Diplomatic Press, 1972. Rev. by J. K.
Emmerson, RR, 32(Apr 1973):204-5; R. Dingman, CHR,
54(Dec 1973):438-9; A. D. Coox, MilAf, 37(Apr 1973):
71-2.

Lensen, George A., ed. War and Revolution: Excerpts from the
Letters and Diaries of Countess Olga Poutiatine. Talla-
hassee, Fla.: Diplomatic Press, 1971. Rev. by W. B.
Walsh, RR, 32(Ja 1973):97-8; M. Patoski, Historian, 35
(Feb 1973):295.

Leonard, Irving A., ed. Colonial Travelers in Latin America. New
York: Knopf, 1972. Rev. by J. E. Rodriguez O., HAHR,
53(May 1973):314-5.

Leone, Mark P., ed. Contemporary Archaeology: A Guide to
Theory and Contributions. Carbondale: S Ill U Press, 1972.
Rev. by J. L. Cotter, Archaeology, 26(Oct 1973):312-13.

Lesch, Ann Mosely see Quandt, William B.

Leslie, Mrs. Frank. California, a Pleasure Trip from Gotham to
the Golden Gate. Nieuwkoop, Netherlands: De Graaf, 1972.
Rev. by J. F. Wheeler, JOW, 12(Apr 1973):437-8.

Lesy, Michael. Wisconsin Death Trip. New York: Pantheon, 1973.
Rev. by P. H. Hass, WMH, 56(Spr 1973):238-41.

Leuzinger, Elsy. The Art of Black Africa. London: Studio Vista,
1972. Rev. by L. Godfrey, AfAf, 72(Oct 1973):460-1; B. M.
Fagan, Archaeology, 26(Apr 1973):150-1.

Levenstein, Harvey A. Labor Organizations in the United States and
Mexico: A History of Their Relations. Westport, Conn.:
Greenwood, 1971. Rev. by J. T. Deiner, HAHR, 53(May
1973):321-2; R. E. Ruiz, JAH, 60(Je 1973):173-4; M. T.
Gilderhus, TAm, 30(Jl 1973):145-6; R. J. Halstead, WMH,
56(Spr 1973):252-3.

Levin, Alexandra Lee. Dare To Be Different: A Biography of
Louis H. Levin of Baltimore. New York: Bloch, 1972. Rev.
by L. S. Levy, MHM, 68(Sum 1973):228-9.

Levin, Harry. The Myth of the Golden Age in the Renaissance.
London: Faber and Faber, 1970. Rev. by D. Baker-Smith,
ESR, 3(Ja 1973):97-8.

Levin, Murray B. Political Hysteria in America. New York: Basic
Books, 1971. Rev. by R. G. Smolka, SS, 64(Nov 1973):277.

Levine, Daniel. Jane Addams and the Liberal Tradition. Madison:
Wis State Historical Society, 1971. Rev. by L. L. Athey,
AHR, 78(Je 1973):739.

Levine, Edward M. The Irish and the Irish Politicians. Notre
Dame, Ind.: U Notre Dame Press, 1966. Rev. by R. T.
Reilly, E-I, 8(Win 1973):129-31.

Levine, Isaac Don. Eyewitness to History: Memoirs and Reflections
of a Foreign Correspondent for Half a Century. New York:
Hawthorn, 1973. Rev. by A. Parry, RR, 32(Oct 1973):437-8.

Levine, Suzanne and Hallie Taylor, trans. Triple Cross. New
York: Dutton, 1972. Rev. by R. D. Souza, HAHR, 53(Nov
1973):732.

Levine, Victor T. The Cameroon Federal Republic. Ithaca, N. Y.:
Cornell U Press, 1971. Rev. by J. F. Bayart, AfAf, 72(Oct
1973):453-4.

Levitan, Sar A. and Barbara Hetrick. Big Brother's Indian Pro-
grams--With Reservations. New York: McGraw-Hill, 1971.
Rev. by R. N. Ellis, Montana 23(Win 1973):64.

Levitt, Morton P. and Saul Field. Bloomsday: An Interpretation of
James Joyce's Ulysses. Greenwich, Conn.: New York
Graphic Society, 1972. Rev. by M. H. Begnal, E-I, 8(Win
1973):142-4.

Levtzion, Nehemia. Ancient Ghana and Mali. London: Methuen,
1973. Rev. by T. Hodgkin, AfAf, 72(Oct 1973):454-5.

Levy, David W. see Urofsky, Melvin I.

Levy, Eugene. James Weldon Johnson: Black Leader, Black Voice.
Chicago: U Chi Press, 1973. Rev. by O. M. Scruggs, JNH,
58(Oct 1973):474-5; P. W. Kennedy, HRNB, 2(Nov/Dec 1973):
52-3.

Levy, Leonard W., ed. The Supreme Court Under Earl Warren.
Chicago: Quadrangle, 1972. Rev. by A. H. Kelly, SS, 64
(Nov 1973):293-4.

Levy, Marion J., Jr. Modernization: Latecomers and Survivors.
New York: Basic Books, 1972. Rev. by R. M. Marsh, SS,
64(Nov 1973):298-9.

Levytsky, Boris. The Uses of Terror--The Soviet Service 1917-
1970. London: Sidgwick and Jackson, 1971; New York:
Coward, McCann and Geoghagan, 1972. Rev. by J. Barber,
History, 58(Feb 1973):144; J. W. Kipp, MilAf, 37(Feb 1973):
31.

Lewin, Ronald. Montgomery. London: Batsford, 1971. Rev. by
B. Bond, History, 58(Feb 1973):142-3.

Lewis, Bernard see Holt, Peter M.

Lewis, Beth Irwin. George Grosz: Art and Politics in the Weimar
Republic. Madison: U Wis Press, 1971. Rev. by P. Selz,
JIH, 4(Sum 1973):146-50.

Lewis, John Wilson, ed. The City in Communist China. Stanford,
Cal.: Stan U Press, 1971. Rev. by A. Briggs, T & C, 14
(Ja 1973):95-6.

Lewis, P. S., ed. The Recovery of France in the Fifteenth Century. London: Macmillan, 1971. Rev. by M. G. A. Vale,
History, 58(Je 1973):270.

Lewis, Paul. The Man Who Lost America: A Biography of Gentleman Johnny Burgoyne. New York: The Dial Press, 1973.
Rev. by R. J. Chaffin, AHI, 8(Oct 1973):49.

Lewis, Willie Newbury. Tapadero: The Making of a Cowboy. Austin: U Tx Press, 1972. Rev. by S. E. Siegel, JAH, 60(Je
1973):152; C. W. Black, JOW, 12(Oct 1973):641; W. Gard,
SWHQ, 76(Ja 1973):348-9.

Lhotsky, Alphons. Das Zeitalter des Hauses Österreich. Die
ersten Jahre der Regierung Ferdinands I. in Österreich (1520-
1527). Vienna: In Kommission bei Hermann Böhlaus Nachf.,
1971. Rev. by S. W. Rowan, JMH, 45(Je 1973):294-6.

Libby, Frederick J. To End War: The Story of the National
Council for the Prevention of War. Nyack, N. Y.: Fellow-
ship, 1969. Rev. by C. Chatfield, AHR, 78(Je 1973):654-5.

Lichtheim, George. From Marx to Hegel. New York: Herder and
Herder, 1971. Rev. by M. Jay, JMH, 45(Sep 1973):502-3.

Lida, Clara and Iris M. Zavala, eds. La Revolucion de 1868: Historia, pensamiento literatura. New York: Las Americas,
1970. Rev. by R. Cardona, HAHR, 53(Feb 1973):167-8; J.
C. Ullman, AHR, 78(Feb 1973):116-17.

Liddell Hart, Basil H. Why Don't We Learn From History? New
York: Hawthorn, 1972. Rev. by R. P. Weinert, MilAf, 37
(Oct 1973):108.

Lieberman, Jethro K. How the Government Breaks the Law. New
York: Stein and Day, 1972. Rev. by D. Carter, Mankind,
4(Aug 1973):41.

Liebhafsky, H. H. American Government and Business. New York:
Wiley, 1971. Rev. by W. O. Wagnon, Jr., JEH, 33(Dec
1973):893-5.

Liebman, Arthur, Kenneth N. Walker and Myron Glazer. Latin
American University Students: A Six-Nation Study. Rev. by
R. H. Ebel, HAHR, 53(May 1973):358-9.

Lierde, Jean Van, ed. Lumumba Speaks: The Speeches and Writings of Patrice Lumumba, 1958-1961. Boston: Little, Brown,
1972. Rev. by O. E. S., CurH, 64(Mar 1973):126.

The Lincolns, the Hanks, and Macon County. Decatur, Ill.: Macon
County Historical Society ... 1971. Rev. by G. R. Planck,
LH, 75(Spr 1973):38-9.

Lindbergh, Charles A. Boyhood on the Upper Mississippi, A Reminiscent Letter. St. Paul: Minn Historical Society, 1972.
Rev. by E. O. C., IS, 29(Win 1973):320.

Lindquist, Emory. An Immigrant's Two Worlds: A Biography of
Hjalmar Edgren. Rock Island, Ill.: Augustana Historical
Society, 1972. Rev. by C. S. Meyer, CHIQ, 46(Sum 1973):93;
C. A. Clausen, JAH, 59(Mar 1973):1027.

Lindsay, Alexander, J., Jr., et al. Survey and Excavation North
and East of Navaho Mountain, Utah, 1959-1962. Flagstaff,
Ariz: Museum of Northern Arizona, 1968. Rev. by W. D.
Lipe, AmAnt, 38(Apr 1973):243-4.

Lindsay, Merrill. The Kentucky Rifle. York, Pa.: Arma Press,
1972. Rev. by R. A. Howard, PH, 40(Oct 1973):479-81.

Link, Arthur S., et al., eds. The Papers of Woodrow Wilson. Vol.
11. 1898-1900. Princeton, N. J.: Prin U Press, 1971.
Rev. by D. W. Grantham, JAH, 60(Je 1973):100-2; H. J.
Bass, AHR, 78(Je 1973):738-9; E. D. Cronon, JSH, 39(Nov
1973):613-17; V. A. Carrafiello, PH, 40(Apr 1973):232-5.

_____ et al., eds. The Papers of Woodrow Wilson. Vol. 12.
1900-1902. Princeton, N. J.: Prin U Press, 1972. Rev.
by D. W. Grantham, JAH, 60(Je 1973):100-2; H. J. Bass,
AHR, 78(Je 1973):738-9; E. D. Cronon, JSH, 39(Nov 1973):
613-17; Melvin Urofsky, AHR, 78(Feb 1973):178-9; R. F.
Durden, NCHR, 50(Win 1973):111-12; J. F. Mahoney, NJH,

91(Aut 1973):198-9; V. A. Carrafiello, PH, 40(Jl 1973):348-9.

Link, Horst Günther. Deutsch-sovjetische Beziehungen bis Rapallo. Köln: Verlag Wissenschaft und Politik, 1970. Rev. by F. T. Epstein, JMH, 45(Mar 1973):171-3.

Linley, John. Architecture of Middle Georgia: The Oconee Area. Athens, Ga.: U Ga Press, 1972. Rev. by G. C. Rogers, Jr., JSH, 39(Nov 1973):631-2; GHQ, 57(Fall 1973):451-2.

Lipking, Lawrence. The Ordering of the Arts in Eighteenth-Century England. Princeton, N. J.: Prin U Press, 1972. Rev. by J. P. Campbell, History, 58(Je 1973):298.

Lipman, Jean. American Folk Art in Wood, Metal, and Stone. New York: Dover, 1972. Rev. by A. Neal, CoMag, 50(Spr 1973): 164-5. NOTE: originally published in 1948.

Lippman, Heinz. Honecker and the New Politics of Europe. New York: Macmillan, 1972. Rev. by A. Z. Rubenstein, CurH, 64(May 1973):224.

Liss, Sheldon B. and Peggy K. Man, State and Society in Latin American History. New York: Praeger, 1972. Rev. by S. B. Heath, Historian, 35(Feb 1973):319-20.

Listowel, Judith. Amin. London and Dublin: Irish U Press, 1973. Rev. by M. Twaddle, AfAf, 72(Jl 1973):344-5.

Litvinov, Pavel, comp. The Trial of the Four. A Collection of Materials on the Case of Galanskov, Ginzburg, Dobrovolsky, and Lashkova, 1967-68. New York: Viking, 1972. Rev. by D. V. Pospielovsky, RR, 32(Oct 1973):441-2.

Livesay, Harold C. and Glenn Porter. Merchants and Manufacturers: Studies in the Changing Structure of Nineteenth-Century Marketing. Baltimore: JHU Press, 1971. Rev. by R. L. Ehrlick, PH, 40(Jl 1973):343-6; R. E. Gallman, AHR, 78 (Je 1973):656-7; M. W. Garber, NJH, 91(Sum 1973):130-1.

Livingston-Little, D. E., ed. The Mexican War Diary of Thomas D. Tennery. Norman: U Ok Press, 1970. Rev. by J. H. Schroeder, JISHS, 66(Aut 1973):354-5.

Llewellyn, Alexander. The Decade of Reform: The 1830's. New York: St. Martin's, 1972. Rev. by W. J Baker, AHR, 78 (Oct 1973):1065; N. Gash, History, 58(Oct 1973):458.

Llewellyn, Peter. Rome in the Dark Ages. London: Faber and Faber, 1971. Rev. by H. Mayr-Harting, Antiquity, 47(Je 1973):154-5.

Lloyd, Alan. The King Who Lost America: A Portrait of the Life and Times of George III. New York: Doubleday, 1971. Rev. by C. R. Ritcheson, AHR, 78(Oct 1973):1015-16; J. J. Heslin, NYHSQ, 57(Oct 1973):350-2.

Lloyd, Christopher. The Search for the Niger. London: Collins, 1973. Rev. by M. Langley, HTo, 23(May 1973):370-2.

Lloyd, Craig. Aggressive Introvert: A Study of Herbert Hoover and Public Relations Management, 1912-1932. Columbus, O.: Ohio St U Press, 1972. Rev. by R. Lowitt, JAH, 60(Dec 1973):833-4.

Lloyd, G. E. R. Greek Science After Aristotle. London: Chatto and Windus, 1973. Rev. by A. Wasserstein, Antiquity, 47 (Dec 1973):331-3.

Lloyd, Howell A. see Connell-Smith, Gordon

Lockhart, James. The Men of Cajamarca: A Social and Biographical Study of the First Conquerors of Peru. Austin: U Tx Press, 1972. Rev. by R. S. Chamberlain, NMHR, 48(Jl 1973):266-7.

Lockwood, Charles. Bricks and Brownstone: The New York Row House, 1783-1929: An Architectural and Social History. New York: McGraw-Hill, 1972. Rev. by R. Porter, NYHSQ, 57 (Oct 1973):363-4.

Loewen, James W. The Mississippi Chinese: Between Black and White. Cambridge, Mass.: Har U Press, 1971. Rev. by G. Barth, AgH, 47(Apr 1973):170; J. R. Skates, Jr., JMiH, 35(May 1973):215-17.

Loewenberg, Bert James. American History in American Thought: Christopher Columbus to Henry Adams. New York: Simon and Schuster, 1972. Rev. by F. H. Matthews, CHR, 54(Dec 1973):463-5; K. I. Polakoff, HT, 6(Feb 1973):325-6; W. H. Hutchinson, AW, 10(Mar 1973):60; D. W. Noble, PHR, 42 (Feb 1973):102-3; M. Kammen, VMHB, 81(Jl 1973):370-1.

Lofchie, Michael, ed. The State of the Nations: Constraints on Development in Independent Africa. Berkeley: U Cal Press, 1972. Rev. by S. C. Nolutshungu, AfAf, 72(Ja 1973):80.

Logan, Oliver. Culture and Society in Venice, 1470-1790: The Renaissance and Its Heritage. New York: Scribner's, 1972. Rev. by P. H. Labalme, AHR, 78(Dec 1973):1493-4; J. J. Renaldo, JMH, 45(Sep 1973):487-8.

Logsdon, Joseph. Horace White: Nineteenth-Century Liberal. Westport, Conn.: Greenwood, 1971. Rev. by J. K. Conway, CHR, 54(Sep 1973):331-2.

Lokken, Roy N. , ed.   The Scientific Papers of James Logan.   Philadelphia: ... American Philosophical Society, 1972.   Rev.
by P. George, PMHB, 97(Apr 1973):253-5.

Lombard, Maurice.   Monnaie et histoire d'Alexandre à Mahomet.
Paris: Mouton, 1971.   Rev. by J. F. McGovern, AHR, 78
(Dec 1973):1421.

Lombardi, John V.   The Decline and Abolition of Negro Slavery in
Venezuela, 1820-1854.   Westport, Conn.: Greenwood, 1971.
Rev. by J. F. King, HAHR, 53(Feb 1973):137-9; J. Nava,
JNH, 58(Apr 1973):228-9.

London, Jack and Herbert Heron.   Gold.   Oakland, Cal.: Holmes,
1972.   Rev. by H. Lachtman, PacH, 17(Spr 1973):94-5.

Long, David F.   Nothing Too Daring: A Biography of Commodore
David Porter, 1780-1843.   Annapolis: U. S. Naval Institute,
1970.   Rev. by C. Boyd, MilAf, 37(Apr 1973):72.

Long, Dorothy, ed.   Medicine in North Carolina: Essays in the
History of Medical Science and Medical Service, 1524-1960.
Vol. I. Development of Medical Science, Medical Adminis-
trative Agencies, and Medical Service Facilities in North
Carolina; Vol. II. Medical Education and Medical Service
in North Carolina.   Raleigh: ... N. C. Medical Society, 1972.
Rev. by G. G. Johnson, NCHR, 50(Sum 1973):322-3.

Long, E. B. and Barbara.   The Civil War Day by Day, 1861-1865.
New York: Doubleday, 1971.   Rev. by R. P. Weinert, Jr.,
MilAf, 37(Feb 1973):33-4.

Longacre, Edward G.   From Union Stars to Top Hat.   Harrisburg,
Pa.: Stackpole, 1972.   Rev. by J. L. McDonough, CWTI,
12(Nov 1973):49; E. B. Long, CWH, 19(Dec 1973):359-60;
F. N. Boney, JAH, 60(Sep 1973):451-2.

Longacre, William A.   Archaeology as Anthropology: A Case Study.
Tucson: U Ariz Press, 1970.   Rev. by M. B. Stanislawski,
AmAnt, 38(Ja 1973):117-22.

Longford, Elizabeth.   Wellington, Pillar of State.   London: Weidenfeld and Nicolson, 1972.   Rev. by H. Kurtz, HTo, 23(Feb
1973):139.

Longstreet, Stephen.   Chicago: 1860-1919.   New York: David Mc-
Kay, 1973.   Rev. by F. I. Olson, HRNB, 2(Nov/Dec 1973):
47-8.

Longworth, Philip.   The Three Empresses: Catherine I, Anne, and
Elizabeth of Russia.   London: Constable, 1972.   Rev. by I.
Grey, HTo, 23(Feb 1973):141-2.

Lopata, Helena Z. Occupation Housewife. New York: Ox U Press, 1971. Rev. by G. Tuchman, T & C, 14(Apr 1973):326-8.

Lopez, Robert S. The Commercial Revolution of the Middle Ages, 950-1350. Englewood Cliffs, N. J.: Prentice-Hall, 1971. Rev. by D. O. Whitten, JEH, 33(Je 1973):495; G. P. Cuttino, SS, 64(Feb 1973):90.

López Guedez, Horacio. Los reyes catolicos y America (1492-1517). Merida, Venezuela: Universidad de los Andes, 1971. Rev. by B. B. Solnick, AHR, 78(Je 1973):745-6.

López-Rey, José. Velázquez' Work and World. Greenwich, Conn.: New York Graphic Society, 1968. Rev. by T. K. Rabb, JIH, 4(Sum 1973):107-17.

Lora, Ronald. Conservative in America. Chicago: Rand McNally, 1971. Rev. by R. A. Skotheim, JAH, 59(Mar 1973):1036-7.

Lord, Walter. The Dawn's Early Light. New York: Norton, 1972. Rev. by R. Horsman, WVH, 34(Ja 1973):213-14; J. S. Pancake, JSH, 39(Feb 1973):114-15; R. L. Hatzenbuehler, NYHSQ, 57(Apr 1973):182-3; F. A. Cassell, WMQ, 3rd ser., 30(Oct 1973):682-3.

Lorenz, Alfred Lawrence. Hugh Gaine: A Colonial Printer-Editor's Odyssey to Loyalism. Carbondale: S Ill U Press, 1972. Rev. by B. Friedman, JAH, 60(Dec 1973):790-1; P. U. Bonomi, NYHSQ, 57(Oct 1973):353-4; R. F. Hixson, NJH, 91 (Aut 1973):204-6; M. B. Norton, PMHB, 97(Oct 1973):537-8; L. R. Gerlach, WMH, 56(Sum 1973):334-5; R. A. Brown, WMQ, 3rd ser., 30(Oct 1973):680-2.

Lorwin, Val R. and Jacob M. Price, eds. The Dimensions of the Past: Materials, Problems and Opportunities for Quantitative Work in History. New Haven, Conn.: Yale U Press, 1972. Rev. by R. P. Swierenga, PHR, 42(Aug 1973):421-3.

Lothar, Gall. Das Bismarck-Problem in der Geschicht-schreibung nach 1945. n. p., n. d. Rev. by M. Sturmer, ESR, 3(Apr 1973):189-91.

Lotman, I. M. Struktura khudozhestvennego teksta. Providence, R. I.: Brown U Press, 1971. Rev. by G. de Mallac, RR, 32(Ja 1973):98.

Lottinville, Savoie see Hine, Robert V.

Lotz, Wolfgang. The Champagne Spy. London: Vallentine, Mitchell, 1972. Rev. by C. C. Rudulph, MEJ, 27(Aut 1973):513-14.

Lougee, Robert W. Mid-Century Revolution, 1848: Society and Revolution in France and Germany. Lexington, Mass.: Heath,

1972. Rev. by R. Anchor, Historian, 36(Nov 1973):109.

Lounsbury, Raymond H. Pennoyer Brothers: Colonization, Com-
    merce, Charity in the Seventeenth Century. Philadelphia:
    Dorrance, 1971. Rev. by J. E. Farnell, AHR, 78(Oct 1973):
    1057.

Love, Jean C., Robert Sharlet and Zigurds L. Zile. The Soviet
    Legal System and Arms Inspection: A Case Study in Policy
    Implementation. New York: Praeger, 1972. Rev. by P. B.
    Maggs, RR, 32(Ja 1973):89-90.

Love, Joseph L. Rio Grande do Sul and Brazillian Regionalism,
    1882-1930. Stanford, Cal.: Stan U Press, 1971. Rev. by
    J. C. Carey, JOW, 12(Jl 1973):501.

Love, Mills, ed. The Rambler in Georgia: Desultory Observations
    on the Situation, Extent, Climate, Population, Manners, Cus-
    toms, Commerce, Constitution, Government, Etc. of the
    State From the Revolution to the Civil War Recorded by
    Thirteen Travelers. Savannah: Beehive, 1973. Rev. in
    GHQ, 57(Fall 1973):448-9.

Lovejoy, David S. The Glorious Revolution in America. New York:
    Harper and Row, 1972. Rev. by D. W. Jordan, AHR, 78
    (Oct 1973):1120-1; S. Adams, NYHSQ, 57(Oct 1973):349-50;
    M. C. Hall, JSH, 39(Aug 1973):435-6; C. Robbins, PMHB,
    97(Apr 1973):252-3; W. M. Billings, VMHB, 81(Oct 1973):
    491-2; T. H Breen, WMQ, 3rd ser., 30(Jl 1973):500-3.

Loveland, Anne C. Emblem of Liberty: The Image of Lafayette in
    the American Mind. Baton Rouge: LSU Press, 1971. Rev.
    by C. E. Burgess, JISHS, 66(Spr 1973):115-16.

Lovett, Robert W. American Economic and Business History Infor-
    mation Sources. Detroit: Gale Research, 1971. Rev. by
    E. S. Ferguson, T & C, 14(Ja 1973):113-15.

Lowe, C. J. and M. L. Dockrill. The Mirage of Power: British
    Foreign Policy, 1902-22. 3 vols. London: Routledge and
    Kegan Paul, 1972. Rev. by Z. Steiner, History, 58(Je 1973):
    318-19.

Lowe, Don and Roberta. One Hundred Southern California Hiking
    Trails. Beaverton, Ore.: Touchstone, 1972. Rev. by K.
    Black, JOW, 12(Jl 1973):510.

Lowe, Norman. The Lancashire Textile Industry in the Sixteenth
    Century. Manchester: Chetham Society, 1972. Rev. by
    G. D. Ramsey, History, 58(Je 1973):279-80.

Lowenstein, Eleanor. Bibliography of American Cookery Books,
    1742-1860. Worcester, Mass.: American Antiquarian So-

ciety, 1972. Rev. by E. S. Weigley, PMHB, 97(Apr 1973):
271-2.

Löwenstein, Julius L. Vision and Wirklichkeit: Marx contra Marxismus. Tubingen: J. C. B. Mohr, 1970. Rev. by W. J.
Brazill, AHR, 78(Feb 1973):67.

Lowenthal, Abrahm F. The Dominican Intervention. Cambridge,
Mass.: Har U Press, 1972. Rev. by D. G. Munro, HAHR,
53(May 1973):320-1.

Lowitt, Richard. George W. Norris: The Persistence of a Pro-
gressive, 1913-1933. Urbana: U Ill Press, 1971. Rev. by
M. Ridge, IMH, 69(Mar 1973):81-2; C. Coate, Montana, 23
(Spr 1973):74-5; R. Stone, JISHS, 66(Win 1973):476-7; R.
M. Abrams, SS, 64(Nov 1973):282-3.

Lubachko, Ivan S. Belorussia Under Soviet Rule, 1917-1957. Lexington: U Press Ky, 1972. Rev. by J. S. Reshetar, Jr.,
AHR, 78(Dec 1973):1502. W. Sukiennicki, RR, 32(Apr 1973):
210.

Lubenow, William C. The Politics of Government Growth: Early
Victorian Attitudes Toward State Intervention, 1833-1848.
Newton Abbot; David and Charles, 1971. Rev. by J. Hart,
History, 58(Je 1973):304-7; R. M. MacLeod, AHR, 78(Dec
1973):1386-1405.

Lucas, Colin. The Structure of the Terror. The Example of
Javogues and the Loire. London: Ox U Press, 1973. Rev.
by B. Behrens, HJ, 16(Sep 1973):641-4.

Lucas, Rex A. Minetown, Milltown, Railtown: Life in Canadian
Communities of Single Industry. Toronto: U Tor Press,
1972. Rev. by R. Cuff, BHR, 47(Sum 1973):286-7.

Luckett, Richard. The White Generals: An Account of the White
Movement and the Russian Civil War. New York: Viking,
1971. Rev. by A. E. Adams, JMH, 45(Mar 1973):168-9.

Ludz, Peter Christian. The German Democratic Republic from the
Sixties to the Seventies: A Socio-Political Analysis. Cam-
bridge, Mass.: Har U Center for International Affairs, 1970.
Rev. by J. S. Wozniak, EEQ, 7(Spr 1973):98-9.

Luebke, Frederick C., ed. Ethnic Voters and the Election of Lincoln. Lincoln: U Neb Press, 1971. Rev. by M. Hough,
WMH, 56(Sum 1973):326-7; N. Lederer, JISHS, 66(Spr 1973):
111-13.

Lukowski, Zygmunt. Polish Participation in the Russian Social
Democratic Movement, 1883-1893. Cracow: Nakladem Uni-

197   LUMBY

versytetu Jagiellonskiego, 1970. Rev. by M. K. Dziewanowski, AHR, 78(Feb 1973):127.

Lumby, E. W. R., ed. Policy and Operations in the Mediterranean,
1912-14. n. p.: the Society, 1970. Rev. by R. A. Courtemanche, AHR, 78(Je 1973):697-8.

Lützow, Henrich Graf von. Im diplomatischen Dienst der k. u. k.
Monarchie. Vienna: Verlag für Geschichte und Politik, 1971.
Rev. by R. A. Kann, JMH, 45(Mar 1973):163-5.

Luvaas, Jay, ed. Dear Miss Em: General Eichelberger's War in
the Pacific, 1942-1945. Westport, Conn.: Greenwood, 1972.
Rev. by C. G. Reynolds, Historian, 36(Nov 1973):133-4;
D. C. James, JAH, 60(Dec 1973):853-4.

Lycan, Gilbert L. Alexander Hamilton and American Foreign Policy:
A Design for Greatness. Norman: U Ok Press, 1971. Rev.
by J. A. Woods, History, 58(Oct 1973):489.

Lydecker, Ryck. Pigboat ... The Story of the Whalebacks. Duluth,
Minn.: Sweetwater, 1973. Rev. by T. A. Sykora, IS, 29
(Win 1973):318-19.

Lydon, J. F. The Lordship of Ireland in the Middle Ages. Toronto: U Tor Press, 1972. Rev. by G. Costigan, Historian,
36(Nov 1973):95.

Lydon, James G. Pirates, Privateers, and Profits. Upper Saddle
River, N. J.: Gregg, 1971. Rev. by L. M. Maloney,
WMQ, 3rd ser., 30(Apr 1973):356-8; J. Judd, NYH, 54(Ja
1973):117-18; C. Ubbelohde, NYHSQ, 57(Ja 1973):76-7.

Lynch, James see Clark, Francis

Lyngstad, Alexandra and Sverre. Ivan Goncharov. New York:
Twayne, 1971. Rev. by T. L. Aman, RR, 32(Apr 1973):
215-16.

Lyons, F. S. L. Ireland Since the Famine. New York: Scribner's, 1971. Rev. by T. E. Hachey, JMH, 45(Mar 1973):
175-6; N. Mansergh, HJ, 16(Je 1973):436-41.

Lyons, Thomas T. Black Leadership in American History. Reading, Mass.: Addison-Wesley, 1971. Rev. by W. F. Mugleston, HT, 7(Nov 1973):127.

Lyons, U. and M. C., eds. Ayyubids, Mamlukes, and Crusaders,
Selections from the Tarīkh al-Duwal wa'l Mulūk of Ibn al
Furāt. Cambridge, Eng.: Heffer, 1971. Rev. by J. M.
Rogers, EHR, 88(Jl 1973):588-90.

Lysaght, A. M. Joseph Banks in Newfoundland and Labrador, 1766:

His Diaries, Manuscripts and Collections. London: Faber
and Faber, 1971. Rev. by G. Williams, History, 58(Feb
1973):148-9.

Mabogunje, A. L. and J. Omer-Cooper. Owu in Yoruba History.
Ibadan: Ibadan U Press, 1971. Rev. by R. Smith, Africa,
43(Ja 1973):83-4.

McCandless, Perry. A History of Missouri, Vol. II. 1820-1860.
Columbia: U Mo Press, 1972. Rev. by J. W. Goodrich,
MoHR, 67(Apr 1973):457-8; E. B. Smith, JSH, 39(Aug 1973):
468-9; D. F. Carmony, JAH, 60(Dec 1973):803; W. H.
Lyon, PHR, 42(Nov 1973):586-7.

McCarthy, Paul, comp. Ralph J. Rivers, U. S. Representative to
Congress from Alaska, 1959-1966; An Inventory of His Con-
gressional Papers in the Archives and Manuscript Collection
of the Elmer E. Rasmuson Library, University of Alaska.
College, Alaska: U Alaska, 1971. Rev. by A. L. Nolen,
AmArch, 36(Ja 1973):76-8.

McCarty, Clara S. McCartys of Virginia, With Emphasis on the
First Four Generations in the Colony. Richmond: Dietz,
1972. Rev. by M. B. D. McCurdy, VMHB, 81(Apr 1973):
215-6.

McClellan, James. Joseph Story and the American Constitution: A
Study in Political and Legal Thought, With Selected Writings.
Norman: U Ok Press, 1971. Rev. by K. Preyer, WMQ,
3rd Ser., 30(Ja 1973):172-4; A. H. Kelly, AHR, 78(Feb
1973):159-60.

McClelland, Charles E. The German Historians and England: A
Study in Nineteenth Century Views. New York: Cam U
Press, 1971. Rev. by D. I. Gaines, AHR, 78(Je 1973):709-
10; G. G. Iggers, JMH, 45(Sep 1973):518-20; K. von Klemperer, H & T, 12(1973):265-7.

McClelland, Vincent Alan. English Roman Catholics and Higher
Education. New York: Ox U Press, 1973. Rev. by S.
Rothblatt, AHR, 78(Dec 1973):1466-7.

McCloskey, Donald N., ed. Essays on a Mature Economy: Britain
After 1840. Princeton, N. J.: Prin U Press, 1971. Rev.
by M. C. Reed, AHR, 78(Je 1973):692-3; W. Ashworth, History, 58(Feb 1973):119-21; F. F. Mendels, JIH, 4(Aut 1973):
328-9; C. K. Hyde, T & C, 14(Apr 1973):313-5; A. Simmons, JEH, 33(Dec 1973):895-6.

McCloskey, Robert G. The Modern Supreme Court. Cambridge,
Mass.: Har U Press, 1972. Rev. by E. A. Purcell, Jr.,
AHR, 78(Feb 1973):180-1; E. Dumbould, JAH, 60(Je 1973):
163-4.

199   MC CORMICK

McCormick, Daniel C.   The Wishbone Fleet.   Massena, N. Y.:
    n. p., 1972. Rev. by G. L. H. IS, 29(Spr 1973):79-80.

McCowen, George Smith, Jr.   The British Occupation of Charleston,
    1780-82. Columbia: U SCar Press, 1972. Rev. by J. L.
    Wright, Jr., FHQ, 52(Oct 1973):193-4.

McCoy, Garnett.   Archives of American Art: A Directory of Re-
    sources. New York: R. R. Bowker, 1972. Rev. by M. F.
    Daniels, AmArc, 36(Jl 1973):403-4.

McCullough, David.   The Great Bridge.   New York: Simon and
    Schuster, 1972. Rev. J. J. Heslin, NYHSQ, 57(Jl 1973):
    272-3; S. R. Wilson, T & C, 14(Jl 1973):506-9.

McCune, Charles Lockhart.   Three Lives and All of Them Are Mine.
    Pittsburgh: Privately printed, n. d. Rev. by J. Markowitz,
    WPHM, 56(Oct 1973):429-31.

MacCurtain, Margaret.   Tudor and Stuart Ireland.   Dublin: Gill and
    Macmillan, 1972. Rev. by R. J. Hunter, E-I, 8(Win 1973):
    121-3.

MacDermot, Violet.   The Cult of the Seer in the Ancient Middle
    East: A Contribution to Current Research on Hallucinations
    Drawn from Coptic and Other Texts.   Berkeley: U Cal
    Press, 1971. Rev. by H. N. Howard, MEJ, 27(Win 1973):
    100.

McDermott, John Francis, ed.   Travelers on the Western Frontier.
    Urbana: U Ill Press, 1970. Rev. by H. R. Lamar, NMHR,
    48(Oct 1973):331-3; W. B. Hendrickson, IMH, 69(Sep 1973):
    289-91.

Macdonald, Major J. R. L.   Soldiering and Surveying in British
    East Africa. London: Dawson's of Pall Mall, 1973. Rev.
    by M. Twaddle, AfAf, 72(Oct 1973):466.

McDonald, William A. and George R. Rapp, Jr., eds.   The Min-
    nesota Messenia Expedition: Reconstructing a Bronze Age
    Regional Environment. Minneapolis: U Minn Press, 1972.
    Rev. by M. H. Jameson, AHR, 78(Oct 1973):1024; J. E.
    Fitting, T & C, 14(Jl 1973):487-8.

MacDonnell, Kevin.   Eadweard Muybridge, the Man Who Invented
    the Moving Picture. Boston: Little, Brown, 1972. Rev. by
    R. O. Dougan, PMHB, 97(Apr 1973):279-81.

McDonough, James L.   Schofield: Union General in the Civil War
    and Reconstruction. Tallahassee: Fla St U Press, 1972.
    Rev. by W. E. Parrish, MoHR, 67(Ja 1973):322-4; J. E.
    Sefton, JISHS, 66(Aut 1973):358-9; R. G. Lowe, JSH, 39
    (Feb 1973):126-7.

MAC DOWELL   200

MacDowell, Dorothy Kelly. Du Bose Genealogy. Columbia: R. L.
    Bryan, 1972. Rev. by C. E. Thomas, SCHM, 74(Oct 1973):
    318-9.

McFaul, John M. The Politics of Jacksonian Finance. Ithaca,
    N. Y.: Cornell U Press, 1972. Rev. by G. L. Browne,
    WMH, 56(Sum 1973):344-6; H. Cohen, IMH, 69(Sep 1973):
    288-9; C. M. Wiltse, AHR, 78(Dec 1973):1529-30; R. P.
    McCormick, JAH, 60(Sep 1973):440-1; J. V. Mering, JSH,
    39(Nov 1973):593-4; D. E. Meerse, NYH, 54(Jl 1973):378-
    80; D. B. Cole, PMHB, 97(Jl 1973):417-8.

McGaw, William Cochrane. Savage Scene: The Life and Times of
    James Kirker, Frontier King. New York: Hastings, 1972.
    Rev. by A. Shoemaker, AW, 10(Jl 1973):57.

McGiffert, Michael, ed. God's Plot: The Paradoxes of Puritan
    Piety: Being the Autobiography of Thomas Shepard. Am-
    herst, Mass.: U Mass Press, 1972. Rev. by M. G. Hall,
    JAH, 60(Je 1973):110-11.

McGimsey, Charles, III. Public Archeology. New York: Seminar
    Press, 1972. Rev. by J. L. Cotter, Archives, 26(Apr 1973):
    148; S. Williams, Antiquity, 47(Mar 1973):85-6.

McGinnis, Dale K. and Floyd W. Sharrock. The Crow People.
    Phoenix: Indian Tribal Series, 1972. Rev. by J. D. Mc-
    Dermott, A & W, 15(Win 1973):372-4; T. B. Hinton, JAriH,
    14(Aut 1973):264-5.

McGloin, John Bernard, S. J. Jesuits by the Golden Gate: The
    Society of Jesus in San Francisco, 1849-1969. San Francisco:
    U SF Press, 1972. Rev. by D. C. Cutter, PHR, 42(Nov
    1973):587-8; S. E. McCaffrey, PacH, 17(Sum 1973):87-8.

McGovern, George S. and Leonard F. Guttridge. The Great Coal-
    field War. Boston: Houghton Mifflin, 1972. Rev. by W. T.
    Eagan, AW, 10(Ja 1973):52; W. Graebner, AHR, 78(Feb
    1973):180; A. Probert, JOW, 12(Ja 1973):178-9.

McGovern, James. To the Yalu: From the Chinese Invasion of
    Korea to MacArthur's Dismissal. New York: Morrow, 1972.
    Rev. by W. G. Hermes, MilAf, 37(Oct 1973):115.

McGreevey, William Paul. An Economic History of Colombia 1845-
    1930. Cambridge: Cam U Press, 1971. Rev. by J. Lynch,
    History, 58(Oct 1973):482-3; J. Wells, HJ, 16(Mar 1973):
    222-4; J. L. Helguera, TAm, 29(Ja 1973):407-9.

MacGreevy, Thomas. Collected Poems. Dublin: Zozimus Books,
    1971. Rev. by F. S. Kiley, E-I, 8(Win 1973):133-5.

201   MC GUIRE

McGuire, E. B. Irish Whiskey. Dublin: Gill and Macmillan, 1973.
     Rev. by R. T. Reilly, E-I, 8(Aut 1973):153-4.

MacHale, Thomas P., ed. Chile: A Critical Survey. Santiago:
     Institute of General Studies, 1972. Rev. by E. H. Corth,
     TAm, 30(Oct 1973):290-1.

McHenry, Paul Graham, Jr. Adobe--Build It Yourself. Tucson: U Ari
     Press, 1973. Rev. by S. Ellinwood, JAriH, 14(Win 1973):392.

Machilek, Franz. Ludolf von Sagan und seine Stellung in der Ause-
     inandersetzung um Konziliarismus und Hussitismus. Munich:
     Verlag Robert Lerche, 1967. Rev. by O. Odlozilik, AHR,
     78(Feb 1973):85.

McHugh, Tom. The Time of the Buffalo. New York: Knopf, 1972.
     Rev. by D. Russell, WHQ, 4(Jl 1973):333-4; M. J. Mattes,
     CoMag, 50(Sum 1973):261-3; R. A. Bartlett, Montana, 23
     (Sum 1973):53; E. N. Moody, NHSQ, 16(Sum 1973):138-9;
     W. Gard, AW, 10(May 1973):50.

Macintyre, Donald. The Naval War Against Hitler. New York:
     Scribners, 1971. Rev. by K. Macksey, JMH, 45(Mar 1973):
     184-6.

MacIntyre, Tom. Blood Relations: Versions of Gaelic Poems of
     the Seventeenth and Eighteenth Centuries. Dublin: Zozimus
     Books, 1972. Rev. by F. S. Kiley, E-I, 8(Win 1973):133-5.

McJimsey, George T. Genteel Partisan: Manton Marble, 1834-
     1917. Ames, Ia.: Ia St U Press, 1971. Rev. by I. Katz,
     JAH, 59(Mar 1973):1026-27.

Mack, Herb see Cook, Ann

McKay, John P. Pioneers for Profit: Foreign Entrepreneurship
     and Russian Industrialization 1885-1913. Chicago: U Chi
     Press, 1970. Rev. by S. Lieberstein, T & C, 14(Oct 1973):
     647-9; H. S. Levine, RR, 32(Ja 1973):86-8.

McKee, Christopher. Edward Preble: A Naval Biography 1761-1807.
     Annapolis: Naval Institute Press, 1972. Rev. by R. E.
     Johnson, JAH, 60(Dec 1973):785-7.

MacKendrick, Paul. Roman France. London: G. Bell, 1972. Rev.
     by O. Brogan, Antiquity, 47(Je 1973):162-3.

McKenney, Thomas L. Sketches of a Tour to the Lakes, of the
     Character and Customs of the Chippeway and of the Incidents
     Connected With the Treaty of Fon du Lac. Barre, Mass.:
     Imprint Society, 1972. Rev. by F. P. Prucha, AHR, 78
     (Oct 1973):1131.

McKenzie, John R. P. Weimar Germany. Totowa, N. J.: Rowman and Littlefield, 1971. Rev. by J. Jacobson, Historian, 35(Feb 1973):290; F. Beck, MilAf, 37(Apr 1973):72-3.

McKie, David and Chris Cook, eds. The Decade of Disillusion: British Politics in the Sixties. New York: St. Martin's, n. d. Rev. by T. Lloyd, AHR, 78(Dec 1973):1472-3.

McKinney, H. Lewis. Wallace and Natural Selection. New Haven, Conn.: Yale U Press, 1972. Rev. by C. J. Schneer, JMH, 45(Sep 1973):504-5.

McKnight, Brian E. Village and Bureaucracy in Southern Sung, China. Chicago: U Chi Press, 1971. Rev. by J. T. C. Liu, AHR, 78(Feb 1973):135-6.

McLaurin, Melton Alonzo. Paternalism and Protest: Southern Cotton Mill Workers and Organized Labor, 1875-1905. Westport, Conn.: Greenwood, 1971. Rev. by H. F. Bedford, AHR, 78(Feb 1973):170-1; W. B. Weare, JNH, 58(Ja 1973): 111-12; C. A. Haulman, FHQ, 51(Apr 1973):456-7; W. M. Dick, CHR, 54(Mar 1973):96-7.

McLemore, Richard Aubrey, ed. A History of Mississippi. 2 vols. Hattiesburg, Miss: U and Coll Press Miss., 1973. Rev. by L. Campbell, Ala Re, 26(Oct 1973):273-5; D. H. Donald, AHR, 78(Dec 1973):1523-5; M. Billington, JAH, 60(Dec 1973): 801-3; A. M. Boom, JSH, 39(Nov 1973):626-8; R. E. Corlew, JMiH, 35(Aug 1973):325-7; W. F. Holmes, NCHR, 50 (Sum 1973):333-5; W. H. Stauffer, VMHB, 81(Oct 1973):504-5.

McLendon, James. Papa: Hemingway in Key West. Miami: E. A. Seeman, 1972. Rev. by K. H. Proby, FHQ, 52(Jl 1973):73-4.

McManus, Edgar J. Black Bondage in the North. Syracuse, N. Y.: Syr U Press, n. d. Rev. by R. Detweiler, HT, 7(Nov 1973):145-6; I. V. Brown, PMHB, 97(Oct 1973):534-5.

Macmillan, David S., ed. Canadian Business History: Selected Studies, 1497-1971. Toronto: McClelland and Stewart, 1972. Rev. by H. G. J. Aitken, BHR, 47(Sum 1973):279-81; M. S. Cross, CHR, 54(Sep 1973):300-2; J. Boudreau. JAH, 60 (Sep 1973):520-1.

Macmillan, Harold. Pointing the Way, 1959-1961. New York: Harper and Row, 1972. Rev. by S. R. Graubard, AHR, 78 (Dec 1973):1471-2.

_____. Riding the Storm, 1956-1959. London: Macmillan, 1971. Rev. by A. Tucker, CHR, 54(Sep 1973):321-2.

McMillen, Neil R. The Citizens Council: Organized Resistance to
the Second Reconstruction 1954-64. Urbana: U Ill Press,
1971. Rev. by A. M. Burns, SS, 64(Oct 1973):234-5.

McNally, Raymond T. Chaadayev and His Friends: An Intellectual
History of Peter Chaadayev and His Russian Contemporaries.
Tallahassee, Fla.: Diplomatic Press, 1971. Rev. by J. A.
Rogers, JMH, 45(Dec 1973):694-5; E. C. Thaden, RR, 32
(Ja 1973):93-4.

McNeal, R. H. Bride of the Revolution: Krupskaya and Lenin.
Ann Arbor: U Mich Press, 1972. Rev. by J. Richardson,
HTo, 23(Mar 1973):216-17; B. Farnsworth, RR, 32(Jl 1973):
324-5.

McNeill, Mary. Vere Foster 1819-1900: An Irish Benefactor.
Newton Abbot: David and Charles, 1971. Rev. by N. Man-
sergh, HJ, 16(Je 1973):436-41; E. D. Steele, History, 58
(Oct 1973):461-2.

McNeill, William H. The Ecumene: Story of Humanity. New York:
Harper and Row, 1973. Rev. by J. Bilello, V. Buscareno
and R. Russo, HT, 7(Nov 1973):108-9.

McNickle, D'Arcy. Indian Man: A Life of Oliver La Farge.
Bloomington: Ind U Press, 1971. Rev. by T. Le Duc, AHR,
78(Je 1973):742-3.

McNitt, Frank. Navajo Wars: Military Campaigns, Slave Raids
and Reprisals. Albuquerque: U NM Press, 1972. Rev. by
H. P. Walker, A & W, 15(Aut 1973):284-5; R. M. Utley,
JAH, 60(Dec 1973):783-4; M. Link, JAriH, 14(Sum 1973):
165-6; L. J. White, JOW, 12(Oct 1973):638; R. L. Nichols,
Montana, 23(Aut 1973):67; L. C. Wyman, NMHR, 48(Apr
1973):173-5; D. E. Worcester, PHR, 42(Nov 1973):584-5.

McSeveney, Samuel T. The Politics of Depression: Political Behavior in the Northeast, 1893-1896. New York: Ox U Press,
1972. Rev. by J. Waksmundski, Historian, 36(Nov 1973):
130-1; E. M. Tobin, NJH, 91(Aut 1973):189-91; S. L.
Jones, NYH, 54(Jl 1973):380-1.

McSherry, James E. Stalin, Hitler and Europe 1939-1941. Vol. II.
The Imbalance of Power. New York: World, 1970. Rev.
by R. J Crampton, History, 58(Feb 1973):141-2.

McWilliams, John P., Jr. Political Justice in a Republic: James
Fenimore Cooper's America. Berkeley: U Cal Press, 1972.
Rev. by A. A. Ekirch, Jr., JAH, 60(Dec 1972):809-10.

McWilliams, Wilson Carey. The Idea of Fraternity in America.
Berkeley: U Cal Press, 1973. Rev. by B. G. Gallagher,
Crisis, 80(Nov 1973):32.

Maddex, Jack P., Jr. The Virginia Conservatives 1867-1879: A
    Study in Reconstruction Politics. Chapel Hill: UNC Press,
    1970. Rev. by R. C. Reinders, History, 58(Feb 1973):152-3.

Maddox, Margaret and Louis Gottschalk. Lafayette in the French
    Revolution: From the October Days Through the Federation.
    Chicago: U Chi Press, 1973. Rev. by G. Downum, HRNB,
    2(Nov/Dec 1973):26-7. SEE ALSO: Gottschalk, Louis and
    Margaret Maddox. Lafayette in the French Revolution....

Maddox, Robert James. The New Left and the Origins of the Cold
    War. Princeton, N. J.: Prin U Press, 1973. Rev. by
    D. M. Smith, JSH, 39(Nov 1973):623-4.

Madhok, Balraj. Murder of Democracy. New Delhi: S. Chand,
    1973. Rev. by V. K. Arora, IQ, 29(Oct-Dec 1973):366-7.

Madwell, Charles R., comp. and trans. The Census Tables for the
    French Colony of Louisiana from 1699 Through 1732. Balti-
    more: Genealogical Publishing Co., 1972. Rev. by M. E.
    Sanders, LaH, 14(Sum 1973):326-7.

Maguire, W. A. The Downshire Estates in Ireland, 1801-1845: The
    Management of Irish Landed Estates in the Early Nineteenth
    Century. New York: Ox U Press, 1972. Rev. by D.
    Spring, AHR, 78(Dec 1973):1473; R. L. Berry, JEH, 33
    (Sep 1973):681-2; E. Larkin, JMH, 45(Dec 1973):654-6.

Mahajani, Usha. Philippine Nationalism: External Challenge and
    Filipino Response, 1565-1946. St. Lucia, Queensland: U
    Queensland Press, 1971. Rev. by G. E. Wheeler, PHR, 42
    (Feb 1973):127-8.

Maheshwari, S. R. The Administrative Reforms Commission. Agra:
    Lakmi Narain Agarwal, 1971. Rev. by A. R. Tyagi, IQ, 29
    (Apr-Je 1973):171-2.

Maheshwari, Shriram. Government Through Consultation. New
    Delhi: Indian Institute of Public Administration, 1972. R.
    Rattan, IQ, 29(Apr-Je 1973):170.

Mahler, Raphael. A History of Modern Jewry, 1780-1815. New
    York: Schocken, 1971. Rev. by S. Reinfeld, AHR, 78(Oct
    1973):1016-17; L. Poliakov, JMH, 45(Mar 1973):124-5.

Mahon, Derek. Lives. London: Ox U Press, 1972. Rev. by
    T. D. Redshaw, E-I, 8(Spr 1973):142-51.

Mahon, John K. The War of 1812. Gainesville: U Fla Press,
    1972. Rev. by A. DeConde, AHR, 78(Dec 1973):1528-9;
    G. D. Lewis, FCHQ, 47(Apr 1973):195-6; R. A. Preston,
    FHQ, 52(Oct 1973):198-200; F. C. Mevers, GHQ, 57(Fall
    1973):439-40; K. I. Polakoff, HT, 6(May 1973):484-5; R. L.

205   MAIER

Hatzenbuehler, IMH, 69(Sep 1973):283-4; R. Horsman, JAH,
60(Dec 1973):804-5; H. P. Jones, JMiH, 35(May 1973):210-
11; F. A. Cassell, JSH, 39(Aug 1973):446-7; P. J. Woehrmann, MHM, 68(Win 1973):462-3; V. Sapio, NCHR, 50(Spr
1973):720-1; E. M. Burton, SCHM, 74(Jl 1973):173-4; F. L.
Owsley, Jr., THQ, 32(Sum 1973):192; M. E. Fletcher,
WMH, 56(Sum 1973):329; P. F. Lambert, WPHM, 56(Jl
1973):321-2.

Maier, Pauline. From Resistance to Revolution: Colonial Radicals
    and the Development of American Opposition to Britain, 1765-
    1776. New York: Knopf, 1972. Rev. by P. U. Bonomi,
    AHR, 78(Feb 1973):154-5; L. H. Leder, JSH, 39(Aug 1973):
    437-8; M. McKay, MHM, 68(Win 1973):456-7; R. A. Ryer-
    son, NYHSQ, 57(Jl 1973):262-4; J. Ferling, PH, 40(Apr
    1973):217-18; R. S. Klein, PMHB, 97(Ja 1973):115-17; G.
    Rude, WMQ, 3rd ser., 30(Ja 1973):152-4.

Mails, Thomas E. The Mystic Warriors of the Plains. Garden
    City, N. Y.: Doubleday, 1972. Rev. by D. Brown, AHI,
    8(Apr 1973):49-50; R. B. Hassrick, CoMag, 50(Spr 1973):
    165-6; D. J. Berthrong, JAH, 60(Sep 1973):462-4; A.
    Cardona-Hine, Mankind, 4(Aug 1973):6, 41; W. Weidert,
    Montana, 23(Aut 1973):72; F. W. Voget, NMHR, 48(Oct
    1973):333-5; W. R. Jacobs, PHR, 42(Aug 1973):425-6; M.
    Utterback, SWHQ, 76(Apr 1973):500.

Main, Jackson Turner. Political Parties Before the Constitution.
    Chapel Hill: UNC Press, 1973. Rev. by J. R. Pole, AHR,
    78(Dec 1973):1525-7; J. H. Silbey, HRNB, 2(Nov/Dec 1973):
    41-2; V. B. Hall, JAH, 60(Dec 1973):793-5; J. L. Humber,
    NCHR, 50(Sum 1973):339-40; C. R. Hanyan, NYHSQ, 57(Oct
    1973):354-6; R. F. Oaks, PH, 40(Oct 1973):483-4; G. S.
    Rowe, PMHB, 97(Oct 1973):541-3; E. J. Ferguson, WMQ,
    3rd ser., 30(Oct 1973):661-3.

_____. The Sovereign States, 1775-1783. New York: New
    Viewpoints ... F. Watts, 1973. Rev. by J. P. Cullen,
    AHI, 8(Dec 1973):50; R. M. Calhoon, VMHB, 81(Oct
    1973):494-5.

Major, John. The Oppenheimer Hearing. London: Batsford, 1971.
    Rev. by H. Brogan, History, 58(Feb 1973):157-8.

Malagon, Javier and Silvio Zavala. Rafael Altanirco y Crevea, El
    Historia y el hombre. Mexico: ANAM, 1971. Rev. by C.
    A. Hale, TAm, 29(Ja 1973):393-4.

Malefakis, Edward E. Agrarian Reform and Peasant Revolution in
    Spain: Origins of the Civil War. New Haven, Conn.: Yale
    U Press, 1970. Rev. by H. Landsberger, CSSH, 15(Je
    1973):378-88; R. M. Blinkhorn, ESR, 3(Ja 1973):81-7; R.
    A. H. Robinson, History, 58(Feb 1973):138.

Malik, Hafeez, ed. Iqbal: Poet-Philosopher of Pakistan. New
York: Columbia U Press, 1971. Rev. by M. Ghaznavi,
MEJ, 27(Win 1973):88.

Malik, Yogendra K. East Indians in Trinidad: A Study in Minority
Politics. New York: Ox U Press, 1971. Rev. by A. Bryan,
HAHR, 53(May 1973):354-5.

Malloy, James M. and Richard S. Thorn, eds. Beyond the Revolution: Bolivia Since 1952. Pittsburgh: U Pittsburgh Press,
1971. Rev. by D. B. Heath, TAm, 29(Ja 1973):409-10.

Malone, Joseph J. The Arab Lands of Western Asia. Englewood
Cliffs, N. J.: Prentice-Hall, 1973. Rev. by A. G. Gerteiny, HRNB, 2(Nov/Dec 1973):37.

Maloney, Walter C. A Sketch of the History of Key West, Florida.
Gainesville: U Fla Press, 1968. Rev. by E. C. Williamson,
AlaRe, 26(Jl 1973):231-2.

Malraux, André. Les Chênes qu'on abat. Paris: Gallimard, 1971.
Rev. by J. C. Cairns, AHR, 78(Dec 1973):1406-20.

Maltby, William S. The Black Legend in England: The Development
of Anti-Spanish Sentiment, 1558-1660. Durham, N. C.: Duke
U Press, 1971. Rev. by J. J. Silke, JMH, 45(Mar 1973):
98-9; R. W. Etulain, SS, 64(Mar 1973):135-6.

Mamatrey, Victor S. and Radomir Luza, eds. A History of the
Czechoslovak Republic, 1918-1948. Princeton, N. J.: Prin
U Press, 1973. Rev. G. Kish, HRNB, 2(Nov/Dec 1973):31.

Mancall, Mark. Russia and China: Their Diplomatic Relations to
1728. Cambridge, Mass.: Har U Press, 1971. Rev. by
J. W. Strong, AHR, 78(Oct 1973):1013-14.

Mandelbaum, Maurice. History, Man, and Reason: A Study in
Nineteenth-Century Thought. Baltimore: JHU Press, 1971.
Rev. by M. Ermarth, JMH, 45(Mar 1973):125-7.

Mandelbaum, Seymour J. Community and Communications. N. Y.:
Norton, 1972. Rev. by J. A. Tarr, JAH, 60(Je 1973):164-5.

Mane, Robert. Henry Adams on the Road to Chartres. Cambridge,
Mass.: Belknap Press, Har U Press, 1971. Rev. by V.
Wagner, NYHSQ, 57(Ja 1973):87-9.

Mangione, Jerre. The Dream and the Deal: The Federal Writers'
Project, 1935-1943. Boston: Little, Brown, 1972. Rev. by
L. Rapport, AHR, 78(Oct 1973):1143-4; S. Persons, JAH,
60(Sep 1973):496-7; L. H. Curry, Jr., JSH, 39(Aug 1973):
463-4.

Mann, Arthur, Neil Harris and Sam Bass Warner, Jr. Indiana His-
    torical Society Lectures: History and the Role of the City in
    American Life. Indianapolis: Ind Historical Society, 1972.
    Rev. by R. A. Mohl, AHR, 78(Oct 1973):1115-16; R. Janis,
    IMH, 69(Sep 1973):278-9.

Mann, J. de L. The Cloth Industry in the West of England, from
    1640-1880. Oxford: Ox U Press, 1971. Rev. by N. B.
    Harte, History, 58(Feb 1973):108-9.

Manning, Maurice. The Blueshirts. Toronto: U Tor Press, 1971.
    Rev. by A. MacLochlainn, JMH, 45(Mar 1973):176-8.

Mansfield, Edwin, John Rapoport, Jerome Schnee, Samuel Wagner
    and Michael Hamburger. Research and Innovation in the
    Modern Corporation. New York: Norton, 1971. Rev. by
    S. J. Mantel, Jr., T & C, 14(Oct 1973):663-5.

Mansfield, J. B., ed. History of the Great Lakes. Vols. I and II.
    Chicago: J. H. Beers, 1899; Cleveland: Freshwater Press
    (Reprint), 1972. Rev. by L. S. B. IS, 29(Sum 1973):158-9.

Mansfield, Peter, ed. The Middle East: A Political and Economic
    Survey. Oxford: Ox U Press, 1973. Rev. by S. K. Lasa-
    rov, NO, 16(Je 1973):49-51.

Mansingh, Surjit and Charles Heimsath. A Diplomatic History of
    Modern India. Bombay: Allied, 1971. Rev. by D. R. Sar-
    Desai, IQ, 29(Oct-Dec 1973):360-1.

Mansoor, Menahem, comp. Political and Diplomatic History of the
    Arab World, 1900-1967: A Chronological Study. Washington,
    D. C.: N C R Microcard Editions, 1972. Rev. by G. N.
    Atiyeh, MEJ, 27(Spr 1973):225-7.

Manypenny, George W. Our Indian Wards. New York: Da Capo,
    1972. (Reprint of 1880) Rev. by C. Reese, JOW, 12(Oct
    1973):657.

Mapunda, O. B. and G. P. Mpangara. The Maji Maji War in Ugoni.
    Nairobi: East African Publishing House, 1969. Rev. by A.
    Redmayne, AfAf, 72(Oct 1973):464-5.

Maquet, Jacques. Civilizations of Black Africa. New York: Ox U
    Press, 1972. Rev. by R. De Gregori, T & C, 14(Ja 1973):
    96-7.

Marambaud, Pierre. William Byrd of Westover, 1674-1744. Char-
    lottesville: U Va Press, 1971. Rev. by A. C. Land, AHR,
    78(Feb 1973):148-9.

Marchand, C. Roland. The American Peace Movement and Social

MARCUS 208

Reform, 1898-1918. Princeton, N. J.: Prin U Press, 1972.
Rev. by D. S. Patterson, AHR, 78(Dec 1973):1538-9; C.
Chatfield, JAH, 60(Dec 1973):830-1.

Marcus, G. J. The Age of Nelson: The Royal Navy 1793-1815.
New York: Viking, 1971. Rev. by C. J. Bartlett, AHR,
78(Feb 1973):101-2; P. K. Crimmin, History, 58(Feb 1973):
112-13; D. A. Baugh, JMH, 45(Mar 1973):112-13.

Marcus, Jacob R. The Colonial American Jew, 1492-1776. Detroit: Wayne St U Press, 1970. Rev. by M. Rischin, WMQ,
3rd ser., 30(Apr 1973):353-5.

_____., ed. An Index to Scientific Articles on American Jewish
History. Cincinnati: American Jewish Archives; New York:
KTAV, 1971. Rev. by W. Kramer, JOW, 12(Jl 1973):509;
M. R. Rubinoff, WPHM, 56(Apr 1973):191-2.

Marcus, Robert D. Grand Old Party: Political Structure in the
Gilded Age 1880-1896. New York: Ox U Press, 1971. Rev.
by N. Macdonald, CHR, 54(Sep 1973):332-3; A. H. Graham,
History, 58(Oct 1973):493-4; J. A. Kehl, PH, 40(Apr 1973):
224-6.

Marcuse, Herbert. Counterrevolution and Revolt. Boston: Beacon,
1972. Rev. by D. W. Shriver, Jr., T & C, 14(Apr 1973):
337-40.

Mardock, Robert Winston. The Reformers and the American Indian.
Columbia, Mo.: U Mo Press, 1971. Rev. by E. J. Dan-
ziger, Jr., CWH, 19(Mar 1973):89-90; H. H. Tanner, FHQ,
51(Ja 1973):333-4.

Marialegui, José Carlos. Seven Interpretative Essays on Peruvian
Reality. Austin: U Tx Press, 1971. Rev. by G. B. Lane,
AHR, 78(Feb 1973):188-9.

Marienhoff, Ira see Sampson, Roy J.

Markensten, Klas. Foreign Investment and Development: Swedish
Companies in India. Lund, Sweden: Student-litteratur, 1972.
Rev. by S. Venu, IQ, 29(Ja-Mar 1973):72-3.

Markowitz, Norman D. The Rise and Fall of the People's Century:
Henry A. Wallace and American Liberalism, 1941-1948. New
York: Free Press, 1973. Rev. by E. W. Hawley, AHR,
78(Dec 1973):1551; T. Buckley, IMH, 69(Dec 1973):282-3;
A. L. Hamby, JAH, 60(Dec 1973):848-9; J. M. McHale,
WMH, 56(Sum 1973):335-6.

Marks, George P., III. The Black Press Views American Imperialism (1898-1900). New York: Arno, 1971. Rev. by E. B.
Tompkins, PHR, 42(Nov 1973):595-6.

Marks, Shula. Reluctant Rebellion: the 1906-8 Disturbances in
    Natal. London: Ox U Press, 1970. Rev. by R. Hyam, HJ,
    16(Sep 1973):616-26.

Marple, Elliot and Bruce H. Olson. The National Bank of Com-
    merce of Seattle, 1899-1969: Territorial to Worldwide Bank-
    ing in Eighty Years.... Palo Alto, Cal.: Pacific, 1972.
    Rev. by V. P. Carosso, JAH, 60(Je 1973):145-7; G. G.
    Suggs, JOW, 12(Jl 1973):513.

Marques, Harland E. see Galler, Meyer

Marriott, Alice and Carol K. Rachlin. American Indian Mythology.
    New York: Crowell, 1967. Rev. by R. N. Ellis, JOW, 12
    (Jl 1973):500.

_____ and _____. Oklahoma: The Forty-Sixth Star. New
    York: Doubleday, 1973. Rev. by O. B. Faulk, AW, 10
    (Jl 1973):59.

Marsden, Arthur. British Diplomacy and Tunis, 1875-1902: A
    Case Study in Mediterranean Policy. New York: Africana,
    1971. Rev. by C. J. Lowe, AHR, 78(Je 1973):695-6.

Marsden, E. W. Greek and Roman Artillery: Technical Treatises.
    Oxford: Clarendon Press, 1971. Rev. by G. D. Young,
    MilAf, 37(Feb 1973):32-3.

Marsh, Andrew J. Letters from Nevada Territory, 1861-1862.
    n. p.: Legislative Counsel [sic] Bureau, State of Nevada,
    1972. Rev. by K. Richards, NHSQ, 16(Fall 1973):193-5.

Marsh, Andrew J., Samuel Clemens and Amos Bowman. Reports
    of the 1863 Constitutional Convention of the Territory of
    Nevada. n. p.: n. d., Rev. by K. Richards, NHSQ, 16
    (Fall 1973):193-5.

Marshal, George and David Poling. Schweitzer: A Biography.
    n. p.: Geoffrey Bles, 1971. Rev. by J. Murray, AfAf, 72
    (Ja 1973):81-2.

Marshall, Dorothy. Industrial England, 1776-1851. New York:
    Scribner's, 1973. Rev. by G. W. Wolff, HT, 7(Nov 1973):
    115-16.

Marshall, Helen E. Mary Adelaide Nutting, Pioneer of Modern
    Nursing. Baltimore: JHU Press, 1972. Rev. by J. Duffy,
    MHM, 68(Spr 1973):112-13.

Marshall, Hugh. Orestes Brownson and the American Republic: An
    Historical Perspective. Washington: Cath U America, 1971.
    Rev. by E. Smith, AHR, 78(Je 1973):735; W. J. Gilmore,
    MHM, 68(Win 1973):463-4.

Marshall, Richard E. and John Edward Wiltz, eds. The Search for Meaning: Viewpoints in American History. New York: Lippincott, 1973. Rev. by F. J. Woeten, HT, 7(Nov 1973):121-2.

Marshall, S. L. A. Crimsoned Prairie: The Wars Between the United States and the Plains Indians During the Winning of the West. New York: Scribner's, 1972. Rev. by J. D. Mc-Dermott, AHI, 8(Oct 1973):50; R. L. Nichols, JAH, 60(Sep 1973):461-2; J. T. King, Montana, 23(Aut 1973):64; K. Philip, WHQ, 4(Jl 1973):335-7.

Marshburn, Joseph H. Murder and Witchcraft in England, 1550-1640, as Recounted in Pamphlets, Ballads, Broadsides and Plays. Norman: U Ok Press, 1971. Rev. by R. H. West, GR, 27(Spr 1973):137-41.

Marsina, Richard. Codex diplomaticus et epistolaris Slovaciae. I. 805-1235. Bratislava: Academia Scientiarum Slovaca, 1971. Rev. by C. R. Cheny, EHR, 88(Jl 1973):582-4.

Marszalek, John F., Jr. Court-Martial: A Black Man in America. New York: Scribner's, 1972. Rev. by M. E. Fletcher, JAH, 60(Dec 1973):823-4; E. M. Coffman, MilAf, 37(Oct 1973):110-11; J. P. Maddex, Jr., NCHR, 50(Sum 1973):341-2; L. A. Glasco, WPHM, 56(Jl 1973):326-9.

Martí Gilabert, Francisco. El motín de Aranjuez. Pamplona: Ediciones Universidad de Navarra ... 1972. Rev. by M. E. Goldstein, JMH, 45(Sep 1973):500-2.

Martin, Albro. Enterprise Denied: Origin of the Decline of American Railroads, 1897-1917. New York: Columbia U Press, 1971. Rev. by C. Ubbelohde, JISHS, 66(Spr 1973):104-5; L. L. Gould, PH, 40(Apr 1973):231-2; J. F. Stover, T & C, 14(Ja 1973):89-90.

Martin, E. W., ed. Comparative Development in Social Welfare. London: Allen and Unwin, 1972. Rev. by P. Stanksy, SS, 64(Dec 1973):339-40.

Martin, G. H. and Sylvia McIntyre. A Bibliography of British and Irish Municipal History. Leicester: Leicester U Press, 1972. Rev. by P. Rutledge, Archives, 11(Aut 1973):106-8.

Martin, Harold H. Starlifter: The C-141, Lockheed's High Speed Flying Truck. Brattleboro, Vt.: Stephen Greene, 1972. Rev. by R. Higham, T & C, 14(Oct 1973):655.

Martin, James Kirby. Men in Rebellion: Higher Governmental Leaders and the Coming of the American Revolution. New Brunswick, N. J.: Rutgers U Press, n. d. Rev. by C. Ubblohde, NCHR, 50(Aut 1973):427-8.

Martin, P. M. The External Trade of the Loango Coast: 1576-
    1870. The Effects of Changing Commercial Relations on the
    Vili Kingdom of Loango. Oxford: Clarendon Press, 1972.
    Rev. by J. Vansina, JAfH, 14(3rd Qr 1973):516-17.

Martin, Richard A. The City Makers. Jacksonville, Fla.: Con-
    vention Press, 1972. Rev. by H. J. Doherty, Jr., FHQ, 51
    (Apr 1973):441-2; M. D. Moore, GHQ, 57(Fall 1973):440-1;
    J. B. Crooks, JSH, 39(May 1973):313-14.

Martineau, La Van. The Rocks Begin to Speak. Las Vegas, Nev.:
    K. C. Publications, 1973. Rev. by F. J. Johnston, JOW,
    12(Oct 1973):658-9; A. C. Wilcox, PacH, 17(Fall 1973):65-6.

Martines, Lauro, ed. Violence and Civil Disorder in Italian Cities,
    1200-1500. Berkeley: U Cal Press, 1972. Rev. by J. R.
    Hale, AHR, 78(Dec 1973):1441-2.

Martínez de Velasco, Angel. La formación de la Junta Central.
    Pamplona: Ediciones Universidad de Navarra ... 1972. Rev.
    by M. E. Goldstein, JMH, 45(Sep 1973):500-2.

Marx, Joseph Laurence. Nagasaki, The Necessary Bomb? New
    York: Macmillan, 1971. Rev. by M. J. Sherwin, WMH, 56
    (Spr 1973):245-6.

Marx, Karl and Max Engels. The Cologne Communist Trial. (Trans-
    lated and edited by Rodney Livingstone). London: Lawrence
    and Wishart, 1971. Rev. by W. O. Henderson, History, 58
    (Feb 1973):121.

Maser, Frederick E. Methodism in Central Pennsylvania, 1771-
    1969. Lebanon: Sowers, 1971. Rev. by C. H. Glatfelter,
    PH, 40(Ja 1973):98-100.

Mason, Davis. Salerno: Foothold in Europe. New York: Ballen-
    tine, 1972. Rev. by R. P. Weinert, Jr., MilAf, 37(Dec
    1973):162.

Mason, Oliver. The Gazeteer of England. (2 vols.) Totowa, N. J.:
    Rowman and Littlefield, 1972. Rev. by F. A. Youngs, Jr.,
    HT, 7(Je 1973):483-4.

Massey, Hector J., ed. The Canadian Military: A Profile. Tor-
    onto: Copp Clark, 1972. Rev. by D. Morton, CHR, 54(Sep
    1973):298-9; D. C. Gordon, MilAf, 37(Feb 1973):36.

Mastellone, Salvo. Venalità e Machiavellismo in Francia (1572-
    1610). All'origine della mentalità politica Borghese. Flor-
    ence: Leo S. Olschki, 1972. Rev. by J. H. M. Salmon,
    JMH, 45(Sep 1973):483-4.

Masterman, Neville. The Forerunner: The Dilemmas, Tom Ellis

1859-1899.   Llandybig: Cristopher Davies, 1972.   Rev. by
S. E. Koss, History, (Je 1973):314-15.

Mastny, Vojtech.   The Czechs Under Nazi Rule: The Failure of
National Resistance, 1939-1942.   New York: Columbia U
Press, 1971.   Rev. by D. H. Perman, AHR, 78(Feb 1973):
124-5; A. Polonsky, History, 58(Feb 1973):140-1.

Mateijka, Ladislav and Krystina Pomorska, eds.   Readings in Russian Poetics: Formalist and Structuralist Views.   Cambridge,
Mass.:   M I T Press, 1971.   Rev. by G. Ivask, RR, 32(Ja
1973):98-9.

Mates, Leo.   Non-Alignment: Theory and Current Policy.   Dobbs
Ferry, N. Y.:   Oceana, 1972.   Rev. by B. N. Mehrish, IQ,
29(Jl-Sep 1973):261-2.

Mather, Cotton.   The Angel of Bethesda.   Barre, Mass.:   Barre
Publishers, 1972.   Rev. by J. Duffy, AHR, 78(Oct 1973):
1118-19.

Mathes, W. Michael, ed.   Californiana II--Documentos para la historia de la explotación comercial de California, 1611-1679.
Vols. 29, 30.   Madrid: Ediciones José Porrúa Turanzas,
1970-71.   Rev. by L. G. Canedo, TAm, 30(Jl 1973):149-50.

Matheson, Peter.   Cardinal Contarini Regensburg.   Oxford: Ox U
Press, 1972.   Rev. by O. Logan, History, 58(Feb 1973):95-6.

Matheson, Sylvia A.   Persia: An Archaeological Guide.   New Jersey:
Noyes, 1973.   Rev. by T. C. Young, Jr., Antiquity, 47(Je
1973):161-2;   D. N. Wilber, Archaeology, 26(Oct 1973):313-14.

Mathew, T.   Economics of Public Expenditure.   Bombay: Vora,
1972.   Rev. by S. Venu, IQ, 29(Apr-Je 1973):174-5.

Mathias, Peter, ed.   Science and Society 1600-1900.   n. p. :   Cam U
Press, 1972.   Rev. by A. Van Helden, History, 58(Oct 1973):
415-16.

Mathy, Helmut.   Die Geschichte des Mainzer Erzkanzlerarchivs
1782-1815:   Bestande--Organisation--Verlagerung.   Wiesbaden:
Franz Steiner Verlag GmbH, 1969.   Rev. by C. G. Anthon,
AHR, 78(Oct 1973):1009-10.

Matis, Herbert.   Osterreichische Wirtschaft 1848-1913:   Konjunk-
turelle Dynamik und Gesellschaftlicher Wandel in Zeitalter
Franz Joseph I.   Berlin: Duncker und Humblot, 1972.   Rev.
by H. Freundenberger, JEH, 33(Dec 1973):897.

Matson, A. T.   Nandi Resistance to British Rule, 1890-1906.   Nairobi: East African Publishing House, 1972.   Rev. by G.
Muriuki, AfAf, 72(Jl 1973):342-3.

213   MATTHEW

Matthew, David. Lady Jane Grey: The Setting of the Reign. London: Eyre Methuen, 1972. Rev. by B. L. Beer, AHR, 78
(Je 1973):679-80; C. V. Graves, Historian 36(Nov 1973):99-
100.

Matthews, Herbert L. Half of Spain Died: A Reappraisal of the
Spanish Civil War. New York: Scribner's, 1973. Rev. by
G. Jackson, AHR, 78(Dec 1973):1484-5.

Matthews, William and Robert Latham, eds. The Diary of Samuel
Pepys, A New and Complete Transcription. (5 vols.) London: Bell, 1970-1. Rev. by V. Pearl, History, 58(Feb
1973):106-8.

_____, and _____, eds. The Diary of Samuel Pepys. Vols.
VI and VII. London: Bell, 1970. Rev. by P. Q., HTo, 23
(Feb 1973):139-40.

Maurice, Nancy, ed. The Maurice Case: From the Papers of
Major-General Sir Frederick Maurice.... Hamden, Conn. :
Archon, 1972. Rev. by P. Guinn, AHR, 78(Oct 1973):1069.

Mavor, James W. , Jr. Voyage to Atlantis. New York: Putnam's,
1969. Rev. by R. A. McNeal, Archaeology, 26(Ja 1973):65.

Maxson, Robert C. and Walter E. Sistrunk. A Practical Approach
to Secondary Social Studies. Dubuque, Ia.: William C.
Brown, 1972. Rev. by D. L. Brubaker, SS, 64(Apr 1973):
185.

Maxwell, Neville. India's China War. New York: Pantheon, 1970.
Rev. by B. G. Gokhale, MilAf, 37(Feb 1973):36.

May, Ernest R. and James O. Thompson, Jr. , eds. American-
East Asian Relations. A Survey. Cambridge, Mass.: Har U
Press, 1972. Rev. by D. H. Bays, HT, 7(Nov 1973):130-1;
E. P. Trani, JAH, 60(Sep 1973):514-5; W. I. Cohen, PHR,
42(Feb 1973):120-1.

May, Philip Ross. On the Mother Lode. Christchurch, New Zealand, 1971. Rev. by W. T. Jackson, AHR, 78(Feb 1973):
168-9; G. R. Stewart, CHQ, 52(Spr 1973):90.

May, W. E. and Leonard Holder. A History of Marine Navigation.
New York: Norton, 1973. Rev. by R. A. Courtemanche,
HRNB, 2(Oct 1973):17.

Mayer, Hans Eberhard. The Crusades. n. p.: Ox U Press, 1972.
Rev. by H. E. J Cowdrey, History, 58(Oct 1973):432-3.

Mayfield, James B. Rural Politics in Nasser's Egypt. Austin: U
Tx Press, 1971. Rev. by S. Kirshner, NO, 16(Ja 1973):29-
30.

Mayr-Harting, Henry.   The Coming of Christianity to Anglo-Saxon
    England. London: Batsford, 1972. Rev. by D. P. Kirby,
    History, 58(Je 1973):252-3.

Mazour, Anatole G.   The Writing of History in the Soviet Union.
    Stanford, Cal.: Hoover Institution Press, 1971. Rev. by
    R. Hellie, JMH, 45(Je 1973):292-3; N. Riasanovsky, PHR,
    42(May 1973):242-3; R. T. Fisher, RR, 32(Jl 1973):320-1.

Meadows, A. J.   Science and Controversy: A Biography of Sir
    Norman Lockyer. Cambridge, Mass.: M I T Press, 1972.
    Rev. by C. C. Martin, Historian, 36(Nov 1973):105-6; L. S.
    Swenson, Jr., HT, 7(Nov 1973):138-9.

Meadows, Lorena Edwards.   A Sage Brush Heritage: The Story of
    Ben Edwards and His Family. San Jose, Cal.: Harlan-
    Young, 1972. Rev. by C. E. Trafzer, JOW, 12(Oct 1973):
    646; H. A. Shamberger, NHSQ, 16(Win 1973):250-2.

Medding, Peter.   Mapai in Israel. New York: Cam U Press, 1972.
    Rev. by CurH, 64(Ja 1973):34; S. D. Johnston, MEJ, 27
    (Spr 1973):239-40.

Megaw, Vincent and Rhys Jones.   The Dawn of Man. London: Way-
    land, 1972. Rev. by R. Place, Antiquity, 47(Sep 1973):252-
    3.

Mehlinger, Howard D. and John M. Thompson.   Count Witte and the
    Tsarist Government in the 1905 Revolution. Bloomington:
    Ind U Press, 1972. Rev. by R. F. Leslie, History, 58(Oct
    1973):465-6; L. Kochan, JMH, 45(Sep 1973):555-7; J. Keep,
    RR, 32(Ja 1973):79-81.

Mehta, G. L.   Dilemmas in Planning. Bombay: Vora, 1971. Rev.
    by N. C. Joshi, IQ, 29(Jan-Mar 1973):71-2.

Mei, Ko-Wang see Singh, Baljit

Meier, August and Elliot Rudwick.   C O R E: A Study in the Civil
    Rights Movement, 1942-1968. n. p.: Ox U Press, n. d.
    Rev. by B. G. Gallagher, Crisis, 80(Nov 1973):322.

Meier, Matt S. and Feliciano Rivera.   The Chicanos: A History of
    Mexican Americans. New York: Hill and Wang, 1972. Rev.
    by J. Gómez-Q, HAHR, 53(Aug 1973):558-60; L. Pitt, TAm,
    30(Oct 1973):283-4.

Meiggs, Russell.   The Athenian Empire. New York: Ox U Press,
    1972. Rev. by J. M. Balcer, AHR, 78(Je 1973):661-2.

Meighan, Clement W. and Francis A. Riddell.   The Maru Cult of
    the Pomo Indians: A California Ghost Dance Survival. Los

Angeles: Southwest Museum Papers, No. 23, 1972. Rev. by
A. B. Elsasser, CHQ, 52(Sum 1973):177-8.

Meigs, John, ed. The Cowboy in American Prints. Chicago: Swallow, 1972. Rev. by J. Burrows, AW, 10(May 1973):52;
C. P. Westermeier, CoMag, 50(Sum 1973):260-1.

Meinardus, Otto F. A. Christian Egypt--Faith and Life. Cairo:
American U Press, 1970. Rev. by A. S. Atiya, MEJ, 27
(Spr 1973):231-2.

Meisner, Heinrich Otto. Archivalienkunde vom 16. Jahrhundert bis
1918. Göttingen: Vandenhoeck and Ruprecht, 1969. Rev.
by C. G. Anthon, AHR, 78(Oct 1973):1009-10.

Meissner, Boris, ed. Social Change in the Soviet Union: Russia's
Path Toward an Industrial Society. Notre Dame, Ind.: U
Notre Dame Press, 1972. Rev. by R. G. Wesson, RR, 32
(Jl 1973):333.

Melada, Ivan. The Captain of Industry in English Fiction, 1821-
1871. Albuquerque: U NM Press, 1970. Rev. by F. M. L.
Thompson, BHR, 47(Spr 1973):130-1.

Melas, Evi, ed. Temples and Sanctuaries of Ancient Greece: A
Companion Guide. London: Thames and Hudson, 1973. Rev.
by B. A. Sparkes, Antiquity, 47(Dec 1973):334-5.

Melendy, H. Brett. The Oriental Americans. New York: Twayne,
1972. Rev. by R. W. Paul, JAH, 60(Dec 1973):838-9; J.
Modell, PHR, 42(May 1973):256-7.

Meleski, Patricia F. Echos of the Past: New Mexico's Ghost
Towns. Albuquerque: U NM Press, 1972. Rev. by S. F.
Kropp, Montana, 23(Win 1973):69; J. B. Pearson, NMHR,
48(Oct 1973):336-7.

Melgunov, S. P. The Bolshevik Seizure of Power. Santa Barbara,
Cal.: A B C--Clio, 1972. Rev. by A. E. Adams, RR, 32
(Oct 1973):440-1.

Mellander, G. A. The United States in Panamanian Politics: The
Intriguing Formative Years. Danville: Interstate Printers,
1971. Rev. by C. D. Ameringer, PHR, 42(May 1973):261-2.

Mellinkoff, Ruth. The Horned Moses in Medieval Art and Thought.
Berkeley: U Cal Press, 1970. Rev. by L. Seidel, AHR, 78
(Feb 1973):79-80.

Meltzer, Milton. Hunted Like a Wolf: The Story of the Seminole
War. New York: Farrar, Straus and Giroux, 1972. Rev.
by J. W. Covington, FHQ, 52(Oct 1973):188-9.

Mendelsohn, Everett and Judson P. Swazey and Irene Taviss.
Human Aspects of Biomedical Innovation. Cambridge, Mass.:
Har U Press, 1971. Rev. by E. V. Perrin, T & C, 14(Apr
1973):340-2.

Meneses García, Emilio, ed. Correspondencia Del Conde de Tendilla. Vol. I. 1508-1509. Madrid: Real Academia de la
Historia, 1972. Rev. by E. Spivakovsky, AHR, 78(Oct 1973):
1082-3.

Menon, K. P. S. Twilight in China. Bombay: Bharatiya Vidya
Bhavan, 1972. Rev. by S. Ganguly, IQ, 29(Jl-Sep 1973):269.

Menon, V. K. N. see Keskar, B. V.

Merk, Frederick. Economic History of Wisconsin During the Civil
War Decade. Madison: State Historical Society of Wisconsin,
1972. Rev. by W. D. Wyman, AgH, 47(Oct 1973):350; R. C.
Nesbit, WMH, 56(Win 1972-73):168.

Merk, Frederick and Lois Barrington Merk. Slavery and the An-
nexation of Texas. New York: Knopf, 1972. Rev. by R. F.
Durden, JAH, 60(Je 1973):135; A. C. Ashcraft, JOW, 12
(Oct 1973):654; H. Hamilton, JSH, 39(May 1973):295-6; L. T.
Ellis, WHQ, 4(Jl 1973):328-9.

Merli, Frank J. Great Britain and the Confederate Navy. Bloomington: Ind U Press, 1970. Rev. by R. P. Weinert, Jr.,
MilAf, 37(Feb 1973):34.

Merrifield, Ralph. Roman London. New York: Praeger, 1969.
Rev. by G. Webster, Archaeology, 26(Ja 1973):72-3.

Merrill, Horace Samuel and Marion G. The Republican Command,
1897-1913. Lexington, Ky.: U Press Ky, 1971. Rev. by
M. I. Scholnick, MHM, 68(Spr 1973):111-12.

Merrill, James M. William Tecumseh Sherman. Chicago: Rand
McNally, 1971. Rev. by R. A. Wooster. JISHS, 66(Spr
1973):114-15.

Meszaros, Istvan, ed. Aspects of History and Class Consciousness.
London: Routledge and Kegan Paul, 1971. Rev. by P. Hollis, History, 58(Feb 1973):160.

Metcalf, Lawrence E., ed. Values Education: Rationale, Strategies
and Procedures (41st Yearbook). Washington, D. C.: National Council for Social Studies, 1971. Rev. by J. L.
Browne, SS, 64(Feb 1973):87-8.

Meyer, Harvey K. Historical Dictionary of Nicaragua. Metuchen,
N. J.: Scarecrow, 1972. Rev. by B. B. Solnick, HAHR,
53(Aug 1973):495-6.

Meyer, Lorenzo. México y los Estados Unidos en el conflicto pe-
trolers 1917-1942. Mexico: El Colegio de México, 1972.
Rev. by R. N. Sinkin, HAHR, 53(Aug 1973):566-7.

Meyer, Mary Keyson. Genealogical Research in Maryland: A Guide.
Baltimore: Md Historical Society, 1972. Rev. by J. Walton,
MHM, 68(Spr 1973):116-17.

Meyer, Michael C. Huerta: A Political Portrait. Lincoln: U Neb
Press, 1972. Rev. by R. E. Quirk, AHR, 78(Je 1973):748-
9; L. L. Blaisdell, HAHR, 53(Aug 1973):519-21; P. J. Van-
derwood, TAm, 30(Jl 1973):141-2.

Meyer, W. Weisgal, gen. ed. The Letters and Papers of Chaim
Weizmann ... Vol. 3. September 1903-December 1904. New
York: Ox U Press, 1972. Rev. by S. Beinfeld, AHR, 78
(Je 1973):659-60.

Meynet, Roland. L'Écriture Arabe en Question: Les Projects de
L'Académie de Langue Arabe du Caire de 1938 à 1968. Beirut: Darel-Machreq, 1971. Rev. by P. F. Abboud, MEJ,
27(Spr 1973):245.

Meyrat, Walter. Das schweizerische Bundesarchiv von 1798 bis zur
Gegenwart. Bern: Bundesarchiv, 1972. Rev. by E. Posner,
AmArch, 36(Jl 1973):406-7.

The Middle East and North Africa, 1972-73. London: Europa, 1972.
Rev. by M. C. Peck, MEJ, 27(Aut 1973):526.

Middlekauff, Robert. The Mathers: Three Generations of Puritan
Intellectuals, 1596-1728. New York: Ox U Press, 1971.
Rev. by A. T. Vaughan, AHR, 78(Feb 1973):140-2; P. Haf-
fenden, History, 58(Oct 1973):485-6.

Middlemas, Keith. Diplomacy of Illusion: The British Government
and Germany, 1937-39. London: Weidenfeld and Nicolson,
1972. Rev. by H. Pelling, History, 58(Oct 1973):474; B.
Lee, HJ, 16(Je 1973):444-6.

Middleton, John see Beattie, John

Middleton, Nigel. When Family Failed: the Treatment of the Child
in the Care of the Community in the First Half of the Twentieth Century. London: Gollancz, 1971. Rev. by G. Sutherland, HJ, 16(Je 1973):420-31.

Midelfort, H. C. Erik. Witch Hunting in Southwestern Germany,
1562-1684: The Social and Intellectual Foundations. Stanford,
Cal.: Stan U Press, 1972. Rev. by H. J. Grimm, AHR, 78
(Dec 1973):1487-8; E. W. Monter, JMH, 45(Sep 1973):476.

Miers, Earl Schenck. The Last Campaign: Grant Saves the Union.

New York: Lippincott, 1972. Rev. by R. Hartje, JAH, 60 (Sep 1973):450-1; W. W. Smith, JSH, 39(Aug 1973):453-4; W. W. Hassler, Jr., NCHR, 50(Sum 1973):340-1; T. R. May, PMHB, 97(Jl 1973):419-21.

Mikhail, E. H. A Bibliography of Irish Literature. Seattle: U Wash Press, 1972. Rev. by D. Romans, E-I, 8(Win 1973): 119.

_____. Sean O'Casey: A Bibliography of Criticism. Seattle: U Wash, 1972. Rev. by D. Romans, E-I, 8(Win 1973):119.

Milani, Lois Darroch. Robert Gourlay, Gadfly: The Biography of Robert (Fleming) Gourlay, 1778-1863, Forerunner of the Rebellion in Upper Canada, 1837. Thornhill, Ontario: Ampersand, 1971. Rev. by E. Jones, CHR, 54(Dec 1973):448-50.

Milfort, Louis Le Clerc. Memoirs of a Quick Glance at My Various Travels and My Sojourn in the Creek Nation. Savannah, Ga.: Beehive, 1972. Rev. in GHQ, 57(Fall 1973):446-7.

Miller, Charles S. and Natalie Joy Ward. History of America: Challenge and Crisis. New York: Wiley, 1971. Rev. by R. M. Fitch, SS, 64(Ja 1973):44.

Miller, George H. Railroads and the Granger Laws. Madison: U Wis Press, 1971. Rev. by D. Crosson, AI, 41(Spr 1973): 1280-2.

Miller, Joseph. The Arizona Rangers. New York: Hastings House, 1972. Rev. by W. Gard, A & W, 15(Aut 1973):299-300; W. A. Duffen, JAriH, 14(Spr 1973):78-9; L. D. Ball, Montana, 23(Sum 1973):51.

Miller, Lillian B., et al. "If Elected...:" Unsuccessful Candidates for the Presidency, 1796-1968. Washington: Smithsonian Institution Press, 1972. Rev. by J. M. Neil, JAH, 59 (Mar 1973):902-3.

Miller, Peggy. James. New York: St. Martin's, 1971. Rev. by G. H. Jones, AHR, 78(Feb 1973):99-100.

Miller, Robert Moats. How Shall They Hear Without a Preacher? The Life of Ernest Fremont Tittle. Chapel Hill: UNC Press, 1971. Rev. by J. A. Dowling, JISHS, 66(Spr 1973):117-18.

Miller, Thomas Lloyd. The Public Lands of Texas, 1519-1970. Norman: U Ok Press, 1972. Rev. by R. N. Richardson, A & W, 15(Spr 1973):96-7; P. E. Isaac, JOW, 12(Ja 1973): 185; R. P. Swierenga, PHR, 42(Feb 1973):103-5; J. B. Pearson, SWHQ, 76(Apr 1973):501-2.

Miller, Townsend. Henry IV of Castile, 1425-1474. Philadelphia:

Lippincott, 1972.   Rev. by W. D. Phillips, Jr. , HAHR, 53 (Feb 1973):150-1.

Miller, Wright. Who Are the Russians? A History of the Russian People. New York: Taplinger, 1973. Rev. by E. K. Volkenier, HRNB, 2(Nov/Dec 1973):32.

Millett, Allan R. and B. Franklin Cooling III. Doctoral Dissertations in Military Affairs: A Bibliography. Manhattan, Ks. : Kan St U Library, 1972. Rev. by M. J. Smith, Jr. , MilAf, 37(Oct 1973):108-9.

Millette, James. The Genesis of Crown Colony Government: Trinidad, 1783-1810. Trinidad: Moko Enterprises, 1970. Rev. by A. J. G. Knox, AHR, 78(Je 1973):750-1.

Milne, Lorus and Margery. The Arena of Life: The Dynamics of Ecology. New York: Doubleday/Natural History Press, 1972. Rev. by D. Cavagnaro, AW, 10(May 1973):51, 57.

Milsom, John. Russian Tanks, 1900-1970. Harrisburg, Pa. Stackpole, 1971. Rev. by S. Lieberstein, T & C, 14(Oct 1973): 649-51.

Milton, John. Complete Prose Works of John Milton. Vol. V. London: Yale U Press, 1971. Rev. by V. Pearl, History, 58(Oct 1973):448-9.

Milward, Alan S. The Fascist Economy in Norway. n. p. : Ox U Press, 1972. Rev. by W. O. Henderson, History, 58(Oct 1973):474-5; H. -D. Loock, JMH, 45(Sep 1973):546-7.

Minces, Juliette see Chaliand, Gérard

Minear, Richard H. Victors' Justice: The Tokyo War Crimes Trial. Princeton, N. J. : Prin U Press, 1971. Rev. by A. D. Coox, MilAf. 37(Feb 1973):35-6.

Miner, H. Craig. The St. Louis-San Francisco Transcontinental Railroad: The Thirty-Fifth Parallel Project, 1853-1890. Lawrence: U Press Kan, 1972. Rev. by C. H. Clark, CWH, 19(Mar 1973):90-1; B. B. Combs, Montana, 23(Win 1973): 70; A. M. Johnson, NMHR, 48(Jl 1973):269-70; K. L. Bryant, Jr. , T & C, 14(Oct 1973):639-40.

Minifie, James M. Homesteader: A Prairie Boyhood Recalled. Toronto: Macmillan, 1972. Rev. by L. G. Thomas, CHR, 54(Sep 1973):305-6.

Ministero della Difesa, Stato Maggiore dell-Esercito-Ufficio Storico. Saggio Bibliografico sulla Seconda Guerra Mondiale. 4 vols. Rome: n. p. , 1955, 1966, 1969, 1971. Rev. by D. Koenig, MilAf, 37(Feb 1973):35.

Minter, William. Portuguese Africa and the West. Harmonsworth:
    Penguin African Library, 1972. Rev. by W. G. Clarence-
    Smith, JAfH, 14(3rd Qr 1973):528-9.

Misra, K. P. The Role of the United Nations in the Indo-Pakistan
    Conflict, 1971. Delhi: Vikas Publishing House, 1973. Rev.
    by B. Mitra, IQ, 29(Oct-Dec 1973):356-7.

Mitchell, Allan. Bismarck and the French Nation 1848-1890. New
    York: Pegasus, 1971. Rev. by R. S. Levy, JMH, 45(Je
    1973):324.

Mitchell, Harvey and Peter N. Stearns. Workers and Protest. The
    European Labor Movement, the Working Classes and the
    Origins of Social Democracy 1890-1914. Itasca, Ill.: F. E.
    Peacock, 1971. Rev. by V. L. Lidtke, BHR, 47(Spr 1973):
    133-4; J. W. Scott, JMH, 45(Mar 1973):152-5.

Mitchell, Joseph B. Military Leaders in the Civil War. New York:
    Putnam's, 1972. Rev. by M. C. Campion, HT, 6(May 1973):
    487.

Mitchell, Robert S. see Morrison, Donald G.

Modelski, George. Principles of World Politics. New York: Free
    Press, 1972. Rev. by A. Z. Rubenstein CurH, 64(May 1973):
    225, 232.

Moeller, Beverly Bowen. Phil Swing and Boulder Dam. Berkeley:
    U Cal Press, 1971. Rev. by D. H. Strong, A & W, 15(Spr
    1973):84-5; P. S. Taylor, CHQ, 52(Spr 1973):86-7; J. S.
    Olson, NHSQ, 16(Sum 1973):131-2.

Moffett, Lee. Water-Powered Mills of Fauquier County, Virginia.
    Warrenton, Va.: Mrs. Meredith J. Moffett, 1972. Rev. by
    D. D. Plater, VMHB, 81(Ja 1973):108-9.

Mohl, Raymond A. Poverty in New York, 1783-1825. Oxford: Ox
    U Press, 1971. Rev. by C. Taylor, History, 58(Feb 1973):
    151-2.

Mohr, E. The Asiatic Wild Horse. London: J. A. Allen, 1971.
    Rev. by S. Bökönyi, Antiquity, 47(Sep 1973):243-4.

Mojumdar, Kanchanmoy. Political Relations Between India and
    Nepal, 1877-1923. New Delhi: Munshiram Menoharlal, 1973.
    Rev. by N. M. Khilnani, IQ, 29(Jl-Sep 1973):269-70.

Molho, Anthony. Florentine Public Finances in the Early Renais-
    sance, 1400-1433. Cambridge, Mass.: Har U Press, 1971.
    Rev. by D. Herlihy, AHR, 78(Oct 1973):1038; A. Antonovics,
    History, 58(Oct 1973):439; D. L. Hicks, JEH, 33(Sep 1973):
    682-3.

Molho, Anthony and John A. Tedeschi, eds. Renaissance. DeKalb: N Ill U Press, 1971. Rev. by L. Martines, AHR, 78(Feb 1973):87-9.

Moline, Norman T. Mobility and the Small Town, 1900-1930: Transportation Change in Oregon, Illinois. Chicago: U Chi Press, 1971. Rev. by R. Janis, JAH, 60(Je 1973):166-7.

Molnar, John W. and Carleton Sprague Smith. Songs from the Williamsburg Theatre: A Selection of Fifty Songs Performed on the Stage in Williamsburg in the Eighteenth Century. Williamsburg: ... U Press Va, 1972. Rev. by E. Emerson, VMHB, 81(Jl 1973):368-70.

Momigliano, Arnaldo. The Development of Greek Biography. Cambridge, Mass.: Har U Press, 1971. Rev. by F. W. Walbank, H & T, 12(1973):230-40.

Mommsen, Karl. Auf dem Wege zur Staatssouveränität: Staatliche Grundbegriffe in Basler Juristischen Doktordisputationen des 17. und 18. Jahrhunderts. Bern: Francke Verlag, 1970. Rev. by C. Rose, AHR, 78(Feb 1973):92-3.

Monaghan, Jay, ed. The Private Journal of Louis McLane, U. S. N., 1844-48. Los Angeles: Dawson's, 1971. Rev. by M. L. Spence, A & W, 15(Spr 1973):85-7.

"Le Monde de L'Automobile." Le Mouvement Social, No. 81, October-December 1972. Paris: Les Editions Ouvrières, 1972. Rev. by R. F. Kuisel, BHR, 47(Win 1973):549-52.

Mondello, Salvatore see Iorizzo, Luciano J.

Monet, Jacques. The Last Cannon Shot: A Study of French-Canadian Nationalism 1837-1850. Toronto: U Tor Press, 1970. Rev. by R. M. Tyzack, History, 58(Oct 1973):484.

Monluc, Blaise de. The Habsburg-Valois Wars and the French Wars of Religion. Hamden, Conn.: Archon, 1972. Rev. by R. D. Linder, MilAf, 37(Feb 1973):33.

Monroe, Elizabeth. The Changing Balance of Power in the Persian Gulf. New York: American Universities Field Staff, 1972. Rev. by R. K. Ramazani, MEJ, 27(Sum 1973):409-10.

Monroe, Haskell M., Jr. and James T. McIntosh, eds. The Papers of Jefferson Davis, Vol. I: 1808-1840. Baton Rouge: LSU Press, 1971. Rev. by M. W. M. Hargreaves, JISHS, 66(Spr 1973):99-100.

Moody, T. W., ed. Irish Historiography, 1936-70. Dublin: Irish Committee of Historical Sciences, 1971. Rev. by J. A. Watt, History, 58(Oct 1973):419-20.

Mookerjee, Girija K. Nehru: The Humanist. New Delhi: Trimurthi, 1972. Rev. by N. M. Khilnani, IQ, 29(Apr-Je 1973):
165-6.

Moon, Penderel, ed. Wavell: The Viceroy's Journal. New York:
Ox U Press, 1973. Rev. by B. Farwell, HRNB, 2(Oct 1973):
5.

Mooney, Booth. Roosevelt and Rayburn: A Political Partnership.
Philadelphia: Lippincott, 1971. Rev. by R. S. Kirkendall,
JISHS, 66(Spr 1973):109-10.

Moore, John Norton. Law and the Indo-China War. Princeton,
N. J.: Prin U Press, 1972. Rev. by P. L. Murphy, JAH,
60(Sep 1973):516-17.

Moore, O. Ernest. Haiti: Its Stagnant Society and Shackled Economy. New York: Exposition, 1972. Rev. by J. E. Bauer,
TAm, 29(Ja 1973):406-7.

Moore, Rayburn S. Paul Hamilton Hayne. New York: Twayne,
1972. Rev. by S. M. Smith, Jr., SCHM, 74(Ja 1973):44.

Moore, Richard. A Question of Survival. Athens, Ga.: U Ga
Press, 1971. Rev. by K. S. Byer, GR, 27(Spr 1973):110-21.

Moorsteen, Richard and Morton Abramowitz. Remaking China
Policy: U. S. -China Relations and Governmental Decision-
making. Cambridge, Mass.: Har U Press, 1971. Rev. by
S. Ganguly, IQ, 29(Apr-Je 1973):163.

Moot, Robert C. The Economics of Defense Spending: A Look at
the Realities. Washington, D. C.: Dept. Defense Publication, 1972. Rev. by J. L. Clayton, JEH, 33(Dec 1973):898-
9.

Moote, A. Lloyd. The Revolt of the Judges: The Parlement of
Paris and the Fronde, 1643-1650. Princeton, N. J.: Prin
U Press, 1971. Rev. by J. M. Hayden, CHR, 54(Sep 1973):
326-7; J. Dent, JMH, 45(Je 1973):301-2.

_____. The Seventeenth Century: Europe in Ferment. Lexing-
ton, Mass.: D. C. Heath, 1971. Rev. by M. Hughes, History, 58(Feb 1973):104-5.

Morden, Robert. The County Maps From William Camden's Britannia, 1695: a Facsimile. Newton Abbot: David and
Charles, 1972. Rev. by S. Tyacke, History, 58(Oct 1973):
418.

Morehouse, Ward. Science in India. Bombay: Popular Prakashan,
1971. Rev. by S. K. Ghaswala, T & C, 14(Apr 1973):351-2.

Moreno, José A. Barrios in Arms: Revolution in Santo Domingo.
   Pittsburgh: U Pittsburgh Press, 1970. Rev. by H. A. Landsberger, CSSH, 15(Je 1973):378-88.

Morgan, David. Suffragists and Democrats: The Politics of Woman
   Suffrage in America. East Lansing: Mich St U Press, 1972.
   Rev. by L. M. Young, AHR, 78(Je 1973):740-1; K. R.
   Johnson, JSH, 39(Feb 1973):133-4.

Morgan, H. Wayne. Unity and Culture: The United States 1877-
   1900. London: Allen Lane, Penguin, 1971. Rev. by P.
   Taylor, History, 58(Feb 1973):153.

Morgan. Kenneth O. The Age of Lloyd George. New York: Barnes
   and Noble, 1971. Rev. by M. Kinnear, AHR, 78(Je 1973):
   697.

Morgan, Margery M. The Shavian Playground. An Exploration of
   the Art of Bernard Shaw. London: Methuen, n. d. Rev. by
   S. Weintraub, E-I, 8(Spr 1973):135-42.

Morgan, Richard E. The Supreme Court and Religion. New York:
   Free Press, 1972. Rev. by D. O. Dewey, JAH, 60(Sep
   1973):508-9.

Morgan, Roger   see   Kaiser, Karl

Morgan, William James, ed. Naval Documents of the American
   Revolution. Vol. V. Washington: U. S. Government Printing
   Office, 1970. Rev. by R. K. MacMaster, VMHB, 81(Apr
   1973):205-6.

Morison, Samuel Eliot. The European Discovery of America: The
   Northern Voyages, A. D. 500-1600. Oxford: Ox U Press,
   1971. Rev. by A. N. Ryan, ESR, 3(Jl 1973):299-301; C. W.
   Arnade, FHQ, 51(Ja 1973):316-18; G. V. Scammell, History,
   58(Feb 1973):93.

_____. Samuel de Champlain: Father of New France. Boston:
   Atlantic-Little Brown, 1972. Rev. by A. Keller, AHI, 7
   (Ja 1973):57; W. J. Eccles, AHR, 78(Oct 1973):1147-8;
   J. C. S. , IS, 29(Fall 1973):233; R. N. Hamilton, JAH, 59
   (Mar 1973):976-8; J. J. Heslin, NYHSQ, 57(Ja 1973):73-4.

Morrill, Sibley S. Ambrose Bierce, F. A. Mitchell-Hedges and the
   Crystal Skull. San Francisco: Cadleon, 1972. Rev. by
   H C. Schmidt, HAHR, 53(Aug 1973):566.

Morris, H. F. and James S. Read. Indirect Rule and the Search
   for Justice: Essays in East African Legal History. Oxford:
   Clarendon Press, 1972. Rev. by R. C. Bridges, JAfH, 14
   (2nd Qr 1973):349-50.

Morris, Joan.   The Lady Was a Bishop: The Hidden History of
    Women With Clerical Ordination and the Jurisdiction of Bish-
    ops.   New York: Macmillan, 1973.   Rev. by A. Tobriner,
    HRNB, 2(Oct 1973):9.

Morris, John.   The Age of Arthur: A History of the British Isles
    from 350-650.   London: Weidenfeld and Nicolson, 1973. Rev.
    by L. Alcock, Antiquity, 47(Dec 1973):329-30.

Morris, Paul C.   American Sailing Coasters of the North Atlantic.
    Chardon, Ohio: Block and Osborn, 1973.   Rev. by N. E. T.,
    IS, 29(Sum 1973):157.

Morris, Richard B.   Seven Who Shaped Our Destiny: The Founding
    Fathers as Revolutionaries.   New York: Harper and Row,
    1973.   Rev. by L. Maganzin, HRNB, 2(Nov/Dec 1973):39-40.

Morris, Wesley.   Toward a New Historicism.   Princeton, N. J. :
    Prin U Press, 1972.   Rev. by B. T. Wilkins, JSH, 39(May
    1973):274-6.

Morrison, Donald G. , Robert S. Mitchell, John N. Paden and Hugh
    M. Stevenson.   Black Africa: A Comparative Handbook.
    New York: Free Press, 1972.   Rev. by O. E. S. , CurH,
    64(Mar 1973):125.

Morrison, George, trans.   Vis and Ramin.   New York: Columbia
    U Press, 1972.   Rev. by P. Avery, MEJ, 27(Win 1973):86-8.

Morrissey, Brenda C.   Abby Hemenway's Vermont: Unique Portrait
    of a State.   Brattleboro, Vt. :   Stephen Greene, 1972.   Rev.
    by B. Bandel, VH, 41(Aut 1973):237-9.

Morse, Richard M. , Michael L. and John Wibel, eds.   The Urban
    Development of Latin America, 1750-1920.   Stanford, Cal. :
    ... Stan U, 1971.   Rev. by H. Browning, HAHR, 53(Nov
    1973):691-3.

Mortenson, William P.   see   Sampson, Roy J.

Morton, Catherine and Hope Muntz, eds.   The Carmen de Hastingae
    Proelio of Guy, Bishop of Amiens.   New York: Ox U Press,
    1972.   Rev. by C. W. Hollister, AHR, 78(Je 1973):671.

Morton, Marian J.   The Terrors of Ideological Politics: Liberal
    Historians in a Conservative Mood.   Cleveland: Press CWR
    U, 1972.   Rev. by J. Higham, AHR, 78(Dec 1973):1556-7;
    L. E. Pennington, JSH, 39(Nov 1973):583-4.

Morton, Miriam.   Pleasures and Palaces: The After-School Activ-
    ities of Russian Children.   New York: Atheneum, 1972.   Rev.
    by P. Dunn, SS, 64(Nov 1973):275.

Moss, Norman. Men Who Play God: The Story of the Hydrogen
     Bomb. Baltimore: Penguin Books, 1972. Rev. by S. L.
     Harrison, MilAf, 37(Oct 1973):113.

Moss, Robert. The War for the Cities. New York: Coward, Mc-
     Cann and Geoghegan, 1971. Rev. by J. B. Bell, MilAf, 37
     (Dec 1973):155-7.

Motto, Sytha. Old Houses of New Mexico and the People Who Built
     Them. Albuquerque: Calvin Horn, 1972. Rev. by F. Rach-
     lin, JOW, 12(Ja 1973):186.

Moulton, Philip P., ed. The Journal and Major Essays of John
     Woolman. New York: Ox U Press, 1971. Rev. by G. W.
     Pilcher, NJH, 91(Aut 1973):269-70; L. Gara, PH, 40(Apr
     1973):215-17.

Moureaux, Philippe. Le Préoccupations Statistiques de Pays-Bas
     Autrichiens et le denombrement des industries dressé en
     1764. Bruxelles: Editions de l'Université de Bruxelles,
     1971. Rev. by R. Alltmont, JEH, 33(Je 1973):496-8.

Mousnier, R. La Vénalité des offices sous les Règnes de Hénri IV
     et Louis XIII. Paris: Presses Universitaires de France,
     1971. Rev. by D. Parker, History, 58(Je 1973):291-3.

Mower, Nancy Alpert and Don Russell. The Plains: Being No Less
     Than a Collection of Veracious Memoranda Taken During the
     Expedition of Exploration in the Year 1845, From the Western
     Settlements of Missouri to the Mexican Border, and from
     Bent's Fort on the Arkansas to Fort Gibson via South Fork
     of the Canadian--North Mexico and North-western Texas, by
     Francois des Montaignes. Norman: U Ok Press, 1972. Rev.
     by R. J. Chaffin, JOW, 12(Ja 1973):182; D. Dean, Montana,
     23(Sep 1973):74.

Mowry, George E. Another Look at the Twentieth-Century South.
     Baton Rouge: LSU Press, 1973. Rev. by A. M. Burns,
     FHQ, 52(Oct 1973):206-8; J. S. Ezell, JAH, 60(Sep 1973):
     492-3; E. Younger, JSH, 39(Aug 1973):424-5; W. F.
     Holmes, WVH, 34(Jl 1973):396-7.

Mowry, Sylvester. Arizona and Sonora. New York: Arno, 1973.
     Rev. by W. A. Duffen, JAriH, 14(Win 1973):390-2.

Mozlish, Bruce. In Search of Nixon: A Psycho-historical Inquiry.
     New York: Basic Books, 1972. Rev. by E. A. Weinstein,
     JAH, 59(Mar 1973):1045-6.

Muench, David. Timberline Ancients. Portland: Charles H. Beld-
     ing, 1972. Rev. by M. McCloskey, AW, 10(Sep 1973):53.

Mugridge, Donald H. and Helen F. Conover. An Album of American

Battle Art, 1755-1918. New York: Da Capo, 1972. Rev.
by D. L. DeBerry, JOW, 12(Oct 1973):648.

Mukherjee, Kartick C. A Comparative Study of Some Educational
Problems. Bombay: Lalvani, 1971. Rev. by A. Ray, IQ,
29(Jl-Sep 1973):274-5.

Mulford, Ami Frank. Fighting Indians! In the Seventh United States
Cavalry, Custer's Favorite Regiment. Fairfield, Wash.: Ye
Galleon, 1972. Rev. by R. M. Utley, JAH, 60(Dec 1973):
819-20.

Muller, Alexander, trans. and ed. The Spiritual Regulation of
Peter the Great. Seattle: U Wash Press, 1972. Rev. by
D. W. Edwards, RR, 32(Oct 1973):451-2.

Muller, Herbert J In Pursuit of Relevance. Bloomington: Ind U
Press, 1971. Rev. by L. B. Cebik, GR, 27(Spr 1973):121-5.

Müller, Rolf. Der Himmel über dem Menschen der Steinzeit,
Astronomie und Mathematik der Megalithkulturen. Berlin:
Springer Verlag, 1970. Rev. by I. Graham, Antiquity, 47
(Sep 1973):248.

Mullin, Gerald W. Flight and Rebellion: Slave Resistance in Eigh-
teenth-Century Virginia. New York: Ox U Press, 1972.
Rev. by A. Meier, AHR, 78(Feb 1973):154; F. N. Boney,
GHQ, 57(Spr 1973):149; H. S. Klein, WMQ, 3rd ser., 30
(Apr 1973):337-9.

Mullin, Robert N. The Strange Story of Wayne Brazel. Canyon,
Tx.: Palo Duro Press, 1971. Rev. by J. B. Frantz, Montana, 23(Win 1973):65.

Mulvaney, D. J. and J. Golson, eds. Aboriginal Man and Environment in Australia. Canberra: Australian National U Press,
1971. Rev. by R. A. Gould, AmAnt, 38(Oct 1973):507-8.

Mumford, Lewis. Interpretations and Forecasts, 1922-1972: Studies
in Literature, History, Biography, Technics, and Contemporary Society. New York: Harcourt, Brace, Jovanovich,
1973. Rev. by H. Bridges, HRNB, 2(Oct 1973):23.

Muncy, Raymond Lee. Sex and Marriage in Utopian Communities:
19th-Century America. Bloomington: Ind U Press, 1973.
Rev. by J. S. Lemons, IMH, 69(Dec 1973):383-5; R. Gal-
breath, JAH, 60(Dec 1973):797-8.

Munden, Kenneth W., ed. The American Film Institute Catalog of
Motion Picture Films Produced in the United States; Feature
Films, 1921-1930. 2 vols. New York: Bowker, 1971. Rev.
by N. Sahli, AmArch, 36(Ja 1973):74-6.

Münkner, Hans-H. Die Organisation der eingetragenen Genossenschaft in den zum englischen Rechtskreis gehärenden Ländern
Schwarzafrikas dargestelt am Beispiel Ghanas. Marburg/
Lahn: n. p., 1971. Rev. by H. F. Illy, AfAf, 72(Oct 1973):
456-7.

Muntanyola, Ramon. Vidal i Barraquer, el cardenal de la paz.
Barcelona: Editorial Estela, 1971. Rev. by P. A. Linehan,
HJ, 16(Sep 1973):652-6.

Murav'eva, L. L. Rural Industry in Central Russia in the Second
Half of the 17th Century. Moscow: Izdatel'stvo "Nauka",
1971. Rev. by T. Esper, AHR, 78(Dec 1973):1499-1500.

Murdock, Eugene C. One Million Men: The Civil War Draft in the
North. Madison: State Historical Society of Wisconsin, 1971.
Rev. by R. E. Sterling, JISHS, 66(Spr 1973):100-1; R. E.
Beringer, JSH, 39(Feb 1973):125-6; R. M. Doolen, MichH,
57(Sum 1973):174-5; P. Johnson, NYH, 54(Ja 1973):114-17;
J. J. Heslin, NHYSQ, 57(Ja 1973):81-3; R. L. Bloom, PH,
40(Apr 1973):221-3.

Murphy, James B. L. Q. C. Lamar, Pragmatic Patriot. Baton
Rouge: LSU Press, 1973. Rev. by R. M. McMurry, AHI,
8(Oct 1973):50; GHQ, 57(Win 1973):601-2; L. M. Sims, Jr.,
HRNB, 2(Oct 1973):16; W. Larsen, JAH, 60(Dec 1973):816-
17; A. J. Going, JSH, 39(Nov 1973):602-4.

Murphy, Lawrence R. Frontier Crusader--William F. M. Arny.
Tucson, U Ariz Press, 1972. Rev. by R. W. Larson, A & W,
15(Aut 1973):289-91; W. T. Hagan, JAH, 60(Sep 1973):468-9;
M. H. Hall, JAriH, 14(Spr 1973):76-8; O. L. Jones, Jr.,
PHR, 42(Aug 1973):427-8; R. W. Delaney, WHQ, 4(Apr
1973):213-4.

Murphy, Paul A. The Meaning of Freedom of Speech. Westport,
Conn.: Greenwood, 1972. Rev. by D. Fellman, WMH, 56
(Spr 1973):248-9.

Murphy, Paul L. The Constitution in Crisis Times, 1918-1969.
New York: ... Harper and Row, 1972. Rev. by R. Lowitt,
JSH, 39(Feb 1973):134-6.

Murray, Albert. South to a Very Old Place. New York: McGraw-
Hill, 1971. Rev. by F. G. Slaughter, FHQ, 51(Ja 1973):
336-7.

Murray, Jacqueline. The First European Agriculture, A Study of
the Osteological and Botanical Evidence Until 2000 B. C.
Edinburgh: Edinburgh U Press, 1970. Rev. by S. Foltiny,
Archaeology, 26(Apr 1973):149-50.

Murray, John J. Antwerp in the Age of Plantin and Brenghel. Newton Abbot: David and Charles, 1972. Rev. by A. C. Carter, History, 58(Je 1973):295-6.

Murray, Lois Smith. Baylor at Independence. Waco, Tx.: Baylor U Press, 1972. Rev. by D. K. Pickens, JSH, 39(Nov 1973): 634.

Murray, Robert K. The Politics of Normalcy: Governmental Theory and Practice in the Harding-Coolidge Era. New York: Norton, 1973. Rev. by W. S. Freeman, IMH, 69(Dec 1973): 379-81; C. J. Tull, JSH, 39(Nov 1973):618-20.

Murray-Brown, J. Kenyatta. London: Allen and Unwin, 1972. Rev. by G. Muriuki, AfAf, 72(Jl 1973):343-4; F. Furedi, JAfH, 14(3rd Qr. 1973):521-2.

Musson, A. E., ed. Science, Technology and Economic Growth in the Eighteenth Century. London: Methuen, 1972. Rev. by S. Pollard, History, 58(Feb 1973):109-10.

Mustafa, Zaki. The Common Law in the Sudan: An Account of the "Justice, Equity and Good Conscience" Provision. London: Ox U Press, 1971. Rev. by S. M. A. El Mahdi, MEJ, 27 (Aut 1973):508-9.

Musto, David F. The American Disease: Origins of Narcotic Control. New Haven, Conn.: Yale U Press, 1973. Rev. by J. Duffy, AHR, 78(Dec 1973):1533.

Mutahaba, G. R. Portrait of a Nationalist: the Life of Ali Migeyo. Nairobi: East African Publishing House, 1969. Rev. by A. Redmayne, AfAf, 72(Ja 1973):91-3.

Mutchler, David E. The Church as a Political Factor in Latin America: With Particular Reference to Colombia and Chile. New York: Praeger, 1971. Rev. by M. T. Williams, HAHR, 53(Nov 1973):715-17.

Muthesius, Stefan. The High Victorian Movement in Architecture, 1850-1870. Boston: Routledge and Kegan Paul, 1972. Rev. by G. Howes, AHR, 78(Oct 1973):1060-2.

Mutwa, Credo Vusa'mazulu. My People, My Africa. New York: John Day, 1969. Rev. by P. L. Vanden Berghe, JAAS, 1 (Ja & Apr 1973):140-1.

Mutz, Alfred. Die Kunst des Metalldrehens bei den Römern. Basel and Stuttgart: Birkhäuser Verlag, 1972. Rev. by R. S. Hartenberg, T & C, 14(Jl 1973):488-91.

Myers, Andrew B., ed. Washington Irving: A Tribute. Tarrytown, N. Y.: Sleepy Hollow Restorations, 1972. Rev. by P. R. Baker, JAH, 60(Dec 1973):808-9.

Myers, David S. Foreign Affairs and the 1964 Presidential Election in the United States. Meerut: Sadhana Prakashan, 1972. Rev. by B. K. Shrivastava, IQ, 29(Ja-Mar 1973):58.

Myers, John Myers. The Alamo. London: U Neb Press, 1973. Rev. by C. E. Trafzer, JOW, 12(Oct 1973):639.

Myers, Richmond E. Lehigh Valley the Unsuspected. Easton, Pa.: Northampton County Historical and Geneaological Society, 1972. Rev. by N. B. W., PMHB, 97(Ja 1973):125.

Myers, Robert Manson, ed. The Children of Pride: A True Story of Georgia and the Civil War. New Haven, Conn.: Yale U Press, 1972. Rev. by L. H. Johnson, CWH, 19(Sep 1973): 280-5.

Naamani, Israel T. Israel: A Profile. New York: Praeger, 1972. Rev. by P. Stern, MEJ, 27(Spr 1973):247.

Nagi, Mostafa H. Labor Force and Employment in Egypt: A Dem- ographic and Socioeconomic Analysis. New York: Praeger, 1971. Rev. by J. B. Mayfield, MEJ, 27(Sum 1973):394-5.

Nair, N. Balakrishna. Systematic Approaches to Indian Socioeco- nomic Development. Delhi: Associated Publishing House, 1971. Rev. by T. K. Oommen, IQ, 29(Jan-Mar):69-71.

Nakayama, Shigeru. A History of Japanese Astronomy: Chinese Background and Western Impact. Cambridge, Mass.: Har U Press, 1969. Rev. by E. C. Forbes, AHR, 78(Feb 1973): 136-7.

Nakayama, Shigeru and Nathan Sivin, eds. Chinese Science: Ex- plorations of an Ancient Tradition. Cambridge, Mass.: M I T Press, 1973. Rev. by N. R. Miner, Historian, 36 (Nov 1973):115-6; C. Furth, HT, 7(Nov 1973):133-4.

Namier, Julia. Lewis Namier, A Biography. n. p.: Ox U Press, 1971. Rev. by H. Butterfield, History, 58(Oct 1973):411; C. R. Ritcheson, WMQ, 3rd ser., 30(Ja 1973):174-6.

Nanda, B. R., ed. Socialism in India. Delhi: Vikas, 1972. Rev. by S. Sarkar, IQ, 29(Ja-Mar 1973):68-9.

Nardi, Enzo. Procurate aborto nel mondo greco romano. Milan: Dott. A. Giuffre Editore, 1971. Rev. by J. Scarborough, AHR, 78(Feb 1973):77.

Nash, Gerald D. The American West in the Twentieth Century: A Short History of an Urban Oasis. Englewood Cliffs, N. J.: Prentice-Hall, 1973. Rev. by E. B. McCluney, HRNB, 2 (Oct 1973):16-17; L. E. Ziewez, HT, 7(Nov 1973):129-30.

Nash, Howard P. , Jr. A Naval History of the Civil War. South
    Brunswick, N. J.: A. S. Barnes, 1972. Rev. by E. C.
    Bearss, CWH, 19(Mar 1973):81-2; R. E. Johnson, JSH, 39
    (May 1973):297-8.

Nash, Roderick. From These Beginnings: A Biographical Approach
    to American History. New York: Harper and Row, 1973.
    Rev. by J. A. Nuenschwander, HT, 7(Nov 1973):116-17.

Nathans, Sydney. Daniel Webster and Jacksonian Democracy. Balti-
    more: JHU Press, 1973. Rev. by L. Harrison, AHI, 8(Dec
    1973):49; R. N. Current, AHR, 78(Dec 1973):1530-1; J. R.
    Sharp, JSH, 39(Nov 1973):594-5; W. G. Shade, PMHB, 97
    (Oct 1973):550-1.

National Library of Scotland. Summary Catalogue of the Advocates'
    Manuscripts. Edinburgh: H. M. S. O., 1971. Rev. by A.
    E. B. Owen, Archives, 11(Spr 1973):59-61.

National Maritime Museum [Great Britain.] Aspects of the History
    of Wooden Shipbuilding. n. p.: Maritime Monographs and
    Reports No. 1, 1970. Rev. by R. H. MilAf, 37(Feb 1973):
    32.

_____. Catalogue of the Library. Vol. III. Atlases and Cart-
    ography, Parts 1 and 2. London: H. M. S. O., 1971. Rev.
    by R. S. Craig, History, 58(Feb 1973):164.

_____. China Station 1859-1864, the Reminiscences of Walter
    White. n. p.: Maritime Monographs and Reports, No. 3,
    1972. Rev. by R. H., MilAf, 37(Feb 1973):32.

_____. The Development of the Boat: A Select Bibliography.
    London: n. p., 1971. Rev. by P. Johnstone, Antiquity, 47
    (Mar 1973):83-4.

The National Park Service [U. S.]. Soldier and Brave: Historic
    Places Associated with Indian Affairs and the Indian Wars in
    the Trans-Mississippi West. Washington, D. C.: Govern-
    ment Printing Office, 1971. Rev. by L. Barry, JISHS, 66
    (Spr 1973):97-8; W. G. Bell, MilAf, 37(Dec 1973):159, W.
    L. Bailey, NDH, 40(Fall 1973):31-2; C. T. McIntosh, PacH,
    17(Sum 1973):83-4; M. W. M. Hargreaves, RKHS, 71(Ja
    1973):110-1; R. E. Smith, WPHM, 56(Ja 1973):93-4.

Navarette, Carlos. The Chiapanec History and Culture. Provo,
    Utah: BYU Press, 1966. Rev. by M. P. Simmons, AmAnt,
    38(Apr 1973):254-5.

Navarro, Moisés González. Raza y tierra. La guerra de castas y
    el henequén. Mexico: El Colegio de México, 1970. Rev.
    by C. A. Hale, TAm, 30(Jl 1973):142-3.

Neal, John. Seventy-Six: "Our Country! Right or Wrong." Bain-
    bridge, N. Y.: York Mail-Print, 1971. Rev. by J. L.
    Wakelyn, MHM, 68(Spr 1973):105-6.

Neale, R. S. Class and Ideology in the Nineteenth Century. Bos-
    ton: Routledge and Kegan Paul, 1972. Rev. by T. R.
    Tholfsen, AHR, 78(Oct 1973):1059-60; G. C. Gunnin, JMH,
    45(Dec 1973):674-5.

Neatby, H. Blair. The Politics of Chaos: Canada in the Thirties.
    Toronto: Macmillan, 1972. Rev. by J. A. Boudreau, CHR,
    54(Dec 1973):451-3.

Nebraska Historical Society. A Guide to the Newspaper Collection
    of the State Archives, Nebraska Historical Society. Lincoln:
    Neb Historical Society, 1969. Rev. by A. L. Nolen, AmArch,
    36(Ja 1973):76-8.

Necheles Ruth F. The Abbe Gregoire, 1787-1831: The Odyssey of
    an Egalitarian. Westport, Conn.: Greenwood, 1971. Rev.
    by P. N. Stearns, AHR, 78(Oct 1973):1074-5; I. Woloch,
    JMH, 45(Mar 1973):139-40.

Needham, Joseph, Wang Ling and Lu Givei-djen. Science and Civi-
    lisation in China. Vol. IV. Physics and Physical Tech-
    nology. Part III. Civil Engineering and Nautics. Cam-
    bridge: Cam U Press, 1971. Rev. by E-tu Zen Sun, T & C,
    14(Apr 1973):289-92.

Needham, Rodney, ed. Rethinking Kinship and Marriage. New York:
    Harper and Row, 1972. Rev. by G. Burkhart, SS, 64(Nov
    1973):286-7.

Negev, Abraham, ed. Archaeological encyclopedia of the Holy Land.
    [London:] Weidenfeld and Nicolson, 1972. Rev. by I. Blake,
    Antiquity, 47(Sep 1973):246-7.

Nelkin, Dorothy. The Politics of Housing Innovation: The Fate of
    the Civilian Industrial Technology Program. Ithaca, N. Y.
    Cornell U Press, 1971. Rev. by W. P. Strassmann, T & C,
    14(Ja 1973):90-1.

    _____. The University and Military Research: Moral Politics at
    M. I. T. Ithaca, N. Y.: Cornell U Press, 1972. Rev. by
    S. L. Harrison, MilAf, 37(Oct 1973):113; D. Greenberg,
    T & C, 14(Ja 1973):99-100.

Nelles, H. V., ed. Philosophy of Railroads and Other Essays by
    T. C. Keefer. Toronto: U Tor Press, 1972. Rev. by
    N. R. Ball, T & C, 14(Oct 1973):632-5.

Nelson, Charles M. The Sunset Creek Site ... and Its Place in
    Plateau Prehistory. Pullman Wash.: Wash St U, 1969. Rev.

by R. Sprague, AmAnt, 38(Jl 1973):369-70.

Nelson, Clifford L. German-American Political Behavior in Nebraska and Wisconsin, 1916-1920. Lincoln: U Neb, 1972.
Rev. by H. W. Allen, JAH, 60(Sep 1973):488-9.

Nelson, E. Clifford. Lutheranism in North America, 1914-1970.
Minneapolis: Augsburg, 1972. Rev. by C. S. Meyer, CHIQ,
46(Sum 1973):93-4; G. E. Arden, JAH, 60(Je 1973):169-70.

Nelson, Lowry. Cuba: The Measure of a Revolution. Minneapolis:
U Minn Press, 1972. Rev. by R. H. Fitzgibbon, AHR, 78
(Oct 1973):1150-1; R. R. Fagen, HAHR, 53(Nov 1973):702-4.

Nemiroff, Robert, ed. Les Blancs: The Collected Last Plays of
Lorraine Hansberry. New York: Random House, 1972. Rev.
by L. Mitchell, Crisis, 80(Ja 1973):31.

Neuberg, Paul. The Hero's Children: The Postwar Generation in
Eastern Europe. New York: Morrow, 1973. Rev. by A.
Z. Rubenstein, CurH, 64(May 1973):224.

Neufeld, E. P. The Financial System of Canada: Its Growth and
Development. Toronto: Macmillan, 1972. Rev. by R. C.
McIvor, BHR, 47(Sum 1973):281-3; W. C. Hood, CHR, 54
(Sep 1973):299-300.

Newby, I. A. Black Carolinians: A History of Blacks in South
Carolina from 1895-1968. Columbia, S. C.: U SCar Press,
1973. Rev. by W. B. Weare, AHR, 78(Dec 1973):1536-7;
A. R. Stoesen, GHQ, 57(Win 1973):594-5; H. Walton, Jr.,
Historian, 36(Nov 1973):128-9; W. J. Cooper, Jr., JAH, 60
(Dec 1973):824-5; P. Daniel, JSH, 39(Aug 1973):460-1; T.
F. Armstrong, NCHR, 50(Sum 1973):327-8; C. W. Joyner,
SCHM, 74(Oct 1973):319-20.

Newcomb, Benjamin H. Franklin and Galloway: A Political Partnership. New Haven, Conn.: Yale U Press, 1972. Rev. by
R. J. Champagne, JAH, 60(Dec 1973):788-9; J. E. Illick,
PMHB, 97(Apr 1973):256-7; W. S. Hanna, WMQ, 3rd ser.,
30(Jl 1973):522-4; R. Detweiler, WPHM, 56(Ja 1973):94-6.

Newell, R. R. and A. P. J. Vroomans. Automatic Artifact Regis-
tration and Systems for Archaeological Analysis With the
Philips P1100 Computer: A Mesolithic Test Case. New
York: Humanities, 1972. Rev. by D. Clarke, Antiquity, 47
(Je 1973):158-60.

Newell, Richard S. The Politics of Afghanistan. Ithaca, N. Y.:
Cornell U Press, 1971. Rev. by R. Rossow, MEJ, 27(Win
1973):78-9.

Newman, Elmer, ed. Lewis Mumford: A Bibliography, 1914-1970.

New York: Harcourt Brace Jovanovich, 1971. Rev. by P.
D. Goist, T & C, 14(Apr 1973):359-60.

Newman, Karl J. European Democracy Between the Wars. Notre
Dame, Ind.: U Notre Dame Press, 1971. Rev. by E.
Weber, JMH, 45(Mar 1973):170.

Newton, Craig A. and James R. Sperry. A Quiet Boomtown: Jami-
son City, Pennsylvania, 1889-1912. Bloomsburg: Columbia
County Historical Society, 1972. Rev. by F. W. Kohlmeyer,
PH, 40(Apr 1973):229-31; W. C. Darrah, PMHB, 97(Ja
1973):122.

Newton, Huey P. Revolutionary Suicide. New York: Harcourt
Brace Jovanovich, n. d. Rev. by B. G. Gallagher, Crisis,
80(Nov 1973):322.

Newton, Milton G., Jr. Atlas of Louisiana: A Guide for Students.
Baton Rouge: LSU Press ... 1972. Rev. by R. M. Crisler,
LaH, 14(Spr 1973):222-3.

Nicholas, David. Town and Countryside: Social, Economic and Political Tensions in Fourteenth-Century Flanders. Bruges: De
Tempel, 1971. Rev. by R. Vaughan, History, 58(Feb 1973):
87-8.

Nicholls, Anthony and Erich Matthias, eds. German Democracy and
the Triumph of Hitler. London: Allen and Unwin, 1971. Rev.
by A. J. Ryder, History, 58(Feb 1973):137-8.

Nicholls, C. S. The Swahili Coast: Politics, Diplomacy and Trade
on the East African Littoral, 1798-1856. London: Allen and
Unwin, 1971. Rev. by J. Lansdale, History, 58(Je 1973):324.

Nicholls, Kenneth. Gaelic and Gaelicized Ireland in the Middle
Ages. Dublin: Gill and Macmillan, 1972. Rev. by K.
Simms, E-I, 8(Sum 1973):149-51; G. W. S. Barrow, His-
tory, 58(Je 1973):257-8.

Nichols, Irby C., Jr. The European Pentarchy and the Congress
of Verona, 1822. The Hague: Martinus Nijhoff, 1971. Rev.
by P. W. Schroeder, JMH, 45(Je 1973):314.

Nichols, Roy F. The Invention of American Political Parties: A
Study of Political Improvisation. New York: Free Press,
1967. Rev. by C. Jackson, RKHS, 71(Apr 1973):195-8.

Nicholson, G. W. L. The Gunners of Canada: The History of the
Royal Regiment of Canadian Artillery. Vol. 2, 1919-1967.
Toronto: McClelland and Stewart, 1972. Rev. by D. J.
Goodspeed, CHR, 54(Sep 1973):303-5.

Nieburg, H. L. Culture Storm: Politics and the Ritual Order.

New York: St. Martin's Press, 1973. Rev. by R. K. Whelan, T & C, 14(Oct 1973):681-3.

Niederhuemer, Rolf, ed. Blätter für Technikgeschichte. Vol. 32/ 33. (1970/71). Vienna: Forschungsinstitute für Technikgeschichte, 1972. Rev. by R. S. Hartenberg, T & C, 14(Apr 1973):356-8.

Nielsen, Waldemar A. The Big Foundations. New York: Columbia U Press, 1972. Rev. by T. C. Reeves, JAH, 60(Sep 1973): 519-20.

Niemeyer, Gerhart. Between Nothingness and Paradise. Baton Rouge: LSU Press, 1971. Rev. by N. Levine, AHR, 78 (Feb 1973):66-7; H. Drucker, History, 58(Feb 1973):160-1.

Niethammer, Lutz. Entnazifizierung in Bayern: Säuberung und Rehabilitierung unter amerikanischer Besatzung. Frankfurt am Main: S. Fischer, 1972. Rev. by G. H. Stein, AHR, 78 (Oct 1973):1094-5.

Niewyk, Donald L. Socialist, Anti-Semite, and Jew: German Social Democracy Confronts the Problem of Anti-Semitism, 1918-1933. Baton Rouge: LSU Press, 1971. Rev. by K. von Klemperer, JMH, 45(Je 1973):344-6.

Nininger, Harvey H. Find A Falling Star. New York: Paul S. Erickson, 1972. Rev. by R. O. Stone, JOW, 12(Oct 1973): 651-2.

Niocaill, G. Mac. Ireland Before the Vikings. Dublin: Gill and Macmillan, 1972. Rev. by A. P. Smyth, History, 58(Je 1973):253.

Nish, Ian H. Alliance in Decline: A Study in Anglo-Japanese Relations, 1908-23. London: Athlone, 1972. Rev. by J. B. Crowley, JMH, 45(Sep 1973):529-30.

Nissenbaum, Stephen, ed. The Great Awakening at Yale College. Belmont, Cal.: Wadsworth, 1972. Rev. by R. W. Beales, Jr., WMQ, 3rd ser., 30(Jl 1973):530-1.

_____ see Boyer, Paul

Noakes, Jeremy. The Nazi Party in Lower Saxony 1921-1933. Oxford: Ox U Press, 1971. Rev. by F. L. Carsten, History, 58(Feb 1973):137; F. C. West, JMH, 45(Sep 1973):541-2.

Nordstrom, Carl. Frontier Elements in a Hudson River Village. Port Washington, N. Y.: Kennikat Press, 1973. Rev. by R. J. Plowman, HRNB, 2(Nov/Dec 1973):46.

Norman, E. R. and J. K. S. St. Joseph. The Early Development of Irish Society: The Evidence of Aerial Photography. London: Cam U Press 1969. Rev. by E. H. Ross, Archaeology, 26(Apr 1973):154-5.

Norman, Edward. A History of Modern Ireland. London: Allen Lane, Penguin, 1971. Rev. by E. D. Steele, History, 58 (Feb 1973):165-6.

North, Douglas C. and Lance Davis. Institutional Change and American Economic Growth. Cambridge: Cam U Press, 1971. Rev. by R. Floud, History, 58(Feb 1973):156. See also: Davis, Lance and Douglas C. North. Institutional Change....

North, Douglas C. and Robert Paul Thomas. The Rise of the Western World: A New Economic History. New York: Cam U Press, 1973. Rev. by J. L. Shneidman, HRNB, 2(Nov/ Dec 1973):38.

Norton, Mary Beth. The British Americans: The Loyalist Exiles in England. Boston: Little, Brown, 1972. Rev. by W. Brown, AHI, 8(Apr 1973):50; P. Smith, AHR, 78(Je 1973): 655-6; G. Stewart, JMH, 45(Sep 1973):492-3; M. S. Down, JSH, 39(Aug 1973):438-40; C. S. Crary, NYHSQ, 57(Jl 1973): 266-7; H. J. Young, PH, 40(Oct 1973):481-2; W. Brown, PMHB, 97(Apr 1973):259-61; E. R. Fingerhut, WMQ, 3rd ser., 30(Jl 1973):506-7.

Norwegian-American Studies. Vols. 24 and 25. Northfield, Minn.: Norwegian-American Historical Assn., 1970, 1972. Rev. by F. D. Scott, AHR, 78(Feb 1973):165-7.

Notable American Women, 1607-1950: A Biographical Dictionary. Ed. by Edward T. James. Cambridge, Mass.: Belknap Press, 1971. Rev. by B. Welter, WMQ, 3rd ser., 30(Jl 1973):518-22.

Notehelfer, F. G. Kōtoku Shūsui: Portrait of a Japanese Radical. New York: Cam U Press, 1971. Rev. by S. D. Brown, AHR, 78(Dec 1973):1514-15.

Notestein, Wallace. The House of Commons 1604-1610. New Haven, Conn.: Yale U Press, 1971. Rev. by L. A. Knafla, CHR, 54(Dec 1973):458-61.

Novinsky, Anita. Cristãos novos na Bahia. São Paulo: Editôra Perspectiva, 1972. Rev. by D. G. Smith, HAHR, 53(Aug 1973):509-10.

Nowlan, Kevin B., ed. Travel and Transport in Ireland. Dublin: Gill and Macmillan, 1973. Rev. by J. D. Conway, E-I, 8 (Win 1973):156-8.

Nunis, Doyce B. , Jr. , ed.   Sketches of a Journey on the Two
Oceans and to the Interior of America and of a Civil War in
Northern Lower California by the Abbe Henry J. A. Alric.
Los Angeles: Dawson's, 1971. Rev. by W. M. Mathes,
CHQ, 52(Apr 1973):88-9.

Nutting, Anthony. Scramble for Africa: The Great Trek to the
Boer War. New York: Dutton, 1971. Rev. by L. H. Gann,
JMH, 45(Sep 1973):514-15.

Oberländer, Ervin, et al. , eds. Russia Enters the Twentieth Century, 1894-1917. New York: Schocken, 1971. Rev. by L.
Kochan, JMH, 45(Sep 1973):555-7.

Oberth, Hermann. Ways to Spaceflight. Washington, D. C. : NASA
Technical Translation ... 1972. Rev. by B. C. Hacker,
T & C, 14(Oct 1973):657-9.

Obolensky, Alexander P. Food-Notes on Gogol. Winnipeg: Trident,
1972. Rev. by L. B. Turkevitch, RR, 32(Oct 1973):453.

O'Brien, D. P. , ed. The Correspondence of Lord Overstone. Vol.
I. June 1804-September 1849. Vol. II. September 1849-
December 1861. Vol. III. December 1861-April 1883. Cam-
bridge: Cam U Press, 1971. Rev. by D. Spring, AHR, 78
(Je 1973):691-2; A. E. Rockwell, JEH, 33(Dec 1973):899-901.

O'Connor, Francis V. The New Deal Art Projects: An Anthology
of Memoirs. Washington: Smithsonian Institute Press, 1972.
Rev. by J. DeH. Mathews, AHR, 78(Dec 1973):1549-50; A.
A. Ekirch, Jr. , NYH, 54(Apr 1973):254-5.

O'Connor, James. The Origins of Socialism in Cuba. Ithaca, N. Y.:
1970. Rev. by L. E. Aguilar, HAHR, 53(Aug 1973):517-8.

O'Connor, Raymond G. Diplomacy for Victory: F D R and Unconditional Surrender. New York: Norton, 1972. Rev. by D. F.
Trask, SS, 64(Nov 1973):278-9.

_____ . Force and Diplomacy: Essays Military and Diplomatic.
Coral Gables, Fla. : U Miami Press, 1972. Rev. by S. R.
Williamson, Jr. , CHR, 54(Sep 1973):333-4; S. J. Kneeshaw,
Historian, 36(Nov 1973):118-19; T. Ropp, SS, 64(Nov 1973):
283-4.

O'Connor, Thomas H. The Disunited States: The Era of Civil War
and Reconstruction. New York: Dodd, Mead, 1972. Rev.
by L. Cox, JAH, 60(Je 1973):135-6.

O'Crouley, Pedro Alonzo. A Description of the Kingdom of New
Spain, 1774. [San Francisco:] Howell, 1972. Rev. by L.
N. McAlister, AHR, 78(Je 1973):747-8; F. D. Almaraz, Jr. ,

JOW, 12(Jl 1973):511-12; K. F. Nutt, WHQ, 4(Apr 1973): 203-4.

Oda, Shigeru, ed. The International Law of the Ocean Development: Basic Documents. Leiden: A. W. Sijthoff, 1972. Rev. by V. K. Arora, IQ, 29(Jan-Mar 1973):61.

Ofari, Earl. "Let Your Motto Be Resistance": The Life and Thought of Henry Highland Garnet. Boston: Beacon, 1972. Rev. by L. F. Litwack, JAH, 60(Dec 1973):811-12.

O'Farrell, Patrick. Ireland's English Question: Anglo-Irish Relations 1534-1970. New York: Schocken, 1971. Rev. by T. Bowden, ESR, 3(Jl 1973):310-12; G. A. Cahill, JMH, 45(Je 1973):296-7.

O'Flaherty, Joseph S. An End and a Beginning: The South Coast and Los Angeles, 1850-1887. New York: Exposition, 1972. Rev. by D. A. Williams, JAH, 60(Sep 1973):475.

Ogot, Bethwell A. War and Society in Africa: Ten Studies. London: Frank Cass, 1972. Rev. by M. Twaddle, JAfH, 14 (Num 2 1973):354.

O'Higgins, James. Anthony Collins: The Man and His Works. The Hague: Martinus Nijhoff, 1970. Rev. by R. N. Stromberg, AHR, 78(Feb 1973):100.

Okada, Yasuo. Public Lands and Pioneer Farmers: Gage County, Nebraska, 1850-1900. Tokyo: Keiv U., 1971. Rev. by M. B. Bogue, WHQ, 4(Ja 1973):73-5.

Okamoto, Shumpei. The Japanese Oligarchy and the Russo-Japanese War. London: Columbia U Press, 1971. Rev. by E. W. Edwards. History, 58(Je 1973):334-5.

Okamoto, Shumpei, Dorothy Borg and Dale K. A. Finlayson, eds. Pearl Harbor as History: Japanese-American Relations, 1931-1941. New York: Columbia U Press, 1973. Rev. by J. Davids, HRNB, 2(Oct 1973):19.

O'Kane, John, trans. The Ship of Sulaimān. New York: Columbia U Press, 1972. Rev. by P. Avery, MEJ, 27(Win 1973):86-8.

Okasha, Elisabeth. Hand-list of Anglo-Saxon Non-runic Inscriptions. London: Cam U Press, 1971. Rev. by J. M. Bately, Antiquity, 47(Je 1973):155-6.

Okladnikov, A. P. Yakutia Before Its Incorporation Into the Russian State. Montreal: McGill-Queen's U Press, 1970. Rev. by E. Dunn, RR, 32(Apr 1973):216-7.

Oliveira Marques, A. H. de see de Oliveira Marques, A. H.

Oliver, Andrew, ed. The Journal of Samuel Curwen, Loyalist. Cambridge, Mass.: Har U Press, 1972. Rev. by M. B. Norton, AHR, 78(Dec 1973):1525; W. Brown, NYHSQ, 57 (Oct 1973):352-3; N. Callahan, PMHB, 97(Oct 1973):535-7; R. D. Brown, WMQ, 3rd ser., 30(Oct 1973):675-6.

Oliver, George. The Rover. [London:] Cassell, 1971. Rev. by R. Church, MH, 2(Spr 1973):58-9.

Oliver, Paul, ed. Shelter in Africa. n. p.: Barrie and Jenkins, 1971. Rev. by N. H. AfAf, 72(Ja 1973):97.

Olivová, V. The Doomed Democracy: Czechoslovakia in a Disrupted Europe, 1914-1938. London: Sidgwick and Jackson, 1972. Rev. by V. Mastny, AHR, 78(Dec 1973):1496-7; K. Robbins, History, 58(Oct 1973):471.

Ollman, Bertell. Alienation: Marx's Concept of Man in Capitalist Society. London: Cam U Press, 1971. Rev. by R. H. W. Theen, JMH, 45(Dec 1973):675-8.

Qloruntimҽhin, B. Q. The Segu Tukulor Empire. London: Longmans, 1972. Rev. by M. Brett, AfAf, 72(Ja 1973):84; A. S. Kanya-Forstner, JAfH, 14(3rd Qr 1973):511-12.

Olson, Alison Gilbert. Anglo-American Politics, 1660-1775: The Relationship Between Parties in England and Colonial America. New York: Ox U Press, 1973. Rev. by D. P. Resnick, HRNB, 2(Nov/Dec 1973):43.

Olson, Ted. Ranch on the Laramie: A Memoir of an American Boyhood. Boston: Atlantic-Little, Brown, 1973. Rev. by S. A. Hicks, AW, 10(Sep 1973):51.

Oman. Musqat, Oman: Dept. of Information, 1972. Rev. by J. D. Anthony, MEJ, 27(Spr 1973):248-9.

Oman, Carola. The Wizard of the North. The Life of Sir Walter Scott. London: Hodder and Stoughton, 1973. Rev. by J. Richardson, HTo, 23(May 1973):363.

Omari, T. Peter. Kwame Nkrumah: The Anatomy of an African Dictatorship. New York: Africana, 1972. Rev. by O. E. S., CurH, 64(Mar 1973):126.

Ó Muirithe, Diarmaid. A Seat Behind the Coachman: Travellers in Ireland 1800-1900. Dublin: Gill and Macmillan, 1972. Rev. by J. D. Conway, E-I, 8(Spr 1973):151-3.

O'Neill, William L. Coming Apart: An Informal History of America in the 1960's. Chicago: Quadrangle, 1971. Rev. by K. Cassidy, CHR, 54(Mar 1973):101-2.

239   O'NEILL

_____. Women at Work. Chicago: Ox U Press, 1971. Rev.
by G. Tuchman, T & C, 14(Apr 1973):326-8.

Ordish, George. The Great Wine Blight. New York: Scribner's,
1972. Rev. by P. H. de Garmo, AgH, 47(Jl 1973):274-5.

Oren, Nissan. Bulgarian Communism: The Road to Power, 1934-
1944. New York: Columbia U Press, 1971. Rev. by W. H.
McNeill, JMH, 45(Mar 1973):186-7.

Oreshkova, S. F. Russian-Turkish Relations at the Beginning of the
18th Century. Moscow: Izdatel'stvo 'Nauka,'' 1971. Rev. by
N. E. Saul, AHR, 78(Oct 1973):1014.

Oroz, Fray Pedro. The Oroz Codex. Washington, D. C.: Academy
of American Franciscan History, 1972. Rev. by B. Keen,
HAHR, 53(Aug 1973):500-1.

Orpen, Neil. War in the Desert. Cape Town and Johannesburg:
Purnell, 1971. Rev. by A. Brett-James, MilAf, 37(Oct
1973):113.

Orr, Douglas M., Jr. see Clay, James W.

Ortega y Gasset, José. An Interpretation of Universal History.
New York: Norton, 1973. Rev. by T. H. Von Love, HRNB,
2(Oct 1973):22-3.

Ortiz, Alfonso, ed. New Perspectives on the Pueblos. Albuquerque: U NM Press, 1972. Rev. by L. Tyler, HAHR, 53(Aug
1973):573-4; C. H. Lange, NMHR, 48(Ja 1973):94-5.

Ortiz, Antonio Dominguez. The Golden Age of Spain: 1516-1659.
New York: Basic Books, 1971. Rev. by R. Kagan, JMH,
45(Mar 1973):95-6.

Osborn, James M. Young Philip Sidney, 1572-1577. New Haven,
Conn.: Yale U Press, 1972. Rev. by N. C. Carpenter,
GR, 27(Spr 1973):141-3.

Osborne, John W. John Cartwright. New York: Cam U Press,
1972. Rev. by E. C. Black, AHR, 78(Dec 1973):1459-60.

Oschinsky, Dorothea, ed. Walter of Henley and Other Treatises on
Estate Management and Accounting. Oxford: Clarendon
Press, 1971. Rev. by E. King, Archives, 11(Aut 1973):101-
2.

Osgood, Cornelius. The Jug and Related Stoneware of Bennington.
Rutland, Vt.: Tuttle, 1971. Rev. by W. B. Pinney, VH, 41
(Win 1973):59.

Osgood, Robert E. The Weary and the Wary: U. S. and Japanese

Security Policies in Transition.   Baltimore: JHU Press,
1972.   Rev. by A. D. Coox, MilAf, 37(Apr 1973):71-2.

Oswald, Delmont R.   The Life and Adventures of James P. Beckwourth, as Told to Thomas D. Bonner.   Lincoln: U Neb
Press, 1972.   Rev. by R. H. Dillon, CHQ, 52(Spr 1973):89-
90;   M. E. Ealy, PacH, 17(Sum 1973):82-3;   J. Burrows,
Montana, 23(Sum 1973):52;   J. E. Wickman, NMHR, 48(Jl
1973):267-9.

Otetea, Andrei.   Tudor Vladimirescu and the Revolution of 1821.
Bucharest: Editura Stiintifica, 1971.   Rev. by J. J. Far-
solas, EEQ, 7(Sum 1973):221-3.

Otis, D. S.   The Dawes Act and the Allotment of Indian Lands.
Norman: U Ok Press, 1973.   Rev. by W. E. Washburn,
JSH, 39(Aug 1973):457-8;   R. W. Mardock, Montana, 23(Aut
1973):76;   H. C. Miner, WHQ, 4(Oct 1973):463-4.

Otto, Volker.   Das Staatsverständnis des Parlamentarischen Rates:
Ein Beitrag zur Entstehungsgeschichte des Grundgesetzes für
die Bundesrepublik Deutschland.   Düsseldorf: Droste Verlag,
1971.   Rev. by P. H. Merkl, JMH, 45(Sep 1973):547-8.

Overseas Museum of Ethnology (Lisbon).   Peoples and Cultures.
Lisbon: The Museum, 1972.   Rev. by M. D. McLeod, AfAf,
72(Oct 1973):461-2.

Owen, A. E. B.   Handlist of the Political Papers of Stanley Baldwin.   Cambridge: Cam U Library, 1973.   Rev. by M. Cow-
ling, Archives, 11(Aut 1973):106.

Owen, D. D. R.   The Vision of Hell: Infernal Journeys in Medieval
French Literature.   Edinburgh ...:   Scottish Academic Press,
1970.   Rev. by C. J. Holdsworth, History, 58(Oct 1973):434.

Owen, David.   Politics of Defense.   New York: Taplinger, 1972.
Rev. by A. R. Millett, MilAf, 37(Dec 1973):157-8.

Owen, Guy.   The White Stallion.   Winston-Salem, N. C.:   John F.
Blair, 1969.   Rev. by K. S. Byer, GR, 27(Spr 1973):110-21.

Owsley, Harriet Chappell, ed.   Guide to the Processed Manuscripts
of the Tennessee Historical Society.   Nashville: Tenn State
Library and Archives, 1969.   Rev. by A. L. Nolen, AmArch,
36(Ja 1973):76-8.

Pachai, Bridglal, ed.   The Early History of Malawi.   London: Longmans, 1972.   Rev. by P. M. Redmond, AfAf, 72(Ja 1973):
95-6.

_____.   Livingstone--Man of Africa: Memorial Essays 1873-1973.

London: Longmans, 1973. Rev. by I. Linden, JAfH, 14(3rd
Qr 1973):518-19.

The Pacific War Research Society. Japan's Longest Day. New York:
Ballantine, 1972. Rev. by A. D. Coox, MilAf, 37(Apr 1973):
71-2.

Padfield, Peter. The Battleship Era. New York: David McKay,
1972. Rev. by C. G. Reynolds, JAH, 60(Dec 1973):825-6.

Page, Evelyn. American Genesis: Pre-Colonial Writing in the
North. Boston: Gambit, 1973. Rev. by L. M. Maloney,
HRNB, 2(Nov/Dec 1973):40.

Page, Joseph A. The Revolution That Never Was, Northeast Brazil
1955-1964. New York: Grossman, 1972. Rev. by J. B.
Bell, MilAf, 37(Dec 1973):155-7.

Page, Stephen. The U S S R in Arabia: The Development of Soviet
Policies and Attitudes Towards the Countries of the Arabian
Peninsula. London: Central Asian Research Centre, 1972.
Rev. by J. D. Anthony, MEJ, 27(Spr 1973):229-31.

Pagès, G. The Thirty Years War, 1618-1648. London: A and C
Black, 1971. Rev. by M. Hughes, History, 58(Feb 1973):
104-5.

Paget, R. F. Central Italy: an Archaeological Guide. London:
Faber, 1973. Rev. by D. Ridgway, Antiquity, 47(Sep 1973):
250-1.

Paher, Stanley W. Las Vegas: As It Began--As It Grew. Las
Vegas: Nev Publications, 1971. Rev. by R. W. Davenport,
Montana, 23(Ja 1973):60.

Paine, T. O. Submarining: Three Thousand Books and Articles.
Santa Barbara, Cal.: General Electric, 1971. Rev. by E.
S. Ferguson, T & C, 14(Ja 1973):112-13.

Paléologue, Maurice. An Ambassador's Memoirs. 3 vols. New
York: Octagon Books, 1972. (reprint). Rev. by S. Ploss,
RR, 32(Oct 1973):454.

Palmade, Guy P. French Capitalism in the Nineteenth Century.
Newton Abbot: David and Charles, 1972. Rev. by D. H.
Aldcroft. History, 58(Feb 1973):124-5.

Palmer, Alan. Metternich. New York: Harper and Row, 1972.
Rev. by G. De Bertier, AHR, 78(Oct 1973):1095.

_____. Russia in War and Peace. London: Weidenfeld and
Nicolson, 1972. Rev. by I. Grey, HTo, 23(Feb 1973):141-2.

Palmer, J. J. N. England, France and Christendom, 1377-99.
    Chapel Hill: UNC Press, 1972. Rev. by F. J. Pegues,
    AHR, 78(Je 1973):666-7; M. G. A. Vale, EHR, 88(Oct 1973):
    848-53.

Pancake, John S. Samuel Smith and the Politics of Business: 1752-
    1839. University, Ala.: U Ala Press, 1972. Rev. by J.
    M. McFaul, HT, 6(May 1973):485-6; C. M. Wiltse, JAH,
    60(Dec 1973):784-5; P. Goodman, JSH, 39(Aug 1973):444-6;
    G. Browne, MHM, 68(Win 1973):460-2; F. A. Cassell,
    PMHB, 97(Jl 1973):415-16; F. C. Mevers, VMHB, 81(Apr
    1973):207-8; R. A. Overfield, WMQ, 3rd ser., 30(Oct 1973):
    678-80.

Panofsky, Erwin. Problems in Titian, Mostly Iconographic. New
    York: NYU Press, 1969. Rev. by T. K. Rabb, JIH, 4(Sum
    1973):107-17.

Papacostea, Şerban. Oltenia Under Austrian Rule (1718-1789). Bu-
    charest: Editura Academiei Republicii Socialiste Rômânia,
    1971. Rev. by C. Bodea, AHR, 78(Oct 1973):1099-1100; S.
    Fisher-Galati, JMH, 45(Mar 1973):122.

Parker, Ben Lee. The Hinges of Destiny: A True Story of Ranch
    Life in the Early Twentieth Century. New York: Exposition,
    1971. Rev. by C. W. Black, JOW, 12(Oct 1973):635-6.

Parker, Franklin. George Peabody: A Biography. Nashville: Van
    U Press, 1971. Rev. by R. A. Davison, AHR, 78(Feb 1973):
    161; M. N. Kay, Historian, 35(Feb 1973):313; K. V. Lot-
    tich, SS, 64(Feb 1973):91-2.

Parker, Geoffrey. The Army of Flanders and the Spanish Road,
    1567-1659. The Logistics of Spanish Victory and Defeat in
    the Low Countries' Wars. New York: Cam U Press, 1972.
    Rev. by S. Ross, HAHR, 53(Aug 1973):534-5; D. L. Jensen,
    JMH, 45(Dec 1973):656-7; B. C. Weber, MilAf, 37(Oct 1973):
    109.

_____. Guide to the Archives of the Spanish Institutions in or
    Concerned with the Netherlands (1556-1706). Brussels: Ar-
    chives et Bibliotheques de Belgique ... 1971. Rev. by A.
    W. Lovett, ESR, 3(Jl 1973):307-9.

Parker, Mattie Erma Edwards, ed. North Carolina Higher Court
    Records, 1697-1701. Raleigh, N. C.: State Dept. of Archives
    and History, 1971. Rev. by J. H. Smith, AHR, 78(Feb 1973):
    150-1.

Parker, W. H. The Superpowers: The United States and the Soviet
    Union Compared. New York: Wiley, 1972. Rev. by R. P.
    Browder, JAH, 60(Dec 1973):866-7.

243   PARKER

Parker, William N., ed. The Structure of the Cotton Economy of
the Antebellum South. Washington, D. C.: Agricultural History Society, 1970. Rev. by J. F. Doster, NCHR, 50(Spr
1973):211-12.

Parkinson, John. A Tour of Russia, Siberia, and the Crimea, 1792-
1794. London: Frank Cass, 1971. Rev. by A. Sinel, AHR,
78(Feb 1973):127-8.

Parkinson, Roger. Blood, Toil, Tears and Sweat: The War History from Dunkirk to Alamein, Based on the War Cabinet
Papers of 1940-1942. New York: David McKay, 1973. Rev.
by D. Fries, HRNB, 2(Oct 1973):5.

_____. Peace for Our Time: Munich to Dunkirk--The Inside
Story. New York: David McKay, 1972. Rev. by T. L.
Thompson, CurH, 64(Apr 1973):179-80; K. Eubank, HT, 6
(May 1973):480.

Parks, Robert J. Democracy's Railroads: Public Enterprise in
Jacksonian Michigan. Port Washington, N. Y.: Kennikat,
1972. Rev. by L. J. Mercer, BHR, 47(Aut 1973):383-5; J.
H. Madison, IMH, 69(Sep 1973):286-7; A. S. Brown, MichH,
57(Spr 1973):72-4; H. Kelsey, WHQ, 4(Oct 1973):466-7.

Parmet, Herbert S. Eisenhower and the American Crusades. New
York: Macmillan, 1972. Rev. by J. C. Vinson, GHQ, 57
(Win 1973):593-4; G. Osborn, Historian, 36(Nov 1973):134-
5; G. H. Mayer, JAH, 60(Je 1973):181-3; D. Lindsay, Mankind, 4(Je 1973):6, 65; A. Yarnell, PHR, 42(May 1973):263-
4; J. F. Heath, WMH, 56(Spr 1973):250-1.

Parmu, R. K. A History of Muslim Rule in Kashmir, 1320-1819.
Delhi: People's Publishing House, 1969. Rev. by F. Lehmann, AHR, 78(Je 1973):721-3.

Parris, Guichard and Lester Brooks. Blacks in the City: A History of the National Urban League. Boston: Little, Brown,
1971. Rev. by A. E. Strickland, JNH, 58(Ja 1973):96-9.

Parris, Henry. Constitutional Bureaucracy: The Development of
British Central Administration Since the Eighteenth Century.
New York: A. M. Kelley, 1969. Rev. by R. M. MacLeod,
AHR, 78(Dec 1973):1386-1405.

Parry, Benita. Delusions and Discoveries: Studies on India in the
British Imagination, 1880-1930. London: Allen Lane; Penguin, 1972. Rev. by P. Mehra, IQ, 29(Ja-Mar 1973):67-8.

Parry, J. H. Trade and Dominion: The European Overseas Em-
pires in the Eighteenth Century. New York: Praeger, 1971.
Rev. by D. F. Lach, AHR, 78(Feb 1973):69-70; D. C.
O'Brien, HT, 6(Feb 1973):323-4.

Parry-Jones, William Ll. The Trade in Lunacy: A Study of Private Madhouses in England in the Eighteenth and Nineteenth Centuries. Toronto: U Tor Press, 1972. Rev. by B. Heeney, AHR, 78(Je 1973):688-9; K. B. Thomas, EHR, 88 (Jl 1973):605-7; M. E. Rose, History, 58(Je 1973):300-1.

Parsegian, V. L. This Cybernetic World of Men, Machines and Earth Systems. New York: Doubleday, 1972. Rev. by S. Beer, T & C, 14(Apr 1973):331-3.

Parsons, Henry McIlvaine. Man-Machine System Experiments. Baltimore: JHU Press, 1972. Rev. by R. E. Bickner, T & C, 14(Jl 1973):521-2.

Partner, Peter. The Lands of St. Peter: The Papal State in the Middle Ages and the Early Renaissance. Berkeley: U Cal Press, 1972. Rev. by E. M. Beame, Historian, 35(Feb 1973):277-8; J. Larner, History, 58(Je 1973):268-9; C. H. Clough, HTo, 23(Mar 1973):213-15.

Pascu, Stefan. Atlas Istoric. Bucharest: Edutura Didactica si Pedagogica, 1971. Rev. by W. H. McNeill, JMH, 45(Sep 1973):471.

Paterson, Thomas G., ed. Containment and the Cold War: American Foreign Policy Since 1945. Reading, Mass.: Addison-Wesley, 1973. Rev. by A. Erlebacher, HRNB, 2(Oct 1973):19-20.

Patrick, Alison. The Men of the First French Republic. Political Alignments in the National Convention of 1792. Baltimore: JHU Press, 1972. Rev. by B. Behrens, HJ, 16(Sep 1973):641-4; M. J. Sydenham, JMH, 45(Sep 1973):497-8; J. I. Shulim, AHR, 78(Oct 1973):1077-8.

Patrick, Max, ed. Complete Prose Works of John Milton. Vol. V, Part II: 1649-1659. London: Yale U Press, 1971. Rev. by V. Pearl, History, 58(Oct 1973):448-9.

Patterson, A. Temple. A History of Southampton, 1700-1914. Vol. 2, The Beginnings of Modern Southampton, 1836-1867. Southampton: Southampton U Press, 1971. Rev. by T. W. Perry, AHR, 78(Feb 1973):105-6.

Patterson, C. L. see Gardner, R. K. A.

Patterson, Edna B. Sagebrush Doctors. Springville, Utah: Art City Publishing, 1972. Rev. by H. Hickson, NHSQ, 16(Fall 1973):195-6.

Patterson, James T. Mr. Republican: A Biography of Robert A. Taft. Boston: Houghton Mifflin, 1972. Rev. by J. S. Chase, ArkHQ, 32(Aut 1973):283-5; C. D. Tompkins, JAH

245   PATTERSON

60(Dec 1973):858-60;   C. M. Mathias, Jr. , MHM, 68(Win
1973):464-5.

Patterson, Thomas C. America's Past: A New World Archaeology.
    Glenview, Ill.: Scott, Foresman, 1973. Rev. by T. F.
    Lynch, HAHR, 53(Aug 1973):531-2.

Patwardhan, Vinayak N. and William J. Darby. The State of Nutri-
    tion in the Arab Middle East. Nashville: U Tenn Press,
    1972. Rev. by R. Asfour, MEJ, 27(Aut 1973):522-3.

Paul, Harry W. The Sorcerer's Apprentice: The French Scientist's
    Image of German Science, 1840-1919. Gainesville: U Fla
    Press, 1972. Rev. by J. M. Laux, AHR, 78(Feb 1973):113.

Paul, Rodman W. , ed. A Victorian Gentlewoman in the Far West:
    The Reminiscences of Mary Hallock Foote. San Marino,
    Cal.: Huntington Library, 1972. Rev. by R. W. Etulain,
    AW, 10(Sep 1973):50; C. Bancroft, CoMag, 50(Sum 1973):
    268-70; T. A. Larson, PHR, 42(Aug 1973):429-30; M. L.
    Spence WHQ, 4(Oct 1973):451-2.

Pauline, Lawrence J. and Howard Weishaus. Ecology: Man's Re-
    lationship to His Environment. New York: Oxford Book Co.,
    1971. Rev. by J. D. McAulay, SS, 64(Feb 1973):89.

Paullin, Charles Oscar. American Voyages to the Orient 1690-1865.
    Annapolis: U. S. Naval Institute, 1971. Rev. by D. A. Ro-
    senberg, MilAf, 37(Apr 1973):73.

Paulson, Ronald. Hogarth: His Life, Art, and Times. 2 vols.
    New Haven, Conn.: Yale U Press, 1971. Rev. by T. K.
    Rabb, JIH, 4(Sum 1973):107-17; F. H. Dowley, JMH, 45
    (Dec 1973):669-72.

Paxton, Robert O. Vichy France: Old Guard and New Order, 1940-
    1944. New York: Knopf, 1972. Rev. by P. C. F. Bank-
    witz, AHR, 78(Oct 1973):1081-2; A. D. Coox, MilAf, 37(Dec
    1973):161.

Payton-Smith, D. J. Oil: A Study of War-Time Policy and Ad-
    ministration. London: H. M. S. O. , 1971. Rev. by W.
    Ashworth, History, 58(Feb 1973):142.

Pearson, Lester B. Mike: The Memoirs of the Right Honourable
    Lester B. Pearson. Vol. 1. 1897-1948. n. p.: Quad-
    rangle, 1972. Rev. by P. B. Waite, AHR, 78(Oct 1973):
    1148; R. A. Preston, Historian, 36(Nov 1973):138-9; G.
    Smith, JAH, 60(Sep 1973):521-2.

Pease, Jane H. and William H. Bound With Them in Chains: A
    Biographical History of the Antislavery Movement. Westport,
    Conn.: Greenwood, 1972. Rev. by R. Mann, Historian, 36

(Nov 1973):126-7; V. B. Howard, JSH, 39(Aug 1973):449-50.

Pease, William H. and Jane H. Austin Steward: Twenty-Two Years a Slave and Forty Years a Freeman. Reading, Mass.: Addison-Wesley, 1969. Rev. by J. L. Franklin, CWH, 19 (Sep 1973):285-7.

Peck, Robert Newton. A Day No Pigs Would Die. New York: Knopf, 1972. Rev. by R. Rath, VH, 41(Aut 1973):239-40.

Peckham, John M. Fighting Fire With Fire. Newfoundland, N. J.: Walter R. Haessner, 1973. Rev. by J. H. White, Jr., T & C, 14(Oct 1973):630-2.

Pedrett, Carlo. Leonardo da Vinci, The Royal Palace at Romorantin. Cambridge, Mass.: Belknap Press, Har U Press, 1973. Rev. by B. C. Pycha, Mankind, 4(Je 1973):65-6.

Peil, Margaret. The Ghanaian Factory Worker: Industrial Man in Africa. Cambridge: Cam U Press, 1972. Rev. by T. R. De Gregori, T & C, 14(Jl 1973):517-8.

Peirce, Neal R. The Megastates of America: People, Politics and Power in the Ten Great States. New York: Norton, 1972. Rev. by W. C. Havard, FHQ, 51(Apr 1973):461-2.

Péladeau, Marius B., coll. and ed. The Prose of Royall Tyler. Rutland, Vt....: Tuttle and Vt. Historical Society, 1972. Rev. by D. L. Cook, VH, 41(Win 1973):50-4.

Pelikán, Jiří, ed. The Secret Vysočany Congress: Proceedings and Documents of the Extraordinary Fourteenth Congress of the Communist Party of Czechoslovakia, 22 August 1968. New York: St. Martin's, 1972. Rev. by V. Mastny, AHR, 78(Dec 1973):1496-7.

Pendergast, James E., et al. Cartier's Hochelaga and the Dawson Site. Montreal: McGill-Queens U Press, 1972. Rev. by J A. Tuck, CHR, 54(Dec 1973):444-5.

Pennington, D. H. Seventeenth-Century Europe. London: Longman, 1970. Rev. by J. R. Jones, History, 58(Oct 1973):445-6.

Perdue, Robert E. The Negro in Savannah, 1865-1900. New York: Exposition, 1973. Rev. by W. B. Weare, JSH, 39(Nov 1973):630-1.

Peretz, Don. The Middle East Today. New York: Holt, Rinehart and Winston, 1971. Rev. by S. Kirshner, NO, 16(Ja 1973): 31-2.

Peretz, Merhav. La Gauche Israelienne. Paris: Editions Anthropos, 1973. Rev. by M. Nahumi, NO, 16(Dec 1973):74-7.

Pericot Garcia, Luis. The Balearic Islands. London: Thames and
    Hudson, 1972. Rev. by L. Grinsell, Antiquity, 47(Je 1973):
    164-5.

Pericot-Garcia, Luis, John Galloway and Andreas Lommel. Prehis-
    toric and Primitive Art. New York: Harry N. Abrams,
    1967. Rev. by E. Pasztory, Archaeology, 26(Ja 1973):76-7.

Perkin, Harold. The Age of the Railway. Newton Abbot: David
    and Charles, 1971. Rev. by F. M. L. Thompson, History,
    58(Feb 1973):116-17.

Perman, Michael. Reunion Without Compromise: The South and
    Reconstruction, 1865-1868. Cambridge: Cam U Press, 1973.
    Rev. by A. Peskin, HT, 7(Nov 1973):147-8.

Pernoud, Régine. Le reine, Blanche. Paris: Editions Albin
    Michel, 1972. Rev. by J. Dahmus, AHR, 78(Je 1973):671-2.

Perrett, Geoffrey. Days of Sadness, Years of Triumph: The
    American People 1939-1945. New York: Coward, McCann
    and Geohegan, 1973. Rev. by W. F. Hellmuth, MilAf, 37
    (Dec 1973):162.

Perrigo, Lynn I. The American Southwest: Its Peoples and Cul-
    tures. New York: Holt, Rinehart and Winston, 1971. Rev.
    by D. E. Berge, SCQ, 54(Sum 1973):285-6.

Perrin, Noel. Dr. Bowdler's Legacy. New York: Atheneum, 1969.
    Rev. by J. L. Kimmey, GR, 27(Spr 1973):135-7.

Perry, Lewis. Radical Abolitionism and the Government of God in
    Antislavery Thought. Ithaca, N. Y.: ... Cornell U Press,
    1973. Rev. by A. S. Kraditor, JSH, 39(Nov 1973):596-8.

Peters, Edward see Kors, Alan C.

Petersen, William J. Steamboating on the Upper Mississippi. n.
    p.: State Historical Society of Iowa, 1968. Rev. by C. W.
    Stoll, FCHQ, 47(Oct 1973):358-9.

Peterson, Charles E., ed. The Rules of Work of the Carpenter's
    Company of the City and County of Philadelphia 1786. Prince-
    ton, N. J.: Pyne, 1971. Rev. by M. R. Smith, PH, 40
    (Apr 1973):218-19; N. R. Ball, T & C, 14(Apr 1973):300-1.

Peterson, Charles S. Take Up Your Mission: Mormon Colonizing
    Along the Little Colorado River 1870-1900. Tucson: U Ariz
    Press, 1973. Rev. by M. S. Ellsworth, JAriH, 14(Aut
    1973):261-2.

_____ et al. Mormon Battalion Trail Guide. Salt Lake City:
    Utah State Historical Society, 1972. Rev. by T. G. Alex-

ander, NSHQ, 16(Spr 1973):30-1.

Peterson, Gale E.   see   Schlebecker, John T.

Peterson, Karen Daniels.   Plains Indian Art from Fort Marion.
   Norman: U Ok Press, 1971. Rev. by C. P. Westermeier,
   Montana   23(Win 1973):64.

Peterson, Roger Tory see Hill, Evan

Peterson, William R.   The View from Courthouse Hill.   Philadelphia: Dorrance, 1972. Rev. by J. B. Swainson, MichH, 57
   (Fall 1973):265.

Pethybridge, Roger.   The Spread of the Russian Revolution: Essays
   on 1917.   New York: St. Martin's, 1972. Rev. by P.
   Kenez, RR, 32(Apr 1973):202-3.

Petras, James and Hugo Zemelman Merino.   Peasants in Revolt: A
   Chilean Case Study, 1965-1971. Austin: U Tx Press, 1972.
   Rev. by A. J. Bauer, AgH, 47(Oct 1973):358-61.

Petrie, Sir Charles.   King Charles III of Spain.   New York: John
   Day, 1971.   Rev. by M. E. Goldstein, JMH, 45(Mar 1973):
   119-20.

Petrie, Glen.   A Singular Iniquity: The Campaigns of Josephine
   Butler.   New York: Viking, 1971. Rev. by J. L. Wunsch,
   JMH, 45(Mar 1973):133-4.

Petroni, Frank A., Ernest A. Hirsch and C. Lillian Petroni.   Two,
   Four, Six, Eight, When You Gonna Integrate? New York:
   Behavioral Publications, 1971. Rev. by C. A. Hildebrandt,
   SS, 64(Apr 1973):185-6.

Petter, Henri.   The Early American Novel.   Columbus: Ohio St U
   Press, 1971. Rev. by W. L. Hedges, WMQ, 3rd ser., 30
   (Jl 1973):516-8.

Phares, Ross.   Cavalier in the Wilderness: The Story of the Ex-
   plorer and Trader Louis Juchereau de St. Denis.   Gloucester,
   Mass.: Peter Smith, 1970. Rev. by P. Moore, LaH, 14
   (Fall 1973):410-11.

Phebus, George, Jr.   Alaskan Eskimo Life in the 1890's As Sketched
   by Native Artists.   Washington: Smithsonian Institution Press,
   1972. Barry M. Gough, JOW, 12(Oct 1973):642.

Phillips, J. R. S.   Aymer de Valence, Earl of Pembroke, 1307-
   1324: Baronial Politics in the Reign of Edward II.   New
   York: Ox U Press, 1972. Rev. by J. R. Lander, AHR,
   78(Oct 1973):1033-4.

Phillips, Philip. Archaeological Survey in the Lower Yazoo Basin,
     Mississippi, 1949-1955. Cambridge, Mass.: Har U Press,
     n. d. Rev. by J. B. Griffin, AmAnt, 38(Jl 1973):374-80.

Phillips, Thomas D. and James E. Wright. The West of the Amer-
     ican People. Itasca, Ill.: F. E. Peacock, 1970. Rev. by
     P. W. Kennedy, HT, 7(Nov 1973):128.

Philosophers and Kings: Studies in Leadership. Bombay: Popular
     Prakasham, 1972. Rev. by Y. Atal, IQ, 29(Jan-Mar 1973):
     58-9.

Picheloup, René. Les ecclésiastiques français émigrés ou deportés
     dans l'Etat Pontifical, 1792-1800. Toulouse: U Toulouse
     Press, 1972. Rev. by D. Higgs, JMH, 45(Sep 1973):499-500.

Pierce, Neal R. The Mountain States of America: People, Politics
     and Power in the Eight Rocky Mountain States. New York:
     Norton, 1972. Rev. by R. G. Athearn, A & W, 15(Aut 1973):
     294-5; G. McGee, Montana, 23(Sum 1973):52-3.

Pierce, Richard A., ed. Rezanov Reconnoiters California, 1806.
     San Francisco: Book Club of California, 1972. Rev. by W.
     L. Sarafian. PHR, 42(Feb 1973):111-12.

Pierre, Andrew J. Nuclear Politics: The British Experience With
     an Independent Strategic Force, 1939-1970. New York: Ox
     U Press, 1972. Rev. by M. Beloff, AHR, 78(Feb 1973):109-
     10.

Pierson, George W. The Moving American. New York: Knopf,
     1973. Rev. by R. Berthoff, JAH, 60(Dec 1973):767-8.

Pierson, Stanley. Marxism and the Origins of British Socialism:
     The Struggle for a New Consciousness. Ithaca, N. Y.: Cor-
     nell U Press, 1973. Rev. by H. Pelling, AHR, 78(Dec 1973):
     1465-6.

Pike, Frederick B. Hispanismo, 1898-1936: Spanish Conservatives
     and Liberals and Their Relations With Spanish America.
     Notre Dame, Ind.: Notre Dame Press, 1971. Rev. by E. I.
     Fox, HAHR, 53(Feb 1973):162-4; S. G. Payne, JMH, 45(Mar
     1973):159-61.

Pike, Ruth. Aristocrats and Traders: Sevillian Society in the Six-
     teenth Century. Ithaca, N. Y.: Cornell U Press, 1972. Rev.
     by M. Weisser, HAHR, 53(Feb 1973):151-3; A. Petrucco,
     Historian, 35(Feb 1973):279-80; W. J. Callahan, JMH, 45
     (Sep 1973):488-9.

Pilsudski, Jozef. Year 1920. New York: Pilsudski Institute of
     America, 1972. Rev. by J. W. Kipp, MilAf, 37(Oct 1973):
     114.

Pinckney, Elise, ed. The Letterbook of Eliza Lucas Pinckney, 1739-1762. Chapel Hill: UNC Press, 1972. Rev. by R. M. Brown, JSH, 39(Feb 1973):104-5.

Pinkney, David H. The French Revolution of 1830. Princeton, N. J.: Prin U Press, 1972. Rev. by P. H. Amann, AHR, 78(Dec 1973):1476-8; J. W. Scott, JMH, 45(Dec 1973):683-4.

Piponnier, Françoise. Costume et vie sociale: La cour d'Anjou XIVe-XVe siècle. Paris: Mouton, 1970. Rev. by F. J. Pegues, AHR, 78(Feb 1973):83.

Pipping, Ella. Soldier of Fortune. Toronto: Macmillan, 1972. Rev. by W. Ormsby, CHR, 54(Sep 1973):302-3.

Pitkin, Thomas M. The Captain Departs: Ulysses S. Grant's Last Campaign. Carbondale: S Ill U Press, 1973. Rev. by D. Lindsey, HRNB, 2(Nov/Dec 1973):50.

Pitzer, Donald E., ed. Robert Owen's American Legacy: Proceedings of the Robert Owen Bicentennial Conference. Indianapolis: Ind Historical Society, 1972. Rev. by L. L. Sylvester, JAH, 60(Sep 1973):443-4.

Plath, David W. Aware of Utopia. Urbana: U Ill Press, 1971. Rev. by L. D. Holmes, SS, 64(Mar 1973):139-40.

Platonov, S. F. Moscow and the West. Hattiesburg, Miss.: Academic International, 1972. Rev. by G. Alef, RR, 32(Ja 1973):99.

Platt, D. C. M. The Cinderella Service: British Consuls Since 1825. London: Longman, 1971. Rev. by V. Cromwell, History, 58(Feb 1973):117-18.

_____. Latin America and British Trade 1806-1914. London: Adam and Charles Black, 1972. Rev. by S. B. Saul, History, 58(Oct 1973):481-2.

Platt, Virginia B. and David C. Skaggs, eds. Of Mother Country and Plantations: Proceedings of the Twenty-Seventh Conference in Early American History. Bowling Green, Ohio: Bowling Green U Press, 1971. Rev. by E. M. Cook, Jr., BHR, 47(Spr 1973):104-5; M. Brunet, CHR, 54(Mar 1973): 82-4; K. Coleman, JAH, 59(Mar 1973):984; J. A. Ernst, WMQ, 3rd ser., 30(Apr 1973):365-6.

Platts, Beryl. A History of Greenwich. Newton Abbot: David and Charles, 1973. Rev. by D. J Olsen, AHR, 78(Dec 1973): 1455-6.

Plowden, David. Floor of the Sky: The Great Plains. New York:

Sierra Club, 1972. Rev. by S. Crouch, AW, 10(May 1973): 49.

Plowden, Gene. Merle Evans: Maestro of the Circus. Miami: E. A. Seeman, 1971. Rev. by M. Murray, FHQ, 51(Apr 1973):463-5.

Plumb, J. H. In the Light of History. London: Allen Lane, 1972. Rev. by D. Allen, MH, 2(Spr 1973):48.

Plummer, Alfred. Bronterre: A Political Biography of Bronterre O'Brien, 1804-1864. Toronto: U Tor Press, 1971. Rev. by J. C. D'Orazio, AHR, 78(Feb 1973):103-4; S. Rothblatt, CHR, 54(Dec 1973):461-3; L. Brown, History, 58(Feb 1973): 115-16.

_____. The London Weavers' Company, 1600-1970. Boston: Routledge and Kegan Paul, 1972. Rev. by D. J. Jeremy, AHR, 78(Je 1973):682-3; J. E. Farnell, JMH, 45(Dec 1973): 653-4; J. deL. Mann, T & C, 14(Oct 1973):620-1.

Pocock, D. F., trans. Essays on the Caste System. Cambridge: Cam U Press, 1971. Rev. by E. Stokes, History, 58(Je 1973):330-1.

Pocock, J. G. A. Politics, Language, and Time; Essays on Political Thought and History. New York: Atheneum, 1971. Rev. by C. Robbins, AHR, 78(Feb 1973):65-6; R. Buel, Jr., H & T, 12(1973):250-64; K. R. Minogue, History, 58(Oct 1973):412.

Pogue, Forrest C. George C. Marshall: Organizer of Victory, 1943-1945. New York: Viking, 1973. Rev. by L. Morton, AHR, 78(Dec 1973):1553-5; H. L. Coles, JAH, 60(Sep 1973): 502-3; N. F. Parrish, JSH, 39(Aug 1973):464-6; W. F. Barber, MilAf, 37(Dec 1973):161.

Pohl, Frederick J. The Viking Settlements of North America. New York: Clarkson N. Potter, 1972. Rev. by V. S. Thomas, WMH, 56(Win 1972-73):162-4.

Pois, Robert A. Friedrich Meinecke and German Politics in the 20th Century. Berkeley: U Cal Press, 1972. Rev. by A. Mitzman, JMH, 45(Dec 1973):708-9.

Polakoff, Keith Ian. The Politics of Inertia: The Election of 1876 and the End of Reconstruction. Baton Rouge: LSU Press, 1973. Rev. by M. F. Holt, HRNB, 2(Nov/Dec 1973):49-50.

Pole, J. R. Foundations of American Independence: 1763-1815. Indianapolis: Bobbs-Merrill, 1972. Rev. by P. Goodman, JAH, 60(Je 1973):116-17; P. J. Furlong, JSH, 39(Feb 1973): 106-7; S. R. Boyd, WMH, 56(Spr 1973):251-2.

Polenberg, Richard. War and Society: The United States, 1941-1945. Philadelphia: Lippincott, 1972. Rev. by A. R. Millett, MilAf, 37(Feb 1973):34-5; P. A. C. Koistinen, PHR, 42(Nov 1973):594-5; R. S. Kirkendall, WMH, 56(Aut 1973):68.

Polisensky, J. V. The Thirty Years' War. Berkeley: U Cal Press, 1971. Rev. by B. Nischan, EEQ, 7(Fall 1973):344-5.

Pollard, S. see Higgins, J. P. P.

Pollig, Hermann, ed. Makonde. n. p.: Institut fur Auslandsbeziehungen, 1971. Rev. by M. D. McLeod, AfAf, 72(Oct 1973):461-2.

Polonsky, Anthony. Politics in Independent Poland, 1921-1939: The Crisis of Constitutional Government. New York: Ox U Press, 1972. Rev. by E. E. Wynot, AHR, 78(Je 1973):715; R. F. Leslie, History, 58(Oct 1973):470-1; A. M. Cienciala, JMH, 45(Sep 1973):559-60.

Poltoratzky, Nikolai P., ed. Russkaia literatura v emigratsii. Pittsburgh: U Pittsburgh Press, 1972. Rev. by H. Muchnic, RR, 32(Oct 1973):446-7.

Pomorska, Krystina see Mateijka, Ladislav

Pomper, Philip. Peter Lavrov and the Russian Revolutionary Movement. Chicago: U Chi Press, 1972. Rev. by P. Avrich, RR, 32(Jl 1973):313.

Ponteil, Félix. Les bourgeois et la démocratie sociale, 1914-1968. Paris: Éditions Albin Michel, 1971. Rev. by N. Greene, AHR, 78(Dec 1973):1480-1.

Ponting, Kenneth G. The Woolen Industry of South West England. New York: Augustus M. Kelley, 1971. Rev. by J. R. Harris, JMH, 45(Dec 1973):651-3.

Pope, Thomas H. The History of Newberry County, South Carolina. Vol. I. 1749-1860. Columbia, S. C.: USCar Press, 1973. Rev. by D. M. McFarland, NCHR, 50(Aut 1973):420-1.

Pope Hennessy, James. Anthony Trollope. Boston: Little, Brown, n. d. Rev. by J. B. Connors, E-I, 8(Sum 1973):157-9.

Poppino, Rollie E. Brazil: The Land and People. New York: Ox U Press, 1973. Rev. by F. J. Munch, HRNB, 2(Nov/Dec 1973):55.

Porambo, Ron. No Cause for Indictment. An Autopsy of Newark. New York: Holt, Rinehart and Winston, 1971. Rev. by S. B. Winters, NJH, 91(Aut 1973):201-4.

Porter, Glenn. The Rise of Big Business, 1860-1910. New York:
    Crowell, 1973. Rev. by G. Porter, BHR, 47(Win 1973):533-
    5.

Porter, H. M. The Celtic Church in Somerset. Bath: Morgan
    Books, 1971. Rev. by W. Davis, History, 58(Feb 1973):80.

Porter, Kenneth W. The Negro on the American Frontier. New
    York: Arno, 1971. Rev. by D. F. Littlefield, Jr., A & W,
    15(Spr 1973):93-4; R. E. Spangler, WHQ, 4(Ja 1973):76-8.

Porter, Raymond J. and James D. Brophy, eds. Modern Irish Lit-
    erature: Essays in Honor of William York Tindall. New
    York: Twayne, 1972. Rev. by E. Brandabur, E-I, 8(Win
    1973):109-14.

Posner, Ernst. Archives in the Ancient World. Cambridge, Mass.:
    Har U Press, 1972. Rev. by L. J. Cappon, AmArch, 36
    (Ja 1973):67-9.

Post, Gaines, Jr. The Civil-Military Fabric of Weimar Foreign
    Policy. Princeton, N. J.: Prin U Press, 1973. Rev. by
    J. Remak, HRNB, 2(Oct 1973):2.

Post, Kenneth W. J and George D. Jenkins. The Price of Liberty;
    Personality and Politics in Colonial Nigeria. Cambridge:
    Cam U Press, 1973. Rev. by D. C. Dorward, JAfH, 14
    (3rd Qr 1973):514-16.

Postan, M. M. Essays on Medieval Agriculture and General Prob-
    lems of the Medieval Economy. New York: Cam U Press,
    1973. Rev. by C. T. Marshall, HRNB, 2(Oct 1973):8.

_____. The Medieval Economy and Society: An Economic His-
    tory of Britain in the Middle Ages, 1100-1500. London:
    Weidenfeld and Nicolson; Berkeley; U Cal Press, 1972.
    Rev. by W. O. Ault, AHR, 78(Oct 1973):1032-3; R. H. Hil-
    ton, History, 58(Oct 1973):424-5; A. Rogers, HTo, 23(May
    1973):369-70.

_____. Medieval Trade and Finance. New York: Cam U Press,
    1973. Rev. by B. W. Scholz, HRNB, 2(Oct 1973):8-9.

Postel, Raner. Johann Martin Lappenberg: Ein Beitrag zur Ges-
    schichte der Geschichtswissenschaft im 19. Jahrhundert.
    Lubeck and Hamburg: Matthiesen Verlag, 1972. Rev. by
    G. G. Iggers JMH, 45(Sep 1973):519-20.

Potholm, Christian and Richard Dale, eds. Southern African in
    Perspective: Essays in Regional Politics. New York: Mac-
    millan, 1972. Rev. by O. E. S., CurH, 64(Mar 1973):125.

Potichnyj, Peter J. Soviet Agricultural Trade Unions 1917-70.

Toronto: U Tor Press, 1972. Rev. by R. D. Laird, AgH,
47(Oct 1973):356-7.

Potter, David M. History and American Society: Essays. New
York: Ox U Press, 1973. Rev. by G. B. Tindall, AHR, 78
(Dec 1973):1519-21; C. Strout, JSH, 39(Aug 1973):425-6; R.
A. Billington, JAH, 60(Dec 1973):762-3.

_____. The South and the Concurrent Majority. Baton Rouge:
LSU Press, 1972. Rev. by W. I. Hair, FHQ, 52(Jl 1973):
86-7; C. W. Crawford, GHQ, 57(Spr 1973):150-1; C. V.
Woodward, JAH, 60(Je 1973):123-4; C. Sallis, JMiH, 35
(Aug 1973):411-13; P. H. Howard, JNH, 58(Jl 1973):361-3;
D. L. Smiley, JSH, 39(May 1973):273-4; D. W. Grantham,
MHM, 68(Sum 1973):227-8; W. B. Gatewood, Jr., NCHR,
50(Spr 1973):214-5; N. B. Bartley, SWHQ, 76(Apr 1973):
496; W. E. Hemphill, WVH, 34(Apr 1973):302-3.

Potter, Edgar R. Cowboy Slang. Seattle: Superior, 1971. Rev.
by C. P. Westermeier, Montana, 23(Win 1973):68.

Poullada, Leon B. Reform and Rebellion in Afghanistan, 1919-1929:
King Amanullah's Failure to Modernize a Tribal Society.
Ithaca, N. Y.: Cornell U Press, 1973. Rev. by R. G. Lan-
den, HRNB, 2(Nov/Dec 1973):35.

Poulton, Helen J. and Marguerite S. Howland. The Historian's
Handbook: A Descriptive Guide to Reference Works. Norman: U Ok, 1972. Rev. by L. Rapport, AmArch, 36(Ja
1973):71-3; C. R. McClure, JOW, 12(Jl 1973):513-14.

Pourade, Richard F. Anza Conquers the Desert: The Anza Expeditions from Mexico to California and the Founding of San Francisco, 1774-1776. San Diego: Copley, 1971. Rev. by K.
McCarty, HAHR, 53(Feb 1973):125-6; R. J. Roske, NHSQ,
16(Win 1973):249-50.

Powell, Donald M. Arizona Gathering II, 1950-1969: An Annotated
Bibliography. Tucson: U Ariz Press, 1973. Rev. by L. C.
Powell, A & W, 15(Aut 1973):292-4; JAriH, 14(Sum 1973):
167-8.

Powell, Fred Wilbur, ed. Hall J. Kelley on Oregon: A Collection
of Five of His Published Works and a Number of Hitherto
Unpublished Letters. New York: Da Capo, 1972. Rev. by
R. Loewenberg, JOW, 12(Jl 1973):516-17.

Powell J. M. The Public Lands of Australia Felix: Settlement
and Land Appraisal in Victoria 1834-91 With Special Reference to the Western Plains. Oxford: Ox U Press, 1970.
Rev. by L. A. Clarkson, History, 58(Je 1973):336.

Powell, John Duncan. Political Mobilization of the Venezuelan Pea-

sant. Cambridge, Mass.: Har U Press, 1971. Rev. by L.
Tullis, HAHR, 53(May 1973):336-8.

Powell, Philip Wayne. Tree of Hate: Propaganda and Prejudices
Affecting United States Relations With the Hispanic World.
New York: Basic Books, 1971. Rev. by B. R. Hamnett,
HAHR, 53(Nov 1973):671-2; J. J. Silke, JMH, 45(Mar 1973):
98-9; S. L. Bailey, SS, 64(Ja 1973):38-9; L. G. Canedo,
TAm, 29(Ja 1973):397-9.

Powell, William S. The First State University: A Pictorial History
of the University of North Carolina. Chapel Hill: UNC
Press, 1972. Rev. by E. L. Kayser, AHR, 78(Oct 1973):
1139; W. U. Solberg, JAH, 59(Mar 1973):989-90; W. B.
O'Neal, VMHB, 81(Ja 1973):110-11.

Powers, Thomas. Balita mula Maynila. Ann Arbor: U Mich Press,
1971. Rev. by K. J. Pike, AmArch, 36(Jl 1973):411-14.

Powley, Edward B. The Naval Side of King William's War. Hamden, Conn.: Archon, 1972. Rev. by N. R. Stout, MilAf, 37
(Feb 1973):33.

Prasad, Dhirenda M. Ceylon's Foreign Policy Under Bandaranaikes.
New Delhi: S. Chand, 1973. Rev. by N. M. Khilnani, IQ,
29(Oct-Dec 1973):355-6.

Prassel, Frank Richard. The Western Peace Officer: A Legacy of
Law and Order. Norman: U Ok Press, 1972. Rev. by W.
Rundell, Jr., CoMag, 50(Sum 1973):259-60; K. L. Steck-
messer, JAH, 60(Sep 1973):465-6; J. D. W. Guice, Montana, 23(Spr 1973):76; W. H. Atherton, PacH, 17(Spr 1973):
103-4; R. Lane, PHR, 42(Nov 1973):589-91; G. L. Roberts,
SWHQ, 76(Apr 1973):494-5; P. T. Nolan, JOW, 12(Jl 1973):
499.

Prawer, Joshua. The Crusader's Kingdom: European Colonialism
in the Middle Ages. New York: Praeger, 1972. Rev. by
B. C. P. Tsangadas, Historian, 36(Nov 1973):93-5.

_____. The Latin Kingdom of Jerusalem: Europeanism in the
Middle Ages. London: Weidenfeld and Nicolson, 1972. Rev.
by S. Na'aman, NO, 16(Jl-Aug 1973):65-77.

Prebisch, Raul. Change and Development--Latin America's Great
Task. New York: Praeger, 1971. Rev. by H. W. Speigel,
TAm, 29(Ja 1973):394-5.

Prescott, Orville. Lords of Italy: Portraits from the Middle Ages.
New York: Harper and Row, 1972. Rev. by R. Price, OQ,
16(Sum 1973):81-3.

Prest, John. Lord John Russell. Columbia, S. C.: USCar Press,

PREST   256

1972. Rev. by D. Spring, AHR, 78(Oct 1973):1067; N. Mc-
Cord, History, 58(Oct 1973):458-9.

Prest, Wilfrid R. The Inns of Court Under Elizabeth I and the Early
Stuarts, 1590-1640. Totowa, N. J.: Rowman and Littlefield,
1972. Rev. by T. G. Barnes, AHR, 78(Oct 1973):1055-7; G.
E. Aylmer, History, 58(Je 1973):285-6.

Prestwich, Michael. War, Politics and Finance Under Edward I.
Totowa, N. J.: Rowman and Littlefield, 1972. Rev. by F.
A. Cazel, Jr., AHR, 78(Dec 1973):1437-8; J. R. L. Maddi-
cott, History, 58(Je 1973):259-60.

Price, Jacob M. France and the Chesapeake: A History of the
French Tobacco Monopoly, 1674-1791, and of Its Relationship
to the British and American Tobacco Trades. (2 vols.) Ann
Arbor: U Mich Press, 1973. Rev. by W. D. Jones, HRNB,
2(Oct 1973):14-15; H. C. Rice, Jr., PMHB, 97(Oct 1973):
532-4; J. C. Robert, VMHB, 81(Oct 1973):488-9.

Price, Richard. An Imperial War and the British Working Class:
Working-Class Attitudes and Reactions to the Boer War, 1899-
1902. Toronto: U Tor Press, 1972. Rev. by M. Hurst,
AHR, 78(Dec 1973):1470; S. E. Koss, History, 58(Je 1973):
316-7; A. J. A. Morris, JMH, 45(Sep 1973):513-4.

Price Roger. The French Second Republic: A Social History.
Ithaca, N. Y.: Cornell U Press, 1972. Rev. by R. D.
Anderson, History, 58(Oct 1973): 460; J. W. Scott, JMH,
45(Je 1973):321-3.

Prieto, Carlos. Mining in the New World. New York: McGraw-
Hill, 1973. Rev. by R. Lenon, P. E., JAriH, 14(Aut 1973):
258-9; R. W. Paul, NMHR, 48(Oct 1973):330-1.

Professor X. This Beats Working for a Living: The Dark Secrets
of a College Professor. New Rochelle, N. Y.: Arlington
House, 1973. Rev. by O. B. Faulk, JOW, 12(Apr 1973):341.

Proffer, Carl R. and Ellendea Proffer, eds. Russian Literature
Triquarterly. Ann Arbor, Mich.: Ardis, Fall 1971, Winter
1972. Rev. by R. A. Maguire, RR, 32(Apr 1973):207-8.

_____ and _____. Russian Literature Triquarterly, No. 3,
Spring 1972. Ann Arbor, Mich.: Ardis, 1972. Rev. by
J. G. Garrard, RR, 32(Jl 1973):327-8.

_____ and _____. Russian Literature Triquarterly, No. 4,
Fall 1972. Ann Arbor, Mich.: Ardis, 1972. Rev. by E.
Bristol, RR, 32(Oct 1973):447-8.

Prokofieff, Vladimir see Harvey, Mose L.

257   PRUCHA

Prucha, Francis Paul, et al. American Indian Policy. Indianapolis: Ind Historical Society, 1971. Rev. by F. W. Turner,
III, AHR, 78(Je 1973):724-6.

Pruitt, Ruth see Rogers, William Warren

Pryce-Jones, David. The Face of Defeat: Palestine Refugees and
Guerrillas. New York: Holt, Rinehart and Winston, 1972.
Rev. by J. B. Bell, MilAf, 37(Dec 1973):155-7.

Public Papers of the Presidents of the United States. Richard
Nixon. Containing the Public Messages, Speeches, and State-
ments of the President. Vol. 1, 1969; Vol. 2, 1970; Vol.
3, 1971. Washington: Government Printing Office, 1971,
1972. Rev. by W. C. Berman, AHR, 78(Dec 1973):1557-9.

Pullan, Brian. A History of Early Renaissance Italy: From the
Mid-Thirteenth to the Mid-Fifteenth Century. New York: St.
Martin's, 1973. Rev. by F. Rosenthal, HRNB, 2(Nov/Dec
1973):27; M. Greenhalgh, HTo, 23(Sep 1973):673-4.

Pulman, M. B. The Elizabethan Privy Council in the Fifteen
Seventies. Berkeley: U Cal Press, 1971. Rev. by P. Williams, History, 58(Je 1973):280.

Purcell, Edward A., Jr. The Crisis of Democratic Theory: Scientific Naturalism and the Problem of Value. Lexington,
Ky.: U Press Ky, 1973. Rev. by N. L. Dawson, FCHQ,
47(Oct 1973):359-61; P. F. Boller, Jr., JAH, 60(Dec 1973):
836-8.

Purdue, Howell and Elizabeth. Pat Cleburne: Confederate General.
Hillsboro, Tx.: Hill Jr. College, 1973. Rev. by J. J. Hud-
son, ArkHQ, 32(Aut 1973):282-3; GHQ, 57(Win 1973):598-9;
H. L. Harper, THQ, 32(Fall 1973):298-9.

Purser, W. F. C. Metal-Mining in Peru, Past and Present. New
York: Praeger, 1971. Rev. by R. Hayn, HAHR, 53(Nov
1973):668-9.

Purves, J. G. and D. A. West, eds. War and Society in the Nineteenth-Century Russian Empire: Selected Papers Presented
in a Seminar Held at McGill University, 1969-1971. Toronto:
New Review Books, 1972. Rev. by J. S. Curtiss, AHR, 78
(Dec 1973):1500; G. Tokmakoff, RR, 32(Jl 1973):334.

Pye, N., ed. Leicester and Its Region. Leicester: Leicester U
Press, ... 1972. Rev. by W. Kirk, MH, 2(Aut 1973):119-21.

Pyne Press Editors, comps. Lamps and Other Lighting Devices,
1850-1906. New York: Scribner's, 1972. Rev. by
N. B. W., PMHB, 97(Ja 1973):125.

_____. Victorian Silverplated Holloware. New York: Scrib-
ner's. 1972. Rev. by N. B. W., PMHB, 97(Ja 1973):
125.

Quam, Alvina, trans. Self Portrayals. By the Zuni People. Albuquerque: U NM Press, 1972. Rev. by A. Bullock, AW,
10(Jl 1973):58; S. Newman, NMHR, 48(Apr 1973):176.

Quandt, William B. Palestinian Nationalism: The Political and
Military Dimensions. Santa Monica, Cal.: Rand, 1971. Rev.
by C. Leiden, MEJ, 27(Win 1973):92; S. Kirshner, NO, 16
(Mar-Apr 1973):43-8.

Quarles, Benjamin, ed. Blacks on John Brown. Urbana: U Ill
Press, 1972. Rev. by L. S. Theisen, IMH, 69(Sep 1973):
291-2; S. Feldstein, JNH, 58(Apr 1973):231-3; M. W. Schlegel, VMHB, 81(Jl 1973):376; J. E Stealey, III, WVH, 34
(Jl 1973):393-4.

Quartim, João. Dictatorship and Armed Struggle in Brazil. New
York: Monthly Review Press, 1971. Rev. by R. M. Schneider, HAHR, 53(Nov 1973):723-5.

Quazza, Guido. La decadenza italiano nella storia europea: Saggai
sui sei-settecento. Turin: Giulio Einaudi Editore, 1971.
Rev. by E. Cochrane, JMH, 45(Mar 1973):108-9.

Quebec. National Archives. Rapport des Archives Nationales du
Québec, 1971. Vol. 49. Quebec: Ministère der Affaires
Culturelles, 1972. Rev. by T. D. Seymour Bassett, Am-
Arch, 36(Jl 1973):420-1.

Quimby, Ian M. G., ed. Winterthur Portfolio 7. Charlottesville:
U Va Press, 1972. Rev. by I. N. Hume, JAH, 59(Mar
1973):990-1; P. C. Welsh, T & C, 14(Jl 1973):527-30; A.
D. Reid, WPHM, 56(Jl 1973):317-9.

Quinn, Charlotte A. Mandingo Kingdoms of the Senegambia: Traditionalism, Islam, and European Expansion. Evanston, Ill.:
Northwestern U Press, 1972. Rev. by R. A. Dunbar, AHR,
78(Dec 1973):1506-7.

Quinn, D. B., see Cumming, W. P.

Quinn, David B. and N. Cheshire. The New Found Land of Stephen
Parmenius. Toronto: U Tor Press, 1972. Rev. by N.
Masterman, HTo, 23(Mar 1973):217-19.

Quinones, Ricardo J. The Renaissance Discovery of Time. Cambridge, Mass.: Har U Press, 1972. Rev. by A. B. Edwards, AHR, 78(Je 1973):649.

Quirk, Robert E. Mexico. Englewood Cliffs, N. J.: Prentice-

Hall, 1971. Rev. by M. D. Bernstein, HAHR, 53(Feb 1973):
114-15; E. B. Couturier, SS, 64(Nov 1973):281-2.

Rabie, Hassanein. The Financial System of Egypt, A. H. 564-741/
A. D. 1169-1341. New York: Ox U Press, 1972. Rev. by
J. L. Bacharach, AHR, 78(Oct 1973):1106-7.

Rabinowitsch, Wolf Zeev. Lithuanian Hasidism. New York:
Schocken, 1971. Rev. by B. D. Weinryb, AHR, 78(Dec
1973):1497-8.

Radkau, Joachim. Die deutsche Emigration in den U S A: Ihr Ein-
fluss auf die amerikanische Europapolitik 1933-1945. Düsseldorf: Bertelsmann Universitatsverlag, 1971. Rev. by M.
Jay, JMH, 45(Je 1973):358-60.

Radoff, Morris L. The State House at Annapolis. Annapolis, Md.:
The Hall of Records Commission, 1972. Rev. by D. Gordon,
MHM, 68(Sum 1973):231-2.

Radvany, Egon. Metternich's Projects for Reform in Austria. The
Hague: Martinus Nijhoff, 1971. Rev. by A. H. Hass, JMH,
45(Je 1973):326-7.

Rae, John B. The Road and the Car in American Life. Cambridge,
Mass.: M I T Press, 1971. Rev. by R. M. Wik, T & C,
14(Apr 1973):308-11.

Raffel, Burton, trans. Russian Poetry Under the Tsars. Albany:
SUNY Press, 1971. Rev. by H. W. Tjalsma, RR, 32(Apr
1973):208-10.

Raffel, Burton and Alla Burago, trans. Selected Works of Nikolai
S. Gumilev. Albany: SUNY Press, 1972. Rev. by H. W.
Tjalsma, RR, 32(Apr 1973):208-10.

Rafroidi, Patrick, Raymonde Popot and William Parker, eds. Aspects of the Irish Theatre. Paris: Editions Universitaires,
1972. Rev. by A. T. L. Parkin, E-I, 8(Sum 1973):137-44.

Raina, K. N. and K. V. Gopala Ratnam, eds. Tej Bahadur Sapru:
Profiles and Tributes. Chandigarh: Tej Bahadur Sapru
Commemoration Volume Committee, 1971. Rev. by S. K.
Saxena, IQ, 29(Apr-Je 1973):186.

Rainey, Anne. Mosaics in Roman Britain. Newton Abbot: David
and Charles. 1973. Rev. by J. Liversidge, Antiquity, 47
(Dec 1973):336-7.

Rainsford, George N. Congress and Higher Education in the Nineteenth Century. Knoxville: U Tenn Press, 1972. Rev. by
J. L. Guth, AgH, 47(Oct 1973):371-3; D. R. Whitnah, HT,
7(Nov 1973):150; D. Madsen, JAH, 60(Dec 1973):798-800.

Raistrick, Arthur. Industrial Archaeology: An Historical Survey. New York: Barnes & Noble, 1972. Rev. by J. Butt, History, 58(Oct 1973):413; J. R. Harris, JMH, 45(Dec 1973): 651-3; M. J. T. Lewis, T & C, 14(Oct 1973):616-8.

Rakshit, Gangadhar. Role of Deficit Financing in the Context of Indian Planning. Calcutta: World Press, 1973. Rev. by N. C. Joshi, IQ, 29(Jl-Sep 1973):278.

Ralston, Leonard F. and Harold H. Negley. The Search for Freedom: Basic American History. Vol. I. Philadelphia: J. B. Lippincott, 1973. Rev. by J. G. Greene, III, HT, 7(Nov 1973):117-18.

Ramazani, Rouhollah K. The Persian Gulf, Iran's Role. Charlottesville: U Press Va., 1972. Rev. by CurH, 64(Ja 1973): 33; M. Khadduri, MEJ, 27(Spr 1973):235-6.

Ramsey, Peter H., ed. The Price Revolution in Sixteenth-Century England. London: Methuen, 1971. Rev. by A. L. Beier, History, 58(Oct 1973):444-5.

Randall, Robert W. Real del Monte: A British Mining Adventure in Mexico. Austin: U Tx Press, 1972. Rev. by R. C. West, HAHR, 53(Nov 1973):693-5; A. Probert, JOW, 12(Ja 1973):180.

Randolph, J. Ralph. British Travelers Among the Southern Indians, 1660-1763. Norman: U Ok Press, 1973. Rev. by GHQ, 57 (Win 1973):603; L. E. Pennington, JAH, 60(Dec 1973):782-3; B. W. Sheehan, JSH, 39(Nov 1973):585-6; L. Lee, NCHR, 50(Sum 1973):335-6; C. J. Milling, SCHM, 74(Jl 1973):175; C. F. Feest, VMHB, 81(Jl 1973):371-2; J. H O'Donnell III, WMQ, 3rd ser., 30(Oct 1973):686-7.

Ranger, T. O. The African Churches of Tanzania. Nairobi: East African Publishing House, n. d. Rev. by A. Redmayne, AfAf, 72(Ja 1973):91-3.

Rapp, Francis. L'Eglise et La Vie Religieuse en Occident à La Fin du Moyen Age. Paris: Presses Universitaires de France, 1971. Rev. by P. Heath, History, 58(Feb 1973):90-1.

Rapp, George R., Jr. see McDonald, William A.

Rapson, Richard L. Britons View America: Travel Commentary, 1860-1935. Seattle: U Wash Press, 1971. Rev. by W. J. Baker, AHR, 78(Je 1973):657.

Ratay, Myra Sauer. Pioneers of the Ponderosa: How Washoe Valley Rescued the Comstock. Sparks, Nev.: Western Printing, 1973. Rev. by K. Richards, NHSQ, 16(Fall 1973):196-8.

Ratcliffe, Robert H. , gen. ed. Great Cases of the Supreme Court
    [and] Vital Issues of the Constitution. 2 booklets. Boston:
    Houghton Mifflin, 1971. Rev. by W. H. Shannon, SS, 64
    (Mar 1973):141.

Ratner, Lorman. Dialogue in American History. New York: Holt,
    Rinehart and Winston, 1972. Rev. by T. R. Wessel, SS, 64
    (Nov 1973):293.

Ratner, Sidney. The Tariff in American History. New York: Van
    Nostrand, 1972. Rev. by P. J. Uselding, BHR, 47(Win
    1973):514-16.

Rauch, R. William, Jr.   Politics and Belief in Contemporary
    France: Emmanuel Mounier and Christian Democracy, 1932-
    1950. The Hague: Martinus Nijhoff, 1972. Rev. by E. T.
    Gargan, AHR, 78(Dec 1973):1481-2; E. Weber, JMH, 45
    (Sep 1973):535-6.

Ravicz, Marilyn Ekdahl. Early Colonial Religious Drama in Mexico:
    From Tzompautli to Golgotha. Washington, D. C.: The
    Catholic U of America Press, 1970. Rev. by H. R. Stone,
    HAHR, 53(May 1973):311-13.

Rawick, George P. The American Slave: A Composite Autobiog-
    raphy. Vol. I. From Sundown to Sunup: The Making of the
    Black Community. Westport, Conn.: Greenwood, 1972. Rev.
    by D. R. Goldfield, AgH, 47(Jl 1973):277-8; M. Fletcher,
    JEH, 33(Je 1973):498-9; S. Feldstein, JSH, 39(Feb 1973):
    115-16.

Rawls, John. A Theory of Justice. Cambridge, Mass.: Har U
    Press, 1971. Rev. by M. Mandelbaum, H & T, 12(1973):
    240-50.

Rawski, Evelyn Sakakida. Agricultural Change and the Peasant
    Economy of South China. Cambridge, Mass.: Har U Press,
    1972. Rev. by W. Eberhard, AgH, 47(Ja 1973):87-8; K. H.
    Hsiao, JEH, 33(Sep 1973):683-5; E-tu Zen Sun, T & C, 14
    (Jl 1973):495-7.

Ray, Grace Ernestine. Wily Women of the West. San Antonio,
    Tx.: Naylor, 1972. Rev. B. B. Jensen, JOW, 12(Apr
    1973):343.

Ray, Jayanta Kumar. Portraits of Thai Politics. New Delhi: Ori-
    ent Longman, 1972. Rev. by S. Dubey, IQ, 29(Apr-Je 1973):
    163-4.

Ray, Dr. Niharranjan. Nationalism in India: an Historical Analysis
    of Its Stresses and Strains. Aligarh: Aligarh Muslim U,
    1973. Rev. by N. M. Khilnani, IQ, 29(Jl-Sep 1973):273-4.

Ray, Sibnarayan, ed. Gandhi, India and the World: An International Symposium. Bombay: Nachiketa, 1970. Rev. by R. Rattan, IQ, 29(Apr-Je 1973):164-5.

Recent Locomotives. Novato, Cal.: Newton K. Gregg, 1972. Rev. by J. H. White, T & C, 14(Oct 1973):635-6.

Reddi, V. M. A History of the Cambodian Independence Movement, 1863-1955. Tirupati: Sri Venkateswara U, n. d. Rev. by B. M. Kaushik, IQ, 29(Oct-Dec 1973):359.

Redford, Donald B. see Grayson, A. Kirk

Redman, Charles A. see Watson, Patty Jo

Reed, John P. and Fuad Baali. Faces of Delinquency. Englewood Cliffs, N. J.: Prentice-Hall, 1972. Rev. by V. Fox, SS, 64(Nov 1973):287.

Reed, John Shelton. The Enduring South: Subcultural Persistence in Mass Society. Lexington, Mass.: Lexington Books, 1972. Rev. by R. A. Hohner, JSH, 39(Aug 1973):421-2; D. W. Grantham, THQ, 32(Sum 1973):193-4.

Reed, Walt. Harold Von Schmidt Draws and Paints the Old West. Flagstaff: Northland Press, 1972. Rev. by M. S. Wolle, AW, 10(Jl 1973):56; V. A. Paladin, WHQ, 4(Oct 1973):452-4.

Reese, George H. and Patricia Hickin, eds. Journal of the Senate of Virginia: November Session, 1793. Richmond: Va. St. Library, 1972. Rev. by W. H. Stauffer, VMHB, 81(Ja 1973):104-5.

Reese, Trevor R., Intro. The Most Delightful Country of the Universe: Promotional Literature of the Colony of Georgia, 1717-1734. Savannah, Ga.: Beehive, 1972. Rev. by F. V. Mills, Sr., JSH, 39(Aug 1973):436-7.

Reeve, Robin M. The Industrial Revolution, 1750-1850. London: U London Press, 1971. Rev. by P. N. Stearns, BHR, 47 (Aut 1973):411-12.

Reeves, P. D., ed. Sleeman in Oudh. Cambridge: Cam U Press, 1971. Rev. by E. Stokes, History, 58(Je 1973):330-1.

Reichert, Günther. Das Scheitern der Kleinen Entente, Internationale Beziehungen im Donauraum von 1933 bis 1938. Munich: Fides-Verlagsgesellschaft, 1971. Rev. by J. Remak, EEQ, 7(Fall 1973):347-8; F. G. Campbell, JMH, 45(Sep 1973):544.

Reichmann, Felix and Josephine Tharpe. Bibliographic Control of Microforms. Westport, Conn.: Greenwood, 1972. Rev. by W. Saffady, AmArch, 36(Jl 1973):404-6.

263   REID

Reid, J. C. Bucks and Bruisers: Pierce Egan and Regency England. Boston: Routledge and Kegan Paul, 1971. Rev. by D. C. Itzkowitz, AHR, 78(Feb 1973):105.

Reid, John Philip. A Law of Blood: The Primitive Law of the Cherokee Nation. New York: NYU Press, 1970. Rev. by L. Lee, WHQ, 4(Apr 1973):208-9.

Reiger, John F., ed. The Passing of the Great West; Selected Papers of George Bird Grinnell. New York: Winchester, 1972. Rev. by J. C. Evers, A & W, 15(Aut 1973):291-2; S. E. Ambrose, AHI, 7(Ja 1973):57; M. D. Husband, JOW 12(Ja 1973):181-2; J T. King, Montana, 23(Spr 1973):75; R. V. Hines, PHR, 42(Feb 1973):114-15; V. H. Treat, SWHQ, 76(Ja 1973):344-5; R. Nash, WHQ, 4(Ja 1973):70-1.

Reigstad Paul. Rölvaag: His Life and Art. Lincoln: U Neb Press, 1972. Rev. by A. Saxton, PHR, 42(Feb 1973):116-17.

Reimers, David see Lankford, John

Reimers, David M., ed. Racism in the United States: An American Dilemma? New York: Holt, Rinehart and Winston, 1972. Rev. by N. Lederer, PH, 40(Oct 1973):496-7.

Reingold, Nathan, ed. The Papers of Joseph Henry, Vol. 1, December 1797-October 1832: The Albany Years. Washington: Smithsonian Press, 1972. Rev. by L. J Cappon, AmArch, 36(Oct 1973):551-2.

Reinhart, Klaus. Turning Point Before Moscow. Stuttgart: Deutsche Verlags-Anstalt 1972. Rev. by E. F. Ziemke, MilAf, 37 (Dec 1973):161.

Remington, Robin Alison. The Warsaw Pact: Case Studies in Communist Conflict Resolution. Cambridge Mass.: M I T Press, 1971. Rev. by R. V. Burks, EEQ, 7(Fall 1973):348-50.

Remini, Robert V., ed. The Age of Jackson. Columbia, S. C.: U SCar Press, 1972. Rev. by P. H. Bergeron, NCHR, 50 (Spr 1973):221-2; J. H. Schroeder, THQ 32(Sum 1973):194-5.

Renfrew, Colin. The Emergence of Civilization: The Cyclades and the Aegean in the Third Millennium B. C. London: Methuen, 1972. Rev. by M. Walker, T & C, 14(Ja 1973):78-81.

Renzulli, L. Marx, Jr. Maryland: The Federalist Years. Rutherford, N. J.: Fairleigh Dickinson U Press, 1973. Rev. by F. A. Cassell, WMQ, 3rd ser., 30(Oct 1973):684-6.

Reps, John W. Tidewater Towns: City Planning in Colonial Vir-

REVELLI 264

ginia and Maryland. Williamsburg, Va.: Colonial Williamsburg Foundation, 1972. Rev. by J. T. Lemon, JAH, 60(Je
1973):115-16; A. C. Land JSH, 39(May 1973):278-9; C. E.
Hatch, Jr., PMHB, 97(Apr 1973):262-4; J. C. Rainbolt,
VMHB, 81(Ja 1973):100-2; F. D. Nichols, WMQ, 3rd ser.,
30(Jl 1973):540-2.

Revelli, Nuto. L'Ultimo Fronte: Lettre di Soldati Caduti o Dispersi
nella Seconda Guerra Mondiale. Turin: Einaudi, n. d. Rev.
by D. Koenig, MilAf, 37(Apr 1973):73.

Revunenkov, V. G. Parisian Sans-Culottes at the Time of the Great
French Revolution. Leningrad: Izdatel'stvo Leningradskogo
U., 1971. Rev. by R. F. Byrnes, AHR, 78(Dec 1973):1476.

Reynolds, Clark W. The Mexican Economy: Twentieth Century
Structure and Growth. New Haven, Conn.: Yale U Press,
1970. Rev. by W. P. Tucker, TAm, 29(Ja 1973):402-3.

Reynolds, Donald E. Editors Make War: Southern Newspapers in
the Secession Crisis. Nashville: Van U Press, 1970. Rev.
by M. Huff, LaH, 14(Win 1973):109-10.

Rhodehamel, Josephine De Witt and Raymond Francis Wood. Ina
Coolbrith, Librarian and Laureate of California. Provo,
Utah: Brigham Young U Press, 1973. Rev. by R. Lamp-
son, PacH, 17(Fall 1973):32-5.

Rhodes, P. J. The Athenian Boule. New York: Ox U Press, 1972.
Rev. by M. Chambers, AHR, 78(Oct 1973):1026-7.

Rhoodie, N. J., ed. South African Dialogue. New York: McGraw-
Hill 1972. Rev. by M. Doxey, AfAf, 72(Oct 1973):457-8.

Rice, Eugene F., Jr. Foundations of Early Modern Europe 1460-
1559. London: Weidenfeld and Nicolson, 1971. Rev. by M.
Hughes, History, 58(Je 1973):274-5.

Rice, Howard C., Jr. and Anne S. K. Brown, trans. and eds. The
American Campaigns of Rochambeau's Army, 1780, 1781,
1782, 1783. 2 vols. Princeton, N. J.: Prin U Press;
Providence R. I.: Brown U Press, 1972. Rev. by A. O.
Victor, NJH, 91(Aut 1973):200-1; B. B. Petchenik, WMQ,
3rd ser., 30(Jl 1973):544-6.

Rich, Norman. The Age of Nationalism and Reform, 1850-1890.
London: Weidenfeld and Nicolson, 1971. Rev. by R. Bullen,
History, 58(Feb 1973):113-14.

_____. Hitler's War Aims: Ideology, the Nazi State, and the
Course of Expansion. New York: Norton, 1973. Rev. by
T. A. Knapp, HRNB, 2(Nov/Dec 1973):31.

Richards, James O. Party Propaganda Under Queen Anne: The
General Elections of 1702-1713. Athens, Ga.: U Ga Press,
1972. Rev. by H. Horwitz, AHR, 78(Feb 1973):99; R. Wal-
cott, JMH, 45(Sep 1973):490-1.

Richards, Peter G. The Backbenchers. New York: Hillary House,
1972. Rev. by M. A. Fitzsimons, HT, 7(Nov 1973):140-1.

Richardson, Kenneth. Twentieth-Century Coventry. [London:] Macmillan, 1972. Rev. by A. Sutcliffe, MH, 2(Spr 1973):56-7.

Richardson, R. C. Puritanism in Northwest England: A Regional
Study of the Diocese of Chester to 1642. Manchester: Manchester U Press, 1972. Rev. by C. Cross, History, 58(Je 1973):286.

Richey, Elinor. Remain to be Seen. Berkeley: Howell-North,
1973. Rev. by P. Butler, CHQ, 52(Win 1973):373-4.

Ridge, Martin, Raymond J. Williamson and George Spiero. Liberty
and Union: A History of the United States. Vol. 1: To 1877.
Boston: Houghton Mifflin, 1973. Rev. by R. Dewing, HT,
7(Nov 1973):118-19; S. Kleiman, HT, 7(Nov 1973):119-21;
J. C. Lawlor, SS, 64(Nov 1973):292-3.

Riegle, John L. Day Before Yesterday: an Autobiography and History of Michigan Schools. Minneapolis: T. S. Denison, 1971.
Rev. by D. W. Disbrow, MichH, 57(Spr 1973):79-81.

Riekhoff, Harald von. German-Polish Relations, 1918-1933. Baltimore: JHU Press, 1971. Rev. by W. Carr, History, 58
(Feb 1973):136-7; Z. J. Gasiorowski, JMH, 45(Je 1973):
347-8.

Riesenberg, Saul M. , ed. James F. O'Connell. A Residence of
Eleven Years in New Holland and the Caroline Islands. Hon-
olulu: U Hawaii Press, 1972. Rev. by S. W. Croker,
PacH, 17(Sum 1973):89-90.

Riezler Kurt. Tagebücher, Aufsätze, Dokumente. Göttingen:
Vandenhoeck and Ruprecht, 1972. Rev. by G. A. Craig,
AHR, 78(Oct 1973):1091-3.

Riker, Dorothy L. see Barnhart, John D.

Riley, Carroll L. Historical and Cultural Dictionary of Saudi
Arabia. Metuchen, N. J.: Scarecrow, 1972. Rev. by M.
C. Peck, MEJ, 27(Spr 1973):246.

Ringe, Donald A. The Pictorial Mode: Space and Time in the Art
of Bryant, Irving and Cooper. Lexington, Ky.: U Press
Ky, 1971. Rev. by E. H. Cady, NYH, 54(Jl 1973):366-7;
W. C. Bryant II, NYHSQ, 57(Ja 1973):86-7.

Ringenbach, Paul T. Tramps and Reformers, 1873-1916: The Discovery of Unemployment in New York. Westpoint, Conn.: Greenwood, 1973. Rev. by J. M. Harrison, HRNB, 2(Nov/Dec 1973):45.

Rippa, S. Alexander. Education in a Free Society: An American History. New York: David McKay, 1971. Rev. by G. A. Knox, SS, 64(Mar 1973):136-7.

Rippy, Merrill. Oil and the Mexican Revolution. Leiden: E. J. Brill, 1972. Rev. by E. J. Hanson, JEH, 33(Dec 1973): 902-3.

Risjord, Norman K. Forging the American Republic, 1760-1815. Reading, Mass.: Addison, Wesley, 1973. Rev. by J. L. Susskind, HT, 7(Nov 1973):122-3.

Ristow, Walter W., comp. À la Carte: Selected Papers on Maps and Atlases. Washington: Library of Congress, 1972. Rev. by J. M. Kinney, AmArch, 36(Oct 1973):560.

Ritter, Eric W., Peter D. Schulz and Robert Kautz, eds. Papers on California and the Great Basin Prehistory. Davis, Cal: U Cal, Davis, 1970. Rev. by G. F. Dalley, AmAnt, 38(Jl 1973):371-2.

Ritter, Gerhard. The Sword and the Sceptre: The Problem of Militarism in Germany. Vols. 1 and 2. Coral Gables, Fla.: U Miami Press, 1972. Rev. by G. Best, History, 58(Oct 1973):421-2; G. E. Rothenberg, MilAf, 37(Oct 1973):111.

Rivera, Feliciano see Meier, Matt S.

Rivkin, Ellis. The Shaping of Jewish History: A Radical New Interpretation. New York: Scribner's, 1971. Rev. by J. Neusner, AHR, 78(Oct 1973):1010-11; S. Rothblatt, JMH, 45 (Sep 1973):465-7; J. L Nethers, OQ, 16(Sum 1973):75-6.

Roach, John. Public Examinations in England 1850-1900. n. p.: Cam U Press, 1971. Rev. by N. B. Harte, History, 58(Oct 1973):462-3.

Roberts, Derrell C. Joseph E. Brown and the Politics of Reconstruction. University, Ala.: U Ala Press, 1973. Rev. by J. C. Bonner, GHQ, 57(Win 1973):590-1.

Roberts, Helen H. Basketry of the San Carlos Apaches. Glorieta, N. M.: Rio Grande Press, 1972. Rev. by C. L. Tanner, JAriH, 14(Win 1973):388-9.

Roberts, J. M. The Mythology of the Secret Societies. New York: Scribner's, 1972. Rev. by E. L. Eisenstein, AHR, 78(Oct

1973):1049-50; M. Johnston, Historian, 36(Nov 1973):107-8.

Roberts, Walter R. Tito, Mihailović and the Allies, 1941-1945.
    New Brunswick, N. J.: Rutgers U Press, 1973. Rev. by
    M. Wheeler, HJ, 16(Dec 1973):878-80.

Robertson, Constance Noyes. Oneida Community: The Breakup,
    1876-1881. Syracuse, N. Y.: Syr U Press, 1972. Rev. by
    L. Filler, JAH, 60(Je 1973):155-6; W. J. Gilmore, NYH,
    54(Jl 1973):371-2; VH, 41(Spr 1973):107-10.

Robertson, William. The Progress of Society in Europe. Chicago:
    U Chi Press, 1972. Rev. by D. Forbes, History, 58(Oct
    1973):416.

Robin, R. La Societé Française en 1789: Semur-en-Auxois. Paris:
    Plon, 1970. Rev. by O. Hufton, ESR, 3(Apr 1973):187.

Robinson, Donald L. Slavery in the Structure of American Politics,
    1765-1820. New York: Harcourt, Brace, Jovanovich, 1971.
    Rev. by E. E. Thorpe, AHR, 78(Oct 1973):1123-4.

Robinson, Jacob S. A Journal of the Santa Fe Expedition Under
    Colonel Doniphan. New York: De Capo, 1972. Rev. by C.
    R. Henderson, JOW, 12(Oct 1973):659-60; J. E. Edwards,
    NHSQ, 16(Fall 1973):188-9.

Robinson, Richard. The Origins of Franco's Spain; The Right, The
    Republic and the Revolution. Newton Abbot: David and
    Charles, 1970. Rev. by R. M. Blinkhorn, ESR, 3(Ja 1973):
    81-7.

Robinson, Ronald, ed. Developing the Third World: The Experience
    of the Nineteen-sixties. Cambridge: Cam U Press, 1971.
    Rev. by L. Barrows, T & C, 14(Apr 1973):347-51.

Robottom, John. Modern Russia. New York: McGraw-Hill, 1971.
    Rev. by D. R. Brower, SS, 64(Apr 1973):182.

Robrecht, John J. and George Anne Daly. An Illustrated Handbook
    of Fire Apparatus. Philadelphia: Insurance Company of North
    America, 1972. Rev. by J. H. White, Jr., T & C, 14(Oct 1973):630-
    2. See also: Daly, George Anne and John J. Robrecht. An
    Illustrated Handbook. . . .

Robson, L. L. The First A. I. F.: A Study of Its Recruitment
    1914-1918. Melbourne: Melbourne U Press; Portland, Ore.:
    International Scholarly Book Services, 1970. Rev. by A. M.
    J. Hyatt, CHR, 54(Dec 1973):454-5.

Rochat, Giorgio. Militari e politici nella preparazione della cam-
    pagua d'Etiopia: Studio e documento 1932-1936. Milan:

Franco Angeli Editore, 1971. Rev. by G. Baer, AHR, 78 (Feb 1973):122-3.

Roche, Jean. A Colonização Alemã e o Rio Grande do Sul. 2 vols. Pôrto Alegre, Brazil: Editôra Globo, 1962, 1969. Rev. by S. Leitman, HAHR, 53(Feb 1973):148-9.

Rodinson, Maxime. Marxisme et le Monde Musulman. Paris: Editions du Seuil, 1972. Rev. by I. L. Gendzier, MEJ, 27(Sep 1973):224-5.

Rodman, Selden. South America of the Poets. Carbondale: S Ill U Press, 1972. Rev. by J. A. Crow, HAHR, 53(May 1973): 361-2.

Rodney, Walter. West Africa and the Atlantic Slave Trade. Nairobi: East African Pub. House, 1967. Rev. by A. Redmayne, AfAf, 72(Ja 1973):91-3.

Rodnick, David. Essays on an America in Transition. Lubbock, Tx.: Caprock, 1972. Rev. by J. Penick, Jr., JAH, 60(Dec 1973):862-3.

Rodrigues, Edgar. Socialismo e Sindicalismo no Brazil, 1675-1913. Rio de Janeiro: Laemmert, 1969. Rev. by J. W. F. Dulles, HAHR, 53(Nov 1973):707-8.

Roe, Derek. Prehistory: An Introduction. Berkeley: U Cal Press, 1970. Rev. by R. M. Rowlett, Archaeology, 26(Jl 1973): 233-5.

Roett, Riordan. The Politics of Foreign Aid in the Brazilian Northeast. Nashville: Van U Press, 1972. Rev. by R. H. Chilcote, HAHR, 53(Feb 1973):155-7; R. Seidel, TAm, 30(Oct 1973):286-7; M. M. A., CurH, 64(Feb 1973):81-2.

_____, ed. Brazil in the Sixties. Nashville, Tenn.: Van U Press, 1972. Rev. by J. D. Wirth, HAHR, 53(Aug 1973): 525-6; M. M. A., CurH, 64(Feb 1973):81.

Rogers, Earl M., comp. A List of References for the History of Agriculture in the Mountain States. Davis, Cal.: U Cal, Davis, 1972. Rev. by R. R. Keller, CoMag, 50(Spr 1973): 169-70.

Rogers, Malcolm J., et al. Ancient Hunters of the Far West. San Diego: Union Tribune, 1966. Rev. by C. C. Colley, JAriH, 14(Sum 1973):168-9.

Rogers Will. Ether and Me or Just Relax. Stillwater, Ok.: Will Rogers Memorial Commission and Ok St U, 1973. Rev. by P. Lester, ChOk, 51(Fall 1973):365.

Rogers, William Warren. Thomas County (Ga.) 1865-1900. Tallahassee: Fla St U Press, 1973. Rev. in GHQ, 57(Win 1973):
599-600.

_____ and Ruth Pruitt. Stephen F. Renfro, Alabama's Outlaw
Sheriff. Tallahassee, Fla.: Sentry, 1972. Rev. by W. S.
Hoole, AlaRe, 26(Ja 1973):74; C. P. Cullop, CWH, 19(Mar
1973):80-1.

_____ and Robert David Ward. August Reckoning: Jack Turner
and Racism in Post-Civil War Alabama. Baton Rouge: LSU
Press, 1973. Rev. by J. L. Wakelyn, HRNB, 2(Nov/Dec
1973):53.

Röhl, John. 1914: Delusion or Design? The Testimony of Two
German Diplomats. New York: St. Martin's, 1973. Rev. by
L. Cecil, HRNB, 2(Nov/Dec 1973):29.

Rohn, Arthur H. Mug House: Mesa Verde National Park--Colo-
rado. Washington, D. C.: National Park Service, 1971.
Rev. by R. C. Euler, AmAnt, 38(Jl 1973):370-1.

Roider, Karl A. The Reluctant Ally: Austria's Policy in the Austro-Turkish War, 1737-1739. Baton Rouge: LSU Press,
1972. Rev. by L. Cassels, JMH, 45(Dec 1973):672-3.

Roiter, Fulvio see Stark, Freya

Rojo, Manuel C. Historical Notes on Lower California With Some
Relative to Upper California Furnished to the Bancroft Li-
brary. Los Angeles: Dawson's, 1972. Rev. by W. M.
Mathes, CHQ, 52(Sum 1973):181-2; R. C. Tyler, HAHR, 53
(May 1973):330-1.

Roller, Duane, H. D., ed. Perspectives in the History of Science
and Technology. Norman: U Ok Press, 1971. Rev. by A.
Thackray, T & C, 14(Apr 1973):287-8.

Romig, Walter. Michigan Place Names. Grosse Point, Mich.:
n. p., 1971. Rev. by E. H. Rankin, IS, 29(Spr 1973):77-8;
D. Chaput, MichH, 57(Spr 1973):70-2.

Romney, A. Kimball see Browne, Robert S.

Ronfeldt David. Atencingo: The Politics of Agrarian Struggle in a
Mexican Ejido. Stanford, Cal.: Stan U Press, 1973. Rev.
by R. Wilkie, HAHR, 53(Nov 1973):718-9.

Roosevelt, Franklin D. Complete Presidential Press Conferences
of Franklin D. Roosevelt. 25 vols. New York: Da Capo,
1972. Rev. by J. R. Wiggins, AHR, 78(Dec 1973):1546-8.

Root, Frank A. and William E. Connelley. The Overland Stage to

ROSAR   270

California. Glorieta, N. M.: Rio Grande, 1970. Rev. by
J. C. Schnell, A & W, 15(Spr 1973):97-8.

Rosar, Wolfgang. Deutsche Gemeinschaft: Seyss-Inquart und der
Anschluss. Vienna: Europa Verlag, 1971. Rev. by H. R.
Ritter, AHR, 78(Oct 1973):1095-6.

Roscoe, Theodore. The Lincoln Assassination ... New York: Franklin Watts, 1971. Rev. by R. D. Hoffsommer, CWTI, 12(Oct
1973):49.

Rose, Lisle A. After Yalta: America and the Origins of the Cold
War. New York: Scribner's, 1973. Rev. by T. M. Leonard, Historian, 36(Nov 1973):136-7; J. L. Gaddis, JAH,
60(Dec 1973):855-7.

Rose, Michael E. The Relief of Poverty 1834-1914. London: Macmillan, 1972. Rev. by P. Thane, History, 58(Feb 1973):117.

Rose, Richard. Governing Without Consensus: An Irish Perspective. Boston: Beacon, 1971. Rev. by T. A. Faughnan,
E-I, 8(Win 1973):126-8.

Roselle, Daniel and Anne P. Young. Our Western Heritage: A
Cultural-Analytic History of Europe Since 1500. Lexington,
Mass.: Ginn, 1972. Rev. by A. M. Kubersky, SS, 64(Nov
1973):279.

Rosenbaum, H. Jon and William G. Tyler, eds. Contemporary
Brazil: Issues in Economic and Political Development. New
York: Praeger, 1972. Rev. by W. Baer, HAHR, 53(May
1973):350-3.

Rosenbaum, Jürgen. Frankreich in Tunesien: Die Anfänge des Pro-
tektorates 1881-1886. Zürich and Freiburg: Atlantis, 1971.
Rev. by R. M. Brace, JMH, 45(Sep 1973):518; H. J.
Liebesny, MEJ, 27(Aut 1973):524-5.

Rosenberg, Carroll Smith. Religion and the Rise of the American
City: The New York City Mission Movement, 1812-1870.
Ithaca, N. Y.: Cornell U Press, 1971. Rev. by S. E.
Ahlstrom, AHR, 78(Oct 1973):1127-30; M. Simpson, History,
58(Oct 1973):490.

Rosenberg, Morton M. Iowa on the Eve of the Civil War: A De-
cade of Frontier Politics. Norman: U Ok Press, 1972.
Rev. by M. B. Husband, Montana, 23(Win 1973):62-3; E. H.
Berwanger, PHR, 42(May 1973):250-1.

Rosenberg, Nathan. Technology and American Economic Growth.
New York: Harper and Row, 1972. Rev. by A. D. Anderson, BHR, 47(Aut 1973):376-8; W. N. Parker, JAH, 60(Je

271   ROSENBERGER

1973):107-9; J. F. Hanieski, JEH, 33(Dec 1973):903-4; H.
F. Williamson, T & C, 14(Ja 1973):83.

Rosenberger, Francis Coleman, ed. Records of the Columbia Historical Society of Washington, D. C. Washington, D. C.:
Columbia Historical Society, 1971. Rev. by M. J. Boyer,
PH, 40(Ja 1973):112-13; D. P. Jordan, WVH, 34(Apr 1973):
303-5.

Rosenberger, Homer T. Adventures and Philosophy of a Pennsylvania Dutchman: An Autobiography in a Broad Setting. Belle-
fonte, Pa.: Pa Heritage, 1971. Rev. by M. E. Gladfelter,
PH, 40(Ja 1973):110-12.

Rosenkrantz, Barbara Gutmann and William A. Koelsch. American
Habitat: An Historical Perspective. New York: Free Press,
1973. Rev. by R. A. Bartlett, HRNB, 2(Nov/Dec 1973):46.

Rosenthal, Donald B. The Limited Elite: Politics and Government
in Two Indian Universities. Chicago: U Chi Press, 1970.
Rev. by R. S. Arora, IQ, 29(Jl-Sep 1973):275-6.

Rosenthal, Eric, comp. and ed. Encyclopedia of Southern Africa.
London: Frederick Warne, 1973. Rev. by J. L., AfAf, 72
(Jl 1973):346-7.

Rosenthal, Joel T. The Purchase of Paradise: Gift Giving and the
Aristocracy, 1307-1485. Toronto: U Tor Press, 1972. Rev.
by J. W. Baldwin, AHR 78(Dec 1973):1438-9.

Rosenwaike, Ira. Population History of New York City. Syracuse,
N. Y.: Syr U Press, 1972. Rev. by R. V. Wells, AHR,
78(Oct 1973):1121; S. J. Mandelbaum, JAH, 60(Je 1973):165-
6; L. Hershkowitz, NYH, 54(Apr 1973):251-2; J. H. Cas-
sedy, PMHB, 97(Apr 1973):282-3.

Roseveare, Henry. The Treasury: The Evolution of a British Institution. New York: Columbia U Press, 1969. Rev. by
R. M. MacLeod, AHR, 78(Dec 1973):1386-1405.

Roskill, Stephen. Hankey: Man of Secrets. Vol. II, 1919-1931.
London: Collins, 1972. Rev. by J. J. Naylor, HJ, 16(Sep
1973):650-2; J. Gooch, History, 58(Je 1973):323.

Ross, B. Joyce. J. E. Spingarn and the Rise of the N A A C P,
1911-1939. New York: Atheneum, 1972. Rev. by J. M.
McPherson, AHR, 78(Oct 1973):1141-2; J. W. Ivy, Crisis,
80(Oct 1973):281-2; D. M. Tucker, JAH, 60(Je 1973):167-8;
C. F. Kellogg, JSH 39(Aug 1973):461-3.

Ross, Dorothy. G. Stanley Hall: The Psychologist as Prophet.
Chicago: U Chi Press, 1972. Rev. by H. Hawkins, AHR,
78(Feb 1973):173; G. N. Grob, JAH, 60(Sep 1973):477-8.

Ross, Eric. Beyond the River and the Bay. Toronto: U Tor
    Press, 1970. Rev. by G. Milburn, HT, 6(Feb 1973):324-5.

Ross, Ian Simpson. Lord Kames and the Scotland of His Day. New
    York: Ox U Press, 1972. Rev. by D. Greene, AHR, 78(Je
    1973):686; D. Forbes, HJ, 16(Dec 1973):868-9.

Ross, Steven T. European Diplomatic History, 1789-1815. New
    York: Anchor, 1969. Rev. by C. C. Sturgill, MilAf, 37
    (Feb 1973):33.

Rossi, Lino. Trajan's Column and the Dacion Wars. Ithaca, N. Y.:
    Cornell U Press, 1971. Rev. by D. W. Wade, AHR, 78(Feb
    1973):78-9.

Rossi, Peter H. see Boesel, David

Rosskam, Edwin. Roosevelt, New Jersey: Big Dreams in a Small
    Town and What Time Did to Them. New York: Grossman,
    1972. Rev. by K. T. Jackson, NJH, 91(Sum 1973):125-9.

Rossmann, Rudolf H. Schuss und Kette: Geschichte der "Sulzer"--
    Webmaschine. Dusseldorf: V D I--Verlag, 1971. Rev. H.
    Freudenberger, T & C, 14(Apr 1973):312-13.

Rostow, W. W. Politics and the Stages of Growth. New York: Cam
    U Press, 1971. Rev. by A. G. Frank, HAHR, 56(Nov 1973):
    663-7.

Roth, Guenther and Reinhard Bendix. Scholarship and Partisanship:
    Essays on Max Weber. Berkeley: U Cal Press, 1971. Rev.
    by J. Kornborg, CHR, 54(Mar 1973):75-9.

Roth, Hal. Two on a Big Ocean. New York: Macmillan, 1972.
    Rev. by D. G. Kelley, AW, 10(Mar 1973):58.

Rothberg, Abraham. The Heirs of Stalin: Dissidence and the Soviet
    Regime, 1953-1970. Ithaca, N. Y.: Cornell U Press, 1972.
    Rev. by W. Leonhard, RR, 32(Ja 1973):85-6.

Rothfels, Hans. Bismarck. Stuttgart: Verlag W. Kohlhammer,
    1970. Rev. by M. Sturmer, ESR, 3(Apr 1973):189-91.

Rothman, David J. The Discovery of the Asylum: Social Order and
    Disorder in the New Republic. Boston: Little, Brown, 1971.
    Rev. by D. M. Reimers, NJH, 91(Aut 1973):270-1; W. D.
    Lewis, PH, 40(Jl 1973):341-2; J. M. Holl, WMQ, 3rd ser.,
    30(Apr 1973):368-70.

Rothstein, William G. American Physicians in the Nineteenth Cen-
    tury: From Sects to Science. Baltimore: JHU Press, 1972.
    Rev. by M. Kaufman, JAH, 60(Je 1973):142-4; G. N. Grob,
    MHM, 68(Fall 1973):346-7.

Rothwell, V. H   British War Aims and Peace Diplomacy 1914-1918.
    Oxford: Ox U Press, 1971. Rev. by K. Robbins, History,
    58(Feb 1973):132; M. Swartz, JMH, 45(Mar 1973):164-6.

Rouse, J. K. The Noble Experiment of Warren C. Coleman. n.
    p.: Crabtree, 1972. Rev. by W. Conrad, NCHR, 50(Spr
    1973):204.

Rouse, Parke, Jr. The Great Wagon Road from Philadelphia to the
    South. New York: McGraw-Hill, 1973. Rev. by O. W.
    Holmes, VMHB, 81(Oct 1973):498-9.

_____. James Blair of Virginia. Chapel Hill: UNC Press, 1971.
    Rev. by A. C. Land, AHR, 78(Feb 1973):148-9.

Rousseau, André see Houtart, Francois

Roussel, Hubert. The Houston Symphony Orchestra, 1913-1971.
    Austin: U Tx Press, 1972. Rev. by W. Rundell, Jr.,
    SWHQ, 76(Apr 1973):497-8.

Rowe, J. G. and W. H. Stockdale, eds. Florilegium Historiale:
    Essays Presented to Wallace K. Ferguson. Toronto: U Tor
    Press 1971. Rev. by D. S. Chambers, History, 58(Feb
    1973):92-3; A. Molho, CHR, 54(Dec 1973):435-7.

Rowland, Peter. The Last Liberal Governments: Unfinished Busi-
    ness, 1911-1914. New York: St. Martin's, 1971. Rev. by
    P. Stansky, JMH, 45(Dec 1973):699-701.

Rowse, A. L. The Elizabethan Renaissance: The Life of the So-
    ciety. New York: Scribner's, 1971. Rev. by M. Lee, Jr.,
    AHR, 78(Feb 1973):97; W. G. Zeeveld, AHR, 78(Je 1973):
    680-1; G. Williams, History, 58(Je 1973):281.

The Royal Commission on Historical Monuments (England). An In-
    ventory of Historical Monuments in the County of Cambridge.
    Vol. 2. North East Cambridgeshire. London: HMSO, 1972.
    Rev. by P. Bicknell, Antiquity, 47(Je 1973):160-1; B. Cun-
    liffe, Antiquity, 47(Sep 1973):242-3.

Royal Institution of Great Britain. Archives. Minutes of Managers'
    Meetings, 1799-1900. Menston, Ilkley, Yorkshire: Scolar
    Press, 1971. Rev. by A. Thackray, T & C, 14(Jl 1973):
    531-2.

Rubin, Israel. Satmar: An Island in the City. Chicago: Quad-
    rangle, 1972. Rev. by M. Rischin, JAH, 59(Mar 1973):
    1042-3.

Rubin, Lillian B. Busing and Backlash: White Against White in an
    Urban California Community. Berkeley: U Cal Press, 1972.
    Rev. by C. Wollenberg, CHQ, 52(Spr 1973):85-6; I. G. Hen-

drick, PHR, 42(Nov 1973):592-4. NOTE: The Hendrick review cites thus: ... an Urban California School District.

Rubin, Louis D., Jr. The Writer in the South: Studies in a Literary Community. Athens, Ga.: U Ga Press, 1972. Rev.
by E. W. Hirshberg, FHQ, 52(Jl 1973):87-9; I. Malin, GR,
27(Spr 1973):128-31.

Rubinoff, Arthur C. India's Use of Force in Goa. Bombay: Popular Prakashan 1971. Rev. by T. G. Ramamurthi, IQ, 29
(Ja-Mar 1973):64-5.

Ruby, Robert H. and John A. Brown. The Cayuse Indians: Imperial Tribesmen of Old Oregon. Norman: U Ok Press,
1972. Rev. by E. Leacock, AHR, 78(Dec 1973):1531-2; J.
C. Bower, AW, 10(Ja 1973):51; D. H. Stratton, Montana,
23(Aut 1973):75; K. A. Murray, PHR, 42(Feb 1973):110-11.

Ruchames, Louis, ed. The Letters of William Lloyd Garrison, II,
A House Dividing Against Itself. Cambridge, Mass.: Belknap
Press, Har U Press, 1971. Rev. by R. G. Walters, MHM,
68(Spr 1973):108-9.

Rudé, George. Europe in the Eighteenth Century: Aristocracy and
the Bourgeois Challenge. New York: Praeger, 1972. Rev.
by L. Gershoy, AHR, 78(Dec 1973):1450-1; J. Richardson,
HTo, 23(Feb 1973):144-5.

_____. The History of London: Hanoverian London, 1714-1808.
London: Secker and Warburg; Toronto: William Heineman,
1971. Rev. by J. Norris, CHR, 54(Sep 1973):317-9.

_____. Paris and London in the Eighteenth Century: Studies in
Popular Protest. New York: Viking, 1971. Rev. by R.
Forster, JMH, 45(Mar 1973):113-15.

Rudolph, S. H. and L. I., eds. Education and Politics in India:
Studies in Organization, Society and Policy. New Delhi: Ox
U Press, 1972. Rev. by J. K. Ray, IQ, 29(Jl-Sep 1973):
271-3.

Rudwick, Elliot see Meier, August

Rudych, F. M., et al., eds. Kiev Province. Kiev: Institut
Istorii Akademii Nauk URSR, 1971. Rev. by J. A. Armstrong, AHR, 78(Je 1973):716.

Rumpler, Helmut. Die Protokolle des österreichischen Ministerrates
(1848-1867): Einleitungsband, Ministerrat und Ministerrats-
protokolle, 1848-1867. Vienna: Österreichischer Bundesver-
lag für Unterricht, Wissenschaft und Kunst, 1970. Rev. by
R. J. Rath, JMH, 45(Je 1973):327-8.

Runkle, Gerald. Anarchism: Old and New. New York: Dell, 1972.
    Rev. by R. L. Hoffman, SS, 64(Nov 1973):282.

Russell, Conrad. The Crisis of Parliament: English History 1509-
    1660. Oxford: Ox U Press, 1971. Rev. by M. E. James,
    History, 58(Feb 1973):94-5.

Russell, Jeffrey Burton. Witchcraft in the Middle Ages. Ithaca,
    N. Y.: Cornell U Press, 1972. Rev. by H. C. E. Midel-
    fort, AHR, 78(Oct 1973):1030-1; R. H. West, GR, 27(Spr
    1973):137-41.

Russell, Josiah Cox. Medieval Regions and Their Cities. Bloom-
    ington: Ind U Press, 1972. Rev. by D. Herlihy, JIH, 4(Aut
    1973):299-302.

Russell, Phillips. These Old Stone Walls. Durham: Seeman ...
    1972. Rev. by A. E. Taylor, NCHR, 50(Spr 1973):199-200.

Russell, Ross. Jazz Style in Kansas City and the Southwest. Berk-
    eley: U Cal Press, 1971. Rev. by E. F. Dyson, JNH, 58
    (Apr 1973):221-2.

Russett, Bruce N. No Clear and Present Danger: A Skeptical View
    of the United States Entry into World War II. New York:
    Harper and Row, 1972. Rev. by D. M. Smith, JAH, 60(Sep
    1973):503-4; J. L. Gaddis, MilAf, 37(Dec 1973):160.

Russian-American Scholars, Association of. Transactions of the
    Association of Russian-American Scholars in the U. S. A.,
    Vol. V. New York: n. p., 1971. Rev. by N. V. Riasa-
    novsky, RR, 32(Ja 1973):103-4.

Rutherford, John. Mexican Society During the Revolution: A Lit-
    erary Approach. New York and London: Clarendon Press,
    1971. Rev. by R. E. Ruiz, HAHR, 53(Aug 1973):518-19; M.
    P. Costeloe, History, 58(Oct 1973):483.

Rutland, Robert A., et al. The Papers of James Madison. Vol. 8.
    10 March 1784-28 March 1786. Chicago: U Chi Press, 1973.
    Rev. by R. L. Ketcham, JSH, 39(Nov 1973):586-8.

Ruttan, Vernon W. see Hayami, Yujiro

Rydjord, John. Kansas Place Names. Norman: U Ok Press, 1972.
    Rev. by H. E. Socolofsky, JOW, 12(Ja 1973):189; J. W.
    Snell, Montana, 23(Sum 1973):54.

Rynin, N. A. Interplanetary Flight and Communication. 9 vols.
    Jerusalem: Israel Program for Scientific Translations, 1970-
    71. Rev. by L. S. Swenson, Jr., T & C, 14(Apr 1973):317-
    23.

Sabean, David Warren. Landbesitz und Gesellschaft am Vorabend des Bavernkriegs: Eine studie der sozialen Verhältnisse im Südlichen Oberschwaben in den Jahren vor 1525. Stuttgart: Gustiv Fischer Verlag, 1972. Rev. by L. K. Berkner, AgH, 47(Apr 1973):176-7.

Sabine, William H. W. Murder, 1776 and Washington's Policy of Silence. Brooklyn: Gaus', n. d. Rev. by A. Keller, AHI, 8(Dec 1973):49-50.

Sable Martin H. Latin American Urbanization: A Guide to the Literature, Organizations and Personnel. Metuchen, N. J.: Scarecrow, 1971. Rev. by F. M. Trueblood, HAHR, 53(Feb 1973):119-20.

Sachar, Abram. The Course of Our Times: Men and Events That Shaped the Twentieth Century. New York: Knopf, 1972. Rev. by B. C. Shafer, Historian, 36(Nov 1973):140-1.

Sachar, Howard M. Europe Leaves the Middle East, 1936-1954. New York: Knopf, 1972. Rev. by J. A. Crabbs, Jr., JMH, 45(Dec 1973):717; H. N. Howard, MEJ, 27(Spr 1973):220-1.

Sacoto, Antonio. El indio en el ensayo de la América Española. New York: Las Americas Publishing Co., 1971. Rev. by I. A. Leonard, HAHR, 53(Aug 1973):557-8.

Sá de Meneses, Francisco de. The Conquest of Malacca. Kuala Lumpar, Malaysia: U Malaysia Press, 1970. Rev. by C. E. Nowell, HAHR, 53(Aug 1973):564-5.

Sage, Bryan L. Alaska and Its Wildlife. New York: Viking, 1973. Rev. by T. C. Hinckley, AW, 10(Nov 1973):49.

Sainty, J. C., comp. Office Holders in Modern Britain. Vol. 1: Treasury Officials, 1660-1870. London: Athlone, 1973. Rev. by H. Pelling, Archives, 11(Spr 1973):53; H. G. Roseveare, History, 58(Oct 1973):418.

Sale, Kirkpatrick. S D S. New York: Random House, 1973. Rev. by S. Lynd, JAH, 60(Dec 1973):863-5.

Salisbury, Harrison E. To Peking--and Beyond: A Report on the New Asia. New York: Quadrangle, 1973. Rev. by A. Z. Rubenstein, CurH, 64(May 1973):225; C. Smith, PacH, 17 (Fall 1973):67-8.

Salsbury, Stephen see Chandler, Alfred, Jr.

Salter, Anne and Phyllis Wolf. The Calendar of the Claude Elliott Collection, 1821-1937. Austin: Texas State Library, 1971. Rev. by A. L. Nolen, AmArch, 36(Ja 1973):76-8.

Salum-Flecha, Antonio. Historia diplomatica del Paraguay: De
1869 a 1938. Asunción, Paraguay: EMASA, 1972. Rev. by
D. J. Vodarsik, HAHR, 53(Feb 1973):142-3.

Sampson, Roy J., William P. Mortenson, and Ira Marienhoff. The
American Economy: Analysis, Issues, Principles. Boston:
Houghton Mifflin, 1972. Rev. by R. M. Fitch, SS, 64(Apr
1973):184-5.

Sand, George X. The Everglades Today: Endangered Wilderness.
New York: Four Winds, 1972. Rev. by T. Peters, FHQ,
51(Ja 1973):314-15.

Sandeen, Ernest. The Roots of Fundamentalism: British and American Millenarianism 1800-1930. Chicago: U Chi Press, 1971.
Rev. by C. Garrett, PH, 40(Ja 1973):105-6.

Sanders, Mary Elizabeth, comp. Annotated Abstracts of the Successions of St. Mary Parish, Louisiana, 1811-1834. n. p.,
1972. Rev. by G. A. Bodin LaH, 14(Fall 1973):404.

Sanderson, M. The Universities and British Industry, 1850-1970.
London: Routledge and Kegan Paul, 1972. Rev. by R. A.
Lowe, MH, 2(Aut 1973):127-8.

Sanderson, Michael and Derek Howse. The Sea Chart, An Histor-
ical Survey Based on the Collections in the National Maritime
Museum. New York: McGraw-Hill, 1973. Rev. by L. A.
P., IS, 29(Fall 1973):234.

Sanger, Marjory Bartlett. Billy Bartram and His Green World: An
Interpretative Biography. New York: Farrar, Straus and
Giroux, 1972. Rev. by W. Blassingame, FHQ, 51(Ja 1973):
310-11.

Sankhdher, M. M. Reflections on Indian Politics. New Delhi:
Kumar, 1973. Rev. by K. C. Kohli, IQ, 29(Jl-Sep 1973):
274.

Sansom, Katherine. Sir George Sansom and Japan, A Memoir.
Tallahassee: Diplomatic Press, 1972. Rev. by G. B. Bikle,
Jr., Historian, 35(Feb 1973):300-1; H. Conroy, AHR, 78
(Dec 1973):1515-16.

Sappington, Roger E. The Brethren in the Carolinas: The History
of the Church of the Brethren in the District of North and
South Carolina. Kingsport, Tenn.: Watson Litho ... n. d.
Rev. by W. H. Allen, Jr., NCHR, 50(Sum 1973):326-7.

_____. Reuel B. Pritchett: Churchman and Antiquarian. Harris-
burg, Va.: Park View Press, for Author, 1972. Rev. by
J. L. Bell, Jr., NCHR, 50(Sum 1973):331-2.

Sarduy, Severo.   From Cuba With a Song.   New York: Dutton,
     1967.   Rev. by R. D. Souza, HAHR, 53(Nov 1973):732.

Sarti, Roland.   Fascism and the Industrial Leadership in Italy, 1919-
     1940.   Berkeley: U Cal Press, 1971.   Rev. by A. Cassels,
     CHR, 54(Mar 1973):108-9;   R. A. H. Robinson, History, 58
     (Feb 1973):135.

Sauer, Carl Ortwin.   Sixteenth-Century North America: The Land
     and the People as Seen by Europeans.   Berkeley: U Cal
     Press, 1971.   Rev. by R. Nash, AgH, 47(Apr 1973):167-8;
     J. D. Ware, FHQ, 51(Apr 1973):447-9.

Saunders, J. J.   The History of the Mongol Conquests.   London:
     Routledge and Kegan Paul, 1971.   Rev. by D. S. M. Wil-
     liams, 58(Je 1973):255-6;   E. D. Phillips, Antiquity, 47(Mar
     1973):81-2.

Sautter, Udo.   Geschichte Kanadas: Das Werden einer Nation.
     Stuttgart: Alfred Kroner Verlag, 1972.   Rev. by L. D.
     Stokes, CHR, 54(Dec 1973):439-40.

Saville, John see Briggs, Asa

Saxena, J. N.   Amending Procedures of the Constituent Instruments
     of International Organizations.   Delhi: Dhanwantra Medical
     and Law Book House, 1972.   Rev. by K. Mathews, IQ, 29
     (Apr-Je 1973):159-60.

Saxton, Alexander.   The Indispensable Enemy: Labor and the Anti-
     Chinese Movement in California.   Berkeley: U Cal Press,
     1971.   Rev. by P. S. Holbo, AHR, 78(Feb 1973):176-7;   R.
     Jeffreys-Jones, History, 58(Feb 1973):154.

Saywell, John.   Quebec 70: A Documentary Narrative.   Toronto: U
     Tor Press, 1971.   Rev. by D. Smiley, CHR, 54(Mar 1973):
     92-3.

Scalapino, Robert A. and Chong-sik Lee.   Communism in Korea.
     Part 1.   The Movement.   Part 2.   The Society.   Berkeley:
     U Cal Press, 1972.   Rev. by A. W. Burks, AHR, 78(Dec
     1973):1516-17.

Scarborough, William Kauffman, ed.   The Diary of Edmund Ruffin.
     Vol. 1.   Toward Independence, October, 1856-April, 1861.
     Baton Rouge: LSU Press, 1972.   Rev. by C. D. Lowery,
     MHM, 68(Sum 1973):225;   N. L. Peterson, JSH, 39(Feb
     1973):121-3;   D. L. Smiley, NCHR, 50(Win 1973):98-9;   T. S.
     Berry, VMHB, 81(Jl 1973):375-6;   GHQ, 57(Spr 1973):158-9;
     J. H. Moore, FHQ, 52(Oct 1973):200-1;   J. H. Dorman,
     JMiH, 35(Aug 1973):329-31;   T. A. Comp, AgH, 47(Oct
     1973):353-4.

Schapsmeier, Edward L. and Frederick H. Prophet in Politics:
Henry A. Wallace and the War Years, 1940-1965. Ames,
Ia.: Ia St U Press, 1970. Rev. by B. Bellush, AHR, 78
(Dec 1973):1550.

Scheips, Paul J. Hold the Fort! The Story of a Song from the Sawdust Trail to the Picket Line. Washington: Smithsonian Institution Press, 1971. Rev. by V. A. Carrafiello, MilAf, 37
(Feb 1973):34.

Schick, Jack M. The Berlin Crisis, 1958-1962. Philadelphia: U Pa
Press, 1971. Rev. by E. Ions, History, 58(Oct 1973):478;
R. W. Carden, JMH, 45(Mar 1973):187-8.

Schieder, Theodor and Peter Burian, eds. Sozialstruktur und Organisation europaischer Nationalbewegun. Munich: R. Oldenbourg, 1971. Rev. by P. N. Stearns, JMH, 45(Mar 1973):
127-8.

Schiffers, Reinhard. Elemente direkter Demokratie im Weimarer
Regierungssystem. Düsseldorf: Droste Verlag, 1971. Rev.
by F. C. West, JMH, 45(Sep 1973):541-2.

Schirmer, Daniel B. Republic or Empire: American Resistence to
the Philippine War. Cambridge, Mass.: Schenkman, 1972.
Rev. by W. Le Feber, JAH, 59(Mar 1973):1022-3; E. B.
Tompkins, PHR, 42(Feb 1973):123-4.

Schiwetz, E. M. "Buck." The Schiwetz Legacy: An Artist's Tribute
to Texas, 1910-1971. Austin: U Tx Press, 1972. Rev. by
B. Delabano, SWHQ, 76(Apr 1973):500-1.

Schlebecker, John T. Agricultural Implements and Machines in the
Collection of the National Museum of History and Technology.
Washington, D. C.: Smithsonian Institution Press 1972. Rev.
by D. P. Kelsey, AgH, 47(Oct 1973):348-9.

_____ and Gale E. Peterson. Living Historical Farms Handbook.
Washington, D. C.: Smithsonian Institution Press, 1972. Rev.
by R. J Romani, AgH, 47(Oct 1973):349-50.

Schleifer, Abdullah. The Fall of Jerusalem. New York: Monthly
Review Press 1972. Rev. in CurH, 64(Ja 1973):34.

Schlenther, Boyd S., ed. The Life and Writings of Francis Makemie.
Philadelphia: Presbyterian Historical Society, 1971. Rev. by
A. W. Genderbien, PH, 40(Ja 1973):97-8.

Schmitt, Karl M., ed. The Roman Catholic Church in Modern Latin
America. New York: Knopf, 1972. Rev. by S. Shapiro,
HAHR, 53(May 1973):345-6.

Schnabel, James F. United States Army in the Korean War: Policy

SCHOENER 280

and Direction: The First Year. Washington, D. C.: Office
of the Chief of Military History, 1972. Rev. by R. R. Simmons, PHR, 42(Nov 1973):597-8.

Schoener, Allon, ed. Portal to America: The Lower East Side,
1870-1925. New York: Holt, Rinehart and Winston, 1972.
Rev. by M. H. Haller, SS, 64(Mar 1973):140-1.

Schoenfeld, Maxwell Philip. The War Ministry of Winston Churchill.
Ames, Ia.: Ia St U Press, 1972. Rev. by S. Roskill,
Archives, 11(Spr 1973):58-9; F. X. J. Homer, HT, 7(Nov
1973):140; A. Gollin, JMH, 45(Dec 1973):703.

Schölch, Alexander. Ägypten den Ägypten!: Die Politische und Ge-
sellschaftliche Krise der Jahre 1878-1882 in Ägypten. Zurich
& Freiburg: Atlantis Verlag, 1973. Rev. by P. Bechtold,
MEJ, 27(Sum 1973):409.

Schonberger, Howard B. Transportation to the Seaboard: The "Communication Revolution" and American Foreign Policy, 1860-
1900. Westport, Conn.: Greenwood, 1971. Rev. by J. P.
Huttman, AgH, 47(Apr 1973):174-6; R. C. Black, III, AHR,
78(Dec 1973):1533-4.

Schorsch, Ismar. Jewish Reactions to German Anti-Semitism, 1870-
1914. New York: Columbia U Press, 1972. Rev. by R. S.
Levy, JMH, 45(Sep 1973):524.

Schottelius, Herbert and Wilhelm Deist, eds. Marine und Marinepolitik im kaiserlichen Deutschland, 1871-1914. Dusseldorf:
Droste Verlag, 1972. Rev. by K. W. Bird, AHR, 78(Dec
1973):1488.

Schou, A. and A. O. Brundtland, eds. Small States in International
Relations. Stockholm: Almqvist and Wiksell, 1971. Rev. by
S. L. Poplai, IQ, 29(Ja-Mar 1973):59-60.

Schroeder, Paul W. Austria, Great Britain and the Crimean War.
Ithaca, N. Y.: Cornell U Press, 1972. Rev. by W. E.
Mosse, HJ, 16(Dec 1973):875-6; E. L. Presseisen, JMH,
45(Dec 1973):692-3.

Schruben, Francis W. Wea Creek to El Dorado: Oil in Kansas,
1860-1920. Columbia, Mo.: U Mo Press, 1972. Rev. by
F. J. Munch JEH, 33(Dec 1973):904-6; G. D. Nash, PHR,
42(Feb 1973):115-16; J. G. Clark, SWHQ, 76(Apr 1973):498-9.

Schücking, Levin L. The Puritan Family: A Social Study From the
Literary Sources. London: Routledge and Kegan Paul, 1969.
Rev. by N. R. N. Tyacke, History 58(Je 1973):287-8.

Schug, Willis E., ed. United States Law and the Armed Forces:

Cases and Materials on Constitutional Law, Courts-Martial
and the Rights of Servicemen. New York: Praeger, 1972.
Rev. by D. F. Harrison, MilAf, 37(Oct 1973):109.

Schüler, Winfried. Der bayreuther Kreis von seiner Entstehung bis
zum Ausgang der wilhelminischen Ära: Wagnerkult und Kulturreform im Geist völkischer Weltanschauung. Münster:
Verlag Aschendorff, 1971. Rev. by W. M. Johnston, JMH,
45(Je 1973):326.

Schull, Joseph. Rebellion: The Rising of French Canada 1837.
Toronto: Macmillan, 1971. Rev. by G. H. Patterson, CHR,
54(Mar 1973):84-5.

Schults, Raymond L. Crusader in Babylon: W. T. Stead and the
"Pall Mall Gazette." Lincoln: U Neb Press, 1972. Rev.
by J. H. Wiener, JMH, 45(Dec 1973):681.

Schultheiss, Thomas, ed. Russian Studies, 1941-1958. A Cumula-
tion of the Annual Bibliographies from The Russian Review.
Ann Arbor, Mich.: Pierian, 1972. Rev. by W. B. Walsh,
RR, 32(Jl 1973):334.

Schultz, George A. An Indian Canaan: Isaac McCoy and the Vision
of an Indian State. Norman: U Ok Press, 1972. Rev. by
J. B. Harte, A & W, 15(Aut 1973):300-2; H. J. Viola, JAH,
60(Sep 1973):435-7; G. Lux, JOW, 12(Oct 1973):650; M.
Young PHR, 42(Nov 1973):580-2; D. Van, WHQ, 4(Oct 1973):
464-6.

Schulz, Gerhard. Revolutions and Peace Treaties, 1917-1920. London: Methuen, 1972. Rev. by V. H. Rothwell, History, 58
(Oct 1973):468; F. G. Campbell, JMH, 45(Sep 1973):536-9.

Schulze, Hagen, ed. Das Kabinett Scheidemann: 13. Februar bis
20. Juni 1919. Boppard am Rhein: Harald Boldt Verlag,
1971. Rev. by H. A. Turner, Jr., AHR, 78(Dec 1973):1489-
90.

Schwabe, Klaus. Deutsche Revolution und Wilson-Frieden: Die
amerikanische und deutsche Friedensstrategie zwischen Ideologie und Machtpolitik 1918/19. Dusseldorf: Droste Verlag,
1971. Rev. by M. Jonas, AHR, 78(Oct 1973):1018-19; H. W.
Koch, History, 58(Je 1973):319-20; F. G. Campbell, JMH,
45(Sep 1973):536-9.

Schwartz, Bernard. From Confederation to Nation: The American
Constitution, 1835-1877. Baltimore: JHU Press, 1973. Rev.
by D. O. Dewey, HRNB, 2(Oct 1973):13.

Schwartz, Pedro. The New Political Economy of J. S. Mill. Durham, Duke U Press, 1972. Rev. by T. W. Hutchinson, AHR,
78(Dec 1973):1452-3.

Schwartz, Richard B. Samuel Johnson and the New Science. Madison: U Wis Press, 1971. Rev. by M. C. Jacob, AHR, 78 (Je 1973):686-7.

Schwarz, Jordan A. The Interregnum of Despair: Hoover, Congress and the Depression. London: U Ill Press, 1971. Rev. by C. Braham, History, 58(Oct 1973):496.

Scobie, J. R. Argentina: A City and a Nation. New York: Ox U Press, 1971. Rev. by T. F. McG., HAHR, 53(Aug 1973): 571-2.

Scott, Roy V. The Reluctant Farmer: The Rise of Agricultural Extension to 1914. Urbana: U Ill Press, 1970. Rev. by W. D. Barns, AHR, 78(Je 1973):728; M. Kuhn, MichH, 57(Spr 1973): 87-8; C. S. Peterson, WHQ, 4(Ja 1973):75-6.

Scott, Winfield Townley. The Literary Notebooks of Winfield Townley Scott, "A Dirty Hand." Austin: U Tx Press, 1969. Rev. by H. G. McCurdy, GR, 27(Spr 1973):132-4.

Scoufopoulos, Niki C. Mycenaean Citadels. Gothenburg: Paul Åström, 1971. Rev. by W. D. Taylor, Antiquity, 47(Mar 1973):83.

Scruggs, Philip Lightfoot. Lynchburg, Virginia ... 'Its Industry, Enterprise and Correct Course." Lynchburg, Va.: J. P. Bell, 1972. Rev. by R. W. Church, VMHB, 81(Ja 1973): 109-10.

Seager, Robin. Tiberias. Berkeley: U Cal Press; London: Eyre Methuen, 1972. Rev. by S. J. Simon, Historian, 35(Feb 1973):276-7; A. E. Astin, History, 58(Je 1973):250.

Sebüktekin, Hikmet. Turkish-English Contrastive Analysis. The Hague: Mouton, 1971. Rev. by T. S. Halman, MEJ, 27(Spr 1973):240-1.

Seckler, David, ed. California Water: A Study in Resource Management. Berkeley: U Cal Press, 1971. Rev. by E. L. Schapsmeier, JOW, 12(Jl 1973):512.

Sedgwick, Romney, et al. The History of Parliament: The House of Commons, 1715-1754. New York: Ox U Press, 1970. Rev. by J. M. Price, JMH, 45(Mar 1973):109-10.

Seebold, Herman de Bachelle. Old Louisiana Plantation Homes and Families. 2 vols. Gretna, La.: Pelican, 1971. Rev. by M. D. Peoples, LAH, 14(Spr 1973):218-9.

Self, Huber see Socolosky, Homer E.

Sellers, Charles Coleman. Dickinson College: A History. Middletown, Conn.: Wes U Press, 1973. Rev. by R. Vassar, JAH, 60(Dec 1973):800-1.

_____. Charles Willson Peale. New York: Scribner's, 1969. Rev. by G. B. Warden, JIH, 4(Sum 1973):135-40.

_____ and Martha Calvert Slotten, comps. Archives and Manuscript Collections of Dickinson College. Carlisle, Pa.: Friends of Dickinson College Library, 1972. Rev. by K. J. Pike, AmArch, 36(Jl 1973):411-14.

Sen, Lalit K., ed. Readings on Micro-Level Planning and Rural Growth Centres. Hyderabad: National Institute of Community Development, 1972. Rev. by S. Venu, IQ, 29(Apr-Je 1973): 176-7.

Sen, S. P., ed. The Sino-Indian Border Question: A Historical Review. Calcutta: Institute of Historical Studies, 1971. Rev. by K. Gupta, IQ, 29(Oct-Dec 1973):367-70.

Senn, Alfred Erich. The Russian Revolution in Switzerland, 1914-1917. Madison: U Wis Press, 1971. Rev. by R. A. Wade, JMH, 45(Mar 1973):166-7.

Senn, Fritz, ed. New Lights on Joyce. Bloomington: Ind U Press, 1972. Rev. by A. O'Doire, E-I, 8(Sum 1973):153-4.

Sergio, Liza. A Measure Filled: The Life of Lena Madesin Phillips. New York: Robert B. Luce, 1972. Rev. by G. J. Roddey, FCHQ, 47(Ja 1973):62-3.

Serle, Geoffrey. The Rush to be Rich: A History of the Colony of Victoria, 1883-1889. Carlton: Melbourne U Press, 1971. Rev. by S. C. McCulloch AHR, 78(Feb 1973):138-9.

Service, John S. The Amerasia Papers: Some Problems in the History of U.S.-China Relations. Berkeley: Center for Chinese Studies, 1971. Rev. by T. L. Kennedy, PHR, 42 (Feb 1973):130-1.

Seth, K. L. Economic Prospects of Bangla Desh. New Delhi: Trimurthi, 1972. Rev. by V. K. Arora, IQ, 29(Jl-Sep 1973): 266-7.

Settle, Raymond W. and Mary L., eds. Overland Days to Montana in 1865: The Diary of Sarah Raymond and Journal of Dr. Ward Howard. Glendale, Cal.: Arthur H. Clark, 1971. Rev. by J. C. Schnell, A & W, 15(Spr 1973):97-8; M. J. Mates, Montana, 23(Spr 1973):66.

_____ and _____. Saddles and Spurs: The Pony Express Saga. Lincoln: U Neb Press, 1972. Rev. by J. H. Fowler, II, JOW, 12(Oct 1973):652.

Seward, Desmond. Prince of the Renaissance: The Golden Life of
    François I. New York: Macmillan, 1973. Rev. by E. I.
    Perry, HRNB, 2(Nov/Dec 1973):28; R. O'Day, HTo, 23(Nov
    1973):821-2.

Shaban, M. A. The Abbasid Revolution. New York: Cam U Press,
    1970. Rev. by R. W. Smith, AHR, 78(Feb 1973):133-4.

_____. Islamic History, A. D. 600-750 (A. H. 132): A New In-
    terpretation. New York: Cam U Press, 1971. Rev. by R.
    W. Smith, AHR, 78(Feb 1973):133-4; F. J. Ziahed, MEJ,
    27(Spr 1973):241-3.

Shade, William G. Banks or No Banks: The Money Issue in West-
    ern Politics, 1832-1865. Detroit: Wayne St U Press, 1972.
    Rev. by G. D. Green, BHR, 47(Win 1973):512-4.

Shafer, Boyd C. Faces of Nationalism: New Realities and Old
    Myths. New York: Harcourt Brace Jovanovich, 1972. Rev.
    by R. M. Berdahl, AHR, 78(Dec 1973):1423-5.

Shales, Tom, et al. The American Film Heritage: Impressions
    From the American Film Institute Archives. Washington:
    Acropolis Press, 1972. Rev. by W. T. Murphy, AmArch,
    36(Jl 1973):414-15.

Shanin, Theodor. The Awkward Class: Political Sociology of Pea-
    santry in a Developing Society: Russia, 1910-1925. Oxford:
    Ox U Press, 1972. Rev. by N. Stone, History, 58(Je 1973):
    322.

Shapp, Martha Glauber, ed. Lands and Peoples: Vol. I. Africa:
    Vol. II. Asia; Australia, New Zealand, Oceania; Vol. III.
    Europe; Vol. IV. Europe; Vol. V. North America; Vol.
    VI. South and Central America. Vol. VII. The World
    Facts and Figures With Index. New York: Grolier, 1972.
    Rev. by J. M. Hunter, SS, 64(Oct 1973):233-4.

Sharf, Andrew. Byzantine Jewry From Justinian to the Fourth
    Crusade. London: Routledge and Kegan Paul, 1971. Rev.
    by R. Browning, History, 58(Feb 1973):77-8.

Sharp, Daniel A. United States Policy and Peru. Austin: U Tx
    Press, 1972. Rev. by L. L. North, HAHR, 53(Aug 1973):
    545-6.

Sharp, Paul F. Whoop-Up Country. The Canadian-American West,
    1865-1885. Norman: U Ok Press, 1973. Rev. by V. R.
    Creel, ChOK, 51(Win 1973-1974):499-500.

Shaw, Bernard. Saint Joan, a Screenplay. Seattle: U Wash Press,
    1968. Rev. by M. Levin, E-I, 8(Win 1973):115-17.

Shaw, Thurston. Igbo Ukwu: An Account of Archaeological Dis-
coveries in Eastern Nigeria. Evanston: Northwestern U
Press, 1970. Rev. by E. Willett, Africa, 43(Ja 1973):88;
M. Posnansky, Archaeology, 26(Oct 1973):309-11.

Shay, C. Thomas. The Itasca Bison Kill Site: An Ecological Analysis. St. Paul: Minn Historical Society, 1971. Rev. by F.
Gorman, AmAnt, 38(Apr 1973):244-6.

Sheehan, Bernard W. Seeds of Extinction: Jeffersonian Philanthropy
and the American Indian. Chapel Hill: UNC Press ... 1973.
Rev. by K. A. Franks, GHQ, 57(Fall 1973):444-5; L. R.
Gerlach, NCHR, 50(Aut 1973):431-3; W. E. Washburn, PHR,
42(Nov 1973):579-80; T. B. Hetzel, PMHB, 97(Oct 1973):
543-4; C. F. Feest, VMHB, 81(Oct 1973):496-7; G. S.
Wood, WMQ, 3rd ser., 30(Oct 1973):658-61.

Sheil-Small Denis see James, Harold

Shenoy, Sudha R. Central Planning in India: A Critical Review.
New Delhi: Wiley Eastern, 1973. Rev. by N. C. Joshi, IQ,
29(Jl-Sep 1973):278.

Shepherd, James F. and Gary M. Walton. Shipping, Maritime
Trade, and the Economic Development of Colonial North
America. Cambridge: Cam U Press, 1972. Rev. by D.
Lindstrom, AgH, 47(Jl 1973):264-6; S. J. Crowther BHR,
47(Spr 1973):101-3; E. R. Green, History, 58(Oct 1973):
483-4; J. G. Lydon, JAH, 60(Sep 1973):424-6; A. C. Land,
JSH, 39(Aug 1973):431-2; R. L. Ehrlich, T & C, 14(Oct
1973):626-7; S. Engerman, WMQ, 3rd ser., 30(Apr 1973):
332-4.

Sheppard, David K. The Growth and Role of U K Financial Institutions, 1880-1962. London: Methuen, 1971. Rev. by J. K.
Horsefield, BHR, 47(Spr 1973):134-6.

Sheppard, Francis. London 1808-1870: The Infernal Wen. London:
Martin, Secker and Warberg; Berkeley: U Cal Press, 1971.
Rev. by G. Best, AHR, 78(Feb 1973):104-5; F. Bedarida,
EHR, 88(Jl 1973):605-12; P. Hollis, History, 58(Feb 1973):
126-7; P. G. Goheen, JMH, 45(Je 1973):316-17.

Sheppard, Thomas F. Lourmarin in the Eighteenth Century: A
Study of a French Village. Baltimore: JHU Press, 1971.
Rev. by T. W. Margadant, AgH, 47(Apr 1973):178-80; O.
Hufton, History, 58(Oct 1973):452.

Shepperson, Wilbur S. Restless Strangers: Nevada's Immigrants
and Their Interpreters. Reno: U Nev Press, 1970. Rev.
by L. J. Arrington, AHR, 78 (Feb 1973):167-8.

Sherman, Howard. Radical Political Economy: Capitalism and

Socialism From the Marxist-Humanist Perspective. New
York: Basic Books, 1972. Rev. by C. Perrow, SS, 64(Apr
1973):183-4.

Shillony, Ben-Ami. Revolt in Japan: The Young Officers and the
February 26, 1936 Incident. Princeton, N. J.: Prin U
Press, 1973. Rev. by A. D. Coox, HRNB, 2(Nov/Dec 1973):
35-6.

Shiloh, Ailon. By Myself I'm a Book! An Oral History of the Immigrant Jewish Experience in Pittsburgh. Waltham, Mass.:
Amer Jewish Historical Society, 1972. Rev. by M. H.
Ebner, AJHQ, 63(Sep 1973):98-100; J. E. Bodnar, WPHM,
56(Ja 1973):90-1.

Shineberg, Dorothy. They Came For Sandalwood: A Study of the
Sandalwood Trade in the Southwest Pacific 1830-1865. Mel-
bourne: Melbourne U Press, 1967. Rev. by J. M. Downs,
BHR, 47(Aut 1973):405-7.

Shipherd, Jacob R. History of the Oberlin-Wellington Rescue. New
York: Da Capo, 1972. Rev. by B. Clayton, WPHM, 56(Ja
1973):96-8.

Shipton, Clifford K. Biographical Sketches of Those Who Attended
Harvard College in the Classes 1764-1767. Boston: Mass
Historical Society, 1972. Rev. by L. J. Cappon, AHR, (Oct
1973):1122-3.

Shklovsky, Viktor. Mayakovsky and His Circle. New York: Dodd,
Mead, 1972; Rev. by R. Sheldon, RR, 32(Oct 1973):445-6.

Shogan, Robert. A Question of Judgment: The Fortas Case and the
Struggle for the Supreme Court. Indianapolis: Bobbs-Merrill, 1972. Rev. by E. A. Purcell, Jr., AHR, 78(Feb 1973):
181.

Shokeid, Moshe. The Dual Heritage: Immigrants from the Atlas
Mountains in an Israeli Village. Manchester: Manchester U
Press, 1971. Rev. by A. Weingrod, MEJ, 27(Spr 1973):
237-9.

Shook, Lawrence K. Catholic Post-Secondary Education in English-
Speaking Canada. Toronto: U Tor Press, 1971. Rev. by
M. R. Lupol, CHR, 54(Mar 1973):88-90.

Shorter, Alfred H. Paper Making in the British Isles. Newton Abbot: David and Charles, 1971. Rev. by T. C. Barker, History, 58(Feb 1973):145.

Shorter, Aylward. Chiefship in Western Tanzania: A Political History of the Kimbu. Oxford: Ox U Press, 1972. Rev. by R.
Abrahams, AfAf, 72(Jl 1973):341-2; A. Roberts, JAfH, 14(Num.
4 1973):701-2.

_____ . Nyungu-ya-Mawe. Nairobi: East African Publishing
House, 1969. Rev. by A. Redmayne, AfAf, 72(Ja 1973):91-3.

Shorter, Edward. The Historian and the Computer. Englewood
Cliffs, N. J.: Prentice-Hall, 1971. Rev. by R. P. Swierenga, CHR, 54(Mar 1973):80-2.

Shular, Antonia Castañeda, et al. Chicano Literature: Text and
Context. (trans. from Spanish). Englewood Cliffs, N. J.:
Prentice-Hall, 1972. Rev. by L. Litvak, HAHR, 53(May
1973):263-5.

Shumaker, Wayne. The Occult Sciences in the Renaissance: A Study
in Intellectual Patterns. Berkeley: U Cal Press, 1972. Rev.
by R. H. West, GR, 27(Spr 1973):137-41.

Shur L. A. To the Shores of the New World: From Unpublished
Reports of Russian Travelers at the Beginning of the 19th
Century. Moscow: Izdatel'stvo "Nauka," 1971. Rev. by
W. L. Sarafian, AHR, 78(Dec 1973):1426.

Sibley, Marilyn McAdams. George W. Brackenridge: Maverick
Philanthropist. Austin: U Tx Press, 1973. Rev. by T. V.
DiBacco, HRNB, 2(Nov/Dec 1973):51-2.

Siddiqi, Noman Ahmad. Land Revenue Administration Under the
Mughals (1700-1750). New York: Asia Publishing House ...
1970. Rev. by F. Lehmann, AHR, 78(Je 1973):721-3.

Siegenthaler, Hansjörg. Das Gewicht Monopolistischer Elemente in
Der Amerikanischen Textilindustrie, 1840-1880. Berlin: Duncker and Humbolt, 1972. Rev. by H. Jaeger, BHR, 47(Aut
1973):525-6.

Sigmann, Jean. 1848. The Romantic and Democratic Revolutions in
Europe. London: Allen and Unwin, 1973. Rev. by J. Richardson, HTo, 23(Je 1973):446.

Silva, Hélio. 1889. A República não esperou o amanhecer. Rio
de Janeiro, Brazil: Editóra Civilazacão Brasileira, 1972.
Rev. by E.-S. Pang, HAHR, 53(Aug 1973):528-9.

_____ . 1939: Véspera de guerra. [Rio de Janeiro:] Editóra
Civilazacão Brasileira, 1972. Rev. by J. W. F. Dulles, AHR,
78(Je 1973):751.

_____ . 1942: Guerra no Continente. Rio de Janeiro: Editóra
Civilazacão Brasileira, 1972. Rev. by J. W. F. Dulles, AHR,
78(Dec 1973):1561-2.

Silverberg, Robert. To the Western Shore. New York: Doubleday,
1972. Rev. by J. P. Cullen, AHI, 7(Feb 1973):49.

Silverio Sainz, Nicasio. Cuba y La Casa de Austria. Miami, Fla.:
Ediciones Universal, 1972. Rev. by U. Lamb, HAHR, 53(Nov
1973):682-4.

Silverlight, John. The Visitors' Dilemma: Allied Intervention in the
Russian Civil War. London: Barrie and Jenkins, 1970. Rev.
by U. H. Rothwell, ESR, 3(Apr 1973):191-3.

Silverman, Dan P. Reluctant Union: Alsace-Lorraine and Imperial
Germany, 1871-1918. University Park: Penn St U Press,
1972. Rev. by J. J. Sheehan, AHR, 78(Je 1973):710-11; R.
J. Ross, JMH, 45(Sep 1973):525-6.

Silverman, Kenneth, comp. Selected Letters of Cotton Mather.
Baton Rouge, LSU Press, 1971. Rev. by A. T. Vaughan,
AHR, 78(Feb 1973):140-2.

Simha, S. L. N., ed. Economic and Social Development: Essays in
honour of Dr. C. D. Deshmukh. Bombay: Vora, 1972. Rev.
by T. N. Madan, IQ, 29(Jan-Mar 1973):72.

Simington, Robert C. The Transplantation to Connacht, 1654-58.
Shannon: Irish U Press, 1970. Rev. by F. G. James, AHR,
78(Feb 1973):102-3.

Simkins, Francis Butler and Charles Pierce Roland. A History of
the South. New York: Knopf, 1972. Rev. by S. E. Hannum,
JSH, 39(Feb 1973):97-8.

Simon, John Y. and Roger D. Bridges, eds. The Papers of Ulysses
S. Grant. Vol. 4: January 8-March 31, 1862. Carbondale:
U S Ill Press, 1972. Rev. by H. H. Simms, FCHQ, 47(Ja
1973):60-2; A. M McMahon, JISHS, 66(Win 1973):477-8; W.
W. Hassler, Jr., JSH, 39(Feb 1973):123-4; R. F. Weigley,
MilAf, 37(Oct 1973):111.

Simonsson, Ragnar. The Constitution of France. Stockholm: Almqvist and Wiksell, 1971. Rev. by E. Ekman, AHR, 78(Oct
1973):1075-6; H. A. Barton, JMH, 45(Dec 1973):703-4.

Simpson, D. D. A., ed. Economy and Settlement in Neolithic and
Early Bronze Age Britain and Europe. Leicester: Leicester
U Press, 1971. Rev. by H. Case, Antiquity, 47(Mar 1973):
78-9.

Simpson, George Eaton. Religious Cults of the Caribbean: Trinidad,
Jamaica, and Haiti. Rio Piedras, Puerto Rico, 1970. Rev.
by R. Abrahams, HAHR, 53(May 1973):357-8.

Sinclair, R. see Cherns, A. B.

Sinclair-Stevenson, Christopher. Inglorious Rebellion: The Jacobite
Risings of 1708, 1715, and 1719. New York: St. Martin's,

1972.   Rev. by G. H. Jones, AHR, 78(Feb 1973):99-100.

Singh, A. K.   Impact of American Aid on Indian Economy.   Bombay:
        Vora, 1973.   Rev. by B. K. Shrivastava, IQ, 29(Oct-Dec
        1973):366.

Singh   Baljit and Ko-Wang Mei.   Theory and Practice of Modern
        Guerilla Warfare.   New York: Asia Publishing House, 1971.
        Rev. by J. B. Bell, MilAf, 37(Dec 1973):155-7.

Singh, Harnam.   Studies in World Order.   Delhi: Kitab Mahal, 1972.
        Rev. by J. K. Ray IQ, 29(Ja-Mar 1973):58.

Singh, S. Nihal.   From the Jhelum to the Volga.   Bombay: Nachi-
        keta, 1972.   Rev. by N. M. Khilnani, IQ, 29(Ja-Mar 1973):
        65-7.

Singhal, Damodar P.   Pakistan.   Englewood Cliffs, N. J.: Prentice-
        Hall, 1972.   Rev. by P. L. Mehra, IQ, 29(Oct-Dec 1973):
        357-8.

Sinha, Nirmal C.   Greater India: Faction, Fiction, and Fetish.
        Bhagalpur: Bhagalpur U, 1973.   Rev. by V. K. Arora, IQ,
        29(Jl-Sep 1973):277.

Sink, M. Jewell and Mary Green Mathews.   Pathfinders, Past and
        Present: A History of Davidson County, North Carolina.   High
        Point, N. C.: Hall, 1972.   Rev. by J. W. Wall, NCHR, 50
        (Spr 1973):201-2.

Sinkler, George.   The Racial Attitudes of American Presidents:
        From Abraham Lincoln to Theodore Roosevelt.   Garden City,
        N. Y.: Doubleday, 1971.   Rev. by R. J. Meister, IMH, 69
        (Mar 1973):79-80.

Siracusa, Joseph M.   New Left Diplomatic Histories and Historians:
        The American Revisionists.   Port Washington, N. Y.: Ken-
        nikat, 1973.   Rev. by W. V. Scholes, HRNB, 2(Oct 1973):13.

Sistrunk, Walter E. and Robert C. Maxson.   A Practical Approach
        to Secondary Social Studies.   Dubuque, Ia.: William C.
        Brown, 1972.   Rev. by D. L. Brubaker, SS, 64(Apr 1973):
        185.

Skaggs, David Curtis.   Roots of Maryland Democracy, 1753-1776.
        Westport, Conn.: Greenwood, 1973.   Rev. by N. S. Cohen,
        HRNB, 2(Nov/Dec 1973):42.

Skaggs, Jimmy M.   The Cattle-Trailing Industry: Between Supply
        and Demand, 1866-1890.   Lawrence: U Press Ks, 1973.
        Rev. by C. H. Morris, ChOk, 51(Fall 1973):366-7; J. B.
        Pearson, HRNB, 2(Nov/Dec 1973):52.

Skardon, Alvin W. Church Leader in the Cities: William Augustus
  Muhlenberg. Philadelphia: U Pa Press, 1971. Rev. by
  S. E. Ahlstrom, AHR 78(Oct 1973):1127-30; B. E. Steiner,
  JAH, 60(Sep 1973):475-7.

Skazkin, S. D., et al., eds. Russia and Italy: On the History of
  Russo-Italian Cultural and Social Relations. Moscow: Izdatel'stvo "Nauka, " 1968. Rev. by R. Wohl, AHR, 78(Je 1973):
  676-7.

Skeltón, R. A. Maps: A Historical Survey of Their Study and Collecting. Chicago: U Chi Press, 1972. Rev. by R. E. Ehren-
  berg, AmArch, 36(Oct 1973):558-9; J. Leighly, JMH, 45(Sep
  1973):470; R. O. Lindsay, WMQ, 3rd ser., 30(Jl 1973):543-
  4.

Skelton, Robin. The Writings of J. M. Synge. Indianapolis: Bobbs-
  Merrill, 1971. Rev. by M. Levin, E-I, 8(Spr 1973):156-8.

Skillings, Helen Wieland. We're Standing on Iron! The Story of
  the Five Wieland Brothers, 1856-1883. Duluth, Minn.: St.
  Louis County Historical Society, 1972. Rev. by G. L. H.,
  IS, 29(Sum 1973):156-7.

Skinner, B. F. Beyond Freedom and Dignity. New York: Knopf,
  1971. Rev. by R. K. Williams, JNH, 58(Ja 1973):101-4.

Skodvin, Magne. Scandinavia or NATO? The Foreign Ministry and
  the Alliance Question, 1947-1949. Oslo: Universitetsforlaget, 1971. Rev. by H. P. Krosby, AHR, 78(Oct 1973):
  1089-90.

Slack, Paul see Clark, Peter

Slaughter, Linda W. From Fortress to Farm: or, Twenty-three
  Years on the Frontier. New York: Exposition; 1972. Rev.
  by B. B. Jensen, JOW, 12(Oct 1973):657-8.

Slavin, Arthur J., ed. Tudor Men and Institutions: Studies in Eng-
  lish Law and Government. Baton Rouge: LSU Press, 1972.
  Rev. by R. W. Kenny, AHR, 78(Dec 1973):1454-5; J. R.
  Rilling, Historian, 36(Nov 1973):98-9.

Sloan, Douglas. The Scottish Enlightenment and the American College Ideal. New York: Teachers Coll Press, Columbia U
  Press, 1971. Rev. by G. P. Schmidt, NJH, 91(Spr 1973):
  57-8.

Slotkin, Richard. Regeneration Through Violence. The Mythology
  of the American Frontier, 1600-1860. Middletown, Conn.:
  Wes U Press, 1973. Rev. by R. A. Billington, AHR, 78
  (Oct 1973):1116-17; J. R. Milton, AW, 10(Nov 1973):50; J.
  Walton, FCHQ, 47(Oct 1973):355-7.

Slottman, William B. see János, Andrew C.

Slusser, Robert M. The Berlin Crisis of 1961: Soviet-American
    Relations and the Struggle for Power in the Kremlin, June-
    November, 1961. Baltimore: JHU Press, 1973. Rev. by
    A. Z. Rubenstein, CurH, 64(May 1973):224-5; D. L. Bark,
    RR, 32(Oct 1973):454-5.

Small, Melvin. Public Opinion and Historians: Interdisciplinary
    Perspectives. Detroit: Wayne St U Press, 1970. Rev. by
    E. Ions, History 58(Feb 1973):158-9.

Smalley, Orange A. and Frederick D. Sturdivant. The Credit Mer-
    chants: A History of Spiegel Inc. Carbondale: S Ill Press,
    1973. Rev. by M. Hough. IMH 69(Dec 1973):374-6.

Smelser, Marshall. The Winning of Independence. Chicago: Quad-
    rangle, 1972. Rev. by D. Gruber, WMQ, 3rd ser., 30(Ja
    1973):170-2.

Smiley, Nixon. Florida: Land of Images. Miami: E. A. See-
    mann, 1972. Rev. by W. M. Goza, FHQ, 52(Jl 1973):72.

Smith, Anthony D. Theories of Nationalism. New York: Harper
    and Row, 1971. Rev. by R. M. Berdahl, AHR, 78(Dec 1973):
    1423-5.

Smith, C. B. Troy State University, 1933-1970. Troy, Ala.: Troy
    St U Press, 1972. Rev. by H. E. Sterkx, AlaRe, 26(Jl
    1973):229-31.

Smith, Clifford Neal. Federal Land Series: A Calendar of Archival
    Materials on the Land Patents Issued by the United States
    Government, With Subject, Tract, and Name Indexes. Vol. I,
    1788-1810. Chicago: Amer Library Assn., 1972. Rev. by
    D. E. Baker, IMH, 69(Mar 1973):73-5; C. A. Hughes, THQ,
    32(Fall 1973):301-2.

_____. Federal Land Series: A Calendar of Archival Materials
    on the Land Patents Issued by the United States Government,
    With Subject, Tract, and Name Indexes. Vol. II, 1799-1835.
    Chicago: Amer Library Assn., 1973. Rev. by C. A. Hughes,
    THQ, 32(Fall 1973):301-2.

Smith, David C. A History of Lumbering in Maine, 1861-1960.
    Orono: U Maine Press, 1972. Rev. by F. W. Kohlmeyer,
    BHR, 47(Spr 1973):115-17; R. W. Hidy, JAH, 60(Sep 1973):
    469-70; W. L. Marr, JEH, 33(Dec 1973):906-7.

_____. A History of Papermaking in the United States (1691-
    1969). New York: Lockwood, 1970. Rev. by R. W. Hidy,
    BHR, 47(Spr 1973):117-18.

Smith, Duane A. see Ubbelohde, Carl

Smith, Ella Williams. Tears and Laughter in Virginia and Else-
where. Verona Va.: McClure, 1972. Rev. by G. G.
Shackelford, VMHB, 81(Ja 1973):115-16.

Smith, Elwyn A. Religious Liberty in the United States: The Development of Church-State Thought Since the Revolutionary
Era. Philadelphia: Fortress, 1972. Rev. by T. L. Smith,
AHR, 78(Oct 1973):1125-6; C. S. Meyer, CHIQ, 46(Sum
1973):93; A. M. Greeley, JAH, 59(Mar 1973):997-8.

Smith, Gaddis. The American Secretaries of State and Their Diplomacy. Vol. XVI: Dean Acheson. New York: Cooper
Square, 1972. Rev. by N. A. Graebner, JAH, 60(Je 1973):
179-81.

Smith, Goldwin. Canada and the Canadian Question. Toronto: U Tor
Press, 1971. Rev. by W. Metcalf, CHR, 54(Mar 1973):90-2.

Smith, H. Shelton. In His Image, But ...: Racism in Southern Religion, 1780-1910. Durham, N. C.: Duke U Press, 1972.
Rev. by C. E. Wynes, FHQ, 52(Jl 1973):80-1; G. M. Frederickson, JAH, 59(Mar 1973):1000-1; J. O. Fish, JNH, 58
(Oct 1973):479-81; D. E. Harrell, Jr., JSH, 39(May 1973):
281-2; W. B. Posy, NCHR, 50(Win 1973):104-5; W. H.
Daniel, VMHB, 81(Ja 1973):106-7.

Smith, Jean Herron. Snickersville: The Biography of a Village.
Miamisburg, Ohio: Miamisburg News, 1970. Rev. by W. J.
Gilmore, VMHB, 81(Ja 1973):113-14.

Smith, Lacey Baldwin. Henry VIII: The Mask of Royalty. Boston:
Houghton Mifflin 1971. Rev. by M. E. James, History, 58
(Oct 1973):444; M. F. Shore, JIH, 4(Aut 1973):306-11.

Smith, Matthew J., comp. An Inventory of the Papers of Dennis J.
Roberts in the Phillips Memorial Library of Providence College. Providence, R. I.: Providence College 1972. Rev.
by K. J. Pike, AmArch, 36(Jl 1973):411-14.

Smith, Michael. Time and Locations. Dublin: Dolman, 1972. Rev.
T. D. Redshaw, E-I, 8(Spr 1973):142-51.

Smith, Norman. A History of Dams. Seacaucus, N. J.: Citadel
Press, 1972. Rev. by C. W. Condit, T & C, 14(Oct 1973):
621-2.

Smith, Paul, ed. Lord Salisbury on Politics: A Selection From His
Articles in the Quarterly Review, 1860-1883. Cambridge: Cam
U Press, 1972. Rev. by V. Bogdaner, History, 58(Je 1973):
313; W. L. Arnstein, JMH, 45(Sep 1973):506-9.

Smith, Paul H., comp. English Defenders of American Freedoms, 1774-1778. Washington, D. C.: American Revolution Bicentennial Office, Library of Congress, 1972. Rev. by B. Z. Ramsome, IMH, 69(Mar 1973):82-4; D. Higgenbotham, NCHR, 50(Win 1973):107-8; T. R. Adams, PMHB, 97(Ja 1973):117-18; R. Alexander, WVH, 34(Jl 1973):389-90.

Smith, R. Harris. O S S: The Secret History of America's First Central Intelligence Agency. Berkeley: U Cal Press, 1972. Rev. by J. A. Huston, JAH, 59(Mar 1973):1041-2; L. Kaufman, JOW, 12(Jl 1973):501.

Smith, Robert Freeman. The United States and Revolutionary Nationalism in Mexico, 1916-1932. Chicago: U Chi Press, 1972. Rev. by J. B. Hunker, AW, 10(Jl 1973):57; M. S. Wionczek, HAHR, 53(May 1973):322-5; K. J. Grieb, PHR, 42(Nov 1973):596-7; M. T. Gilderhus, TAm, 29(Ja 1973): 403-4; R. Zeitlin, WMH, 56(Sum 1973):337-8.

Smith, Susan see Dean, Jill. Also: Wisconsin: A State for All Seasons.

Smith, W. H. C. Napoleon III. New York: St. Martin's, 1973. Rev. by N. Greene, HRNB, 2(Nov/Dec 1973):28-9.

Smith, Watson. Painted Ceramics of the Western Mound at Awatovi. Cambridge, Mass.: Har U Press, 1971. Rev. by G. J. Gumerman, AmAnt, 38(Apr 1973):248-9.

Smith, Wilfred I. (Intro.). Archives: Mirror of Canada Past.... Toronto: U Tor Press, 1972. Rev. by G. Martin, Archives 11(Aut 1973):111-12.

Smith, William, Jr. The History of the Province of New York. 2 Vols. Cambridge, Mass.: Belknap Press (Har U Press), 1972. D. R. Gerlach, JAH, 60(Je 1973):112-14; M. M. Klein, NYH, 54(Ja 1973):104-6; R. J. Champagne, PMHB, 97(Ja 1973):112-14; N. Varga, WMQ, 3rd ser., 30(Jl 1973):535-7.

Smith, William R. The Rhetoric of American Politics: A Study of Documents. Westport, Conn.: Greenwood, 1969. Rev. by C. Coate, JOW, 12(Ja 1973):186.

Smithsonian Institution. Preliminary Guide to the Smithsonian Archives. Washington: The Institution Press, 1971. Rev. by K. J. Pike, AmArch, 36(Jl 1973):411-14.

Smock, Audrey. Ibo Politics: The Role of Ethnic Unions in Eastern Nigeria. Cambridge, Mass.: Har U Press, 1971. Rev. by P. A. C. Isichea, AfAf, 72(Ja 1973):86-7.

Smock, Raymond W., Louis R. Harlan, John W. Blassingame, Pete Daniel, Stuart B. Kaufman and William M. Welty. The

Booker T. Washington Papers. Vol. I. The Autobiographical Writings. Vol. II. 1860-89. Urbana: U Ill Press, 1972. Rev. by A. H. Spear, JAH, 60(Dec 1973):753-5.

Smoot, Mrs. Betty Carter. Days in an Old Town. King George, Va.: Lewis Egerton Smoot Memorial Library, 1972. Rev. by R. L. Montague III, VMHB, 81(Ja 1973):117.

Smythe, Donald, S. J. Guerilla Warrior: The Early Life of John J. Pershing. New York: Scribner's, 1973. Rev. by J. G. Clifford, IMH, 69(Dec 1973):376-7; L. Anders, MoHR, 67 (Jl 1973):621-3; R. Price, OQ, 16(Win 1973):148-50.

Snow, Peter G. Political Forces in Argentina. Boston: Allyn and Bacon, 1971. Rev. by P. Ranis, HAHR, 53(Aug 1973):555-6.

Soares de Souza, José Antônio. A Missão Bellgarde ao Paraguai, 1849-1852. 3 vols. Rio de Janeiro: Departamento da Imprensa Nacional, Divisão de Documentacão ... 1966, 1968, 1970. Rev. by P. D'Eca, HAHR, 53(Feb 1973):140-2.

Sobel, Robert. The Age of Giant Corporations: A Microeconomic History of American Business, 1914-1970. Westport, Conn.: Greenwood, 1972. Rev. by T. C. Cochran, AHR, 78(Dec 1973):1543-4.

_____. Annex: A History of the American Stock Exchange, 1921-1971. New York: Weybright and Talley, 1972. Rev. by D. S. Levin, JAH, 60(Dec 1973):842-3.

Sochen, June. The New Woman: Feminism in Greenwich Village, 1910-1920. New York: Quadrangle, 1972. Rev. by K. S. Lynn, AHR, 78(Je 1973):741; J. R. McGovern, JAH, 60(Je 1973):160-1.

_____. The Unbridgeable Gap: Blacks and Their Quest for the American Dream, 1900-1930. Chicago: Rand McNally, 1972. Rev. by E. D. Cronon, JAH, 60(Sep 1973):512-13; A. Gilmore, JNH, 58(Oct 1973):485-6; R. G. Sherer JSH, 39(May 1973):306-7.

Sociedad Bolivariana de Venezuela. Comisión Editora. Escritos del Libertador. Vol. 8. Caracas, Venezuela: Cuatricentenario de la Ciudad de Caracas, 1972. Rev. by D. Bushnell, HAHR, 53(Aug 1973):513.

Socolosky, Homer E. and Huber, Self. Historical Atlas of Kansas. Norman: U Ok Press, 1972. Rev. by L. E. Rickard, AgH, 47(Oct 1973):351; B. Petchenik, JAH, 60(Sep 1973):460-1; R. Beach, JOW, 12(Oct 1973):633.

Solomon, Howard M. Public Welfare, Science and Propaganda in Seventeenth-Century France: The Innovations of Theophraste

Renaudot. Princeton, N. J.: Prin U Press, 1972. Rev. by
H. Brown, AHR, 78(Oct 1973):1072.

Solow, Barbara Lewis. The Land Question and the Irish Economy,
1870-1903. Cambridge, Mass.: Har U Press, 1971. Rev.
by J. P. Huttman, AgH, 47(Ja 1973):91-2; L. J. McCaffrey,
AHR, 78(Je 1973):699; A. Cohen, E-I, 8(Win 1973):128-9.

Soltow, Lee. Patterns of Wealthholding in Wisconsin Since 1850.
Madison: U Wis Press, 1971. Rev. by J. L. Barr, BHR,
47(Spr 1973):118-20; E. J. Watts, IMH, 69(Mar 1973):71-2.

Somekh, Sasson. The Changing Rhythym: A Study of Najib Mahfuz's Novels. Leiden: E. J. Brill, 1973. Rev. by S.
Somekh, NO 16(Jl-Aug 1973):78-9.

Somers, Dale A. The Rise of Sports in New Orleans: 1850-1900.
Baton Rouge: LSU Press, 1972. Rev. by D. A. Riley, JAH,
59(Mar 1973):1009-10; B. A. Brownell, JSH, 39(Feb 1973):
120-1.

Sonneck, Oscar. Report on "The Star-Spangled Banner," "Hail Columbia," "America," and "Yankee Doodle." New York:
Dover, 1972. (reprint). Rev. by S. A. Linscome, CoMag
50(Spr 1973):172-3.

Sonnichsen, C. L. Billy King's Tombstone: The Private Life of an
Arizona Boom Town. Tucson: U Ariz Press, 1972. Rev. by
H. P. Walker, JAriH, 14(Spr 1973):80-1.

Sontag, Frederick and John K. Roth. The American Religious Experience: The Roots, Trends, and Future of American Theology. New York: Harper and Row, 1972. Rev. by W. R.
Hutchison, JAH, 59(Mar 1973):998-9.

Sorin, Gerald. Abolitionism: A New Perspective. New York:
Praeger, 1972. Rev. by N. Lederer, Historian, 35(Feb
1973):311-12; A. M. McMahon, JSH, 39(Feb 1973):116-17.

_____. The New York Abolitionists: A Case Study of Political
Radicalism. Westport, Conn.: Greenwood 1971. Rev. by
R. Trendel, JNH, 58(Ja 1973):112-14.

Soucy, Robert. Fascism in France: The Case of Maurice Barrès.
Berkeley: U Cal Press, 1972. Rev. by E. R. Tannenbaum,
AHR, 78(Dec 1973):1478-80; E. Weber, JMH, 45(Dec 1973):
685-7.

Spann, Edward K. Ideals and Politics: New York Intellectuals and
Liberal Democracy, 1820-1880. Albany: SUNY Press, 1972.
Rev. by J. H. Schroeder, NYH, 54(Jl 1973):365-6; E. Pes-
sen, NYHSQ, 57(Oct 1973):361-2.

SPARKES   296

Sparkes, Brian A. and Lucy Talcott. The Athenian Agora: Results
    of Excavations Conducted by the American School of Classical
    Studies at Athens. Vol. XII. Black and Plain Pottery of the
    6th, 5th, and 4th Centuries B. C. Part 1, Text. Part 2, In-
    dexes and Illustrations. Princeton, N. J.: American School
    of Classical Studies at Athens, 1970. Rev. by C. G. Boulter,
    Archaeology, 26(Ja 1973):67-8.

Spicer, Edward H., et al. Impounded People: Japanese-Americans
    in Relocation Centers. Tucson: U Ariz Press, 1969. Rev.
    by J. V. Metzgar, NHSQ, 16(Sum 1973):143-7.

Spiegel, John. Transactions: The Interplay Between Individual,
    Family, and Society. New York: Science House, 1972.
    Rev. by E. J Nichols, SS, 64(Nov 1973):291-2.

Spiero, George see Wilson, Raymond J.

Spindler, Max, ed. Handbuch der bayerischen Geschichte. Vol. 5.
    Franken, Schwaben, Oberpfalz, bis zum Ausgang des 18.
    Jahrhundert. Munich: C. W. Beck'sche Verlagbuchhandlung,
    1971. Rev. by G. Strauss, AHR, 78(Feb 1973):117-18.

Spini, Georgio. L'Evangelo e il Berretto Frigio. Turin: Editrice
    Claudiana, 1971. Rev. by J. Whittam, History, 58(Feb 1973):
    123-4.

Spinner, Thomas J., Jr. George Joachim Goschen: The Transform-
    ation of a Victorian Liberal. New York: Cam U Press, 1973.
    Rev. by P. Scherer, HRNB, 2(Oct 1973):4-5.

Spitaels, P. see DeLaet, S. J.

Spitzer, Alan B. Old Hatreds and Young Hopes: The French Car-
    bonari Against the Bourbon Restoration. Cambridge, Mass.:
    Har U Press, 1971. Rev. by V. W. Beach, AHR, 78(Feb
    1973):111-13.

Spivakovsky, Erika. Son of the Alhambra: Don Diego Hurtado de
    Mendoza 1504-1575. Austin: U Tx Press, 1970. Rev. by
    A. W. Lovett, ESR 3(Apr 1973):181-2.

Sprague, Rosamond Kent, ed. The Older Sophists. Columbia, S. C.:
    U SCar Press, 1972. Rev. by S. J. Becroft, Historian, 36
    (Nov 1973):92-3.

Spriano, Paolo. Storia del Partito comunista italiano ... 3 vols.
    Turin: Giulio Einaudi Editore, 1967, 1969, 1970. Rev. by
    E. Craver, JMH, 45(Dec 1973):706-8.

Sprunger, Keith L. The Learned Doctor William Ames: Dutch Back-
    grounds of English and American Puritanism. Urbana: U Ill
    Press, 1972. Rev. by H. G. Swanhart, Historian, 36(Nov

297   SPULER

1973):101-2; S. Bercovitch, JAH, 60(Je 1973):111-12; J.
Tanis, WMQ, 3rd ser., 30(Jl 1973):538-40.

Spuler, Bertold. History of the Mongols, Based on Eastern and West-
ern Accounts. London: Routledge and Kegan Paul, 1971.
Rev. by D. S. M. Williams, History, 58(Je 1973):255-6; E.
Allworth, MEJ, 27(Aut 1973):500-1.

Squibb, G. D. Founder's Kin: Privilege and Pedigree. Oxford:
Clarendon Press, 1972. Rev. by F. Jones, Archives, 11
(Aut 1973):108-9.

Staar, Richard F., ed. 1972 Yearbook on International Communist
Affairs. Stanford, Cal.: Hoover Institution, 1971. Rev. by
A. J. Rubenstein, CurH, 64(May 1973):225; S. Kirshner, NO,
16(Mar-Apr 1973):48-50.

Staccioli, Romolo A. Modelli di Edifici Etrusco-Italici: I Modelli
Votivi. Florence: Sansoni, 1968. Rev. by K. M. Phillips,
Jr., Archaeology, 26(Ja 1973):68-9.

Stacey, C. P. Historical Documents of Canada. Vol. 5. The Arts
of War and Peace, 1914-1945. Toronto: Macmillan, 1972.
Rev. by M. Prang, CHR, 54(Sep 1973):306-8.

Stackpole, Edouard A. Whales and Destiny: The Rivalry Between
America, France, and Britain for Control of the Southern
Whale Fishery, 1785-1825. Amherst: U Mass Press, 1972.
Rev. by S. C. Sherman, WMQ, 3rd ser., 30(Oct 1973):677-8.

Stadler, Karl R. Austria. London: Ernest Benn, 1971. Rev. by
J. Dreijmanis, EEQ, 7(Sum 1973):226-7.

Stadler, Peter. Karl Marx: Ideologie und Politik. Goettingen:
Musterschmidt-Verlag, 1966. Rev. by R. H. W. Theem,
JMH 45(Dec 1973):675-8.

Stadtfeld, Curtis K. From the Land and Back. New York: Scribner's, 1972. Rev. by R. Kirk, GR, 27(Spr 1973):125-8.

Stafford, David. From Anarchism to Reformism: A Study of the
Political Activities of Paul Brousse Within the First International and the French Socialist Movement 1870-90. Toronto:
U Tor Press, 1971. Rev. by H. Mitchell, CHR, 54(Mar
1973):106-8.

Stagg, Brian L. The Distant Eden, Tennessee's Rugby Colony.
Knoxville: Paylor, 1973. Rev. by U. S. Beach, THQ, 32
(Sum 1973):191.

Stagg, J M. Forecast for Overlord, June 6, 1944. New York:
Norton, 1971. Rev. by M. Blumenson, JAH, 59(Mar 1973):
1038-9.

STANFORD 298

Stanford, W. B. and R. B. McDowell. Mahaffy: A Biography of an
Anglo-Irishman. Boston: Routledge and Kegan Paul, 1971.
Rev. by M. R. O'Connell, AHR, 78(Dec 1973):1473-4.

Stansky, Peter and William Abrahams. The Unknown Orwell. New
York: Knopf 1972. Rev. by G. Beadle, JMH 45(Dec 1973):
701-3.

Stark, Freya and Fulvio Roiter. Gateways and Caravans: A Portrait of Turkey. New York: Macmillan, 1971. Rev. by P.
Nulty, MEJ, 27(Aut 1973):525.

Starobin, Joseph R. American Communism in Crisis: 1943-57.
Cambridge, Mass.: Har U Press, 1972. Rev. by G. Char-
ney, WMH 56(Spr 1973):234-6.

Starr, Kevin. Americans and the California Dream, 1850-1915.
New York: Ox U Press, 1973. Rev. by C. Wollenberg,
CHQ, 52(Win 1973):374-5.

Starr, S. Frederick. Decentralization and Self-Government in Rus-
sia, 1830-1870. Princeton, N. J.: Prin U Press, 1972.
Rev. by D. Field, JMH, 45(Sep 1973):526-7; W. M. Pintner,
RR, 32(Apr 1973):200-1.

Stasack, Edward see Cox, J. Halley

Stauder, Jack. The Majangir: Ecology and Society of a Southwest
Ethiopian People. London: Cam U Press, 1971. Rev. by
H. Blackhurst, Africa, 43(Ja 1973):84-5.

Stauff, Faye and W. Bradley Twitty. Sacred Chitimacha Indian Beliefs. Pompano Beach, Fla.: Twitty and Twitty, 1971. Rev.
by J. L. Gibson, LaH, 14(Fall 1973):410.

Stauridou-Zaphrada, Alkemene. The Meeting of Symeon and Nicholas
Mysticus (August 913) in the Context of the Byzantino-Bulgar-
ian Struggle. Thessaloniki: Center of Byzantine Studies,
1972. Rev. by P. Charanis, AHR, 78(Dec 1973):1445.

Stearns, Monroe. Julius Caesar: Master of Men. New York:
Franklin Watts, 1971. Rev. by A. J. Christopherson, SS,
64(Feb 1973):92, 94.

Stedman, John Gabriel. Narrative of a Five Years' Expedition
Against the Revolted Negroes of Surinam in Guiana on the
Wild Coast of South America from 1772-1777.... 2 vols.
Amherst: U Mass Press, 1972. Rev. by R. Moore, HAHR,
53(Nov 1973):729-30; C. Levy, JNH, 58(Ja 1973):109-10.

Stedman Jones, Gareth. Outcast London: A Study in the Relationship Between Classes in Victorian Society. Oxford: Clarendon
Press, 1971. Rev. by G. Himmelfarb, AHR, 78(Dec 1973):

1467-8; F. Bédarida, EHR, 88(Jl 1973):605-12; P. Hollis,
History, 58(Feb 1973):126-7.

Steel, D. J., et al. National Index of Parish Registers, Vol. 2:
     Sources for Nonformist Genealogy and Family History. Chi-
     chester: Phillimore.... 1973. Rev. by A. M. Wherry,
     Archives, 11(Aut 1973):109-10.

Steensgaard, Niels. Carracks, Caravans, and Companies: The
     Structural Crisis in the European-Asian Trade in the Early
     17th Century. Copenhagen: Scandinavian Institute of Asian
     Studies, 1973. Rev. by C. R. Boxer, HTo, 23(Dec 1973):
     898-9.

Stegenga, James A., ed. Towards a Wiser Colossus. Lafayette,
     Ind.: Purdue U Press, 1972. Rev. by S. L. P., IQ, 29(Jl-
     Sep):260-1.

Stegner, Wallace. The Big Rock Candy Mountain. Garden City,
     N. Y.: Doubleday, 1973. Rev. by T. H. Watkins, AW, 10
     (May 1973):55.

Stehl, William F. see Hill, Evan

Stein, Charles Francis, Jr. Origin and History of Howard County.
     Baltimore: Published by Author, Printed by Schneidereith,
     1972. Rev. by H. W. Newman, MHM, 68(Sum 1973):232.

Stein, R. A. Tibetan Civilization. London: Faber and Faber, 1972.
     Rev. by 'P. R. S., IQ, 29(Jan-Mar 1973):62-3.

Steinberg, Albert. The First Ten: The Founding Presidents and
     Their Administrations. New York: Doubleday, 1967. Rev.
     by C. N. Tyson, ChOk, 51(Win 1973-74):501-2.

Steinberg, Alfred. The Bosses. New York: Macmillan, 1972. Rev.
     by H. R. Grant, CoMag, 50(Sum 1973):251-2; A. R. Havig,
     JSH, 39(May 1973):317-18; D. W. Grantham, NCHR, 50(Sum
     1973):343.

Steiner, Bruce E. Samuel Seabury, 1729-1796: A Study in the High
     Church Tradition. Athens, Ohio: Ohio U Press, 1971. Rev.
     by G. J. Goodwin, JAH, 59(Mar 1973):982-3; M. B. Norton,
     NYHSQ, 57(Jl 1973):261-2; A. C. Loveland, PMHB, 97(Jl
     1973):408-9; G. E. Hartdagen, WMQ 3rd ser., 30(Jl 1973):
     537-8.

Stelmack, Carole B. and J. K. Johnson, eds. The Papers of the
     Prime Ministers. The Letters of Sir John A. Macdonald.
     2 vols. Ottawa: Public Archives of Canada, 1968, 1969.
     Rev. by B. W. Hodgins, CHR, 54(Mar 1973):85-8.

Stempel, Wolf-Dieter, ed. Texte der russischen Formalisten. Vol.

STENDEL   300

II. Munich: Wilhelm Fink Verlag, 1972. Rev. by V. Ter-
ras, RR, 32(Ja 1973):92-3.

Stendel, Ori. The Minorities in Israel: Trends in the Development
of the Arab Droz Communities 1948-1973. n. p., n. d. Rev.
by K. Nakhleh, NO, 16(Dec 1973):78-9.

Stenzel, Franz. Cleveland Rockwell, Scientist and Artist, 1837-1907.
Portland: Oregon Historical Society, 1972. Rev. by R.
Hitchman, AW, 10(Ja 1973):55.

Stephan, John J. Sakhalin: A History. Oxford: Ox U Press, 1971.
Rev. by I. H. Nish, History, 58(Je 1973):334.

Stephens, W. B. Sources for English Local History. [Manchester:]
Manchester U Press 1973. Rev. by F. G. Emmison, MH,
2(Aut 1973):118-19.

Sterkx H. E. The Free Negro in Ante-Bellum Louisiana. Rutherford, N. J.: Fairleigh Dickinson U Press, 1972. Rev. by
J. G. Sproat, JSH, 39(May 1973):292-3; J. G. Taylor, LaH,
14(Spr 1973):220-1.

_____. Partners in Rebellion: Alabama Women in the Civil War.
Madison, Wis.: Fairleigh Dickinson U Press, 1970. Rev.
by L. N. Allen, AlaRe, 26(Ja 1973):73-4.

Stern, Fritz. The Failure of Illiberalism: Essays on the Political
Culture of Modern Germany. New York: Knopf, 1972. Rev.
by P. Lowenberg, AHR, 78(Feb 1973):118-19.

Stern, J. P. Idylls and Realities, Studies in Nineteenth-Century
German Literature. London: Methuen, 1971. Rev. by M.
C. Ives, ESR, 3(Ja 1973):98-101.

Stern, S. M., et al., eds. Islamic Philosophy and the Classical
Tradition: Essays Presented by His Friends and Pupils to
Richard Walzer on His Seventieth Birthday. Columbia, S. C.:
U SCar Press, 1973. Rev. by F. E. Peters, AHR, 78(Oct
1973):1102-3; M. Fakhry, MEJ, 27(Sum 1973):408-9.

Sternhell, Zeev. Maurice Barrès et le nationalisme français. Paris:
Armand Colin, 1972. Rev. by E. R. Tannenbaum, AHR, 78
(Dec 1973):1478-80; E. Weber, JMH 45(Dec 1973):685-7.

Stern-Taeubler, Selma. Der Preussische Staat und de Juden. 2
vols. Tübingen: J. C. B. Mohr, 1971. Rev. by G. R.
Mork, AJHQ 63(Sep 1973):103-5.

Stevens, G. R. History of the Canadian National Railways. New
York: Macmillan, 1973. Rev. by J. A. Boudreau, HRNB,
2(Oct 1973):20-1.

Stevens, Richard P., ed. Zionism and Palestine Before the Mandate:
A Phase of Western Imperialism. Beirut: Institute for Palestine Studies, 1972. Rev. by A. M. Lesch, MEJ, 27(Spr
1973):249-50.

Stevens, Rosemary. American Medicine and the Public Interest.
New Haven, Conn.: Yale U Press 1971. Rev. by T. N.
Bonner, AHR, 78(Feb 1973):143-4.

Stevens, S. K., Donald H. Kent, and Autumn L. Leonard, eds.
The Papers of Henry Bouquet. Vol. 1. December 11, 1755-
May 31, 1758. Harrisburg, Pa.: Pa Historical and Museum
Commission, 1972. Rev. by W. E. A. Bernhard, AmArch,
36(Ja 1973):69-70; J. W. Huston, PH, 40(Oct 1973):476-7;
G. C. Rogers, Jr., SCHM, 74(Ja 1973):42-3; J. R. Sellers,
WMQ, 3rd ser., 30(Ja 1973):185-6; E. G. Williams, WPHM,
56(Apr 1973):195-7.

Stevenson, Mary. The Diary of Clarissa Adger Bowen, Ashtabula
Plantation, 1865, With Excerpts from Other Family Diaries
and Comments by Her Granddaughter, Clarissa Walton Taylor,
and Many Other Accounts of the Pendleton, Clemson Area,
South Carolina, 1776-1889. Pendleton, S. C.: Foundation for
Historic Restoration in Pendleton Area, 1973. Rev. by E. M.
Lander, Jr., SCHM, 74(Oct 1973):317-18.

Stewart, Mrs. Catesby Willis. The Life of Brigadier General William Woodford of the American Revolution. 2 vols. Richmond, Va.: Whittet and Shepperson, 1973. Rev. by M. W.
Fishwick, JSH, 39(Nov 1973):591; R. B. Davis, NCHR, 50
(Sum 1973):328-9.

Stewart, George R. American Place Names. A Concise and Selective Dictionary for the Continental United States of America.
New York: Ox U Press, 1970. Rev. by H. H. Bisbee, NJH,
91(Sum 1973):133-4.

_____. Committee of Vigilance: Revolution in San Francisco,
1851. An Account of the Hundred Days When Certain Citizens
Undertook the Supression of the Criminal Activities of the
Sydney Ducks. New York: Ballantine, 1971. Rev. by M. J.
Brodhead, JOW, 12(Ja 1973):177-8.

Stewart, Gordon and George Rawlyk. A People Highly Favored of
God: The Nova Scotia Yankees and the American Revolution.
Hamden, Conn.: Archon, 1972. Rev. by W. H. Nelson,
AHR, 78(Feb 1973):182-3; M. B. Norton, CHR, 54(Dec 1973):
447-9; W. Brown, JAH, 59(Mar 1973):986-7; G. S. French,
WMQ, 3rd ser., 30(Jl 1973):524-6.

Stewart, James Brewer. Joshua R. Giddings and the Tactics of
Radical Politics. Cleveland, Ohio: Press, CWRU, 1970.
Rev. by H. Aptheker, AHR, 78(Feb 1973):161-3.

Stewart, Robert. The Politics of Protection: Lord Derby and the Protectionist Party, 1841-1852. Cambridge: Cam U Press, 1971. Rev. by F. A. Dreyer, JMH, 45(Mar 1973):130-1.

Stewart, Rosemary. How Computers Affect Management. Cambridge: Mass.: M I T Press, 1972. Rev. by J. Diebold, T & C, 14(Jl 1973):518-20.

Stigler, G. J. and J. K. Kindahl. The Behavior of Industrial Prices. New York: National Bureau of Economic Research, 1970. Rev. by A. Spencer, JEH, 33(Sep 1973):685-6.

Still, William N., Jr. Iron Afloat: The Story of the Confederate Ironclads. Nashville: Van U Press, 1971. Rev. by R. Luraghi, VMHB, 81(Jl 1973):377-8.

Stites, Francis N. Private Interest and Public Gain: The Dartmouth College Case, 1819. Amherst: U Mass Press, 1972. Rev. by G. H. Evans, Jr., BHR, 47(Win 1973):524-5; K. Newmyer, Historian, 36(Nov 1973):123-4; R. E. Ellis, JAH, 60(Dec 1973):807-8.

Stockdale, W. H. see Rowe, J. G.

Stockholm International Peace Research Institute. World Armaments and Disarmament: Sipri Yearbook, 1972. London: Paul Elek, 1972. Rev. by K. P. Misra, IQ, 29(Ja-Mar 1973):60-1.

Stols, Eddy. De Spaanse Brabanders of de handelsbetrekkingen der Zuidelijke Nederlanden met de Iberische wereld, 1598-1648. 2 vols. Brussels: ... Royal Flemish Academy of Sciences, Letters, and Fine Arts of Belgium ... 1971. Rev. by E. Sluiter, HAHR, 53(Aug 1973):511-12.

Stoltman, James B. The Laurel Culture in Minnesota. St. Paul: Minn Historical Society. Rev. by J. E. Fitting, MichH, 57 (Fall 1973):266-7.

Stone, Gerald. The Smallest Slavonic Nation: The Sorbs of Lusatia. London: Athlone, 1972. Rev. by C. A. Macartney, ESR, 3 (Jl 1973):310; N. C. Masterson, History, 58(Je 1973):309-10.

Stone, John. Colonist or Uitlander? Oxford: Clarendon Press, 1973. Rev. by J. Levin, AfAf, 72(Jl 1973):345-6.

Stone, Lawrence. The Causes of the English Revolution, 1529-1642. London: Routledge and Kegan Paul. Rev. by R. Schlatter, AHR, 78(Oct 1973):1052-5; C. Russell, EHR, 88(Oct 1973): 856-61; G. R. Elton, HJ, 16(Mar 1973):205-8; G. E. Aylmer, History, 58(Je 1973):288-9.

_____. Family and Fortune: Studies in Aristocratic Finance in

the Sixteenth and Seventeenth Centuries. New York: Ox U
Press, 1973. Rev. by B. B. Gilbert, HRNB, 2(Oct 1973):6.

Stouff, Louis. Ravitaillement et alimentation en Provence aux XIVe
et XVe siècles. Paris: Mouton, 1970. Rev. by R. F.
Kierstead, AHR, 78(Feb 1973):89-91; R. L. De Lavigne,
CHR, 54(Mar 1973):102-3.

Stout, Joseph Allen, Jr. The Liberators: Filibustering Expeditions
into Mexico 1848-1862, and the Last Thrust of Manifest Destiny. Los Angeles: Westernlore, 1973. Rev. by J. B.
Harte, JAriH, 14(Sum 1973):166-7; D. L. DeBerry, JOW,
12(Oct 1973):653-4.

Strauss, Gerald, ed. Manifestations of Discontent in Germany on
the Eve of the Reformation. Bloomington: Ind U Press, 1971.
Rev. by P. C. Matheson, History, 58(Je 1973):275-6.

_____. Pre-Reformation Germany. London: Macmillan, 1972.
Rev. by H. S. Offler, History, 58(Je 1973):267-8.

Strong, Major General Sir Kenneth. Men of Intelligence: A Study
of the Roles and Decisions of Chiefs of Intelligence from
World War I to the Present Day. New York: Giniger/St.
Martin's, 1972. Rev. in MilAf, 37(Feb 1973):31.

Strong, Roy. The English Icon: Elizabethan and Jacobean Portraiture. New Haven, Conn.: Yale U Press, 1970. Rev. by
L. B. Smith, JIH, 4(Sum 1973):119-27.

_____. Holbein and Henry VIII. New Haven, Conn.: Yale U
Press, 1970. Rev. by L. B. Smith, JIH, 4(Sum 1973):119-
27.

Struever Nancy S. The Language of History in the Renaissance.
Princeton, N. J.: Prin U Press, 1971. Rev. by J. K.
Hyde, History, 58(Feb 1973):90.

Struik, Bridglal Pachai C. The South African Indian Question, 1860-
1971. n. p.: Capetown 1971. Rev. by H. Tinker, JAfH,
14(3rd Qr 1973):523-7.

Struve, Gleb. Russian Literature Under Lenin and Stalin, 1917-33.
London: Routledge and Kegan Paul, n. d. Rev. by M. Latey,
HTo, 23(Ja 1973):66-7.

Stuart, Jesse. The Land Beyond the River. New York: McGraw-
Hill, 1973. Rev. by E. W. Bentley, FCHQ, 47(Jl 1973):
292-3.

Stuart, Peter. Edward Gibbon Wakefield in New Zealand: His Political Career, 1853-4. Wellington: Price Milburn ... 1971.
Rev. by H. T. Manning, AHR, 78(Je 1973):723.

Stubbings, Frank N. Prehistoric Greece. London: Rupert Hart-
Davis, 1972. Rev. by P. Warren Antiquity, 47(Sep 1973):
244-5.

Stump, Wolfgang. Geschichte und Organisation der zentrumspartei
in Düsseldorf, 1917-1933. Düsseldorf: Droste Verlag, 1971.
Rev. by F. C. West, JMH, 45(Sep 1973):541-2.

Sturdivant, Frederick D. see Smalley, Orange A.

Styan, J. L. Chekhov in Performance: A Commentary on the Major Plays. Cambridge: Cam U Press, 1971. Rev. by T.
G. Winner, RR, 32(Jl 1973):326-7.

Suárez, Ramón Darío. Historial genealógico del Doctor Cristóbal
Mendoza, 1772-1829. Caracas, Venezuela: Ediciones de la
Sociedad Bolivariana, 1972. Rev. by C. J. Fleener, HAHR,
53(Aug 1973):565.

Subramanian, K. K. Import of Capital and Technology: A Study of
Foreign Collaborations in Indian Industry. New Delhi:
People's Publishing House, 1972. Rev. by N. C. Joshi, IQ,
29(Apr-Je 1973):178-9.

Suchlicki, Jaime, ed. Cuba, Castro, and Revolution. Coral Gables,
Fla.: U Miami Press 1972. Rev. by R. H. Fitzgibbon,
AHR, 78(Oct 1973):1150-1.

Suggs, George G., Jr. Colorado's War on Militant Unionism: James
H. Peabody and the Western Federation of Miners. Detroit:
Wayne St U Press, 1972. Rev. by J. Turner, A & W, 15
(Aut 1973):298-9; W. T. Egan, AW, 10(Jl 1973):55; J. P.
Mitchell, CoMag, 50(Sum 1973):266-7; J. M. Cooper, JAH,
60(Sep 1973):466-7; H. Weintraub, PHR, 42(Aug 1973):430-1;
J. E. Brinley, Jr., WHQ, 4(Oct 1973):467-8.

Sullivan, Walter. Death by Melancholy: Essays on Modern Southern
Fiction. Baton Rouge: LSU Press, 1972. Rev. by I. Malin,
GR, 27(Spr 1973):128-31.

Sundarlal, Pandit. British Rule in India. Bombay: Popular Prakashan, 1972. Rev. by A. Prasad, IQ, 29(Oct-Dec 1973):365-6.

Suny, Ronald Grigor. The Baku Commune 1917-1918: Class and
Nationality in the Russian Revolution. Princeton, N. J.: Prin
U Press, 1972. Rev. by J. M. Thompson, JMH, 45(Sep
1973):557-8.

Supple, Barry. The Royal Exchange Assurance: A History of
British Insurance 1720-1970. Cambridge: Cam U Press,
1970. Rev. by L. S. Pressnell, History 58(Feb 1973):167.

Suret-Canale, Jean. French Colonialism in Tropical Africa, 1900-

1945. New York: Pica, 1971. Rev. by M. A. Klein, JMH, 45(Je 1973):333-4.

Sutcliffe, Bob see Glyn, Andrew

Sutherland, C. H. V. English Coinage, 600-1900. London: Batsford, 1973. Rev. by D. F. Allen, Antiquity, 47(Dec 1973): 328-9.

Sutherland, Gillian, ed. Studies in the Growth of Nineteenth-Century Government. Totowa, N. J.: Rowman and Littlefield, 1972. Rev. by R. M. MacLeod, AHR, 78(Dec 1973):1386-1405.

Sutherland Nicola M. The Massacre of St. Bartholomew and the European Conflict 1559-1572. New York: Macmillan, 1973. Rev. by C. Wilson, HJ, 16(Sep 1973):635-7; A. L. Rowse, HTo, 23(Apr 1973):293-4.

Sutton, Anthony C. Western Technology and Soviet Economic Development, 1917 to 1930. Stanford, Cal.: Hoover Institution Press, 1968. Rev. by S. Lieberstein, T & C, 14(Ja 1973): 92-3.

_____. Western Technology and Soviet Economic Development, 1930 to 1945. Stanford, Cal.: Hoover Institution Press, 1971. Rev. by S. Lieberstein, T & C, 14(Ja 1973):92-3.

Sutton, J. E. The East Africa Coast: An Historical and Archaeological Review. Nairobi: East African Publishing House, 1966. Rev. by A. Redmayne, AfAf, 72(Ja 1973):91-3.

Suzuki, Peter, trans. and ed. Aspects of Modern Society: Six Papers. Wiesbaden, Germany: wds--Schnelldruck GmBh, 1971. Rev. by P. Nulty, MEJ, 27(Win 1973):99.

Sveino, Per. Orestes A. Brownson's Road to Catholicism. New York: Humanities, 1971. Rev. by W. J. Gilmore, JAH, 60 (Je 1973):128-9.

Swan, James G. The Northwest Coast: or Three Years' Residence in Washington Territory. Seattle: U Wash Press, 1972. Rev. by R. M. Logan, JOW, 12(Jl 1973):503-4.

Swanberg, W. A. Luce and His Empire. New York: Scribner's, 1972. Rev. by O. Knight, WMH, 56(Sum 1973):331-2.

Swedenberg, H. T., Jr., ed. England in the Restoration and Early Eighteenth Century: Essays on Culture and Society. Berkeley: U Cal Press, 1972. Rev. by J. H. Middendorf, AHR, 78(Je 1973):684-5.

Swenson, Loyd S., Jr. The Ethereal Aether: A History of the Michelson--Morley--Miller Aether-Drift Experiments, 1880-

1930. Austin: U Tx Press, 1972. Rev. by J. L. Heilbron, AHR, 78(Feb 1973):70.

Swomley, John M., Jr. Liberation Ethics. New York: Macmillan, 1973. Rev. by N. Levine, JNH, 58(Oct 1973):482-3.

Sykes, Christopher. Nancy: the Life of Lady Astor. London: Collins, 1972. Rev. by Sowle, VMHB, 81(Apr 1973):213-5.

Syman, Vinson. The Holiness-Pentecostal Movement in the United States. Grand Rapids, Mich.: Eerdmans, 1971. Rev. by C. S. Meyer, CHIQ, 46(Sum 1973):94.

Symons, R. D. Where the Wagon Led: One Man's Memories of the Cowboy's Life in the Old West. Garden City, N. Y.: Doubleday, 1973. Rev. by M. Shatraw, AW, 10(Nov 1973):59.

Syrett, Harold C., et al., eds. The Papers of Alexander Hamilton. Vol. XVI. February 1794-July 1794. New York: Columbia U Press, 1972. Rev. by E. J. Ferguson, JAH, 60(Sep 1973):409-11.

_____. The Papers of Alexander Hamilton. Vol. XVII. August 1794-December 1794. New York: Columbia U Press, 1972. Rev. by E. J. Ferguson, JAH, 60(Sep 1973):409-11; N. E. Cunningham, Jr., JSH, 39(Aug 1973):441-2.

Sywottek, Arnold. Deutsche Volksdemokratie: Studien zur politischen konzeption der K P D 1935-1946. Düsseldorf: Bertelsmann Universitätsverlag, 1971. Rev. by P. H. Merkl, JMH, 45 (Sep 1973):547-8.

Tabor, Thomas T. III. The Rock-A-Bye Baby. n. p. 1972. Rev. by W. S. Webber, NJH, 91(Aut 1973):206.

Tackenberg, K. Die Jüngere Bronzezeit in Nordwestdeutschland, Vol. 1: Die Bronzen. Hildesheim: August Lax, 1971. Rev. by H. Thrane, Antiquity, 47(Sep 1973):241-2.

Takaki, Ronald T. A Pro-Slavery Crusade: The Agitation to Reopen the African Slave Trade. New York: Free Press, 1971. Rev. by H. Aptheker, AHR, 78(Feb 1973):162-3; D. G. Matthews, JNH, 58(Apr 1973):224-5; K. F. Kiple, FHQ, 51(Ja 1973):332-3; J. M. Richardson, CWH, 19(Mar 1973):83-4.

Talbot, Theodore see Hine, Robert V.

Tamuno, T. N. The Evolution of the Nigerian State: The Southern Phase: 1898-1914. New York: Humanities, 1972. Rev. by L. G. Cowan, AHR, 78(Dec 1973):1507-8; J. D. Hargreaves, JAfH, 14(3rd Qr 1973):512-14; A. H. M. Kirk-Greene, AfAf, 72(Oct 1973):455-6.

Tan, Lek see Caldwell, Malcolm

Tandon, Y. A. ed. Readings in African International Relations.
    Nairobi: East African Literature Bureau, 1972. Rev. by P.
    W., AfAf, 72(Oct 1973):465.

Tandrup, Leo. A Swedish Agent at the Sound: The Dispatches of
    the Customs' Commissar and Agent Anders Svensen at Elsi-
    nore to Gustavus II Adolphus and Axel Oxenstierna. Aarhus:
    Universitetsforlaget, 1971. Rev. by W. Kirchner, AHR, 78
    (Oct 1973):1086-8.

Tanham, George. Contribution à l'histoire de la Résistance belge,
    1940/1944. Brussels: Presses Universitaires de Bruxelles,
    1971. Rev. by W. Warmbrunn, JMH, 45(Sep 1973):550-1.

Tann, Jennifer. The Development of the Factory. London: Corn-
    market Press, 1970. Rev. by J. R. Harris, MH, 2(Aut
    1973):124-5; D. O. Whitten, JEH, 33(Dec 1973):907-8.

Tanner, Clara Lee. Southwest Indian Painting. Tucson: U Ariz
    Press, Rev. by J. N. Young JAriH, 14(Spr 1973):79-80.

Tantaquidgeon Gladys. Folk Medicine of the Delaware and Related
    Algonkian Indians. Harrisburg: Pa Historical and Museum
    Commission, 1972. Rev. by C. A. Weslager, PMHB, 97
    (Apr 1973):264-5; J. Duffy, WPHM, 56(Apr 1973):193-5.

Tarling, Nicholas. Britain, the Brookes, and Brunei. Oxford: Ox U
    Press, 1972. Rev. by T. J. Barron, History, 58(Je 1973):
    333.

Tarr, Joel Arthur. A Study of Boss Politics: William Lorimer of
    Chicago. Urbana: U Ill Press, 1971. Rev. by B. McKelvey,
    SS, 64(Ja 1973):39.

Tate, D. J. M. The Making of Modern Southeast Asia. Vol. 1:
    The European Conquest. Kuala Lumpur, Singapore: Ox U
    Press, 1971. Rev. by R. T Smith, Jr., Historian, 35(Nov
    1973):117; M. Caldwell, History, 58(Je 1973):333.

Tate, H. Clay. The Way It Was in McLean County. Bloomington,
    Ill.: McLean County History Assn., 1972. Rev. by A.
    O'Rourke JISHS, 66(Aut 1973):356-7.

Taylor, A. J. P. Beaverbrook. London: Hamish Hamilton, 1972.
    Rev. by K. O. Morgan, History, 58(Oct 1973):475-6; C. R.
    Cole, JMH, 45(Sep 1973):531-3.

Taylor, Maxwell D. Swords and Plowshares. New York: Norton,
    1972. Rev. by L. J. Korb, MilAf, 37(Oct 1973):114-5.

Taylor, Philip. The Distant Magnet: European Emigration to the

TAYLOR   308

United States of America. New York: Harper and Row, 1971.
    Rev. by R. Ernst, AHR, 78(Feb 1973):164-5.

Taylor, Robert J., ed. The Susquehannah Company Papers. Vol. X:
    1789-1800; Vol. XI: 1801-1808. Ithaca, N. Y.: Cornell U
    Press, 1971. Rev. by L. R. Gerlach, PH, 40(Ja 1973):103-
    5; I. Richman, PH 40(Jl 1973):337-8; W. S. Hanna, WMQ,
    3rd ser., 30 (Ja 1973):176-8.

Taylor, Samuel W. Nightfall at Nauvoo. New York: Macmillan,
    1971. Rev. by J. Shipps, Historian, 35(Feb 1973):312.

Taylor, Welford Dunaway, et al., eds. Virginia Authors: Past and
    Present. Farmville, Va.: Longwood College, 1972. Rev.
    by F. C. Rosenberger, NCHR, 50(Win 1973):99-100; R. B.
    Davis, VMHB, 81(Ja 1973):121-3.

Taylor, William B. Landlord and Peasant in Colonial Oaxaca. [Stan-
    ford, Cal.]: Stan U Press, 1972. Rev. by J. Fisher, His-
    tory, 58(Oct 1973):480; M. J. Penton, CHR, 54(Sep 1973):
    314; J. Lockhart, AHR, 78(Oct 1973):1151-2; G. M. Riley,
    HAHR, 53(Aug 1973):502-4.

Taylor, William Leonhard. A Productive Monopoly: The Effect of
    Railroad Control on New England Coastal Steamship Lines,
    1870-1916. Providence, R. I.: Brown U Press, 1970. Rev.
    by A. E Rokwell, JEH, 33(Sep 1973):687-8.

Teale, Edwin Way. Photographs of American Nature. New York:
    Dodd, Mead, 1972. Rev. by R. M. Pyle, AW, 10(Nov 1973):
    52.

Tebbel, John. A History of Book Publishing in the United States.
    Vol. I. The Creation of an Industry, 1660-1865. New York:
    R. R. Bowker, 1972. Rev. by M. B. Stern, BHR, 47(Win
    1973):522-3.

Tebeau, Charlton W. Synagogue in the Central City: Temple Israel
    of Greater Miami. Miami, Fla.: U Miami Press, 1972.
    Rev. by J. F. Reiger, FHQ, 51(Apr 1973):444-5.

Te-K'un, Cheng. Archaeology in Sarawak. Toronto: U Tor Press,
    1969. Rev. by R. C. Rudolf, Archaeology, 26(Ja 1973):75-6.

Témine, Émile see Broué, Pierre

Temkin, Polly Brody. Discovering Wisconsin. Madison: Wisconsin
    House, 1973. Rev. by J. O. Holzhueter, WMH, 56(Sum 1973):
    327-8.

Temperley, Howard. British Antislavery, 1833-1870. Columbia,
    S. C.: U SCar Press, 1972. Rev. by W. A. Green, AHR,
    78(Je 1973):690-1; B. Harrison, History, 58(Oct 1973):459-

-60; P. C. Lipscomb III, JSH, 39(Aug 1973):447-8; J. L.
Godfrey, NCHR, 50(Spr 1973):222-3.

Temu, A. J. British Protestant Missions. London: Longmans,
1972. Rev. by I. Linden, JAfH, 14(3rd Qr 1973):520-1.

Teng, S. Y. The Taiping Rebellion and the Western Powers: A
Comprehensive Survey. Oxford: Clarendon Press, 1971.
Rev. by A. Iriye, JMH, 45(Mar 1973):150-2.

Terrell, John Upton. American Indian Almanac. New York: World,
1971. Rev. by H. E. Driver, AHR, 78(Je 1973):723-4.

_____. Apache Chronicle: The Story of the People. New York:
World, 1972. Rev. by D. L. Thrapp, A & W, 15(Win 1973):
375-6; O. L. Jones, Montana, 23(Sum 1973):58; R. F.
Locke, AW, 10(Jl 1973):51, 56.

_____. Bunkhouse Papers: Reminiscences of a Distinguished
Western Historian. New York: Dial, 1971. Rev. by E.
West, Montana, 23(Win 1973):61.

_____. Land Grab: The Truth About "The Winning of the West."
New York: Dial, 1972. Rev. by L. B. Lee, AW, 10(Mar
1973):57.

Terrill, Ross. R. H. Tawney and His Times: Socialism as Fellow-
ship. Cambridge, Mass.: Har U Press, 1973. Rev. by
W. H. Dunham, Jr., HRNB, 2(Nov/Dec 1973):30-1.

Tewari, R. N. Agricultural Planning and Cooperatives. Delhi: Sul-
tan Chand, 1972. Rev. by B. N. Nair, IQ, 29(Apr-Je 1973):
177-8.

Thale, Mary, ed. The Autobiography of Francis Place, 1771-1854.
New York: Cam U Press, 1970. Rev. by T. M. Kemnitz,
AHR, 78(Feb 1973):100-1; R. A. Smith, Historian, 36(Nov
1973):103-4; P. Hollis, History, 58(Oct 1973):458.

Thane, Elswyth. The Fighting Quaker: Nathaniel Greene. New
York: Hawthorn, 1972. Rev. by J. E. Hendricks, NCHR,
50(Sum 1973):338; G. W. Kyte, PMHB, 97(Ja 1973):118-19.

Theberge, J. D., ed. Soviet Seapower in the Caribbean: Political
and Strategic Implications. New York: Praeger, 1972. Rev.
by R. W. Herrick, RR, 32(Apr 1973):217-8.

Theisen, Gerald see Bandelier, Fanny

Thelen, David P. The New Citizenship: Origins of Progressivism
in Wisconsin 1885-1900. Columbia, Mo.: U Mo Press, 1972.
Rev. by R. M. Wurner, MichH, 57(Sum 1973):178-81.

THEODOLOU 310

Theodolou, Christos. Greece and the Entente: August 1, 1914-
September 25, 1916. Thessaloniki: Institute of Balkan Studies,
1971. Rev. by W. H. McNeill, JMH, 45(Sep 1973):555; H. N.
Howard, MEJ, 27(Sum 1973):410.

Theoharis, Athan. Seeds of Repression: Harry S. Truman and the
Origins of McCarthyism. Chicago: Quadrangle, 1971. Rev.
by D. Albertson, JAH, 60(Sep 1973):506-8.

Theoharis, Athan G. The Yalta Myths: An Issue in United States
Politics, 1945-1955. Columbia, Mo.: U Mo Press, 1970.
Rev. by R. D. Schulzinger, H & T, 12(1973):146-62.

Thésée, Françoise. Négociants bordelais et colons de Saint-Dom-
ingue: Liaisons d'habitations: La maison Henry Rombert,
Bapst et Cie, 1783-1793. Paris: Paul Geuthner, 1972. Rev.
by J. F. Bosher, JMH, 45(Sep 1973):497.

Thirsk, Joan and J. P. Cooper, eds. Seventeenth-Century Economic
Documents. Oxford: Clarendon Press, 1972. Rev. by J.
Appleby, JEH, 33(Sep 1973):689; R. O'Day, MH, 2(Spr 1973):
50-1.

Thomas, Brinley. Migration and Urban Development: A Reappraisal
of British and American Long Cycles. London: Methuen,
1972. Rev. by P. George, JEH, 33(Dec 1973):909-10.

Thomas, Charles. Britain and Ireland in Early Christian Times.
London: Thames and Hudson, 1971. Rev. by P. Rahtz, History, 58(Feb 1973):75-6.

_____. The Early Christian Archaeology of North Britain. Ox-
ford: Ox U Press, 1971. Rev. by P. Rahtz, History, 58
(Feb 1973):75-6.

_____, ed. The Iron Age in the Irish Sea Province. London:
Council for British Archaeology, 1972. Rev. by T. G. E.
Powell, Antiquity, 47(Mar 1973):74-5.

Thomas, D. Aneurin, ed. The Welsh Elizabethan Catholic Martyrs.
Cardiff: U Wales Press, 1971. Rev. by B. Howells, History, 58(Je 1973):282.

Thomas, Hugh. Cuba. The Pursuit of Freedom. New York: Harper and Row, 1971. Rev. by R. W. Gronet, TAm, 30(Oct
1973):288-90; F. Laubert, History, 58(Feb 1973):145-6.

_____. John Strachey. New York: Harper and Row, 1973. Rev.
by L. Bisceglia, HRNB, 2(Nov/Dec 1973):29-30.

Thomas, John. The Rise of the Staffordshire Potteries. New York:
Augustus M. Kelley, 1971. Rev. by J. R. Harris, JMH, 45
(Dec 1973):651-3.

Thomas, Lately. The Astor Orphans: A Pride of Lions: The
   Chanler Chronicle. New York: Morrow, 1971. Rev. by V.
   Buranelli, NYHSQ, 57(Apr 1973):187-8.

_____. When Even Angels Wept: The Senator Joseph McCarthy
   Affair--A Story Without a Hero. New York: Morrow, 1973.
   Rev. by T. C. Reeves, JAH, 60(Dec 1973):860-1.

Thomas, Norman C., et al., eds. The Institutional Presidency.
   Dobbs Ferry, N. Y.: Oceana, 1972. Rev. by S. Warren,
   JAH 59(Mar 1973):1044-5.

Thomas, William H. B. Orange, Virginia: Story of a Courthouse
   Town. Verona, Va.: McClure, 1972. Rev. by J. T. Moore,
   VMHB, 81(Ja 1973):116-7.

Thomis, Malcolm I. The Luddites: Machine-Breaking in Regency
   England. New York: Schocken, 1972. Rev. by G. Rude, SS,
   64(Nov 1973):284-5.

_____., ed. Luddism in Nottinghamshire. n. p. : Phillimore
   ... 1972. Rev. by B. K. Crawford, MH, 2(Spr 1973):53-4.

Thompson, Daniel C. Private Black Colleges at the Crossroads.
   Westport, Conn.: Greenwood, 1973. Rev. by D. L. Watson,
   Crisis, 80(Dec 1973):322-3.

Thompson, E. A. The Goths in Spain. [Oxford:] Ox U Press, 1969.
   Rev. by R. J. H. Collins, History, 58(Oct 1973):423-4.

Thompson, Erwin N. Modoc War: Its Military History and Topography. Sacramento, Cal.: Argus, 1971. Rev. by O.
   Knight, A & W, 15(Spr 1973):94-5.

Thompson, Ewa M. Russian Formalism and Anglo-American New
   Criticism. The Hague: Mouton, 1971. Rev. by L. G.
   Leighton, RR, 32(Ja 1973):100.

Thompson, Gregory Coyne. Southern Ute Lands, 1848-1899; The
   Creation of a Reservation. Durango, Colo.: Ft. Lewis College, 1972. Rev. by S. L. Tyler, NMHR, 48(Apr 1973):180-
   181.

_____. The Southern Utes: ... see Jefferson, James.

Thompson, Homer A. and R. E. Wycherley. The Agora of Athens:
   The History, Shape and Uses of an Ancient City Center.
   Princeton, N. J.: American School of Classical Studies at
   Athens, 1972. Rev. by M. Hammond, AHR, 78(Oct 1973):
   1025-6.

Thompson, J. A. and Arthur Mejia, Jr. The Modern British Monarchy. New York: St. Martin's, 1971. Rev. by G. Smith,

THOMPSON 312

AHR, 78(Feb 1973):106-7.

Thompson, John M. see Mehlinger, Howard D.

Thompson, Lawrence S. Books in Our Time (Essays). Washington,
D. C.: Consortium Press, 1972. Rev. by J. R. Bentley,
FCHQ, 47(Jl 1973):291-2.

Thompson, Lawrence. The Enthusiasts: A Biography of John and
Katherine Bruce Glazier. London: Gollancz, 1971. Rev. by
A. Markwick, History, 58(Feb 1973):130.

Thompson, Paul. William Butterfield. Cambridge, Mass.: M I T
Press, 1971. Rev. by G. Howes, AHR, 78(Oct 1973):1060-2.

Thompson, R. W. D-Day: Spearhead of Invasion. New York: Ballantine, 1968. Rev. by R. P. Weinert, Jr., MilAf, 37(Dec
1973):162.

Thomsen, Erich. Deutsch Besatzungspolitik in Dänemark 1940-1945.
Düsseldorf: Bertelsmann Universitätsverlag, 1971. Rev. by
V. Mastny, JMH, 45(Je 1973):361-3.

Thomson, George Malcolm. Sir Francis Drake. New York: Morrow, 1972. Rev. by L. B. Wright, AHR, 78(Je 1973):681.

Thornbrough, Emma Lou, ed. Black Reconstructionists. Englewood
Cliffs, N. J.: Prentice-Hall, 1972. Rev. by W. H. Daniel,
HT, 6(May 1973):487-8.

_____. T. Thomas Fortune: Militant Journalist. Chicago: U
Chi Press, 1972. Rev. by J. H. Shofner, FHQ, 51(Ja 1973):
315-16; L. R. Harlan, JSH, 39(Feb 1973):129-31.

Thornbrough, Gayle, ed. The Diary of Calvin Fletcher. Vol. I.
1817-1838: Including Letters of Calvin Fletcher and Diaries
and Letters of His Wife, Sarah Hill Fletcher. Indianapolis:
Ind Historical Society, 1972. Rev. by J. H. Rodabaugh, IMH,
69(Mar 1973):65-6; J. F. Stover, JAH, 60(Je 1973):133-4.

Thornton, Richard C. The Bear and the Dragon: Sino-Soviet Relations and the Evolution of the Chinese People's Republic, 1949-
1971. New York: American Asian Educational Science, 1972.
Rev. by R. L. Walker, RR, 32(Apr 1973):189-192.

Thorpe, Earl E. The Old South: A Psychohistory. Durham, N. C.:
The Author, 1972. Rev. by M. Billington, RKHS, 71(Ja 1973):
121-3; R. McColley, JSH, 39(May 1973):290-2; A. Rolle,
JAH, 60(Sep 1973):448-9.

Thrapp, Dan L. General Crook and the Sierra Madre Adventure.
Norman: U Ok Press, 1972. Rev. by R. Brandes, WHQ, 4
(Oct 1973):456-7; O. Knight, A & W, 15(Spr 1973):94-5; R.

L. Nichols, Montana, 23(Spr 1973):68; W. G. Bell, MilAf, 37(Oct 1973):111-12; R. N. Ellis, CoMag, 50(Sum 1973):255-6; R. M. Utley, NMHR, 48(Apr 1973):181-2; R. C. Carriker, PHR, 42(May 1973):255-6.

Throckmorton, Peter. Shipwrecks and Archaeology: The Unharvested Sea. Boston: Little, Brown, 1970. Rev. by M. L. Katzev, Archaeology, 26(Ja 1973):72.

Tibawi, A. L. Islamic Education: Its Traditions and Modernization into the Arab National Systems. London: Luzac, 1972. Rev. by F. I. Qubain, MEJ, 27(Aut 1973):519-21.

Tibbles, Thomas Henry and Kay Graber eds. The Ponca Chiefs: An Account of the Trial of Standing Bear. Lincoln: U Neb Press, 1972. Rev. by L. J. White, JOW, 12(Oct 1973):640.

Tien, Hung-Mao. Government and Politics in Kuomintang China, 1927-1937. Stanford, Cal.: Stan U Press, 1972. Rev. by A. Feuerwerker, AHR, 78(Dec 1973):1510-11.

Tierney, Brian. Origins of Papal Infallibility, 1150-1350: A Study on the Concepts of Infallibility, Sovereignty, and Tradition in the Middle Ages. Leiden: E. J. Brill, 1972. Rev. by H. S. Offler, AHR, 78(Je 1973):664-6.

Till, Barry. The Churches Search for Unity. Baltimore: Penguin, 1972. Rev. by C. E. McClelland, JMH, 45(Sep 1973):528-9.

Timberlake, Charles E., ed. Essays on Russian Liberalism. Columbia, Mo.: U Mo Press, 1972. Rev. by A. G. Mazour, RR, 32(Apr 1973):218.

Timur, Serim. Family Structure in Turkey. Ankara: Dogus Maatbacilik, 1972. Rev. by P. Nulty, MEJ, 27(Win 1973):101.

Tindall, George Brown. The Disruption of the Solid South. Athens, Ga.: U Ga Press, 1971. Rev. by J. W. Silver, FHQ, 51 (Apr 1973):452-4; D. H. Donald, JNH, 58(Apr 1973):207-9; J. H. Wilkinson III, VMHB, 81(Apr 1973):210-12; J. R. Skates, Jr., JMiH, 35(Feb 1973):102-4.

Titiev, Mischa. The Hopi Indians of Old Oraibi, Change and Continuity. Ann Arbor: U Mich Press, 1972. Rev. by F. Eggan, JAriH, 14(1973):257-8.

Titow, J. Z. Winchester Yields: A Study in Medieval Agricultural Productivity. Cambridge: Cam U Press, 1972. Rev. by R. H. Hilton, EHR, 88(Jl 1973):590-2; W. O. Ault, AgH, 47(Jl 1973):273-4.

Tobias, Henry J. The Jewish Bund in Russia From Its Origins to 1905. Stanford, Cal.: Stan U Press 1972. Rev. by H.

Shukman, RR, 32(Apr 1973):201-2; R. G. Suny, Historian,
35(Feb 1973):292-3.

Todd, John M. Reformation. London: Darton, Longman and Todd,
1972. Rev. by P. C. Matheson, History, 58(Je 1973):275-6.

Todd, Malcolm. Everyday Life of the Barbarians: Goths, Franks,
and Vandals. New York: Putnam's, 1972. Rev. by O.
Klindt-Jenson, Antiquity, 47(Sep 1973):240-1.

Todd, William. History as Applied Science: A Philosophical Study.
Detroit: Wayne St U Press, 1972. Rev. by T. Langan,
T & C, 14(Jl 1973):525-7.

Toland, John. The Rising Sun: The Decline and Fall of the Japanese Empire, 1936-1945. New York: Random House, 1970.
Rev. by E. Andrade, Jr., Historian, 35(Feb 1973):301-2.

Tolley, Kemp. Yangtze Patrol. The U. S. Navy in China. Annapolis: Naval Institute Press, 1971. Rev. by O. J. Caldwell,
Historian, 36(Nov 1973):132-3.

Tomasi, S. M. see Wenk Michael

Tompkins, E. Berkeley, ed. The United Nations in Perspective.
Stanford, Cal.: Hoover Institute Press, 1972. Rev. by G. B.
Ostrower, JAH, 60(Je 1973):178-9.

Toole, K. Ross. Twentieth Century Montana: A State of Extremes.
Norman: U Ok Press, 1972. Rev. by F. R. Peterson,
A & W, 15(Aut 1973):285-6; R. Athearn, Montana, 23(Win
1973):59; R. T. Ruetten, PHR, 42(Aug 1973):431-2.

Toplin, Robert Brent. The Abolition of Slavery in Brazil. New
York: Atheneum, 1972. Rev. by F. W. Knight, AHR, 78
(Dec 1973):1561; D. B. Cooper, Historian, 36(Nov 1973):140;
P. L. Eisenberg, HAHR, 53(Nov 1973):704-7; R. E. Conrad,
JSH, 39(Aug 1973):452-3.

Toponce, Alexander. (Robert A. Griffin, intro.). Reminiscences
of Alexander Toponce, Written by Himself. Norman: U Ok
Press, 1971. Rev. by P. I. Earl, NHSQ, 16(Sum 1973):135-
7.

Toppin, Edgar A. A Biographical History of Blacks in America Since
1528. New York: David McKay, 1971. Rev. by R. P.
Carlisle, SS, 64(Feb 1973):86-7.

Tovar, Frederico Ribes. Albizu Campos: Puerto Rican Revolutionary. New York: Plus Ultra Educational Publishers, 1971.
Rev. by W. Bratter, HAHR, 53(Feb 1973):161-2.

Townsend, Dorothy Edwards. The Life and Works of John Wilson

Townsend. Lexington, Ky.: Keystone Printery, 1972. Rev.
by B. Milward, RKHS, 71(Apr 1973):194-5; T. D. Clark,
FCHQ, 47(Apr 1973):193-4.

Toynbee, J. M. C. Animals in Roman Life and Art. Ithaca, N. Y.:
Cornell U Press, 1973. Rev. by S. I. Oost, HRNB, 2(Nov/
Dec 1973):34.

Tragle, Henry Irving. The Southampton Revolt of 1831: A Compilation of Source Material. Amherst, Mass.: U Mass Press,
1971. Rev. by D. P. Jordan, MHM, 68(Spr 1973):106-7; P.
M. Mitchell, Historian, 35(Feb 1973):309-10.

Trask, David F. Captains and Cabinets: Anglo-American Naval
Relations, 1917-1918. Columbia, Mo.: U Mo Press, 1972.
Rev. by G. E. Wheeler, MilAf, 37(Dec 1973):160.

Trease, Geoffrey. Samuel Pepys and His World. New York: Putnam's, 1972. Rev. by G. R. Abernathy, Jr., HT, 6(May
1973):482.

Treasure, G. R. R. Cardinal Richelieu and the Development of Absolutism. New York: St. Martin's, 1972. Rev. by J. H. M.
Salmon, JMH, 45(Sep 1973):481-3.

Treganza, Adam E. see Heizer, Robert F.

Treharne, R. F. The Baronial Plan of Reform, 1258-1263. New
York: Barnes and Noble, 1971. Rev. by E. J. Kealey, Historian, 35(Feb 1973):282-3.

Trelease, Allen W. White Terror. The Ku Klux Klan Conspiracy
and Southern Reconstruction. New York: Harper and Row,
1971. Rev. by C. Bolt, History, 58(Oct 1973):492; E. Swin-
ney, CWH, 19(Mar 1973):87-8.

Trench, Charles Chenevix. The Western Rising. London: Longmans, 1969. R. A. Beddard, History, 58(Oct 1973):450-1.

Trentlein, Theodore E. San Francisco Bay: Discovery and Colonization, 1769-1776. San Francisco: Cal Historical Society,
1968. Rev. by T. F. Andrews, JAH, 59(Mar 1973):983-4.

Trevor Arnett Library, Atlanta University. Guide to Manuscripts
and Archives in the Negro Collection of Trevor Arnett Library, Atlanta University. Atlanta: Atlanta U, 1971. Rev.
by A. L. Nolen, AmArch, 36(Ja 1973):76-8.

Trevor-Roper, H. The Plunder of the Arts in the Seventeenth Century. London: Thames and Hudson, 1971. Rev. by L. O.
Boynton, History, 58(Oct 1973):449-50.

Tribe, David President Charles Bradlaugh, M. P. Hamden, Conn.:

Archon, 1971. Rev. by W. L. Arnstein, JMH, 45(Mar 1973): 131-3; C. K. Krantz, AHR, 78(Je 1973):694-5.

Trivers, Howard. Three Crises in American Foreign Affairs and a Continuing Revolution. Carbondale: S Ill U Press, 1972. Rev. by L. Gardner, JAH, 60(Je 1973):185-6.

Trogdon, Katherine Curtis, ed. and comp. The History of Stephens County, Georgia. Toccoa, Ga.: Toccoa Women's Club, 1973. Rev. in GHQ, 57(Fall 1973):450-1.

Trotsky, Leon. Military Writings. New York: Merit, 1969. Rev. by J. W. Kipp, MilAf, 37(Oct 1973):114.

_____. The Spanish Revolution (1931-39). New York: Pathfinder, 1973. Rev. by G. Jackson, AHR, 78(Dec 1973):1484-5.

_____. 1905. New York: Random House, 1971. Rev. by A. G. Mazour, RR, 32(Ja 1973):100-1.

Trovaioli, August P. and Raulhac B. Toledano. William Aiken Walker: Southern Genre Painter. Baton Rouge: LSU Press, 1972. Rev. by H. Wayne Morgan, JAH, 60(Sep 1973):485; R. B. Harwell, JSH, 39(Aug 1973):472-3.

Trueblood, Elton. Abraham Lincoln: Theologian of American Anguish. New York: Harper and Row, 1973. Rev. by T. H. Williams, CWH, 19(Dec 1973):361-2.

Truman, Margaret. Harry S. Truman. New York: Morrow, 1973. Rev. by K. McNaught, AHR, 78(Dec 1973):1555-6.

Tsvetayeva, Marina. Selected Poems. New York: Ox U Press, 1971. Rev. by S. Karlinsky, RR, 32(Ja 1973):101-2.

Tucker, David M. Lieutenant Lee of Beale Street. Nashville: Van U Press, 1971. Rev. M. D. Eberling, THQ, 32(Sum 1973): 189-90

Tucker, Glen. Mad Anthony Wayne and the New Nation: The Story of Washington's Front-Line General. Harrisburg, Pa.: Stackpole, 1973. Rev. by A. R Sunseri, HRNB, 2(Nov/Dec 1973):44; GHQ, 57(Win 1973):598-9; L. Brewster, NCHR, 50(Aut 1973):428-9.

Tucker, Robert. The Radical Left and American Foreign Policy. Baltimore: JHU Press, 1971. Rev. by R. L. Roe, WMH, 56(Sum 1973):336-7.

Tucker, Robert C. Stalin as a Revolutionary, 1879-1929: A Study in History and Personality. New York: Norton, 1973. Rev. by S. M. Horak, HRNB, 2(Oct 1973):2.

Tugwell, Rexford G.   In Search of Roosevelt.   Cambridge, Mass.:
    Har U Press, 1972.   Rev. by F. Freidel, AHR, 78(Dec 1973):
    1548-9.

_____. Off Course: From Truman to Nixon.   New York:
    Praeger, 1971.   Rev. by F. Freidel, AHR, 78(Dec 1973):
    1548-9.

Tulchin, Joseph S.   The Aftermath of War: World War I and U. S.
    Policy Toward Latin America.   New York: NYU Press, 1971.
    Rev. by K. J. Grieb, TAm, 30(Jl 1973):146-7; D. K. Adams,
    History, 58(Oct 1973):495-6.

Tullis, F. Lamond.   Politics and Social Change in Third World
    Countries.   New York: Wiley, 1973.   Rev. by W. Clark,
    Jr., MEJ, 27(Aut 1973):526-7.

Tuma, Elias H.   Economic History and the Social Sciences: Prob-
    lems of Methodology.   Berkeley: U Cal Press, 1971.   Rev.
    by L. Galambos, BHR, 47(Aut 1973):374-5.

Tümertekin, Erol.   Analysis of the Location of Industry in Istanbul.
    Istanbul: Istanbul U, 1972.   Rev. by P. Nulty, MEJ, 27(Spr
    1973):244-5.

Turin, Yvonne.   Affrontements culturels dans l'Algérie coloniale:
    Écoles, medecines, religion, 1830-1880.   Paris: Francois
    Maspero, 1971.   Rev. by J. Ruedy, AHR, 78(Je 1973):720-1.

Turki, Fawaz.   The Disinherited, Journal of a Palestinian Exile.
    New York: Monthly Review Press, 1972.   Rev. in CurH, 64
    (Ja 1973):34.

Turnbull, C. M.   The Straits Settlements, 1826-67: Indian Presi-
    dency to Crown Colony.   London: Athlone, 1972.   Rev. by
    E. Stokes, History, 58(Je 1973):331-2.

Turner, Barry A.   Exploring the Industrial Subculture.   New York:
    Herder and Herder, 1972.   Rev. by E. Kurzweil, T & C, 14
    (Oct 1973):672-3.

Turner, Hilary L.   Town Defences in England and Wales: An Archi-
    tectural and Documentary Study, AD 900-1500.   London: John
    Baker, 1971.   Rev. by G. H. Martin, History, 58(Oct 1973):
    429-30.

Turner, Josephine M.   The Happy Years.   Louisville, Ky.: Litho-
    craft, n. d.   Rev. by R. D. Deiss, RKHS, 71(Apr 1973):198-
    9.

Turner, Justin G. and Linda Levitt Turner.   Mary Todd Lincoln,
    Her Life and Letters.   New York: Knopf, 1972.   Rev. by
    F. C. McLaughlin, WPHM, 56(Apr 1973):187-90; R. A.

Walker, JISHS, 66(Spr 1973):96-7; F. L. Byrne, JAH, 60 (Sep 1973):454-5.

Turner, Martha Anne. William Barret Travis: His Sword and His Pen. Waco, Tx.: Texian, 1972. Rev. by E. H. Phillips, JSH, 39(Nov 1973):596.

Tutorow, Norman E. Leland Stanford: Man of Many Careers. Menlo Park, Cal.: Pacific Coast Publishers, 1971. Rev. by R. J. Roske, NHSQ, 16(Spr 1973):32.

Tuttleton, James W. The Novel of Manners in America. Chapel Hill: UNC Press, 1972. Rev. by H. Kaplan, JAH, 60(Je 1973):141-2.

Twain, Mark. (Franklin R. Rogers, ed.). Roughing It. Berkeley: U Cal Press, 1972. Rev. by R. Stewart, NHSQ, 16(Sum 1973):137-8.

Tweeten, Luther G. Foundations of Farm Policy. Lincoln: U Neb Press, 1970. Rev. by D. E. Anderson, NDH, 40(Fall 1973): 31.

Twenty-Five Years of Indian Independence. Calcutta: Oxford and I B H, 1972. Rev. by V. Machwe, IQ, 29(Apr-Je 1973):183.

Tweton, D. Jerome. The Marquis de Mores: Dakota Capitalist, French Nationalist. Fargo: N D Institute for Regional Studies, 1972. Rev. by L. Atherton, NDH, 40(Sum 1973):34-5; T. Hinckley, JAH, 60(Dec 1973):821-2; J. W. Whitaker, AgH, 47(Oct 1973):369-70.

Tyler, R. L. Walter Reuther. Grand Rapids, Mich.: Eerdmans, 1973. Rev. by V. J. Vogel, MichH, 57(Fall 1973):271-3.

Tymn, Marshall B. , comp. and ed. Thomas Cole's Poetry: The Collected Poems of America's Foremost Painter of the Hudson River School Reflecting His Feelings for Nature and the Romantic Spirit of the Nineteenth Century. York, Pa.: Liberty Cap Books, 1972. Rev. by S. S. Smith NYH, 54 (Jl 1973):367-70; E. S. Vesell, NYHSQ, 57(Jl 1973):271-2.

Ubbelohde, Carl, Maxine Benson and Duane A. Smith. A Colorado History. Boulder, Colo.: Pruett, 1972. Rev. by R. C. Black III, CoMag, 50(Spr 1973):163-4.

Ulam, Adam B. The Rivals: America and Russia Since World War II. New York: Viking, 1971. Rev. by D. F. Fleming, JMH, 45(Je 1973):363-4.

Ullman, Victor. Martin R. Delaney: The Beginnings of Black Nationalism. Boston: Beacon, 1971. Rev. by O. M. Scruggs, JNH, 58(Apr 1973):229-31.

Ullman, Walter. A Short History of the Papacy in the Middle Ages.
London: Methuen, 1972. Rev. by C. H. Lawrence, History,
58(Oct 1973):428-9; C. Morris, EHR, 88(Oct 1973):842-4.

Ulloa, Berta. La Revolución intervenida. Relaciones diplomáticas
entre México y Estados Unidos (1910-1914). Guanajuato: El
Colegio de Mexico, 1971. Rev. by S. B. Liss, TAm, 30(Jl
1973):139-40.

Unbeqaun, B. O. Russian Surnames. New York: Ox U Press,
1972. Rev. by D. S. Worth, RR, 32(Oct 1973):444-5.

Unione regionale della province Toscane, Provincia di Firenze, and
Instituto storico per la Resistenza in Toscana, La Toscana
nel regime fascista (1922-1939). Florence: Leo S. Olschki
Editore, 1971. Rev. by R. A. Webster, JMH, 45(Je 1973):
342-4.

UNESCO. World Guide to Technical Information and Documentation
Services. New York: UNIPUB, 1969. Rev. by J. R. Good-
stein, AmArch, 36(Jl 1973):419-20.

University College of Wales, Aberystwyth. Centenary Exhibition,
1872-1972. Aberystwyth: The College, 1972. Rev. J. Varley, Archives, 11(Aut 1973):110-11.

Unrau, William E. The Kansa Indians: A History of the Wind
People, 1673-1873. Norman: U Ok Press, 1971. Rev. by
A. M. Gibson, PHR, 42(May 1973):243-5.

Upton, Richard, ed. and comp. Fort Custer on the Big Horn, 1877-
1898: Its History and Personalities as Told and Pictured by
Its Contemporaries. Glendale, Cal.: Arthur H. Clark, 1973.
Rev. by R. M. Utley, WHQ, 4(Oct 1973):455-6.

Urban, G. R. and Michael Glenny, eds. Can We Survive Our Future? New York: St. Martin's, 1972. Rev. by H. J. Muller, T & C, 14(Ja 1973):100-8.

Urfer, Sylvani. Ujamaa, espoir du socialisme africain en Tanzania.
n. p.: Aubier Montaigne, 1971. Rev. by G. Kitching, AfAf,
72(Ja 1973):93-4.

Urofsky, Melvin I. and David W. Levy, eds. Letters of Louis D.
Brandeis. Vol. I. 1870-1907: Urban Reformer. Albany:
SUNY, 1971. Rev. by J. B. Crooks, MHM, 68(Spr 1973):
110-11.

_____ and _____. Letters of Louis D. Brandeis. Vol. II.
1907-1912. People's Attorney. Albany: SUNY, 1972. Rev.
by M. K. B. Tachau, FCHQ, 47(Jl 1973):287-9; E. V. Mit-
tlebeeler, RKHS, 71(Apr 1973):218-9.

Urquhart, Brian. Hammarskjold. New York: Knopf, 1972. Rev.

by E. M. Wilson, MEJ, 27(Spr 1973):245-6.

Urrutia, Carlos Lopez. Las Escuadra chilena en México, 1822. Los Carsarios chilenos y argentinos en los mares del norte. Buenos Aires, Argentina: Editorial Francisco de Aguirra, 1971. Rev. by D. E. Worcester, HAHR, 53(Feb 1973):127-8.

Urrutia, Miguel M. and Mario Arrubla, eds. Compendio de Esladísticas historicas de Colombia. Bogata: Universidad Nacional de Colombia, 1970. Rev. by R. H. Dalkart, HAHR, 53(Feb 1973):139-40.

Ussery, Huling E. Chaucer's Physician: Medicine and Literature in Fourteenth-Century England. New Orleans: Tulane U, 1971. Rev. by P. Kibre, AHR, 78(Je 1973):668-9.

Vail, Philip. The Great American Rascal: The Turbulent Life of Aaron Burr. New York: Hawthorn, 1973. Rev. by A. Bakshian, Jr., Mankind, 4(Aug 1973):6; R. Van Zandt, NYHSQ, 57(Oct 1973):356-7.

Valdés, Nelson P. see Bonachea, Rolando E.

Vali, Ferenc A. Bridge Across the Bosporus. Baltimore: JHU Press, n. d. Rev. by S. Kirshner, NO, 16(May 1973):49-52.

_____. The Turkish Straits and NATO. Stanford, Cal.: Hoover Institution Press, 1972. Rev. by R. W. Herrick, RR, 32 (Ja 1973):102.

Van Caenegen, R. C. The Birth of the English Common Law. New York: Cam U Press, 1973. Rev. by S. E. Prall, HRNB, 2(Oct 1973):3-4.

Van Cleve, Thomas Curtis. The Emperor Frederick II of Hohenstaufen. New York: Ox U Press, 1972. Rev. by P. Munz, AHR, 78(Oct 1973):1037-8; M. Latey, HTo, 23(May 1973): 365, 367.

Vandenbosch, Amry. South Africa and the World: The Foreign Policy of Apartheid. Lexington, Ky.: U Press, Ky, 1970. Rev. by G. M. Carter, AHR, 78(Feb 1973):135.

VanDerBeets, Richard, ed. Held Captive by Indians: Selected Narratives, 1642-1836. Knoxville: U Tenn Press, 1973. Rev. by E. B. McCluney, HRNB, 2(Nov/Dec 1973):41.

Van Der Wal, S. L., ed. Official Documents Concerning Dutch-Indonesian Relations, 1945-1950. The Hague: Martinus Nijhoff, 1971. Rev. by J. R. W. Smail, AHR, 78(Oct 1973):1114.

Vanderwerth, W. C., comp. Indian Oratory: Famous Speeches by Noted Indian Chieftains. Norman: U Ok Press, 1971. Rev.

321   VAN DER WOUDE

by R. L. Nichols, A & W, 15(Spr 1973):88-9.

Van Der Woude, A. M. The Noorderkwartier: A Study in the Dem-
    ographic and Economic History of Western parts of the Neth-
    erlands from the end of the Middle Ages till the Beginning of
    the Nineteenth Century. Wageningen: Afdeling Agrarisch
    Geschiedenis, Landbouwhogeschool, 1972. Rev. by J. de
    Vries, AHR, 78(Je 1973):705-6; P. Burke, History, 58(Je
    1973):296-7.

Van Der Zee, Henri and Barbara. William and Mary. New York:
    Macmillan, 1973. Rev. by J. Richardson, HTo, 23(Je 1973):
    443-4.

Vande Vere, Emmett K. The Wisdom Seekers. Nashville: Southern
    Publishing, 1972. Rev. by V. P. DeSantis, MichH, 57(Spr
    1973):81-3.

Van Duyn, Janet. The Egyptians: Pharaohs and Craftsmen. n. p.:
    McGraw-Hill, 1971. Rev. by L. R. Johnson, SS, 64(Feb
    1973):92.

Van Dyken, Seymour. Samuel Willard, 1640-1707: Preacher of
    Orthodoxy in an Era of Change. Grand Rapids, Mich.: Eerd-
    mans, 1972. Rev. by E. B. Holifield, WMQ, 3rd ser., 30
    (Ja 1973):181-3.

Van Koevering, Adrian. Legends of the Dutch. Zeeland: Zeeland
    Record, 1960. Rev. by J. H. Yzenbaard, MichH, 57(Spr
    1973):77-9.

Van Lierde, Jean, ed. Lumumba Speaks: The Speeches and Writ-
    ings of Patrice Lumumba, 1958-1961. Boston: Little, Brown,
    1972. Rev. by O. E. S., CurH, 64(Mar 1973):126.

Van Nieuwenhuijze, C. A. O. Sociology of the Middle East: A
    Stocktaking Interpretation. Leiden: E. J. Brill, 1971. Rev.
    by R. Van Dusen, MEJ, 27(Win 1973):97-8.

Vanstone, James W. Akulivikchuk: A Nineteenth-Century Eskimo
    Village on the Nushagak River, Alaska. Chicago: Field
    Museum of Natural History, 1970. Rev. by D. E. Dumond,
    AmAnt 38(Apr 1973):247-8.

_____ and Joan B. Townsend. Kijik: An Historic Tanaina Indian
    Settlement. Chicago: Field Museum of Natural History, 1970.
    Rev. by D. E. Dumond, AmAnt, 38(Apr 1973):247-8.

Van Til, L. John. Liberty of Conscience: The History of a Puri-
    tan Idea. Philadelphia: Craig, 1972. Rev. by G. M. Wal-
    ler, JAH, 60(Dec 1973):776-7.

Van Zandt, Roland. Chronicles of the Hudson: Three Centuries of

VARLEY   322

Travelers' Accounts. New Brunswick, N. J.: Rutgers U
Press, 1971. Rev. by S. Rezneck, NYH, 54(Apr 1973):247-
9; E. R. Ellis, NYHSQ, 57(Jan 1973):80-1; K. A. Job,
NJH, 91(Sum 1973):131-3.

Varley, H. Paul. Imperial Restoration in Medieval Japan. New
York: Columbia U Press, 1971. Rev. by D. M. Brown,
AHR, 78(Dec 1973):1513.

Vartsos, Ioannis A. Athenian Cleruchies. Athens: M. Pechlivanides,
1972. Rev. by L. Pearson, AHR, 78(Oct 1973):1028.

Vassen, Florian. Georg Weerth. Ein Politischer Dichter des
Vomärz und der Revolution von 1848-49. Stuttgart: J. B.
Metzlersche, 1971. Rev. by W. O. Henderson, ESR, 3(Oct
1973):400-1.

Vasyl'ev, V. O., et al., eds. Nikolaev Province. Kiev: Institut
Istorii Akademii Nauk URSR, 1971. Rev. by J. A. Armstrong, AHR, 78(Je 1973):716.

Vatikiotis, P. J., ed. Revolution in the Middle East: And Other
Case Studies. Totowa, N. J.: Rowman and Littlefield, 1972.
Rev. by R. L. Tignor, AHR, 78(Oct 1972):1021-3; M. Hal-
pern, MEJ, 27(Sum 1973):381-2.

Vaughan, Alden T. and George Athan Billias, eds. Perspectives on
Early American History: Essays in Honor of Richard B.
Morris. New York: Harper and Row, 1973. Rev. by D. E.
Leach, JSH, 39(Nov 1973):584-5; A. H. Shaffer, VMNB, 81
(Oct 1973):492-3.

Vaughan, Michalina and Margaret Scotford Archer. Social Conflict
and Educational Change in England and France, 1789-1848.
New York: Cam U Press, 1971. Rev. by S. Meacham, JIH,
4(Aut 1973):323-7.

Vaughan, Richard. Philip the Good: the Apogee of Burgundy. London: Longmans 1970. Rev. by K. Fowler, History, 58(Je
1973):265-6.

Venkataramani, M. S. Bengal Famine of 1943: The American Response. Delhi: Vikas, 1973. Rev. by S. Ganguly, IQ, 29
(Oct-Dec 1973):354-5.

Venturi, Franco. Europe des Lumierès: Recherches sur le 18e
siècle. Paris: Mouton, 1971. Rev. by M. Wilks, EHR, 88
(Jl 1973):599-605.

_____. Utopia and Reform in the Enlightenment. Cambridge:
Cam U Press, 1971. Rev. by M. Wilks, EHR, 88(Jl 1973):
599-605.

Verlinden, Charles. The Beginnings of Modern Colonization. London: Cornell U Press, 1970. Rev. by J. H. Elliott, History, 58(Oct 1973):439-40.

Vernadsky, George, et al., eds. A Source Book for Russian History From Early Times to 1917. 3 vols. New Haven, Conn.: Yale U Press, 1973. Rev. by I. Grey, HTo, 23(May 1973): 372-3.

Vernadsky, George. Kievan Russia: A History of Russia. New Haven, Conn.: Yale U Press, 1971. Rev. by A. V. Muller, HT, 6(May 1973):479.

Vernam, Glenn R. Man on Horseback: The Story of the Mounted Man From the Scythians to the American Cowboy. Lincoln: U Neb Press, 1972. Rev. by S. A. Winfree, JOW, 12(Oct 1973):647.

Vernant, Jacques and J. C. Hurewitz, eds. Intérets et Politiques de la France et des Etats-Unis au Moyen-Orient et en Afrique du Nord. Special Issue of Politique Etrangere, Vol. 36, Numbers 5-6, 1971. Rev. by W. Zartman, MEJ, 27(Aut 1973):516-7. See also: Hurewitz, J. C. and Jacques Vernant. Intérets et Politiques....

Vicinus, Martha, ed. Suffer and Be Still: Women in the Victorian Age. Bloomington: Ind U Press, 1972. Rev. by A. F. Scott, IMH 69(Mar 1973):84-5; R. J. Helmstadter, AHR, 78 (Je 1973):693-4.

Vignobles et Vins d'Aquitaine Histoire: Economie: Art. Bordeaux: Federation historique du Sud Ouest, 1970. Rev. by J. Le Patourel, EHR, 88(Jl 1973):592-4.

Vila, Manuel Pérez. La formación intellectual del Libertador. Caracas: Ministerio de Educación, 1971. Rev. by P. K. Liss, AHR, 78(Feb 1973):187-8.

Villalobos, R. Sergio. El comercio y la crisis colonial Un mito de la independencia. Santiago de Chile: Ediciones de la Universidad de Chile, 1968. Rev. by S. Collier, HAHR, 53(Nov 1973):686-9.

Villanueva, Víctor. 100 años del ejército peruano: frustraciones y cambios. Lima, Peru: Editorial Juan Mejía Baca, 1971. Rev. by F. M. Nunn, HAHR, 53(Aug 1973):521-3.

Villard, Henry. The Past and Present of the Pike's Peak Gold Regions. New York: Da Capo, 1972. Rev. by O. E. Young, NMHR, 48(Apr 1973):182-3; B. G. Ramsey, JOW, 12(Oct 1973):649. NOTE: This work was originally published in 1860.

Villegas, Daniel Casío. Historia moderna de México. Vol. IX. El Parfiriato. La Vida política interior. Mexico and Buenos Aires: Editorial Hermes, 1972. Rev. by J. Womack, Jr., HAHR, 53(May 1973):328-30.

Vincent, J. and M. Stenton. McCalmont's Parliamentary Poll Book. British Electoral Results 1832-1918. 8th ed. Brighton: Harvester, 1971. Rev. by P. F. Clarke, History, 58(Feb 1973): 143.

Vincent, J. R. see Cooke, A. B.

Viner, Jacob. The Role of Providence in the Social Order: An Essay in Intellectual History. Philadelphia: American Philosophical Society, 1972. Rev. by A. W. Coats, AHR, 78(Oct 1973):1005.

Vishnyakova-Akimova, Vera. Two Years in Revolutionary China, 1925-1927. Cambridge, Mass.: Har U Press, 1971. Rev. by E. P. Trani, RR, 32(Ja 1973):102-3.

Vita-Finzi, Claudio. The Mediterranean Valleys: Geological Changes in Historical Times. Cambridge: Cam U Press, 1969. Rev. by E. S. Higgs, Antiquity, 47(Je 1973):158.

Vivan, Itala. Caccia alle streghe nell' America puritana. [Milan:] Rizzoli, 1972. Rev. by E. W. Monter, AHR, 78(Oct 1973): 1118.

Vogel, Virgil J., ed. This Country Was Ours: A Documentary History of the American Indian. New York: Harper and Row, 1972. Rev. by R. S. Nelson, Jr., WMH, 56(Sum 1973):346-7; M. Gormly, AW, 10(Nov 1973):50.

Vogt, Adolph Max. Art of the Nineteenth Century. New York: Universe Books, 1973. Rev. by L. B. Miller, HRNB, 2(Nov/Dec 1973):38.

Vogt, Martin, ed. Das Kabinett Müller I and II. 2 volumes. Boppard am Rhein: Harald Boldt Verlag, 1971. Rev. by H. A. Turner, Jr., AHR, 78(Dec 1973):1489-90.

Volgyes, Ivan, ed. Hungary in Revolution, 1918-19; Nine Essays. Lincoln: U Neb Press, 1971. Rev. by M. Fenyo, EEQ, 7 (Sep 1973):94-5.

vom Brocke, Bernhard. Kurt Breysig: Geschichtswissenschaft zwischen Historismus und Soziologie. Lübeck and Hamburg: Matthiesen Verlag, 1971. Rev. by H. White, JMH, 45(Mar 1973):161-3.

Von der Porten, Edward P. The German Navy in World War II. New York: Crowell, 1969. Rev. by C. Burdick, JMH, 45

(Sep 1973):544-5.

Von Fritz, Kurt. Grundprobleme der Geschichte der Autiken Wissenschaft. Berlin: Walter de Gruyter, 1971. Rev. O. Neu-
genbauer, AHR, 78(Feb 1973):76-7.

von Haxthausen, August. Studies on the Interior of Russia. Chicago:
U Chi Press, 1972. Rev. by J. P. Posey, Historian, 36
(Nov 1973):112-13; G. E. Snow, RR, 32(Apr 1973):214.

Von Klemperer, Klemens. Ignaz Seipel: Christian Statesman in a
Time of Crisis. Princeton, N. J.: Prin U Press, 1972.
Rev. by F. E. Hirsch, AHR, 78(Oct 1973):1096.

Von Lazar, Arpad. Latin American Politics: A Primer. Boston:
Allyn and Bacon, 1971. Rev. by P. Taylor, HAHR, 53(Aug
1973):537-8.

Von Nostitz, Siegfried. Die Vernichtung des Roten Mannes: Dokumentarbericht. Dusseldorf: Eugen Diederichs Verlag, 1970.
Rev. by F. W. Turner, III, AHR, 78(Je 1973):724-6.

von Rauch, G. Geschichte der baltischen-Staaten. Stuttgart: Verlag
W. Kohlhammer, 1970. Rev. by D. Kirby, ESR, 3(Oct 1973):
401-3.

Vorpahl, Ben Merchant. My Dear Wister: The Frederic Remington-
Owen Wister Letters. Palo Alto, Cal.: American West, 1972.
Rev. by T. Wilkins, A & W, 15(Win 1973):371-2; R. V.
Hine, JAH, 59(Mar 1973):1016; P. Bonnifield, JOW, 12(Oct
1973):642; R. E. Lee, Montana, 23(Spr 1973):70; G. E.
White, PMHB, 97(Ja 1973):120-1.

Vovelle, Michel. La chute de la Monarchie, 1787-1792. Paris:
Editions du Seuil, 1972. Rev. by O. A. Hufton, JMH, 45
(Dec 1973):666-8.

Vucinich, Wayne S., ed. Russia and Asia: Essays on the Influence
of Russia on the Asian Peoples. Stanford, Cal.: Hoover Institution Press, Stan U, 1972. Rev. by G. E. Wheeler, MEJ,
27(Aut 1973):501-2; R. A. Pierce, AHR, 78(Dec 1973):1498-
9; G. Tokmakoff, RR, 32(Oct 1973):443-4.

Wade, Mason. Francis Parkman, Heroic Historian. Hamden, Conn.:
Archon, 1972. Rev. by H. S. Marks, JOW, 12(Oct 1973):640.

Wagar, W. Warren. Good Tidings: The Belief in Progress from
Darwin to Marcuse. Bloomington: Ind U Press, 1972. Rev.
by C. L. Stanford, T & C, 14(Apr 1973):333-7.

Wagner, Sir Anthony Richard. English Genealogy. Oxford: Clarendon Press, 1972. Rev. by G. D. Squibb, Archives, 11(Spr
1973):61-2.

WAGNER 326

_____. Heralds of England: A History of the Office and College of Arms. London: H. M. S. O., 1967. Rev. by J. P. Cooper, History, 58(Feb 1973):164-5.

_____, ed. Aspilogia II: Rolls of Arms, Henry III. London: Society of Antiquaries, 1967. Rev. by J. P. Cooper, History, 58(Feb 1973):164-5.

Wagner, Dieter and Gerhard Tomkowitz. Anschluss: The Week Hitler Siezed Vienna. New York: St. Martin's, 1972. Rev. by J. Remak, EEQ, 7(Sum 1973):227-8.

Wagner, Walter. Geschichte des k. k. Kriegsministeriums. Vol. 1: 1848-1866, Vol. 2: 1866-1888. Graz: Verlag Hermann Böhlaus Nachf., 1966-71. Rev. by L. A. Gebhard, JMH, 45 (Je 1973):328-30.

Waite, P. B. Canada 1874-1896. Arduous Destiny. n. p.: Mc-Clelland and Stewart, 1971. Rev. by I. M. Cumpston, History, 58(Oct 1973):484-5.

Wake, Joan and Deborah Champion Webster, eds. The Letters of Daniel Eaton to the Third Earl of Cardigan 1725-1732. Northampton: The Northamptonshire Record Society, 1971. Rev. by H. J. Habakkuk, MH, 2(Spr 1973):52-3.

Wakelyn, Jon L. The Politics of a Literary Man: William Gilmore Simms. Westport, Conn.: Greenwood, 1973. Rev. by J. F. Pacheco, HRNB, 2(Oct 1973):17-18; GHQ, 57(Win 1973):604-5.

Wakin, Jeannette A., ed. The Function of Documents in Islamic Law: The Chapters on Sale from Tahāwī's "Kitāb al-Shurut al Kabīr." Albany: SUNY Press, 1972. Rev. by H. J. Liebesny, MEJ, 27(Aut 1973):509-10.

Walker, Kenneth R. A History of the Middle West: From the Beginning to 1970. Little Rock, Ark.: Pioneer, 1972. Rev. by H. R. Stevens, IMH, 69(Dec 1973):366-7; C. F. Williams, ArkHQ, 32(Aut 1973):290-2; G. S. May MichH, 57(Sum 1973):182-4.

Walker, Mack. German Home Towns: Community, State, and General Estate, 1648-1871. Ithaca, N. Y.: Cornell U Press, 1971, Rev. by J. J. Sheehan, JMH, 45(Mar 1973):104-5; D. McKay, History, 58(Oct 1973):451.

Wall, Joseph Frazier. Andrew Carnegie. New York: Ox U Press, 1970. Rev. by A. C. Davies, History, 58(Oct 1973):494-5.

Wall, Robert Emmet, Jr. Massachusetts Bay: The Crucial Decade, 1640-1650. New Haven, Conn.: Yale U Press, 1972.

Rev. by R. C. Simmons, WMQ, 3rd ser., 30(Apr 1973):342-3; S. Bush, Jr., WMH, 56(Sum 1973):342-3; J. M. Poteet, Historian, 36(Nov 1973):119; C. K. Shipton, PMHB, 97(Apr 1973):250-1; R. R. Lucas, VH, 41(Sum 1973):175-7.

Walsh, Margaret. The Manufacturing Frontier: Pioneer Industry in Antebellum Wisconsin, 1830-1860. Madison: State Historical Society of Wisconsin, 1972. Rev. by S. Karges, JAH, 60(Sep 1973):444-5; F. Bateman, BHR, 47(Aut 1973):381-3; P. W. Gates, WMH, 56(Sum 1973):325-6.

Walsh, Richard, ed. Archives of Maryland. Vol. LXXII. Journal and Correspondence of the Council of Maryland. Baltimore: Md Historical Society, 1972. Rev. by J. Haw, MHM 68(Win 1973):457; R. N. Olsberg, AHR, 78(Dec 1973):1527-8.

Walton, Hanes, Jr. Black Political Parties: An Historical and Political Analysis. New York: Free Press, 1972. Rev. by N. R. McMillen, JNH, 58(Jl 1973):367-9; D. S. Strong, JSH, 39 (Aug 1973):466-7; S. M. Lemmon, NCHR, 50(Spr 1973):225-6; R. Gavins, JSH, 39(Feb 1973):143-4; F. M. Wirt, JNH, 58 (Ja 1973):99-101.

Walton, Richard J. Cold War and Counter Revolution: The Foreign Policy of John F. Kennedy. New York: Viking, 1972. Rev. by T. M. Leonard, Historian, 35(Feb 1973):317-8; J. Spanier, PHR, 42(Feb 1973):134-5.

Walton, Robert C. Over There: European Reaction to Americans in World War I. Itasca, Ill.: F. E. Peacock, 1972. Rev. by C. Boyd, MilAf, 37(Oct 1973):112.

Walvin, James. The Black Presence: A Documentary History of the Negro in England, 1555-1860. New York: Schocken, 1972. Rev. by R. W. Winks, SS, 64(Apr 1973):182-3.

Wandel, Eckhard. Die Bedeutung der Vereinigten Staaten von Amerika für das deutsche Reparationsproblem, 1924-1929. Tübingen: J. C. B. Mohr (Paul Siebeck), 1971. Rev. by D. Felix, JMH, 45(Je 1973):349-50.

Wangermann, Ernst. The Austrian Achievement, 1700-1800. London: Thames and Hudson, 1973. Rev. by J. Richardson, HTo, 23(Mar 1973):213.

Ward, Anne G., ed. The Quest for Theseus. New York: Praeger, 1970. Rev. by I. K. Raubitschek, Archaeology, 26(Ja 1973): 65-6.

Ward, David. Cities and Immigrants, a Geography of Change in Nineteenth-Century America. New York: Ox U Press, 1971. Rev. by S. B. Warner, Jr., T & C, 14(Ja 1973):94.

WARD   328

Ward, Harry M.   Statism in Plymouth Colony.   Port Washington,
N. Y.: Kennikat, 1973.   Rev. by J. Parker, HRNB, 2(Nov/
Dec 1973):40.

_____.   "Unite or Die":   Intercolony Relations, 1690-1763.   Port
Washington, N. Y.: Kennikat, 1971.   Rev. by S. S. Webb,
AHR, 78(Feb 1973):149.

Ward, J. T. and R. G. Wilson.   Land and Industry: The Landed
Estate and the Industrial Revolution: A Symposium.   Newton
Abbot: David and Charles, 1971.   Rev. by N. McCord, His-
tory, 58(Feb 1973):115.

Ward, W. E. F. and L. W. White.   East Africa: A Century of
Change, 1870-1970.   n. p.: Africana, 1972.   Rev. by M. D.
Newitt, AfAf, 72(Ja 1973):90-1.

Ward, W. R., ed.   The Early Correspondence of Jabez Bunting,
1820-1829.   London: The Society, 1972.   Rev. by R. J.
Helmstadter, AHR, 78(Dec 1973):1460-1.

_____.   Religion and Society in England, 1790-1850.   New York:
Schocken, 1973.   Rev. by R. J. Helmstadter, AHR, 78(Dec
1973):1460-1; O. Chadwick, HJ, 16(Dec 1973):870-4.

Warder, A. K.   An Introduction to Indian Historiography.   Bombay:
Prakashan, 1972.   Rev. by R. P. Dua, IQ, 29(Apr-Je 1973):
184.

Wardle, David.   Education and Society in Nineteenth-Century Not-
tingham.   Cambridge: Cam U Press, 1971.   Rev. by J.
Whittam, History, 58(Feb 1973):122-3.

Ware, Joseph E.   The Emigrant's Guide to California.   New York:
Da Capo, 1972.   (First published, 1849).   Rev. by O. E.
Young, NMHR, 48(Apr 1973):182-3; E. Best, JOW, 12(Oct
1973):639.

Wark, K. R.   Elizabethan Recusancy in Cheshire.   Manchester:
Chetham Society, 1971.   Rev. by B. W. Beckinsale, History,
58(Feb 1973):99.

Warner, Marina.   'The Dragon Empress.'   Life and Times of Tz'u
Hsi (1835-1908).   Empress Dowager of China.   London: Weidenfeld and Nicolson, 1972.   Rev. by S. Harcourt-Smith, HTo,
23(Feb 1973):137-9.

Warner, Sam Bass, Jr.   The Urban Wilderness: A History of the
American City.   New York: Harper and Row, 1972.   Rev. by
P. A. Kalisch, IMH, 69(Sep 1973):295-7; R. A. Mohl, AHR,
78(Oct 1973):1115-6; R. C. Wade, JAH, 60(Sep 1973):471-4;
W. A. Bullough, PHR, 42(Nov 1973):578-9.

Warren, Peter. Myrtos: An Early Bronze-Age Settlement in
Crete. London: Thames and Hudson, 1972. Rev. by C.
Renfrew, Antiquity, 47(Dec 1973):325-7.

Warrett, W. P., ed. A Calendar of the Register of Henry Wakefield, Bishop of Worcester, 1375-1395. Worcester: Worcester: Worcester Historical Society and Worcester Record
Office, 1972. Rev. by M. J. Kennedy, MH, 2(Aut 1973):121-
3.

Warten, Mary Curtis, ed. Thomas Hart Benton: A Personal Commemorative. Kansas City: Burd and Fletcher, 1973. Rev.
by S. Larson, MoHR, 67(Jl 1973):623-4.

Warzeski, Walter C. Byzantine Rite Rusins in Carpatho-Ruthenia
and America. Pittsburgh: Byzantine Seminary Press, 1971.
Rev. by J. Bodnar, PaH, 40(Apr 1973):226-8.

Washburn, Wilcomb E., ed. Proceedings of the Vinland Map Conference. Chicago: U Chi Press, 1971. Rev. by M. E.
Kaups, JIH, 4(Sum 1973):154-9.

_____. Red Man's Land/White Man's Law: A Study of the Past
and Present Status of the American Indian. New York: Scribner's, 1971. Rev. by F. W. Turner, III, AHR, 78(Je 1973):
724-6; H. R. Grant, NDH, 40(Win 1973):34; D. M. Roper,
NYHSQ, 57(Ja 1973):89-91; E. Tooker, PH, 40(Apr 1973):
214-5.

Wasson, R. Gordon. The Hall Carbine Affair: An Essay in Historiography. Danbury, Conn.: Privately printed, 1971. Rev.
by I. Katz, BHR, 47(Spr 1973):109-11.

Waterbury, John. North for the Trade: The Life and Times of a
Berber Merchant. Berkeley: U Cal Press, 1972. Rev. by
M. Gilsenan, MEJ, 27(Aut 1973):507-8.

Waters, Frank. Midas of the Rockies: The Story of Stratton and
Cripple Creek. Chicago: Sage Books, Swallow Press, 1972.
Rev. by J. L. Dodson, JOW, 12(Ja 1973):188; D. A. Smith,
Montana, 23(Spr 1973):66-7.

Waters, Harold. Smugglers of Spirits: Prohibition and the Coast
Guard Patrol. New York: Hastings House, 1971. Rev. by
L. O. Prior, FHQ, 51(Apr 1973):463.

Waters, John J., Jr. The Otis Family in Provincial and Revolutionary Massachusetts. n. p.: North Carolina Press, 1970.
Rev. by D. B. Swinfen, History, 58(Oct 1973):488.

Watkins, C. Malcolm. The Cultural History of Marlborough, Virginia. Washington: Smithsonian Institution, 1968. Rev. by
L. J. Abel, AmAnt, 38(Apr 1973):253-4.

Watkins, Owen C. The Puritan Experience. London: Routledge and
     Kegan Paul, 1972. Rev. by R. C. Simmons, History, 58(Je
     1973):287.

Watkins, T. H. California, an Illustrated History. Palo Alto,
     Cal.: American West, 1973. Rev. by W. Bean, CHQ, 52
     (Win 1973):372.

Watlington, Patricia. The Partisan Spirit: Kentucky Politics, 1779-
     1792. New York: Atheneum ... 1972. Rev. by R. M. Ire-
     land, WMQ, 3rd ser., 30(Ja 1973):163-6; C. C. Bonwick,
     History, 58(Oct 1973):491; R. N. Ellis, MHM, 68(Sum 1973):
     220-1; T. D. Clark, VMHB, 81(Ja 1973):102-4; V. B. Hall,
     AHR, 78(Je 1973):727-8.

Watson, Robert. Christmas in Las Vegas. New York: Atheneum,
     1971. Rev. by K. S. Byer, GR, 27(Spr 1973):110-21.

Watson, S. Arthur. Penn College: A Product and a Producer.
     Oskaloosa, Ia.: William Penn College, 1971. Rev. by L. G.
     Geiger, AHR, 78(Oct 1973):1137-9.

Watson, Thomas Shelby. The Silent Riders. Louisville, Ky.:
     Beechmont, n. d. Rev. by F. G. Rankin, FCHQ, 47(Apr
     1973):199-200.

Watt, D. C. Survey of International Affairs, 1962. London: Ox U
     Press, 1970. Rev. by W. H. NcNeill, JMH, 45(Je 1973):
     364-6.

Watt, J. A. The Church and the Two Nations in Medieval Ireland.
     n. p.: Cam U Press, 1970. Rev. by W. L. Warren, His-
     tory, 58(Oct 1973):436-7.

Watters, Pat. Down to Now: Reflections on the Southern Civil
     Rights Movement. New York: Pantheon Books, 1971. Rev.
     by D. Chalmers, FHQ, 51(Ja 1973):334-6.

Watters, William E. An International Affair: Non-Intervention in
     the Spanish Civil War, 1936-1939. New York: Exposition,
     1971. Rev. by G. Jackson, AHR, 78(Dec 1973):1484-5.

Waung, W. S. K. Revolution and Liberation: A Short History of
     Modern China 1900-1970. London: Heinemann, 1972. Rev. by
     P. Lowe, History, 58(Je 1973):335.

Wax, Rosalie H. Doing Fieldwork: Warnings and Advice. Chicago:
     U Chi Press, 1971. Rev. by R. Daniels, PHR, 42(Feb 1973):
     119-20.

Wayman, John Hudson. A Doctor on the California Trail: The
     Diary of Dr. John Hudson Wayman from Cambridge City, In-
     diana to the Gold Fields in 1852. Denver: Old West, 1971.

Rev. by S. L. Tyler, WHQ, 4(Ja 1973):78-9.

Weare, Walter B.   Black Business in the New South: A Social History of the North Carolina Mutual Life Insurance Company. Urbana: U Ill Press, 1973. Rev. by R. C. Puth, BHR, 47 (Sum 1973):535-7.

Weatherill, Lorna.   The Pottery Trade of North Staffordshire, 1660-1760.   New York: Augustus M. Kelley, 1971. Rev. by J. R. Harris, JMH, 45(Dec 1973):651-3; M. W. Greenslade, History, 58(Je 1973):293-4.

Weatherly, A. Earl.   The First Hundred Years of Historic Guilford, 1771-1871. Greensboro, N. C.: for the Author by Greensboro Printing, 1972. Rev. by M. D. Moore, NCHR, 50(Sum 1973):325.

Weaver, Herbert and Paul H. Bergeron, eds.   Correspondence of James K. Polk. Vol. II. 1833-1834. Nashville: Van U Press, 1971. Rev. by J. H. Parks, FHQ, 51(Apr 1973):450-1; W. G. Shade, PH, 40(Oct 1973):493-4; J. E. Murphy, AmArch, 36(Oct 1973):562-3; E. A. Miles, JSH, 39(Feb 1973):117-19; R. V. Remini, JAH, 60(Sep 1973):416-17.

Weaver, Mike.   William Carlos Williams: The American Background. Cambridge: [Cam] U Press, 1971. Rev. by E. Rosenberg, NJH, 91(Spr 1973):61-2.

Weaver, Warren, Jr.   Both Your Houses: The Truth About Congress. New York: Praeger, 1972. Rev. by R. F. Fenno, SS, 64(Nov 1973):288-9.

Weber, David J.   The Taos Trappers: The Fur Trade in the Far Southwest, 1540-1846. Norman: U Ok Press, 1971. Rev. by J. B. Pearson, AHR, 78(Je 1973):726-7.

Weber, Francis J., ed. and trans.   A Letter of Junipero Serra: A Bicentennial Discovery. Boston: David R. Goldine, 1970. Rev. by W. Kramer, JOW, 12(Ja 1973):184.

Weber, Ralph E.   see Hachey, Thomas E.

Webster, Deborah Champion see Wake, Joan

Webster, T. B. L.   Potter and Patron in Classical Athens. London: Methuen, 1972. Rev. by E. Vermeule, AHR, 78(Dec 1973):1432.

Wector, Dixon.   The Hero in America. New York: Scribner's, 1972. Rev. by M. Klein, AHI, 8(Apr 1973):50.

Wedderburn, Dorothy and Rosemary Crompton.   Workers' Attitudes and Technology. New York: Cam U Press, 1972. Rev. by

R. H. Guest, T & C, 14, (Jl 1973):515-7.

Weddle, Robert S. Wilderness Manhunt: The Spanish Search for
    La Salle. Austin: U Tx Press, 1973. Rev. by J. P. Moore,
    HRNB, 2(Nov/Dec 1973):40-1.

Wedgwood, C. V. Oliver Cromwell. London: Duckworth, 1939.
    Rev. by M. Ashley, HTo, 23(Sep 1973):669.

Weems, John Edward. Dream of Empire: A Human History of the
    Republic of Texas, 1836-1846. New York: Simon and Schus-
    ter, 1971. Rev. by R. N. Conger, SWHQ, 76(Ja 1973):346-7.

Wefald, Jon. A Voice of Protest: Norwegians in American Poli-
    tics, 1890-1917. Northfield, Minn.: Norwegian-American
    Historical Assn., 1971. Rev. by F. D. Scott, AHR, 78(Feb
    1973):165-7.

Wehlage, Gary and Eugene M. Anderson. Social Studies Curricu-
    lum in Perspective: A Conceptual Analysis. Englewood
    Cliffs, N. J.: Prentice-Hall, 1972. Rev. by S. Kleiman,
    SS, 64(Nov 1973):292.

Weigley, Russell F. The American Way of War: A History of the
    United States Military Strategy and Policy. New York: Mac-
    millan, 1973. Rev. by J. K. Mahon, JSH, 39(Nov 1973):624-
    6.

Weill, Herman N. , ed. European Diplomatic History 1815-1914.
    Jericho, N. Y.: Exposition, 1972. Rev. by J. A. Lynch,
    Jr. , CurH, 64(Apr 1973):179.

Weinberg, Gerhard L. Germany and the Soviet Union, 1939-1941.
    Leiden: n. p., 1972. Rev. by R. G. Wesson, RR, 32(Apr
    1973):218-9.

Weinberg, Julius. Edward Alsworth Ross and the Sociology of Pro-
    gressivism. Madison: State Historical Society of Wisconsin,
    1972. Rev. by B. Curtis, JAH, 60(Je 1973):152-4.

Weinsinger, Arthur S. and W. B. Coley, eds. and trans. Hogarth
    on High Life. Middletown, Conn.: Wes U Press, 1970. Rev.
    by T. K. Rabb, JIH, 4(Sum 1973):107-17.

Weinstein, Allen and Frank Otto Gatell, eds. American Negro
    Slavery: A Reader. New York: Ox U Press, 1973. Rev.
    by D. D. Joyce, HT, 7(Nov 1973):125-6.

Weinstein, Brian. Eboué. New York: Ox U Press, 1972. Rev.
    by R. W. Johnson, AfAf, 72(Jl 1973):341.

Weinstein, Donald. Savonarola and Florence: Prophecy and Patri-
    otism in the Renaissance. Princeton, N. J.: Prin U Press,
    1971. Rev. by J. Larner, History, 58(Je 1973):269-70.

Weiss, Harry B.   The Personal Estates of Early Farmers and
    Tradesmen of Colonial New Jersey, 1670-1750. Trenton: N J
    Agricultural Society, 1971. Rev. by J. T. Lemon, AgH, 47
    (Oct 1973):354-5.

Weitz, Raanan.   From Peasant to Farmer: A Revolutionary Strategy
    for Development. New York: Columbia U Press, 1971. Rev.
    by J. P. Huttman, AgH, 47(Oct 1973):364-5.

Welch, d'Alté A., comp. A Bibliography of American Children's
    Books Printed Prior to 1821. Worcester and Barre, Mass.:
    American Antiquarian Society, 1972. Rev. by E. Heyl, MHM,
    68(Sum 1973):223; H. J. Heaney, PMHB, 97(Jl 1973):426-7.

Welch, Holmes.   Buddhism Under Mao. Cambridge, Mass.: Har U
    Press, 1972. Rev. by J. M. Kitagawa, AHR, 78(Dec 1973):
    1511-12.

Welch, June Rayfield and J. Larry Nance.   The Texas Courthouse.
    Dallas: G. L. A. Press, 1971. Rev. by W. B. Robinson,
    SWHQ, 76(Ja 1973):347-8.

Wellenreuther, Hermann.   Glaube und Politik in Pennsylvania 1681-
    1776: Die Wandlungen der Obrigkeitsdoktrin und des Peace
    Testimony der Quäker. Cologne: Böhlau Verlag, 1972. Rev.
    by G. Moltmann, JAH, 60(Sep 1973):422-3; U. Sautter,
    PMHB, 97(Apr 1973):283-4.

Wellman, Manly Wade.   The Kingdom of Madison: A Southern
    Mountain Fastness and Its People. Chapel Hill: UNC Press,
    1973. Rev. by M. Russell, NCHR, 50(Aut 1973):416.

Welsch, Roger.   Shingling the Fog and Other Plains Lies: Tall
    Tales of the Great Plains. Chicago: Swallow, 1972. Rev.
    by Editor, NDH, 40(Spr 1973):39.

Wenk, Michael, S. M. Tomasi, and Geno Baroni, eds. Pieces of
    a Dream: The Ethnic Workers' Crisis with America. New
    York: Center for Migration Studies, 1972. Rev. by B. B.
    Caroli, JAH, 60(Dec 1973):861.

Wenzel, Marian.   House Decoration in Nubia. [London:] Duck-
    worth, n. d. Rev. by M. Shinnie, JAfH, 14(No. 2 1973):353.

Weslager, Clinton A.   The Delaware Indians: A History. New
    Brunswick, N. J.: Rutgers U Press, 1972. Rev. by R. E.
    Smith, NJH, 91(Sum 1973):129-30; B. Graymont, NYH, 54(Jl
    1973):375-6; F. Jennings, PH, 40(Jl 1973):328-31; J. H.
    Howard, PH, 40(Jl 1973):331-2; J. A. Greene, JOW, 12(Jl
    1973):507-8; T. B. Hetzel, PMHB, 97(Ja 1973):108-10; Y.
    Kawashima, WMQ, 3rd ser., 30(Ja 1973):183-5.

Wessels, Antonie.   A Modern Arabic Biography of Muhammad: A

Critical Study of Muhammad Husayn Haykal's Hayāt Muhammed.
Leiden: E. J. Brill, 1972. Rev. by J. Kritzeck, MEJ, 27
(Aut 1973):506-7.

Wesson, Robert G. The Soviet Russian State. New York: Wiley,
1972. Rev by J. A. Armstrong, RR, 32(Ja 1973):81-2.

West, Richard. Congo. Holt, Rinehart and Winston, 1972. Rev.
by O. E. S., CurH, 64(Mar 1973):126.

Western, J. R. Monarchy and Revolution: The English State in
the 1680's. London: Blandford, 1972. Rev. by J. P. Kenyon, History, 58(Je 1973):294-5.

Weston, Rubin Francis. Racism in U. S. Imperialism: The Influence of Racial Assumptions on American Foreign Policy,
1893-1896. Columbia, S. C.: U SCar Press, 1972. Rev.
by P. W. Kennedy, AHR, 78(Feb 1973):177; R. E. Weber,
JNH, 58(Apr 1973):217-19; J. G. Utley, Historian, 36(Nov
1973):131-2; L. L. Gould, PHR, 42(Feb 1973):121-3.

Westrich, Sal Alexander. The Ormèe of Bordeaux: A Revolution
During the Fronde. Baltimore: J H U Press, 1972. Rev.
by W. H. Beik AHR, 78(Oct 1973):1072-3.

Whaley, Barton. Codeword Barbarossa. Cambridge, Mass.: M I T
Press, 1973. Rev. by J. E. McSherry, AHR, 78(Dec 1973):
1491.

Whaley, Thomas. Consignments to El Dorado: A Record of the
Voyage of the Sutton. New York: Exposition, 1972. Rev.
by S. Jackson, JAH, 59(Mar 1973):1006-7; J. W. Caruthers,
JOW, 12(Ja 1973):184.

Wharton, David. The Alaska Gold Rush. Bloomington: Ind U
Press, 1972. Rev. by D. Lindsey, AHI, 8(Jl 1973):50; O.
W. Miller, Montana, 23(Aut 1973):66; R. W Paul, PHR,
42(Aug 1973):428-9.

Wheeler, Richard. Voices of 1776: The Story of the American
Revolution in the Words of Those Who Were There. New
York: Crowell, 1972. Rev. by R. E. Harper WVH, 34(Apr
1973):301-2; T. Thayer, NJH, 91(Aut 1973):273; J. P. Cullen, AHI, 8(Oct 1973):49.

Wheeler-Bennett, Sir John and Anthony Nicholls. The Semblance
of Peace: The Political Settlement After the Second World
War. New York: St. Martin's, 1972. Rev. by G. A. Craig,
JMH, 45(Dec 1973):714-5; G. Wright, AHR, 78(Oct 1973):
1019-21.

Whisnant, David E. James Boyd. New York: Twayne, 1972.
Rev. by R. W. Etulain, JAH, 60(Sep 1973):495-6.

Whitcombe, Elizabeth. Agrarian Conditions in Northern India. London: U Cal Press, 1972. Rev. by R. C. Mullett, History, 58(Je 1973):331.

White, B. R. The English Separatist Tradition From the Marian Martyrs to the Pilgrim Fathers. Oxford: Ox U Press, 1971. Rev. by P. Collinson, History, 58(Feb 1973):99-100.

White, Christopher. Rembrandt and His World. New York: Viking, 1964. Rev. by T. K. Rabb, JIH, 4(Sum 1973):107-17.

White, Eugene E. Puritan Rhetoric: The Issue of Emotion in Religion. Carbondale: S Ill U Press, 1972. Rev. by D. Hall, JAH, 60(Je 1973):110.

White, Helen and Redding S. Sugg, eds. From the Mountain. Memphis: Memphis St U Press, 1972. Rev. by M. Sosna, WMH, 56(Sum 1973):333-4.

White, J. R. From Peterloo to the Crystal Palace. London: Heinemann, 1972. Rev. by G. B. A. M. Finlayson, History, 58(Je 1973):303.

White, L. W. see Ward, W. E. F.

White, Lonnie J., et al., eds. Hostiles and Horse Soldiers. Boulder, Colo.: Pruett, 1972. Rev. by R. C. Carriker, Montana, 23(Win 1973):67; L. E. Oliva, AW, 10(Ja 1973):52.

White, Lynn, Jr., ed. Viator: Medieval and Renaissance Studies. Vol. I. Berkeley: U Cal Press, 1972. Rev. by B. S. Smith, JIH, 4(Sum 1973):132-5.

White, R. J., ed. Lay Sermons. London: Routledge and Kegan Paul, 1972. Rev. by J. Richardson, HTo, 23(Jl 1973):517-8.

White, William Gee see Cummins, Duane.

Whiteman, Anne, J. W. Bromley, and P. G. M. Dickson, eds. Statesmen, Scholars, and Merchants: Essays in Eighteenth-Century History.... New York: Ox U Press, 1973. Rev. by S. Hanft, HRNB, 2(Oct 1973):4.

Whiteman, Maxwell. Copper for America: The Hendricks Family and a National Industry, 1755-1939. New Brunswick, N. J.: Rutgers U Press, 1971. Rev. by J. P. Baughman, AHR, 78 (Oct 1973):1121-2; W. Graebner, NYH, 54(Jl 1973):377-8; J. W. Osborne, PH, 40(Oct 1973):438-9.

Whitrow, Magda, ed. ISIS Cumulative Bibliography: A Bibliography of the History of Science Formed from ISIS Critical Bibliographies 1-90, 1913-1965. Part 1. Personalities. Part 2. Personalities and Institutions. 2 vols. London: Mansell,

WHITTLESEY 336

1971. Rev. by R. V. Jenkins, T & C, 14(Apr 1973):354-6.

Whittlesey, Walter R. and O. G. Sonneck. Catalogue of First Editions of Stephen C. Foster (1826-1864). New York: Da Capo, 1971. Rev. by G. T. McWhorter, FCHQ, 47(Jl 1973):291.

Whyte, Donald. A Dictionary of Scottish Emigrants to the U. S. A. Baltimore: Magna Carta Book Co. 1972. Rev. by T. F. Beard, VMHB, 81(Oct 1973):505-6.

Whyte, J. H. Church and State in Modern Ireland. New York: Barnes and Noble, 1971. Rev. by L. J. McCaffrey, JMH, 45(Mar 1973):178-9.

Wicker, Rassie E. Miscellaneous Ancient Records of Moore County, North Carolina. n. p.: ... Moore County Historical Assn., [1972]. Rev. by F. D. Gatton, NCHR, 50(Spr 1973):202-3.

Wickham, Glynne. Early English Stages, 1300-1660. Vol. 2, 1576-1660. Part 2. New York: Columbia U Press, 1972. Rev. by F. D. Hoeniger, AHR, 78(Je 1973):678-9.

Wickwire, Franklin and Mary. Cornwallis and the War of Independence. London: Faber and Faber, 1971. Rev. by R. Middleton, History, 58(Feb 1973):150-1.

Widder, Keith R. Reveille Till Taps. Lansing, Mich.: Mackinac Island State Park Commission, n. d. Rev. by J. L. Tevebaugh, MichH, 57(Fall 1973):267-8.

Widick, B. J. Detroit: City of Race and Class Violence. Chicago: Quadrangle, 1972. Rev. by M. G. Holli, WMH, 56(Win 1972-73):166-7.

Wiecek, William M. The Guarantee Clause of the United States Constitution. Ithaca, N. Y.: Cornell U Press, 1972. Rev. by L. A. Pereyra, CWH, 19(Mar 1973):88-9; W. F. Zornow, Historian, 35(Feb 1973):307-8.

Wielandt, Rotraud. Offenbarung und Geschichte im Denken Moderner Muslime. Wiesbaden: Franz Steiner, 1971. Rev. K. Stowasser, MEJ, 27(Sum 1973):411.

Wiener, Martin J. Between Two Worlds: The Political Thought of Graham Wallas. New York: Ox U Press, 1971. Rev. by F. M. Schweitzer, AHR, 78(Je 1973):696; P. F. Clarke, History, 58(Feb 1973):130-1; M. Richter, JMH, 45(Mar 1973):155-6.

Wieruszowski, Helene. Politics and Culture in Medieval Spain and Italy. Roma: Edizioni de Storia e Letteratura, 1971. Rev. by P. A. Linehan, History, 58(Mar 1973):261-2.

Wiesendanger, Martin and Margaret. 19th-Century Louisiana

Painters and Paintings from the Collection of W. E. Graves.
Gretna, La.: Pelican, 1971. Rev. by W. M. Lowrey, LaH,
14(Spr 1973):219-20.

Wiesflecker, Hermann. Kaiser Maximilian I: Das Reich Österreich
und Europa an der Wende zur Neuzeit. Vol. I. Jugend, bur-
gundisches Erbe und Römisches Königtum bis zur Alleinherr-
schaft 1459-1493. Munich: R. Oldenbourg Verlag, 1971. Rev.
by H. J. Cohn, ESR, 3(Jl 1973):301-3; S. W. Rowan, JMH,
45(Je 1973):294-6.

Wightman, Edith Mary. Roman Trier and the Treveri. London:
Rupert Hart-Davis, 1970. Rev. by M. H. Bräude, Antiquity,
47(Mar 1973):69-70.

Wik, Reynold M. Henry Ford and Grass-Roots America. Ann
Arbor: U Mich Press, 1972. Rev. by G. C. Fite, T & C,
14(Oct 1973):645-7; A. R. Travis, MichH 57(Spr 1973):74-6;
O. L. Graham, Jr., AgH, 47(Oct 1973):346-7; J. W. Eastman, BHR, 47(Spr 1973):122-3.

Wilding, Paul see George, Victor

Wiles, P. J. D., ed. The Prediction of Communist Economic Performance. London: Cam U Press, 1971. Rev. by N. M.
Khilnani, IQ, 29(Jl-Sep 1973):262.

Wilke, Wendell. The End of the Corn Belt Fleet. The Great Lakes
Reserve Destroyer Division. Algoma, Wis.: West End Publications, 1972. G. L. H., IS, 29(Fall 1973):234-5.

Wilkins, Mira. The Emergence of Multinational Enterprise: American Business Abroad From the Colonial Era to 1914. Cambridge, Mass.: Har U Press, 1970. Rev. by J. S. Nye, JIH,
4(Aut 1973):336-7.

Wilkinson, Alix. Ancient Egyptian Jewellery. London: Methuen,
1971. Rev. by J. Ruffle, Antiquity, 47(Mar 1973):72-4.

Wilkinson, Norman B. E. I. du Pont, Botaniste: The Beginning of
a Tradition. Charlottesville: U Press Va., 1972. Rev. by
J. Ewan, PH, 40(Oct 1973):489-90; K. R. Bowling, MHM, 68
(Sum 1973):222; E. Berkeley, JAH, 60(Sep 1973):426; R. M.
Sargent, PMHB, 97(Jl 1973):416-7.

Will, Edouard. Le monde grec et l'Orient. Vol. 1. Le Ve siecle
(510-603). Paris: Presses Universitaires de France, 1972.
Rev. by D. Kagan, AHR, 78(Oct 1973):1028-9.

Will, H. A. Constitutional Change in the British West Indies, 1880-
1903: With Special Reference to Jamaica, British Guiana and
Trinidad. Oxford: Ox U Press, 1970. Rev. by D. A. G.
Waddell, History, 58(Feb 1973):147-8; P. Marshall, AHR, 78
(Je 1973):750.

Willcox, William B., et al., eds. The Papers of Benjamin Franklin. Vol. 15, January 1 Through December 31, 1768. New Haven, Conn.: Yale U Press, 1972. Rev. by A. Owen Aldridge, AHR, 78(Feb 1973):155-6; O. L. Graham, Jr., JAH, 60(Je 1973):96-8; J. H. Hutson, PMHB, 97(Jl 1973):410-11.

_____, ed. The Papers of Benjamin Franklin: Vol. 17, January 1-December 31, 1770. New York: Yale U Press, 1973. Rev. by J. B. Whisker, HRNB, 2(Nov/Dec 1973):43.

Williams, Burton J. Senator John James Ingalls: Kansas' Iridescent Republican. Lawrence: U Press Ks, 1972. Rev. by P. H. Argersinger, WMH, 56(Win 1972-73):167-8; M. T. Downey, Montana, 23(Win 1973):68-9; F. H. Schapsmeier, JOW, 12(Oct 1973):648-9.

Williams, Donovan and E. Daniel Potts, eds. Essays in Indian History: In Honour of Cuthbert Collin Davies. Bombay: Asia Publishing House, 1973. Rev. by N. M. Khilnani, IQ, 29(Jl-Sep 1973):273-4.

Williams, Forrest see Lang, Berel

Williams, Glynder, ed. Peter Skene Ogden's Snake Country Journals, 1827-28 and 1828-29. London: Hudson's Bay Record Society, 1971. Rev. by F. D. Haines, Jr., Montana, 23(Win 1973):71; B. Sawyer, NHSQ 16(Spr 1973):39-41.

Williams, Gwyn. Eastern Turkey: A Guide and History. London: Faber and Faber, 1972. Rev. by D. P. Williams, MEJ, 27 (Sum 1973):400-1.

Williams, Harold A. Bodine: A Legend in His Time. Baltimore: Bodine and Associates, 1971. Rev. by W. G. Rose, MHM, 68(Spr 1973):116.

Williams, Isabel M. and Leora H. McEachern. Salt--That Necessary Article. Wilmington: Authors, 1973. Rev. by G. Troxler, NCHR, 50(Aut 1973):418-19.

Williams, Judith Blow. British Commerical Policy and Trade Expansion, 1750-1850. New York: Ox U Press, 1972. Rev. by W. Ashworth, AHR, 78(Dec 1973):1456-7; D. C. M. Platt, HJ, 16(Je 1973):435-6; J. H. Parry, BHR, 47(Win 1973):542-4.

Williams, Lee E. and Lee E. Williams II. Anatomy of Four Race Riots: Racial Conflict in Knoxville, Elaine (Arkansas), Tulsa and Chicago, 1919-1921. Hattiesburg, Miss.: U & Coll Press, Miss., 1972. Rev. by I. A. Newby, JAH, 60(Je 1973):170-1; J. W. Roberson, ChOk, 51(Fall 1973):368-9; F. V. Mills, Sr., GHQ, 57(Fall 1973):441; R. V. Haynes, JMiH, 35(Feb 1973):104-6; M. Wolff, NCHR, 50(Win 1973):105-6.

Williams, Neville. All the Queen's Men. Elizabeth I and Her
   Courtiers. London: Weidenfeld and Nicolson, 1972. Rev. by
   A. L. Rowse, HTo, 23(Mar 1973):211, 213.

_____. Henry VIII and His Court. London: Weidenfeld and
   Nicolson, 1971. Rev. by M. E. James, History, 58(Oct 1973):
   444.

Williams, Robert C. Culture in Exile: Russian Emigrés in Germany,
   1881-1941. Ithaca, N. Y.: Cornell U Press, 1972. Rev. by
   R. Pethybridge, History, 58(Oct 1973):472-3; N. V. Riasanovsky, JMH, 45(Je 1973):326; R. Sheldon, RR, 32(Ja 1973):
   90-1.

Williams, Roger L. The Mortal Napoleon III. Princeton, N. J.:
   Prin U Press, 1971. Rev. by W. F. Spencer, AHR, 78(Feb
   1973):113-114.

Williams, William Appleman, ed. From Colony to Empire: Essays
   in the History of American Foreign Relations. New York:
   Wiley, 1972. Rev. by A. Rappaport, PHR, 42(Nov 1973):576-
   8; R. G. O'Connor, SS, 64(Nov 1973):294-5.

Willoughby, C. A., ed. The Guerrilla Resistance Movement in the
   Philippines. New York: Vantage, 1972. Rev. by J. B. Bell,
   MilAf, 37(Dec 1973):156.

Wilson, Arthur M. Diderot. New York: Ox U Press, 1972. Rev.
   by H. Dieckmann, AHR, 78(Je 1973):649-51.

Wilson, Edmund. A Window on Russia. New York: Farrar, Straus
   and Giroux, 1972. Rev. by R. Gregg, RR, 32(Apr 1973):219-
   20.

Wilson, Elinor. Jim Beckwourth: Black Mountain Man and War
   Chief of the Crows. Norman: U Ok Press, 1972. Rev. by
   K. W. Porter, A & W, 15(Aut 1973):279-80; N. J. Bender,
   Historian, 36(Nov 1973):125-6; L. Carranco, JOW, 12(Oct
   1973):634; J. Burrows, Montana, 23(Sum 1973):52; J. E.
   Sunder, PHR, 42(Nov 1973):585-6; R. A. Trennert, AW, 10
   (May 1973):56.

Wilson, Francis. Labour in the South African Gold Mines, 1911-
   1969. Cambridge: Cam U Press, 1972. Rev. by J. A.
   Casada, JEH, 33(Dec 1973):912.

Wilson, Frank L. The French Democratic Left, 1963-1969: Toward a Modern Party System. Stanford, Cal.: Stan U Press,
   1971. Rev. by A. R. Zolberg, JMH, 45(Mar 1973):190-1.

Wilson, Garff B. Three Hundred Years of American Drama and
   Theatre: From ye Bear and ye Cubb to Hair. Englewood
   Cliffs, N. J.: Prentice-Hall, 1973. Rev. by G. T. Tan-

selle, JAH, 60(Sep 1973):418-20.

Wilson, Joan Hoff. American Business and Foreign Policy, 1920-1933. Lexington: U Press Ky, 1971. Rev. by P. P. Abrahams, JEH, 33(Je 1973):499-500; S. J. Kneashaw, Historian, 35(Feb 1973):315-6; C. Parrini, PHR, 42(Aug 1973):436-7.

Wilson, Kenneth M. New England Glass and Glassmaking. New York: Crowell, 1972. Rev. by J. Strauss, Archaeology, 26 (Jl 1973):236.

Wilson, Leonard G. Charles Lyell. The Years to 1841: The Revolution in Geology. New Haven, Conn.: Yale U Press, 1972. Rev. by G. L. Davies, AHR, 78(Dec 1973):1461-2; R. Porter, JMH, 45(Sep 1973):503-4.

Wilson, Monica. Religion and the Transformation of Society: A Study of Social Change in Africa. London: Cam U Press, 1971. Rev. by R. G. Willis, Africa, 43(Ja 1973):82-3.

Wilson, Monica and Leonard Thompson, eds. The Oxford History of South Africa. Vol. 2: South Africa, 1870-1966. Oxford: Clarendon, 1971. Rev. by A. H. Jeeves, CHR, 54(Sep 1973): 323-4; R. Hyam, HJ, 16(Sep 1973):616-26.

Wilson, R. G. see Ward, J. T.

Wilson, Roger Burdett, ed. Sir Daniel Gooch: Memoirs and Diary. Newton Abbot: David and Charles, 1972. Rev. by B. F. Duckham, History, 58(Je 1973):313-4.

Wilson, Samuel, Jr. The Vieux Carré, New Orleans: Its Plan, Its Growth, Its Architecture. New Orleans: ... Bureau of Governmental Research, ... 1968. Rev. R. W. Heck, LaH, 14 (Win 1973):110-11.

Wiltz, John Edward see Marshall, Richard E.

Windolph, F. Lyman. Selected Essays. Lancaster, Pa.: Franklin and Marshall College, 1972. Rev. by R. M. Landis, PMHB, 97(Apr 1973):281-2.

Winkler, Heinrich August. Mittelstand, Demokratie und Nationalsozialismus: Die politische Entwicklung von Handwerk und Kleinhandel in der Weimarer Republik. Cologne: Kiepenheuer and Witsch, 1972. Rev. by H. Lebovics, JMH, 45(Sep 1973): 539-50.

Winks, Robin W. An Autobiography of the Reverend Josiah Henson. Reading, Mass.: Addison-Wesley, 1969. Rev. by J. L. Franklin, CWH, 19(Sep 1973):285-7.

_____. The Blacks in Canada: A History. New Haven, Conn.:

341   WINKS

Yale U Press, 1971. Rev. by J. T. Talman MichH, 57(Sum 1973):181-2.

_____, ed. The Historian as Detective: Essays on Evidence. New York: Harper and Row, 1969. Rev. by M. Brichford, AmArc, 36(Jl 1973):397-402.

_____, ed. Slavery: A Comparative Perspective. New York: NYU Press, 1972. Rev. by R. McColley, AgH 47(Oct 1973): 363-4.

Winner, Irene. A Slovenian Village: Zerovnica. Providence, R. I.: Brown U Press, 1971. Rev. by C. Rogel, EEQ, 7(Sum 1973):228-30.

Wint, Guy see Calvocoressi, Peter

Winter, J. M. and D. M. Joslin, ed. R. H. Tawney's Commonplace Book. Cambridge: Cam U Press, 1972. Rev. by P. F. Clarke, History, 58(Feb 1973):130-1.

Winters, Howard Dalton. The Riverton Culture: A Second-Millennium Occupation in the Central Wabash Valley. Springfield: Ill Archeological Survey and Ill State Museum, 1969. Rev. by J. E. Fitting, AmAnt, 38(Jl 1973):368-9.

Wirth, Arthur G. Education in the Technological Society: The Vocational-Liberal Studies Controversy in the Early Twentieth Century. Scranton, Pa.: Intext Education, 1972. Rev. by L. Veysey, AHR, 78(Oct 1973):1136-7.

Wirz, Albert. Vom Sklavenhandel zum Kolonialen Handel; Wirtschaftsräume und Wirtschaftsformen in Kamerun vor 1914. Zürich and Freiburg: Atlantis Verlag, n. d. Rev. by C. Newbury, JAfH, 14(3rd Qr 1973):528.

Wise, J. C. The Red Man in the New World Drama: A Politico-Legal Study With a Pageantry of American Indian History. New York: Macmillan, 1971. Rev. by F. W. Turner III, AHR, 78(Je 1973):724-6.

Wittlin, Thaddeus. Commissar, The Life and Death of Lavrenty Pavolich Beria. New York: Macmillan, 1972. Rev. by J. L. Nogee, Historian, 36(Nov 1973):113-4.

Woehrlin, William F. Chernyshevskii: The Man and the Journalist. Cambridge, Mass.: Har U Press, 1971. Rev. by R. Wortman, JMH, 45(Mar 1973):148-50; T. Emmons, AHR, 78(Je 1973):718-9.

Woehrmann, Paul. At the Headwaters of the Maumee: A History of the Forts of Fort Wayne. Indianapolis: Ind Historical Society, 1971. Rev. by D. L. Parman, WHQ, 4(Jl 1973):331-3; O. Knight, AHR, 78(Feb 1973):159.

Wolf, Eric R.   Peasant Wars of the Twentieth Century.   Scranton,
    Pa.:   Harper and Row, 1970.   Rev. by H. A. Landsberger,
    CSSH, 15(Je 1973):378-88.

_____ and Edward C. Hansen.   The Human Condition in Latin
    America.   New York: Ox U Press, 1972.   Rev. by M. M.
    Anderberg, CurH, 64(Feb 1973):82;   E. B. Burns, HAHR, 53
    (Feb 1973):112-13.

Wolf, Phyllis see Salter, Anne

Wolfe, Martin.   The Fiscal System of Renaissance France.   New
    Haven, Conn.:   Yale U Press, 1972.   Rev. by M. B. Becker,
    JEH, 33(Je 1973):500-2;   F. J. Pegues, AHR, 78(Dec 1973):
    1443-4;   R. Major, JMH, 45(Sep 1973):480-1.

Wolff, Philippe.   Western Languages A. D. 100-1500.   London:
    Weidenfeld and Nicolson, 1971.   Rev. by D. Hay, History, 58
    (Oct 1973):425-6.

Wolff, Tatiana.   Pushkin on Literature.   London: Methuen, 1971.
    Rev. by A. D. Briggs, ESR, 3(Oct 1973):398-400.

Wolffe, B. P.   The Royal Demesne in English History: The Crown
    Estate in the Governance of the Realm From the Conquest to
    1509.   Athens: Ohio U Press, 1971.   Rev. by J. Rosenthal,
    AHR, 78(Feb 1973):81;   G. L. Harriss, History, 58(Feb 1973):
    86-7.

Wolk, Donald J. , ed.   Drugs and Youth.   Washington, D. C.: Na-
    tional Council for the Social Studies, 1971.   Rev. by J. L.
    Browne, SS, 64(Feb 1973):87-8.

Wolpin, Miles D.   Military Aid and Counterrevolution in the Third
    World.   Lexington, Mass.:   D. C. Heath, 1972.   Rev. by E.
    E. Beauregard, MilAf, 37(Dec 1973):157.

Woltring, J. , ed.   Selected Documents on the Foreign Policy of the
    Netherlands.   The Hague: Martinus Nijhoff, 1970.   Rev. by
    P. -H. Laurent, AHR, 78(Oct 1973):1084-5.

Wood, Leonard C. and Ralph H. Gabriel.   America: Its People and
    Values.   New York: Harcourt Brace Jovanovich, 1971.   Rev.
    by J. V. Ellis, SS, 64(Apr 1973):179.

Wood, Virginia Steele.   McIntosh County Academy, McIntosh County,
    Georgia....   Belmont, Mass.:   Virginia Steel Wood, n.d. Rev.
    by Mrs. E. A. Stanley, GHQ, 57(Fall 1973):445-6.

Woodburn, James.   Hunters and Gatherers: The Material Culture
    of the Nomadic Hadza.   London: British Museum, 1970.   Rev.
    by J. Kesby, AfAf, 72(Oct 1973):462-3.

Woodham-Smith, Cecil.   Queen Victoria: From Her Birth to the
   Death of the Prince Consort.   New York: Knopf, 1972.   Rev.
   by G.   Costigan, AHR   78(Dec 1973):1463-4.

Woodhouse, C. M.   Capodistra.   The Founder of Greek Independence.
   Oxford: Ox U Press, 1973.   Rev. by J. A. Hodge, HTo, 23
   (Sep 1973):672.

Woods, Sister Frances Jerome.   Marginality and Identity: A Colored Creole Family Through Ten Generations.   Baton Rouge:
   LSU Press, 1972.   Rev. by D. H. Brogaw, FHQ, 52(Oct
   1973):208-10;   L. Schneider, JSH, 39(Aug 1973):470-1.

Woods, Ted H.   Caldwell Parish in Slices: Beginning a Brief History of Caldwell Parish, Louisiana.   Baton Rouge: Claitor's,
   1972.   Rev. by H. Humphreys, LaH   14(Fall 1973):408-9.

Woodsworth, J. S.   My Neighbour.   Toronto: U Tor Press, 1972.
   Rev. by W. Metcalf, CHR, 54(Mar 1973):90-2.

Woodward, C. Vann.   American Counterpoint: Slavery and Racism
   in the North-South Dialogue.   Boston: Little, Brown, 1971.
   Rev. by G. M. Fredrickson, JAH, 60(Sep 1973):456-7.

Woodward, Carl R.   Plantation in Yankeeland: The Story of Co-
   cumscussoc, Mirror of Colonial Rhode Island.   Chester,
   Conn.:   Pequot, 1971.   Rev. by D. P. Kelsey, AgH, 47(Apr
   1973):184-5.

Woodward, Sir Llewellyn.   British Foreign Policy in the Second
   World War.   3 vols.   London: H. M. S. O., 1970-71.   Rev.
   by P. L. Mehra, IQ, 29(Oct-Dec 1973):353-4;   C. Howard,
   History, 58(Oct 1973):475;   W. N. Meddicott, EHR, 88(Oct
   1973):866-9.

Woodward, William P.   The Allied Occupation of Japan, 1945-1952,
   and Japanese Religions.   Leiden, The Netherlands: E. J.
   Brill, 1972.   Rev. by L. Houchins, MilAf, 37(Dec 1973):162;
   J. Williams, PHR, 42(Feb 1973):126.

Woolf, S. J., ed.   The Rebirth of Italy, 1943-50.   New York:
   Humanities, 1972.   Rev. by S. B. Clough, AHR, 78(Oct 1973):
   1097-8.

Wootton, Barbara.   Contemporary Britain.   London: George Allen
   and Unwin, 1971.   Rev. by P. Stansky, SS, 64(Mar 1973):
   137-8.

World Bank, The.   Economic Growth of Colombia: Problems and
   Prospects.   Baltimore: JHU Press, 1972.   Rev. by M. Ur-
   rutia, HAHR, 53(Nov 1973):731-2;   C. O. Andrew, AgH, 47
   (Jl 1973):269-70.

Woronoff, Denis. La république bourgeoise thermidor à brumaire, 1794-1799. Paris: Editions du Seuil, 1972. Rev. by O. H. Hufton, JMH, 45(Dec 1973):666-8.

Woronoff, Jon. West African Wager: Houphouet Versus Nkrumah. Metuchen, N. J.: Scarecrow, 1972. Rev. by O. V. Madu, Crisis, 80(Feb 1973):69-70, N. Chazan, NO, 16(Oct-Nov 1973): 63-8.

Worsley, Peter, ed. Two Blades of Grass: Rural Cooperatives in Agricultural Modernization. Manchester: Manchester U Press, 1971. Rev. by R. M. Finley, AgH, 47(Oct 1973):365-6.

Wraith, Ronald. Local Administration in West Africa. New York: Africana, 1972. Rev. by O. E. S., CurH, 64(Mar 1973):135.

Wren, Daniel A. The Evolution of Management Thought. New York: Ronald Press, 1972. Rev. by A. D. Chandler, Jr., BHR, 47 (Aut 1973):393-5.

Wreszin, Michael. The Superfluous Anarchist: Albert J. Nock. Providence, R. I.: Brown U Press, 1972. Rev. by C. Forcey, JAH, 60(Je 1973):171-2.

Wright, Constance. Fanny Kemble and the Lovely Land. New York: Dodd, Mead, 1972. Rev. by C. Ashby, PMHB, 97(Apr 1973): 275-6.

Wright, George see Goldberg, Gerry

Wright, Helen, Joan N. Warnow and Charles Weiner, eds. The Legacy of George Ellery Hale: Evolution of Astronomy and Scientific Institutions, in Pictures and Documents. Cambridge, Mass.: M I T Press, 1972. Rev. L. S. Swenson, Jr., JAH, 60(Sep 1973):480-1.

Wright, J. Leitch, Jr. Anglo-Spanish Rivalry in North America. Athens, Ga.: U Ga Press, 1971. Rev. by R. Magnaghi, WHQ, 4(Apr 1973):204-5; L. B. Wright, HAHR, 53(Feb 1973): 153-4; E. K. Eckert, MilAf, 37(Feb 1973):32; C. Shammas, AHR, 78(Feb 1973):140; J. G. Lydon, NYHSQ, 57(Apr 1973): 174-5.

Wright, John S. Lincoln and the Politics of Slavery. Reno: U Nev Press, 1970. Rev. by R. D. Rietveld, CWH, 19(Dec 1973):362-4.

Wright, John W. D., comp. and ed. Jackson County, Illinois Residents in 1850. Carbondale, Ill.: Jackson County Historical Society, 1972. Rev. by B. B. Hubbs, JISHS, 66(Aut 1973): 357-8.

Wright, Maurice. Treasury Control of the Civil Service, 1854-

1874. New York: Ox U Press, 1969. Rev. by R. M. Mac-
Leod, AHR, 78(Dec 1973):1386-1405.

Wright, Theon. The Disenchanged Isles: The Story of the Second
Revolution in Hawaii. New York: Dial 1972. Rev. by M.
Tate, AHR, 78(Je 1973):745; B. Melendy, AW, 10(May 1973):
58.

Wulf, Peter, ed. Das Kabinett Fehrenbach: 25. Juni 1920 bis 4
Mai 1921. Boppard am Rhein: Harald Boldt Verlag, 1972.
Rev. by H. A. Turner, Jr., AHR, 78(Dec 1973):1489-90.

Wyatt-Brown, Bertram. The American People in the Antebellum
South. West Haven, Conn.: Pendulum Press, 1973. Rev. by
W. K. Scarborough, NCHR, 50(Aut 1973):424.

Wyckoff, Peter. Wall Street and the Stock Markets. New York:
Chilton, 1972. Rev. by R. Sobel, BHR, 47(Aut 1973):398-400;
L. L. Murray, NYH, 54(Jl 1973):374.

Wyman, Walker D., ed. Frontier Woman: The Life of a Woman
Homesteader on the Dakota Frontier. River Falls, Wis.: U
Wis, River Falls, n. d. Rev. by B. B. Jensen, JOW, 12
(Apr 1973):339.

Yakir, Pyotr. A Childhood in Prison. New York: Coward, Mc-
Cann and Geoghegan, 1973. Rev. by D. V. Pospielovsky, RR,
32(Oct 1973):441-2.

Yaney, George L. The Systemization of Russian Government: Social Evolution in the Domestic Administration of Imperial Russia, 1711-1905. Rev. by A. E. Adams, HRNB, 2(Oct 1973):
26.

Yardeni, Myriam. La Conscience Nationale en France Pendant Les
Guerres de Religion, 1559-1598. Rev. by N. M. Sutherland,
History, 58(Je 1973):284-5; R. M. Kingdom, JMH, 45(Je
1973):300-1.

Yates, Frances A. The Rosicrucian Enlightenment. Boston: Routledge and Kegan Paul, 1972. Rev. by O. Odlozilik, AHR, 78
(Dec 1973):1448.

Yearns, W. Buck, ed. The Papers of Thomas Jordan Jarvis. Vol.
I: 1869-1882. Raleigh, N. C.: State Dept, Archives and
History, 1969. Rev. by J. F. Doster, JAH, 59(Mar 1973):
1011-12.

Yerushalmi, Yosef Hayim. From Spanish Court to Italian Ghetto.
Isaac Cardosa: A Study in Seventeenth-Century Marranism
and Jewish Apologetics. New York: Columbia U Press, 1971.
Rev. by A. A. Sicroff, JMH, 45(Dec 1973):658-60; F. Rosenthal. AHR, 78(Oct 1973):1048-9.

YIN 346

Yin, John. Sino-Soviet Dialogue on the Problem of War. The Hague: Martinus Nijhoff, 1971. Rev. by R. L. Walker, RR, 32(Apr 1973):189-92.

Yoder, C. P. Delaware Canal Journal: A Definitive History of the Canal and the River Valley Through Which It Flows. Bethlehem, Pa.: Canal Press, 1972. Rev. by L. F. Ellsworth, BHR, 47(Win 1973):527-8; W. D. Lewis, PH, 40(Oct 1973): 491-3.

Yodfat, Aryeh. Arab Politics in the Soviet Mirror. Jerusalem: Israel U Press, 1973. Rev. by S. Page, MEJ, 27(Aut 1973): 512-3.

Yokelson, Doris see Armbruster, Frank E.

Young, Arthur. China's Nation-Building Effort, 1927-1937: The Financial and Economic Record. Stanford, Cal.: Hoover Institution Press, Stan U, 1971. Rev. by J. Ch'en, CHR, 54 (Sep 1973):311-13.

Young, Donald. American Roulette: The History and Dilemma of the Vice-Presidency. New York: Holt, Rinehart and Winston, 1972. Rev. by M. Borden, SS, 64(Nov 1973):275-6.

Young, Otis E., Jr. Western Mining: An Informal Account of Precious-Metals Prospecting, Placering, Lode Mining, and Milling on the American Frontier From Spanish Times to 1893. Norman: U Ok Press, 1970. Rev. by W. Parker, WHQ, 4(Jl 1973):344-5; W. T. Jackson, AHR, 78(Feb 1973):168-9.

Younger, Carlton. A State of Disunion: Arthur Griffith, Michael Collins, James Craig, Eamon de Valera. London: Frederick Muller, 1972. Rev. by J. M. Curran, JMH, 45(Sep 1973):533.

Zaller, Robert. The Parliament of 1621: A Study in Constitutional Conflict. Berkeley: U Cal Press, 1971. Rev. by C. Russell, JMH, 45(Mar 1973):100.

Zampaglione, Gerardo. The Idea of Peace in Antiquity. Notre Dame, Ind.: U Notre Dame Press, 1973. Rev. by T. Kelly, HRNB, 2(Oct 1973):11.

Zavala, Iris M. Ideologia y politica en la novela española del Siglo XIX. Salamanca, Spain: Anaya, 1971. Rev. by T. Kaplan, HAHR, 53(Feb 1973):165-7.

_____. Masones, comuneros y carbonarios. Madrid: Siglo XXI de España Editores, 1971. Rev. by J. C. LaForce, HAHR, 53(Feb 1973):164-5; G. M. Addy, AHR, 78(Je 1973):702.

_____ and Clara Lida, eds. La Revolución de 1868: Historia, literatura. New York: Las Americas, 1970. R. Cardona,

347   ZEFF

HAHR, 53(Feb 1973):167-8.

Zeff, Stephen A. Forging Accounting Principles in Five Countries:
A History and an Analysis of Trends. Champaign, Ill.: Stipes,
1972. Rev. by H. T. Johnson, BHR, 47(Spr 1973):139-40.

Zeitlin, Irving M. Liberty, Equality, and Revolution in Alexis de
Tocqueville. Boston: Little, Brown, 1971. Rev. by S.
Drescher, AHR, 78(Feb 1973):93-4.

Zelnik, Reginald E. Labor and Society in Tsarist Russia: The
Factory Workers of St. Petersburg, 1855-1870. Stanford,
Cal.: Stan U Press, 1971. Rev. by C. A. Ruud. CHR, 54
(Mar 1973):105-6; J. Keep, JMH, 45(Mar 1973):147-8.

Zeman, Z. A. B. A Diplomatic History of the First World War.
London: Weidenfeld and Nicolson, 1971. Rev. by Z. Steiner,
History, 58(Feb 1973):133.

Zerinque, Earlene L. see Forsyth, Alice D.

Ziegler, Philip. King William IV. New York: Harper and Row,
1973. Rev. by G. B. Cooper, AHR, 78(Dec 1973):1462-3.

Zielonka, David M. and Robert J. Wechman. The Eager Immigrants. Champaign, Ill.: Stipes, 1972. Rev. by H. Schwartz, SS, 64(Nov 1973):283.

Zikmund, Joseph II and Miriam Ershkowitz, eds. Black Politics
in Philadelphia. New York: Basic Books, 1973. Rev. by H.
Sitkoff, HRNB, 2(Nov/Dec 1973):54-5.

Zimmerman, Karl R. C Z: The Story of the California Zephyr.
Starucca, Pa.: Starucca Valley Publications, 1972. Rev. by
G. Chappell, CoMag, 50(Sum 1973):254-5.

Zimmerman, Ludwig. Frankreichs Ruhrpolitik: Von Versailles bis
zum Dawesplan. Gottingen: Musterschmidt, 1971. Rev. by
D. Felix, AHR, 78(Oct 1973):1080-1.

Zinn, Howard. Postwar America, 1945-1971. Indianapolis: Bobbs-
Merrill, 1973. Rev. by J. T. Patterson, JAH, 60(Sep 1973):
513-4.

Zins, Henryk. England and the Baltic in the Elizabethan Era.
Manchester: Manchester U Press, 1972. Rev. by G. A.
Janus, JMH, 45(Dec 1973):649-51.

Zophy, Jonathan W. and Lawrence P. Buck, eds. The Social His-
tory of the Reformation. Columbus: Ohio St U Press, 1972.
Rev. by C. -P. Clasen, AHR, 78(Dec 1973):1445-8; N. L.
Roelker, JMH, 45(Dec 1973):647-9.

Zuckerman, Arthur J. A Jewish Princedom in Feudal France, 768-
900. New York: Columbia U Press, 1972. Rev. by B. S.
Bachrach, AHR, 78(Dec 1973):1440-1.

Zulaliai, M. K. Armenia in the First Half of the Sixteenth Century.
Moscow: Izdatel'stvo "Nauka, " 1971. Rev. by A. W. Fisher,
AHR, 78(Dec 1973):1504.

Zwinger, Ann H. and Beatrice E. Willard. Land Above the Trees:
A Guide to American Alpine Tundra. New York: Harper and
Row 1972. Rev. by R. M. Pyle, AW, 10(Jl 1973):52.

TITLE INDEX

The Age of Giant Corporations: A
Microeconomic History of Amer-
ican Business, 1914-1970. Robert
Sobel.

The Age of Humanism: Europe in
the 14th, 15th and 16th Centuries.
A. G. Dickens.

The Age of Jackson. Robert V.
Remini, ed.

The Age of Nationalism and Reform
1850-1890. Norman Rich.

The Age of Nelson: The Royal
Navy 1793-1815. G. J. Marcus.

The Age of Patronage: The Arts
in England, 1660-1750. Michael
Foss.

The Age of Religious Wars 1559-
1689. Richard S. Dunn.

The Age of Revolution and Reaction
1789-1850. Charles Breunig.

The Age of the Railway. Harold
Perkin.

Aggressive Introvert: A Study of
Herbert Hoover and Public Rela-
tions Management, 1912-1932.
Craig Lloyd.

The Agony of Vietnam: The Origin
and Background of American Intervention in Vietnam. Susheela
Kaushik.

The Agora of Athens: The History,
Shape and Uses of an Ancient
City Center. Homer A. Thomp-
son and R. E. Wycherley.

Agrarian Conditions in Northern
India. Elizabeth Whitcombe.

The Agrarian History of England
and Wales. H. P. R. Finberg, ed.

Agrarian Reform and Peasant Revolution in Spain: Origins of the
Civil War. Edward E. Malefakis.

Agricultural Change and the Peasant
Economy of South China. Evelyn
Sakakida Rawski.

Agricultural Change in Modern Tanganyika: An Outline History.
John Iliffe.

The Agricultural Community in Southwest Wales at the Turn of the
Century. David Jenkins.

Agricultural Development: An International Perspective. Yujiro
Hayami and Vernon Ruttan.

Agricultural Implements and Ma-
chines in the Collection of the
National Museum of History and
Technology. John T. Schlebecker.

Agricultural Planning and Cooperatives. R. N. Tewari.

Ägypten den Ägypten!: Die Politische und Gesellschaftliche Krise
der Jahre 1878-1882 in Ägypten.
Alexander Schölch.

Aid to Russia 1941-1946: Strategy,
Diplomacy, the Origins of the
Cold War. George C. Herring,
Jr.

Air Power--A Concise History.
Robin Higham.

Air Travel: A Social History. Kenneth Hudson.

Aircraft Hijacking and International
Law. S. K. Agarwal.

Akten zur Deutschen Auswärtigen
Politik 1918-1945.

Akulivikchuk: A Nineteenth-Century
Eskimo Village on the Nushagak
River, Alaska. James W. Van-
stone.

The Alamo. John Myers Myers.

Alaska and Its Wildlife. Bryan S.
Sage.

The Alaska Gold Rush. David
Wharton.

Alaska: The Last Frontier. Bryan
Cooper.

Alaskan Eskimo Life in the 1890's
as Sketched by Native Artists.
George Phebus, Jr.

Alabama: A Documentary History
to 1900. Lucille Griffith.

Albizu Campos: Puerto Rican Revolutionary. Frederico Ribes
Tovar.

An Album of American Battle Art,
1755-1918. Helen F. Conover
and Donald H. Mugridge.

Alexander Hamilton and American
Foreign Policy: A Design for
Greatness. Gilbert L. Lycan.

Alexander of Tunis. W. G. F.
Jackson.

Alfonso Reyes and Spain. Barbara
Bockus Aponte.

The Algonquins: Indians of That
Part of the New World First
Visited by the English. 2 vols.
F. Roy Johnson.

The Alien Invasion: The Origins
of the Aliens Act of 1905.
Bernard Gainer.

Alienation: Marx's Concept of Man
in Capitalist Society. Bertell
Ollman.

The All India Muslim Conference (1928-35). K. K. Aziz.

All the Queen's Men. Elizabeth I and Her Courtiers. Neville Williams.

Allal El Fassi: Ou l'histoire de l'Istiqlal. Gaudio Attilio.

Alliance in Decline: A Study in Anglo-Japanese Relations, 1908-23. Ian H. Nish.

The Allied Occupation of Japan, 1945-1952, and Japanese Religions. William P. Woodward.

Al-Manar English-Arabic Dictionary. Hasan S. Karmi.

Al Smith: Hero of the Cities. Matthew and Hannah Josephson.

Amadeo Bordiga. Andreina de Clementi

An Ambassador's Memoirs. 3 vols. Maurice Paléologue.

L'Ambivalence dans la culture Arabe. Jean-Paul Charnay, ed.

Ambrose Bierce, F. A. Mitchell-Hedges and the Crystal Skull. Sibley S. Morill.

The Amerasia Papers: Some Problems in the History of the U. S. - China Relations. John S. Service.

America at 1750: A Social Portrait. Richard Hofstadter.

America: Its People and Values. Leonard C. Wood and Ralph H. Gabriel.

American Axes: A Survey of Their Development and Their Makers. Henry J. Kauffman.

American Business and Foreign Policy, 1920-1933. Joan Hoff Wilson.

American Business in the Twentieth Century. Thomas C. Cochran.

The American Campaigns of Rochambeau's Army, 1780, 1781, 1782, 1783. Howard C. Rice, Jr. and Anne S. K. Brown, trans. and eds.

American Convictions: Cycles of Public Thought 1600-1850. Charles A. Barker.

American Counterpoint: Slavery and Racism in the North-South Dialogue. C. Vann Woodward.

The American Disease: Origins of Narcotic Control. David F. Musto.

American Economic and Business

History Information Sources. Robert W. Lovett.

The American Economy: Analysis, Issues, Principles. Roy J. Sampson, William P. Mortenson, Ira Marienhoff.

American Enterprise: Free and Not So Free. Clarence H. Cramer.

The American Film Heritage: Impressions from the American Film Institute Archives. Tom Shales, et al.

The American Film Institute Catalog of Motion Picture Films Produced in the United States; Feature Films, 1921-1930. 2 vols. Kenneth W. Munden, ed.

The American Fishing Schooners, 1825-1835. Howard I. Chapelle.

American Folk Art in Wood, Metal, and Stone. Jean Lipman.

The American Frontier: Readings and Documents. Robert V. Hine and Edwin R. Bingham, eds.

American Genesis: Pre-Colonial Writing in the North. Evelyn Page.

American Government and Business. H. H. Liebhafsky.

American Habitat: An Historical Perspective. Barbara Gutmann Rosenkrantz and William A. Koelsch.

The American Heritage Book of Natural Wonders.

American Heroine: The Life and Legend of Jane Addams. Allen F. Davis.

American History in American Thought: Christopher Columbus to Henry Adams. Bert James Loewenberg.

American Indian Almanac. John Upton Terrell.

American Indian Ceremonial Dances. John Collier.

American Indian Mythology. Alice Marriott and Carol K. Rachlin.

American Indian Policy. Francis Paul Prucha, et al.

The American Left: Radical Political Thought in the 20th Century. Loren Baritz, ed.

The American Mail: Enlarger of the Common Life. Wayne E. Fuller.

American Medicine and the Public

Interest. Rosemary Stevens.
American Negro Slavery: A Reader.
Allen Weinstein and Frank Otto
Gatell, eds.
The American Newsreel, 1911-1967.
Raymond Fielding.
The American Peace Movement and
Social Reform, 1898-1918. C.
Roland Marchand.
The American People in the Antebel-
lum South. Bertram Wyatt-
Brown.
American Philanthropy in the Near
East, 1820-1960. Robert L.
Daniel.
American Physicians in the Nine-
teenth Century: From Sects to
Science. William G. Rothstein.
American Place Names: A Concise
and Selective Dictionary for the
Continental United States of
America. George R. Stewart.
American Policy and the Division
of Germany: The Clash with
Russia Over Reparations. Bruce
Kuklick.
American Policy Toward Communist
China: The Historical Record,
1949-1969. Foster Rhea Dulles.
American Presidents and the Presi-
dency. Marcus Cunliffe.
The American Primitive: The
Words of John and Abigail Adams.
William Gibson.
The American Religious Experience:
The Roots, Trends and Future of
American Theology. Frederick
Sontag and John K. Roth.
The American Revolution, 1775-1783.
An Atlas of 18th-Century Maps
and Charts. W. Bart Green-
wood and Edwin B. Hopper, comps.
American Sailing Coasters of the
North Atlantic. Paul C. Morris.
The American Sectetaries of State
and Their Diplomacy. Gaddis
Smith.
The American Shakers: From Neo-
Christianity to Presocialism.
Henri Desroche.
American Silver, 1655-1825, in the
Museum of Fine Arts, Boston.
2 vols. Kathryn C. Buhler.
The American Slave: A Composite
Autobiography. Vol. I: From
Sundown to Sunup: The Making
of the Black Community. George
P. Rawick.

American Society and Black Revolu-
tion. Frank Hercules.
The American Southwest: Its
Peoples and Cultures. Lynn I.
Perrigo.
American Space: The Centennial
Years, 1865-1876. John Brinck-
erhoff Jackson.
American Still-Life Painting. Wil-
liam H. Gerdts and Russell
Burke.
American Transcendentalism: An
Anthology of Criticism. Brian
M. Barbour, ed.
American Utopianism. Robert S.
Fogarty, ed.
American Voyages to the Orient
1690-1865. Charles Oscar
Paullin.
The American Way of War: A His-
tory of the United States Military
Strategy and Policy. Russell F.
Weigley.
The American West: An Interpre-
tative History. Robert V. Hine.
The American West in the Twenti-
eth Century: A Short History of
an Urban Oasis. Gerald D. Nash.
The American Woman: Her Chang-
ing Social, Economic, and Polit-
ical Roles, 1920-1970. William
Henry Chafe.
The Americanization of Alaska,
1867-1897. Ted C. Hinckley.
The Americanization of the Gulf
Coast, 1803-1850. Lucius F.
Ellsworth, et al., eds.
Americans and the California Dream,
1850-1915. Kevin Starr.
The Americans: The Democratic
Experience. Daniel J. Boorstin.
America's Past: A New World
Archaeology. Thomas C. Patter-
son.
Amin. Judith Listowel.
Among the Indians: Four Years on
the Upper Missouri, 1858-1862.
Henry A. Boller.
Among the Mescalero Apaches: The
Story of Father Albert Braun,
O. F. M. Dorothy Emerson.
The Amphibians Came to Conquer:
The Story of Admiral Richmond
Kelly Turner. 2 vols. George
Carroll Dyer.
Anabaptism: A Social History, 1525-
1618. Claus-Peter Clasen.
Analysis of the Location of Industry

in Istanbul. Erol Tümertekin.

Anamur Nekropolü: The Necropolis of Anemurium. E. Alföldi-Rosenbaum.

Anarchism in Germany. Vol. 1: The Early Movement. Andrew R. Carlson.

Anarchism: Old and New. Gerald Runkle.

The Anatomy of a Scientific Institution, The Paris Academy of Sciences, 1666-1803. Richard Hahn.

Anatomy of Four Race Riots: Racial Conflict in Knoxville, Elaine (Arkansas), Tulsa and Chicago, 1919-1921. Lee E. Williams and Lee E. Williams II.

The Anatomy of the Confederate Congress: A Study of the Influence of Member Characteristics on Legislative Voting Behavior, 1861-1865. Thomas B. Alexander and Richard E. Beringer.

The Ancient American Civilizations. Frederick Katz.

The Ancient Civilization of Germanic Peoples. Rolf Hachmann.

Ancient Egyptian Jewellery. Alix Wilkinson.

Ancient Ghana and Mali. Nehemia Levtzion.

Ancient Hunters of the Far West. Malcolm J. Rogers, et al.

And ... I'll Throw in the Socks. William M. Jenkins, Jr.

Andamans and Nicobars. C. Boden Kloss.

Andrew Carnegie. Jospeh Frazier Wall.

Anecdotes of Public Men. John W. Forney.

Anglo-Saxon England. Vol. I. Peter Clemoes, et al., eds.

Anglo-Saxons and Celts: A Study of Anti-Irish Prejudice in Victorian England. L. Perry Curtis, Jr.

Anglo-Spanish Rivalry in North America. J. Leitch Wright, Jr.

Animals in Roman Life and Art. J. M. C. Toynbee.

Anne Royall's U. S. A. Bessie Rowland James.

Annex: A History of the American Stock Exchange, 1921-1971. Robert Sobel.

Annotated Abstracts of the Successions of St. Mary Parish, Louisiana, 1811-1834. Mary Elizabeth Sanders.

Annual Studies of America, 1971.

Anonymous Americans: Explorations in 19th-Century Social History. Tamara K. Hareven.

Another Look at the Twentieth-Century South. George E. Mowry.

Anthony Collins: The Man and His Works. James O'Higgins.

Anthony Trollope. James Pope Hennessy.

Antichrist in Seventeenth-Century England. Christopher Hill.

Antonio Gramsci: Life of a Revolutionary. Giuseppe Fiori.

Antwerp in the Age of Plantin and Breughel. John J. Murray.

Anza Conquers the Desert: The Anza Expeditions from Mexico to California and the Founding of San Francisco, 1774-1776. Richard F. Pourade.

Apache Chronicle: The Story of the People. John Upton Terrell.

The Apache People (Coyotero). Henry F. Dobyns.

Apes and Angels: The Irishman in Victorian Caricature. L. P. Curtis.

The Appeal of Fascism: A Study of Intellectuals and Fascism 1919-1945. Alistair Hamilton.

Arab Attitudes Toward Israel. Yehoshafat Harkabi.

Arab Civilization to A. D. 1500. D. M. Dunlop.

The Arab Lands of Western Asia. Joseph J. Malone.

Arab Politics in the Soviet Mirror. Aryeh Yodfat.

Arab Village: A Social Structural Study of a Transjordanian Peasant Community. Richard T. Antoun.

The Arabian Peninsula: Society and Politics. Derek Hopwood, ed.

Archaeological Encyclopaedia of the Holy Land. Abraham Negev, ed.

Archaeological Explorations on San Nicholas Island. Bruce Bryan.

Archaeological Survey Annual Report. Vol. 10. T. F. King, J. P. Carpenter, and N. N. Leonard, III, eds.

Archaeological Survey in the Lower Yazoo Basin, Mississippi, 1949-1955. Philip Phillips.

Archaeology and the Landscape: Essays for L. V. Grinsell. P. J. Fowler, ed.

-B-

A Basic Course in Iraqi Arabic.
Wallace M. Erwin.
Basic Documents on African Affairs.
Ian Brownlie, ed.
Basic Problems of the Internal De-
velopment of Byzantine Cities in
the 4th-7th Centuries. G. L.
Kurbatov.
Basketry of the Papago and Pima
Indians. Mary Lois Kissell.
Basketry of the San Carlos Apaches.
Helen H. Roberts.
Das Basler Arztrelief: Studien zum
griechischen Grab- und Votivre-
lief um 500v. Chr. und zur
vorhippokratischen Medizin.
Ernst Berger.
The Battle of Leyte Gulf: The
Death Knell of the Japanese
Fleet. Edwin P. Hoyt.
The Battleship Era. Peter Padfield.
Baylor at Independence. Lois
Smith Murray.
The Bayou Chene Story: A History
of the Atchafalaya Basin and Its
People. Gladys Calhoon Case.
Der bayreuther Kreis von seiner
Entstehung bis zum Ausgang der
wilhelminischen Ära: Wagnerkult
und Kulturreform im Geiste vol-
kischer Weltanschauung. Win-
fried Schüler.
The Bear and the Dragon: Sino-
Soviet Relations and the Evolution
of the Chinese People's Republic,
1949-1971. Richard C. Thronton.
The Bear at the Gate: Chinese
Policy-Making Under Soviet Pres-
sure. Harold C. Hinton.
Beaverbrook. A. J. P. Taylor.
A Becon [sic] Across Asia: A Bi-
ography of Subhas Chandra Bose.
Sisir K. Bose, ed.
Die Bedeutung der Vereinigten
Staaten von Amerika für das
deutsche Reparationsproblem,
1924-1929. Eckhard Wandel.
Before the Bawdy Court. Paul
Hair, ed.
Before the Deluge: A Portrait of
Berlin in the 1920's. Otto
Friedrich.
Der Beginn der Gold-und Dickmunzen
pragung Munz-und Geldgeschichte
de 15 Jahrhunderts. Hans-Ulrich
Geiger.
The Beginning of the West: Annals
of the Kansas Gateway to the

American West, 1504-1854.
Louise Barry.
The Beginnings of the American
People. Volume II: No Peace
Beyond the Line: The English
in the Caribbean, 1624-1690.
Carl and Roberta Bridenbaugh.
The Beginnings of Modern Coloniza-
tion. Charles Verlinden.
The Behavior of Industrial Prices.
G. J. Stigler and J. K. Kindahl.
A Behavorial Approach to Historical
Analysis. Robert F. Berkhofer.
Die belgische Neutralist als Prob-
lem der europaischen Politik,
1830-1914. Horst Ladenacher.
Belgium's Return to Neutrality: An
Essay in the Frustrations of
Small-Power Diplomacy. David
Owen Kieft.
Bellièvre and Villeroy: Power in
France Under Henry III and
Henry IV. Edmund H. Dicker-
man.
Belorussia Under Soviet Rule, 1917-
1957. Ivan S. Lubachko.
Benedict Arnold: The Dark Eagle.
Brian Richard Boylan.
Benedict Kiely. Grace Eckley.
Bengal Famine of 1943: The Amer-
ican Response. M. S. Venkata-
ramani.
Benjamin Franklin: A Biography in
His Own Words. Thomas Flem-
ing, ed.
Benjamin Rush: Revolutionary
Gadfly. David Freeman Hawke.
The Berlin Crisis, 1958-1962. Jack
M. Schick.
The Berlin Crisis of 1961: Soviet-
American Relations and the
Struggle for Power in the Krem-
lin, June-November 1961. Robert
M. Slusser.
Berliner Unternehmer Waehrend der
Fruhen Industrialisierung. Hart-
mut Kaelble.
Bernard Shaw. Collected Letters
1898-1910. Dan H. Laurence,
ed.
Bernard Shaw, Director. Bernard
F. Dukore.
Bernardo de Galvez in Louisiana,
1776-1783. John Walton Caughey.
The Best Poor Man's Country: A
Geographical Study of Early
Southeastern Pennsylvania.
James T. Lemon.

Between Harvard and America: The
Educational Leadership of Charles
W. Eliot. Hugh Hawkins.
Between Nothingness and Paradise.
Gerhart Niemeyer.
Between Two Worlds: The Political
Thought of Graham Wallas.
Martin J. Wiener.
Beyond Freedom and Dignity.
B. F. Skinner.
Beyond the Oxus: Archaeology,
Art and Architecture of Central
Asia. Edgar Knobloch.
Beyond the Revolution: Bolivia
Since 1952. James M. Malloy
and Richard S. Thorn, eds.
Beyond the River and the Bay.
Eric Ross.
A Bias for Hope: Essays on De-
velopment and Latin America.
Albert O. Hirschman.
Bibliographic Control of Microforms.
Felix Reichmann and Josephine
Tharpe.
A Bibliography of American Child-
ren's Books Printed Prior to
1821. d'Alté A. Welch, comp.
Bibliography of American Cookery
Books, 1742-1860. Eleanor
Lowenstein.
A Bibliography of British and Irish
Municipal History. G. H. Mar-
tin and Sylvia McIntyre.
A Bibliography of Irish Literature.
E. H. Mikhail.
Bibliography of José Figueres.
Harry Kantor.
A Bibliography of Mesopotamian
Archaeological Sites. Richard
S. Ellis.
A Bibliography of Yeats Criticism.
K. G. W. Cross and R. T.
Dunlop.
Bicycling, a History. Frederick
Alderson.
Big Brother's Indian Programs--
With Reservations. Sar A.
Levitan and Barbara Hetrick.
The Big Foundations. Waldemar
A. Nielsen.
The Big Rock Candy Mountain.
Wallace Stegner.
The Big Thicket: A Challenge for
Conservation. A. Y. Gunter.
Billy Bartram and His Green
World: An Interpretative Biog-
raphy. Marjory Bartlett Sanger.
Billy King's Tombstone: The Pri-
vate Life of an Arizona Boom

Town. C. L. Sonnichsen.
A Biographical Dictionary of Amer-
ican Civil Engineers. Antoinette
Lee and Harold Skramsted.
A Biographical History of Blacks in
America Since 1528. Edgar A.
Toppin.
Biographical Sketches of Those Who
Attended Harvard College in the
Classes 1764-1767. Clifford K.
Shipton.
Biracial Politics: Conflict and Co-
alition in the Metropolitan South.
Chandler Davidson.
The Birth of a Union Local: The
History of U A W Local 674,
Norwood, Ohio, 1933-1940. John
G. Kruchko.
The Birth of Mass Political Part-
ies: Michigan, 1827-1861.
Ronald P. Formisano.
The Birth of the English Common
Law. R. C. Van Caenegem.
Bishop Heber in Northern India:
Selections From Heber's Journal.
M. A. Laird, ed.
Bismarck. Hans Rothfels.
Bismarck and the French Nation:
1848-1890. Allan Mitchell.
Das Bismarck-Problem in der
Geschicht-schreibung. Gall
Lothar.
Black Africa: A Comparative
Handbook. Donald G. Morrison,
Robert S. Mitchell, John N.
Paden and Hugh M. Stevenson.
Black Bondage in the North. Edgar
J. McManus.
Black Business in the New South:
A Social History of the North
Carolina Mutual Life Insurance
Company. Walter B. Weare.
Black Carolinians: A History of
Blacks in South Carolina from
1895 to 1968. I. A. Newby.
Black English: Its History and
Usage. J. L. Dillard.
The Black Experience in America.
Norman Coombs.
Black Ghettos, White Ghettos, and
Slums. Robert E. Forman.
The Black Image in the White
Mind: The Debate on Afro-
American Character and Destiny,
1817-1914. George M. Fred-
erickson.
Black Images in the American
Theatre. Leonard C. Archer.
Black Labor in America. Milton
Cantor, ed.

Black Leadership in American
History. Thomas T. Lyons.
The Black Legend in England: The
Development of Anti-Spanish
Sentiment, 1558-1660. William
S. Maltby.
The Black Man of Zinacantan: A
Central American Legend.
Sarah C. Blaffer.
Black Mesa: Survey and Excava-
tion in Northeastern Arizona,
1968. George J. Gumerman.
The Black Military Experience in
the Middle West. John M.
Carroll, ed.
Black Mountain: An Exploration in
Community. Martin Duberman.
Black New Orleans, 1860-1880.
John W. Blassingame.
Black Political Parties: An His-
torical and Political Record.
Hanes Walton, Jr.
Black Politics in Philadelphia.
Miriam Ershkowitz and Joseph
Zikmund, II, eds.
The Black Press Views American
Imperialism (1898-1900). George
P. Marks, III.
The Black Prophet: A Tale of
Irish Famine. Willian [sic]
Carleton.
Black Psyche: The Modal Person-
ality Patterns of Black Americans.
Stanley S. Guterman.
Black Reconstructionists. Emma
Lou Thornbrough, ed.
Black Resistance/White Law: A
History of Constitutional Racism
in America. Mary Frances
Berry.
The Black West. William Loren
Katz.
The Blacks in Canada: A History.
Robin W. Winks.
Blacks in the City: A History of
the National Urban League.
Guichard Parris and Lester
Brooks.
Blacks in White America Before
1865: Issues and Interpretations.
Robert V. Haynes.
Blacks on John Brown. Benjamin
Quarles, ed.
The Black Presence: A Documen-
tary History of the Negro in Eng-
land 1555-1860. James Walvin.
Les Blancs: The Collected Last
Plays of Lorraine Hansberry.
Robert Nemiroff, ed.

Blasted, Beloved Breckenridge.
Mark Fiester.
Blätter für Technikgeschichte. Vol.
32/33 (1970/71). Rolf Nieder-
huemer, ed.
Blaze of Glory: The Fight for New
Orleans, 1814-1815. Samuel
Carter, III.
The Blitzkrieg Era and the German
General Staff, 1865-1941. Larry
H. Addington.
Blood Relations: Versions of Gaelic
Poems of the Seventeenth and
Eighteenth Centuries. Tom Mac-
Intyre.
Blood, Toil, Tears and Sweat: The
War History from Dunkirk to
Alamein, Based on the War
Cabinet Papers of 1940 to 1942.
Roger Parkinson.
The Bloody Bozeman: The Perilous
Trail to Montana's Gold. Dor-
othy W. Johnson.
Bloomsday. An Interpretation of
James Joyce's Ulysses. Saul
Field and Morton P. Levitt.
The Blueshirts. Maurice Manning.
The B'nai Khaim in America.
Joseph M. Gillman.
Bodine: A Legend in His Time.
Harold A. Williams.
Bohemia: Jahrbuch des. Collegium
Carolinum. Volume X.
The Bog People: Iron-Age Man
Preserved. P. V. Glob.
Bolivia: A Profile. William
Carter.
Bolivia: Land, Location, and Pol-
itics Since 1825. J. Valerie
Fifer.
The Bolshevik Seizure of Power.
S. P. Melgunov.
Bonnin and Morris of Philadelphia:
The First American Porcelain
Factory, 1770-1772. Graham
Hood.
The Bonus March: An Episode of
the Great Depression. Roger
Daniels.
Book of the Gods and Rites and the
Ancient Calendar. Fray Diego
Duran.
The Booker T. Washington Papers.
Vols. 1 and 2. Louis R. Har-
lan, et al., eds.
The Booker T. Washington Press,
Volume I.... Louis R. Harlan,
ed.
Booker T. Washington: The Mak-

ing of a Black Leader, 1856-
1901. Louis R. Harlan.
Books in Our Time (Essays).
Lawrence S. Thompson.
Books on Asia from the Near East
to the Far East: A Guide for
the General Reader. Eleazar
Birnbaum.
The Bosses. Alfred Steinberg.
The Booth Site: A Late Archaic
Campsite. Walter E. Klippel.
Bordeaux au XXe siècle. Joseph
La Juge, et al., eds.
The Born-Einstein Letters....
Irene Born, trans.
Born Sober: Prohibition in Okla-
homa, 1907-1959. Jimmie
Lewis Franklin.
Both Your Houses: The Truth
About Congress. Warren
Weaver, Jr.
Les bourgeois et la démocratie
sociale, 1914-1968. Félix
Ponteil.
Boyhood on the Upper Mississippi,
a Reminiscent Letter. Charles
A. Lindbergh.
The Bracero Program: Interest
Groups and Foreign Policy.
Richard B. Craig.
Brand Book Two of the Tucson
Corral of Westerners.... Otis
B. Chidester, ed.
Brazil in the Sixties. Riordan
Roett, ed.
Brazil: The Land and People.
Rollie E. Poppino.
Brazil: The People and the Power.
Miguel Arraes.
Brazza explorateur: Les traites
Makoko, 1880-1882. Henri
Brunschwig, et al.
Bread and Roses Too: Studies of
the Wobblies. Joseph Robert
Conlin.
The Brethren in the Carolinas: The
History of the Church of the
Brethren in the District of North
and South Carolina. Roger E.
Sappington.
Bricks and Brownstone: The New
York Row House, 1783-1929....
Charles Lockwood.
Bride of the Revolution: Krupskaya
and Lenin. R. H. McNeal.
Bridge Across the Bosporus.
Ferenc A. Vali.
Brierfield, Plantation Home of Jef-
ferson Davis. Frank Edgar
Everett, Jr.

Britain and Ireland in Early
Christian Times. Charles Thomas.
Britain and the Netherlands. Vol.
IV. J. S. Bromley and E. H.
Kossmann, eds.
Britain and the Western Seaways.
E. G. Bowen.
Britain and West Germany: Chang-
ing Societies and the Future of
Foreign Policy. Karl Kaiser and
Roger Morgan, eds.
Britain in the Nineteen Thirties.
Noreen Branson and Margot
Heineman.
Britain, the Brookes, and Brunei.
Nicholas Tarling.
British Admirals of the Eighteenth
Century: Tactics in Battle. John
Creswell.
The British Americans: The Loyal-
ist Exiles in England. Mary
Beth Norton.
British and Soviet Politics: Legiti-
macy and Convergence. Jerome
M. Gilison.
British Antislavery, 1833-1870.
Howard Temperley.
British Chartists in America 1839-
1900. Ray Boston.
British Commercial Policy and
Trade Expansion, 1750-1850.
Judith Blow Williams.
British Diplomacy and Tunis, 1875-
1902: A Case Study in Mediter-
ranean Policy. Arthur Marsden.
British Economic Fluctuations 1790-
1939. Derek H. Aldcroft and
Peter Fearon, eds.
British Emigration Policy, 1815-
1830: "Shoveling Out the
Paupers." H. J. M. Johnston.
British Foreign Policy in the
Second World War. Vols. I, II,
III. Sir Llewellyn Woodward.
The British in the Caribbean.
Cyril Hamshere.
British Investment in American
Railways, 1834-1898. Dorothy
R. Adler.
British Labour Struggles: Contem-
porary Pamphlets, 1727-1850.
Kenneth E. Carpenter, ed.
British Maps of the American Rev-
olution. Peter J. Guthorn.
The British Occupation of Charles-
ton, 1780-82. George Smith
McCowen, Jr.
British Parliamentary Election Re-
sults 1950-1970. F. W. S. Craig,
comp. and ed.

British Pioneers in Geography.
Edmund W. Gilbert.
British Protestant Missions.
A. J. Temu.
British Rule in India. Pandit
Sundarlal.
British Social Policy 1914-1939.
Bentley B. Gilbert.
British Travelers among the South-
ern Indians, 1660-1763. J.
Ralph Randolph.
British War Aims and Peace Diplo-
macy 1914-1918. V. H. Rothwell.
Britons View America: Travel
Commentary, 1860-1935.
Richard L. Rapson.
Broken K Pueblo: Prehistoric So-
cial Organization in the Amer-
ican Southwest. James N. Hill.
Brokenburn: The Journal of Kate
Stone, 1861-1868. John Q.
Anderson, ed.
Bronterre: A Political Biography
of Bronterre O'Brien, 1804-1864.
Alfred Plummer.
The Brownsville Affair: National
Crisis and Black Reaction. Ann
J. Lane.
Bruno Bauer: Studien und Materi-
alien. Ernst Barnikol.
Bryan: A Political Biography of
William Jennings Bryan. Louis
W Koenig.
Bucks and Bruisers: Pierce Egan
and Regency England. J. C.
Reid.
Buddhism in Hawaii--Its Impact on
a Yankee Community. Louise
Hunter.
Buddhism Under Mao. Holmes Welch.
The Buffalo Head: A Century of
Mercantile Pioneering in the
Southwest. Daniel T. Kelly and
Beatrice Chauvenet.
Building the Organizational Society:
Essays on Associational Activities
in Modern America. Jerry Israel,
ed.
Bulgarian Communism: The Road to
Power, 1934-1944. Nissan Oren.
The Bunkhouse Man: Life and
Labour in the Northern Work
Camps. Edmund Bradwin.
Bunkhouse Papers: Reminiscences
of a Distinguished Western His-
torian. John Upton Terrell.
The Bureau of Land Management.
Marion Clawson.

Burnt-Out Fires: California's Modoc
Indian War. Richard Dillon.
Bushcraft: A Serious Guide to Sur-
vival and Camping. Richard
Graves.
Business and Politics in America
from the Age of Jackson to the
Civil War: The Career Biography
of W. W. Corcoran. Henry
Cohen.
Business in American Life: A His-
tory. Thomas C. Cochran.
Busing and Backlash: White Against
White in an Urban California
School District. Lillian B. Rubin.
The Butterfly Caste: A Social His-
tory of Pellagra in the South.
Elizabeth W. Etheridge.
By Myself I'm a Book: An Oral
History of the Immigrant Jewish
Experience in Pittsburgh. Ailon
Shiloh, Dir.
"By South Cadbury is that Camelot.
... " Leslie Alcock.
Byzantine Jewry from Justinian to
the Fourth Crusade. Andrew
Sharf.
Byzantine Rite Rusins in Carpatho-
Ruthenia and America. Walter
C. Warzeski.

-C-

CORE: A Study in the Civil Rights
Movement, 1942-1968. August
Meier and Elliot Rudwick.
C Z: The Story of the California
Zephyr. Karl R. Zimmerman.
The Cable Car in America. George
W. Hilton.
Caccia alle streghe nell' America
puritana. Itala Vivan.
Cairo: 1001 Years of the City Vic-
torious. Janet L. Abu-Lughod.
Caldwell Parish in Slices: Begin-
ning a Brief History of Caldwell
Parish, Louisiana. Ted. H.
Woods.
The Calendar of the Claude Elliott
Collection, 1821-1937. Anne
Salter and Phyllis Wolf.
A Calendar of the Egan Family Col-
lection. Katherine Bridges.
A Calendar of the Register of Henry
Wakefield, Bishop of Worcester,

1375-1395. W. P. Warrett, ed.
A Calendar of the Shrewsbury and
Talbot Papers. G. R. Batho, ed.
California: A History of the
Golden State. Warren A. Beck
and David A. Williams.
California, a Pleasure Trip from
Gotham to the Golden Gate.
Mrs. Frank Leslie.
California, an Illustrated History.
T. H. Watkins
California In-Doors and Out: Or,
How We Farm, Mine and Live
Generally in the Golden State.
Eliza W. Farnham.
California: Land of New Begin-
nings. David Lavender.
California: Two Centuries of Man,
Land and Growth in the Golden
State. W. H. Hutchinson.
Californiana II--Documentos para
la historia de la explotación
comercial de California, 1611-
1679. W. Michael Mathes, ed.
California Water: A Study in Re-
source Management. David W.
Seckler, ed.
Cambodia in the Southeast Asian
War. Malcolm Caldwell and
Lek Tan.
The Cambridge Ancient History.
Vol. I, Part 2. Early History
of the Middle East. I. Edwards,
C. Gadd, N. Hammond, eds.
The Cambridge History of Islam.
Volumes I and II. Peter M.
Holt, A. K. S. Lambton and
Bernard Lewis, eds.
The Cameroon Federal Republic.
Victor T. LeVine.
The Cameroon Federation: Polit-
ical Integration in a Fragmentary
Society. Willard R. Johnson.
Les Camerounais Occidentaux: la
minorité dans un état bicom-
munautaire. Jacques Benjamin.
Can We Survive Our Future? G.
R. Urban and Michael Glenny,
eds.
Canada and the Canadian Question.
Goldwin Smith.
Canada 1874-1896: Arduous Des-
tiny. P. B. Waite.
Canadian Business History: Selected
Studies, 1497-1971. David S.
Macmillan, ed.
The Canadian Military: A Profile.
Hector J. Massey, ed.

The Canals of Pennsylvania and the
System of Internal Improvement.
Theodore B. Klein.
Cannon Smoke: The Letters of Cap-
tain John J. Good, Good-Douglas
Texas Battery, C. S. A. Lester
Newton Fitzhugh, ed.
Capital Cities of Arab Islam.
Philip K. Hitti.
Capital Formation in the Industrial
Revolution. Francois Crouzet,
ed.
Capitalism in Crisis. Andrew Glyn
and Bob Sutcliffe.
Le Capitalisme "Sauvage" aux
Etats-Unis (1860-1900). Mari-
anne Debouzy.
Capodistra. The Founder of Greek
Independence. C. M. Woodhouse.
Capone: The Life and World of Al
Capone. John Kobler.
The Captain Departs: Ulysses S.
Grant's Last Campaign. Thomas
M. Pitkin.
The Captain of Industry in English
Fiction, 1821-1871. Ivan Melada.
Captains and Cabinets: Anglo-
American Naval Relations, 1917-
1918. David F. Trask.
The Caption of Seisin of the Duchy
of Cornwall (1337) P. L. Hull,
ed.
El Cardenal Gomá: Primado de
España. Anastasio Granados.
Cardinal Contarini Regensburg.
Peter Matheson.
Cardinal Richelieu and the Develop-
ment of Absolutism. G. R. R.
Treasure.
The Care of Historical Collections:
A Conservation Handbook for the
Nonspecialist. Per E. Guldbeck.
The Career of Aleksei S. Suvorin,
Russian Journalism and Politics,
1861-1881. Effie Ambler.
The Career of Mrs. Anne Brunton
Merry in the American Theatre.
Gresdna Ann Doty.
The Caribbean Community: Chang-
ing Societies and United States
Policy. Robert D. Crasweller.
Carleton's Pah-Ute Campaign.
Dennis Casebier.
The Carmen de Hastingae Proelio
of Guy, Bishop of Amiens.
Catherine Morton and Hope
Muntz, eds.
Caro: The Fatal Passion. Henry
Blyth.

Carolina Quakers: Our Heritage,
Our Hope; Tercentenary, 1672-
1972. Seth B. and Mary Edith
Hinshaw, eds.
Carracks, Caravans, and Companies:
The Structural Crisis in the Euro-
pean-Asian Trade in the Early
17th Century. Niels Steens-
gaard.
Carson Valley: "Historical Sketches
of Nevada's First Settlement. "
Grace Dangberg.
Cartier's Hochelaga and the Dawson
Site. James E. Pendergast, et
al.
Case of Marcus A. Reno. Barry
C. Johnson.
Cast for a Revolution: Some Amer-
ican Friends and Enemies, 1728-
1814. Jean Fritz.
A Catalog of Manuscripts in Lam-
beth Palace Library: Mss. 1222-
1860. E. G. W. Bill.
Catalog of the Sophia Smith Collec-
tion.
Catalogue of Manuscripts in the Li-
brary of the Honourable Society
of the Inner Temple. 3 vols. J.
Conway Davies, ed.
Catalogue of the First Editions of
Stephen C. Foster (1826-1864).
Walter R. Whittlesey and O. G.
Sonneck.
Catalogue of the Library. Vol. III.
Atlases and Cartography. Parts
1 and 2. National Maritime
Museum.
Catherine May: An Indexed Register
of Her Congressional Papers,
1959-1970, in the Washington
State University Library.
Catholic Post-Secondary Education
in English-Speaking Canada.
Lawrence K. Shook.
The Catholic Priest in the United
States: Historical Investigations.
John Tracy Ellis, ed.
The Catskills: From Wilderness to
Woodstock. Alf Evers.
The Cattle-Trailing Industry: Be-
tween Supply and Demand, 1866-
1890. Jimmy M. Skaggs.
The Causes of the English Revolu-
tion, 1529-1642. Lawrence Stone.
Cavalier in the Wilderness: The
Story of the Explorer and Trader
Louis Juchereau de St. Denis.
Ross Phares.

Cave Dwellers and Citrus Growers:
A Jewish Community in Libya
and Israel. Harvey Goldberg.
Caves of God: The Monastic En-
vironment of Byzantine Cappa-
docia. Spiro Kostof.
The Cayuse Indians: Imperial
Tribesmen of Old Oregon.
Robert H. Ruby and John A.
Brown.
The Celtic Church in Britain. Leslie
Hardinge.
The Celtic Church in Somerset.
H. M. Porter.
The Census Tables for the French
Colony of Louisiana from 1699
Through 1732. Charles R.
Maduell, comp. and trans.
Central Africa: The Former British
States. Lewis H. Gann.
Central Italy: An Archaeological
Guide. R. F. Paget.
Central Planning in India: A Crit-
ical Review. Sudha R. Shenoy.
Century of Innovation: A History
of European Theatre and Drama
Since 1870. Oscar G. Brockett
and Robert R. Findlay.
Ceylon's Foreign Policy Under
Bandaranaikes (1956-65). Dhirenda
M. Prasad.
Chaadayev and His Friends: An In-
tellectual History of Peter
Chaadayev and His Russian Con-
temporaries. Raymond T.
McNally.
Chairman or Chief? The Role of
Taoiseach in Irish Government.
Brian Farrell.
The Champagne Spy. Wolfgang Lotz.
Champion of Southern Federalism:
Robert Goodloe Harper of South
Carolina. Joseph W. Cox.
Change and Conflict in the Indian
University. Joseph Di Bona.
Change and Development--Latin
America's Great Task. Raul
Rebisch.
Change and Uncertainty in a Pea-
sant Economy: The Maya Corn
Farmers of Zinacantan. Frank
Cancian.
Change at Park Street Under: The
Story of Boston's Subways.
Brian J. Cudahy.
Changement et continuité chez les
mayas du mexique. Henri Faure.
The Changing Balance of Power in

the Persian Gulf   Elizabeth
Monroe.
The Changing Economy of the Lower
Volta, 1954-67.   Rowena Lawson.
Changing Latin America: New In-
terpretations of Its Politics and
Society.   Douglas A. Chalmers.
The Changing Pattern of Political
Power in Iraq, 1958-1971.
Lorenzo Kent Kimball.
The Changing Politics of the South.
William C. Harvard, ed.
The Changing Rhythm: A Study of
Najib Mahfuz's Novels.   Sasson
Somekh.
The Character of the Good Ruler,
Puritan Political Ideas in New
England 1630-1730.   T. H.
Breen.
Charles II: The Man and the
Statesman.   Maurice Ashley.
Charles X of France: His Life
and Times.   Vincent W. Beach.
Charles F. Lummis: Crusader in
Corduroy.   Dudley Gordon.
Charles James Fox.   John W.
Derry.
Charles Lyell.   The Years to
1841: The Revolution in Geology.
Leonard G. Wilson.
Charles Sumner Slichter: The
Golden Vector.   Mark H. Ingra-
ham.
Charles Willson Peale.   Charles
Coleman Sellers.
Charters of the House of Mowbray,
1107-1191.   D. E. Greenway, ed
Chaucer's Physician: Medicine and
Literature in Fourteenth-Century
England.   Huling E. Ussery.
Chekhov in Performance: A Com-
mentary on the Major Plays.
J. L. Styan.
Chemins de l'hérésie.   Vol. 2.
Eugénie Droz.
Les chênes qu'on abat.   André
Malraux.
Chernyshevskii: The Man and the
Journalist.   William F. Woehrlin.
The Chiapanec History and Culture.
Carlos Navarette.
Chicago: 1860-1919.   Stephen Long-
street.
Chicano Literature: Text and Con-
text.   Antonia Castañeda Shular,
et al.
The Chicanos: A History of Mex-
ican Americans.   Matt S. Meier
and Feliciano Rivera.

The Chickasaws.   Arrell M.
Gibson.
Chief Bowles and the Texas Chero-
kees.   Mary Whatley Clarke.
Chiefship in Western Tanzania: A
Political History of the Kimbu.
Aylward Shorter.
A Childhood in Prison.   Pyotr
Yakir.
Children in Urban Society: Juvenile
Delinquency in Nineteenth-Century
America.   Joseph M. Hawes.
Children of Nashville ... Lineages
from James Robertson.   Sarah
Foster Kelley.
The Children of Pride: A True
Story of Georgia and the Civil
War.   Robert Manson Myers, ed.
Chile: A Critical Survey.   Thomás
P. MacHale, ed.
China.   Hyman Kublin.
China: Selected Reading.   Hyman
Kublin, ed.
China and Japan at War, 1937-1945:
The Politics of Collaboration.
John Hunter Boyle.
China and Russia: The "Great
Game." O. Edmund Clubb.
China Station 1859-1864, the Re-
miniscences of Walter White.
National Maritime Museum.
The China Trade: Export Paintings,
Furniture, Silver, and Other
Objects.   Carl L. Crossman and
Ernest S. Dodge.
China's Nation-Building Effort, 1927-
1937: The Financial and Eco-
nomic Record.   Arthur Young.
The Chinese Helped Build America.
Dorothy and Joseph Dowdell.
Chinese Science: Explorations of
an Ancient Tradition.   Shigeru
Nakayama and Nathan Sivin, eds.
The Chippewa and Their Neigh-
bours: A Study in Ethnohistory.
Harold Hickerson.
The Chorus of History: Literary-
Historical Relations in Renais-
sance Britain 1485-1558.   A. M.
Kinghorn.
Christendom Divided: The Protes-
tant Reformation.   Hans J.
Hillerbrand.
Christian Egypt--Faith and Life.
Otto F. A. Meinardus.
Die Christliche Demokratie Chiles:
Partei, Ideologie, revolutionäre
Bewegung.... Alf Ammon.
Christmas Eve at Rancho Los

Alamitos.   Katharine Bixby
Hotchkiss.
Christmas in Las Vegas.   Robert
Watson.
Chronicle into History.   Louis Green.
Chronicles of the Hudson: Three
Centuries of Travelers' Accounts.
Roland Van Zandt.
The Church and Revolution: From
the French Revolution of 1789 to
the Paris Riots of 1968.   Fran-
çois Houtart and André Rousseau.
The Church and Social Change in
Latin America.   Henry A. Lands-
berger, ed.
Church and State in Modern Ire-
land.   J. H. Whyte.
The Church and the Two Nations in
Medieval Ireland.   J. A. Watt.
The Church as a Political Factor
in Latin America: With Partic-
ular Reference to Colombia and
Chile.   David E. Mutchler.
Church History in the Age of Sci-
ence: Historiographical Patterns
in the United States, 1876-1918.
Henry Warner Bowden.
Church Leader in the Cities: Wil-
liam Augustus Muhlenberg.
Alvin W. Skardon.
The Church of Ireland: Ecclesi-
astical Reform and Revolution,
1800-1885.   Donald Harmon
Akenson.
The Church of the Brethren: Past
and Present.   Donald F. Durn-
baugh, ed.
The Church Reform of Peter the
Great.   James Cracraft.
Churches in Cultural Captivity: A
History of the Social Attitudes
of Southern Baptists.   John Lee
Eighmy.
The Churches Militant: the War of
1812 and American Religion.
William Gribbin.
The Churches Search for Unity.
Barry Till.
Churchmen and the Condition of
England 1832-1885.   G. Kitson
Clark.
La chute de la monarchie, 1787-
1792.   Michel Vovelle.
The Cinderella Service: British
Consuls Since 1825.   D. C. M.
Platt.
Cities and Immigrants, a Geography
of Change in Nineteenth-Century
America.   David Ward.

Cities Under Siege: An Anatomy of
the Ghetto Riots, 1964-1968.
David Boesel and Peter H. Rossi,
eds.
The Citizen Soldiers: The Platts-
burg Training Camp Movement,
1913-1920.   John Garry Clifford.
The Citizens Council: Organized
Resistance to the Second Recon-
struction 1954-64.   Neil R.
McMillen.
The City in Communist China.   John
Wilson Lewis, ed.
The City in the Ancient World.
Mason Hammond.
City Life, 1865-1900:   Views of
Urban America.   Ann Cook,
Marilyn Gittell and Herb Mack,
eds.
The City Makers.   Richard A.
Martin.
City Politics: A Study of Leopold-
ville, 1962-63.   J. S. La Fon-
taine.
The Civil-Military Fabric of Weimar
Foreign Policy.   Gaines Post,
Jr.
Civil Pleas of the Wiltshire Eyre,
1249.   M. T. Clanchy, ed.
Civil Strife in Latin America: A
Legal History of U. S. Involve-
ment.   William Everett Kane.
The Civil War Day by Day, 1861-
1865.   E. B. and Barbara Long.
Civil War in Russia, 1918:   The
First Year of the Volunteer
Army.   Peter Kenez.
Civil Wars in the Twentieth Cen-
tury.   Robin Higham, ed.
Civilization and Science: In Con-
flict or Collaboration.
Civilizations of Black Africa.
Jacques Maquet.
Class and Ideology in the Nineteenth
Century.   R. S. Neale.
The Classical Tradition in West
European Farming.   G. E. Fus-
sell.
Classified Files: The Yellowing
Pages; A Report on Scholars'
Access to Government Documents.
Carol M. Barker and Matthew
H. Fox.
Clay Gods: The Neolithic Period
and Copper Age in Hungary.
Nándor Kalicz.
Cleveland Rockwell,   Scientist and
Artist, 1837-1907.   Franz
Stenzel.

The Cliff: America's First Great
Copper Mine. Donald Chaput.
The Clifton-Morenci Strike: Labor
Difficulties in Arizona, 1915-1916.
James R. Kluger.
The Clocks of Columbus: The Lit-
erary Career of James Thurber.
Charles S. Holmes.
The Cloth Industry in the West of
England, from 1640 to 1880.
J. deL. Mann.
Cluniac Monasticism in the Central
Middle Ages. Noreen Hunt, ed.
Coalmining. A. R. Griffin.
Cobbler in Congress: The Life of
Henry Wilson, 1812-1875.
Richard H. Abbott.
Code No. 72, Ben Franklin: Pa-
triot or Spy?. Cecil B. Currey.
Codeword Barbarossa. Barton
Whaley.
Codex diplomaticus et epistolaris
Slovaciae. I. 805-1235.
Richard Marsina.
Coins and Archaeology. Lloyd
Laing.
Cold War and Counter Revolution:
The Foreign Policy of John F.
Kennedy. Richard J. Walton.
Collected Papers on the Jacobite
Risings, vol. 2. Rupert C.
Jarvis.
Collected Poems. Thomas Mac-
Greevy.
The Collected Poetry of Abraham
Lincoln. Paul M. Angle.
Collected Works of Count Rumford,
5, Public Institutions. Sanborn
C. Brown, ed.
Collecting Greek Antiquities. Her-
bert Hoffman.
College Literary Societies: Their
Contribution to Higher Education
in the United States, 1815-1876.
Thomas S. Harding.
Collegium Carolinum. Vol. X.
Jahrbuch des Bohemia.
Colloque universitaire pour la com-
mémoration du centenaire de la
commune de 1871.
The Cologne Communist Trial.
Kark Marx and Max Engels.
Colonial America. Allan Keller.
The Colonial American Jew, 1492-
1776. Jacob R. Marcus.
The Colonial Legacy. Vol. II.
Some Eighteenth-Century Com-
mentaries. Lawrence H. Leder,
ed.

The Colonial Office, 1868-1892.
Brian L. Blakeley.
Colonial Roots of Modern Brazil:
Papers of the Newberry Library
Conference. Dauril Alden, ed.
The Colonial System: America in
the Sixteenth and Seventeenth
Centuries. William H. Goetz-
mann, ed.
Colonial Travelers in Latin Amer-
ica. Irving A. Leonard, ed.
Colonialism in Africa, 1870-1960.
Vol. 3. Profiles of Change:
African Society and Colonial
Rule. Peter Duignan, Victor
Turner, and L. H. Gann, eds.
Colonies into Nation: American
Diplomacy, 1763-1801. Law-
rence S. Kaplan.
Colonist or Uitlander? John Stone.
A Colonização Alemã e o Rio
Grande do Sul. 2 vols. Jean
Roche.
A Colorado History. Carl Ubbe-
lohde, Maxine Benson, and
Duane A. Smith.
Colorado's War on Militant Union-
ism: James H. Peabody and the
Western Federation of Miners.
George G. Suggs, Jr.
The Columbian Exchange: Biolog-
ical and Cultural Consequences
of 1492. Alfred W. Crosby, Jr.
El combate homérico, 21 de mayo
de 1879. Vincente Grez.
Comercio colonial y guerras revo-
lucionarias.... Antonio García-
Baquero González.
El comercio y la crisis colonial.
Un mito de la independencia.
Sergio Villalobos R.
Coming Apart: An Informal History
of America in the 1960's. Wil-
liam L. O'Neill.
The Coming of Age of American
Business: Three Centuries of
Enterprise, 1600-1900. Elisha
P. Douglass.
The Coming of Christianity to
Anglo-Saxon England. Henry
Mayr-Harting.
Command and Commanders in
Modern Warfare: The Proceed-
ings of the Second Military His-
tory Symposium, United States
Air Force Academy 2-3 May
1968. William Geffen, ed.
Commentarios sobre el catechismo
christiano. Vols. 1 and 2.

Bartolome Carranza de Mirando.

The Commercial Revolution of the
Middle Ages, 950-1350. Robert
S. Lopez.

Commissar, the Life and Death of
Lavrenty Pavolich Beria. Thaddeus Wittlin.

Committee of Vigilance: Revolution
in San Francisco, 1851. An Account of the Hundred Days When
Certain Citizens Undertook the
Suppression of the Criminal Activities of the Sydney Ducks. George
R. Stewart.

The Common Law in the Sudan: An
Account of the "Justice, Equity
and Good Conscience" Provision.
Zaki Mustafa.

Commonwealth: A History of the
British Commonwealth of Nations.
H. Duncan Hall.

The Communards of Paris, 1871.
Stewart Edwards, ed.

Communism in Indian Politics.
Bhabani Sen Gupta.

Communism in Korea. Part 1.
The Movement; Part 2, The
Society. Robert A. Scalapino
and Chong-sik Lee.

Communist China and Latin America.
Cecil Johnson.

Community and Communications.
Seymour J. Mandelbaum.

Community Culture and National
Change. Richard N. Adams
et al.

A Community in Search of Itself: A
Case History of Cairo, Illinois.
Herman R. Lantz.

The Compact History of the United
States Army. R. Ernest Dupuy.

Comparative Development in Social
Welfare. E. W. Martin, ed.

A Comparative Study of Some Educational Problems. Kartick C.
Mukherjee.

Compendio de Estadísticas historicas
de Colombia. Miguel M. Urrutia
and Mario Arrubla, eds.

Competition and Collective Bargaining in the Needle Trades, 1910-
1917. Jesse Thomas Carpenter.

Complete Presidential Press Conferences of Franklin D. Roosevelt. [Franklin D. Roosevelt].

Complete Prose Works of John Milton. Vol. V, Part I: 1648?-
1671. The History of Britain;
Part II: 1649-1659. The Miltonic

State Papers. John Milton.
(French Fogle and Max Patrick,
eds.)

The Complete Sourdough Cookbook:
For Camp, Trail and Kitchen--
Authentic and Original Sourdough
Recipes from the Old West. Don
and Myrtle Holm.

Le comte d'Anjou et son entourage
au XIe siècle. 2 vols. Olivier
Guillot.

Concentration Camps U. S. A.: Japanese Americans and World War
II. Roger Daniels.

Conflict in the Congo. Thomas
Kanza.

Confrontación Transpacífica. El
Japón y el Nuevo Mundo Hispánico 1542-1639. Lothar Knauth.

Congo. Richard West.

Congress and Higher Education in
the Nineteenth Century. George
N. Rainsford.

The Connecticut River. Evan Hill,
William F. Stehl and Roger Tory
Peterson.

Conococheague: A History of the
Greencastle-Antrim Community,
1736-1971. W. P. Conrad.

The Conquest of Malacca. Francisco de Sá de Meneses.

La Conquista de Constantinopoli
(1198-1216). Roberto Di Clari.

La Conscience Nationale en France
Pendant Les Guerres de Religion;
1559-1598. Myriam Yardeni.

Conservation of Library Materials:
A Manual and Bibliography on
the Care, Repair and Restoration
of Library Materials. Vol. 2.
George Martin Cunha and Dorothy Grant Cunha.

Conservative in America. Ronald
Lora.

Conserving Life on Earth. David
W. Ehrenfeld.

Consignments to El Dorado: A
Record of the Voyage of the
Sutton. Thomas Whaley.

Conspiracy in American Politics,
1787-1815. J. Wendell Knox.

Constantine the Great. Hermann
Dörries.

Constantinople and the Latins: The
Foreign Policy of Andronicus II,
1282-1328. Angeliki E. Laiou.

The Constitution in Crisis Times,
1918-1969. Paul L. Murphy.

Constitution Making in Illinois, 1818-

1970. Janet Cornelius.
The Constitution of France. Ragnar Simonsson.
Constitutional Bureaucracy: The Development of British Central Administration Since the Eighteenth Century. Henry Parris.
Constitutional Change in the British West Indies, 1880-1903: With Special Reference to Jamaica, British Guiana, and Trinidad. H. A. Will.
Containment and the Cold War: American Foreign Policy Since 1945. Thomas G. Paterson, ed.
Contemporary Archaeology: A Guide to Theory and Contributions. Mark P. Leone, ed.
Contemporary Brazil: Issues in Economic and Political Development. H. Jon Rosenbaum and William G. Tyler, eds.
Contemporary Britain. Barbar Wootton.
Contemporary Inter-American Relations: A Reader in Theory and Issues. Yale H. Ferguson, ed.
Contradiction and Dilemma: Orestes Brownson and the American Idea. Leonard Gilhooley.
Contribution à l'histoire de la Résistance belge, 1940/1944. George Tanham.
The Conventions of Crisis: A Study in Diplomatic Management. Coral Bell.
Copper for America: The Hendricks Family and a National Industry, 1755-1939. Maxwell Whiteman.
Cornwallis and the War of Independence. Franklin and Mary Wickwire.
El Corregimiento de la Paz, 1548-1600. Alberto Crespo R.
Correio Marítimo Hispano-Americano. A Carreira de Buenos Aires, 1767-1779. Manoel Lelo Bellotto.
The Correspondence of George, Prince of Wales, 1770-1812. Vol. VIII, 1811-1812. A. Aspinall, ed.
Correspondence of James K. Polk. Vol. II, 1833-1834. Herbert Weaver and Paul H. Bergeron, eds.
The Correspondence of Jeremy Bentham. Vol. 3, January 1781 to October 1788. Ian B. Christie, ed.
The Correspondence of Lord Overstone. 3 vols. D. P. O'Brien, ed.
Correspondencia Del Conde de Tendilla. Vol. 1 (1508-1509). Emilio Meneses García, ed.
The Corrupt Kingdom: The Rise and Fall of the United Mine Workers. Joseph E. Finley.
Costume et vie sociale: La cour d'Anjou XIVe-XVe siècle. Françoise Piponnier.
A Cotton Enterprise, 1795-1840: A History of McConnel and Kennedy, Fine Cotton Spinners. C. H. Lee.
Coulomb and the Evolution of Physics and Engineering in Eighteenth-Century France. C. Stewart Gillmor.
Coulomb's Memoir on Statics: An Essay in the History of Civil Engineering. Jacques Heyman.
Count Witte and the Tsarist Government in the 1905 Revolution. Howard D. Mehlinger and John M. Thompson.
Countee Cullen and the Negro Renaissance. Blanche E. Ferguson.
Counterrevolution and Revolt. Herbert Marcuse.
The County Courts in Ante-Bellum Kentucky. Robert M. Ireland.
The County Maps from William Camden's Britannia 1695: A Facsimile. Robert Morden.
The Course of Our Times: Men and Events That Shaped the Twentieth Century. Abram Sachar.
Court Martial: A Black Man in America. John F. Marszalek, Jr.
Covered Bridges of Lamoille County. Robert L. Hagerman.
The Cowboy Capital of the World: The Saga of Dodge City. Samuel Carter, III.
The Cowboy in American Prints. John Meigs, ed.
Cowboy Lore. Jules Verne Allen.
Cowboy Slang. Edgar R. Potter.
The Cowman Says It Salty. Ramon F. Adams.
Craftsmen in Greek and Roman Society. Alison Burford.

Creative Imagination in the Sufism of Ibn 'Arabí. Henry Corbin.
The Credit Merchants: A History of Spiegel, Inc. Orange A. Smalley and Frederick D. Sturdivant.
Creole Families of New Orleans. Grace King.
Crime and Public Order in England in the Later Middle Ages. John Bellamy.
The Crimean War. R. L. V. Ffrench-Blake.
Crimsoned Prairie: The Wars Between the United States and the Plains Indians During the Winning of the West. S. L. A. Marshall.
La crisi del 1907: Una Tappa della Sviluppo industriale in Italia. Franco Bonelli.
Crisis and Conflict in Nigeria: A Documentary Sourcebook, 1966-1969. 2 vols. A. H. M. Kirk-Greene.
Crisis and Order in English Towns, 1500-1700: Essays in Urban History. Peter Clark and Paul Slack, eds.
Crisis in Costa Rica: The 1948 Revolution. John Patrick Bell.
The Crisis of Democratic Theory: Scientific Naturalism and the Problem of Value. Edward A. Purcell, Jr.
The Crisis of Parliament: English History 1509-1660. Conrad Russell.
Crisis of the House Divided: An Interpretation of the Issues in the Lincoln-Douglas Debates. Harry V. Jaffa.
Cristãos novos na Bahia. Anita Novinsky.
The Croatian-Slavonian Kingdom, 1526-1792. Stanko Guldescu.
The Cross of Culture: A Social Analysis of Midwestern Politics, 1850-1900. Paul Kleppner.
The Crow People. Dale K. McGinnis and Floyd W. Sharrock.
Crowfoot, Chief of the Blackfeet. Hugh A. Dempsey.
The Crown of Mexico: Maximilian and His Empress Carlota. Joan Haslip.
The Cruel Choice: A New Concept in the Theory of Development. Denis Goulet.
Crusade Against Radicalism: New

York During the Red Scare, 1914-1924. Julian F. Jaffe.
Crusade for Justice: The Autobiography of Ida B. Wells. Alfreda M. Duster, ed.
Crusader in Babylon: W. T. Stead and the Pall Mall Gazette. Raymond L. Schults.
The Crusader's Kingdom: European Colonialism in the Middle Ages. Joshua Prawler.
The Crusades. Hans Eberhard Mayer.
Crush India or Pakistan's Death Wish. G. S. Bhargava.
Cry from the Cotton: The Southern Tenant Farmers' Union and the New Deal. Donald Grubbs.
Cry of the Thunderbird. Charles Hamilton, ed.
Cuba, Castro, and Revolution. Jaime Suchlicki, ed.
Cuba, 1933: Prologue to Revolution. Luis E. Aguilar.
Cuba: The Measure of a Revolution. Lowry Nelson.
Cuba. The Pursuit of Freedom. Hugh Thomas.
Cuba y La Casa de Austria. Nicasio Silverio Sainz.
The Cult of Kingship in Anglo-Saxon England: The Transition from Paganism to Christianity. William A. Chaney.
The Cult of the Seer in the Ancient Middle East: A Contribution to Current Research on Hallucinations Drawn from Coptic and Other Texts. Violet MacDermot.
The Cultural History of Marlborough, Virginia. C. Malcolm Watkins.
Culture and Life: Essays in Memory of Clyde Kluckhorn.
Culture and Nationality. A. G. Bailey.
Culture and Society in France, 1848-1898: Dissidents and Philistines. F. W. J. Hemmings.
Culture and Society in Italy, 1290-1420. John Larner.
Culture and Society in Renaissance Italy, 1420-1540. Peter Burke.
Culture and Society in Venice, 1470-1790: The Renaissance and Its Heritage. Oliver Logan.
Culture Confrontation in the Lower Congo: From the Old Congo Kingdom to the Congo Independ-

ent State, With Special Reference
to the Swedish Missionaries in
the 1880's and 1890's. Sigbert
Axelson.

Culture in Exile: Russian Emigrés
in Germany, 1881-1941. Robert
C. Williams.

Culture Storm: Politics and the
Ritual Order. H. L. Nieburg.

Curia Regis Rolls of the Reign of
Henry III Preserved in the Public
Record Office. Vol. 15.

Current Africanist Research International Bulletin.

The Curse of Cromwell: A History
of the Ironside Conquest of Ireland, 1649-53. D. M. R. Esson.

A Cycle of Power: The Career of
Jersey City Mayor Frank Hague.
Richard J. Connors.

The Czech Renascence in the Nineteenth Century: Essays Presented to Otokar Odlozilek.
Peter Brock and H. G. Skilling,
eds.

The Czechoslovak Reform Movement:
Communism in Crisis, 1962-1968.
Galia Golan.

The Czechs Under Nazi Rule: The
Failure of National Resistance,
1939-1942. Vojtech Mastny.

-D-

D-Day: Spearhead of Invasion.
R. W. Thompson.

Da Adua a Sarajevo: La politica
estera italiana e la Francia, 1896-
1914. Enrico Decleva.

Daniel Lee, Agriculturist: His Life
North and South. E. Merton
Coulter.

Daniel Webster and Jacksonian Democracy. Sydney Nathans.

Daniel Webster and the Trial of
American Nationalism, 1843-1852.
Robert F. Dalzell, Jr.

Dare to be Different: A Biography
of Louis H. Levin of Baltimore.
Alexandra Lee Levin.

Darkness at the Dawning: Race and
Reform in the Progressive South.
Jack Temple Kirby.

Dartmouth Medical School: The
First 175 Years. Carleton B.
Chapman.

The Dawes Act and the Allotment
of Indian Lands. D. S. Otis.

The Dawn of Empire: Rome's Rise
to World Power. Robert M.
Errington.

The Dawn of Man. Vincent Megaw
and Rhys Jones.

The Dawn's Early Light. Walter
Lord.

Day Before Yesterday: An Autobiography and History of Michigan
Schools. John L. Riegle.

A Day No Pigs Would Die. Robert
Newton Peck.

Days in an Old Town. Mrs. Betty
Carter Smoot.

Days of Sadness, Years of Triumph:
The American People 1939-1945.
Geoffrey Perrett.

Dear Israelis, Dear Arabs: A
Working Approach to Peace.
Roger Fisher.

"Dear Lady": The Letters of Fred-
erick Jackson Turner and Alice
Forbes Perkins Hooper. Ray
Allen Billington, ed.

Dear Miss Em: General Eichelberger's War in the Pacific,
1942-1945. Jay Luvaas, ed.

Death by Melancholy: Essays on
Modern Southern Fiction. Walter
Sullivan.

Death in New England: Regional
Variations in Mortality. John
W. Florin.

De Brahm's Report of the General
Survey in the Southern District
of North America. Louis De
Vorsey, Jr.

The Decade of Disillusion: British
Politics in the Sixties. David
McKie and Chris Cook, eds.

A Decade of Progress; The United
States Army Medical Department
1959-1969. Rose C. Engelman,
ed.

The Decade of Reform: The 1830's.
Alexander Llewellyn.

La decadenza italiano nella storia
europea: Saggai sui sei-settecento. Guido Quazza.

Decentralization and Self-Government in Russia, 1830-1870. S.
Frederick Starr.

Decision by Default: Peacetime
Conscription and British Defence,
1919-39. Peter Dennis.

The Decline and Abolition of Negro
Slavery in Venezuela, 1820-1854.

The Diary of Calvin Fletcher. Vol.
I. Gayle Thornbrough, ed.
The Diary of Clarissa Adger Bowen,
Ashtabula Plantation, 1865....
Mary Stevenson.
The Diary of Edmund Ruffin. Vol.
1. Toward Independence, Octo-
ber 1856-April, 1861. William
Kauffman Scarborough, ed.
The Diary of Samuel Pepys. Vols.
VI and VII. Robert Latham and
William Matthews, eds.
The Diary of Sir Edward Walter
Hamilton, 1880-1885. Dudley
W. R. Bahlman, ed.
Dickinson College: A History.
Charles Coleman Sellers.
Dictatorship and Armed Struggle in
Brazil. João Quartim.
Dictionary of Canadian Biography.
Vol. 10. 1871-1880. Marc La
Terreur, ed.
Dictionary of Scientific Biography.
2 vols. Charles Coulston Gillis-
pie, ed. in chief.
A Dictionary of Scottish Emigrants
to the U. S. A. Donald Whyte.
Diderot. Arthur M. Wilson.
Diderot's Letters to Sophie Volland.
Peter France, trans.
Dilemmas of Growth in Pre-War
Japan. George M. Beckmann,
et al.
Dilemmas in Planning. G. L.
Mehta.
The Dimensions of Quantitative Re-
search in History. William O.
Aydelotte, Allan G. Bogue, and
Robert William Fogel. eds.
The Dimensions of the Past: Ma-
terials, Problems, and Oppor-
tunities for Quantitative Work
in History. Val R. Lorwin and
Jacob M. Price, eds.
Diplomacy for Victory: F D R and
Unconditional Surrender. Ray-
mond G. O'Connor.
Diplomacy of Illusion: The British
Government and Germany, 1937-
39. Keith Middlemas.
The Diplomacy of the Mexican Em-
pire, 1863-1867. Arnold Blum-
berg.
The Diplomatic Diaries of Oliver
Harvey, 1937-1940. John Harvey,
ed.
Diplomatarium Danicum. C. A.
Christensen and Herluf Nielsen,
eds.

A Diplomatic History of Modern
India. Charles Heimsath and
Surjit Mansingh.
A Diplomatic History of the First
World War. Z. A. B. Zeman.
Diplomats and Demagogues. Spruille
Braden.
Discovering Wisconsin. Polly Brody
Temkin.
The Discovery of North America.
W. P. Cumming, R. A. Skelton
and D. B. Quinn.
The Discovery of the Asylum: Social
Order and Disorder in the New
Republic. David J. Rothman.
The Disenchanted Isles: The Story
of the Second Revolution in
Hawaii. Theon Wright.
The Disinherited, Journal of a
Palestinian Exile. Fawaz Turki.
Disparités Régionales et Aménage-
ment du Territoire en Afrique.
Jacques Bugnicourt.
Dispossessing the American Indian:
Indians and Whites on the Co-
lonial Frontier. Wilbur R.
Jacobs.
The Disrupted Decades: The Civil
War and Reconstruction Years.
Robert H. Jones.
The Disruption of the Solid South.
George Brown Tindall.
The Distant Eden, Tennessee's
Rugby Colony. Brian L. Stagg.
The Distant Magnet: European
Emigration to the U. S. A.
Philip Taylor.
The Disunited States: The Era of
Civil War and Reconstruction.
Thomas H. O'Connor.
Diverging Parallels: A Comparison
of American and European
Thought and Action. A. N. J.
Den Hollander, ed.
The Dividing of Christendom.
Christopher Dawson.
Divine Kingship in Africa. William
Fagg.
Dixie After the War. Myrta Lock-
ett Avary.
Dr. Bowdler's Legacy. Noel Per-
rin.
Doctor Kane of the Arctic Seas.
George W. Corner.
A Doctor on the California Trail:
The Diary of Dr. John Hudson
Wayman from Cambridge City,
Indiana, to the Gold Fields in
1852. John Hudson Wayman.

Doctoral Dissertations in Military Affairs: A Bibliography. Allan R. Millett and B. Franklin Cooling, III.

Doctoral Students in Social Sciences. Inter-University Board of India and Ceylon and Indian Council of Social Science Research.

Documentary History of the First Federal Congress, March 4, 1789-March 3, 1791. Vol. 1: Senate Legislative Journal. Linda Grant De Pauw, ed.

Documents Concerning the Foreign Policy of the USSR. Vols. 16 and 17. A. A. Gromyko, et al., eds.

Documents of Southwestern History: A Guide to the Manuscript Collections of the Arizona Historical Society. Charles C. Colley, comp.

Documents on Canadian External Relations. Vol. 4: 1926-1930. Alex I. Inglis.

Documents Relative to the Manufactures in the United States. U. S. Congress.

Dod's Electoral Facts, 1832-1853 (1853). H. J Hanham, ed.

Doing Fieldwork: Warnings and Advice. Rosalie H. Wax.

Doing History. John H. Hexter.

Dokumente zur Kirchenpolitik des Dritten Reiches. Band I: Das Jahr 1933.

The Doll. Carl Fox.

The Domination of Nature. William Leiss.

The Dominican Intervention. Abraham F. Lowenthal.

Domingo Faustino Sarmiento. Frances G. Crowley.

The Donner Party. George Keithley.

The Doomed Democracy: Czechoslovakia in a Disrupted Europe, 1914-38. Věra Olivová.

The Downshire Estates in Ireland, 1801-1845: The Management of Irish Landed Estates in the Early Nineteenth Century. W. A. Maguire.

Down to Now: Reflections on the Southern Civil Rights Movement. Pat Watters.

"The Dragon Empress." Life and Times of Tz'u Hsi (1835-1908). Marina Warner.

The Dream and the Deal: The Federal Writers' Project, 1935-1943. Jerre Mangione.

Dream of Empire: A Human History of the Republic of Texas, 1836-1846. John Edward Weems.

Drink and the Victorians: The Temperance Question in England, 1815-1872. Brian Harrison.

Das Dritte Feich und Argentinien. Arnold Ebel.

Du Droit des Magistrates. Theodore de Bèze. (Robert M. Kingdon, ed.).

Drugs and Youth. Donald J. Wolk, ed.

The Dual Heritage: Immigrants from the Atlas Mountains in an Israeli Village. Moshe Shokeid.

Du Bose Genealogy. Dorothy Kelly MacDowell.

Ducal Brittany. Michael Jones.

Le duc de Saint-Simon et la monarchie. Jean-Pierre Brancourt.

Duce! A Biography of Benito Mussolini. Richard Collier.

The Duchy of Lancaster's Estates in Derbyshire 1485-1540. I. S. W. Blanchard, ed.

Les ducs et pairs de France au XVIIᵉ siecle: Étude sociale. Jean-Pierre Labatut.

The Duel: De Gaulle and Pompidou. Philippe Alexandre.

Dumbarton Oaks Conference on Chavin. Elizabeth P. Benson, ed.

Dumbarton Oaks Papers. No. 25.

The Dutch in the Seventeenth Century. K. D. Haley.

Dzieje Rosji, 1801-1917. Ludwik Bazylow.

-E-

E. I. DuPont, Botaniste: The Beginning of a Tradition. Norman B. Wilkinson.

Eadweard Muybridge, the Man Who Invented the Moving Picture. Kevin MacDonnell.

The Eager Immigrants. David M. Zielonka and Robert J. Wechman.

Early American Bookbindings from the Collection of Michael Papantonio.

The Early American Novel. Henri Petter.

Early Buddhist Japan. J. Edward Kidder.

The Early Christian Archaeology of North Britain. Charles Thomas.

Early Christian Ireland: Introduction to the Sources. Kathleen Hughes.

Early Colonial Religious Drama in Mexico from Tzompantli to Golgotha. Marilyn Ekdahl Ravicz.

The Early Correspondence of Jabez Bunting, 1820-1829. W. R. Ward, ed.

The Early Development of Irish Society: The Evidence of Aerial Photography. E. R. Norman

Early English Stages, 1300-1660. Vol. 2, 1576-1660. Part 2. Glynne Wickham. and J. K. S. St. Joseph.

Early Gardening Catalogues. John H. Harvey.

Early Greek Warfare. P. A. L. Greenhalgh

The Early History of Malawi. B. Pachai, ed.

Early Registers of Writs. Elsa de Haas and G. D. G. Hall, eds.

Early Settlement in the Lake Counties. Clare Fell.

The Earthen Long Barrow in Britain: An Introduction to the Study of the Funerary Practice and Culture of the Neolithic People of the Third Millennium B. C. Paul Ashbee.

East Across the Pacific: Historical and Sociological Studies of Japanese Immigration and Assimilation. Hilary Conroy and T. Scott Miyokawa, eds.

East Africa: A Century of Change, 1870-1970. W. E. F. Ward and L. W. White.

The East Africa Coast: An Historical and Archaeological Review. J. E. G. Sutton.

The East African Slave Trade. E. A. Alpers.

East and West of Suez: The Suez Canal in History, 1854-1956. D. A. Farnie.

East Indians in Trinidad: A Study in Minority Politics. Yogendra K. Malik.

Eastern Turkey: A Guide and History. Gwyn Williams.

Eboué. Brian Weinstein.

Les ecclésiastiques français émigrés ou deportés dans l'Etat Pontifical, 1792-1800. René Picheloup.

Economic Beginnings in Colonial South Carolina, 1670-1730. Converse D. Clowse.

Economic Development and Population Growth in the Middle East. Charles A. Cooper and Sidney S. Alexander.

Economic Development: Ends and Means. L. K. Jha.

Economic Development in Iran: 1900-1970. Julian Bharier.

The Economic Development of Medieval Europe. Robert-Henri Bautier.

Economic Growth and Development: The Less Developed Countries. Eva Garzouzi.

Economic Growth of Colombia: Problems and Prospects. The World Bank.

Economic History and the Social Sciences: Problems of Methodology. Elias H. Tuma.

An Economic History of Colombia, 1845-1930. William Paul McGreevey.

The Economic History of Iran, 1800-1914. Charles Issawi, ed.

An Economic History of Ireland Since 1660. L. M. Cullen.

Economic History of Wisconsin During the Civil War Decade. Frederick Merk.

Economic Opportunity and White American Fertility Ratios, 1800-1860. Colin Forster and G. S. L. Tucker.

Economic Prospects of Bangla Desh. K. L. Seth.

The Economics of Defense Spending: A Look at the Realities. Robert C. Moot.

Economics of Public Expenditure. T. Mathew.

Economy and Settlement in Neolithic and Early Bronze Age Britain and Europe. D. D. A. Simpson, ed.

Economy and Society in Early Modern Europe: Essays from Annales. Peter Burke, ed.

The Economy of the War on the Continent: Studies in the Financing of War in the Period When Sweden Was a Great Power.

Cyclades and the Aegean in the Third Millennium B. C. Colin Renfrew.

The Emergence of Multinational Enterprise: American Business Abroad from the Colonial Era to 1914. Mira Wilkins.

Emerging Nationalism in Portuguese Africa: Documents. Ronald H. Chilcote.

The Emigrant's Guide to California. Joseph E. Ware.

L'emigration de Canadiens aux Etats-Unis avant 1930: Mesure du Phénomène. Yolande Lavoie.

Émile Durkheim: Sociologist and Philosopher. Dominick La Capra.

The Emperor Frederick II of Hohenstaufen. Thomas Curtis Van Cleve.

Empire and Communications. Harold A. Innis.

The Empresario: Don Martin de León (The Richest Man in Texas). A. B. J. Hammett.

Encomenderos y estancieros: Estudios acerca de constitución social aristocratica de Chile después de la conquista, 1580-1660. Mario Góngora.

Encyclopedia of American Shipwrecks. Bruce D. Berman.

Encyclopedia of Southern Africa. Eric Rosenthal, comp. and ed.

An End and a Beginning: The South Coast and Los Angeles, 1850-1887. Joseph S. O'Flaherty.

The End of the Corn Belt Fleet. The Great Lakes Reserve Destroyer Division. Wendell Wilke.

The End of the European Era. 1890 to the Present. Felix Gilbert.

Das Ende auf dem Balkan 1944/45: Die militarische Raumung Jugoslaviens durch die deutsche Wehrmacht. Karl Hnilicka.

The Enduring South: Subcultural Persistence in Mass Society. John Shelton Reed.

Engagieter Expressionismus. Eva Kolinsky.

England and the Baltic in the Elizabethan Era. Henryk Zins.

England Before the Conquests: Studies in Primary Sources Presented to Dorothy Whitelock. P. Clemoes and Kathleen Hughes, eds.

England, France and Christendom,

1377-99. J. J. N. Palmer.

England in the Later Middle Ages. M. H. Keen.

England in the Restoration and Early Eighteenth Century: Essays on Culture and Society. H. T. Swedenberg, Jr., ed.

The English Bastille: A History of Newgate Gaol and Prison Conditions in England, 1188-1902. Anthony Babington.

English Civic Pageantry. David M. Bergeron.

English Defenders of American Freedoms, 1774-1778. Paul H. Smith, comp.

English Coinage 600-1900. C. H. V. Sutherland.

The English Defense of the Commune 1871. Royden Harrison, ed.

English Diplomacy, 1422-1461. John Ferguson.

English Diplomatic Administration. G. P. Cuttino.

The English Essays of Edward Gibbon. Patricia B. Craddock, ed.

English Genealogy. Anthony Richard Wagner.

The English Icon: Elizabethan and Jacobean Portraiture. Roy Strong.

The English in the Caribbean. Carl and Roberta Bridenbaugh.

English Local Administration in the Middle Ages. Helen M. Jewell.

English Money and Irish Land: The "Adventurers" in the Cromwellian Settlement of Ireland. Karl S. Bottigheimer.

English Roman Catholics and Higher Education. Vincent Alan McClelland.

English Royal Documents: King John--Henry IV, 1199-1461. Pierre Chaplais.

English-Russian General Economic and Foreign Trade Dictionary. E. E. Israilevich, comp.

The English Separatist Tradition from the Marian Martyrs to the Pilgrim Fathers. B. R. White.

An Englishman in the American Civil War: The Diaries of Henry Yates Thompson: 1863. Sir Christopher Chancellor, ed.

The Enigma of Mary Stuart. Ian B. Cowan, ed.

Enjoying Archives. David Iredale.

L'Evangelo e il Bercetto Frigio.
Georgio Spini.
The Everglades Today: Endangered
Wilderness. George X. Sand.
Everyday Life of the Barbarians:
Goths, Franks, and Vandals.
Malcolm Todd.
Evolución histórica de los partidos
políticos chilenos. René León
Echaiz.
The Evolution of a Medical Center:
A History of Medicine at Duke
University to 1941. James F.
Gifford, Jr.
The Evolution of an Urban School
System. Carl F. Kaestle.
The Evolution of Management
Thought. Daniel A. Wren.
The Evolution of the Nigerian State:
The Southern Phase, 1898-1914.
T. N. Tamuno.
Excavations at Navdatoli: 1957-59.
H. D. Sankalia, Z. B. Deo, and
Z. D. Ansari.
Excavations at Saliagos Near Anti-
paros. J. D. Evans and Colin
Renfrew.
Explanation in Archaeology: An Ex-
plicitly Scientific Approach. Patty
Jo Watson, Steven A. LeBlanc,
and Charles A. Redman.
Explorations of Kamchatka, North
Pacific Scimitar: Opsanie Kemli
Kamchatki, a Journey Made to
Explore Eastern Siberia in 1735-
1741. Stephan Petrovich Krash-
ennikov.
Exploring the Industrial Subculture.
Barry A. Turner.
Exploring the Social Sciences. O.
L. Davis, Jr., et al.
Exploring Yellowstone. Ruth Kirk.
The Extension of Man: A History of
Physics Before the Quantum.
J. D. Bernal.
The External Trade of the Loango
Coast: 1576-1870. P. M. Martin.
Eyewitness to History: Memoirs and
Reflections of a Foreign Corres-
pondent for Half a Century. Isaac
Don Levine.

-F-

The Face of Defeat: Palestine Ref-

ugees and Guerrillas. David
Pryce-Jones.
Faces of Delinquency. John P.
Reed and Fuad Baali.
Faces of Nationalism: New Realities
and Old Myths. Boyd C. Shafer.
Faces of the Wilderness. Harvey
Broome.
Factions No More. Attitudes to
Party in Government and Opposi-
tion in the Eighteenth Century.
J. A. W. Gunn.
A Factious People: Politics and
Society in Colonial New York.
Patricia U. Bonomi.
Fafr El-Elow: An Egyptian Village
in Transition. Hani Fakhouri.
The Failure of Illiberalism: Essays
on the Political Culture of Mod-
ern Germany. Fritz Stern.
The Failure of Independent Liberal-
ism, 1930-1941. R. Alan Law-
son.
The Failure of South African Expan-
sion, 1909-1939. Ronald Hyam.
The Faithful Shepherd: A History
of the New England Ministry in
the Seventeenth Century. David
D. Hall.
The Fall of Jerusalem. Abdullah
Schleifer.
Family and Fortune: Studies in
Aristocratic Finance in the Six-
teenth and Seventeenth Centuries.
Lawrence Stone.
Family Letters of Robert and Elinor
Frost. Arnold Grade, ed.
Family Structure in Nineteenth-Cen-
tury Lancashire. Michael Ander-
son.
Family Structure in Turkey. Serim
Timur.
Famine in China and the Missionary:
Timothy Richard as Relief Ad-
ministrator and Advocate of Na-
tional Reform, 1876-1884. Paul
Richard Bohr.
Fanny Kemble and the Lovely Land.
Constance Wright.
Faraday as a Natural Philosopher.
Joseph Agassi.
Farewell to the South. Robert Coles.
Farm Bureau in Mississippi. Ed-
ward L. Blake.
Farming and Food Supply: The In-
terdependence of Countryside and
town. Sir Joseph Hutchinson.
Farming in the New Nation: Inter-

preting American Agriculture,
1790-1840. Darwin P. Kelsey,
ed.

Fascism and the Industrial Leadership in Italy, 1919-1940. Roland Sarti.

Fascism in France: The Case of Maurice Barrès. Robert Soucy.

The Facist Economy in Norway. Alan S. Milward.

The Fate of the Lakes, a Portrait of the Great Lakes. James P. Barry.

FDR: The Beckoning of Destiny, 1882-1928: A History. Kenneth S. Davis.

Federal Land Series: A Calendar of Archival Materials on the Land Patents Issued by the United States Government, With Subject, Tract, and Name Indexes. 2 vols. Clifford Neal Smith.

Federal Reserve System. Benjamin Haggott Beckhart.

Feeding the Russian Fur Trade: Provisionment of the Okhotsk Seaboard, 1639-1856. James R. Gibson.

The Feitosas and the Sertão dos Inhamuns: The History of a Family and a Community in Northeast Brazil, 1700-1930. Billy Jaynes Chandler.

Felipe de Neve: First Governor of California. Edwin A. Beilharz.

Les Fermiers Généraux au XVIIIe Siècle. Yves Durand.

Fermín Francisco de Lasuén (1736-1803): A Biography. Francis F. Guest.

Festschrift für Hermann Heimpel. Hermann Heimpel.

Fidel in Chile: A Symbolic Meeting Between Two Historical Processes. Selected Speeches of Major Fidel Castro During His Visit to Chile, November, 1971. Fidel Castro.

Field Archaeology in Britain. John Coles.

The Fifth Monarchy Men: A Study in Seventeenth-Century English Millenarianism. B. S. Capp.

The Fifth World of Forster Bennett: Portrait of a Navaho. Vincent Crapanzano.

Fighting Fire with Fire. John M. Peckham.

Fighting Indians! In the Seventh United States Cavalry, Custer's Favorite Regiment. Ami Frank Mulford.

The Fighting Quaker: Nathaniel Greene. Elswyth Thane.

Fighting Ships and Prisons: The Mediterranean Galleys of France in the Age of Louis XIV. Paul W. Bamford.

The Figure of Arthur. Richard Barber.

Finance and Economic Development in the Old South: Louisiana Banking, 1804-1861. George D. Green.

The Finance of the Commune of Siena, 1285-1355. William M. Bowsky.

A Financial History of the New Japan. T. F. M. Adams and Iwao Hoshii.

The Financial System of Canada: Its Growth and Development. E. P. Neufeld.

The Financial System of Egypt, A. H. 564-741/A. D. 1169-1341. Hassanein Rabie.

Find a Falling Star. Harvey H. Nininger.

La fine del potere temporale e il ricongiungimento di Roma all'-Italia. . . .

The Finds from the Site of La Téne. Vol. I. J. M. de Navarro.

The Fingerhut Guide: Sources in American History. Eugene R. Fingerhut.

Fire in the Lake: The Vietnamese and the Americans in Vietnam. Frances Fitzgerald.

The First A. I. F.: A Study of Its Recruitment, 1914-1918. L. L. Robson.

The First European Agriculture: A Study of the Osteological and Botanical Evidence Until 2000 B. C. Jacqueline Murray.

First Freedom: The Responses of Alabama's Blacks to Emancipation and Reconstruction. Peter Kolchin.

The First Hundred Years of Historic Guilford, 1771-1871. A. Earl Weatherly.

The First Hundred Years of Nino Cochise: The Untold Story of an Apache Indian Chief. Ciyé

"Nino" Cochise and A. Kenny Griffith.

The First One Hundred: A Catalog of Manuscripts and Special Collections [in the John C. Pace Library].

The First One Hundred Years: A History of Virginia Polytechnic Institute and State University. Duncan Lyle Kinnear.

The First State University: A Pictorial History of the University of North Carolina. William S. Powell.

The First Ten: The Founding Presidents and Their Administrations. Albert Steinberg.

The First West. Ruby Addison Henry.

The Fiscal System of Renaissance France. Martin Wolfe.

Fit and Proper Persons: Ideal and Reality in Nineteenth-Century Urban Government. E. P. Hennock.

The Flamboyant Judge, James D. Hamlin. J. Evetts Haley and William Curry Holden.

Flight and Rebellion: Slave Resistance in Eighteenth-Century Virginia. Gerald W. Mullin.

The Flight to America: Motives for the Mass Emigration from Denmark, 1868-1914. Kristian Hvidt.

Flood Tide of Empire: Spain and the Pacific Northwest, 1543-1819. Warren L. Cook.

Floor of the Sky: The Great Plains. David Plowden.

Florence in the Forgotten Centuries, 1527-1800: A History of Florence and the Forentines in the Age of the Grand Dukes. Eric Cochrane.

Florentine Public Finances in the Early Renaissance, 1400-1433. Anthony Molho.

Florida: Land of Images. Nixon Smiley.

Florida's Promoters: The Men Who Made It Big. Charles E. Harner.

Florilegium Historiale: Essays Presented to Wallace K. Ferguson. J. G. Rowe and W. H. Stockdale, eds.

Folk Medicine of the Delaware and Related Algonkian Indians. Gladys Tantaquidgeon.

Folklore and Folklife. An Introduction. Richard M. Dorson, ed.

Food-Notes on Gogol. Alexander P. Obolensky.

For Better or For Worse: The Ecology of an Urban Area. Harold Gilliam.

For the President--Personal and Secret: Correspondence Between Franklin D. Roosevelt and William C. Bullitt. Orville H. Bullitt, ed.

For the Reputation of Truth: Politics, Religion and Conflict Among the Pennsylvania Quakers, 1750-1800. Richard Bauman.

Force and Diplomacy: Essays Military and Diplomatic. Raymond G. O'Connor.

Forecast for Overlord, June 6, 1944. J. M. Stagg.

Foreign Affairs and the 1964 Presidential Election in the United States. David S. Myers.

Foreign Aid and Industrial Development in Pakistan. Irving Brecher and S. A. Abbas.

Foreign Investment and Development: Swedish Companies in India. Klas Markensten.

The Foreign Policy of Victorian England, 1830-1902. Kenneth Bourne.

The Foreign Policy System of Israel. Michael Brecher.

The Foreign Powers in Latin America. Herbert Goldhamer.

Foreign Relations of the United States, 1947. Vols. II, IV, V, VI, VIII, X.

Foreign Relations of the United States. The Conferences at Washington and Quebec, 1943; The Conference at Quebec, 1944.

The Forerunner: The Dilemmas, Tom Ellis 1859-1899. Neville Masterman.

Forerunners of Black Power: The Rhetoric of Abolition. Ernest G. Bormann, ed.

Forging Accounting Principles in Five Countries: A History and an Analysis of Trends. Stephen A. Zeff.

Forging the American Republic, 1760-1815. Norman K. Risjord.

The Forgotten Americans: A Survey of Values, Beliefs, and Concerns of the Majority. Frank B. Armbruster and Doris Yokelson.

La formación de la Junta Central.

Angel Martínez de Velasco.
La formación intellectual del Libertador. Manuel Pérez Vila.
Forrest 1847-1918. I: 1847-1891, Apprenticeship to Premiership. F. K. Crowley.
Fort Custer on the Big Horn, 1877-1898: Its History and Personalities as Told and Pictured by Its Contemporaries. Richard Upton, ed. and comp.
The Fortunes of the West: The Future of the Atlantic Nations. Theodore Geiger.
Foundations of a Planned Economy, 1926-1929. Vol. I, Parts I and II. Edward Hallett Carr and R. W. Davies.
The Foundations of American Economic Freedom: Government and Enterprise in the Age of Washington. E. A. J. Johnson.
Foundations of American Independence: 1763-1815. J. R. Pole.
Foundations of Colonial America. 3 vols. W. Keith Kavenagh, ed.
Foundations of Early Modern Europe 1460-1559. Eugene F. Rice, Jr.
Foundations of Farm Policy. Luther G. Tweeten.
Foundations of Pennsylvania Prehistory. Barry C. Kent, Ira F. Smith, III, and Catherine McCann.
Founder's Kin: Privilege and Pedigree. G. D. Squibb.
Foundlings on the Frontier: Racial and Religious Conflict in Arizona Territory, 1904-1905. A. Blake Brophy.
Four Years With the Boys in Gray. Gervis D. Grainger.
Fourteen Thousand Feet: A History of the Naming and Early Ascents of the High Colorado Peaks. John L. Jerome Hart
The Fourth World of the Hopis. Harold Courlander.
France and Britain in Africa: Imperial Rivalry and Colonial Rule. P. Gifford and William Roger Louis, eds.
France and Europe in 1848: A Study of French Foreign Affairs in Time of Crisis. Lawrence C. Jennings.
France and the Chesapeake: A History of the French Tobacco Monopoly, 1674-1791 and of Its Rela-

tionship to the British and American Tobacco Trades. 2 vols. Jacob M. Price.
France and the Eighteenth-Century Corsican Question. Thadd E. Hall.
La France et la Hongrie au début du XVIIIe siècle.... Béla Kopeczi.
France in America. W. J. Eccles.
Francis Drake, Privateer: Contemporary Narratives and Documents. John Hampden, ed.
Francis Lee Jaques: Artist of the Wilderness World. Florence Page Jaques.
Francis Parkman, Heroic Historian. Mason Wade.
Franklin and Galloway: A Political Partnership. Benjamin H. Newcomb.
Frankreich in Tunesien: Die Anfänge des Protektorates 1881-1886. Jürgen Rosenbaum.
Frankreichs Ruhrpolitik: Von Versailles bis zum Dawesplan. Ludwig Zimmerman.
Frantz Fanon: A Critical Study. Irene L. Gendzier.
Französischer Imperialismus in Vietnam: Die koloniale Expansion und die Errichtung des Protektorates Anam-Tongking 1880-1885. Dieter Brötel.
Frederic William Maitland: A Life. C. H. S. Fifoot.
Frederick Denison Maurice: Rebellious Conformist. Olive J. Brose.
Frederick Jackson Turner: Historian--Scholar--Teacher. Ray Allen Billington.
Frederick Law Olmsted and the American Environmental Tradition. Albert Fein.
The Free Negro in Ante-Bellum Louisiana. H. E. Sterk.
Free Negroes in the District of Columbia: 1790-1846. Letitia Woods Brown.
The Free Soilers: Third Party Politics, 1848-54. Frederick J. Blue.
Free Trade and Slavery: Calhoun's Defense of Southern Interests Against British Interference, 1811-1848. Bruno Gujer.
The French and the Dardanelles: A Study of Failure in the Conduct of War. George H. Cassar.

French Capitalism in the Nine-
teenth Century. Guy P Palmade.
French Colonialism in Tropical
Africa, 1900-1945. Jean Suret-
Canale.
The French Communists: Profile of
a People. Annie Kriegel.
The French Democratic Left, 1963-
1969: Toward a Modern Party
System. Frank L. Wilson.
The French Economy, 1913-1939.
Tom Kemp.
French Finances 1770-1795: From
Business to Bureaucracy. J. F.
Bosher.
The French Legation in Texas.
Volume II: Mission Miscarried.
Nancy Nichols Barker, tr. and ed.
The French Revolution. Selected
Documents. Paul H Beik, ed.
The French Revolution of 1830.
David H. Pinkney.
The French Second Republic: A
Social History. Roger Price.
French Society and Culture: Back-
ground for 18th Century Litera-
ture. Lionel Gossman.
Der Friede von Paris 1856: Studien
zum Verhältnis von Kriegsfuh-
rüng, Politik, und Friedensbe-
wahrung. Winfried Baumgart.
Friedrich Meinecke and German
Politics in the Twentieth Century.
Robert A. Pois.
Friesland Over Three Centuries:
Economic and Social Develop-
ments from 1500 to 1800. 2 vols.
J. A. Faber.
From Anarchism to Reformism: A
Study of the Political Activities
of Paul Brousse Within the First
International and the French So-
cialist Movement 1870-90. David
Stafford.
From Castlereach to Gladstone:
1815-1885. Derek Beales.
From Colony to Empire: Essays in
the History of American Foreign
Relations. William Appleman
Williams, ed.
From Confederation to Nation: The
American Constitution, 1835-1977.
Bernard Schwartz.
From Contraband to Freedman: Fed-
eral Policy Toward Southern
Blacks, 1861-1865. Louis E.
Gerteis.
From Cuba with a Song. Severo
Sarduy.

From Fortress to Farm: or,
Twenty-Three Years on the Fron-
tier. Linda W. Slaughter.
From Kingdom to Commonwealth:
The Development of Civic Con-
sciousness in English Public
Thought. Donald W. Hanson.
From Ivy Street to Kennedy Center:
Centennial History of the Atlanta
Public School System. Melvin W.
Ecke.
From Marx to Hegel. George Lich-
theim.
From Ottomanism to Arabism: Es-
says on the Origins of Arab Na-
tionalism. C. Ernest Dawn.
From Peasant to Farmer: A Revo-
lutionary Strategy for Develop-
ment. Raanan Weitz.
From Peterloo to the Crystal Palace.
J. R. White.
From Resistance to Revolution: Co-
lonial Radicals and the Develop-
ment of American Opposition to
Britain, 1765-1776. Pauline
Maier.
From Sadowa to Sarajevo: The For-
eign Policy to Austria-Hungary.
1866-1914. F. R. Bridge.
From Spanish Court to Italian
Ghetto. Isaac Cordosa: A Study
in Seventeenth-Century Marrianism
and Jewish Apologetics. Yosef
Hayim Yerushalmi.
From Stonehenge to Modern Cos-
mology. Fred Hoyle.
From the Jhelum to the Volga. S.
Nihal Singh.
From the Land and Back. Curtis K.
Stadtfeld.
From the Missouri to the Great Salt
Lake: An Account of Overland
Freighting. William E. Lass.
From the Molly Maguires to the
United Mine Workers: The Social
Ecology of an Industrial Union,
1869-1897. Harold W. Aurand.
From the Mountain. Helen White
and Redding S. Sugg, ed.
From the Revolution Through the
Age of Jackson: Innocence and
Empire in the Young Republic.
John R. Howe.
From the Rio Grande to the Arctic:
The Story of the Richfield Oil
Corporation. Charles S. Jones.
From These Beginnings: A Bio-
graphical Approach to American
History. Roderick Nash.

From Trappers to Tourists: Fremont County, Colorado, 1830-1950. Rosemae Wells Campbell.

From Union Stars to Top Hat: A Biography of the Extraordinary General James Harrison Wilson. Edward G. Longacre.

From Village to State in Tanzania. Clyde R. Ingle.

Frontier Crusader--William F. M. Arny. Lawrence R. Murphy.

Frontier Elements in a Hudson River Village. Carl Nordstrom.

Frontier Woman: The Life of a Woman Homesteader on the Dakota Frontier. Walker D. Wyman, ed.

Führerideologie und Parteiorganisation in der NSDAP (1919-1933). Wolfgang Horn.

The Function of Documents in Islamic Law: The Chapters on Sale from Tahāwī's "Kitāb al-Shurut al Kabir." Jeanette A. Wakin, ed.

-G-

G. Stanley Hall: The Psychologist as Prophet. Dorothy Ross.

El Gabierno de las Vacas, 1933-1956. Daniel Drosdoff.

Gaelic and Gaelicized Ireland in the Middle Ages. Kenneth Nicholls.

The Gallup Poll: Public Opinion, 1935-1971. 3 volumes. George H. Gallup.

Gandhi in South Africa: British Imperialism and the Indian Question, 1860-1914. Robert A. Huttenback.

Gandhi, India and the World: An International Symposium. Sibnarayan Ray, ed.

Garcilaso de la Vega, el Inca and His Sources in Commentarios Reales de los Incas. Frances G. Crowley.

La Garde nationale et les debuts de la revolution en Ille-et-Vilaine (1789-mars 1793). Roger Dupuy.

Gateways and Caravans: A Portrait of Turkey. Freya Stark and Fulvio Roiter.

Le Gauche Israelienne. Merhav Peretz.

Gaullism: The Rise and Fall of a Political Movement. Anthony Hartley.

Genealogical Research in Maryland: A Guide. Mary Keysor Meyer.

General Crook and the Sierra Madre Adventure. Dan L. Thrapp.

A General History of the Pyrates. Daniel Defoe.

General Pope and U. S. Indian Policy. Richard N. Ellis.

Genèse de la frontière franco-belge: Les variations des limites septentrionales de la France de 1659 à 1789. Nelly Girard D'Albissin.

The Genesis of Crown Colony Government: Trinidad, 1783-1810. James Millette.

The Genesis of the Frontier Thesis: A Study in Historical Creativity. Genteel Partisan: Manton Marble, 1834-1917. George T. McJimsey.

George C. Marshall: Organizer of Victory, 1943-1945. Forrest C. Pogue.

George Grosz: Art and Politics in the Weimar Republic. Beth Irwin Lewis.

George Joachim Goschen: The Transformation of a Victorian Liberal. Thomas J. Spinner, Jr.

George Peabody: A Biography. Franklin Parker.

George Rapp's Successors and Material Heirs (1847-1916). Karl J. R. Arndt.

George Sylvester Viereck: German-American Propagandist. Niel M. Johnson.

George the Third. Stanley Ayling.

George W. Brackenridge: Maverick Philanthropist. Marilyn McAdams Sibley.

George W. Norris: The Persistence of a Progressive, 1913-1933. Richard Lowitt.

George Washington: A Biography in His Own Words. Ralph K. Andrist, ed.

George Washington and the New Nation (1783-1793). James Thomas Flexner.

George Washington; Volume IV: Anguish and Farewell (1793-1799). James Thomas Flexner.

George Washington: Soldier and Man. North Callahan.

Georg Weerth. Ein politischer Dichter des Vomärz und der Rev-

olution von 1848-49. Florian
Vassen.

Georgia's Last Frontier. James C.
Bonner.

German-American Pioneers in Wisconsin and Michigan. Louis F.
Frank.

German-American Political Behavior
in Nebraska and Wisconsin 1916-
1920. Clifford L. Nelson.

German Antiquity in Renaissance
Myth. Frank L. Borchardt.

German Democracy and the Triumph
of Hitler. Anthony Nicholls and
Erich Matthias, eds.

The German Democratic Republic
from the 60's to the 70's: A
Socio-Political Analysis. Peter
Christian Ludz.

The German Dictatorship: The Ori-
gins, Structure and Effects of
National Socialism. Karl Dietrich
Bracher.

German Diplomacy 1919-1945, An
Outline Sketch. Henryk Batowski.

The German Historians and England:
A Study in Nineteenth-Century
Views. Charles E. McClelland.

German Home Towns: Community,
State, and General Estate, 1648-
1871. Mack Walker.

German Intelligence Activities in
Pomerania 1920-1933. Henryk
Kopczyk.

The German Navy in World War II.
Edward P. Von der Porten.

German "Pest Ships." Alice D.
Forsyth and Earlene L. Zeringue,
comps. and trans.

German-Polish Relations, 1918-1933.
Harald von Riekhoff.

German Strategy Against Russia,
1939-1941. Barry A Leach.

Germany. Ernest K. Bramstead.

Germany and the East: Selected
Essays. Fritz T. Epstein.

Germany and the Soviet Union, 1939-
1941. Gerhard L. Weinberg.

Germany's Drive to the East and the
Ukrainian Revolution, 1917-1918.
Oleh H. Fedyshyn.

Geronimo: A Biography. Alexander
B. Adams.

Geschichte der baltischen-Staaten.
G. von Rauch.

Geschichte des Konzils von Trient.
Band III. Hubert Jedin.

Geschichte des k. k. Kriegsminis-

teriums. 2 vols. Walter Wagner.

Die Geschichte des Mainzer Erzkanzlerarchivs 1782-1815....
Helmut Mathy.

Geschichte Kanadas: Das Werden
einer Nation. Udo Sautter.

Geschichte und Organisation der
zentrumspartei in Düsseldorf
1917-1933. Wolfgang Stump.

Das Gewicht Monopolistischer Elemente in Der Amerikanischen
Textilindustrie, 1840-1880. Hansjörg Siegenthaler.

The Ghanaian Factory Worker: Industrial Man in Africa. Margaret
Peil.

Gibbon and His Roman Empire.
David P. Jordan.

The Gilcrease-Hargrett Catalog of
Imprints. Lester Hargrett, comp.

Ginn Social Science Series. 8 vols.
Leonard S. Kenworthy.

The Gladstones: A Family Biography,
1764-1851. S. G. Checkland.

Glaube und Politik in Pennsylvania
1681-1776: Die Wandlungen der
Obrigkeitsdoktrin und des Peace
Testimony der Quäker. Hermann
Wellenreuther.

Gli Investimenti Finanziari Genovesi
In Europa Tra Il Seicento e la
Restaurazione. Guiseppe Felloni.

The Glorious Failure: Congressman
Robert Brown Elliott and the Re-
construction in South Carolina.
Peggy Lamson.

The Glorious Revolution in America.
David S. Lovejoy.

"God Save This Honorable Court!"
Louis M. Kohlmeier, Jr.

The Gods of Revolution. Christopher
Dawson.

God's Plot: The Paradoxes of Puritan Piety Being the Autobiography
of Thomas Shepard. Michael
McGiffert, ed.

Goebbels. Helmuth Heiber.

Going to America. Terry Coleman.

Gold. Jack London and Herbert
Heron.

Gold in the Blue Ridge. The True
Story of the Beale Treasure.
P. B. Innis and Walter Dean
Innis.

Gold Rush. James Blower.

The Golden Age of Spain: 1516-1659.
Antonio Domínguez Ortiz.

The Golden Century: Europe 1598-

385 Guerrilla

Willoughby, ed.
Guerrilla Struggle in Africa: An
Analysis and Preview. Kenneth
W. Grundy.
Guerrilla Warfare, Analysis and
Projections. N. I. Klonis.
Guerrilla Warrior: The Early Life
of John J. Pershing. Donald
Smythe.
The Guerrillas. Jean Lartéguy.
Guide to Historical Manuscripts in
the National Archives of Rhodesia.
T. W. Baxter and E. E. Burke.
Guide to Manuscripts and Archives
in the Negro Collection of Trevor
Arnett Library, Atlanta Univer-
sity. (Trevor Arnett Library,
Atlanta University.)
Guide to Research and Reference
Works on Sub-Saharan Africa.
Peter Duignan, ed.
Guide to the Archives of the Spanish
Institutions in or Concerned With
the Netherlands (1556-1706).
Geoffrey Parker.
A Guide to the Historical Geography
of New Spain. Peter Gerhard.
A Guide to the Industrial Archae-
ology of Europe. Kenneth Hudson.
A Guide to the Manuscript Collec-
tions of the Bancroft Library.
Vol. 2. George P. Hammond, ed.
A Guide to the Microfilm Edition of
the William Wirt Papers. John
B. Boles.
A Guide to the Newspaper Collection
of the State Archives, Nebraska
Historical Society. (Nebraska
Historical Society.)
Guide to the Processed Manuscripts
of the Tennessee Historical So-
ciety. Harriet Chappell Owsley,
ed.
Guide to the Records of Parliament.
Maurice F. Bond.
A Guide to the Sources of British
Military History. Robin Higham,
ed.
The Gunners of Canada: The His-
tory of the Royal Regiment of
Canadian Artillery. Vol. 2, 1919-
1967. G. W. L. Nicholson.

-H-

The Habsburg-Valois Wars and the
French Wars of the Religion.
Blaise de Monluc.
Haiti: Its Stagnant Society and
Shackled Economy. O. Ernest
Moore.
Half-Bitter, Half Sweet: An Excur-
sion into Italian-American His-
tory. Alexander De Conde.
Half of Spain Died: A Reappraisal
of the Spanish Civil War. Her-
bert L. Matthews.
The Hall Carbine Affair: An Essay
in Historiography. R. Gordon
Wasson.
Hall J. Kelley on Oregon: A Col-
lection of Five of His Published
Works and a Number of Hitherto
Unpublished Letters. Fred Wil-
bur Powell, ed.
Hall's Breechloaders: John H.
Hall's Invention and Development
of a Breechloading Rifle With
Precision-Made Interchangeable
Parts, and Its Introduction into
the United States Service. R. T.
Huntington.
Hammarskjold. Brian Urquhart.
Handbook for History Teachers.
W. H. Burston and C. W.
Green, eds.
Handbook of Latin American Studies,
32: Humanities. Henry E.
Adams, ed.
Handbuch der bayerischen Ges-
chichte.... Max Spindler, ed.
Hand-list of Anglo-Saxon Non-runic
Inscriptions. Elisabeth Okasha.
Handlist of the Political Papers of
Stanley Baldwin. A. E. B. Owen.
Hankey: Man of Secrets. Vol. II,
1919-1931. Stephen Roskill.
Hap Arnold: Architect of American
Air Power. Flint O. DuPre.
The Harlem Renaissance Remem-
bered. Arna Bontemps, ed.
Harmsen's Western Americana: A
Collection of One Hundred West-
ern Paintings With Biographical
Profiles of the Artists. Dorothy
B. Harmsen.
Harold von Schmidt Draws and
Paints the Old West. Walt Reed.
Harry Bridges: The Rise and Fall
of Radical Labor in the United

States. Charles P. Larrowe.
Harry Ferguson, Inventor and Pioneer. Colin Fraser.
Harry S. Truman. Margaret Truman.
Harry Truman and the Crisis Presidency. Bert Cochran.
Haunted by God. James McBride Dabbs.
The Havasupai People. Henry F. Dobyns and Robert C. Euler.
Hawaii: An Uncommon History. Edward Joesting.
Hawaiian Petroglyphs. J. Halley Cox and Edward Stasack.
The Heirs of Stalin: Dissidence and the Soviet Regime, 1953-1970. Abraham Rothberg.
The Hejaz Railway and the Muslim Pilgrimage: A Case of Ottoman Political Propaganda. Jacob M. Landau
Held Captive by Indians: Selected Narratives, 1642-1836. Richard VanDerBeets, ed.
Hell Has No Limits. José Donoso.
Helmuth von Moltke: A Leader Against Hitler. Michael Balfour and Julian Frisby.
Henri Mercier and the American Civil War. Daniel B. Carroll.
Henrietta Maria: Queen of the Cavaliers. Quentin Bone.
Henry IV of Castile, 1425-1474. Townsend Miller.
Henry VII. S. B. Chrimes.
Henry VIII and His Court. Neville Williams.
Henry VIII: The Mask of Royalty. Lacey Baldwin Smith.
Henry VIII's Scottish Diplomacy, 1513-1524. Richard Glen Eaves.
Henry Adams on the Road to Chartres. Robert Mane.
Henry Alline, 1748-1784. J. M. Bumsted.
Henry Ford and Grass-Roots America. Reynold M. Wik.
Henry Home, Lord Kames and the Scottish Enlightenment: A Study in National Character and the History of Ideas. William C. Lehmann.
Henry Labouchere and the Empire, 1880-1905. R. J. Hind.
Heralds of England: A History of the Office and College of Arms. Sir Anthony Wagner.

Heresy and Obedience in Tridentine Italy: Cardinal Pole and the Counter Reformation. Dermot Fenlon.
The Hero in America. Dixon Wector.
The Hero's Children: The Postwar Generation in Eastern Europe. Paul Neuberg.
Herzog Albrecht von Preussen und der Osiandrismus, 1522-1568. Jörg Rainer Fligge.
Der Herzogstitel in Frankreich und Deutschland (9. bis 12. Jahrhundert) mit Listen der Ältesten deutschen Herzogsurkunden. W. Kienast.
The Hessian View of America, 1776-1783. Ernst Kipping.
Heute sprach ich mit....: Tagebücher eines berliner Publizisten, 1926-1932. Ernst Feder.
The High Court of Delegates. G. I. O. Duncan.
High Victorian Gothic: A Study in Associationism. George L. Hersey.
The High Victorian Movement in Architecture, 1850-1870. Stefan Muthesius.
Hillbilly Women. Kathy Kahn.
Der Himmel über dem Menschen der Steinzeit, Astronomie und Mathematik der MegalithKulturen. Rolf Müller.
Hindus and Family Planning: A Socio-Political Demography. Sudhir Laxman Hendre.
Hindus of the Himalayas: Ethnography and Change. Gerald D. Berreman.
The Hinges of Destiny: A True Story of Ranch Life in the Early Twentieth Century. Ben Lee Parker.
Hiram Martin Crittenden: His Public Career. Gordon B. Dodds.
His Day is Marching On: A Memoir of W. E. B. DuBois. Shirley Graham DuBois.
Hispanismo, 1898-1936: Spanish Conservatives and Liberals and Their Relations With Spanish America. Frederick B. Pike.
Histoire de l'enseignement au Quebec, 1608-1971. 2 vols. Louis-Philippe Audet.
Histoire de l'imprimerie. Radioscopie d'une ère: De Gutenberg

à l'Informatique. Maurice Audin.
Histoire des Juifs en France.
Bernhard Blumenkranz.
Histoire des Usines Renault: Nais-
sance de la Grande Enterprise,
1898-1939. Patrick Fridenson.
Histoire du plus grand quotidien de
la IIIe République: Le Petit
Parisien, 1876-1944. 2 vols.
Francine Amaury.
Histoire générale de l'Afrique noire,
de Madagascar, et des archi-
pelo.... Hubert Deschamps, ed.
Historia contemporanea de Ibero-
américa. 3 vols. José Bel-
monte.
Historia de la educación en Guate-
mala. Carlos González Ore-
llana
Historia diplomatica del Paraguay:
De 1869 a 1938. Antonio Salum-
Flecha.
Historia geral da civilizacão brasile-
ira, Tomo II: O Brasil mon-
arquico, Vol. IV: Declinio e
quedo do império. Myriam Ellis,
et al.
Historia moderna de México. Vol.
IX: El Parfiriato. La Vida po-
lítica interior. Daniel Casio
Villegas.
Historial genealógico del Doctor
Cristóbal Mendoza, 1772-1829.
Ramón Darío Suárez.
The Historian and the Computer.
Edward Shorter.
The Historian as Detective: Essays
on Evidence. Robin W. Winks,
ed.
Historians' Fallacies: Toward a
Logic of Historical Thought.
David H. Fischer.
The Historian's Handbook: A Des-
criptive Guide to Reference Works.
Helen J. Poulton and Marguerite
S. Howland.
The Historian's Workshop: Original
Essays by Sixteen Historians. L.
P. Curtis, Jr., ed.
Historical and Cultural Dictionary of
Saudi Arabia. Carroll L. Riley.
Historical Atlas of Kansas. Homer
E. Socolosky and Huber Self.
Historical Base Map: Proposed
Lincoln Home National Historical
Park, Springfield, Illinois. Edwin
C. Bearss.
Historical Demography. T. H. Hol-
lingsworth.

Historical Dictionary of Chile. Sal-
vatore Bizzarro.
Historical Dictionary of El Salvador.
Philip F. Flemion.
Historical Dictionary of Nicaragua.
Harvey K. Meyer.
Historical Documents of Canada.
Vol. 5: The Arts of War and
Peace, 1914-1945. C. P. Stacey.
Historical Notes on Lower California,
With Some Relative to Upper Cal-
ifornia Furnished to the Bancroft
Library. Manuel C. Rojo.
Historical Studies Today. Felix Gil-
bert and Stephen R. Graubard,
eds.
Historique ... du Comite des travaux
historiques des sociétés savan-
tes....
History and American Society: Es-
says of David M. Potter. Don E.
Fehrenbacher, ed.
History and Development of Engin-
eering. Malcolm S. Gregory.
The History and Present Condition
of St. Domingo. 2 vols. Jona-
than Brown.
History and the Role of the City in
American Life. Arthur Mann,
et al.
History as Applied Science: A Phil-
osophical Study. William Todd.
History as Social Science. David S.
Landes, et al., eds.
History in Geographic Perspective:
The Other France. Edward
Walling Fox.
History, Man, and Reason: A Study
in Nineteenth-Century Thought.
Maurice Mandelbaum.
History of America: Challenge and
Crisis. Charles S. Miller and
Natalie Joy War.
The History of American Business
and Industry. Alex Groner.
A History of American Political
Thought. A. J. Beitzinger.
A History of Book Publishing in the
United States. Vol. I. John
Tebbel.
A History of Buganda, from the
Foundation of the Kingdom to
1900. M. S. M. Semakula Ki-
wanuka.
A History of Dams. Norman Smith.
A History of Early Renaissance
Italy: From the Mid-Thirteenth
to the Mid-Fifteenth Century.
Brian Pullan.

History of Erie County, 1870-1970.
Walter S. Dunn, Jr., ed.
A History of Federal Water Re-
sources Programs, 1800-1960.
Beatrice Hort Holmes.
A History of Florida Baptists.
Edward E. Joiner.
A History of Greenwich. Beryl
Platts.
A History of Ireland in the Eight-
eenth Century. W. E. H. Lecky.
A History of Japanese Astronomy:
Chinese Background and Western
Impact. Shigeru Nakayama.
History of Kershaw's Brigade....
D. Augustus Dickert.
A History of Literary Aesthetics in
America. Max I. Baym.
The History of London: Hanoverian
London, 1714-1808. George Rudé.
A History of Louisiana, Vol. II.
Alcee Fortier.
A History of Lumbering in Maine,
1861-1960. David C. Smith.
A History of Malayalam Literature.
Krishna Chaitanya.
A History of Marine Navigation. W.
E. May and Leonard Holder.
History of Mennonites in Virginia,
1900-1960. Harry Anthony Brunk.
A History of Meredith College.
Mary Lynch Johnson.
A History of Mississippi. 2 volumes.
Richard Aubrey McLemore, ed.
A History of Missouri, Vol. II,
1820-1860. Perry McCandless.
A History of Modern Ireland. Ed-
ward Norman.
A History of Modern Jewry, 1780-
1815 Raphael Mahler.
A History of Modern Norway, 1814-
1972. T. K. Derry.
A History of Muslim Rule in Kash-
mir, 1320-1819. R. K. Parmu.
The History of My Contemporary.
Vladimir G. Korolenko.
History of Nevada. Russell R.
Elliott.
The History of Newberry County,
South Carolina. Vol. I: 1749-
1860. Thomas H. Pope.
History of Papermaking in the United
States (1691-1969). David C.
Smith
The History of Parliament: The
House of Commons, 1715-1754.
Romney Sedgwick, et al.
A History of Pennsylvania. Philip
S. Klein and Ari Hoogenboom.

History of Persia Under Qājār Rule.
Heribert Busse, trans.
History of Portugal. Vol. I: From
Lusitania to Empire. A. H. De
Oliveira Marques.
History of Portugal. Vol. II: From
Empire to Corporate State. A.
H. de Oliveira Marques.
A History of Public Speaking in
Pennsylvania. De Witte Holland
and Robert Oliver, eds.
History of Russian Non-Marxian
Thought. Boris Ischboldin.
History of Seafaring: Based on
Underwater Archaeology. George
F. Bass, ed.
A History of Southampton, 1700-1914.
Vol. 2, The Beginnings of Modern
Southampton, 1836-1867. A.
Temple Patterson.
The History of Springfield, Vermont,
1885-1961. Keith Richard Barney.
History of Standard Oil Company
(New Jersey), 1927-1950: New
Horizons. Henrietta M. Larson,
Evelyn H. Knowlton, and Charles
S. Popple.
The History of Stephens County,
Georgia. Katherine Curtis Trog-
don, ed. and comp.
A History of the Alans in the West:
From Their First Appearances
in the Sources of Classical Anti-
quity Through the Early Middle
Ages. Bernard S. Bachrach.
A History of the Cambodian Inde-
pendence Movement, 1863-1955.
V. M. Reddi.
History of the Canadian National
Railways. G. R. Stevens.
History of the Cities and Villages of
the Ukrainian SSR. O. O. Cher-
nov, et al., eds.
History of the Cossacks. Wasili G.
Glaskow.
A History of the Czechoslovak Re-
public, 1918-1948. Victor S.
Mamatrey and Radomir Luza, eds.
History of the Freedom Movement
in India. (Vols. 3 and 4). Tara
Chand.
History of the Great Lakes. Vols.
I and II. J. B. Mansfield, ed.
History of the Indies. Bartolome
de las Casas.
A History of the Irish Working Class.
P. Berresford Ellis.
A History of the Kingdom of Nkore
in Western Uganda to 1896. S. R.

Karngiere.
The History of the Liberal Party,
1805-1970. Roy Douglas.
History of the Louisville and Nash-
ville Railroad. Maury Klein.
A History of the Maghrib. Jamil
M. Abun-Nasr.
A History of the Middle West: From
the Beginning to 1970. Kenneth
R. Walker.
The History of the Mongol Conquests.
J. J. Saunders.
History of the Mongols   Based on
Eastern and Western Accounts.
Bertold Spuler.
A History of the "National Intelli-
gencer." William E. Ames.
History of the Oberlin-Wellington
Rescue. Jacob R. Shipherd.
The History of the Province of New
York. 2 vols. William Smith,
Jr.
The History of the Reign of King
Henry the Seventh. Francis
Bacon.
A History of the Royal College of
Physicians of London. Vol. III.
A. M. Cooke.
A History of the Russian Empire.
Vol. I. Nicholas L Chirovsky.
A History of the South. Francis
Butler Simkins and Charles Pierce
Roland.
The History of the South Tyrol Ques-
tion. A. E. Alcock.
History of the Supreme Court of the
United States. Vol. I. Antece-
dents and Beginnings to 1801.
Julius Goebel, Jr.
History of the Supreme Court of the
United States. Vol. VI: Recon-
struction and Reunion, 1864-88.
Charles Fairman.
The History of West Africa, Volume
I. J. F. Ade Ajayi and Michael
Crowder, eds.
The History of Working-Class Hous-
ing--a Symposium. S. D. Chap-
man, ed.
A History of Zionism. Walter
Laqueur.
Hitler and Middle Sea. Walter Ansel.
Hitler and the Beer Hall Putsch.
Harold J. Gordon, Jr.
Hitler, Horthy, and Hungary: Ger-
man-Hungarian Relations, 1941-
1944. Mario D. Fenyo.

Hitler: The Last Ten Days. Ger-
hard Boldt.
Hitler's War Aims: Ideology, the
Nazi State, and the Course of
Expansion. Norman Rich.
Hog Meat and Hoecake: Food Supply
in the Old South, 1840-1860.
Sam Bowers Hilliard.
Hogarth: His Life, Art, and Times.
2 vols. Ronald Paulson.
Hogarth on High Life. Arthur S.
Weinsinger and W. B. Coley,
eds. and trans.
Holbein and Henry VIII. Roy Strong.
Hold the Fort! The Story of a Song
from the Sawdust Trail to the
Picket Line. Paul J. Scheips.
The Holiness-Pentecostal Movement
in the United States. Vinson
Syman.
The Holocaust: From a Survivor of
Verdun. William Hermanns.
Homeopathy in America: The Rise
and Fall of a Medical Heresy.
Martin Kaufman.
Homesteader: A Prairie Boyhood
Recalled. James M. Minifie.
Les Hommes et la mort en Anjou
aux 17e et 18e siècles. Fran-
çois LeBrun.
Honor, Commerce, and Industry in
Eighteenth-Century Spain. Wil-
liam J. Callahan.
Hopes and Fears of Israelis: Con-
sensus in a New Society. Aaron
Antonovsky and Alan Arian.
The Hopi Indians of Old Oraibi,
Change and Continuity. Mischa
Titiev.
Horace White: Nineteenth-Century
Liberal. Joseph Logsdon.
Horan's Field and Other Reserva-
tions. Valentin Iremonger.
The Horizon History of Africa.
Alvin M. Josephy, Jr., ed.
The Horned Moses in Medieval Art
and Thought. Ruth Mellinkoff.
Hostiles and Horse Soldiers. Lon-
nie J. White, et al., eds.
The House and Home. M. W. Bar-
ley.
House Decoration in Nubia. Marian
Wenzel.
A House for all Peoples: Ethnic
Politics in Chicago. John M.
Allswang.
The House of Commons, 1604-1610.

Wallace Notestein.
The House of Saulx-Tavanes: Versailles and Burgundy, 1700-1830. Robert Forster.
Household and Family in Past Time. P. Laslett, ed.
The Household Book of Queen Isabella of England. F. D. Blackley and G. Hermansen, eds.
The Houston Symphony Orchestra, 1913-1971. Hubert Roussel.
How Computers Affect Management. Rosemary Stewart.
How It Happened. Frank E. Huggett.
How Shall They Hear Without a Preacher? The Life of Ernest Fremont Tittle. Robert Moats Miller.
How the Government Breaks the Law. Jethro K. Lieberman.
How the U. S. Cavalry Saved Our National Parks. H. Duane Hampton.
The Howe Brothers and the American Revolution. Ira D. Gruber.
Huerta: A Political Portrait. Michael C. Meyer.
Hugh Gaine: A Colonial Printer-Editor's Odyssey to Loyalism. Alfred Lawrence Lorenz.
Hugo Black: The Alabama Years. Virginia Van Der Veer Hamilton.
Hull in the Eighteenth Century: A Study in Economic and Social History. Gordon Jackson.
Human Aspects of Biomedical Innovation. Everett Mendelsohn, Judson P. Swazey and Irene Taviss.
The Human Condition in Latin America. Eric R. Wolf and Edward C. Hansen.
Hungary. Paul Ignatus.
Hungary in Revolution, 1018-19; Nine Essays. Ivan Volgyes, ed.
Hunted Like a Wolf: The Story of the Seminole War. Milton Meltzer.
Hunters and Gatherers: The Material Culture of the Nomadic Hadza. James Woodburn.

-I-

I Am a Sensation. Gerry Goldberg and George Wright, eds.
I Have Spoken: American History Through the Voices of the Indians. Virginia I. Armstrong comp.
Ibo Politics: The Role of Ethnic Unions in Eastern Nigeria. Audrey Smock.
The Idea of Fraternity in America. Wilson Carey McWilliams.
The Idea of Landscape and the Sense of Place, 1730-1840: An Approach to the Poetry of John Clare. John Barrell.
The Idea of Peace in Antiquity. Gerardo Zampaglione.
Ideals and Politics: New York Intellectuals and Liberal Democracy, 1820-1880. Edward K. Spann.
Ideologia y política en la novela española del Siglo XIX. Iris M. Zavala.
Idéologies au Canada Français, 1850-1900. Fernand Dumont, Jean-Paul Montminy et Jean Hamelin.
Idylls and Realities, Studies in Nineteenth-Century German Literature. J. P. Stern.
"If Elected...": Unsuccessful Candidates for the Presidency, 1796-1968. Lillian B. Miller, et al.
Igbo Ukwu: An Account of Archaeological Discoveries in Eastern Nigeria. Thurston Shaw.
Ignaz Seipel: Christian Statesman in a Time of Crisis. Klemens Von Klemperer.
Ignition! An Informal History of Liquid Rocket Propellants. John D. Clark.
Ikhnaton: Legend and History. F. J. Giles.
The Ile-de-France: The Country Around Paris. Marc Bloch.
Illinois: A History of the Prairie State. Robert P. Howard.
Illusions of Security: North Atlantic Diplomacy, 1918-22. Michael G. Fry.
An Illustrated Handbook of Fire Apparatus. George Anne Daly and John J. Robrecht.
Im diplomatischen Dienst der k. u. k. Monarchie. Henrich Lutzow.

Ideas. Vol. II. Peter K. Christoff.

An Introduction to Quantitative Methods for Historians. Roderick Floud.

An Introduction to the Abercorn Letters (As Relating to Ireland 1736-1816). John H. Gebbie.

An Introduction to the Principles of Morals and Legislation. Jeremy Bentham.

Introduction to Traditional Art of Western Africa. E. V. Asihene.

The Invention of American Political Parties: A Study of Political Improvisation. Roy F. Nichols.

An Inventory of Historical Monuments in the County of Dorset. Royal Commission on Historical Monuments (England).

An Inventory of the Papers of Dennis J. Roberts in the Phillips Memorial Library of Providence College. Matthew J. Smith, comp.

Investigaciones Contemporáneas sobre Historia de México.

The Invisible Immigrants: The Adaptation of English and Scottish Immigrants in Nineteenth-Century America. Charlotte Erickson.

Iowa on the Eve of the Civil War: A Decade of Frontier Politics. Morton M. Rosenberg.

Iqbal: Poet-Philosopher of Pakistan. Hafeez Malik, ed.

Iran. Yahya Armajani.

Iran: Continuity and Variety. Peter J. Chelkowski, ed.

Iran: Economic Development Under Dualistic Conditions. Jahangir Amuzegar and M. Ali Fekrat.

Ireland Before the Normans. D. O. Corráin.

Ireland Before the Vikings. G. Mac Niocaill.

Ireland in the Empire, 1688-1770: A History of Ireland from the Williamite Wars to the Eve of the American Revolution. Francis Godwin James.

Ireland Since the Famine. F. S. L. Lyons.

Ireland's English Question. Anglo-Irish Relations 1534-1970. Patrick O'Farrell.

Die irische Nationalbewegung zwischen Parlament und Revolution: Der konstitutionelle Nationalismus in

Irland, 1880-1918.... Peter Alter.

The Irish and the Irish Politicans. Edward M. Levine.

Irish Art in the Romanesque Period, 1020-1170, A. D. Henry Françoise.

Irish Historiography 1936-70. T. W. Moody, ed.

Irish Unionism. Patrick Buckland.

Irish Whiskey. E. B. McGuire.

Iron Afloat: The Story of the Confederate Ironclads. William N. Still, Jr.

The Iron Age in the Irish Sea Province. Charles Thomas, ed.

The Iron Century: Social Change in Europe, 1550-1660. Henry Kamen.

The Iroquois in the American Revolution. Barbara Graymont.

Irrigation and Society in Medieval Valencia. Thomas F. Glick.

Isaac Williams and His Circle. O. W. Jones.

ISIS Cumulative Bibliography: A Bibliography of the History of Science Formed from ISIS.... Magda Whitrow, ed.

L'Islam des Origines au Début de l'Empire Ottoman. Claude Cohen.

Islam in Egypt Today. Social and Political Aspects of Popular Religion. Morroe Berger.

Islamic Education: Its Traditions and Modernization Into the Arab National Systems. A. L. Tibawi.

Islamic History, A. D. 600-750 (A. H. 132): A New Interpretation. M. A. Shaban.

Islamic Philosophy and the Classical Tradition.... S. M. Stern, et al., eds.

Israel: A Profile. Israel T. Naamani.

Israeli, Democracy, and the Tory Party: Conservative Leadership and Organization After the Second Reform Bill. E. J. Feuchtwanger.

It Began With Zade Usher. Yaffa Draznin.

The Italian-Americans. Luciano J. Iorizzo and Salvatore Mondello.

The Itasca Bison Kill Site: An Ecological Analysis. C. Thomas Shay.

Ivan Goncharov. Alexandra and Sverre Lyngstad.

Joe Louis. A. O. Edmonds.
Johann Martin Lappenberg: Ein
Beitrag zur Geschichte der
Geschichtswissenschaft im 19.
Jahrhundert. Rainer Postel.
John Brown. Richard Warch and
Jonathan F. Fanton, eds.
John Cartwright. John W. Osborne.
John Dee. The World of an Eliza-
bethan Magus. Peter J. French.
John D. Rockefeller. The Cleve-
land Years. Grace Goulder.
John Foster Dulles: A Statesman
and His Times. Michael A.
Guhin.
John Gorrie, M. D.: Father of
Air Conditioning and Mechanical
Refrigeration. Raymond B.
Becker.
John McIntosh Kell of the Raider
Alabama. Norman C. Delaney.
John Quincy Adams: A Personal
History of an Independent Man.
Marie B. Hecht.
John Strachey. Hugh Thomas.
John Woolman in England, 1772: A
Documentary Supplement. Henry
J. Cadbury.
Jordan: A Study in Political De-
velopment (1921-1965). Naseer
H. Aruri.
Joseph Addison's Sociable Animal:
In the Market Place on the Hust-
ings, in the Pulpit. Edward A.
and Lillian D. Bloom.
Joseph Banks in Newfoundland and
Labrador, 1766: His Diaries,
Manuscripts and Collections.
A. M. Lysaght.
Joseph E. Brown and the Politics of
Reconstruction. Derrell C.
Roberts.
Joseph Eötvös and the Modernization
of Hungary, 1840-1870: A Study
of Ideas of Individuality and So-
cial Pluralism in Modern Politics.
Paul Bödy.
Joseph Fels and the Single-Tax
Movement. Arthur Power Dudden.
Joseph Fourier, 1768-1830. I.
Grattan-Guinness.
Joseph Smith's New England Heri-
tage: Influences of Grandfathers
Solomon Mack and Asael Smith.
Richard Lloyd Anderson.
Joseph Story and the American Con-
stitution: A Study in Political
and Legal Thought With Selected

Writings. James McClellan.
Joshua R. Giddings and the Tactics
of Radical Politics. James
Brewer Stewart.
Josiah Royce: An Intellectual Bi-
ography. Bruce Kuklik.
The Journal and Major Essays of
John Woolman. Philip P. Moul-
ton, ed.
Journal of Glass Studies, Volume 13.
The Journal of John Fontaine: An
Irish Hugenot Son in Spain and
Virginia, 1710-1719. Edward
Porter Alexander, ed.
The Journal of Madam Knight. Mal-
colm Freiberg and Michael Mc-
Crudy.
The Journal of Samuel Curwen,
Loyalist. 2 volumes. Andrew
Oliver, ed.
A Journal of the Santa Fe Expedition
Under Colonel Doniphan. Jacob S.
Robinson.
Journal of the Senate of Virginia:
November Session, 1793. George
H. Reese and Patricia Hickin,
eds.
The Journals and Letters of Sir
Alexander Mackenzie. W. Kaye
Lamb, ed.
Journey Through a Part of the United
States of North America in the
Years 1844 to 1846. Albert C.
Koch.
The Joyous Journey of LeRoy R. and
Ann W. Hafen: An Autobiography.
LeRoy R. and Ann W. Hafen.
Juarez of Mexico. Wendell Blanché.
Die Juden und die deutsche Linke in
der Weimarer Republik. Hans-
Helmuth Knütter.
Judicial Politics in the Old Régime:
The Parlement of Paris During
the Regency. James D. Hardy,
Jr.
Judicial Review in Mexico: A Study
of the Amparo Suit. Richard D.
Baker.
The Jug and Related Stoneware of
Bennington. Cornelius Osgood.
Julius Caesar: Master of Men.
Monroe Stearns.
Die Jüngere Bronzezeit in Nordwest-
deutschland, Vol. 1: Die Bron-
zen. K. Tackenberg.
Jungle Alliance: Japan and Indian
National Army. Joyce C. Lebra.
Justice Joseph Story and the Rise

of the Supreme Court. Gerald
T. Dunne.
Juvenile Reform in the Progressive
Era: William R. George and the
Junior Republic Movement. Jack
M. Holl.

-K-

Das Kabinett Fehrenbach: 25. Juni
1920 bis 4. Mai 1921. Peter
Wulf, ed.
Das Kabinett Müller I and II. 2
volumes. Martin Vogt, ed.
Das Kabinett Scheidemann: 13.
Februar bis 20. Juni 1919.
Hagen Schulze, ed.
Kahlil Gibran: His Background,
Character and Works. Khalil
S. Hawi.
Kaiser Maximilian I, Band I. Her-
mann Wiesflecker.
Kamloops Cattlemen: One Hundred
Years of Trail Dust! T. Alex
Bulman.
The Kansa Indians: A History of
the Wind People, 1673-1873.
William E. Unrau.
Kansas Place Names. John Rydjord.
Karl Marx: Ideologie und Politik.
Peter Stadler.
Die Katholische Universität in Latein
amerika. André Delobelle.
Katyn: A Crime Without Parallel.
Louis FitzGibbon.
Kentucky Court and Other Records.
Julia Spencer Ardery.
The Kentucky Rifle. Merrill Lind-
say.
Kenyatta. Jeremy Murray-Brown.
Kiev Province. F. M. Rudych, et
al., eds.
Kievan Russia: A History of Russia.
George Vernadsky.
Kijik: An Historic Tanaina Indian
Settlement. James W. Vanstone
and Joan B. Townsend.
King Charles III of Spain. Sir
Charles Petrie.
King George III. John Brooke.
The King Strang Story: A Vindica-
tion of James J. Strang, The
Beaver Island Mormon King.
Doyle C. Fitzpatrick.
The King Who Lost America: A

Portrait of the Life and Times of
George III. Alan Lloyd.
King William IV. Philip Ziegler.
The Kingdom of Madison: A South-
ern Mountain Fastness and Its
People. Manly Wade Wellman.
The Kingdom of the Netherlands in
the Second World War. Vol. 4.
May 1940-March 1941. L. De
Jong.
Kingdoms and Strongholds of the
Crusades. T. S. R. Boase.
Kings and Philosophers 1689-1789.
Leonard Krieger.
Kino and Manje: Explorers of
Sonora and Arizona, Their Vision
of the Future.... Ernest J.
Burros.
Kirby Smith's Confederacy: The
Trans-Mississippi South, 1861-
1865. Robert L. Kerby.
The Korean War. Dean Acheson.
The Korean War. Lloyd C. Gard-
ner, ed.
Kōtoku Shūsui: Portrait of a Japa-
nese Radical. F. G. Notehelfer.
Die K P D von 1933 bis 1945. Horst
Duhnke.
Kumbukumbu za Vita uya Maji Maji,
1905-1907. G. C. K. Gwassa,
ed. and trans.
Die Kunst des Metalldrehens bei den
Römern. Alfred Mutz.
The Kurbskii--Groznyi Apocrypha:
The Seventeenth-Century Genesis
of the "Correspondence" Attrib-
uted to Prince A. M. Kurbskii
and Tsar Ivan IV. Edward L.
Keenan.
Kurt Breysig: Geschichtswissen-
schaft zwischen Historismus und
Soziologie. Bernhard vom Brocke.
Kuwait: Prospect and Reality.
Zahra Freeth and Victor Winstone.
Kwame Nkrumah: The Anatomy of
an African Dictatorship. T.
Peter Omari.
Kythera: Excavations and Studies
Conducted by the University of
Pennsylvania Museum and the
British School at Athens. J. N.
Coldstream and G. L. Huxley,
eds.

-L-

L. Q. C. Lamar: Pragmatic Patriot. James B. Murphy.
Labor and Socialism in America: The Gompers Era. William M. Dick.
Labor and Society in Tsarist Russia: The Factory Workers of St. Petersburg, 1855-1870. Reginald E. Zelnik.
Labor Force and Employment in Egypt: A Demographic and Socioeconomic Analysis. Mostafa H. Nagi.
Labor Organizations in the United States and Mexico: A History of Their Relations. Harvey A. Levenstein.
Laboratory for Liberty: The South Carolina Legislative Committee System, 1719-1776. George Edward Frakes.
Labour in the South African Gold Mines, 1911-1969. Francis Wilson.
Lacquer of the West: The History of a Craft and an Industry, 1550-1950. Hans Huth.
The Ladners of Ladner: By Covered Wagon to the Welfare State. Leon J. Ladner.
Lady Jane Grey: The Setting of the Reign. David Mathew.
The Lady Was a Bishop: The Hidden History of Women With Clerical Ordination and the Jurisdiction of Bishops. Joan Morris.
Lafayette in the French Revolution: From the October Days Through the Federation. Louis Gottschalk and Margaret Maddox.
Lame Deer, Seeker of Visions: The Life of a Sioux Medicine Man. John Lame Deer and Richard Erdoes.
Lamps and Other Lighting Devices, 1850-1906. Editors of Pyne Press, comps.
L'an 40. La Belgique Occupée. J. Gérard-Libois and José Gotovitch.
The Lancashire Textile Industry in the Sixteenth Century. Norman Lowe.
Land Above the Trees: A Guide to American Alpine Tundra. Ann H. Zwinger and Beatrice E. Willard.

Land and Industry: The Landed Estate and the Industrial Revolution: A Symposium. J. T. Ward and R. G. Wilson.
Land and People in Holywell-cum-Needingworth, Structures of Tenure and Patterns of Social Organization in an East Midlands Village: 1252-1457. Edwin Brezetto Dewindt.
The Land Beyond the River. Jesse Stuart.
Land Beyond the Rivers: The Southern Sudan, 1898-1918. Robert Collins.
Land Grab: The Truth About "The Winning of the West." John Upton Terrell.
The Land Question and the Irish Economy, 1870-1903. Barbara Lewis Solow.
Land Reform in Latin America: Issues and Cases. Peter Dorner, ed.
Land Revenue Administration Under the Mughals (1700-1750). Noman Ahmad Siddiqi.
Landbesitz und Gesellschaft am Vovabend des Bauernkriegs: Eine Studie der sozialen Verhältnisse im südlichen Oberschwaben in den Jahren vor 1525. David Warren Sabean.
Landlord and Peasant in Colonial Oaxaca. William B. Taylor.
Lands and Peoples: Vol. I, Africa; Vol. II, Asia, Australia, New Zealand, Oceania; Vol. III, Europe; Vol. IV, Europe; Vol. V, North America; Vol. VI, South and Central America; Vol. VII, The World Facts and Index. Martha Glauber Shapp, ed.
The Lands of St. Peter: The Papal State in the Middle Ages and Early Renaissance. Peter Partner.
Language and History in Africa. David Dalby, ed.
The Language of History in the Renaissance. Nancy S. Struever.
Las Vegas: As It Began--As It Grew. Stanley W. Paher.
The Last Boom. James A. Clark and Michel T. Halbouty.
The Last Campaign: Grant Saves the Union. Earl Schenck Miers.
The Last Cannon Shot: A Study of French-Canadian Nationalism

Jacques Monet.

The Last Captive. A. C. Greene.

The Last Foray: The South Carolina
Planter of 1860: A Sociological
Study. Chalmers Gaston David-
son.

The Last Liberal Governments:
Unfinished Business, 1911-1914.
Peter Rowland.

The Last Voyage of Drake and
Hawkins. Kenneth R. Andrews,
ed.

Late Roman Pottery: A Catalogue
of Roman Fine Wares. J. W.
Hayes.

Latimer: Belgic, Roman, Dark
Age, and Early Modern Farm.
K. Branigan, et al.

Latin America: A Concise Interpretative History. E. Bradford
Burns.

Latin America: A Guide to the Historical Literature. Charles C.
Griffin, ed.

Latin America and British Trade
1806-1914. D. C. M. Platt.

Latin America: New World, Third
World. Stephen Clissold.

The Latin American Military as a
Socio-Political Force: A Case
Study of Bolivia and Argentina.
Charles D. Corbett.

Latin American Politics: A Primer.
Arpad Von Lazar.

Latin American Thought: A Historical Interpretation. Harold
Eugene Davis.

Latin American University Students:
A Six-Nation Study. Arthur Kenneth Liebman.

Latin American Urbanization: A
Guide to the Literature, Organi-
zations and Personnel. Martin
H. Sable.

The Latin Americans: Past and
Present. Helen Miller Bailey
and Frank H. Cruz.

The Latin Kingdom of Jerusalem:
Europeanism in the Middle Ages.
Joshua Prawer.

The Laurel Culture in Minnesota.
James B. Stoltman.

Law and Disorder. James A. Forman.

Law and Society in the Visigothic
Kingdom. P. D. King.

Law and the Indo-China War. John
Norton Moore.

A Law of Blood: The Primitive
Law of the Cherokee Nation. John
Phillip Reid.

Law, Politics and Birth Control.
C. Thomas Dienes.

Lay Sermons. R. J. White, ed.

Lazare Carnot, Savant. Charles
Coulson Gillispie.

Leaders of the Church of England,
1828-1944. David L. Edwards.

Leadership and National Development
in North Africa: A Comparative
Study. Elbaki Hermassi.

Leadership in Crisis: FDR and the
Path to Intervention. Gloria J.
Barron.

The Learned Doctor William Ames:
Dutch Backgrounds of English and
American Puritanism. Keith L.
Sprunger.

Learned Letters From and To P. A.
Munch. Vol. 3.... Trygve
Knudsen and Per Sveaas Ander-
son, eds.

Leben und Taten der türkischen
Kaiser: Die anonyme vulgärgrie-
chische Chronik Codes Barberin-
ianus Graecus III (Anonymus
Zoras). Richard F. Kreutel, ed.
and trans.

The Legacy of Egypt. J. R. Harris,
ed.

The Legacy of George Ellery Hale:
Evolution of Astronomy and Sci-
entific Institutions in Pictures and
Documents. Helen Wright, Joan
N. Warnow and Charles Weiner,
eds.

Legacy of Glory: The Bonaparte
Kingdom of Spain, 1808-1813.
Michael Glover.

The Legacy of the German Refugee
Intellectuals. Robert Boyers, ed.

The Legend of John Brown: A Biography and a History. Richard
O. Boyer.

Legends of the Dutch. Adrian Van
Koevering.

Leges Henrici Primi. L. J.
Downer, ed.

Lehigh Valley the Unsuspected.
Richmond E. Myers.

Leicester and Its Region. N. Pye,
ed.

Leland Stanford: Man of Many
Careers. Norman C. Tutorow.

Lenin and the Communist International. Vol. I. Branko Lazitch

and Milorad M. Drachkovitch.
Leofric of Exeter: Essays in Com-
memoration of the Foundation of
Exeter Cathedral Library in
A. D. 1072. Frank Barlow, et
al.
Leon Trotsky and the Politics of
Economic Isolation. Richard B.
Day.
Leon Trotsky's 1905. Anya Bos-
tock, trans.
Leonard Wood and Cuban Independ-
ence, 1898-1902. James H.
Hitchman.
Leonardo da Vinci, The Royal
Palace at Romorantin. Carlo
Pedrett.
Lerna, a Preclassical Site in the
Argolid.... Lawrence J. Angel.
"Let Your Motto Be Resistance":
The Life and Thought of Henry
Highland Garnet. Earl Ofari.
Letcher County's Pine Mountain
Caves. Gary D. Jessey.
A Letter of Junipero Serra: A Bi-
centennial Discovery. Francis
J. Weber, ed. and trans.
The Letterbook of Eliza Lucas Pinck-
ney, 1739-1762. Elise Pinckney,
ed.
The Letterbook of Robert Pringle.
2 vols. Walter B. Edgar, ed.
The Letters and Papers of Chaim
Weizmann ... Vol. 3: September
1903-December 1904. W. Weisgal
Meyer, gen. ed.
Letters from Nevada Territory, 1861-
1862. Andrew J. Marsh.
The Letters of Daniel Eaton to the
Third Earl of Cardigan, 1725-
1732. Joan Wake and Deborah
Champion Webster, eds.
Letters of Louis D. Brandeis. 2
vols. Melvin I. Urofsky and
David W. Levy, eds.
The Letters of William Lloyd Gar-
rison.... Louis Ruchames, ed.
Lewis Evans and His Maps. Walter
Klinefelter.
Lewis Mumford: A Bibliography,
1914-1970. Elmer Newman, ed.
Lewis Namier, A Biography. Julia
Namier.
Liang Chi-ch'ao and Modern Chinese
Liberalism. Philip C. Huang.
Libellus de diversis ordinibus et
professionibus qui sunt in aec-
clesia. G. Constable and B.

Smith, eds. and trans.
Liberal Politics in the Age of Glad-
stone and Rosebery: A Study in
Leadership and Policy. D. A.
Hamer.
Liberation Ethics. John M. Swom-
ley, Jr.
The Liberation Movement in Russia
1900-1905. Shmuel Galai.
The Liberators: Filibustering Ex-
peditions into Mexico, 1848-1862,
and the Last Thrust of Manifest
Destiny. Joseph Allen Stout, Jr.
Liberty and Union: A History of the
United States. Martin Ridge,
Raymond J. Wilson and George
Spiero.
Liberty, Equality and Revolution in
Alexis de Tocqueville. Irving M.
Zeitlin.
Liberty of Conscience: The History
of a Puritan Idea. L. John Van
Til.
Library and Archives Conservation.
George Martin Cunha and Norman
Paul Tucker, eds.
Lieutenant Lee of Beale Street.
David M. Tucker.
The Life and Adventures of James
P. Beckwourth as Told to Thomas
D. Bonner. Delmont R. Oswald.
Life and Leisure in Ancient Rome.
J. P. V. D. Balsdon.
The Life and Times of Joseph Fish,
Mormon Pioneer. John H.
Krenkel, ed.
The Life and Works of John Wilson
Townsend. Dorothy Edwards
Townsend.
The Life and Writings of Francis
Makemie. Boyd S. Schlenther,
ed.
Life in Prairie Land. Eliza W.
Farnham.
The Life of Benjamin Banneker.
Silvio A. Bendini.
The Life of Brigadier General Wil-
liam Woodford of the American
Revolution. 2 vols. Mrs.
Catesby Willis Stewart.
The Life of George William Gordon.
Ansell Hart.
The Life of Saladin: From the
Works of Imad ad-Din and Bahá
ad-Din. Sir Hamilton A. R. Gibb.
The Limited Elite: Politics and
Government in Two Indian Univer-
sities. Donald B. Rosenthal.

sion, Insurgency, and Peacekeeping. Frank Kitson.

The Loyal Conspiracy: The Lords Appellant Under Richard II. Anthony Goodman.

Luce and His Empire. W. A. Swanberg.

Luddism in Nottinghamshire. M. I. Thomis, ed.

The Luddites: Machine-Breaking in Regency England. Malcolm I. Thomis.

Ludolf von Sagan und seine Stellung in der Auseinandersetzung um Konziliarismus und Hussitismus. Franz Machilek.

Ludvig Holberg's Memoirs: An Eighteenth-Century Danish Contribution to International Understanding. Stewart E. Fraser, ed.

Lumumba Speaks: The Speeches and Writings of Patrice Lumumba 1958-1961. Jean Van Lierde, ed.

Lutheranism in North America, 1914-1970. E. Clifford Nelson.

Lynchburg, Virginia ... "Its Industry, Enterprise and Correct Course." Philip Lightfoot Scruggs.

-M-

M. H. Baillie Scott and the Arts and Crafts Movement. James D. Kornwolf.

Macaulay: The Shaping of the Historian. John Clive.

McCartys of Virginia, With Emphasis on the First Four Generations in the Colony. Clara S. McCarty.

MacDonald of the 42nd. Donald Featherstone.

Machiavelli and the Nature of Political Thought. Martin Fleisher, ed.

McIntosh County Academy, McIntosh County, Georgia. Virginia Steele Wood.

The McKenny-Hall Portrait Gallery of American Indians. James D. Horan.

Mackinnon and East Africa, 1878-1895: A Study in the "New Imperialism." John S. Galbraith.

Mad Anthony Wayne and the New Nation: The Story of Washington's Front-Line General. Glen Tucker.

Magallanes, Sintesis de tierra y gentes. Mateo Martinč Beros.

The Magic War, the Battle for North Burma. Ian Fellow-Gordon.

The Magic World: American Indian Songs and Poems. William Brandon, ed.

The Magnificent West: Yosemite. Milton Goldstein.

Magyarorszag kulpolitikaja, 1919-1945. Gyula Juhasz.

Mahaffy: A Biography of an Anglo-Irishman. W. B. Stanford and R. B. McDowell.

Maharashtra in the Age of Shivaji. A. R. Kulkarni.

Main basse sur le Cameroun: Autopsie d'une de'colonisation. Mongo Beti.

The Majangir: Ecology and Society of a Southwest Ethiopian People. Jack Stauder.

The Maji Maji War in Ugoni. O. B. Mapunda and G. P. Mpangara.

Major Middle Eastern Problems in International Law. Majid Khadduri, ed.

Major Writers of Early American Literature. Everett Emerson, ed.

The Making and Limitations of the Yorkshire Domesday. R. Welldon Finn.

The Making of a Conglomerate. Charles Gilbert, ed.

The Making of an Arab Nationalist: Ottomanism and Arabism in the Life and Thought of Satic al-Husri. William L. Cleveland.

The Making of Black Revolutionaries: A Personal Account. James Forman.

The Making of Medieval Spain. Gabriel Jackson.

The Making of Modern Southeast Asia. Vol. 1: The European Conquest. D. J. M. Tate.

The Making of the Australian Constitution. J. A. La Nauze.

The Making of the Karagwe Kingdom: Tanzanian History from Oral Traditions. Israel K. Katoke.

The Making of the Modern World. Douglas Johnson, ed.

Makonde. Hermann Pollig, ed.

The Mallorys of Mystic. James P. Baughman.

Man and Culture in the Late Pleistocene: A Case Study. Richard

G. Klein.
Man and His Habitat--Essays Presented to Emyr Estyn Evans.
R. H. Buchanan, et al.
Man and the Computer. John G. Kemeny.
Man-Machine System Experiments. Henry McIlvaine Parsons.
Man of the Woods. Herbert F. Keith.
Man on Fire: John Brown and the Cause of Liberty. Jules Abels.
Man on Horseback: The Story of the Mounted Man from the Scythians to the American Cowboy. Glenn R. Vernam.
Man, State, and Society in Latin American History. Sheldon B. and Peggy K. Liss.
Man, State and Society in the Contemporary Middle East. Jacob M. Landau, ed.
The Man Who Lost America: A Biography of Gentleman Johnny Burgoyne. Paul Lewis.
The Man Who Searched for Henry Hudson. Richard A Belford.
The Managerial Revolution Reassessed: Family Control in America's Large Corporations. Philip H. Burch, Jr.
Managing the Modern Economy. Jan S. Hogendorn.
The Manchester Guardian: Biography of a Newspaper. David Ayerst.
Mandingo Kingdoms of the Senegambia: Traditionalism, Islam, and European Expansion. Charlotte A. Quinn.
Manifestations of Discontent in Germany on the Eve of the Reformation. Gerald Strauss, ed.
The Manufacturing Frontier: Pioneer Industry in Antebellum Wisconsin, 1830-1860. Margaret Walsh.
Many Pasts: Readings in American Social History. 2 volumes. Herbert G. Gutman and Gregory S. Kealey, eds.
Mao Tse-Tung and Gandhi. Jayantanuja Bandyopadhyaya.
Mapai in Israel. Peter Medding.
Maps: A Historical Survey of Their Study and Collecting. R. A. Skelton.
The March to the Right--A Case Study in Political Repression. Thomas Ford Hoult.

Marcus Garvey. Daniel S. Davis.
Margaret Bourke-White, Photojournalist. Theodore M. Brown.
Marginality and Identity: a Colored Creole Family Through Ten Generations. Sister Frances Jerome Woods.
Marine und Marinepolitik im kaiserlichen Deutschland, 1871-1914. Herbert Schottelius and Wilhelm Deist, eds.
Marlborough as Military Commander. David Chandler.
Marquette's Explorations: The Narratives Reexamined. Raphael N. Hamilton.
The Marquis de Custine and His Russia in 1839. George F. Kennan.
The Marquis de Mores: Dakota Capitalist, French Nationalist. D. Jerome Tweton.
Marshall Versus Jefferson: The Political Background of Marbury v. Madison. Donald O. Dewey.
Martí y su concepcion del mundo. Roberto D. Agramonte.
Martin R. Delany: The Beginnings of Black Nationalism. Victor Ullman.
The Maru Cult of the Pomo Indians: A California Ghost Dance Survival. Clement W. Meighan and Francis A. Riddell.
Marx and Marxism. Iring Fetscher.
Marxism and Art: Writings in Aesthetics and Criticism. Berel Lang and Forrest Williams, eds.
Marxism and the Origins of British Socialism: The Struggle for a New Consciousness. Stanley Pierson.
Marxisme et le Monde Musulman. Maxime Rodinson.
Mary Adelaide Nutting, Pioneer of Modern Nursing. Helen E. Marshall.
Mary Kingsley ... Explorer in West Africa. Signe Höjer.
Mary Todd Lincoln: Her Life and Letters. Justin G. and Linda Levitt Turner.
Maryland in Africa: The Maryland State Colonization Society, 1831-1857. Penelope Campbell.
Maryland: The Federalist Years. L. Marx. Renzulli, Jr.
Masones comuneros y carbonarios.

Iris M. Zavala.

Masquerade Peace: America's UN Policy, 1944-1945. Thomas M. Campbell.

Massachusetts Bay: The Crucial Decade, 1640-1650. Robert E. Wall, Jr.

The Massacre of St. Bartholomew and the European Conflict, 1559-1572. Nicola M. Sutherland.

Master Planning the Aviation Environment. Angelo J. Cerchione, Victor E. Rothe and James Vercellina, eds.

Matanza, El Salvador's Communist Revolt of 1932. Thomas P. Anderson.

Mathematics in the Archaeological and Historical Sciences: Proceedings of the Anglo-Romanian Conference, Mamaia, 1970.... F. R. Hodson, et al., eds.

The Mathers: Three Generations of Puritan Intellectuals, 1596-1728. Robert Middlekauff.

Maurice Barrès et le nationalisme français. Zeev Sternhell.

The Maurice Case: From the Papers of Major-General Sir Frederick Maurice.... Nancy Maurice, ed.

Mayakovsky and His Circle. Viktor Shklovsky.

Mbiru: Popular Protest in Colonial Tanzania. I. N. Kimambo.

The Meaning of Freedom of Speech. Paul A. Murphy.

A Measure Filled: The Life of Lena Madesin Phillips. Lisa Sergio.

Médecins, climat et epidémies à la fin du XVIIIe siècle. Jean-Paul Desaive, et al.

Medical Education in Oklahoma: The University of Oklahoma School of Medicine and Medical Center, 1900-1931. Mark R. Everett.

Medicine in North Carolina ... 2 volumes. Dorothy Long, ed.

Medicine on the Santa Fe Trail. Thomas B. Hall.

The Medieval Architect. John Harvey.

The Medieval Economy and Society: An Economic History of Britain in the Middle Ages, 1100-1500. M. M. Postan.

Medieval Ireland c. 1170-1495: A Bibliography of Secondary Works.

P. W. A. Asplin.

Medieval London. Timothy Baker.

Medieval Monarchy in Action: The German Empire from Henry I to Henry IV. Boyd H. Hill, Jr.

Medieval Portraits from East and West. Eleanor Duckett.

Medieval Regions and Their Cities. Josiah Cox Russell.

Medieval Trade and Finance. M. M. Postan.

Medieval Wales. R. Ian Jack.

A Mediterranean Society, the Jewish Community of the Arab World as Portrayed in the Documents of the Cairo Geniza. Vol. II. The Community. S. D. Goitein.

The Mediterranean Valleys: Geological Changes in Historical Times. Claudio Vita-Finzi.

The Meeting of Symeon and Nicholas Mysticus (August 913).... Alkemene Stauridou-Zaphrada.

Megaliths in History. Glyn Daniel.

The Megastates of America: People, Politics and Power in the Ten Great States. Neal R. Peirce.

The Meiji Restoration. W. G. Beasley.

Memoirs, 1950-1963. Vol. II. George F. Kennan.

Memoirs of a Quick Glance at My Various Travels and My Sojourn in the Creek Nation. Louis Le Clerc Milfort.

Memoirs of a Swiss Officer in the American Civil War. Rudolph Aschmann.

Memoirs of Hope: Renewal and Endeavor. Charles De Gaulle.

Memoriales o Libro de las casas de la Nueva Espana y de las Naturales de Ella. Fray Taribio de Benavente o Mololinía.

Memoriales y discursos de Francisco Martinez de Mata. Gonzalo Anes, ed.

The Memphis "Commercial Appeal": The History of a Southern Newspaper. Thomas Harrison Baker.

Men, Beasts, and Gods: A History of Cruelty and Kindness to Animals. Gerald Carson.

The Men of Cajamarca: A Social and Biographical Study of the First Conquerors of Peru. James Lockhart.

Men of Intelligence: A Study of the

Roles and Decisions of Chiefs of
Intelligence from World War I to
the Present Day.   Kenneth Strong.
Men of Letters in Colonial Mary-
land.   J. A. Leo Lemay.
The Men of the First French Repub-
lic.   Political Alignments in the
National Convention of 1792.
Alison Patrick.
Men Who Play God: The Story of
the Hydrogen Bomb.   Norman
Moss.
Merchant Congressmen in the Young
Republic: Samuel Smith of Mary-
land, 1752-1839.   Frank A. Cas-
sell.
Merchants and Manufacturers: Stud-
ies in the Changing Structure of
Nineteenth-Century Marketing.
Glenn Porter and Harold C. Live-
say.
Merchants and Moneymen: The Com-
mercial Revolution, 1000-1500.
Joseph and Frances Gies.
Merle Evans: Maestro of the Circus.
Gene Plowden.
Merovingian Military Organization,
481-751.   Bernard S. Bachrach.
Metal-Mining in Peru, Past and
Present.   W. F. C. Purser.
Metal Uniform Insignia of the Fron-
tier U. S. Army 1846-1902.
Sidney B. Brinckerhoff.
Methodism in the City of Lincoln.
W. Leary.
Methodism in Central Pennsylvania,
1771-1969.   Frederick E. Maser.
Methodism in the Town of Boston.
W. Leary.
Metrolina Atlas   James W. Clay
and Douglas M. Orr, Jr., eds.
Metternich.   Alan Palmer.
Metternich et al France après le
Congrès de Vienne.   Vol. 3. Guil-
laume de Bertier de Sauvigny.
Metternich's Projects for Reform in
Austria.   Egon Radvany.
Mexican Americans: Sons of the
Southwest.   Ruth S. Lamb.
The Mexican Economy: Twentieth-
Century Structure and Growth.
Clark W. Reynolds.
Mexican Revolution: The Constitu-
tionalist Years.   Charles C. Cum-
berland.
Mexican Society During the Revolu-
tion: A Literary Approach.   John
Rutherford.

The Mexican War Diary of Thomas
D. Tennery.   D. E. Livingston-
Little, ed.
Mexico.   Robert E. Quirk.
Mexico and the Old Southwest:
People, Palaver, and Places.
Haldeen Braddy.
México y los Estados Unidos en el
Conflicto petrolero, 1917-1942.
Lorenzo Meyer.
Michael Collins--The Lost Leader.
Margaret Forester.
Michigan Place Names.   Walter
Romig.
Midas of the Rockies: The Story of
Stratton and Cripple Creek.
Frank Waters.
Midcentury America: Life in the
1850's.   Carl Bode, comp. and
ed.
Mid-Century Revolution, 1848:   So-
ciety and Revolution in France
and Germany.   Robert W. Lougee.
The Middle East: A Political and
Economic Survey.   Peter Mans-
field, ed.
The Middle East and North Africa,
1972-73.
The Middle East Today.   Don
Peretz.
Midnight Was My Cry: New and
Selected Poems.   Carolyn Kizer.
Mid-Victorian Britain, 1851-1875.
Geoffrey Best.
Migration and Urban Development:
A Reappraisal of British and
American Long Cycles.   Brinley
Thomas.
Mike: The Memoirs of the Right
Honourable Lester B. Pearson.
Vol. 1.   1897-1948.   Lester B.
Pearson.
Mikhail Kuzmin's Wings: Prose and
Poetry.   Neil Granoien and
Michael Green, eds. and trans.
Militari e politici nella preparazione
della campagna d'Etiopia: Studio
e documento, 1932-1936.   Giorgio
Rochat.
Military Aid and Counterrevolution
in the Third World.   Miles D.
Wolpin.
Military Bibliography of the Civil
War.   Vol. 3.   C. E. Dorn-
busch, comp.
Military Leaders in the Civil War.
Joseph B. Mitchell.
The Military Life of Abraham Lin-

coln: Commander-in-Chief.
Trevor Nevitt Dupuy.
Military Professionalization and
Political Power. Bengt Abra-
hamsson.
Military Writings. Leon Trotsky.
Millénaire monastique du Mont Saint-
Michel. Vol. 3. Marcel Baudot,
ed.
Milligan's Fight Against Lincoln.
Darwin Kelley.
La Mineria Hispana e Iberoam-
erica.... 7 numbered vols.
Mines and Quarries of the Indians
of California. Robert F. Heizer
and Adam E. Treganza.
Minetown, Milltown, Railtown: Life
in Canadian Communities of Single
Industry. Rex A. Lucas.
Miniature Wood Carvings of Africa.
William Fagg.
The Minnesota Messenia Expedition:
Reconstructing a Bronze Age Re-
gional Environment. William A.
McDonald and George R. Rapp,
Jr., eds.
Minnesota's Major Historic Sites: A
Guide. June Drenning Holmquist
and Jean A. Brookins.
The Minoans: The Story of Bronze
Age Crete. Sinclair Hood.
The Minorities in Israel: Trends in
the Development of the Arab and
Droz Communities 1948-1973. Ori
Stendel.
Minutes of Managers' Meetings,
1799-1900. Royal Institution of
Great Britain. Archives.
Le mirage égyptien dans la littéra-
ture grecque d'Homère à Aristotle.
Christian Froidefond.
The Mirage of Power: British For-
eign Policy, 1902-22. 3 vols.
C. J. Lowe and M L. Dockrill.
Mirza Malkum Khan: A Biographical
Study of Iranian Modernism. Hamid
Algar.
Miscellaneous Ancient Records of
Moore County, North Carolina.
Rassie E. Wicker.
A Missão Bellgarde ao Paraguai,
1849-1852. 3 vols. José Antônio
Soares de Souza.
Mission Among the Blackfeet. Howard
L. Harrod.
Mission and Liturgie in Mexiko.
Jakob Baumgartner.
La mission de Jean Mounet à Alger:

mars-octobre 1943. André Kaspi.
Mission San Antonio de Padua: The
Mission in the Sierras. Zephyrin
Engelhardt.
Mission to the Cherokees. O. B.
Campbell.
The Mississippi Chinese: Between
Black and White. James W.
Loewen.
Mississippi Folklore: A Research
Bibliography and Discography.
William R. Ferris, Jr.
Mr. Jefferson, Architect. Desmond
Guinness and Julius Trousdale
Sadler, Jr.
Mr. Joyce is Leaving Paris. Tom
Gallacher.
Mr. Republican: A Biography of
Robert A. Taft. James T. Pat-
terson.
Mitninske knifge 16. in 17. stoletja
na Slovenskem. Ferdo Gestrin.
Mittelstand, Demokratie und Na-
tionalsozialismus.... Heinrich
August Winkler.
Mobile Americans: Residential and
Social Mobility in Omaha, 1880-
1920. Howard P. Chudacoff.
Mobility and the Small Town, 1900-
1930: Transportation Change in
Oregon, Illinois. Norman T.
Moline.
Modelli di Edifici Estrusco-Italici:
I Modelli Votivi. Romolo A.
Staccioli.
A Modern Arabic Biography of Mu-
hammad: A Critical Study of
Muhammad Husayn Haykal's
Hayāt Muhammed. Antonie Wes-
sels.
Modern British Farming Systems:
An Introduction. Frank H. Gar-
ner, ed.
The Modern British Monarchy. J.
A. Thompson and Arthur Mejia,
Jr.
Modern European Social History.
Robert J. Bezucha.
Modern Irish Literature: Essays in
Honor of William York Tindall.
Raymond J. Porter and James D.
Brophy, eds.
Modern Revolutions: An Introduction
to the Analysis of a Political
Phenomenon. John Dunn.
Modern Russia. John Robottom.
The Modern Supreme Court. Robert
G. McCloskey.

Modernization: Latecomers and Survivors. Marion J. Levy, Jr.

The Modernization of Irish Society 1848-1918. Joseph Lee.

Modoc War: Its Military History and Topography. Erwin N. Thompson.

Monarchy and Revolution: The English State in the 1680's. J. R. Western.

Le Monde de L'Automobile.

Le monde grec et l'Orient. Volume 1. Le Ve siècle (510-603). Edouard Will.

Monnaie et histoire d'Alexandre a Mahomet. Maurice Lombard.

Monographs and Papers in Maya Archaeology. William R. Bullard, Jr. ed.

Montgomery. Ronald Lewin.

Montgomery College: Maryland's First Community College, 1946-1970. William Lloyd Fox.

The Mooney Case. Richard H. Frost.

Moralphilosophie und Naturrecht bei Samuel Pufendorf.... Horst Denzer.

The Moravian Potters in North Carolina. John Bivins, Jr.

The Morleys: Young Upstarts on the Southwest Frontier. Norman Cleaveland.

Mormon Battalion Trail Guide. Charles S. Peterson, et al.

The Mortal Napoleon III. Roger L. Williams.

Mosaics in Roman Britain. Anne Rainey.

Moscow and the West. S. F. Platonov.

The Most Delightful Country of the Universe: Promotional Literature of the Colony of Georgia, 1717-1734. Trevor R. Reese, intro.

Motherless Families. Victor George and Paul Wilding.

El motín de Aranjuez. Francisco Martí Gilabert.

The Mountain States of America: People, Politics, and Power in the Eight Rocky Mountain States. Neal R. Pierce.

Le mouvement syndical au Liban (1919-1946)... Jacques Couland.

The Movement for Peace Without a Victory During the Civil War. Elbert J. Benton.

Movements in European History. D. H. Lawrence.

Movimentos revolucionarios de Latin America. Alejandro Del Corro.

The Moving American. George W. Pierson.

Mudie's Circulating Library and the Victorian Novel. Guinevere L. Griest.

Mug House: Mesa Verde National Park--Colorado. Arthur H. Rohn.

La Mujer Paraguaya: Su Participación en la Guerra Grande. Olinda Massare de Kostianovsky.

Murder and Witchcraft in England, 1550-1640, as Recounted in Pamphlets, Ballads, Broadsides and Plays. Joseph H. Marshburn.

Murder in Baghdad. Salāh 'Abd al-Sabūr.

Murder of Democracy. Balraj Madhok.

Murder, 1776 and Washington's Policy of Silence. William H. W. Sabine.

Music and Society in Lowland Scotland in the Eighteenth Century. David Johnson.

Music in the Service of the King: France in the Seventeenth Century. Robert M. Isherwood.

Music of the Americas: An Illustrated Music Ethnology of the Eskimo and American Indian Peoples. Paul Collaer, ed.

Muslim Rule in India: The Assessments of British Historians. J. S. Grewal.

The Muslims of British India. P. Hardy.

Mussolini and Fascism: The View from America. John P. Diggins.

Mussolini's Italy: Twenty Years of the Fascist Era. Max Gallo.

My Beloved Zebulon: The Correspondence of Zebulon Baird Vance and Harriet Newell Espy. Elizabeth Roberts Cannon, ed.

My Dear Wister: The Frederic Remington-Owen Wister Letters. Ben Merchant Vorpahl.

My Life and Experiences Among Our Hostile Indians: A Record of Personal Observations, Adventures, and Campaigns Among the Indians of the Great West. Oliver O. Howard.

ist Appeals to German Labor,
1919-1933. Max H. Kele.
The Near East in Modern Times.
Vol. I. George G. Arnakis.
The Near East in Modern Times.
Vol. II. George C. Arnakis
and Wayne S. Vucinich.
La Nécropole Gallo-Romaine de
Blicquy. Vol. XIV. S. J. De
Laet, A. Van Doorselaer, P.
Spitaels and H. Thoen.
Négociants bordelais et colons de
Saint-Dominque.... Françoise
Thésée.
The Negro in American Culture.
Margaret Just Butcher.
The Negro in Savannah, 1865-1900.
Robert E. Perdue.
Negro Ironworkers of Louisiana,
1718-1900. Marcus Christian.
The Negro on the American Frontier.
Kenneth W. Porter.
Nehru: A Political Biography.
Michael Edwardes
Nehru: The Humanist. Girijo K.
Mookerjee.
Neighbors on Separate Roads: Fin-
nish-Swedish Cooperation in the
Finnish and Swedish Foreign Pol-
cies, 1921-1923. Jorma Kalela.
Neither Black Nor White: Slavery
and Race Relations in Brazil and
the United States. Carl N. Degler.
Neither Slave nor Free: The Freed-
man of African Descent in the
Slave Societies of the New World.
David W. Cohen and Jack P.
Greene, eds.
Nelson the Commander. Geoffrey
Bennett.
The Neolithic and Bronze Ages.
S. A. Immerwahr.
The New Cambridge Modern History.
Vol. IV. The Decline of Spain
and the Thirty-Years' War, 1609-
48/59. J. P. Cooper, ed.
The New Citizenship: Origins of
Progressivism in Wisconsin, 1885-
1900. David P. Thelen.
The New Deal Art Projects: An
Anthology of Memoirs. Francis
V. O'Connor.
The New Deal in the Suburbs: A
History of the Greenbelt Town
Program, 1935-1954. Joseph L.
Arnold.
New England Glass and Glassmaking.
Kenneth M. Wilson.

The New Found Land of Stephen
Parmenius. David B. Quinn and
Noel Cheshire.
A New History of Ireland. R. Dud-
ley Edwards.
A New History of the Countries of
Latin America. M. S. Al'Pero-
vich and L. IU. Slezkin.
The New Left and the Origins of the
Cold War. Robert James Mad-
dox.
New Left Diplomatic Histories and
Historians: The American Revi-
sionists. Joseph M. Siracusa.
New Lights on Joyce. Fritz Senn,
ed.
New Mexico Past and Present: A
Historical Reader. Richard N.
Ellis, ed.
New Orleans Architecture. Vol. II.
The American Sector. Mary
Louise Christovich, et al., comps.
and eds.
New Perspectives on the Pueblos.
Alfonso Ortiz, ed.
The New Political Economy of J. S.
Mill. Pedro Schwartz.
The New Tsars: Russia Under
Stalin's Heirs. John Dornberg.
The New Woman: Feminism in
Greenwich Village, 1910-1920.
June Sochen.
The New York Abolitionists: A Case
Study of Political Radicalism.
Gerald Sorin.
The New York Public Library: A
History of Its Founding and Early
Years. Phyllis Dain.
The New York Volunteers in Cali-
fornia. Francis Clark and James
Lynch.
The Niagara. Donald Braider.
The Nicaragua Route. David I.
Folkman, Jr.
Niger Delta Rivalry: Itsekiri-Urhobo
Relations and the European Pres-
ence 1884-1936. Obaro Ikime.
The Night Unstones. George Ellen-
bogen.
Nightfall at Nauvoo. Samuel W.
Taylor.
Nikolaev Province. V. O. Vasyl'ev,
et al., eds.
1942: Guerra no Continente. Hélio
Silva.
1914. Delusion or Design? The
Testimony of Two German Diplo-
mats. John Röhl.

1905. Leon Trotsky.
1972: Yearbook on International
Communist Affairs. Richard F.
Starr, ed.
1939: Véspera de guerra. Hélio
Silva.
The Nineteenth-Century Foreign
Office: An Administrative His-
tory. Ray Jones.
Nineteenth-Century Louisiana Paint-
ers and Paintings from the Col-
lection of W. E. Graves. Martin
and Margaret Wiesendanger.
No Cause for Indictment: An
Autopsy of Newark. Ron Porambo.
No Clear and Present Danger: A
Skeptical View of the United
States Entry Into World War II.
Bruce M. Russett.
No Peace Beyond the Line: The
English in the Caribbean, 1624-
1690. Carl and Roberta Briden-
baugh.
The Noble Experiment of Warren C.
Coleman. J. K. Rouse.
Noch ist Deutschland nicht verloren:
Eine historisch-politische Analyse
unterdrückter Lyrik von der
Französischen Revolution bis zur
Reichsgründung. Walter Grab
and Uwe Friesel.
Non-Alignment: Theory and Current
Policy. Leo Mates.
The Noorderkwartier: A Study in
the Demographic and Economic
History of Western Parts of the
Netherlands from the end of the
Middle Ages till the Beginning of
the Nineteenth Century. A. M
Van Der Woude.
North America Divided: The Mex-
ican War, 1846-1848. Seymour
V. Connor and Odie B. Faulk.
North Carolina Higher Court Records,
1697-1701. Mattie Erma Ed-
wards Parker, ed.
North-Central Washington Prehistory.
G. F. Grabert.
North for the Trade: The Life and
Times of a Berber Merchant.
John Waterbury.
Northern Italy Before Rome. Lawr-
ence Barfield.
The Northwest Coast: Or Three
Years' Residence in Washington
Territory. James G. Swan.
Norwegian-American Studies. Vols.
24 and 25. Kenneth O. Bjork, ed.

Not Slaves, Not Citizens. Peter
Biskup.
Notable American Women, 1607-
1950. ... Edward T. and Janet
Wilson James and Paul S. Boyer,
eds.
Il notaio a Genova tra prestigio e
potere. Giorgio Costamagna.
Notaries Public in England. C. R.
Cheney.
Notes from the Land of the Dead.
Thomas Kinsella.
Nothing Too Daring: A Biography
of Commodore David Porter 1780-
1843. David F. Long.
The Novel of Manners in America.
James W. Tuttleton.
Novoe naznachenie. Alexander Bek.
Novy kolokol. ... Nadezhda Be-
linkov, et al., eds.
Nuba Personal Art. James C.
Faris.
Nuclear Politics: The British Ex-
perience With an Independent
Strategic Force, 1939-1970.
Andrew J. Pierre.
The Nyoro State. John Beattie.
Nyungu-ya-Mawe. Aylward Shorter.

-O-

O Jerusalem! Larry Collins and
Dominique Lapierre.
O Recrutamento politico em Minos,
1890-1918. ... David M. Flei-
scher.
Oak and Ivy: A Biography of Paul
Laurence Dunbar. Addison
Gayle.
Oboronnaia promyshlennost' sovet-
skoi Rossii v 1918-1920 gg. D.
A. Kovalenko.
The Occult Sciences in the Renais-
sance: A Study in Intellectual
Patterns. Wayne Shumaker.
Occupation Housewife. Helena Z.
Lopata.
Occupied America: The Chicano's
Struggle Toward Liberation.
Rodolfo Acuña.
The Oder-Neisse Boundary and Po-
land's Modernization: The Socio-
economic and Political Impact.
Anthony Z. Kruszewski.
Of Laws in General. Jeremy Bentham.

Of Mother Country and Plantations:
Proceedings of the Twenty-Seventh
Conference in Early American
History. Virginia Bever Platt
and David Curtis Skaggs, eds.
Off Course: From Truman to Nixon.
Rexford G. Tugwell.
Offenbarung und Geschichte im
Denken Moderner Muslime.
Rotraud Wielandt.
Office-Holders in Modern Britain.
Vol. 1: Treasury Officials, 1660-
1870. J. C Sainty, comp.
Official Documents Concerning
Dutch-Indonesian Relations, 1945-
1950. S. L. Van Der Wal, ed.
Oil: A Study of War-Time Policy
and Administration. D. J. Pay-
ton-Smith.
Oil and the Mexican Revolution.
Merrill Rippy.
Oil Rivers Trader. Raymund Gore
Clough.
Okla Hannali. R. A. Lafferty.
Oklahoma: The Forty-Sixth Star.
Alice Marriott and Carol K.
Rachlin.
Old Brownsville Days: An Historical
Sketch of Early Times in Jackson
County, Illinois. Will W. Hus-
band.
The Old Dominion and the New
Nation, 1788-1801. Richard R.
Beeman.
The Old-Fashioned Dutch Oven Cook
Book: Complete With Authentic
Sourdough Baking, Smoking Fish
and Game, Making Jerky, Pem-
mican and Other Lost Campfire
Arts. Don Holm.
Old Hatreds and Young Hopes: The
French Carbonari Against the
Bourbon Restoration. Alan B.
Spitzer.
Old Houses of New Mexico and the
People Who Built Them. Sytha
Motto.
Old Louisiana Plantation Homes and
Families. 2 vols. Herman de
Bachelle Seebold.
Old Santa Fe Today. The Historic
Santa Fe Foundation.
The Old South: A Psychohistory.
Earl E. Thorpe.
The Old World Background of the
Irrigation System of San Antonio,
Texas. Thomas F. Glick.
The Older Sophists. Rosamond Kent

Sprague, ed.
Oliver Cromwell. C. V. Wedg-
wood.
Oltenia Under Austrian Rule (1718-
1739). Serban Papacostea.
Oman.
On Doing Good: The Quaker Ex-
periment. Gerald Jonas.
On the Border With Crook. John
C. Bourke.
On the Mother Lode. Philip Ross
May.
One Hundred California Hiking Trails.
Don and Roberta Lowe.
100 años del ejército peruano.
Victor Villanueva.
One Million Men: The Civil War
Draft in the North. Eugene C.
Murdock.
Oneida Community: The Breakup,
1876-1881. Constance Noyes
Robertson.
Oneida: Utopian Community to
Modern Corporation. Maren
Lockwood Carden.
Only a Miner: Studies in Recorded
Coal-Mining Songs. Archie
Green.
The Only Good Indian: The Holly-
wood Gospel. Ralph and Natasha
Friar.
The "Open" Commonwealth. M.
Margaret Ball.
Open Field Farming in Medieval
England. Warren O. Ault.
Open Shelves and Open Minds: A
History of the Cleveland Public
Library. C. H. Cramer.
Open Veins of Latin America: Five
Centuries of the Pillage of a
Continent. Eduardo Galeano.
The Oppenheimer Hearing. John
Major.
The Optional Society: An Essay on
Economic Choice and Bargains
of Communication in an Affluent
World. Folke and Karin Dovring.
Orange, Virginia: Story of a Court-
house Town. William H. B.
Thomas.
The Ordeal of Nationhood: A Social
Study of India Since Independence.
Krishnan Bhatia.
The Ordering of the Arts in Eight-
eenth-Century England. Lawr-
ence Lipking.
The Oregon Trail Revisited. Greg-
ory M. Franzwa.

Orestes A. Brownson's Road to
Catholicism.   Per. Sveino.
Orestes Brownson and the American
Republic: An Historical Perspec-
tive.   Hugh S. T. Marshall.
Die Organisation der eingetragenen
Genossenschaft in den zum eng-
lischen Rechtskreis gehörenden
Ländern Schwarzafrikas dargestelt
am Beispiel Ghanas.   Hans-H.
Münkner.
The Oriental Americans.   H. Brett
Melendy.
Origin and History of Howard
County.   Charles Francis Stein,
Jr.
The Origin of Homo sapiens: Pro-
ceedings of the Paris Symposium
on Ecology and Conservation.   F.
Bordes, ed.
The Origins and Growth of Archae-
ology.   Glyn Daniel.
The Origins of American Intervention
in the First World War.   Ross
Gregory.
The Origins of Capitalism in Russia:
Industry and Progress in the Six-
teenth and Seventeenth Centuries.
Joseph T. Fuhrmann.
The Origins of Franco's Spain: The
Right, the Republic and the Revo-
lution.   Richard Robinson.
Origins of Papal Infallibility, 1150-
1350: A Study on the Concepts of
Infallibility, Sovereignty and Tra-
dition in the Middle Ages.   Brian
Tierney.
The Origins of Socialism in Cuba.
James O'Connor.
The Origins of Polish Socialism:
The History and Ideas of the First
Polish Socialist Party, 1878-1886.
Lucjan Blit.
Origins of the Chinese Revolution,
1915-1949.   Lucien Bianco.
The Origins of the Civil War.   Duane
Cummins and William Gee White.
The Origins of the Peloponnesian
War.   G. E. M. De Ste Croix.
Origins of the Urban School: Public
Education in Massachusetts 1870-
1915.   Marvin Lazerson.
The Ormèe of Bordeaux: A Revolu-
tion During the Fronde.   Sal Alex-
ander Westrich.
The Oroz Codex.   Fray Pedro Oroz.
The Oroz Codex....   Angelico
Chavez, ed. and trans.

The Osage People.   W. David Baird.
OSS: The Secret History of Amer-
ica's First Central Intelligence
Agency.   R. Harris Smith.
Ostatnie Lata Rosji Carskiej: Rzady
Stolypina.   Ludwik Bazylow.
Osterreich: Ein Jahrtausend
Geschichte im Herzen Europas.
Rolf Bauer.
Osterreichische Wirtschaft 1848-
1913....   Herbert Matis.
The Otis Family in Provincial and
Revolutionary Massachusetts.
John J. Waters, Jr.
La Otra verdad.   La Independencia
Americana vista por los es-
pañoles.   Juan Friede.
Ottoman Diplomacy in Hungary.
Gustav Bayerle.
The Ottoman Empire and the Arabian
Peninsula, 1840-1909.   Rajab
Harrāz.
The Ottoman Empire, the Great
Powers, and the Straits Question,
1870-1887.   Barbara Jelavich.
Ottoman Imperialism During the Ref-
ormation: Europe and the Cau-
casus.   Carl Max Kortepeter.
Our Indian Wards.   George W.
Manypenny.
Our People and Our History.
Rodolphe Lucien Desdunes.
Our Western Heritage: A Cultural-
Analytic History of Europe Since
1500.   Daniel Roselle and Anne
P. Young.
Outcast London: A Study in the Re-
lationship Between Classes in
Victorian Society.   Gareth Sted-
man Jones.
Out of the Blue: United States Army
Airborne Operations in World
War II.   James A. Huston.
Over There: European Reaction to
Americans in World War I.
Robert C. Walton.
Overland Days to Montana in 1865:
The Diary of Sarah Raymond and
Journal of Dr. Ward Howard.
Raymond and Mary L. Settle, eds.
The Overland Stage to California.
Frank A. Root and William E.
Connelley.
The Overproduction Trap in U. S.
Agriculture: A Study of Resource
Allocation from World War I to
the Late 1960's.   Glenn L. John-
son and C. Leroy Quance, eds.

Owu in Yoruba History. A. L.
Mabogunje and J. Omer-Cooper.
The Oxford History of South Africa.
Vol. 2: South Africa, 1870-1966.
Monica Wilson and Leonard
Thompson, eds.

-P-

Pacific Circle 2: Proceedings of
the Third Biennial Conference of
the Australian and New Zealand
American Studies Association.
Norman Harper, ed.
Pacific Estrangement: Japanese and
American Expansion, 1897-1911.
Akira Iriye.
The Pacific Then and Now. Bruce
Bahrenburg.
Pacifism in Europe to 1914. Peter
Brock.
Pages From a Colorful Life: An
Autobiographical Sketch. Melech
Epstein.
Painted Ceramics of the Western
Mound at Awatovi. Watson Smith.
The Painter and the Photograph
from Delacroix to Warhol. Van
Deren Coke.
A Pair of Lawn Sleeves: A Biog-
raphy of William Smith (1727-
1803). Thomas Firth Jones.
Pakistan. Damodar P. Singhal.
Le paléolithique inférieur et moyen
du midi méditerranean dans son
cadre géologique. Henry de
Lumley-Woodyear.
Palestine Before and After. Yusuf
Haikal.
Palestine Papers, 1917-1922: Seeds
of Conflict. Doreen Ingrams,
comp.
Palestinian Nationalism: The Polit-
ical and Military Dimensions.
William B. Quandt.
Pan Africanism and Education: A
Study of Race Philanthropy and
Education in the Southern States
of America and East Africa. Ken-
neth James King.
Papa: Hemingway in Key West.
James McLendon.
Paper Making in the British Isles.
Alfred H. Shorter.
Papers in Economic Prehistory.

E. S. Higgs, ed.
The Papers of Adlai Stevenson. 2
vols. Walter Johnson and Carol
Evans, eds.
The Papers of Alexander Hamilton.
Vols. XVI and XVII. Harold C.
Syrett, et al., eds.
The Papers of Andrew Johnson.
Vol. III. LeRoy P. Graf, Ralph
W. Haskins and Patricia P.
Clark, eds.
The Papers of Benjamin Franklin.
Vol. 14. January 1 through De-
cember 31, 1767. Leonard W.
Labaree, et al., eds.
The Papers of Benjamin Franklin.
Volumes 15 and 17. William B.
Willcox, et al., eds.
The Papers of Henry Bouquet. Vol.
1. S. K. Stevens, et al., eds.
The Papers of Henry Clay. Vol. 4.
Secretary of State, 1825. James
F. Hopkins, et al., eds.
The Papers of Henry Laurens. Vols.
2 and 3. Philip M. Hamer, et
al., eds.
The Papers of James Madison. Vol.
8. Robert A. Rutland, et al.,
eds.
The Papers of Jefferson Davis,
Volume I: 1808-1840. Haskell
M. Monroe, Jr. and James T.
McIntosh, eds.
The Papers of John C. Calhoun.
Vols. 5 and 6. W. Edwin Hemp-
hill, ed.
The Papers of Joseph Henry. Vol.
1. Nathan Reingold, ed.
The Papers of the Prime Ministers.
The Letters of Sir John A. Mac-
donald. 2 vols. J. K. Johnson
and Carole B. Stelmack, eds.
The Papers of Thomas Jefferson.
Vols. 17 and 18. Julian P.
Boyd, ed.
The Papers of Thomas Jordan Jar-
vis. Vol. I. W. Buck Yearns,
ed.
The Papers of Ulysses S. Grant.
Vol. 4. John Y. Simon and
Roger D. Bridges, eds.
The Papers of Woodrow Wilson.
Volumes 11 and 12. Arthur S.
Link, et al., eds.
Papers on California and the Great
Basin Prehistory. Eric W. Rit-
ter, Peter D. Schulz and Robert
Kautz, eds.

tution. Jackson Turner Main.
Political Relations Between India
and Nepal, 1877-1923. Kanchan-
moy Mojumdar.
The Political Status of the Negro in
the Age of FDR. Ralph J. Bunche.
Political Tendencies in Louisiana.
Perry H. Howard.
The Political Thought of Bolivar:
Selected Writings. Gerald E.
Fitzgerald, ed.
Political Trends in the Arab World:
The Role of Ideas and Ideals in
Politics. Majid Khadduri.
Politics and Belief in Contemporary
France: Emmanuel Mounier and
Christian Democracy, 1932-1950.
R. William Rauch, Jr.
Politics and Culture in Medieval
Spain and Italy. Helene Wieru-
szowski.
Politics and History in the Soviet
Union. Nancy Whittier Heer.
Politics and Privilege in a Mexican
City. Richard R. Fagen and
William S. Tuohy.
Politics and Social Change in Third
World Countries. F. Lamond
Tullis.
Politics and the Bench. W. J. Jones.
Politics in the Gilded Age: A New
Perspective on Reform. John
M. Dobson.
Politics and the Labour Movement
in Chile. Alan Angell.
Politics and the Stages of Growth.
W. W. Rostow.
Politics in Independent Poland, 1921-
1939. The Crisis of Constitu-
tional Government. Anthony
Polonsky.
Politics, Language, and Time: Es-
says on Political Thought and
History. J. G. A. Pocock.
The Politics of a Literary Man:
William Gilmore Simms. Jon
L. Wakelyn.
The Politics of Afghanistan. Richard
S. Newell.
The Politics of Chaos: Canada in
the Thirties. H. Blair Neatby.
The Politics of Command: Factions
and Ideas in Confederate Strategy.
Thomas Lawrence Connelly and
Archer Jones.
The Politics of Continuity: Mary-
land Political Parties from 1858-
1870. Jean H. Baker.

Politics of Defense. David Owen.
The Politics of Depression: Polit-
ical Behavior in the Northeast,
1893-1896. Samuel T. McSeveney.
The Politics of Economic Reform in
the Soviet Union. Abraham Katz.
The Politics of Foreign Aid in the
Brazilian Northeast. Riordan
Roett.
The Politics of German Protestant-
ism: The Rise of the Protestant
Church Elite in Prussia, 1815-
1848. Robert M. Bigler.
The Politics of Government Growth:
Early Victorian Attitudes Toward
State Intervention, 1833-1848.
William C. Lubenow.
The Politics of Housing Innovation:
The Fate of the Civilian Industrial
Technology Program. Dorothy
Nelkin.
The Politics of Inertia. The Elec-
tion of 1876 and the End of Re-
construction. Keith Ian Polakoff.
The Politics of Iran: Groups,
Classes and Modernization. James
Alban Bill.
The Politics of Irish Literature.
Malcolm Brown.
The Politics of Jacksonian Finance.
John M. McFaul.
The Politics of Land Reform in
Chile, 1950-1970: Public Policy,
Political Institutions and Social
Change. Robert R. Kaufman.
The Politics of Mexican Develop-
ment. Roger D. Hansen.
The Politics of Normalcy: Govern-
mental Theory and Practice in
the Harding-Coolidge Era. Robert
K. Murray.
The Politics of Protection: Lord
Derby and the Protectionist
Party, 1841-1852. Robert
Stewart.
The Politics of Reform 1884.
Andrew Jones.
The Politics of Rescue: The Roose-
velt Administration and the Holo-
caust, 1938-1945. Henry L.
Feingold.
The Politics of Soviet Agriculture,
1960-1970. Werner G. Hahn.
Politics Without Parties: Massa-
chusetts, 1780-1791. Van Beck
Hall.
Die Politik des schwedischen Reich-
skanzlers Axel Oxenstierna

gegenüber Kaiser und Reich.
Sigmund Goetze.
Politische Partei und Parlamenta-
rische Opposition. Eine Studie
zum Politischen Denken von Lord
Bolingbroke und David Hume.
Wolfgang Jäger.
Der politische Widerstand gegen Rom
in Griechenland, 217-86 v. Chr.
Jürgen Deininger.
Polls: Their Use and Misuse in
Politics. Charles W. Roll, Jr.
and Albert H. Cantril.
Polygamy Was Better Than Monotony.
Paul Bailey.
The Ponca Chiefs: An Account of
the Trial of Standing Bear.
Thomas Henry Tibbles and Kay
Graber, eds.
Pont-de-Montvert: Social Structure
and Politics in a French Village,
1700-1914. Patrice L.-R. Higon-
net.
Poor Scholar: A Study of the Works
and Days of William Carleton
(1794-1869). Benedict Kiely.
The Popish Plot. John Kenyon.
Pops Foster: The Autobiography of
a New Orleans Jazzman....
La population Française au XIXe
siècle. André Armengaud.
Population Growth and Economic De-
velopment Since 1750. H. J.
Habakkuk.
Population History of New York City.
Ira Rosenwaike.
Population Pressure in Rural Ana-
tolia, 1450-1600. M. A. Cook.
Populations of the Middle East and
North Africa: A Geographical
Approach. J. I. Clarke and W.
B. Fisher, eds.
Portal to America: The Lower East
Side, 1870-1925. Allon Schoener,
ed.
Portrait of a Decade: Roy Stryker
and the Development of Documen-
tary Photography in the Thirties.
F. Jack Hurley.
Portrait of a Nationalist: The Life
of Ali Migeyo. G. R. Mutahaba.
Portraits of Thai Politics. Jayanta
Kumar Ray.
Portuguese Africa and the West.
William Minter.
Portuguese Plain Architecture: Be-
tween Spices and Diamonds.
George Kubler.

Postwar America, 1945-1971.
Howard Zinn.
Potter and Patron in Classical
Athens. T. B. L. Webster.
The Potter's Art in Africa. William
Fagg and John Picton.
The Pottery Trade of North Staf-
fordshire, 1660-1760. Lorna
Weatherill.
Pour une histoire de l'alimentation.
Jean-Jacques Hémardinquer, ed.
Poverty, Ethnic Identity, and Health
Care. Bonnie and Vern L. Bul-
lough.
Poverty in New York, 1783-1825.
Raymond A. Mohl.
Power and Diplomacy in Northern
Nigeria, 1804-1906: the Sokoto
Caliphate and Its Enemies. R.
A. Adeleye.
A Practical Approach to Secondary
Social Studies. Walter E. Sis-
trunk and Robert C. Maxson.
The Practice of History. Geoffrey
R. Elton.
Prähistorische Goldfunde aus Europa.
Axel Hartmann.
The Prairie School: Frank Lloyd
Wright and His Midwest Contem-
poraries. H. Allen Brooks.
The Pre-Columbian Mind. Fran-
cisco Guerra.
The Prediction of Communist Eco-
nomic Performance. P. J. D.
Wiles, ed.
Pré-história brasileiro.... Renato
Castelo Branco.
Prehistoric and Primitive Art.
Luis Pericot-Garcia, John Gallo-
way and Andreas Lommel.
The Prehistoric Antiquities of the
Maltese Islands: A Survey. J.
D. Evans.
Prehistoric Greece. Frank H.
Stubbings.
Prehistoric Villages in Eastern
Nebraska. David Mayer Grad-
wohl.
Prehistory: An Introduction. Derek
Roe.
The Pre-Industrial Economy in Eng-
land, 1500-1750. Leslie A.
Clarkson.
Preliminary Guide to the Smithsonian
Archives. Smithsonian Institu-
tion.
Le Préoccupations Statistiques de
Pays-Bas Autrichiens et le

denombrement des industries dresse' en 1764. Philippe Moureaux.

Pre-Reformation Germany. Gerald Strauss, ed.

Presence and Possibility: Louisville Catholicism and Its Cathedral. Clyde F. Crews.

The Presidency of Rutherford B. Hayes. Kenneth E. Davison.

The Presidency of William Howard Taft. Paolo E. Coletta.

President Charles Bradlaugh, M. P. David Tribe.

Presidents, Bureaucrats and Foreign Policy: The Politics of Organizational Reform. I. M. Destler.

The Press in the French Revolution. J. Gilchrist and W. J. Murray, eds.

The Preussische Staat und de Juden. 2 vols. Selma Stern-Taeubler.

The Price of Liberty; Personality and Politics in Colonial Nigeria. Kenneth W. J. Post and George D. Jenkins.

The Price Revolution in Sixteenth-Century England. Peter H. Ramsey, ed.

The Prime Ministers' Papers: W. E. Gladstone. I. Autobiographica. William Evart Gladstone.

Prince George's Heritage: Sidelights on the Early History of Prince George's Country from 1696 to 1800. Louise Joyner Hienton.

Prince of the Renaissance. The Golden Life of François I. Desmond Seward.

The Principality of Wales in the Later Middle Ages: The Structure and Personnel of Government. I. South Wales. Ralph A. Griffiths.

Principles of World Politics. George Modelski.

Printed Books to 1800. Vol. I. Margaret Canney and David Knott, comps.

Privacy in Colonial New England. David H. Flaherty.

Private Black Colleges at the Crossroads. Daniel C. Thompson.

Private Interest and Public Gain: The Dartmouth College Case, 1819. Francis N. Stites.

Private Investment in India, 1900-1939. Amiya Kumar Bagchi.

The Private Journal of Louis McLane, U. S. N. , 1844-48. Jay Monaghan, ed.

Privilege and Creative Destruction: The Charles River Bridge Case. Stanley I. Kutler.

Problems in Titian, Mostly Iconographic. Erwin Panofsky.

Proceedings of the Vinland Map Conference. Wilcomb E. Washburn, ed.

Procurate aborto nel mondo greco romano. Enzo Nardi.

A Productive Monopoly: The Effect of Railroad Control on New England Coastal Steamship Lines, 1870-1916. William Leonhard Taylor.

Productivity and Industrial Growth. The Irish Experience. Kiernan A. Kennedy.

The Profession of Dramatist in Shakespeare's Time 1590-1642. Gerald Eades Bentley.

Professional Forestry in the United States. Henry Clepper.

Profiles from the Susquehanna Valley. Paul B. Beers.

Progress in Historical Geography. Alan R. H. Baker.

The Progress of Society in Europe. William Robertson.

Progressives and Prohibitionists: Texas Democrats in the Wilson Era. Lewis L. Gould.

Prohibitions and Restraints in War. Sidney D. Bailey.

Project Paperclip: German Scientists and the Cold War. Clarence G. Lasby.

A Proof of Eminence: The Life of Sir John Hawkins. Bertram H. Davis.

The Prophet Harris--A Study of an African Prophet and His Mass Movement in the Ivory Coast and the Gold Coast, 1913-1915. Gordon M. Haliburton.

Prophet in Politics: Henry A. Wallace and the War Years, 1940-1965. Edward L. Schapsmeier and Frederick H. Schapsmeier.

A Pro-Slavery Crusade: The Agitation to Reopen the African Slave Trade. Ronald T. Takaki.

The Prose of Royall Tyler. Marius

Race and Races. Richard A.
Goldsby.
Race and the American Roman-
tics. Vincent Freimark and
Bernard Rosenthal, eds.
The Racial Attitudes of American
Presidents: From Abraham Lin-
coln to Theodore Roosevelt.
George Sinkler.
Racism in the United States: An
American Dilemma? David M.
Reimers, ed.
Racism in U. S. Imperialism: The
Influence of Racial Assumptions
on American Foreign Policy,
1893-1896. Francis Rubin Weston.
Radical Abolitionism: Anarchy and
the Government of God in Anti-
slavery Thought. Lewis Perry.
The Radical Brethren: Anabaptism
and the English Reformation to
1558. Irvin B. Horst.
The Radical Left and American For-
eign Policy. Robert Tucker.
Radical Political Economy: Capit-
alism and Socialism from the
Marxist-Humanist Perspective.
Howard Sherman.
The Radical Programme. Joseph
Chamberlain, et al.
The Raft Fishermen: Tradition and
Change in the Brazilian Peasant
Economy. Shephard Forman.
Railway Development in the Ottoman
Empire 1856-1914. Yaqub N.
Karbar.
Ralph J. Rivers, U. S. Representa-
tive to Congress from Alaska,
1959-1966.... Paul McCarthy,
comp.
The Rambler in Georgia.... Mills
Love, ed.
Ramon Lull and Lullism in Four-
teenth-Century France. J. N.
Hillgarth.
Ranch on the Laramie: A Memoir
of an American Boyhood. Ted
Olson.
The Randolphs of Virginia. Jonathan
Daniels.
The Rape of Ethiopia, 1936. A. J.
Barker.
The Rape of the Peasantry: Latin
America's Landholding System.
Ernest Feder.
Rapport des Archives Nationales du
Québec, 1971. Vol. 49. Quebec,
National Archives.

Raza y tierra. La guerra de castas
y el henequén. Moisés González
Navarro.
Readings in African International Re-
lations. Y. A. Tandon, ed.
Readings in Russian Poetics: Form-
alist and Structuralist Views.
Ladislav Mateijka and Krystina
Pomorska, eds.
Readings in the Latin American
Policy of the United States.
Thomas L. Karnes, ed.
Readings on Micro-Level Planning
and Rural Growth Centres. Lalit
K. Sen, ed.
Real del Monte: A British Mining
Adventure in Mexico. Robert W.
Randall.
Realignment of World Power: The
Russo-Chinese Schism. 2 vols.
Oton Ambroz.
Rebel Leadership, Commitment and
Charisma in the Revolutionary
Process. James V. Downton.
Rebellion: The Rising of French
Canada, 1837. Joseph Schull.
The Rebirth of Italy, 1943-50. S.
J. Woolf, ed.
Recent Locomotives.
Reconstruction in Indian Territory:
A Story of Avarice, Discrimina-
tion, and Opportunism. M.
Thomas Bailey.
Reconstruction to Reform: Texas
Politics 1876-1906. Alwyn Barr.
Recording East Africa's Past: A
Brief Guide for the Amateur His-
torian. Andrew Roberts.
Records of the Columbia Historical
Society of Washington, D. C.
Francis Coleman Rosenberger, ed.
Records of the Maji Maji Rising
(Part 1). G. C. K. Gwassa and
John Iliffe, eds.
The Recovery of France in the Fif-
teenth Century. P. S. Lewis, ed.
The Red Arrow: A History of One
of the Most Successful Suburban
Transit Companies in the World.
Ronald De Graw.
Red Capitali$m: An Analysis of the
Navajo Economy. Kent Gil-
breath.
The Red Man in the New World
Drama: A Politico-Legal Study
with a Pageantry of American
Indian History. Jennings C. Wise.
Red Man's Land/White Man's Law:

A Study of the Past and Present
Status of the American Indian.
Wilcomb E. Washburn.
Red Power on the Rio Grande: The
Native American Revolution of
1680. Franklin Folsom.
Reference Materials and Periodicals
in Economics.... Emma Lila
Fundaburk.
Reflections on Indian Politics.
M. M. Sankhdher.
Reform and Rebellion in Afghanis-
tan, 1919-1929: King Amanul-
lah's Failure to Modernize a
Tribal Society. Leon B. Poullada.
Reform Rule in Czechoslovakia: The
Dubček Era, 1968-1969. Galia
Golan.
Reform, War and Reaction: 1912-
1932. Stanley Coben, ed.
A Reforma agraria no Brasil. José
Gomes Da Silva.
Reformation. John M. Todd.
The Reformers and the American
Indian. Robert Winston Mardock.
Reframing the Constitution: An
Imperative for Modern America.
Leland Baldwin.
The Refugee: A North-side View
of Slavery. Benjamin Drew.
Regeneration Through Violence: the
Mythology of the American Fron-
tier, 1600-1860. Richard Slotkin.
Regesta Regum Scottarum: Vol.
II: The Acts of William I.
G. W. S. Barrow, ed.
Regional Development: Experiences
and Prospects in South and Southeast
Asia. Louis Lefeber and Mrinal
Datta-Chaudhuri.
The Reign of Richard II: Essays in
Honour of May McKisack. F. R.
H. du Boulay and Caroline Bar-
ron, eds.
La reine, Blanche. Régine Pernoud.
Reinhard Heydrich und die Früh-
geschichte von Gestapo und SD.
Shlomo Aronson.
The Relevance of General Systems
Theory. Ervin Lazlo, ed.
The Relevance of History. Gordon
Connell-Smith and Howell A. Lloyd.
The Relief of Poverty, 1834-1914.
Michael E. Rose.
Religion and Society in England
1790-1850. W. R. Ward.
Religion and the Rise of the Amer-
ican City: The New York City

Mission Movement, 1812-1870.
Carroll Smith Rosenberg.
Religion and the Solid South. Samuel
S. Hill, Jr.
Religion and the Transformation of
Society: A Study of Social Change
in Africa. Monica Wilson.
Religion in the American Experi-
ence: The Pluralistic Style.
Robert T. Handy, ed.
Religious Cults of the Caribbean:
Trinidad, Jamaica, and Haiti.
George Eaton Simpson.
A Religious History of the American
People. Sydney E. Ahlstrom.
Religious Liberty in the United
States: The Development of
Church-State Thought Since the
Revolutionary Era. Elwyn A.
Smith.
The Religious Minorities of Chios:
Jews and Roman Catholics.
Philip P. Argenti.
The Reluctant Ally: Austria's Policy
in the Austro-Turkish War, 1737-
1739. Karl A. Roider.
The Reluctant Farmer: The Rise
of Agricultural Extension to 1914.
Roy V. Scott.
Reluctant Rebellion: The 1906-8
Disturbances in Natal. Shula
Marks.
Reluctant Union: Alsace-Lorraine
and Imperial Germany, 1871-1918.
Dan P. Silverman.
Remain to be Seen. Elinor Richey.
Remaking China Policy: U. S.-China
Relations and Governmental De-
cision-Making. Richard Moors-
teen and Morton Abramowitz.
Rembrandt and His World. Christo-
pher White.
Reminiscences of Alexander Toponce,
Written by Himself. Robert A.
Griffin, intro.
The Reminiscences of John B. Jer-
vis, Engineer of the Old Croton.
Neal FitzSimmons, ed.
Renaissance. Anthony Molho and
John A. Tedeschi, eds.
The Renaissance Discovery of Time.
Ricardo J. Quinones.
Renaissance Europe: Individual and
Society, 1480-1520. J. R. Hale.
Report on "The Star-Spangled Ban-
ner, " "Hail Columbia, " "Amer-
ica, " and "Yankee Doodle. "
Oscar Sonneck.

Reports of the 1863 Constitutional Convention of the Territory of Nevada. Andrew J. Marsh, Samuel Clemens and Amos Bowman.

The Republic and the Civil War in Spain. Raymond Carr, ed.

The Republic of Armenia. Vol. I: 1918-1919. Richard G. Hovannisian.

Republic or Empire: American Resistance to the Philippine War. Daniel B. Schirmer.

A Republica Velha. 2 vols. Edgar D. Carone.

The Republican Command, 1897-1913. Horace Samuel and Marion G. Merrill.

La république bourgeoise thermidor à brumaire, 1794-1799. Denis Woronoff.

La république jacobine, 10 août 1792-9 thermidor an II. Marc Bouloiseau.

Requiem for a People: The Rogue Indians and the Frontiersmen. Stephen Dow Beckham.

The Rescue of Emin Pasha. Roger Jones.

Research and Innovation in the Modern Corporation. Edwin Mansfield, John Rapoport, Jerome Schnee, Samuel Wagner, and Michael Hamburger.

Restless Strangers: Nevada's Immigrants and Their Interpreters. Wilbur S. Shepperson.

Rethinking Kinship and Marriage. Rodney Needham, ed.

Reuel B. Pritchett: Churchman and Antiquarian. Roger E. Sappington.

Reunion without Compromise: The South and Reconstruction, 1865-1868. Michael Perman.

Reveille Till Taps. Keith R. Widder.

Revitaillement et alimentation en Provence aux XIVe et XVe siècles. Louis Stouff.

Revolt in Athens: The Greek Communist "Second Round", 1944-1945. John O. Iatrides.

Revolt in Japan: The Young Officers and the February 26, 1936 Incident. Ben-Ami Shillony.

The Revolt of the Judges: The Parlement of Paris and the Fronde, 1643-1650. A. Lloyd Moote.

A Revolução Francesca e a vida de

José Bonifácio. Gondin Da Fonseca.

La Revolución de 1868: Historia Pensamiento, Literatura. Clara Lida and Iris M. Zavala, eds.

La Revolución intervenida. Relaciones diplomáticas entre México y Estados Unidos (1910-1914). Berta Ulloa.

La revolution dans le Puy-de-Dômi. G. Gerbaud, A. Lamadon, D. Martin, and J. Pételet.

Revolution and Intervention: The Diplomacy of Taft and Wilson With Mexico, 1910-1917. P. Edward Haley.

Revolution and Liberation: A Short History of Modern China 1900-1970. W. S. K. Waung.

The Revolution and the Civil War in Spain. Pierre Broué and Émile Témine.

La révolution espagnole (1931-1939). Pierre Broué.

Revolution in Central Europe: 1918-1919. F. L. Carsten.

Revolution in Perspective: Essays on the Hungarian Soviet Republic. Andrew C. János and William B. Slottman, eds.

Revolution in Peru: Mariategui and the Myth. John M. Baines.

Revolution in the Middle East: And Other Case Studies. P. J. Vatikiotis, ed.

The Revolution That Never Was, Northeast Brazil, 1955-1964. Joseph A. Page.

Revolution und internationale Politik: Zur kommunistischen Interpretation der kapitalistischen Welt 1921-1925. Wolfgang Eichwede.

Revolutionary Justice: The Social and Political Theory of P. -J. Proudhon. Robert L. Hoffman.

Revolutionary Struggle, 1947-1958: Vol. 1 of the Selected Works of Fidel Castro. Rolando E. Bonachea and Nelson P. Valdés, eds.

Revolutionary Suicide. Huey P. Newton.

Revolutions and Peace Treaties, 1917-1920. Gerhard Schulz.

Los reyes catolicos y America (1492-1517). Horacio Lopez Guedez.

Rezanov Reconnoiters California, 1806. Richard A. Pierce, ed.

The Rhetoric of American Politics: A Study of Documents. William R. Smith.

Richard Bourke. Hazel King.

Richelieu and His Age. Vol. III: Power Politics and the Cardinal's Death. Carl J. Burckhardt.

Rideau Waterway. Robert Legget.

Riding the Storm. Harold Macmillan.

Righteous Conquest: Woodrow Wilson and the Evolution of the New Diplomacy. Sidney Bell.

Rio Grande do Sul and Brazillian Regionalism. Jospeh L. Love.

The Rise and Decline of Fidel Castro: An Essay in Contemporary History. Maurice Halperin.

The Rise and Fall of the New Roman Empire: Italy's Bid for World Power, 1890-1943. Glen St. J. Barclay.

The Rise and Fall of the People's Century: Henry A. Wallace and American Liberalism, 1941-1948. Norman D. Markowitz.

The Rise of a Central Authority for English Education. A. S. Bishop.

The Rise of Big Business, 1860-1910. Glenn Porter.

The Rise of Sports in New Orleans: 1850-1900. Dale A. Somers.

The Rise of Teamster Power in the West. Donald Garnel.

The Rise of the Atlantic Economies. Ralph Davis.

The Rise of the Monophysite Movement. W. H. C. Frend.

The Rise of the Staffordshire Potteries. John Thomas.

The Rise of the Western World: A New Economic History. Douglas North and Robert Paul Thomas.

Rise to Globalism. Stephen E. Ambrose.

The Rising Sun: The Decline and Fall of the Japanese Empire, 1936-1945. John Toland.

The Rivals: America and Russia Since World War II. Adam B. Ulam.

River of the Golden Ibis. Gloria Jahoda.

The Riverton Culture: A Second Millennium Occupation in the Central Wabash Valley. Howard Dalton Winters.

The Road and the Car in American Life. John B. Rae.

The Road to Aba. Harry A. Gailey.

The Road to Secession: A New Perspective on the Old South. William Barney.

The Road to Yalta: Soviet Foreign Relations, 1941-1945. Louis Fischer.

Robert Gourlay, Gadfly: The Biography of Robert Fleming Gourlay, 1778-1863, Forerunner of the Rebellion in Upper Canada, 1837. Lois Darroch Milani.

Robert Owen's American Legacy: Proceedings of the Robert Owen Bicentennial Conference. Donald E. Pitzer, ed.

Robespierre, The Force of Circumstances. John Laurence Carr.

The Rocks Begin to Speak. La Van Martineau.

The Rocky Mountain Bench: The Territorial Supreme Courts of Colorado, Montana and Wyoming, 1861-1890. John D. W. Guice.

Roger of Salisbury: Viceroy of England. Edward J. Kealey.

Roger Sherman's Connecticut: Yankee Politics and the American Revolution. Christopher Collier.

Le rôle des experts à la conférence de la paix de 1919: Gestation d'une technocratie en politique internationale. Dimitri Kitsikis.

Role of Deficit Financing in the Context of Indian Planning. Gangadhar Rakshit.

The Role of Group Action in the Industrialization of Rural Areas. Joseph Klatzman, et al., eds.

The Role of Providence in the Social Order: An Essay in Intellectual History. Jacob Viner.

The Role of the United Nations in the Indo-Pakistan Conflict, 1971. K. P. Misra.

The Role of the Yankee in the Old South. Fletcher M. Green.

Rölvaag: His Life and Art. Paul Reigstad.

La "Roma dei Romani." Fiorella Bartoccini.

Roman Bath Discovered. Barry Cunliffe.

The Roman Catholic Church in Modern Latin America. Karl M. Schmitt, ed.

The Roman Forum. Michael Grant.

Roman France. Paul MacKendrick.

The Roman Land-Surveyors: An Introduction to the Agrimensores.

O. A. W. Dilke.
Roman London. Ralph Merrifield.
Roman Trier and the Treveri. Edith Mary Wightman.
The Romanovs: The Rise and Fall of a Russian Dynasty. Ian Grey.
Rome in the Dark Ages. Peter Llewellyn.
Rome in Erituria and Umbria. W. V. Harris.
Roosevelt and Rayburn: A Political Partnership. Booth Mooney.
Roosevelt, New Jersey: Big Dreams in a Small Town and What Time Did to Them. Edwin Rosskam.
The Roots of Ancient India. Walter A. Fairservis, Jr.
The Roots of Fundamentalism: British and American Millenarianism 1800-1930. Ernest Sandeen.
Roots of Maryland Democracy, 1753-1776. David Curtis Skaggs.
The Roots of Southern Writing: Essays on the Literature of the American South. C. Hugh Holman.
Roots of War. Richard J. Barnet.
Roscoe Conkling of New York: Voice in the Senate. David M. Jordan.
The Rosicrucian Enlightenment. Frances A. Yates.
Roughing It. Mark Twain. Franklin R. Rogers, ed.
The Rover. George Oliver.
The Royal Demesne in English History: The Crown Estate in The Governance of the Realm from the Conquest to 1509. B. P. Wolffe.
The Royal Exchange Assurance: A History of British Insurance 1720-1970. Barry Supple.
Royal Navy on the Northwest Coast of North America, 1810-1914: A Study of the British Maritime Ascendency. Barry M. Gough.
The Royal Provincial Intendants: A Governing Elite in Eighteenth-Century France. Vivian R. Gruder.
Royal Taxation in Fourteenth-Century France: The Development of War Financing 1322-1356. John Bell Henneman.
Rulers of Empire: The French Colonial Service in Africa. William B. Cohen.
The Rules of Work of the Carpen-

ters' Company of the City and County of Philadelphia 1786. Charles E. Peterson, ed.
Rum Road to Spokane. Edmund Fahey.
Rural Hausa: A Village and a Setting. Polly Hill.
Rural Industry in Central Russia in the Second Half of the Seventeenth Century. L. L. Murav'eva.
Rural Politics and Social Change in the Middle East. Richard Antoun and Iliya Harik, eds.
Rural Politics in Nasser's Egypt. James B. Mayfield.
The Rush to Be Rich: A History of the Colony of Victoria, 1883-1889. Geoffrey Serle.
Russia and Asia: Essays on the Influence of Russia on the Asian Peoples. Wayne S. Vucinich, ed.
Russia and China: Their Diplomatic Relations to 1728. Mark Mancall.
Russia and Italy: On the History of Russo-Italian Cultural and Social Relations. S. D. Skazkin, et al., eds.
Russia and the Austin State Treaty: A Case Study of Soviet Policy in Europe. Sven Allard.
Russia and the U. S. A., 1914-1917: Essays on the History of Russian-American Relations. R. Sh. Ganelin.
Russia Enters the Twentieth Century, 1894-1917. Erwin Oberländer, et al., eds.
Russia in War and Peace. Alan Palmer.
Russian Embassies to the Georgian Kings (1589-1605). 2 vols. W. E. D. Allen, ed.
Russian Formalism and Anglo-American New Criticism. Ewa M. Thompson.
Russian Journalism and Politics: The Career of Aleksei S. Suvorin, 1861-1881. Effie Ambler.
Russian Poetry Under the Tsars. Burton Raffel, trans.
Russian Literature Triquarterly. Carl R. and Ellendea Proffer, eds.
Russian Literature Under Lenin and Stalin, 1917-33. Gleb Struve.
Russian Rebels, 1600-1800. Paul

Avrich.
The Russian Revolution. Robert V. Daniels, ed.
The Russian Revolution and Italy, March-October, 1917. K. Z. Kirova.
The Russian Revolution in Switzerland, 1914-1917. Alfred Erich Senn.
Russian Studies, 1941-1958. A Cumulation of the Annual Bibliographies from the Russian Review. Thomas Schultheiss, ed.
Russian Surnames. B. O. Unbegaun.
Russian Tanks, 1900-1970. John Milsom.
Russian-Turkish Relations at the Beginning of the Eighteenth Century. S. F. Oreshkova.
Die russisch-österreichische militärische Zusammenarbeit.... Dieter Ernst Bangert.
Die russische Justizreform von 1864.... Friedhelm Berthold Kaiser.
Russkaia literatura vemigratsii. Nikolai P. Poltoratzky, ed.
Russo-Indian Relations, 1466-1917. David N. Druhe.

-S-

S D S. Kirkpatrick Sale.
Sacajawea. Harold P. Howard.
The Sack of Rome, 1527 Judith Hook.
Sacred Chitimacha Indian Beliefs. Faye Stauff and W. Bradley Twitty.
Saddles and Spurs: The Pony Express Saga. Raymond W. and Mary Lund Settle.
Saga of the Soo: West from Shoreham. John A. Gjevre.
Sage Brush Doctors. Edna B. Patterson.
A Sage Brush Heritage: The Story of Ben Edwards and His Family. Lorena Edwards Meadows.
Saggio Bibliografico sulla Seconda Guerra Mondiale. Ministero della Difesa....
Saint Joan, A Screenplay. Bernard Shaw.
The St. Louis-San Francisco Transcontinental Railroad: The Thirty-

Fifth Parallel Project, 1853-1890. H. Craig Miner.
Sakhalin: A History. John J. Stephan.
Saladin. Andrew S. Ehrenkreutz.
Salem-Village Witchcraft: A Documentary Record of Local Conflict in Colonial New England. Paul Boyer and Stephen Nissenbaum, eds.
Salerno: Foothold in Europe. Davis Mason.
Salt--That Necessary Article. Isabel M. Williams and Leora H. McEachern.
"Salutary Neglect": Colonial Administration Under the Duke of Newcastle. James A. Henretta.
Samuel Beckett. Francis Doherty.
Samuel de Champlain: Father of New France. Samuel Eliot Morison.
Samuel Johnson and the New Science. Richard B. Schwartz.
Samuel Pepys and His World. Geoffrey Trease.
Samuel Seabury, 1729-1796: A Study in the High Church Tradition. Bruce E. Steiner.
Samuel Smith and the Politics of Business. John S. Pancake.
Samuel Willard, 1640-1707: Preacher of Orthodoxy in an Era of Change. Seymour Van Dyken.
San Francisco Bay: Discovery and Colonization, 1769-1776. Theodore E. Trentlein.
Sand in a Whirlwind: The Paiute Indian War of 1860. Ferol Egan.
Sardar Patels' Correspondence 1945-50. 5 vols. Durga Das, ed.
Satmar: An Island in the City. Israel Rubin.
The Savage Ideal. Intolerance and Intellectual Leadership in the South, 1890-1914. Bruce Clayton.
Savage Scene: The Life and Times of James Kirker, Frontier King. William Cochrane McGaw.
Savonarola and Florence: Prophecy and Patriotism in the Renaissance. Donald Weinstein.
Sayyid Jamāl ad-Dīn "Al-Afghānī": A Political Biography. Nikki R. Keddie.
The Scandal of the Andover Workhouse. Ian Anstruther.
Scandinavia or NATO? The Foreign

Ministry and the Alliance Question, 1947-1949. Magne Skodvin.
Scenery of the Plains, Mountains and Mines. Franklin Langworthy.
Das Scheitern der Kleinen Entente: Internationale Beziehungen im Donauraum von 1933 bis 1938. Günter Reichert.
The Schiwetz Legacy: An Artist's Tribute to Texas, 1910-1971. E. M. "Buck" Schiwetz.
Schofield: Union General in the Civil War and Reconstruction. James L. McDonough.
Scholarship and Partisanship: Essays on Max Weber. Reinhard Bendix and Guenther Roth.
School Desegregation in the Carolinas: Two Case Studies. William Bagwell.
Schoolbooks and Krags: The United States Army in the Philippines, 1898-1902. John M. Gates.
The Schultz Site at Green Point. James E. Fitting.
Schuss und Kette: Geschichte der "Sulzer"--Webmaschine. Rudolf H. Rossmann.
Schweitzer: A Biography. George Marshal and David Poling.
Die Schweiz seit 1945: Beitrage zur Zeitgeschichte.... Erich Gruner.
Das schweizerische Bundesarchiv von 1798 bis zur Gegenwart. Walter Meyrat.
Science and Archaeology. Robert H. Brill, ed.
Science and Civilisation in China. Vol. IV, Part 3. Joseph Needham, and Wang Ling and Lu Gwei-djen.
Science and Controversy: A Biography of Sir Norman Lockyer. A. J. Meadows.
Science and Philosophy in the Soviet Union. Loren R. Graham.
Science and Society 1600-1900. Peter Mathias, ed
Science and Technology as an Instrument of Soviet Policy. Mose L. Harvey, Leon Goure, and Vladimir Prokofieff.
Science and Technology in Art Today. Jonathan Benthall.
Science in India. Ward Morehouse.
Science, Technology, and Economic Growth in the Eighteenth Century. A. E. Musson, ed.
Scientific Instruments of the Seventeenth and Eighteenth Centuries and Their Makers. Maurice Daumas.
The Scientific Origins of National Socialism. Daniel Gasman.
The Scientific Papers of James Logan. Roy N. Lokken, ed.
Scientific-Technical Progress: Essence of Basic Tendencies. G. S. Gudozhnik.
Scotland Under Mary Stuart. Madeleine Bingham.
The Scottish Enlightenment and the American College Ideal. Douglas Sloan.
Scottish Parish Clergy at the Reformation, 1540-1574. Charles H. Haws, ed.
Scramble for Africa: The Great Trek to the Boer War. Anthony Nutting.
The Sea Chart, An Historical Survey Based on the Collections in the National Maritime Museum. Derek Howse and Michael Sanderson.
The Seabright Skiff and Other Jersey Shore Boats. Peter J. Guthorn.
Sean O'Casey: A Bibliography of Criticism. E. H. Mikhail.
The Search for an American Identity, Modern Pan-Indian Movements. Hazel W. Hertzberg.
The Search for Freedom: Basic American History. Vol. 1. Leonard F. Ralston and Harold H. Negley.
The Search for Meaning: Viewpoints in American History. Richard E. Marshall and John Edward Wiltz, eds.
The Search for Steam. Joe G. Collias.
The Search for the Niger. Christopher Lloyd.
The Search for the Well-Dressed Soldier, 1865-1890. Gordon Chappell.
A Seat Behind the Coachman: Travellers in Ireland 1800-1900. Diarmaid Ó Muirithe.
The Secret Vysočany Congress.... Jiří Pelikán, ed.

427   Secret

A Secret War: Americans in
China, 1944-1945. Oliver J.
Caldwell.
Le Secrétariat d'Etat et le Conseil
Espagnol des Indes (1700-1808).
Bernard Gildas.
Securing the Revolution: Ideology
in American Politics, 1789-1815.
Richard Buel, Jr.
Seeds of Extinction, Jeffersonian
Philanthropy and the American
Indian. Bernard W. Sheehan.
Seeds of Repression: Harry S. Tru-
man and the Origins of McCarthy-
ism. Athan Theoharis.
The Segu Tukulor Empire. B.
Olatunji Oloruntimehin.
Seigneurie et Féodalité: L'Apogée
(XIe-XIIIe siècles). Robert
Boutruche.
Seis años de vacaciones. Recuerdos
de la Guerra del Pacifico, Chile
contra Perú y Bolivia, 1879-1884.
Santos Benavides.
Die Selbstbehauptung einer Nation....
Christoph Klessmann.
Selected Documents on the Foreign
Policy of the Netherlands. J.
Woltring, ed.
Selected Essays. F. Lyman Windolph.
Selected Letters of Cotton Mather.
Kenneth Silverman, comp.
Selected Papers of Will Clayton.
Frederick J. Dobney, ed.
Selected Poems. Brian Coffey.
Selected Poems. Marina Tsvetayeva.
Selected Works. Zinaida Gippius.
Selected Works of Nikolai S. Gumi-
lev. Burton Raffel and Alla
Burago, trans.
Self-Determination and History in
the Third World. David C.
Gordon.
Self-Portrayals. By the Zuni People.
Alvina Quam, trans.
The Semblance of Peace: The Po-
litical Settlement After the Second
World War. Sir John Wheeler-
Bennett and Anthony Nicholls.
Semnan: Persian City and Region.
John Connell, ed.
Senate Legislative Journal. Vol. I.
Linda Grant De Pauw, Charlene
Bangs Bickford and La Vonne
Marlene Siegel, eds.
Senator John James Ingalls: Kansas
Iridescent Republican. Burton
J. Williams.

The Senatorial Aristocracy in the
Later Roman Empire. M. T. W.
Arnheim.
The Sephardi Heritage: Essays on
the History and Cultural Contri-
bution of the Jews of Spain and
Portugal. Vol. I. R. D. Bar-
nett, ed.
The Sephardic Tradition: Ladino
and Spanish Literature. Moshe
Lazar, ed.
The Sepoy and the Cossack. Pierce
G. Frederick.
Septimus Severus, the African Em-
peror. A. Birley.
Sessions of the Peace in the City of
Lincoln, 1351-1354 and the
Borough of Stamford, 1351.
E. G. Kimball, ed.
Seth Low: The Reformer in an
Urban and Industrial Age. Gerald
Kurland.
Seven Interpretative Essays on Peru-
vian Reality. José Carlos
Mariálegui.
Seven Who Shaped Our Destiny: The
Founding Fathers as Revolution-
aries. Richard B. Morris.
Seventeenth-Century Economic Doc-
uments. Joan Thirsk and J. P.
Cooper, eds.
Seventeenth-Century Europe. D.
H. Pennington.
The Seventeenth Century: Europe
in Ferment. A. Lloyd Moote.
Seventy-Six: "Our Country! Right
or Wrong. " 2 vols. John Neal.
Sex and Marriage in Utopian Com-
munities: Nineteenth-Century
America. Raymond Lee Muncy.
The Shadow of Slavery: Peonage in
the South, 1901-1969. Pete
Daniel.
The Shadow of the Parthenon:
Studies in Ancient History and
Literature. Peter Green.
Shakespeare and the Bawdy Court
of Stratford. E. R. C. Brink-
worth.
Shaping a New World: An Orien-
tation to Latin America. Ed-
ward L. Cleary, ed.
The Shaping of Jewish History: A
Radical New Interpretation.
Ellis Rivkin.
The Shaping of the American High
School. Edward A. Krug.
The Shavian Playground: An Ex-

429   Slovenian

A Slovenian Village: Zerovnica.
Irene Winner.
Small States in International Rela-
tions. A. Schou and A. O.
Brundtland, eds.
The Smallest Slavonic Nation.
Gerald Stone.
Smoked Yankees and the Struggle
for Empire: Letters from Negro
Soldiers, 1898-1902. Willard
B. Gatewood, Jr.
Smugglers of Spirits: Prohibition
and the Coast Guard Patrol.
Harold Waters.
Snickersville: The Biography of a
Village. Jean Herron Smith.
A Social and Economic History of
Medieval Europe. Gerald A. J.
Hodgett.
A Social and Religious History of
the Jews: Late Middle Ages and
the Era of European Expansion,
1200-1650. Vols. 13 and 14.
Salo Wittmayer Baron.
Social Change in Industrial Society.
Thomas C. Cochran.
Social Change in the Soviet Union:
Russia's Path Toward an Indus-
trial Society. Boris Meissner, ed.
Social Conflict and Educational
Change in England and France,
1789-1848. Michalina Vaughan
and Margaret Scotford Archer.
Social Control in Slave Plantation
Societies: A Comparison of St.
Dominique and Cuba. Gwendolyn
Midlo Hall.
The Social Dimensions of Work.
Clifton D. Bryant, ed.
The Social Foundations of German
Unification, 1858-1871: Struggles
and Accomplishments. Theodore
S. Hamerow.
The Social History of the Reforma-
tion: In Honor of Harold J.
Grimm. Lawrence P. Buck and
Jonathan W. Zophy, eds.
Social Movements in America.
Roberta Ash.
The Social Scene. Robert S.
Browne, Howard E. Freeman,
Charles V. Hamilton, Jerome
Kagan, and A. Kimball Romney.
Social Science and Government: Pol-
icies and Problems. A B.
Cherns, R. Sinclair and W. L.
Jenkins, eds.
Social Studies Curriculum in Per-

spective: A Conceptual Analysis.
Gary Wehlage and Eugene M
Anderson.
Socialism in Britain From the In-
dustrial Revolution to the Present
Day. Thomas L. Jarman.
Socialism and the Great War: The
Collapse of the Second Interna-
tional. Georges Haupt.
Socialism in India. B. R. Nanda,
ed.
Socialismo e Sindicalismo no Brazil,
1675-1913. Edgar Rodriguez.
Socialist, Anti-Semite, and Jew:
German Social Democracy Con-
fronts the Problem of Anti-
Semitism, 1918-1933. Donald
L. Niewyk.
La Societé Française en 1789:
Semur-en-Auxois. R. Robin.
Sociology of the Middle East: A
Stocktaking Interpretation. C. A.
O. Van Nieuwenhuijze.
Society and Government 1760-1780:
The Power Structure in Massa-
chusetts Townships. Dirk
Hoerder.
Sociocultural Changes in American
Jewish Life as Reflected in Se-
lected Jewish Literature. Bern-
ard Cohen.
Sociology: An Introduction. Charles
Allyn.
Soldier and Brave: Historic Places
Associated With Indian Affairs
and the Indian Wars in the Trans-
Mississippi West. Robert G.
Ferris, ed.
Soldier and Civilian in Roman York-
shire. R. M. Butler, ed.
Soldier in the West: Letters of
Theodore Talbot During His
Services in California, Mexico,
and Oregon, 1845-53. Robert V.
Hine and Savoie Lottinville, eds.
Soldier of Fortune. Ella Pipping.
Soldiering and Surveying in British
East Africa. J. R. L. Macdonald.
Some More Horse Tradin'. Ben K.
Green.
Some Things I Did. Roxy Gordon.
Some Who Passed This Way. Ira
A. Hutchinson.
Somerset Assize Orders, 1640-1659.
J. S. Cockburn, ed.
Son of the Alhambra: Don Diego
Hurtado de Mendoza 1504-1575.
Erika Spivakovsky.

Songs from the Williamsburg The-
atre: A Selection.... John W.
Molnar and Carleton Sprague
Smith.
Sophie Dorothea. Ruth Jordan.
The Sorcerer's Apprentice: The
French Scientist's Image of Ger-
man Science, 1840-1919. Harry
W. Paul.
A Source Book For Russian History
From Early Times to 1917.
George Vernadsky, et al., eds.
Source Material on the South African
Economy, 1860-1970. Vol. I.
D. Hobart Houghton and Jennifer
Dagut, eds.
Sources and Studies for the History
of the Americas. Vol. 9....
Eusebio Francisco Kino.
Sources and Studies for the History
of the Jesuits. Vol. III....
Hubert Jacobs, ed. and trans.
Sources for English Local History.
W. B. Stephens.
South Africa and the World. The
Foreign Policy of Apartheid.
Amry Vandenbosch.
South African Dialogue. N. J.
Rhoodie, ed.
The South African Indian Question,
1860-1971. Bridglal Pachai C.
Struik.
South Africa's Foreign Policy, 1945-
1970. James Barber.
South America of the Poets. Selden
Rodman.
The South and the Concurrent Ma-
jority. David M. Potter.
South to a Very Old Place. Albert
Murray.
The Southampton Revolt of 1831: A
Compilation of Source Material.
Henry Irving Tragle.
Southern Africa in Perspective:
Essays in Regional Politics.
Christian Potholm and Richard
Dale, eds.
Southern Arabia. Brian Doe.
Southern Italy: An Archaeological
Guide. Margaret Guido.
Southern Ute Lands, 1848-1899; The
Creation of a Reservation. Greg-
ory Coyne Thompson.
The Southern Utes: A Tribal His-
tory. James Jefferson, Robert
W. Delaney, and Gregory C.
Thomson.
Southwest Indian Painting. Clara

Lee Tanner.
The Sovereign States, 1775-1783.
Jackson Turner Main.
Soviet Agricultural Trade Unions
1917-70. Peter J. Potichnyj.
Soviet Nationality Problems. Edward
Allworth, ed.
Soviet Political Indoctrination: De-
velopments in Mass Media and
Propaganda Since Stalin. Gayle
Durham Hollander.
Soviet Prison Camp Speech: A Sur-
vivor's Glossary. Meyer Galler
and Harland E. Marques, comps.
The Soviet Quest for Economic
Efficiency: Issues, Controversies
and Reforms. George R. Feiwel.
Soviet Russia and the Hindustan
Subcontinent. Vijay Sen Budhraj.
The Soviet Russian State. Robert
G. Wesson.
Soviet Seapower in the Caribbean:
Political and Strategic Implica-
tions. J. D. Theberge, ed.
Sozialstruktur und Organisation
europaischer Nationalbewegun.
Theodor Schieder and Peter
Burian, eds.
De Spaanse Brabanders of de hand-
elsbetrekkingen der Zuidelijke
Nederlanden met de Iberische
wereld, 1598-1648. Eddy Stols.
Spain. Richard Herr.
Spain and Her Rivals on the Gulf
Coast. Ernest F. Dibble and
Earle W. Newton, eds.
Spain in the Fifteenth Century.
Roger Highfield, ed.
Spain in the Philippines: From
Conquest to Revolution. Nicholas
P. Cushner.
The Spain of Fernando de Rojas:
The Intellectual and Social Land-
scape of La Celestina. Stephen
Gilman.
The Spaniards: An Introduction to
Their History. Américo Castro.
Die Spanisch-Indianisch auseinander-
setzund in der nördlichen Sierra
Nevada de Santa Marta, 1501-
1600. Henning Bischof.
Spanish America in the Struggle for
Independence. M. S. Al'Perovich.
Spanish and Mexican Land Grants in
the Chihuahuan Acquisition. J.
J. Bowden.
The Spanish Company. Pauline
Croft.

The Spanish-Cuban-American War
and the Birth of American Im-
perialism, 1895-1902. 2 vols.
Philip S. Foner.
Spanish Islam: A History of the
Moslems in Spain. Reinhart Dozy.
Spanish Military Weapons in Colonial
America, 1700-1821. Sidney B.
Brinckerhoff and Pierce A.
Chamberlain.
The Spanish Revolution (1931-39).
Leon Trotsky.
Spanish Texas: Yesterday and To-
day. Gerald Ashford.
The Speaking Tree: A Study of
Indian Culture and Society.
Richard Lannoy.
The Spearless Leader: Senator
Borah and the Progressive Move-
ment in the 1920's. Le Roy
Ashby.
Spirit Mediumship and Society in
Africa. John Beattie and John
Middleton.
The Spiritual Regulation of Peter
the Great. Alexander Muller,
trans. and ed.
Spirits of the Deep: A Study of an
Afro-Brazilian Cult. Seth and
Ruth Leacock.
The Spiritual Crisis of the Gilded
Age. Paul A. Carter.
Spiritualite Franciscaine en Flandre
au XVIe Siècle: L'Homéliaire de
Jean Vitrier. Andre Godin.
The Spoils of Progress: Environ-
mental Pollution in the Soviet
Union. Marshall I. Goldman.
Sport in Greece and Rome. H. A.
Harris.
The Spread of the Russian Revolu-
tion: Essays on 1917. Roger
Pethybridge.
The Squire's Sketches of Lexington.
J. Winston Coleman, Jr.
Das Staatsverständnis des Parla-
mentarischen Rates.... Volker
Otto.
Staatsverwaltung und kirchliche auto-
rität im 18. Jahrhundert....
Grete Klingenstein.
Stalin as Revolutionary, 1879-1929:
A Study in History and Personality.
Robert C. Tucker.
Stalin, Hitler and Europe 1939-1941.
Vol. II. The Imbalance of Power.
James E. McSherry.
Stalin: The History of a Dictator.

H. Montgomery Hyde.
Star-Spangled Books: Books, Sheet
Music, Newspapers, Manuscripts,
and Persons Associated With
"The Star-Spangled Banner."
P. W. Filby and Edward G.
Howard, comps.
Staretz Amvrosy: Model for
Dostoevsky's Staretz Zossima.
John B. Dunlop.
Starlifter: The C-141, Lockheed's
High-Speed Flying Truck. Harold
H. Martin.
The State House at Annapolis.
Morris L. Radoff.
State Legislatures in India: The
Rajasthan Legislative Assembly,
A Comparative Study. C. M.
Jain.
A State of Disunion: Arthur Griffith,
Michael Collins, James Craig,
Eamon de Valera. Carlton
Younger.
The State of Nutrition in the Arab
Middle East. Vinayak N. Pat-
wardhan and William J. Darby.
The State of the Nations: Con-
straints on Development in Inde-
pendent Africa. Michael Lofchie,
ed.
Stately Mansions: Eighteenth-Cen-
tury Paris Architecture. Michel
Gallet.
Statesmen in Disguise: The Chang-
ing Role of the Administrative
Class of the British Home Civil
Service, 1853-1966. Geoffrey
Kingdon Fry.
Statesmen, Scholars, and Merchants:
Essays in Eighteenth-Century
History.... Anne Whiteman,
J. S. Bromley and P. G. M.
Dickson, eds.
Statism in Plymouth Colony. Harry
M. Ward.
Steamboating on the Upper Missis-
sippi. William J. Petersen.
The Steel Bonnets: The Story of
the Anglo-Scottish Border. George
MacDonald Fraser.
Steinstücken: A Study in Cold War
Politics. Honoré M. Catudal, Jr.
Stephen A. Douglas. Robert W.
Johannsen.
Stephen F. Renfro, Alabama's Out-
law Sheriff. William Warren
Rogers and Ruth Pruitt.
Storia dell'Anabattismo, dalle origini

a Münster (1525-1535). Ugo
Gastaldi.
Storia del Partito comunista italiano.
3 vols. Paolo Spriano.
The Straits Settlements, 1826-67:
Indian Presidency to Crown
Colony. C. M. Turnbull.
The Strange Neutrality: Soviet-Jap-
anese Relations During the Second
World War, 1941-1945. George
A. Lensen.
The Strange Story of Wayne Brazel.
Robert N. Mullin.
Strategy and Transaction in an
African Factory. B. Kapferer.
Streams in a Thirsty Land: A His-
tory of the Turlock Region.
Helen Alma Hohenthal, et al.
Structure of Financial Institutions.
V. V. Bhatt.
The Structure of the Cotton Economy
of the Antebellum South. William
N. Parker, ed.
The Structure of the Terror. The
Example of Javogues and the
Loire. Colin Lucas.
Struggle for a Continent: The Dip-
lomatic History of South America,
1919-1945. Glen Barclay.
The Struggle for the Ministry of
Health. Frank Honigsbaum.
Struktura khudozhestvennego teksta.
Iu. M. Lotman.
Studi sul XVIII secolo: Le Prime
manifestazioni della rivoluzione
d'occidente in Francia e nella re-
pubbliche oligarchiche (1748-1775).
Carlo Baudi di Vesme.
Studies in Greek History, a Com-
panion Volume to A History of
Greece to 322 B. C. N. G. L.
Hammond.
Studies in Judaica Americana.
Rudolf Glanz.
Studies in the Documents of the
Customs Accounts at the Begin-
ning of the Sixteenth Century. ...
2 vols. Poul Enemark.
Studies in the Growth of Nineteenth-
Century Government. Gillian
Sutherland, ed.
Studies in the History of Civilization.
Julian A. Joffe.
Studies in the History of the Near
East. P. M. Holt.
Studies in the Medieval Wine Trade.
Margery Kirkbride James.
Studies in World Order. Harnam Singh.

Studies on Machiavelli. Myron P.
Gilmore, ed.
Studies on the Interior of Russia.
August von Haxthausen.
Studies on the Demography of the
Byzantine Empire: Collected
Studies. Peter Charanis.
Study Circle on Diaspora Jewry at
the Home of the President of
Israel. Moshe Davis, ed.
The Study of Architectural History.
Bruce Allsop.
A Study of Boss Politics: William
Lorimer of Chicago. Joel
Arthur Tarr.
The Study of Medieval Records: Es-
says in Honour of Kathleen Major.
D. A. Bullough and R. L.
Storey, eds.
Submarining: Three Thousand Books
and Articles. T. O. Paine.
Success or Surrender?: The Simla
Summit. G. S. Bhargava.
Successful Management in Develop-
ing Countries. Vol. 3 and 4.
Douglas W. Foster.
The Successors of Genghis Khan.
Rashīd Al-dīn.
Suffer and Be Still: Women in the
Victorian Age. Martha Vicinus,
ed.
Suffragists and Democrats: The
Politics of Woman Suffrage in
America. David Morgan.
Sufis, Scholars and Saints: Muslim
Religious Institutions Since 1500.
Nikkie Keddie, ed.
Sugar and Slaves: The Rise of the
Planter Class in the English West
Indies, 1624-1713. Richard S.
Dunn.
The Sugar Hacienda of the Mar-
quesses del Valle. Ward J.
Barrett.
Sugar Without Slaves: The Political
Economy of British Guiana, 1838-
1904. Alan H. Adamson.
The Sumerians: Inventors and
Builders. Elizabeth Lansing.
Summary Catalogue of the Advocates'
Manuscripts. National Library
of Scotland.
Summer on the Lakes. Margaret
Fuller.
The Sun Dance Religion: Power for
the Powerless. Joseph G. Jor-
genson.
The Sunset Creek Site ... : And

Against Moisture in Industrial Building in the Polish Kingdom of the First Half of the XIXth Century. Jerzy Gorewicz.

Technological Change in Regulated Industries. William M. Capron, ed.

Technology and American Economic Growth. Nathan Rosenberg.

Technology and Copyright: Annotated Bibliography and Source Materials. George P. Bush, ed.

Technology, Science and History. D. S. L. Cardwell.

Technology and Culture: An Anthology. Melvin Kransberg and William H. Davenport, eds.

Tej Bahadur Sapru: Profiles and Tributes. K. N. Raina and K. V. Gopala Ratnam, eds.

Tell Them They Lie, The Sequoyah Myth. Traveller Bird.

Telling Tongues: Language Policy in Mexico, Colony to Nation. Shirley Brice Heath.

Temperate Freedom: An Essay on the Relationship of the Church and State in the Republic of the United Netherlands and on Freedom of Expression in Religion, Press, and Education During the Seventeenth Century. Enno Van Gelder.

Temples and Sanctuaries of Ancient Greece: A Companion Guide. Evi Melas, ed.

The Terrors of Ideological Politics: Liberal Historians in a Conservative Mood. Marian J. Morton.

Tertullian: A Historical and Literary Study. Timothy David Barnes.

Texas: A History. Seymour V. Connor.

The Texas Courthouse. June Rayfield Welch and J. Larry Nance.

Texte der russischen Formalisten. Vol. II. Wolf-Dieter Stempel, ed.

That All May Learn: New Mexico State University, 1888-1964. Simon F. Kropp.

That Greece Might Still Be Free: The Philhellenes in the War of Independence. William St. Clair.

That Most Distressful Nation: The Taming of the American Irish. Andrew M. Greeley.

The Theatre in Early Kentucky, 1790-1820. West T. Hill, Jr.

Their Solitary Way: The Puritan Social Ethic in the First Century of Settlement in New England. Stephen Foster.

Théorie économique du système féodal: Pour un modèle de l'economie polonaise 16ᵉ-18ᵉ siècles. Witold Kula.

Theories of Nationalism. Anthony D. Smith.

Theory and Practice of Modern Guerrilla Warfare. Baljit Singh and Ko-Wang Mei.

A Theory of Justice. John Rawls.

These Are the Great Lakes. Phil Ault.

These Old Stone Walls. Phillips Russell.

They Came for Sandalwood: A Study of the Sandalwood Trade in the Southwest Pacific, 1830-1865. Dorothy Shineberg.

They Rode Into Europe: The Fruitful Exchange in the Arts of Horsemanship Between East and West. Miklós Jankovich.

Things to Come: Thinking About the 70's and 80's. Herman Kahn and B. Bruce-Briggs.

Think Big. Str. Mary Carmel Browning.

Think Tanks. Paul Dickson.

Third International Conference of Economic History, Munich, 1965. Vol. 4. Demography and Economy. D. E. C. Eversley and Jane S. Williams, eds.

The Thirty Years War. J. V. Polisensky.

The Thirty Years War, 1618-1648. G. Pages.

This Beats Working for a Living: The Dark Secrets of a College Professor. Professor X.

This Country Was Ours: A Documentary History of the American Indian. Virgil J. Vogel.

This Cybernetic World of Men, Machines and Earth Systems. V. L. Parsegian.

This Is the Coast Guard. H. R. Kaplan and ... James F. Hunt.

Thomas Cole's Poetry: The Collected Poems of America's Foremost Painter of the Hudson River School.... Marshall B. Tymn, comp. and ed.

Thomas County, 1865-1900. William
Warren Rogers.
Thomas Hart Benton: A Personal
Commemorative. Mary Curtis
Warten, ed.
Those Incredible Methodists: A
History of the Baltimore Confer-
ence of the United Methodist
Church. Gordon Pratt Baker, ed.
Three Crises in American Foreign
Affairs and a Continuing Revolu-
tion. Howard Trivers.
The Three Empresses: Catherine I,
Anne and Elizabeth of Russia.
Philip Longworth.
Three Hundred Years of American
Drama and Theatre.... Garff B.
Wilson.
Three Lives and All of Them Are
Mine. Charles Lockhart McCune.
Three Ranches West. Clarence S.
Adams and Tom E. Brown, Sr.
Things to Come: Thinking About the
70's and 80's. Herman Kahn and
B. Bruce-Briggs.
Tiberias. Robin Seager.
Tibetan Civilization. R. A. Stein.
Tidewater Towns: City Planning in
Colonial Virginia and Maryland.
John W. Reps.
Timber Roots: The Laird Norton
Story, 1885-1905. Fred W.
Kohlmeyer.
Time and Locations. Michael Smith.
Time as History. George Grant.
The Time of the Buffalo. Tom
McHugh.
Der Tirpitz Plan.... Volker R.
Berghahn.
Tito, Mihailović and the Allies, 1941-
1945. Walter R. Roberts.
To Be an Indian: An Oral History.
Joseph H. Cash and Herbert T.
Hoover, eds.
To End War: The Story of the Na-
tional Council for the Prevention
of War. Frederick J. Libby.
To Kill a Child's Spirit: The Tragedy
of School Segregation in Los An-
geles. John and La Ree Caughey.
To Live on This Earth: American
Indian Education. Estelle Fuchs
and Robert J. Havighurst.
To Peking--and Beyond: A Report
on the New Asia. Harrison E.
Salisbury.
To the Maginot Line: The Politics
of French Military Preparations

in the 1920's. Judith Hughes.
To the Shores of the New World:
From Unpublished Reports of Rus-
sian Travelers at the Beginning of
the Nineteenth Century. L. A.
Shur.
To the Western Shore. Robert
Silverberg.
To the Yalu: From the Chinese In-
vasion of Korea to MacArthur's
Dismissal. James McGovern.
Tombstone: Myth and Reality. Odie
B. Faulk.
Total War: The Story of World War
II. Peter Calvocoressi and Guy
Wint.
A Touchstone For Greatness: Es-
says, Addresses and Occasional
Pieces about Abraham Lincoln.
Roy P. Basler.
A Tour of Russia, Siberia, and the
Crimea, 1792-1794. John Park-
inson.
Toward a New Historicism. Wesley
Morris.
Toward the Scientific Study of His-
tory: Selected Essays. Lee
Benson.
Towards a Wiser Colossus. James
A. Stegenga, ed.
Towards the Discovery of Canada.
Donald Creighton.
Town and Countryside: Social, Eco-
nomic and Political Tensions in
Fourteenth-Century Flanders.
David Nicholas.
Town Defences in England and Wales:
An Architectural and Documentary
Study, A. D. 900-1500. Hilary
L. Turner.
Town Into City: Springfield, Massa-
chusetts and the Meaning of Com-
munity, 1840-1880. Michael H.
Frisch.
Towns and Minerals in Southeastern
Kansas, 1890-1930. John G.
Clark.
Trade and Dominion: The European
Overseas Empires in the Eight-
eenth Century. J. H. Parry.
The Trade in Lunacy: A Study of
Private Madhouses in England in
the Eighteenth and Nineteenth Cen-
turies. William Ll. Parry-Jones.
Tradition and Modernization in Jap-
anese Culture. Carmen Blacker,
et al.
Tragic Cavalier: Governor Manuel

pendence. Indian Oxygen Ltd.
Twilight in China. K. P. S. Menon.
Two Blades of Grass: Rural Co-
operatives in Agricultural Mod-
ernization. Peter Worsley, ed.
Two Centuries of Costume in
America: 1620-1820. Alice
Morse Earle.
Two, Four, Six, Eight, When You
Gonna Integrate? Frank A. Pe-
troni, Ernest A. Hirsch, and C.
Lillian Petroni.
Two Hundred Years of Methodism
in Messingham. W. Leary.
Two on a Big Ocean. Hal Roth.
Two Years in Revolutionary China,
1925-1927. Vera Vishnyakova-
Akimova.

-U-

U-Boottaktik: Zur deutschen U-
Boottaktik 1900-1945. Hubert
Jeschke.
Uganda: a Case Study in African
Political Development. Peter M.
Gukiina.
Ujamaa, espair du socialisme Afri-
cain en Tanzania. Sylvani Urfer.
Ulster: a Case Study in Conflict
Theory. R. S. P. Elliot and
John Hickie.
L'Ultimo Fronte: Lettre di Soldati
Caduti o Dispersi nella Seconda
Guerra Mondiale. Nuto Revelli.
The Unbridgeable Gap: Blacks and
Their Quest for the American
Dream 1900-1930. June Sochen.
Uncle Tom's Campus. Ann Jones.
Uncommon Obdurate: the Several
Public Careers of J. F. W. Des
Barres. G. N. D. Evans.
The Undeclared War: the Story of
the Indonesian Confrontation 1962-
1966. Harold James and Denis
Sheil-Small.
Under the Guns-New York: 1775-
1776. Bruce Bliven, Jr.
Under the Stone. Conleth Ellis.
Une entreprise horlogère du Val-de-
Travers: Fleurier Watch Co. SA.
De l'atelier familial du XIXe aux
concentrations du XXe siècle.
François Jequier.
Une politique étrangère, 1958-1969.

Maurice Couve DeMurville.
Unemployment and Politics: a Study
in English Social Policy, 1886-
1914. José Harris.
The Unholy Land. A. C. Forrest.
Unidad y testimonio de las grandes
letras hispanomericanas. José
María Bulnes Aldunate.
The Unification of Greece, 1770-
1923. Douglas Dakin.
Unification of the Romanian National
State: the Union of Transylvania
With Old Romania. Miron Con-
stantinescu, et al.
Uniforms of the American, British,
French and German Armies in
the War of the American Revolu-
tion 1775-1783. Charles M.
Lefferts.
The USSR in Arabia: the Develop-
ment of Soviet Policies and Atti-
tudes Towards the Countries of
the Arabian Peninsula. Stephen
Page.
Unione regionale della province Tos-
cane, Provincia di Firenze, and
Istituto storico per la Resis-
tenza....
"Unite or Die": Intercolony Rela-
tions, 1690-1763. Harry M.
Ward.
The United Nations in Perspective.
E. Berkeley Tompkins, ed.
U. N. Meditation in Kashmir: a
study in power politics. Surendra
Chopra.
United Nations: Past, Present, and
Future. James Barros, ed.
United Nations Peacemaking: the
Conciliation Commission for Pal-
estine. David P. Forsythe.
The United States and Revolutionary
Nationalism in Mexico, 1916-1932.
Robert Freeman Smith.
The United States and the Origins of
the Cold War, 1941-1947. John
Lewis Gaddis.
United States Army in the Korean
War: Policy and Direction: the
First Year. James F. Schnabel.
United States Army in World War II:
The Technical Services--the Corps
of Engineers: Construction in the
United States. Lenore Fine and
Jesse A. Remington.
The United States, Communism, and
the Emergent World. Bernard P.
Kiernan.

The United States in Panamanian
Politics: the Intriguing Formative
Years. G. A. Mellander.
United States Law and the Armed
Forces: Cases and Materials on
Constitutional Law, Courts-Mar-
tial, and the Rights of Service-
men. Willis E. Schug, ed.
The United States Navy in the Pacific,
1909-1922. William Reynolds
Braisted.
U. S. Policy and Peru. Daniel A.
Sharp.
United States-Spanish Relations,
Wolfram and World War II.
James W. Cortada.
Unity and Culture: the United States,
1877-1900. H. Wayne Morgan.
Universalism in America: a Docu-
mentary History. Ernest Cas-
sara, ed.
The Universities and British Industry,
1850-1970. M. Sanderson.
Universities in Politics: Case Stud-
ies from the Late Middle Ages
and Early Modern Period. John
W. Baldwin and Richard A. Gold-
thwaite, ed.
The University and Military Research:
Moral Politics at M.I.T. Dorothy
Nelkin.
The University College of Wales,
Aberystwyth: 1872-1972 (E. L.
Ellis). University College of
Wales, Aberystwyth.
University in the Forest: the Story
of Drew University. John T.
Cunningham.
The University of Wisconsin-Mil-
waukee: An Urban University.
J. Martin Klotsche.
The Unknown Orwell. Peter Stansky
and William Abrahams.
An Unsettled People: Social Order
and Disorder in American History.
Rowland Berthoff.
Uomini e terre di um borgo collinare
dal XVI al XVIII secolo. Giorgio
Doria.
Upper Beaver Creek: Pioneer Life
in Early Colorado. Mabel Hall.
The Uprooted. Oscar Handlin.
The Urban Development of Latin
America, 1750-1920. Richard M.
Morse, Michael and John Wibel,
eds.
Urban Leadership in Western India.
Christine Dobbin.

The Urban Wilderness: A History
of the American City. Sam Bass
Warner, Jr.
Urbanisierte Ortschaften und lateinu-
sche Terminologie: Studien zur
Geschichte des norslemropaischen
Stadte Wesens Nor 1350. Hans
Anderson.
The Uses of Terror--The Soviet Serv-
ice 1917-1970. Boris Levytsky.
Utah's Heritage. S. George Ells-
worth.
Utopia and Reform in the Enlighten-
ment. Franco Venturi.

-V-

Values and Youth. Robert D. Barr,
ed.
Values Education: Rationale, Stra-
tegies and Procedures. Lawrence
E. Metcalf, ed.
Values in Transition: A Handbook.
Gail M. Inlow.
Velázquez' Work and World. Jóse
López-Rey.
Venalita e Machiavellismo in Fran-
cia (1572-1610). All'origine della
mentalità politica Borghese. Salvo
Mastellone.
La vénalité des offices sous les
Règnes de Hénri IV et Louis XIII.
R. Mousnier.
The Venezuelan Armed Forces in
Politics, 1935-1959. Winfield J.
Burggraaff.
The Verderers and Forest Laws of
Dean. Cyril Hart.
Die Vernichtung des Roten Mannes:
Dokumentarbericht. Siegfried Von
Nostitz.
Vere Foster 1819-1900: An Irish
Benefactor. Mary McNeill.
Verulamium Excavations I. Shep-
pard Frere, I. W. Cornwall, R.
Goodburn, B. R. Hartley, K. F.
Hartley, W. H. Manning, H.
Waugh and M. G. Wilson.
Viator: Medieval and Renaissance
Studies. Vol. 1. Lynn White,
Jr., ed.
Vichy France: Old Guard and New
Order, 1940-1944. Robert O.
Paxton.
Vicky: Princess Royal of England

and German Empress. Daphne
Bennett.
Victims of Groupthink: A Psycho-
logical Study of Foreign-Policy
Decisions and Fiascoes. Irving
L. Janis.
The Victorian Army and the Staff
College, 1854-1914. Brian Bond.
Victorian Attitudes to Race.
Christine Bolt.
A Victorian Gentlewoman in the Far
West: The Reminiscences of
Mary Hallock Foote. Rodman
W. Paul, ed.
Victorian Inventions. Leonard de
Vries and Ilonka van Amstel.
Victorian Silverplated Holloware.
Pyne Press, comps.
The Victorian Underworld. Kellow
Chesney.
Victor's Justice: The Tokyo War
Crimes Trial. Richard H. Minear.
Vidal i Barraquer el cardenal de la
paz. Ramon Muntanyola.
The Vieux Carré, New Orleans: Its
Plan, Its Growth, Its Architecture.
Samuel Wilson, Jr.
The View from Courthouse Hill.
William R. Peterson.
Vignobles et Vins d'Aquitaine His-
toire: Economie: Art.
The Viking Settlements of North
America. Frederick J. Pohl.
Village Bureaucracy in Southern
Sung, China. Brian E. McKnight.
Le Village merovingien de Brebieres
(VIe-VIIe siècles). Pierre De-
molon.
Violence and Civil Disorder in
Italian Cities, 1200-1500. Lauro
Martines, ed.
Virginia Authors: Past and Present.
Welford Dunaway Taylor, gen. ed.
The Virginia Conservatives 1867-
1879: A Study in Reconstruction
Politics. Jack P. Maddex, Jr.
Virginia: The New Republic. Vir-
ginius Dabney.
Virginians Out Front. Pocahontas
Wight Edmunds.
The Vision of Hell: Infernal Jour-
neys in Medieval French Litera-
ture. D. D. R. Owen.
Vision und Wirklichkeit: Marx
contra Marxismus. Julius Löw-
enstein.
The Visitors' Dilemma: Allied In-
tervention in the Russian Civil

War. John Silverlight.
Vita Karoli Magni: The Life of
Charlemagne. Einhard.
A Voice of Protest: Norwegians in
American Politics, 1890-1917.
Jon Wefald.
Voices of Revolution. Thomas E.
Hachey and Ralph E. Weber.
Voices of 1776: The Story of the
American Revolution in the Words
of Those Who Were There.
Richard Wheeler.
Vol. I. Printed Books to 1800.
Margaret Canney and David
Knott, comps.
Vom Chaoszur Katastrophe: Vati-
kanische Gespräche 1918 bis
1938; vornehmlich auf Grund der
Berichte der osterreichen Gesand-
ten beim heiligen Stuhl. Fred-
erich Engel-Janosi.
Vom Sklavenhandel zum Kolonialen
Handel. Albert Wirz.
Voyage to Atlantis. James W.
Mavor, Jr.
The Voyages of Frederick Williams.
Eleanor P. Cross, ed.

-W-

Wage Patterns and Wage Policy in
Modern China, 1919-1972. Chris-
topher Howe.
Waiting for the Morning Train: An
American Boyhood. Bruce Catton.
Wake Up Dead Man: Afro-American
Worksongs from Texas Prisons.
Bruce Jackson.
Wall Street and the Stock Markets.
Peter Wyckoff.
Wallace and Natural Selection. H.
Lewis McKinney.
Walter of Henley and Other Treatises
on Estate Management and Account-
ing. Dorothea Oschinsky, ed.
Walter Reuther. R. L. Tyler.
War and Revolution: Excerpts from
the Letters and Diaries of
Countess Olga Poutiatine. George
Alexander Lensen, ed. and trans.
War and Society in Africa: Ten
Studies. Bethwell A. Ogot.
War and Society in the Nineteenth
Century Russian Empire. J. G.
Purves and D. A. West, ed.

When Even Angels Wept: the Senator
Joseph McCarthy Affair-A Story
Without a Hero. Lately Thomas.
When Family Failed: The Treat-
ment of the Child in the Care of
the Community in the First One
Half of the 20th Century. Nigel
Middleton.
Where the Wagon Led: One Man's
Memories of the Cowboy's Life
in the Old West R. D. Symons.
White Eagle, Red Star: the Polish-
Soviet War, 1919-20. Norman
Davies.
The White Generals: An Account of
the White Movement and the Rus-
sian Civil War. Richard Luckett.
White, Red and Black: The 17th
Century Virginian. Wesley Frank
Craven.
White Savage: the Case of John
Dunn Hunter. Richard Drinnon.
White Silence: Greenough, Powers
and Crawford, American Sculp-
tors in 19th Century Italy. Sylvia
E. Crane.
The White Stallion. Guy Owen.
White Terror: the Ku Klux Klan
Conspiracy and Southern Recon-
struction Allen W. Trelease.
Who Are the Russians? A History
of the Russian People. Wright
Miller.
Who Owns America? Walter J.
Hickel.
Who Rules Lebanon. Iliya Harik.
Whoop-Up Country, the Canadian-
American West, 1865-1885.
Paul F. Sharp.
Why Don't We Learn From History?
Basil H. Liddell Hart.
Wilderness Bonanza: the Tri-State
District of Missouri, Kansas, and
Oklahoma. Arrell M. Gibson.
Wilderness Manhunt: The Spanish
Search for LaSalle. Robert S.
Weddle.
William Aiken Walker: Southern
Genre Painter. August P. Tro-
vaioli and Raulhac B. Toledano.
William and Mary. Henri and Bar-
bara van der Zee.
William Barret Travis: His Sword
and His Pen. Martha Anne Turner.
William Butterfield. Paul Thompson.
William Byrd of Westover, 1674-
1744. Pierre Maramband.
William Carlos Williams: The Amer-

ican Background. Mike Weaver.
William Cullen Bryant. Charles H.
Brown.
William Grant Still and the Fusion
of Cultures in American Music.
Robert Bartlett Haas, ed.
William Tatham, 1752-1819: Amer-
ican Versatile. G. Melvin
Herndon.
William Tecumseh Sherman. James
M. Merrill.
William Tecumseh Sherman: Gold
Rush Banker. Dwight L. Clarke.
William's Mary. Elizabeth Hamilton.
Wily Women of the West. Grace
Ernestine Ray.
Winchester Yields: A Study in
Medieval Agricultural Produc-
tivity. J. Z. Titanm.
The Wind that Swept Mexico: the
History of the Mexican Revolu-
tion, 1910-1942. Anita Brenner.
A Window on Russia. Edmund
Wilson.
Wings: Prose and Poetry. Mikhail
Kuzmin. See also Neil Granoien
and Michael Green, eds. and tr.
The Winning of Independence.
Marshall Smelser.
The Winning of the Midwest: Social
and Political Conflict, 1888-1896.
Richard Jensen.
Winston S. Churchill. Vol. 3,
1914-1916. Martin Gilbert.
The Winter Soldiers. Richard
Ketchum.
Winter's Tales from Ireland. Kevin
Casey, ed.
Winterthur Portfolio 7 and 8. Ian
M. Quimby, ed.
Wisconsin: A State for All Seasons.
Jill Dean and Susan Smith, ed.
Wisconsin Death Trip. Michael
Lesy.
The Wisdom Seekers. Emmett K.
Vande Vere.
The Wishbone Fleet. Daniel C.
McCormick.
Witch Hunting in Southwestern Ger-
many, 1562-1684: the Social and
Intellectual Foundations. H. C.
Erik Midelfort.
Witchcraft Confessions and Accusa-
tions. Mary Douglas, ed.
Witchcraft in Europe, 1100-1700: A
Documentary History. Alan C.
Kors and Edward Peters, ed.
Witchcraft in the Middle Ages.

Jeffrey Burton Russell.
With Macdonald in Uganda. Major
H. H. Austin.
With Malice Towards None: the
Musings of a Retired Politician.
James M. Hare.
Witness to Revolution: Letters from
Russia, 1916-1919. Edward T.
Heald.
The Wizard of the North. The Life
of Sir Walter Scott. Carola Oman.
The Woman Citizen: Social Femi-
nism in the 1920's. J. Stanley
Lemons.
Women at Work. William L. O'Neill.
Women Who Spied for the Blue and
Gray. Oscar A. Kinchen.
The Woolen Industry of South West
England. Kenneth G. Ponting.
The Woolsey Sisters of New York:
a Family's Involvement in the
Civil War and a New Profession
(1860-1900): Anne L. Austin.
Workers and Protest: The European
Labor Movement, the Working
Classes and the Origins of Social
Democracy 1890-1914. Harvey
Mitchell and Peter N. Stearns.
Workers' Attitudes and Technology.
Dorothy Wedderburn and Rosemary
Crompton.
The Works of Sir Roger Williams.
John X. Evans.
World Armaments and Disarmament:
Sipri Yearbook 1972. Stockholm
International Peace Research In-
stitute.
The World Between the Eyes. Fred
Chappell.
World Guide to Technical Information
and Documentation Services.
UNESCO.
The World of Europe. Neil J.
Hackett, et al.
The World of Late Antiquity. Peter
Brown.
The World of the Vikings. Ole
Klindt-Jensen.
The World Petroleum Market. M. A.
Adelman.
The World Turned Upside Down:
Radical Ideas During the English
Revolution. Christopher Hill.
Worship and Theology in England:
From Cranmer to Hooker, 1534-
1603. Horton Davies.
The Writer in the South: Studies in
a Literary Community. Louis D.
Rubin, Jr.

Writing American History: Essays
on Modern Scholarship. John
Higham.
The Writing of History in the Soviet
Union. Anatole G. Mazour.
The Writings of J. M. Synge. Robin
Skelton.

-X-Y-Z-

X-Ray of the Pampa. Ezequiel
Martinez Estrada.
Yachting, A Pictorial History.
Peter Heaton.
Yakutia Before Its Incorporation Into
the Russian State. A. P. Oklad-
nikov.
Yalta. Diane Shaver Clemens.
The Yalta Myths: An Issue in U. S.
Politics, 1945-1955. Athan G.
Theoharis.
Yamagata Aritomo in the Rise of
Modern Japan, 1838-1922. Roger
F. Hackett.
Yangtze Patrol. The U. S. Navy
in China. Kemp Tolley.
Yankee Quaker Confederate General:
The Curious Career of Bushrod
Rust Johnson. Charles M. Cum-
mings.
Yesterday and Today in the Life of
the Apaches. Irene Burlinson.
Year 1920. Jozef Pilsudski.
The Yorubas of Nigeria. John
Ferguson.
You Can't Eat Magnolias. H. Brandt
Ayers and Thomas H. Naylor, eds.
Young Philip Sidney, 1572-1577.
James M. Osborn.
Your Dear Letter: Private Corres-
pondence of Queen Victoria and
the Crown Princess of Prussia,
1865-1871. Roger Fulford, ed.
Yugoslavs in Nevada 1859-1900.
Adam S. Eterovich.
Yvon at the Quai D'Orsay, French
Foreign Policy During the Popular
Front, 1936-1938. John E.
Dreifort.
Das Zeitalter des Hauses Öster-
reich.... Alphons Lhotsky.
Die Zeremonialzentren der Maya:
Ein Beitrag zur Untersuchung der
Planungsprinzipien. Horst
Hartung.
Zionism and Palestine Before the

Mandate: A Phase of Western
Imperialism. Richard P. Stevens,
ed.